MW01124777

Library of Congress Cataloging-in-Publication Data

Names: Hessler, James A., author. | Isenberg, Britt C., author.
Title: Gettysburg's Peach Orchard: Longstreet, Sickles, and the Bloody Fight for the "Commanding Ground" Along the Emmitsburg Road / by James A. Hessler and Britt C. Isenberg.
Description: El Dorado Hills, California: Savas Beatie, 2019
Identifiers: LCCN 2019002519| ISBN 9781611214550 (hardcover: alk. paper) | ISBN 9781611214567 (ebk)
Subjects: LCSH: Gettysburg, Battle of, Gettysburg, Pa., 1863. | Sickles, Daniel Edgar, 1819-1914—Military leadership. | Lee, Robert E. (Robert Edward), 1807-1870—Military leadership. | Longstreet, James, 1821-1904—Military leadership.
Classification: LCC E475.53 .H477 2019 | DDC 973.7/349—dc23
LC record available at https://lccn.loc.gov/2019002519

First Edition, First Printing

SB

Published by
Savas Beatie
989 Governor Drive, Suite 102
El Dorado Hills, CA 95762

Phone: 916-941-6896
(web) www.savasbeatie.com
(E-mail) sales@savasbeatie.com

Proudly published, printed, and warehoused in the United States of America.

To our family, friends, historians, and fellow Gettysburg Licensed Battlefield Guides who assisted in the completion of this book.

James A. Hessler:

To Michele, Alex, and Aimee. Thank you for sharing our time and space with Dan Sickles for too many years.

Britt C. Isenberg:

To Snezana and Una. Thank you for supporting this sacrifice of our time for theirs. Any shortcomings are of the head and not of the heart.

Table of Contents

List of Photographs and Illustrations

List of Maps

Abbreviations

ACHS: Adams County Historical Society
CCW: Joint Committee on the Conduct of the War
GNMP: Gettysburg National Military Park
HSP: Historical Society of Pennsylvania
LOC: Library of Congress
NARA: National Archives and Records Administration
OR: Official Records of the War of the Rebellion
SHSP: Southern Historical Society Papers
USAHEC: United States Army Heritage and Education Center
VHS: Virginia Historical Society

Preface

Gettysburg's Peach Orchard is not new to either author. Both of us have written previous books that touched upon it. James Hessler penned *Sickles at Gettysburg* (Savas Beatie, 2009), a detailed biography of Union General Daniel E. Sickles that includes analysis of his decision to occupy the Peach Orchard. Britt Isenberg wrote *The Boys Fought Like Demons* (CreateSpace, 2016), a complete regimental history of the 105th Pennsylvania, one of the many regiments that fought near the orchard.

We embarked individually on those projects because we appreciated the significance of the Peach Orchard to the battle. We also realized there was much left to tell about this landmark, the action there, and the people involved than was possible in our original books. In many ways, the book you are now reading is a sequel to our earlier work. However, completing the story of the Peach Orchard was surprisingly difficult. The fighting was confusing, at best, and has escaped the scrutiny of many Gettysburg historians. The numerous controversies surrounding Longstreet and Sickles muddied post-battle and contemporary perceptions. Conflicting accounts and differing opinions existed then and now. The Peach Orchard was both a reward and a challenge to interpret, but we are honored to tell the stories of those who fought there.

James A. Hessler and Britt C. Isenberg

Introduction: A Fatal Mistake

"In front of General Longstreet the enemy held a position from which, if he could be driven, it was thought our artillery could be used to advantage in assailing the more elevated ground beyond."

– General Robert E. Lee,
Army of Northern Virginia (July 31, 1863)[1]

The battle at Gettysburg on July 2, 1863, is primarily remembered as one fought for control of Little Round Top, a small hill on the Army of the Potomac's left flank. Although other terrain features also proved significant that day, including a farmer's wheat field and a rocky ridge later known as "Devil's Den," Little Round Top overshadows all others in Gettysburg historiography. Confederate forces struck the position and Union forces repulsed the attack. The Northern army's heroic defense saved the day and prevented the Southerners from capturing the high ground. This is the typical interpretation of the second day at Gettysburg.

In reality, another location played a greater part in Confederate General Robert E. Lee's plan of attack, and inadvertently defined Union Major General George G. Meade's defense. Major General Daniel E. Sickles, the controversial commander of the Army of the Potomac's Third Corps, had orders to occupy Little Round Top, but he apparently considered another

1 *The War of the Rebellion: A Compilation of the Official Records of the Union and Confederate Armies*, 128 vols. (Washington, DC, 1880-1901), Series 1, vol. 27, pt. 2, 308. Hereafter cited as *OR*. All references are to Series 1 unless otherwise noted.

position more important. Lee and Sickles both valued roughly four acres of elevated terrain along the Emmitsburg Road as a key artillery platform. A farmer's fruit orchard, forever afterwards known as the Peach Orchard, sat on this elevation and became the scene of brutal combat on the afternoon of July 2. Not only did the Peach Orchard heavily influence the second day's fighting, but it also partially persuaded Lee to launch the disastrous assault known as "Pickett's Charge" on July 3. Clearly, the Peach Orchard was vital to both armies at Gettysburg. Yet, the story has often been overlooked by Gettysburg historians.

From a military perspective, a battle's outcome is often determined by effective evaluation of terrain and the resulting selection of positions. Terrain is defined as a "geographic area, a piece of land, ground" or "the physical features of a tract of land." The physical features of terrain include ridgelines, roads, fences, woodlots, and open farm fields. The works of military theorist Antoine-Henri Jomini and West Point instructor Dennis Hart Mahan influenced many Civil War commanders who studied at institutions such as the United States Military Academy at West Point. Both Jomini and Mahan prescribed rules for selecting offensive and defensive positions. Mahan considered topography, "or the study of the natural features of positions" as one of "the most important modern additions to the military art."[2]

While allowing for some evolution and terminology changes, many of the basic principles accepted by Civil War officers still exist today. A modern concept of terrain assessment expects leaders to evaluate ground through five aspects: key terrain that can give a marked advantage to combatants; observation to see and maintain effective fields of fire; cover and concealment to protect against enemy fire; obstacles to impede troop movements; and avenues of approach to reach an objective. General officers from both armies utilized similar concepts to varying degrees of success in and around the Peach Orchard.[3]

This terrain evaluation process is one of the few parallels between civilians and soldiers. Civilians use their own form of terrain assessment when deciding

2 Mahan, *An Elementary Treatise on Advanced Guard, Out-Post, and Detachment Service of Troops*, 63-65; Jomini, *Art of War*, 163-166. "Terrain," *Merriam-Webster.com. 2018*. https://www.merriam-webster.com/dictionary/terrain (July 25, 2018).

3 This terrain assessment technique is often referred to as KOCOA, or also OKCOA. This practice is also used in modern battlefield preservation. These same analytic techniques help the National Park Service at Gettysburg National Military Park determine "exactly which terrain features were significant to the outcome of the Battle of Gettysburg. By definition then, those features which were significant to the outcome of the Battle of Gettysburg automatically became the most significant features of the historic landscapes of the battlefield, and became our highest priority for preservation and rehabilitation." See "Battlefield Rehabilitation at Gettysburg National Military Park," https://www.nps.gov/gett/learn/news/gett-battlefield-rehab.htm.

where to build their homes and their lives. Is the land accessible? What obstacles exist? Are there open fields for farming? Is there shelter for concealment from the elements? This was particularly true in nineteenth century America when a family's livelihood often literally depended on their land.

The intersection of these assessments frequently causes collisions between armies and civilians. This was true at the Peach Orchard in Gettysburg. The roads and ridgelines that convinced an enterprising fruit dealer to build a better life for his family also cost the lives of countless soldiers. Military historians emphasize command decisions made by the general officers. The stories of civilians who lived there are often forgotten, but they too valued the same terrain and often for the same reasons.

* * *

Confederate General Robert E. Lee had commanded the Army of Northern Virginia since June 1862. For more than one year, Lee's army provided the Confederacy with hope through a series of victories that frustrated the Northern army and the Lincoln Administration. The morale in Lee's army soared during the opening days of May 1863. Lee secured another success against the Army of the Potomac and Major General Joseph Hooker at the battle of Chancellorsville, in the wilderness of Spotsylvania County, Virginia. Lee fought with aggressive audacity, divided his outnumbered army, and stole the initiative from Hooker with a series of feints and marches.

Lee's aggressiveness culminated in a surprise flank attack unleashed by Lieutenant General Thomas J. "Stonewall" Jackson on May 2. Jackson marched 30,000 of his men over narrow and circuitous country roads, and massed opposite the Army of the Potomac's exposed right flank. However, members of General Sickles's Third Corps discovered Jackson's flanking march while in progress but misinterpreted the movement as a Confederate retreat. This mistake contributed greatly to a general lack of preparedness within Federal lines. Major General Oliver Howard's Eleventh Corps held the Federal right flank. When Jackson launched the attack, the sight of thousands of screaming Rebels pouring out of the woods and undergrowth sent many of Howard's men to flight. Negative feelings against Howard's corps ran strong in the Army of the Potomac after this debacle, and every Union general hoped to avoid being caught in a similar situation the next time these two armies met.[4]

4 *OR*, 25/1: 386; Dodge, *The Campaign of Chancellorsville*, 70; Howard, "The Eleventh Corps at Chancellorsville," *Battles and Leaders*, 3:196-197; De Trobriand, *Four Years With the Army of the Potomac*, p. 440; Sears, *Chancellorsville*, 239, 256, 262, 264, 269. For a deeper discussion

Sickles's Third Corps was in a critical position again on the following morning, May 3. His infantry and artillery initially occupied a salient position in advance of the army's main line. Hooker decided to consolidate his lines into a defensive posture and reduce the chances of the Confederates catching Sickles in a crossfire from multiple sides. Hooker ordered the Third Corps to abandon Hazel Grove, an open grassy ridge of several hundred yards in length. Confederate artillerist Colonel Edward Porter Alexander later described Hazel Grove as simply "a beautiful position for artillery."[5]

Brigadier General Charles Graham's infantry brigade and one battery fought as the rear guard during the Federals' evacuation of Hazel Grove. Advancing Southerners quickly outflanked Graham's men, and the Northerners withdrew. After their departure, Southern artillery rolled in as many as 28 cannon under Colonel Alexander. His gunners could see much of the Federal line from Hazel Grove, including Hooker's headquarters at the Chancellor house. Alexander placed an additional 14 guns in positions nearby and opened fire on Hooker's beleaguered army.[6]

"A converging fire of the enemy's guns from front, right, and left swept the ground," near the Chancellor house wrote New Yorker Josiah Favill, "round shot and shell filled the air about us, and confusion reigned supreme." Alexander considered Hooker's decision to remove Sickles from Hazel Grove "a fatal mistake." The Southern artillerist added, "There has rarely been a more gratuitous gift of a battle-field."[7]

There was little doubt about Lee's tactical victory and "Fighting Joe" Hooker's humiliating defeat. Strategically speaking, however, the Confederate cause was no better after the battle than it was before. They had suffered dearly in terms of casualties, including the mortal wounding of the irreplaceable General Jackson. Both armies afterwards returned to a stalemate along the

---

of Sickles and the Third Corps's role in Jackson's attack and Howard's defense, see James Hessler, *Sickles at Gettysburg* (El Dorado Hills, CA, 2009), 55-58.

5 *OR*, 25/1: 390; *Report of the Joint Committee on the Conduct of the War*, 8 (hereafter *CCW*); Dodge, *The Campaign of Chancellorsville*, 126-128; Alexander, *Military Memoirs*, 342, 345; Sears, *Chancellorsville,* 193, 286, 312-313. Historian Stephen Sears, critical of Sickles's overall Chancellorsville performance, admitted that there was danger at Hazel Grove, but thought Sickles might have been capable of holding the position with seven brigades and 38 artillery pieces. Sears wrote, "And whatever Dan Sickles might have lacked in military judgment he could make up for with military pugnaciousness." See Sears, 313.

6 *CCW*, 8; De Trobriand, *Four Years with the Army of the Potomac*, 457; Doubleday, *Chancellorsville and Gettysburg*, 46; Dodge, *The Campaign of Chancellorsville*, 128; Sears, *Chancellorsville*, 316-320.

7 Favill, *Diary of a Young Army Officer*, 234-235; Alexander, *Military Memoirs*, 345.

Rappahannock River near Fredericksburg, Virginia. Nevertheless, the combatants learned lessons and many officers, including General Sickles, did not forget their experiences at Chancellorsville. As a result, Chancellorsville significantly influenced the combat that occurred at Gettysburg later that summer.

After subsequent meetings in Richmond, Lee proposed and received permission to undertake a summer campaign in Pennsylvania. His objectives included removal of occupying enemy armies from Virginia, resupply of his own army via the Northern economy, and alleviating Federal pressure in the western theater. Although a journey into enemy territory was risky, Lee wrote, "It was determined to draw it [Hooker's army] from this position, and, if practicable, to transfer the scene of hostilities beyond the Potomac." If the Army of Northern Virginia was "unable to attain the valuable results which might . . . follow a decided advantage gained over the enemy in Maryland or Pennsylvania, it was hoped that we should at least so far disturb his plan for the summer campaign."[8]

Meanwhile, the final days of June 1863 were overcast and unseasonably cool in Cumberland Township, Pennsylvania. The prized peach trees of Joseph and Mary Sherfy, whose farm was roughly two miles south of the town of Gettysburg, displayed their scraggly limbs and blossoming fruit. The Sherfys' mature peach orchard of four acres rewarded their years of dedicated care. The orchard sat about 300 yards south of their residence at the southeast corner of two intersecting country roads, the Emmitsburg and Millerstown roads. The more prominent of these two thoroughfares was the Emmitsburg Road, which ran on a roughly southwest to northeast axis between Gettysburg and Emmitsburg, Maryland. The Millerstown Road was an artery to nearby Fairfield, Pennsylvania. These roads conveniently located the Sherfys in an era of travel and commerce that was reliant on foot, horse, and wagon traffic.[9]

The Sherfys recently added another six-acre orchard to their holdings just across the Emmitsburg Road from their house. This lot consisted of 500 young trees that were not yet producing. The new orchard held great promise, however, and the family might soon double their annual peach harvest. This

8 *OR*, 27/2: 313; Longstreet, *From Manassas to Appomattox*, 335 -337; Coddington, *Gettysburg Campaign*, 5-9.

9 Elmore, "A Meteorological and Astronomical Chronology of the Gettysburg Campaign," *Gettysburg Magazine 13*, 20. Daily high temperatures recorded between June 25 and June 30 ranged 63 to 79 degrees. The east to west Millerstown Road is referred to as the Wheatfield Road once east of the Emmitsburg Road intersection. It will be referred to as such in this text. The Wheatfield Road then connected the Emmitsburg and Taneytown roads, which was another path from Gettysburg to Maryland.

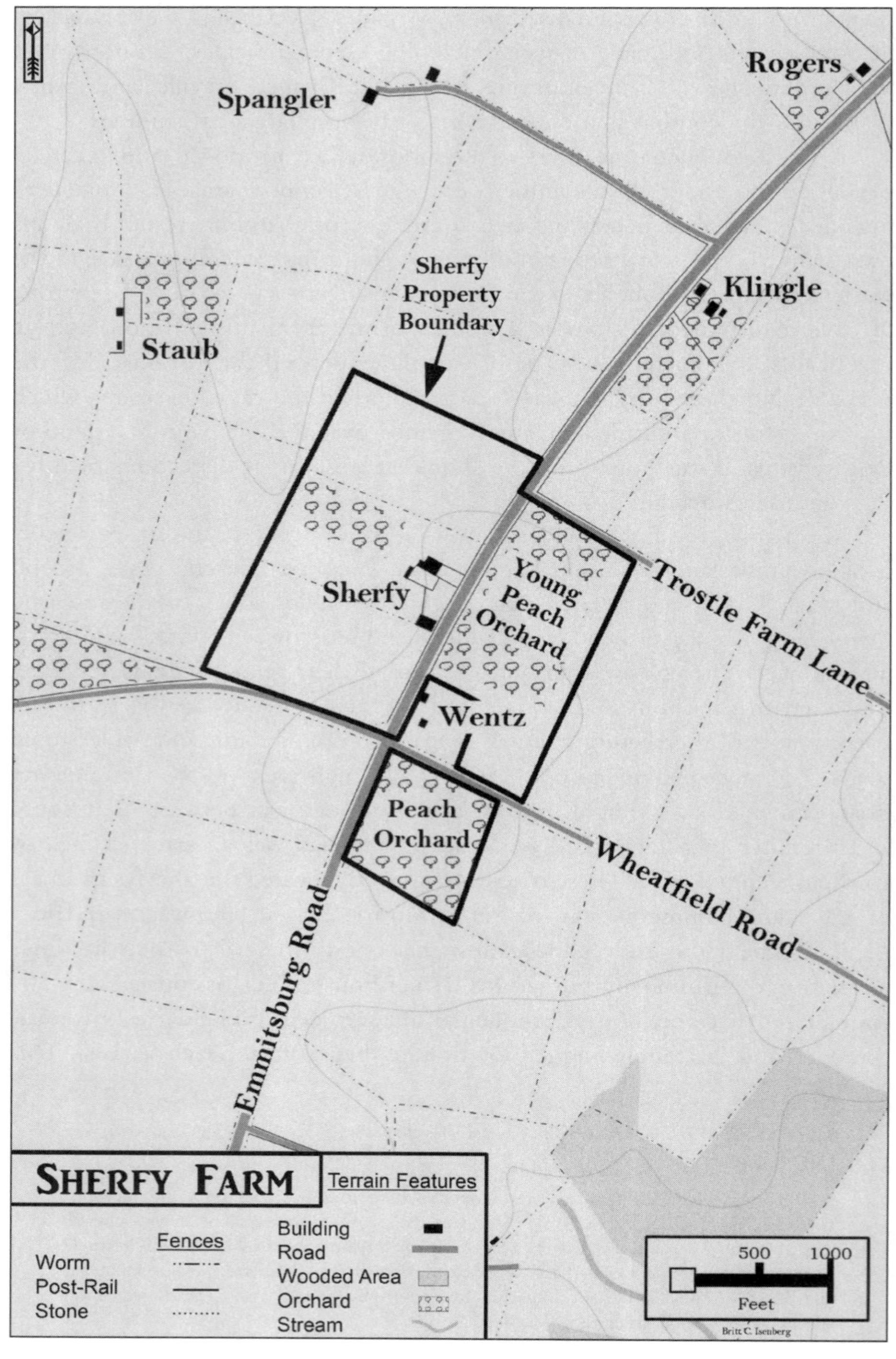
Rogers
Spangler
Sherfy
Property
Boundary
Klingle
Staub
Sherfy
Young
Peach
Orchard
Trostle Farm Lane
Wentz
Peach
Orchard
Wheatfield Road
Emmitsburg Road
SHERFY FARM
Terrain Features
Fences
Worm
Post-Rail
Stone
Building
Road
Wooded Area
Orchard
Stream
500
1000
Feet
Britt C. Isenberg

Postwar photo by William Tipton of the Sherfy house from the Emmitsburg Road looking southwest. Warfield Ridge can be seen in the background.
Sue Boardman Collection

was important because Joseph's primary means of supporting his family was as a "fruit dealer." Although horticultural techniques for peach trees had been around for generations, the practice was generally untapped in Adams County, Pennsylvania. The Sherfys undoubtedly looked forward to a productive summer of 1863.[10]

10 Copy of the Claims of Joseph Sherfy, National Archives, RG 92, Records of the Quartermaster General (hereafter Sherfy Claims), on file at Gettysburg National Military Park (hereafter GNMP), Library Box B-5; Georg, "The Sherfy Farm and the Battle of Gettysburg," GNMP, 6; United States Census of 1860, Cumberland Township, Adams County, Pennsylvania, house number 546. The Millerstown (or Wheatfield Road) has also been referred to as "The Peach Orchard Road" in some sources.

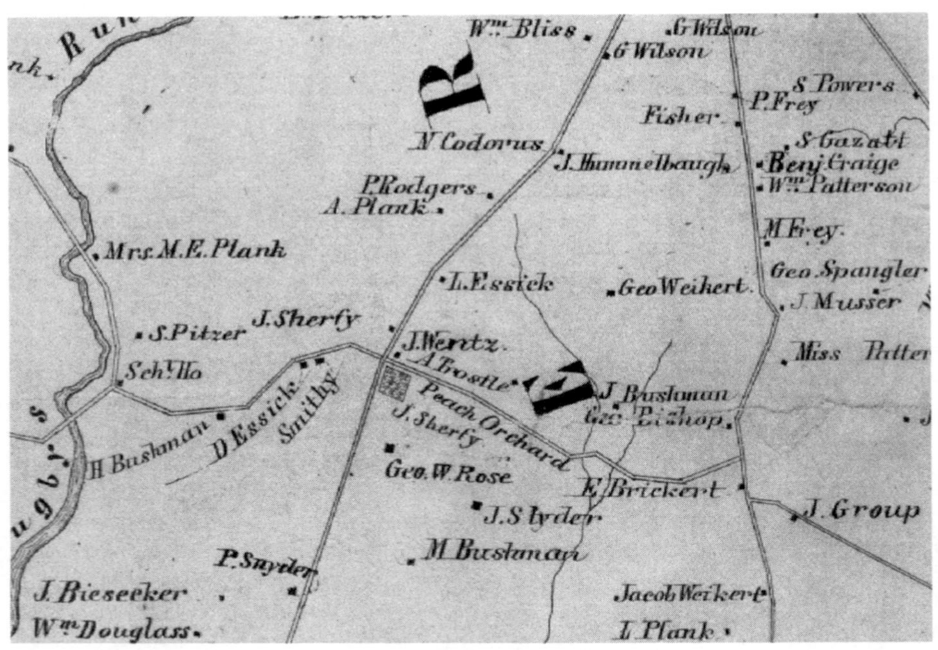

The Peach Orchard on the 1858 Adams County Map.
LOC

Joseph Sherfy was born in 1812 and grew up only about 400 yards south of his peach trees, in a stone house built by his father Jacob. Gettysburg historians would later know Sherfy's childhood home as the Rose farm, named for George Rose who owned it during the 1863 battle. In 1840, Joseph married Mary Heagen. They purchased some tracts of his father's property and portions of an adjacent farm previously owned by a family named Woods. Fruit trees had deep roots on Joseph Sherfy's new farm. The Woods planted several large English cherry trees on the property, probably as early as the 1750s. These sat just north of the site where Joseph and Mary built their two-story brick farmhouse in the early 1840s. The brick house, with some post-war modifications, still stands today.[11]

11 Georg, "The Sherfy Farm and the Battle of Gettysburg," 2-6. Prior ownership by Thomas Woods and his brother Joseph has been traced back to the 1820s. During the battle, several soldiers mentioned an "outdoor cellar" and National Park Service historian Kathleen Georg proposed in her report on the Sherfy farm that this may have been the foundations of the old Woods home near the Sherfy House. Based on soldier's accounts, it would have been within a few hundred yards of the house and barn. The Heagen family name also appears as Hagen.

The Sherfys' peach orchard was prominent enough that it appeared as a separate entity, labeled "Peach Orchard," in the commercially popular 1858 Adams County wall map. Crops and orchards were otherwise not included on this map so the inclusion of "Peach Orchard" was something of a curiosity. Significantly, the map was the most readily available guide to Adams County, and both armies made use of it during the 1863 Gettysburg campaign. Due to the presence of the Peach Orchard on the map, generals became aware of its location in relation to the surrounding road network, and perhaps mistook it as an individual settlement of farms.[12]

By 1863, the prosperous 50-acre Sherfy farm had everything necessary for a self-sufficient and profitable agricultural business. Sherfy's acreage was not particularly large, but his real estate value of $3,000 and personal property of approximately $600 both surpassed the average. In addition to the house, other buildings included a barn, hog stable, corn crib, and windmill. Woodlots surrounded the periphery of the property, providing not only lumber but also foliage for grazing livestock. Hundreds of feet of fencing crisscrossed the property. Along the Emmitsburg Road ridge, the Peach Orchard sat as a crown at the center of it all.[13]

Sherfy built his modest empire in the years after his property purchases. He also practiced as a German Baptist Brethren minister at the Lower Marsh Creek Brethren Church. Whether they were participating in religious activities or working the farm, their close proximity to Gettysburg made Reverend Joseph and Mary's busy daily routine easier. The town provided a market to sell their fruit and also offered plenty of social opportunities.[14]

Joseph Sherfy celebrated his 51st birthday on June 12, 1863. He and his 46-year-old wife could easily boast of their relative prosperity, but their faith kept them from such indulgences. Together the couple had six children by 1863, three boys and three girls. They ranged in age from two to 20 years old. Mary's widowed mother, Catherine, also lived with the family since her husband's passing. The entire Sherfy family was well respected in the Gettysburg community.[15]

12 For a history of the development of the 1858 Adams County map and its importance to both armies, see Frassanito, *Early Photography at Gettysburg*, 7-10. The map could have been available either in its original form or as a tracing on other maps.

13 Georg, "The Sherfy Farm and the Battle of Gettysburg," 3, 6.

14 The German Baptist Brethren church is also known as Dunkard or Dunker.

15 Sherfey, *The Sherfey Family in the United States*, 195, 204, 207; Georg, "The Sherfy Farm and the Battle of Gettysburg," 4. The six children were Raphael (born 1843), Otelia (born 1845), Mary (born 1847), Anna (born 1850), John (born 1853), and Ernest (born 1860).

Reverend Joseph Sherfy
ACHS

The planting of a new orchard demonstrated Joseph's ambitions for expansion. Every member of the household played a part in successfully sustaining the operations. The Sherfy children's chores left little time for daydreaming about personal aspirations, but eldest son Raphael fostered ambition for something more than farming. He loved books, attended the local schools, and pursued a classical education to become a teacher. The uncertainty of unfolding events threatened Raphael's educational goals. He could choose not to fight in the war, but only if the war avoided him.[16]

The Sherfys' closest neighbors were John and Mary Wentz, an elderly couple both in their mid-seventies. Their one-and-a-half-story log and weatherboard home and other structures were roughly 200 yards from the Sherfy house, on the opposite side of the Emmitsburg Road. The Wentz house stood on a small lot just north of the mature peach orchard, along the Wheatfield Road. John Wentz acquired these modest holdings in 1836. John and Mary's children were all adults, and only one daughter still lived at home. Their oldest son Henry had long since left the Gettysburg area, but his circumstances were noteworthy.[17]

Henry Wentz was likely born in 1827 when the family lived in neighboring York County, Pennsylvania. As a young man, Henry apprenticed in Gettysburg's growing carriage manufacturing industry. Around 1852, he migrated to Martinsburg, Virginia, to work and perhaps start his own carriage business. How his parents felt about the move remains unknown, but by 1860 Henry was working in Martinsburg as a plasterer. Wentz joined the local militia, and he enlisted into Confederate service with the outbreak of the Civil War.

16 Bradsby, *History of Adams County*, 403.

17 McMillan, *Gettysburg Rebels*, 8-9.

He joined what eventually became the Wise Artillery from Berkeley County. The unit served throughout the war, and Henry earned a promotion to first sergeant in February 1862. Wentz transferred in October of that year to what later became Osmond B. Taylor's Virginia Battery. Henry's promotion and length of service suggest that he was well regarded and devoted to his job. There is no evidence of any wartime correspondence between Henry and his parents, but John and Mary surely worried about their son's safety as the war continued into 1863.[18]

Unfortunately, the opening days of July 1863 put an end to all hopes for a prosperous and peaceful summer. The Sherfys and their neighbors soon learned that two powerful armies in transition, and holding the fate of their respective countries in hand, were about to collide at Gettysburg.

18 Ibid., xiii-xiv, 10-13; Clouse, "Whatever Happened to Henry Wentz?" *The Battlefield Dispatch* (October 1998): 6-10; United States Census of 1860, Martinsburg, house number 1195; *Survey Report for Restoration and Rehabilitation of Historic Structures: Wentz Buildings*, GNMP. Henry Wentz's birth year is estimated by the dates from his tombstone at Green Hill Cemetery in Martinsburg, West Virginia. His stone states that he died December 10, 1875 at the age of 48 years, suggesting an 1827 birth.

Chapter 1

War Comes to the Sherfy Farm

Lieutenant General James Longstreet was a career military man. Longstreet was born on January 8, 1821, in South Carolina. At age nine his parents sent him to Augusta, Georgia, to live with his uncle and receive an education. A military career appealed to young Longstreet, and he received an appointment to West Point where he was generally a poor student. He graduated in the class of 1842, ranked 54 out of 56 cadets. Despite his low ranking, he was still better educated than most Americans of that period. During his time at West Point, Longstreet forged lifelong relationships with many other cadets including Ulysses S. Grant and future subordinate Lafayette McLaws. Army life suited Longstreet. He received a commission in the infantry, where the prospects for promotion were slow, and saw combat in the Mexican War. Longstreet was wounded at Chapultepec, where he fought alongside another future subordinate named George Pickett, and received a brevet promotion for his gallantry. After returning from Mexico, Longstreet married Maria Louisa "Louise" Garland in 1848. It was a good match as she was the daughter of an army officer. Lieutenant Richard Ewell described Louise and her sister as the only attractive girls in the state of Missouri. The Longstreet marriage produced 10 children, not all of whom survived to adulthood, and lasted until her death in 1889.[1]

1 Wert, *General James Longstreet*, 22-23, 30-31, 45-46, 90-91, 421; Piston, "Petticoats, Promotions, and Military Assignments," *James Longstreet*, 54-55; DiNardo, "James Longstreet, the Modern Soldier," *James Longstreet*, 40. Longstreet was appointed to West Point from Alabama, where his mother lived following his father's death. See Wert, *General James Longstreet*, 25-26.

Lieutenant General James Longstreet
LOC

Major Longstreet was a paymaster in the United States Army when the Civil War began. He resigned his commission to join the Confederacy, and was appointed a brigadier general in June 1861. The Rebellion gave new life to numerous military careers, including Longstreet's. By October, he received promotion to major general and command of his own division. His professional accomplishments were marred by the deaths of three of his young children from scarlet fever in early 1862. Longstreet returned to the army within days of their deaths, and although he led his troops throughout 1862, the tragedy left him "very low spirited." Longstreet quickly gained General Robert E. Lee's confidence when the Virginian received a promotion to army command. Lee referred to Longstreet as "my old war-horse" and "the staff in my right hand."[2]

At Second Manassas, Longstreet led a massive 25,000 man counter-attack against the left flank of Major General John Pope's Union Army of Virginia. Longstreet's offensive of August 30, 1862, swept the Northern forces from the field and is considered one of the war's most successful assaults, but some controversy ensued afterwards. Longstreet had arrived at the battlefield on the prior day, but he obtained Lee's permission to conduct a lengthy reconnaissance that ultimately delayed his attack for one day. Some of Longstreet's post-war critics argued that this event created the impression that he could make Lee yield to his views. However, on the actual battlefield, this illustrated Longstreet's deliberateness and care in committing his troops. The final results proved his judgment to be sound, and Lee appeared to harbor no concerns. Only weeks later, after Longstreet performed capably again at the battle of Antietam, Lee reorganized his army into two corps under Longstreet and Jackson. Both

2 Wert, *General James Longstreet*, 53, 58, 90, 97; Cutrer, *Longstreet's Aide*, 72, 98. For a discussion regarding the date of Longstreet's actual army resignation, see Wert, *General James Longstreet*, 53-54.

officers received promotions to lieutenant general. Longstreet's was dated one day prior to Jackson's, which officially made him Lee's senior ranking subordinate.[3]

At Fredericksburg in December 1862, Longstreet had his men prepare extensive fortifications at the foot of Marye's Heights. He also employed his artillery as a combat multiplier, and covered the field in front of the heights so effectively that Colonel Alexander memorably observed, "A chicken could not live on that field when we open on it." As a result, Longstreet's infantry and artillery successfully repulsed repeated assaults made by Union forces against his strong position. Lee became momentarily concerned by the enemy's repeated attempts to break his lines, but Longstreet assured his commander that if every man in the Federal army made that same assault, "I will kill them all before they reach my line." Longstreet afterwards admired the courage and daring displayed by his opponent, but realized that their charges were "utterly hopeless." There is no debate over Longstreet's Fredericksburg success, but the battle has helped him gain a reputation among some historians and students as a "defensive" general. This perception ignores Longstreet's offensive at Second Manassas, and similar post-Gettysburg successes at Chickamauga and the Wilderness. Those battles demonstrated his ability to move his column, adapt to terrain, and strike powerful blows.[4]

The losses Lee's army suffered at Chancellorsville created a shortage of experienced officers. This predicament necessitated a restructuring of the Army of Northern Virginia. While Longstreet retained command of his First Corps, Lee handed the reins of Jackson's old Second Corps to recently promoted Lieutenant General Richard Ewell. Lee realized that the structure of two infantry corps no longer suited the army, as each corps had grown too large. He created the Third Corps and assigned recently promoted Lieutenant

3 *OR*, 16: 557, 564-566; Wert, *General James Longstreet*, 168-177, 204-205; Piston, *Lee's Tarnished Lieutenant*, 24; DiNardo, "James Longstreet, the Modern Soldier," *James Longstreet*, 36-37; Eckenrode and Conrad, *James Longstreet*, 105-106. Lee and Longstreet's ORs did not address any extended August 29 reconnaissance or hesitation on Lee's part to allow it. Longstreet's critics thought that Longstreet's handling "when he at least elected to do something, was admirable; but his long delay had imperiled Jackson and caused the latter heavy losses. Also in waiting until the afternoon to move, he had lessened the chances of decisive victory." See Eckenrode and Conrad *James Longstreet*, 110-111.

4 Longstreet, "The Battle of Fredericksburg," *Battles and Leaders*: 3:79, 81-82; DiNardo, "James Longstreet, the Modern Soldier," *James Longstreet*, 31-44; Knudsen, *General James Longstreet*, 28-30. The perception of Longstreet as a "defensive general" has been amplified by Michael Shaara's classic and popular novel, *The Killer Angels*. Although Shaara's book is based on historical accounts and has contributed considerably to the modern positive reassessment of Longstreet, it is ultimately a work of fiction.

General A. P. Hill to command. While both Ewell and Hill had demonstrated their ability to lead a division, neither had experience at the level of corps command. At every level of Lee's army, other officers advanced up the chain of command to fill vacancies. Major General Lafayette McLaws, who led a division under Longstreet, and Brigadier General Cadmus Wilcox, who had a brigade in Hill's new corps, were among those overlooked in the reorganization.[5]

In the summer of 1863, a British military observer described Longstreet as "a thickset, determined-looking man. . . . He is never far from General Lee, who relies very much upon his judgment." As his only proven corps commander, Lee depended on Longstreet's experience for the upcoming Pennsylvania campaign. Lee also needed his three corps commanders to cooperate with one another. Longstreet and A. P. Hill had quarreled following the Seven Days in 1862, although such disputes were admittedly not uncommon in either army. Thomas Goree, one of Longstreet's staff officers, insisted that Longstreet and Hill's relations "were strained for a short time only, and they were warm friends until the day of General Hill's death." Conversely, historian Douglas Southall Freeman described the relationship as "not cordial and may not even have been genuinely co-operative in spirit." Longstreet's command missed Chancellorsville while on detached service, but he justifiably had great confidence in their abilities. "The First Corps was as solid as a rock – a great rock," he wrote proudly in later years.[6]

Longstreet later insisted he and Lee agreed on fighting a defensive battle "in a position of our own choosing" as the "ruling idea" for the Pennsylvania campaign. Accordingly, Longstreet realized by mid-1863 that "a mere victory without decided fruits was a luxury we could not afford. Our numbers were less than the Federal forces, and our resources were limited while theirs were not." The example of Fredericksburg had indeed shown the "advantage of receiving instead of giving attack." Heavy losses from offensive operations would deplete Southern manpower to such an extent that "we should not be able to hold a force in the field to meet our adversary." Lee was unlikely to have entered into such a limiting agreement with his subordinate beforehand, although he later acknowledged in his own post-battle report, "It had not been

5 Freeman, *Lee's Lieutenants*, 3:202; Wert, *General James Longstreet*, 248-249; Oeffinger, *A Soldier's General*, 38.

6 Fremantle, *Three Months in the Southern States*, 237; Cutrer, *Longstreet's Aide*, 168; Freeman, *Lee's Lieutenants*, 3: 147, 185; Longstreet, *From Manassas to Appomattox*, 334.

intended to fight a general battle at such a distance from our base, unless attacked by the enemy."[7]

While Longstreet may have harbored personal reservations regarding the invasion, or magnified them later, he confided in Confederate Senator Louis Wigfall on May 13, that he was optimistic of success if Lee's army received reinforcements. "If we could cross the Potomac with one hundred + fifty thousand men I think we could demand of Lincoln to declare his purpose." Longstreet forecasted "a grand effort," and emphasized that if "every available man and means" were put into the field against the Yankees then "we could either destroy them or bring them to terms before the Summer is ended."[8]

Although two of the three Confederate corps commanders remained untested, veteran soldiers still comprised the nucleus of the army. "We can take care of any Yankee force which may come at us in our present position," one Southerner confidently told his wife. He continued, "If we get into Maryland or Pennsylvania and Hooker engages us you may be certain that he will be severely whipped."[9]

The Army of Northern Virginia began their move north on June 3, 1863. Leaving behind the familiar surroundings of the Rappahannock River near Fredericksburg, they tramped west toward the Blue Ridge Mountains. Confidence quickened the step, but most men had no idea where they were headed. Lieutenant William M. Owen of the Washington (Louisiana) Artillery Battalion in Longstreet's First Corps Artillery Reserve recorded, "We are all in the dark as to what our summer campaign is to be."[10]

General Hooker's Army of the Potomac launched its pursuit on June 10, in hopes of discovering Lee's intended objective. Confederate cavalry blocked gaps in the Bull Run Mountains and the Blue Ridge to prevent their Federal counterparts from penetrating Lee's extended lines of communications. The Union probes resulted in fights that scarred the landscape at Aldie, Middleburg and Upperville. Moving down the Shenandoah Valley, Lee's army wiped out

7 James Longstreet to Lafayette McLaws, July 25, 1873, Lafayette McLaws Papers #472, Southern Historical Collection, Wilson Library, University of North Carolina at Chapel Hill; Longstreet, "Lee's Invasion of Pennsylvania," *Battles and Leaders*, *3*: 246-247; *OR*, 27/2: 318.

8 James Longstreet to Louis T. Wigfall, May 13, 1863, Louis T. Wigfall Papers, LOC. Longstreet added, "When I agreed with the Secy + yourself about sending troops west it was under the impression that we would be obliged to remain on the defensive here. But the prospect of an advance changes the aspect of affairs to us entirely." See Ibid.

9 Welch, *A Confederate Surgeon's Letters to His Wife*, 54, 56.

10 Owen, *In Camp and Battle with the Washington Artillery of New Orleans*, 236.

Union garrisons at Winchester, Berryville and Martinsburg, and then crossed the Potomac River into Maryland. Arriving on the northern shore to the tune of "My Maryland," the Confederates then pressed forward into Pennsylvania. Lee's army fanned out like a giant umbrella across the southern portion of the Keystone State in order to take advantage of Pennsylvania's bountiful farms. Ewell's Second Corps led the Army of Northern Virginia toward the farming communities on the east side of South Mountain, the northern extension of the Blue Ridge range, and into south central Pennsylvania.[11]

Rumors of an enemy invasion had rippled across the Pennsylvania countryside so many times before that the citizens "lost faith in their coming, and it grew to be an old story." These rumors became so repetitive among the people of Adams County that "we even laughed and joked among ourselves, little dreaming they were really so near." On June 26, elements of Lee's army arrived and the reality of the Rebel invasion came into clear, sharp focus. This day was also Raphael Sherfy's 20th birthday.[12]

Major General Jubal Early's Division scattered overmatched local militia along the Chambersburg Pike west of Gettysburg. Fortunately for the townsfolk, the Rebel visit was short-lived. The Confederates entered Gettysburg and levied a substantial requisition on the town, but the local elders could not meet the demands. Early decided to spare Gettysburg in favor of potential targets further east and his men soon departed. Gettysburg resident Sarah Broadhead remembered, "They came with such horrid yells that it was enough to frighten us to death." Broadhead considered them "miserable-looking" and recalled, "how bad I felt to hear them, and to see the traitors' flag floating overhead."[13]

Word of the temporary Confederate occupation undoubtedly created much excitement among the Sherfy family. After two years of unfulfilled threats, it seemed that Lee's army had finally arrived to wreak havoc in Pennsylvania. Many townspeople fled, often taking their most valuable possessions with them, but not the Sherfys. They had worked too hard to abandon their home. The immediate threat of battle subsided, albeit temporarily, with Jubal Early's departure and surely the Army of the Potomac, wherever they were, would not allow these degradations upon the Northern people to pass unnoticed.

11 *OR*, 27/2: 306-307, 439-443; Dickert, *History of Kershaw's Brigade*, 229.

12 Buehler, *Recollections of the Rebel Invasion and One Woman's Experience during the Battle of Gettysburg*, 6, 9-10.

13 Skelly, *A Boy's Experiences During the Battles of Gettysburg*, 9; Jacobs, *The Rebel Invasion of Maryland & Pennsylvania and Battle of Gettysburg*, 17; Broadhead, *The Diary of a Lady of Gettysburg*, 9-10.

The Army of the Potomac was indeed in pursuit of these unwelcomed intruders. Hooker's army, like Lee's, underwent a reorganization following Chancellorsville. The Union Army's battle-hardened Third Corps, under colorful General Dan Sickles, headed north as one of many units with their share of changes and question marks.

Daniel Edgar Sickles was not a military man. The former United States congressman turned general had a checkered past that included womanizing, fast living, questionable business ethics, and even murder. He was born in New York City on October 20, 1819, and grew up as an only child in a relatively affluent household. He was an attorney in the mid-1840s when he became an active Democrat at Tammany Hall, the political machine that controlled New York City politics and was notorious for patronage and corruption. Sickles was elected to the New York State Assembly in 1847 and proudly called himself, "a tough Democrat; a fighting one; a Tammany Hall Democrat."[14]

In 1852, Sickles married Teresa Bagioli, the teenage daughter of a family friend. She was an exotic Italian beauty but also 17 years his junior and likely pregnant at the time of the wedding. Seven moths later she gave birth to a daughter, but nonetheless, this unconventional union did not derail Sickles's political career. In 1853, he accepted a post as assistant to James Buchanan, the new American Minister in London and future President of the United States. Buchanan took a liking to Sickles and became something of a mentor to the rising New Yorker. While they were abroad, Sickles caused an incident when, on July 4, 1854, he refused to toast the Queen's health. He also maintained a long-term relationship with a prostitute named Fanny White, and he allegedly introduced the quean to the Queen. Sickles's political career peaked with his election to the United States Congress in 1856 and he moved his family to Washington in early 1857. They took up residence in fashionable and expensive Lafayette Square, while President Buchanan assumed office literally across the street in the White House. The future looked bright for Dan Sickles.[15]

14 Hessler, *Sickles at Gettysburg*, 1-4; Brandt, *The Congressman Who Got Away With Murder*, 20-22; *Dedication of the New York Auxiliary State Monument*, 107. For a discussion of Sickles's disputed birth year, see Hessler, *Sickles at Gettysburg*. For an overview of Tammany Hall's role in New York City politics, see Strausbaugh, *City of Sedition*, 41-47, 64-71, 346-347.

15 Hessler, *Sickles at Gettysburg*, 6-8; *Life and Death of Fanny White*, 8; New York *Times*, March 15, 1859; Brandt, *The Congressman Who Got Away With Murder*, 26-36. A "quean" is "a disreputable woman" or more specifically, a "prostitute." https://www.merriam-webster.com/dictionary/quean. While "Fanny White" may seem an improbable name for a prostitute, that was only her professional name. She was actually born as Jane Augusta Funk; she is also referenced as Jane Augusta Blankman after she married Edmon Blankman in 1859. White

Sickles was a lifelong philanderer and his marriage was a stormy one. The schoolgirl-like Teresa Sickles soon embarked on an affair of her own with a U.S. Attorney for the District of Columbia named Phillip Barton Key, who was a friend of her husband's. Key was the son of Francis Scott Key and known throughout the city as a dashing ladies man. Congressman Sickles eventually learned of the infidelity and, on February 27, 1859, murdered Key in Lafayette Square. Authorities arrested and jailed Sickles, but with public opinion strongly in his favor, he assembled a team of high-powered lawyers. The accomplished attorney James T. Brady led the defense team that included future Secretary of War Edwin Stanton and a friend from New York named John Graham. The defense strategy combined elements of "self-defense," since a husband had a right to protect his wife from an adulterer, with "crime of passion" into what became known as "temporary insanity." The jury acquitted Sickles after a sensational, scandalous, and brief trial.[16]

Although Sickles enjoyed the public support of his many friends throughout the ordeal, he outraged New York and Washington society by reconciling with Teresa several months after the trial. Their reunion, more than the murder itself, torpedoed his once promising political career. In many ways, the American Civil War came at the best possible time for Daniel Sickles.[17]

Sickles had no military background or training, other than a brief stint in the early 1850s with the New York State Militia. He felt betrayed by Southern Democrats who led the secession movement, and he saw an opportunity for a new career when the war started. He recruited and raised troops in New York that soon became known as the Excelsior Brigade. Lincoln needed fighting Democrats, even sullied ones, to support his unpopular war effort and the President enabled Sickles's rapid rise to brigadier general. The roguish Sickles also became one of Mrs. Lincoln's personal favorites and, as a result, he became a frequent visitor to the White House. Sickles saw little combat during 1862 and missed battles at Second Manassas and Antietam while away

was unique in that she owned and managed high-end brothels in an age when the "working" women did not always do so.

16 For coverage of the trial and aftermath see Hessler, *Sickles at Gettysburg*, 8-20 and Brandt, *The Congressman Who Got Away With Murder*, 162-199.

17 Besides the murder, as another example of Sickles's emotional outbursts, during the 1840 funeral of friend and then-mentor Lorenzo L. Da Ponte, a "spasm of grief" overcame Sickles and he was carried from the graveyard while raving, shrieking, and yelling. During the trial itself, he broke down several times while listening to testimony about Teresa and Key's liaisons, and had to be led from the courtroom on at least one occasion. Clearly, Dan Sickles was an emotional man. See Brandt, *The Congressman Who Got Away With Murder*, 19-20, 175-176.

Congressional Portrait of Daniel Sickles
LOC

from the army. Yet he still received promotion to division command prior to Fredericksburg, where he saw minor action. Sickles's military rise continued, due in part to his new friendship with Joseph Hooker. Hooker took command of the Army of the Potomac in January 1863, and upon reorganizing the army, promoted Sickles to major general and gave him command of the Third Corps.[18]

Sickles's first test as a corps commander came at Chancellorsville. The Third Corps found itself in the thickest of the fighting and sustained the largest number of casualties of any Federal corps fighting around Chancellorsville. Sickles learned hard lessons at Chancellorsville. For better or worse, those lessons resonated with him at Gettysburg.[19]

Sickles embarked on the Gettysburg campaign as the only non-West Point corps commander in either army. He lacked military training and his battlefield experience was limited, yet many of his men loved him and a large number of his partisans served in the Third Corps officer ranks. He also relied heavily on good relationships with those above him. Unfortunately for Sickles, in late June, Hooker resigned as commander of the Army of the Potomac. As the armies maneuvered from Maryland into Pennsylvania, the question emerged as to whether Sickles could manage a corps independently under a less friendly commanding officer.

18 Hessler, *Sickles at Gettysburg*, 21-35; Warner, *Generals in Blue*, 227-228; Stevenson, *History of the Excelsior or Sickles's Brigade*, 8-9; *Dedication of the New York State Auxiliary Monument*, 107-109. Republicans in the Senate, questioning his Democrat loyalty and probably his qualifications, resisted in appointing him a Major General. They finally confirmed him in March 1863 and the commission was dated to November 1862.

19 *OR*, 25/1: 177-191. Third Corps losses have been estimated at 4,119 men. The Sixth Corps suffered the most casualties (4,590) in the Army of the Potomac during the Chancellorsville campaign, but actually fought in the vicinity of Fredericksburg as a detached unit.

At Chancellorsville, the Third Corps consisted of three divisions. The massive losses incurred at that battle included the deaths of division commanders Amiel Whipple and Hiram Berry. This necessitated a consolidation of the corps into two divisions. The First Division remained under Major General David Bell Birney. The 38- year-old Birney was the son of prominent abolitionist James Birney, who was twice an unsuccessful Presidential candidate for the anti-slavery Liberty Party in the 1840s. David Birney was born in Alabama, but his family moved frequently, including stops in Cincinnati and Philadelphia. He received a good education and was practicing law in Philadelphia in 1861. Birney inherited his father's patriotism but not his radical abolitionism. At the beginning of the Civil War, Birney recruited the 23rd Pennsylvania Volunteer Infantry, forever known as "Birney's Zouaves," and received a commission as the regiment's lieutenant colonel. Birney was promoted to brigadier general in February 1862, and took command of a Third Corps brigade.[20]

At Fredericksburg, Birney became embroiled in a dispute with Major General George Gordon Meade, then a First Corps division commander and a fellow Philadelphian. Meade's men had exploited a gap in Stonewall Jackson's line, and he requested Birney's support in order to take advantage of the breakthrough. However, Birney considered himself under orders from First Corps commander John Reynolds to withdraw from the field. Consequently, Birney did not assist Meade and the Confederates repulsed the promising assault. A furious Meade reportedly tore into Birney verbally on the battlefield, and bad blood between the generals continued long afterward, even though Meade later acknowledged privately that Reynolds was partially responsible for the episode. The upshot of this incident was that it sparked animosity between Meade and the officers of the Third Corps that continued into Gettysburg.[21]

20 Wray, *History of the Twenty Third Pennsylvania Volunteer Infantry Birney's Zouaves*, 29-32; *The Union Army*, Volume VIII, Biographical, 32; Davis, *Life of David Bell Birney*, 1-18, 25-27, 30-31, 44-45, 73.

21 *OR*, 21: 58, 358-360, 362, 454, 511-512; Biddle, "General Meade at Gettysburg," *The Annals of the War*, 205; Rable, *Fredericksburg! Fredericksburg!* 215-216. In his report, Meade neither censured nor praised Birney, but acknowledged that he requested Birney's support early in the attack. Meade later elaborated that he sent to Birney three times to come to his assistance. (Also see Rable, 513, n. 38.) Writing privately to his wife on December 16, Meade blamed his failure on a lack of support and the enemy's strong "redoubts." Again in private correspondence on December 30, Meade also blamed John Reynolds as "he knows I think he was in some measure responsible for my not being supported on the 13th as he was commanding the corps & had the authority to order up other troops- and it was his business

Birney received a promotion to major general in late May of 1863, but he remained a division commander since Sickles was then leading the corps. Birney accepted life under Sickles, who the Pennsylvanian thought "has many qualities to commend him as a soldier." In short time, Sickles and Birney became friends.[22]

History has not always been kind to Birney's image. Theodore Lyman, who served on Meade's staff after Gettysburg, later described Birney as a professionally competent officer but a personally cold man:

> Birney was one who had many enemies, but, in my belief, we had few officers who could command 10,000 men as well as he. He was a pale, Puritanical figure, with a demeanor of unmovable coldness; only he would smile politely when you spoke to him. He was spare in person, with a thin face, light-blue eye, and sandy hair. As a General he took very good care of his Staff and saw they got due promotion. He was a man, too, who looked out for his own interests sharply and knew the mainsprings of military advancement. His unpopularity among some persons arose partly from his promotion, which, however, he deserved; and partly from his cold covert manner. I always felt safe when he had the division; it was always well put in and safely handled.[23]

Brigadier General Andrew Atkinson Humphreys received command of the fallen general Hiram Berry's Second Division. Born in Philadelphia in 1810, Humphreys was the opposite of both Sickles and Birney in terms of military training. He graduated from the United States Military Academy at West Point in the Class of 1831. Humphreys's first assignments were in artillery and against Seminole Indians, but like many of the old army officers he had little combat experience prior to the Civil War. In 1836, he resigned from the army to work as a civilian engineer, but returned in 1838 with an appointment to the Corps of Topographical Engineers. Despite his expertise in scientific disciplines, Humphreys bristled at the notion that he was anything but a soldier. "Why, anyone who knows me intimately knows that I had more of the soldier than a man of science in me." Humphreys

to have seen that I was properly supported . . . This is all confidential & for you alone." The passage was later omitted from the publication of Meade's *Life and Letters*. Yet Meade seems to have held the longest grudge against Birney. Seventeen months later, long after Reynolds had apparently been forgiven, Meade would tell his wife that he and Birney would "always" have Fredericksburg "between us." George Meade to Margaret Meade, December 16, 20, 30, 1862 and April 11, 1864, George Meade Collection, HSP.

22 David Birney to George Gross, March 16, 1863, David B. Birney Papers, USAHEC.

23 Agassiz, *Meade's Headquarters*, 266.

Major General David Birney
LOC

frequently expressed his preference to command troops over serving in staff capacities. His first real experience at leading large bodies of men under fire came at Fredericksburg. He commanded a division in the Fifth Corps that suffered more than 1,000 casualties in the last of several futile assaults against Marye's Heights.[24]

Humphreys again led his Fifth Corps division at Chancellorsville, but saw little combat. His division was composed of nine-month regiments that were due to muster out of service at the end of May. The Third Corps casualties created opportunities, however, and Humphreys welcomed his new assignment to command Berry's old division, which he considered "one of the best in the whole army."[25]

Like countless seasoned military men, Humphreys was often a profane and strict disciplinarian. Assistant Secretary of War Charles Dana considered him "one of the loudest swearers" he had ever met, and a man of "distinguished and brilliant profanity." Yet, despite his constant use of vulgarity, Humphreys otherwise gave off a surprisingly scholarly appearance. Theodore Lyman, one of Meade's staff officers, described Humphreys as "an extremely neat man, and is continually washing himself and putting on paper dickeys." According to Birney, Humphreys was "what we call an old granny, a charming, clever gentleman, fussy." Humphreys joined Meade and Brigadier General Gouverneur K. Warren in what Birney mockingly called the army's engineer clique. George Meade, then still commanding the Fifth Corps, was sorry to lose his friend to another corps. Meade considered Humphreys, "a most valuable officer,

24 *The Union Army*, Volume VIII, Biographical, 135; *OR*, 21: 137; Humphreys, *Andrew Atkinson Humphreys*, 25, 30-45, 156-177, 183-185, 194, 197; Stackpole, *The Fredericksburg Campaign*, 217-218. General Whipple's Third Division was consolidated with the other two divisions.

25 *The Union Army*, Volume VIII, Biographical, 135; Humphreys, *Andrew Atkinson Humphreys*, 183-184, 194, 197.

Brigadier General Andrew Humphreys
LOC

besides being an associate of the most agreeable character." Upon taking his new assignment, Humphreys held the distinction of being the only West Point graduate in the upper echelon of the Third Corps. However, his personal bond with Meade undoubtedly hindered his relations with Sickles and Birney.[26]

In addition to his animosity with Birney, or as a partial result of it, Meade's relations with Sickles floundered through most of 1863. During the past winter, Hooker, Sickles, and chief of staff Major General Dan Butterfield had created a raucous atmosphere of loose women and free flowing alcohol at army headquarters. The happily married Meade, however, found himself excluded from their inner circle. In mid-February, Meade complained to his wife, "I do not like his [Hooker's] *entourage.* Such gentlemen as Dan Sickles and Dan Butterfield are not the persons I should select as my intimates, however worthy and superior they may be."[27]

The relationships deteriorated further after Chancellorsville. Hooker accused Meade of favoring a retreat following the defeat; something the Pennsylvanian denied vehemently. An angry Meade polled the other corps commanders to obtain their recollections of his expressed views. Not surprisingly, Sickles backed his friend Hooker instead of Meade. Sickles acknowledged that Meade, "expressed the opinion that General Hooker should attack the enemy," but after discussing the matter in war council, "my impression was that [Meade's] original preferences appeared to have been surrendered to the clear conviction

26 Agassiz, *Meade's Headquarters*, 6-7; Tagg, *Generals of Gettysburg*, 73; Humphreys, *Andrew Atkinson Humphreys*, 183-184, 194, 197; David Birney to George Gross, October, 28, 1863, *David B. Birney Papers*, USAHEC; Meade, *Life and Letters*, 1:378.

27 Meade, *Life and Letters*, 1:354, 357.

of the commanding general." Coincidence or not, this portrayal of a seemingly indecisive Meade emerged as a theme that Sickles returned to repeatedly for decades to come.[28]

After weeks of squabbling with Washington over his authority following Chancellorsville, Hooker offered his resignation. Both Lincoln and general-in-chief Henry Halleck promptly accepted it. On June 28, while encamped near Frederick, Maryland, Meade awoke to orders placing him in command of the Army of the Potomac. He was as surprised as anyone and largely unknown to soldiers outside of his Fifth Army Corps. One of Birney's staff officers, Levi Bird Duff, confided to his wife about the new commander, "Of Meade I know but very little. . . . He looks like an earnest patient man. I do not expect that we will meet with any great disaster under his command nor do I expect any great victories." The new commander's first order of business was to gather intelligence regarding his scattered army, and then to resume moving toward the enemy.[29]

Meade determined that the Army of Northern Virginia had crossed the Potomac and was moving north through the Cumberland Valley. He decided to move north from Frederick to Harrisburg with the army's left and right wings spread as far as possible, in order to keep Baltimore and Washington covered. The objective was to halt Lee's probable advance toward Harrisburg, Pennsylvania, and bring on a battle "at some point." Further developments were dependent upon Lee's movements, but by June 29, the Union army's seven infantry corps were moving north.[30]

Shortly thereafter, Meade expressed unhappiness with the marching performance of the Third Corps. On June 30, he notified his new subordinate Sickles, "The commanding general noticed with regret the very slow movement of your corps yesterday." The distance travelled was "far from meeting the expectation of the commanding general," and as a final reminder Meade "looks for rapid movements of the troops." This terse message served an

28 Ibid., 1: 377; *OR*, 25/1: 511.

29 Helmreich, *To Petersburg with the Army of the Potomac*, 128; Meade, *Life and Letters*, 2: 11-12; *OR*, 27/1: 114; 27/3: 374.

30 *OR*, 27/1: 61-62, 114; 27/3: 398; *CCW*, 329-330; Hyde, *The Union Generals Speak*, 103; Meade, *Life and Letters*, 2:3,8,11; Callihan, "Passing the Test...", *Gettysburg Magazine 30*, 32; Pfanz, *Gettysburg: The First Day*, 32; Smith, *A Famous Battery and Its Campaigns*, 98-100; Scott, *History of the One Hundred and Fifth Regiment of Pennsylvania Volunteers*, 81; Craft, *History of the 141st Regiment Pennsylvania Volunteers*, 111.

early reminder to Sickles that he no longer had the confidence of headquarters that he enjoyed under Hooker.[31]

Despite the censure from headquarters, the *esprit de corps* remained strong among the veterans of Dan Sickles's corps. Major Israel Spaulding of the 141st Pennsylvania proudly wore the red-diamond Third Corps emblem of the First Division on his uniform. Spaulding boasted to his family, "Our men are in fine spirits and the long marches have only made them more hardy and strong than ever. . . . The men felt they were going to defend their native State and drive back the invaders of their homes." For many Federal soldiers the benefits of marching toward loyal Union territory bolstered their confidence. Private Egbert Lewis, in the Excelsior Brigade's 120th New York, never forgot the "bread, pies, cakes, biscuits, milk, fruit, and vegetables, which were given to them or purchased at very low prices." The outpouring of the citizenry was so great that "some of these loyal people did not keep enough for themselves to eat."[32]

Meanwhile, Meade attempted to ascertain Lee's whereabouts and intended destination.[33] Much of the intelligence that Meade received about Confederate movements came from his cavalry, including Brigadier General John Buford's First Division of the Cavalry Corps. It was sometime before noon on June 30 when Buford's cavalrymen came up the Emmitsburg Road toward the Sherfy farm. The family members witnessed the arrival of these friendly forces. It must have been quite a sight since the largest crowds they encountered previously were those at community gatherings. The Sherfys "gazed with interest and satisfaction as the long column of veteran troopers, with trampling horses and fluttering guidons" rode past their farmstead. Buford's horsemen did not dawdle, but continued on into Gettysburg. The arrival of Union cavalry must have brought mixed signals to the local citizenry. The danger of war had not yet passed, but at least their protectors in blue were on the scene should the Rebels decide to come back.[34]

31 *OR*, 27/1: 482, 530, 542, 27/3: 375, 399, 420; Meade, Life and Letters, 2:9-10.

32 Craft, *History of the One Hundred and Forty-First Regiment*, 112, 128-129; Van Santvoord, *The One Hundred and Twentieth New York State Volunteers*, 66.

33 Meade transmitted his understanding to General Howard, "from present information, Longstreet and Hill are at Chambersburg, partly toward Gettysburg; Ewell at Carlisle and York. Movements indicate a disposition to advance from Chambersburg to Gettysburg." To Meade, this indicated that Harrisburg and Philadelphia were relieved of any immediate threat, while his own movements continued to protect Washington. See *OR*, 27/3: 415, 427.

34 *OR*, 27/1: 926, 27/3: 415, 427; Besley, *History of the Sixth New York Cavalry*, 133. The 6th New York Cavalry history claims they entered Gettysburg by 11:00 a.m., but Buford's official report, filed on August 27, 1863, says it was in the afternoon. Other unit histories from the division simply state that it was before dark.

During the march northward, Lee and the Army of Northern Virginia's main body lost contact with Major General J.E.B. Stuart's cavalry and were increasingly uninformed on Federal movements.[35] However, thanks to intelligence acquired by a spy that Longstreet hired, Lee learned on June 28 that the Federal army had crossed the Potomac River. The enemy was advancing northward and threatened to cut Lee's lines of communication and supply. Although Lee was initially skeptical of the report, he decided to deter the enemy "from advancing farther west, and intercepting our communication with Virginia" by concentrating his own forces "on the east side" of South Mountain. As a result, he ordered Ewell's Second Corps to fall back from the outskirts of Harrisburg and "either move directly on Gettysburg or turn down to Cashtown." The small village of Cashtown was located about ten miles west of Gettysburg, and near a key gap in the South Mountain range. Lee added, "Longstreet and Hill were directed to proceed from Chambersburg to Gettysburg." Clearly, Lee intended to concentrate his three scattered infantry corps before engaging in battle. Perhaps an opportunity even existed to pursue Longstreet's preferred strategy. A defensive fight on a chosen battlefield remained plausible should the Army of Northern Virginia arrive and concentrate ahead of the Army of the Potomac.[36]

On June 30, as Buford's cavalry rode toward Gettysburg via the Emmitsburg Road, a Confederate force approached the town from the west along the Chambersburg Pike. Brigadier General James Johnston Pettigrew's Brigade, from A. P. Hill's Third Corps, moved toward Gettysburg from Cashtown to "procure supplies." Pettigrew did not have orders to fight and upon seeing Buford's men, withdrew his troops back to Cashtown. Both sides knew something was amiss near Gettysburg. For Buford, this sighting confirmed that Confederate infantry was concentrating west of town. That evening, Pettigrew's superior officer, Major General Henry Heth, reported the encounter to General Hill.

35 An analysis of Stuart's role in the campaign is beyond the scope of this work. For information on Stuart consult Wittenberg and Petruzzi, *Plenty of Blame to Go Around: Jeb Stuart's Controversial Ride to Gettysburg*.

36 *OR*, 27/2: 307, 317, 358; 27/3: 933-934; Longstreet, *From Manassas to Appomattox*, 333, 346-348; Longstreet, "Lee's Invasion of Pennsylvania," *Battles and Leaders*, 3: 249-250; Freeman, *Lee's Lieutenants*, 3: 35, 49. According to Hill's report, on the morning of June 29, while "encamped on the road from Chambersburg to Gettysburg, near the village of Fayetteville. I was directed to move on this road in the direction of York, and to cross the Susquehanna, menacing the communications of Harrisburg with Philadelphia, and to co-operate with General Ewell, acting as circumstances might require." See *OR*, 27/2: 606-607. The plan to menace Harrisburg was negated by Lee's decision to concentrate east of South Mountain, and this subsequently placed Hill in Cashtown on June 30.

Both Heth and Hill questioned the veracity of Pettigrew's report. "I intended to advance the next morning," wrote a somewhat skeptical Hill to Lee, "and discover what was in my front." Heth's Division began preparations for an early morning march to Gettysburg, this time in greater force.[37]

On that same day, Meade added a new layer to the structure of the Army of the Potomac. He directed Major General John Reynolds to exercise command over three corps and in doing so, created the army's left wing. This gave Reynolds control of Sickles's Third Corps, Oliver Howard's Eleventh Corps, and his own First Corps. Meade also instructed Sickles to advance the Third Corps from Taneytown to Emmitsburg. However, Sickles received conflicting instructions from Reynolds that directed him to stop before reaching Emmitsburg. Sickles sent a message to Meade's headquarters conveying his uncertainty and requesting clarification. The head of his column, Birney's First Division, was only about one mile from Emmitsburg and they stopped close enough to town to meet the spirit of Meade's directive. Humphreys's Second Division halted near the "Cat Tail Branch" of the Monocacy River, in compliance with Reynolds's orders, and Sickles made his headquarters at nearby Bridgeport, Maryland. Already, Meade and Sickles displayed an inability to communicate effectively with one another in the field.[38]

In the hours after dark, June 30 proved a busy night for Buford's cavalrymen at Gettysburg. His outposts scanned the countryside to the west and north, as he had decided upon "entertaining" Lee's army "until General Reynolds could reach the scene." Reynolds was only a short distance south of Gettysburg. Earlier, he moved his First Corps to Marsh Creek and established his headquarters at the Moritz Tavern, a residence along the Emmitsburg Road that stood roughly four miles from the Sherfy farm. Howard's Eleventh Corps was at Emmitsburg and Sickles camped nearby.[39]

The sun rose red, sending forth the first streaks of daylight at 4:35 a.m. on July 1. Two Confederate infantry divisions from General Hill's Third Corps departed Cashtown and marched in column along the Chambersburg Pike

37 *OR*, 27/1: 922-923, 27/2: 317, 358, 606-607, 637, 27/3: 400, 402, 414-415.

38 *OR*, 27/1: 482, 530, 542, 27/3: 414-416, 422, 424-425; Meade, *Life and Letters*, 2: 15-16; Brown, *History of the Third Regiment, Excelsior Brigade*, 104. A historical marker placed along modern MD-140 by the Maryland Civil War Centennial Commission reads, "Bridgeport. As part of General Meade's screen for Washington as the Confederates invaded Maryland and Pennsylvania, the Third Corps, Army of the Potomac, arrived here June 30, 1863 from Taneytown. Next day General Daniel E. Sickles marched this corps to Emmitsburg."

39 *OR*, 27/1: 701, 758, 927, 27/3: 417-419; Howard, *Autobiography of Oliver Otis Howard*, 1: 403-404.

toward Gettysburg. They encountered Buford's cavalry videttes blocking the pike about three miles northwest of town. Just after 7:00 a.m., the two sides greeted each other with a smattering of small arms fire. Over the next several hours, the combatants increasingly "became hotly engaged," as Buford reported. As the fighting escalated, the advance elements of Confederate General Henry Heth's infantry division pushed Buford's men back slowly toward Gettysburg.[40]

Reynolds's First Corps approached Gettysburg from the south along the Emmitsburg Road. They heard the booming sounds of Buford's engagement a few miles ahead. The head of Reynolds's column approached the Sherfy farm sometime before 10:00 a.m. Impressive as Buford's cavalry was when they rode past the place on the previous afternoon, the large number of Federal infantry dwarfed that spectacle.[41]

The excited Sherfy family probably cheered the troops on, knowing that a battle had erupted somewhere beyond the town. Many soldiers broke ranks to get water from wells and trampled nearby crops. According to Sherfy family lore:

> The soldier boys who marched along the Emmitsburg Road on their way to their position in the battle on July 1 drew grateful [sic] refreshment from a tub of water which grandf. [sic-Joseph] Sherfy kept replenishing with two large pails- drawing the water from the well near the house. Here two [sic] grandmother [Mary] Sherfy kept to her post baking bread & dealing it out with liberal Hand to the hungry & weary soldiers passing by the 100s.[42]

The artillery "rang out upon the still morning air" while the men of the First Corps "were slaking their thirst and filling their canteens" with water from the Wentz well just across the Emmitsburg Road. Captain Robert Walsh Mitchell, Reynolds's aide de camp, soon raced down the Emmitsburg Road with orders "to push forward as rapidly as possible" and the men swept northward almost as quickly as they arrived. The increasing danger spurred Joseph Sherfy into action. He instructed his son Raphael to take the other children to the John Trostle farm southeast of Big Round Top, "for safer environments." Their departure left only Joseph, Mary, and her mother Catherine at home.[43]

40 *OR*, 27/1: 927, 934, 1030-1031, 27/2: 317; Elmore, "Gettysburg Campaign Weather," *Gettysburg Magazine 13*, 10.

41 *OR*, 27/1: 265, 267; Hyde, *The Union Generals Speak*, 229.

42 Civilian Accounts of the Battle of Gettysburg (Sherfy), ACHS, Typescript of a handwritten account, possibly 1916, of the Sherfy farm "written by a family member."

43 "Water from Wentz's well," *Gettysburg Compiler*, January 23, 1900; Georg, "The Sherfy Fam and the Battle of Gettysburg," 8; Sherfy Claims, GNMP; Sherfey, *The Sherfey Family in the United States*, 207.

Near Emmitsburg, General Howard received early morning orders from Meade to "move the Eleventh Corps to within supporting distance of the First Corps, which was to move to Gettysburg." Howard intended to follow with one division on the Emmitsburg Road, while directing the others to keep the road clear for Reynolds's ammunition trains. Unless Reynolds objected, Howard planned to encamp near the Wentz farm and the Millerstown-Emmitsburg Road intersection. Thus, the Sherfys increasingly found themselves strategically located along the route taken to Gettysburg by a large portion of the Army of the Potomac.[44]

At Bridgeport, Sickles dispatched Captain Henry Tremain, his most trusted staff officer, to locate Reynolds and ask for instructions. Tremain approached Gettysburg after a difficult and circuitous ride, largely because the First and Eleventh Corps troops tramped northward in his path. Finally getting ahead of this mass of humanity, Tremain came to "a slight elevation" near Sherfy's orchards that offered a panoramic view of the surrounding country. Tremain noticed a road "leading off to the west," and he "did not like the idea of its not being occupied." He soon met some locals who informed him that this byway was the Millerstown Road.[45]

As he approached Reynolds near the edge of town, Tremain heard artillery thundering in the distance. He found Reynolds and his mounted contingent on the southwestern side of Cemetery Hill, along the Emmitsburg Road. The general scanned the horizon as he pondered his options. When elements of the First Corps began to arrive, Reynolds instructed the column to turn left off the Emmitsburg Road, and cut across the fields to the west in order to support Buford. Shortly thereafter, Reynolds acknowledged Tremain's presence and directed the staff officer, "Tell General Sickles I think he had better come up." With a somewhat vague understanding of the situation, Tremain turned back and rode south toward Emmitsburg in all haste.[46]

Reynolds quickly dispatched a staff officer to Meade's headquarters in Taneytown, Maryland, with a message informing his commander of his intent

44 *OR*, 27/1: 701, 27/3: 457. Howard did not receive Meade's circular of June 30 detailing the movements of each corps until 3:30 in the morning of July 1, but it is apparent that he was already aware of his supporting role because of meeting with Reynolds the previous night.

45 Tremain, *Two Days of War*, 9.

46 Ibid., 10-14; *OR*, 27/1: 265. Brigadier General James Wadsworth, commanding Reynolds's First Division, later testified, "It was a matter of momentary consultation between General Reynolds and myself whether we would go into the town or take a position in front of the town. He decided that if we went into the town the enemy would shell it and destroy it, and that we had better take a position in front of the town." See Hyde, *The Union Generals Speak*, 229.

to "fight them inch by inch." Reynolds vowed that "if driven into the town, I will barricade the streets and hold them back as long as possible." At that time, Meade was unfamiliar with Gettysburg and was considering a defensive position along Pipe Creek in Maryland. Reynolds, in pledging to "hold them back as long as possible," likely intended to buy time for Meade to concentrate the army. Unfortunately, Reynolds soon rode into the fray and was cut down by an enemy bullet. His untimely demise left a vacuum in the Union Army's field command; subordinate Major General Abner Doubleday and then General Howard increasingly committed themselves to the fields west and north of Gettysburg. The die had been cast.[47]

Captain Tremain's direct route from Gettysburg to Emmitsburg measured less than 10 miles. He arrived at Sickles's temporary headquarters and offered a summary of the state of affairs in Gettysburg. Sickles considered himself in a dilemma. The problem was, Sickles later claimed, that he had conflicting orders from Meade and Reynolds. Was Sickles to hold Emmitsburg or rush to Reynolds's support? After deliberating for several hours, at about 2:00 p.m., he sent staff officer Captain Alexander Moore to reestablish communications with Reynolds. Before Moore returned, however, messages began to arrive from Howard at Gettysburg.[48]

47 *OR*, 27/3: 458; Meade, *Life and Letters*, 2: 35-36. On July 1, Meade drafted what is known as the "Pipe Creek Circular" in which he outlined plans for the army to fall back to a line along Pipe Creek in Maryland. See *OR*, 27/3: 458 – 459. The time of morning in which the Circular was distributed is unclear, but Reynolds did not receive it before he went into action and was immediately killed. However, Reynolds and Meade had been in frequent contact on the prior day, and among other things, Reynolds was instructed to fall back to Emmitsburg if attacked. See ibid., 27/3: 420. A message from Meade's headquarters to Reynolds on the morning of July 1 further illuminates Meade's thoughts on Gettysburg. "If the enemy is concentrating to our right of Gettysburg, that point would not at first glance seem to be a proper strategic point of concentration for this army. If the enemy is concentrating in front of Gettysburg or to the left of it, the general is not sufficiently well informed of the nature of the country to judge of its character for either an offensive or defensive position." See ibid., 27/3: 460-461. Again, Reynolds may not have received that message but it seems likely that if he was attuned to Meade's thinking then he knew that Meade preferred other locations from which to fight. A modern analysis of the Pipe Creek Circular's timing suggested that it was issued shortly before noon on July 1. See Himmer, "A Matter of Time: The Issuance of the Pipe Creek Circular," *Gettysburg Magazine 46*, 7-18. Discussion of Sickles's claim that he received the Circular around mid-day on July 1 appears in the subsequent note.

48 *OR*, 51/1: 200; Tremain, *Two Days of War*, 15-18. Henry Tremain referenced *OR*, 27/3: 416-419, 422 as the source of Sickles's belief that he must continue to "hold" Emmitsburg. The last of these orders, found in ibid., 27/3: 422, was dated June 30, 12:45 p.m. and ordered the Third Corps to Emmitsburg. Sickles's critics argue that circumstances had certainly evolved such that there should have been no conflict in rushing to Gettysburg. But Sickles later compounded the confusion by claiming to be in possession of Meade's Pipe Creek Circular. Under this plan, the Third Corps was to withdraw to Middleburg, Maryland. Sickles testified

Oliver Howard had marched one division of his corps up the Emmitsburg Road in the wake of the First Corps. As he reached the Wentz house and Sherfy's peach orchard, one of Reynolds's staff officers advised, "Stop anywhere about here." This location allowed Howard several options. Depending upon circumstances, he could either cut across fields to the west, as the First Corps had done, or continue north on the Emmitsburg Road into town. He could even fall back to Emmitsburg if necessary. The din of battle quickly diverted his attention. Howard rode into Gettysburg and observed fighting to the northwest from atop a building in the town. While there, he received word that General Reynolds had fallen, and as the ranking officer on the field, he immediately assumed command. Howard established his headquarters on Cemetery Hill, high ground that commanded the southern end of town, and it was there that he posted a reserve. He deployed the majority of his Eleventh Corps into open fields north of town, and at an angle to the right and rear of the First Corps. He then sent couriers to Twelfth Corps commander Major General Henry Slocum, who was about five miles to the south at Two Taverns along the Baltimore Pike, and to Sickles at Emmitsburg.[49]

By mid-afternoon, Sickles received multiple communications from Howard imploring him to move to Gettysburg. These messages finally spurred him into action. Sickles replied to Howard at 3:15 p.m., "I shall move to Gettysburg immediately." Sickles once again sent Tremain to Gettysburg, this time to notify Howard that the Third Corps was on the way. He also wrote to Meade notifying the army commander of his planned movements. By 3:30 p.m., Birney had orders to move his division to Gettysburg "with the least possible delay." Sickles rode with Birney along the Emmitsburg Road, marking the third time that day that a Union infantry corps used that important route into Gettysburg.[50]

---

before the Joint Committee on the Conduct of the War in 1864, "On that morning I received a circular from General Meade's headquarters having reference to the occupation of a new line." See Hyde, *The Union Generals Speak*, 32-33. Gettysburg students debate whether Meade's circular could have actually been in Sickles's possession at this hour, but if Himmer's analysis (see above) is accurate then Sickles should have at least received his copy from Taneytown by the time he departed Emmitsburg after 3:00 p.m.

49 *OR*, 27/1: 696, 701; Howard, *Autobiography*, 1:408-409. Howard's other two divisions were sent off the Emmitsburg Road to Horner's Mill (modern day Barlow) and then northward along the Taneytown Road toward Gettysburg.

50 *OR*, 27/1: 530, 27/3: 463-465; Tremain, *Two Days of War*, 18; Howard, *Autobiography*, 1:413. Sickles later explained to the Joint Committee on the Conduct of the War: "My preliminary orders in going to Gettysburg [sic- Emmitsburg] were to go there and hold that position with

Reconsidering the decision to vacate Emmitsburg entirely, Sickles sent a follow-up note to Meade indicating that two brigades and two batteries would remain there to protect the approaches to the army's left flank. The brigades of Colonel Philip Regis de Trobriand and Colonel George Burling, approximately 2,700 men, along with twelve artillery pieces from the batteries of captains James Smith and George Winslow stayed behind while their comrades marched toward Gettysburg.[51]

Sickles's hesitation to abandon Emmitsburg was confirmed by a subsequent message from Meade. At 4:45 p.m., Meade had his chief of staff Dan Butterfield fire off a note to Sickles expressly stating, "The general does not wish the approaches through Emmitsburg left unguarded, as they cover our left and rear. He desires you to hold on until you shall hear from General Hancock, leaving a division at Emmitsburg, as it is a point not to be abandoned excepting in an extremity." This established the importance of Emmitsburg in Meade's evolving strategy, and likely impressed upon Sickles the need to maintain control of the road network leading to the town.[52]

While most of Sickles's Third Corps was finally in motion by mid-afternoon, Ewell and Hill's two Confederate corps overwhelmed the Federals' First and Eleventh Corps positions north and west of Gettysburg. By 4:30 p.m., the disorganized Yankees were in full retreat through the town of Gettysburg, falling back to their rallying point at Cemetery Hill. As one Wisconsin man recalled, "It was the most humiliating step I ever took," after proudly marching as saviors through those same streets only hours earlier.[53]

Major General Winfield Scott Hancock of the Second Corps also arrived on Cemetery Hill at this hour. Earlier that afternoon in Taneytown, upon learning of Reynolds's death, Meade ordered Hancock to Gettysburg directing him to "assume command of the corps there assembled." The commanding

---

my corps, as it was regarded as a very important flanking position, to cover our rear and line of communication. Then on the other hand was this order of General Meade which I had received that morning, contemplating another and entirely different line of operations. Then there was this new fact which I assumed was not known to General Meade, who was ten miles or so distant. I therefore determined to take the principal part of my corps and move as promptly as possible to Gettysburg." See *CCW*, 296-297.

51 *OR*, 27/1: 519, 570, 581, 586, 27/3: 464, 468; Busey, *Regimental Strengths and Losses at Gettysburg*, 132-133.

52 *OR*, 27/3: 466. In the same message, Meade (Butterfield) added, "General Hancock has been ordered up to assume command of the three corps --First, Eleventh, and Third. . . . Please put yourself in communication with him."

53 Pfanz, *Gettysburg Culp's Hill and Cemetery Hill*, 45.

general trusted Hancock's judgment and left much to his discretion. "If you think the ground and position there a better one to fight a battle under existing circumstances," Meade proposed, "you will so advise the general, and he will order all the troops up."[54]

Hancock reached Cemetery Hill and worked with Howard to reorganize the assembled masses at their disposal. By 5:25 p.m. Hancock established communications with Meade in Taneytown, notifying the commanding general, "We have now taken up a position in the cemetery, and cannot well be taken. It is a position, however, easily turned." He expected General Slocum's Twelfth Corps, then arriving via the Baltimore Pike, to protect the right and the Third Corps, which had not yet reached Gettysburg, to "in a degree protect our left flank."[55]

Meade sent Hancock a message of his own at 6:00 p.m. "I thought it prudent to leave a division of the Third Corps at Emmitsburg, to hold in check any force attempting to come through there. It can be ordered up to-night, if necessary." Major General John Sedgwick's Sixth Corps was also on the march and Meade pledged to push them forward through the night, if necessary. "It seems to me we have so concentrated that a battle at Gettysburg is now forced on us," he concluded, adding that "if we get up all our people, and attack with our whole force to-morrow, we ought to defeat the force the enemy has."[56]

Within the next 90 minutes, Meade ordered his remaining forces forward, including the Third Corps brigades that he earlier directed to remain in

54 *OR*, 27/3: 461; Meade, *Life and Letters*, 2:36-37. There was later a disagreement over the wording of this order. At the Joint Committee hearings in 1864, Meade submitted a version of this order that read, "If you think the ground and position there a (better) suitable one to fight a battle..." Hancock's widow and others later asserted that "better" indicated that Hancock had been given responsibility for choosing Gettysburg, while the insertion of "suitable" was afterwards designed to downplay the impression that Meade had not wanted to fight at Gettysburg and also served to minimize Hancock's part in choosing Gettysburg. See Hancock, *Reminiscences of Winfield S. Hancock*, 186-187 and Hyde, *The Union Generals Speak*, 209.

55 *OR*, 27/1: 366. Hancock was junior in rank to all of the army's corps commanders, including Howard. Generals Hancock, Howard, and Sickles were all promoted to major general dated 11/29/62, but Hancock was junior due to the date of his brigadier promotion. However, Meade had authority to place anyone he chose in command. Hancock showed Meade's orders to Howard, and this sticky matter was addressed with the understanding that the senior General Slocum would assume command when he arrived. See ibid., 27/3: 461; *CCW*, 330, 377; Hyde, *The Union Generals Speak*, 104, 166-167, 209; Pfanz, *Gettysburg: The First Day*, 337.

56 *OR*, 27/3: 466. Meade addressed this note to both Hancock and Abner Doubleday, who replaced Reynolds in command of the First Corps on that day. General Henry Halleck, Meade's superior officer, was likewise notified at 6:00 p.m. that the army was concentrating at Gettysburg. See ibid., 27/1: 71-72.

Emmitsburg. Sickles was unaware of this, but Meade addressed a dispatch at 7:30 p.m. to "Commanding Officer at Emmitsburg," instructing the troops to "join their corps at the field in the vicinity of Gettysburg with the greatest dispatch." Meade expected these men "to be up by daylight" on July 2. This indicates that Emmitsburg, which Meade earlier considered of extreme importance, became less significant due to the concentration of forces at Gettysburg.[57]

Hancock turned his attention to the army's left flank. He recognized the elevation, later known as Little Round Top, was an important piece of terrain, particularly if the army remained south of Gettysburg. As Brigadier General John Geary's division from the Twelfth Corps arrived, Hancock acknowledged that "the immediate need of a division on the left was imperative." He ordered Geary "to the high ground to the right of and near Round Top Mountain," which potentially commanded both the Emmitsburg and Taneytown roads. Geary described placing some of his troops on a "range of hills south and west of the town, which I occupied with two regiments of the First Brigade. These hills I regarded as of the utmost importance, since their possession by the enemy would give him an opportunity of enfilading our entire left wing and center with a fire which could not fail to dislodge us from our position."[58]

Protection of the Union left also fell upon John Buford's cavalry. After regrouping from the morning's actions, his men went into bivouac on the extreme left with pickets extending west along the Millerstown Road. The 6th New York Cavalry picketed in Sherfy's peach orchard throughout the night of July 1, "watching the enemy, and directing the different commands where to go."[59]

It was near 7:00 p.m. when Sickles and Birney's division approached Gettysburg along the Emmitsburg Road. A member of Captain Judson Clark's Battery B, 1st New Jersey Light Artillery, recalled meeting "panic-stricken"

57 Ibid., 27/3: 467-468; Meade, *Life and Letters*, 2: 40. In issuing orders to bring up John Sedgwick's large Sixth Corps, which had earlier been directed toward Taneytown, Meade thought they would be "largely outnumbered without your [Sedgwick's] presence." This was inaccurate but the perception of the enemy's greater strength continued to influence Meade's strategy into the following day.

58 *OR*, 27/1: 368, 825; *CCW*, 405. Geary noted that the enemy "was reported to be attempting to flank it, and cavalry were already skirmishing in front of that position." See *OR*, 27/1: 825.

59 *OR*, 27/1: 927, 934-935; Hall, *History of the Sixth New York Cavalry*, 142; Wittenberg, *John Buford at Gettysburg*, 158. For an excellent overview of Buford's protection of the Union left on the late afternoon of July 1, see Wittenberg, *John Buford at Gettysburg*, 148-156. The 6th New York Cavalry's Gettysburg battlefield monument also states that they bivouacked in the Peach Orchard that evening.

civilians fleeing in the opposite direction with their household goods and warnings that "our army was defeated; Gettysburg was sacked." Approaching from the south, the elevation upon which Sherfy's peach trees sat would have appeared fairly prominent to the men of the Third Corps. This was likely Dan Sickles's first visual impression of the Gettysburg battlefield.[60]

The morning's light rain and heavy traffic made the road "almost impassable by mud." Nevertheless, affirmed General Birney, the men marched onward with "enthusiasm and alacrity." Lieutenant John Bucklyn of Battery E, 1st Rhode Island Light Artillery, rode toward Gettysburg astride his horse and many of his men had the luxury of riding on their battery limbers. The Third Corps infantry, Bucklyn recalled, "moved so rapidly that we were frequently compelled to trot to keep pace with them." The column halted momentarily at the Peach Orchard to close up ranks. The soldiers then turned right, or eastward, and followed the narrow Wheatfield Road down into a low valley. They crossed a small stream known as Plum Run, and headed uphill toward a slight ridgeline. This modest elevation extends from Cemetery Hill, on the northern end, to Little Round Top, on the southern end, and is known as Cemetery Ridge. Before reaching the ridge itself, the troops veered to the left (north) for a few hundred yards and set up their bivouac in fields south of farmer George Weikert's small stone house.[61]

Things did not go quite as smoothly for General Humphreys's division. Perhaps this was symbolic of Humphreys's status as an outsider in the Third Corps, but his brigades under Brigadier General Joseph Carr and Colonel William Brewster departed Emmitsburg without him. Humphreys had been absent while fulfilling a direct request from Meade to examine the terrain around Emmitsburg. When he returned from this assignment at about 4:00 p.m., he discovered that Carr ordered the troops to leave without him.[62]

60 Tremain, *Two Days of War*, 22-23, 27-28, 30-32; *CCW*, 297; *OR*, 27/1: 482; Meade, *Life and Letters*, 2:56; Hanifen, *History of Battery B*, 66-67. The division vanguard arrived at the intersection of the Millerstown and Emmitsburg roads probably around 7:00 p.m., although some regimental histories (such as the 141st Pennsylvania) recorded that they did not go into camp until "about dark." See Craft, *History of the 141st Regiment Pennsylvania Volunteers*, 117. Birney reported that he arrived at 5:30; but Hancock wrote at 5:25 that the Third Corps had not yet arrived. Both Howard and Meade reported that Sickles arrived about 7:00. See *OR*, 27/1: 704.

61 Meade, *Life and Letters*, 2: 39-41; *OR*, 27/1:482, 27/3: 466-468; Hanifen, *History of Battery B*, 67; Rhode Island Historical Society, Soldiers and Sailors Historical Society Records, MSS 723, Box 2, f 6, Bucklyn, John K. "Battery E" [First Light Artillery], undated. 4 pages.

62 *OR*, 27/1: 530, 542-543, 27/3: 465; *CCW*, 388-389; Hyde, *The Union Generals Speak*, 184-185; Humphreys, *Andrew Atkinson Humphreys*, 187-188.

Shortly after departing Emmitsburg, Humphreys met two of Sickles's staff officers, each of whom directed him to march on an alternate road west of the Emmitsburg Road and to "look out for his left." Twilight was fading quickly when another courier arrived and instructed Humphreys "to take position on the left of Gettysburg." The column should have turned right, or east, upon reaching the Millerstown Road to head toward Cemetery Ridge. Yet, one of the couriers was certain that Sickles wanted the division to move by way of the Black Horse Tavern along the Fairfield Road. Such a movement was in the opposite direction of where Meade's army was concentrating. As a result, Humphreys's column veered to their left instead of their right and moved toward the Black Horse Tavern, a location that was well behind enemy lines. In what must have been an increasingly unsettling journey, Humphreys cautiously halted the column while guides went ahead to reconnoiter the area. It was fortunate that they did so. Near the Black Horse Tavern, the guides found themselves in the "immediate vicinity" of the enemy. With great stealth, they made their way back to Humphreys, and the general ordered the column to retrace its steps as quickly and quietly as possible. Luckily, the Confederates near the tavern remained unaware that the Yankees had come so close.[63]

The Second Division wearily countermarched back to the Millerstown Road, and then east toward the Emmitsburg Road. They crossed over the Emmitsburg Road and onto the Wheatfield Road, passing between the Wentz house on their left and Sherfy's peach orchard on the right. These movements demonstrated how easily these roads led toward the Union's left flank. The men finally arrived at the area where Birney's division had already gone into camp. Humphreys's men set up their bivouac just north of the Weikert farm on the gentle western slope of Cemetery Ridge. Sickles assured Humphreys that their guide had erred in taking them along such a "circuitous route." Humphreys

63 *OR*, 27/1: 531, 543; Hyde, *The Union Generals Speak*, 185-186; Brown, *History of the Third Regiment Excelsior Brigade 72nd New York Volunteer Infantry 1861-1865*, 104. The historian of the 72nd New York claimed that as a party of foragers neared the Black Horse Tavern, they could see light streaming from the windows and within "a number of rebel artillerymen eating." Thomas Rafferty of the Excelsior's 71st New York claimed that the error was discovered only because "one of the bummers of my own regiment (I must admit we had our share of them) had been straggling from the line of march on a foraging expedition" and captured a "rebel bummer, who was on the same errand." See Rafferty, "Gettysburg," *Personal Recollections of the War of the Rebellion*, 5. In still another version, Humphreys rode ahead toward the tavern with a small staff. The tavern keeper, Mr. Bream, told the party that 36 pieces of Rebel artillery had been seen on a nearby hill just before sundown, and also pointed out Lee's nearby sentinels. See Humphreys, *Andrew Atkinson Humphreys*, 188-190.

lamented, "It shows what can be done by accident." It was after midnight when most of the men bedded down for their first night at Gettysburg.[64]

While awaiting Humphreys's wayward column that evening, Sickles remained unaware that Meade had ordered the remainder of the Third Corps to come up from Emmitsburg. Sickles undoubtedly felt the strain of his awkward relationship with his new commanding officer. At 9:30 p.m., he decided it might be prudent to explain his actions and wrote, "I left two brigades and two batteries at Emmitsburg, assuming that the approaches through Emmitsburg toward our left and rear must not be uncovered." Sickles also offered Meade an assessment of the situation and with deference to the commanding general wrote, "My impression is, if I may be allowed to make a suggestion, that our left and rear are not sufficiently guarded. . . . If my corps is to remain in position here, I hope my brigades at Emmitsburg (and batteries) may be relieved and ordered to join me. This is a good battle-field."[65]

Sometime that evening, Sickles and Birney posted a skirmish line along the Emmitsburg Road, facing west toward Seminary Ridge. They were undoubtedly concerned about the men and trains of the Third Corps still in Emmitsburg and hoped to secure the road. This skirmish line also carried the benefit of protecting the army's worrisome left flank. Birney selected the 63rd Pennsylvania infantry for the assignment and posted the regiment at the fence line along the road. The left of the 63rd rested on the Millerstown crossroad and their right extended past the Sherfy house.[66]

64 *OR*, 27/1: 531, 543, 547, 549; Hyde, *The Union Generals Speak*, 185-186; Humphreys, *Andrew Atkinson Humphreys*, 191-192. Third Corps officers place their arrival time at Gettysburg from midnight to 2:30 a.m. on July 2.

65 *OR*, 27/3: 468. When testifying before the Committee on the Conduct of the War, in the spring of 1864, Sickles claimed that his note had been prompted by a difference in opinion between the assembled corps commanders as to whether they should remain at Gettysburg. He also mischaracterized the tone of his message. "I wrote to General Meade . . . begging him by all means to concentrate his army there and fight a battle, stating in my judgment that it was a good place to fight; that the position of General Howard was an admirably chosen one, and that the enemy would undoubtedly mass there in great force, and that in my judgment it would be most destructive to the morale of the army to fall back, as was apparently contemplated in his order of that morning." See *CCW*, 297.

66 *OR*, 27/1: 498. Sickles's critics sometimes point to this skirmish line as proof that Sickles was, even at this hour, already planning a forward move to the Emmitsburg Road. While that argument cannot be proven or disproven, the Official Records' reports and communications provide ample evidence that the Union high command was worried about covering approaches to their left. With troops still in Emmitsburg, and expected eventually, a picket line along the road was a logical move.

Around 11:00 p.m., still in the dark as to Meade's intentions, Sickles and Birney ordered General Charles Graham to return to Emmitsburg and assume command of those troops left behind. Sickles instructed Graham accordingly, "The position is of the utmost importance, as it covers the left and rear of this army, and must be held at all hazards." He also reminded Graham to give special care to the corps ammunition and headquarter trains. When Graham was approximately one mile from Emmitsburg, he met one of Meade's aides who delivered orders to assemble the troops and "march to Gettysburg without delay."[67]

General Meade left Taneytown for Gettysburg around 10:00 p.m., and arrived on Cemetery Hill between midnight and 1:00 a.m. On arrival, a number of officers including Sickles, Howard, Slocum, and Gouverneur Warren, the army's chief engineer, greeted Meade. The commanding general asked his subordinates, "Is this the place to fight the battle?" According to Howard, he and Slocum were conferring with Meade near the cemetery gatehouse when Sickles, who was nearby, "piped up: 'It's a good place to fight from, Sir!'" Meade was pleased that his generals were in agreement on the position's strength. "I am glad to hear you say so, gentlemen. I have already ordered the other corps commanders to concentrate here and it is too late to change."[68]

Joseph and Mary Sherfy, along with her mother, likely enjoyed little sleep that night. Buford's cavalry and Sickles's infantry were picketing on their property. Robert E. Lee's army was out there somewhere in the darkness. No one knew what the following day would bring.

67 Ibid., 27/3: 464; Charles Graham account, 16 February 1865, Participant Accounts File 5, GNMP. Graham was told to retreat toward Taneytown if unable to hold Emmitsburg.

68 CCW, p. 405; Hyde, *The Union Generals Speak*, 213; Meade, *Life and Letters*, 2:41; Hunt, "The Second Day at Gettysburg," *Battles and Leaders*, 3: 291-292; Styple, *Generals in Bronze*, 177.

Chapter 2

Commanding Ground

Despite the battlefield successes of July 1, that night was still a restless one for many members of Robert E. Lee's army. While Richard Ewell's Second Corps and A. P. Hill's Third Corps contributed to the day's victory, James Longstreet's First Corps spent most of the afternoon and evening hours on the march.

The preceding days had been long ones for Longstreet's boys. Although a select few like Henry Wentz were returning to familiar territory, the majority had never before seen Pennsylvania. "The most beautiful I ever beheld," was how Taliaferro "Tally" Simpson of the 3rd South Carolina described the countryside. He found the citizens, however, "grim and sullen." Simpson elaborated, "They have the fattest horses and the ugliest women I ever saw. . . . The gals are ugly, broad-mouthed specimens of humanity." Young men on the march had a tendency to be hungry, but Lee issued orders that prohibited plundering the locals. "Most of the soldiers seem to harbor a terrific spirit of revenge and steal and pillage in the most sinful manner," Simpson confessed in a letter to his aunt, adding that the men, "paid no more attention to them [Lee's orders] than they would to the cries of a screech owl." Simpson observed that most officers simply ignored the indifference to Lee's orders, while the farmers obliged the Rebels under fear of retribution. "The citizens are certainly hostile to our case," observed Simpson, "but in the presence of our army, they are defenceless [sic]."[1]

Longstreet's trusted chief of staff, Moxley Sorrel, concurred with Simpson's assessment of Pennsylvania women. Sorrel also added a dig at local men who were not serving in the military, such as Raphael Sherfy. "The drain of war had not here shown itself- none of the men out of this populous region seemed to have gone to the front. There was no need."[2]

On July 1, Longstreet's First Corps trudged east along the Chambersburg Pike behind Hill's Third Corps. Private John S. McNeily of the 21st Mississippi regiment described heading "for Gettysburg, of which we then had never heard." The men waited on the side of the road for hours while they were stuck behind the supply wagons from other commands. "Passing through the South mountain defiles shortly after noon, our trained ears caught the 'low and distant muttering of the cannon's opening roar' ushering in the unordered, unexpected, and fateful battle."[3]

Colonel Henry Cabell was a former attorney from Richmond, Virginia, who commanded the artillery battalion in General Lafayette McLaws's Division. "Our army was full of confidence," Cabell thought, "that some decisive blow was now to be struck that would on Northern soil result in a complete and crushing victory and thus restore peace. No one doubted it, no one thought of the possibility of failure." Cabell agreed with the observations of other Confederates and was less than impressed by the locals. "The people themselves seemed to indicate by their looks and bearing that they regarded the contest on their side hopeless."[4]

1 Everson and Simpson, *Far, Far From Home*, 250-251; Wyckoff, *A History of the 3rd South Carolina Regiment*, 163-164.

2 Sorrel, *At the Right Hand of Longstreet*, 179. Gilbert Moxley Sorrel joined Longstreet in 1861 as a volunteer aide-de-camp. By late 1862, he was serving as Longstreet's chief of staff. See Sorrel, 125, 129. Regarding the women, Sorrel noted, "The women of the country were a hard-featured lot. The population, principally Pennsylvania Dutch, are an ignorant offshoot of a certain class of Germans long settled there. Many can speak no English. A hard-working, thrifty class, with, it seems, no thought but for their big horses and barns, huge road-wagons like ships at sea, and the weekly baking, and apple-butter."

3 McNeily, "Barksdale's Mississippi Brigade at Gettysburg," 233. John Seymour McNeily's account was published by the *Mississippi Historical Society* under the byline of "J.S. McNeily." Compiled Military Service Record (CMSR) shows Private J.S. McNeely (alternately Seymour McNeely) with Company E, 21st Mississippi at Gettysburg. See CMSR, M232, Roll 27. For a biographical sketch of John S. McNeily, see *Publications of the Mississippi Historical Society*, Vol. VI (1902): 129, note 1.

4 Cabell, "A Visit to the Battle-Field of Gettysburg," Cabell family papers, 1774-1941 (Mss1 C1118 a), Virginia Historical Society, 1.

In addition to marching behind Hill's column, Longstreet's journey to Gettysburg was further delayed by Major General Edward Johnson's infantry division and supply wagons that entered into the road ahead of the First Corps. "The march was much impeded by too many troops and trains on one road. . . . [We] heard the lively fire of cannon and rifles," remembered Moxley Sorrel. Longstreet rode ahead to locate Lee's headquarters, and by late afternoon found the commanding general camped on Seminary Ridge, west of the town. According to Longstreet, he observed Lee, "watching the enemy concentrate on the opposite hill."[5]

Longstreet was quite pleased by the developments. "All we have to do is to throw our army around by their left," he suggested to his superior officer, "and we shall interpose between the Federal army and Washington." Although there were several logistical challenges to such a movement in the enemy's presence, Longstreet considered it advantageous to "get a strong position and wait, and if they fail to attack us we shall have everything in condition to move back tomorrow night in the direction of Washington, selecting beforehand a good position into which we can place our troops to receive battle next day."[6]

Lee, however, surprised Longstreet when he responded decisively to the contrary. "No, the enemy is there, and I am going to attack him there." Lee rejected reminders of "our original plans" from Longstreet, who also noticed that the lack of communication from General Stuart's cavalry caused Lee considerable anxiety. Seeing that Lee was "in no frame of mind to listen to further argument," Longstreet deferred the matter until the following morning.[7]

5 Sorrel, *At the Right Hand of Longstreet*, 165; Longstreet, "Lee's Right Wing at Gettysburg," *Battles and Leaders*, 3: 339.

6 Longstreet, "Lee's Right Wing at Gettysburg," *Battles and Leaders*, 3: 339-340. Longstreet wrote in *Battles and Leaders* (3: 340) that this meeting occurred about 5:00 p.m. Longstreet's historical critics note that we primarily only have Longstreet's version of this conversation. However, Lee's military secretary Armistead Long, *Memoirs of Robert E. Lee*, 277, said that the conversation occurred in his presence. "Longstreet gave it as his opinion that the best plan would be to turn Meade's left flank and force him back to the neighborhood of Pipeclay Creek. To this General Lee objected, and pronounced it impracticable under the circumstances." According to Long, Lee then ordered Long to reconnoiter the Federal position, after which Lee allegedly told both Longstreet and Hill, "Gentlemen, we will attack the enemy in the morning as early as practicable."

7 Longstreet, "Lee's Right Wing at Gettysburg," *Battles and Leaders*, 3: 339-340. A slightly different Lee emerges in Longstreet's memoirs, likely the reflection of Longstreet's 1890s frustration with years of attacks from Lee's supporters. In this later version, Longstreet portrayed a Lee who punctuated his remarks by "striking the air with his closed hand." In

Longstreet and his staff departed Lee's headquarters sometime after dark. They rode west toward Marsh Creek to make camp while Confederate men and materiel continued to clog the Chambersburg Pike leading into Gettysburg. British military observer Arthur Fremantle was present and found "the universal feeling in the army was one of profound contempt for an enemy whom they have beaten so constantly, and under so many disadvantages." Only Longstreet appeared to counter the jubilation with a dose of reality. That evening at dinner, Fremantle recorded, "General Longstreet spoke of the enemy's position as being 'very formidable'. He also said that they [the enemy] would doubtless intrench [sic] themselves strongly during the night."[8]

Later that evening, after Longstreet's departure, Lee considered launching an offensive against the enemy's right at Culp's and Cemetery hills. The Federals had not yet secured either position and Lee sensed an opportunity to press his advantage. However, Ewell and his division commanders, particularly Major General Jubal Early, convinced Lee that the terrain in their front did not favor such an assault.[9]

Lee then proposed contracting his extended lines by drawing Ewell's corps back toward the west of Gettysburg. Ewell, Early, and company also rejected this plan as they did not want to abandon the hard-fought ground their men had already gained in the town. They argued instead, that the best chance for success was an attack against the Federal left flank. Later that night, Lee told Ewell again that he wanted to move the Second Corps away from the Federals' right. Once again, Ewell persuaded Lee to leave him in position. The lack of consensus among his subordinates undoubtedly concerned Lee, but with the wheels already in motion, plans for an attack on Meade's left took shape as July 2 dawned.

The Confederate high command resumed deliberations after a few hours of sleep. "The stars were shining brightly on the morning of the 2nd when I reported to General Lee's head-quarters and asked for orders," Longstreet later wrote. His post-war critics, including Confederate generals William N.

From Manassas to Appomattox, 357-359, Longstreet also specifically refers to Lee's "impatience," "his nervous condition," and "his uneven temper."

8 Fremantle, *Three Months in the Southern States*, 255-256. See Freeman, *Lee's Lieutenants*, 3: 110, including notes 19-20, for a discussion around the time of Longstreet's departure.

9 Subsequent events essentially proved this argument valid, particularly because the terrain north and east of Gettysburg provided minimal opportunities for Confederate artillery to support any large-scale infantry assaults.

Pendleton and Jubal Early, later made false accusations that Longstreet was expected to attack at sunrise. But as Longstreet noted correctly, the fact that Lee was still consulting with his subordinates at this hour indicated that the commanding general was "was not ready with his plans."[10]

There was uncertainty over how far south along Cemetery Ridge the Federal position extended, and whether Union troops occupied the heights now known as Big Round Top and Little Round Top. Sickles's Third Corps was bivouacked in the low ground on the southern end of Cemetery Ridge. However, the Emmitsburg Road's ridgeline blocked Lee's view of that sector. This ridge was situated between, and roughly parallel to, Seminary and Cemetery ridges. In order to learn more about the Federal position, Lee sent out several reconnaissance parties. Captain Samuel Johnston, an engineer on Lee's staff, led the most significant of these expeditions. According to Johnston, Lee summoned him at about daybreak and his small party of three or four departed around 4:00 a.m.[11]

Meanwhile, Longstreet's infantry began to approach Gettysburg. The lead division under Major General John Bell Hood consisted of hard-hitting infantry regiments from Texas, Alabama, Arkansas, and Georgia. Hood arrived after daybreak and joined Lee, Longstreet, and Hill in consultation while his men pulled off the road to rest. Hood remembered Lee as "seemingly anxious" for Longstreet to attack. "The enemy is here and if we do not whip him," Lee remarked to Hood, "he will whip us." Longstreet remained hesitant, however, in part because one of his divisions, that of Major General George Pickett, remained several hours from Gettysburg. "The General [Lee] is a little nervous this morning," Longstreet told Hood, "he wishes me to attack; I do not wish to do so without Pickett. I never like to go into battle with one boot off."[12]

10 Longstreet, *From Manassas to Appomattox*, 362. The so-called "sunrise attack" has been discredited by most modern Gettysburg historians, and a debate on the topic is not required here. It is worthy, however, to consider whether Lee ultimately hoped for an attack to occur earlier in the day than it actually did.

11 Samuel Johnston to Fitzhugh Lee, February 11, 1878; Johnston to Lafayette McLaws, June 27, 1892. Copies of both letters are on file at GNMP; Hyde, "Did You Get There?"*Gettysburg Magazine* 29, 86-88. Armistead Long and William N. Pendleton performed other reconnaissance for the Confederates. All of these missions contributed toward Lee's decision to attack Meade's left. See Pfanz, *Gettysburg: The Second Day*, 105-107.

12 "Letter From General John B. Hood," *SHSP*, 4: 147-148; Fremantle, *Three Months in the Southern States*, 257. Arthur Fremantle was in a nearby tree and observed, "Just below us were seated Generals Lee, Hill, Longstreet, and Hood, in consultation—the two latter assisting their deliberations by the truly American custom of whittling sticks."

Major General Lafayette McLaws
LOC

General Lafayette McLaws commanded Longstreet's other available division. The Georgia native was a stout man with a round face and full beard. McLaws and Longstreet were long-time colleagues. Both men were members of the West Point Class of 1842, where neither distinguished themselves academically. McLaws actually finished higher in the class, graduating 48th to Longstreet's 54th. While ensuing events hurt their relationship, McLaws confided to his wife in 1862 that Longstreet "stands high as a very gallant soldier." McLaws thought of Longstreet as more than his commanding officer; he considered him an "old friend."[13]

McLaws rose to the rank of major general early in the war, but the Maryland and Chancellorsville campaigns earned him a reputation for being slow of movement. Moxley Sorrel described McLaws as "an officer of much experience and most careful. Fond of detail, his command was in excellent condition, and his ground and position well examined and reconnoitered; not brilliant in the field or quick in movement there or elsewhere, he could always be counted on and had secured the entire confidence of his officers and men."[14] When Lee reorganized the army following Stonewall Jackson's death, McLaws was disappointed to be passed over for corps command by the junior A. P. Hill. Longstreet blamed this on Virginia nepotism, but acknowledged that McLaws's lack of "vigorous health" also influenced the decision.[15]

13 Oeffinger, *A Soldier's General*, 139.

14 Tagg, *The Generals of Gettysburg*, 204, 209-211; Wert, *General James Longstreet*, 28, 209; Sorrel, *At the Right Hand of Longstreet*, 135.

15 Longstreet, "Lee's Invasion of Pennsylvania," *Battles and Leaders*, 3: 245; Piston, *Lee's Tarnished Lieutenant*, 38-40; Oeffinger, *A Soldier's General*, 38.

McLaws's division consisted of four experienced infantry brigades and artillery that numbered roughly 7,100 men. The largest brigade was that of Brigadier General Joseph Kershaw, who led five regiments and a battalion from South Carolina. Fiery Brigadier General William Barksdale commanded four experienced Mississippi units. Brigadier General William Wofford had five Georgia regiments and an attached battalion of sharpshooters. The smallest brigade was the four Georgia regiments under Brigadier General Paul Semmes. As with all Confederate infantry divisions, an artillery battalion supported McLaws. Four batteries of 16 guns were under Colonel Henry Cabell.[16]

McLaws arrived on Seminary Ridge while Lee and Longstreet were still conferring. Lee was sitting on a fallen tree with a map beside him when McLaws reported. The commanding general pointed to the Emmitsburg Road on the map and instructed McLaws, "General, I wish you to place your division across this road, and I wish you to get there if possible without being seen by the enemy." He wanted McLaws to position his men perpendicular to the road, just south Sherfy's peach orchard. Lee asked, "Can you get there?" Since McLaws had just arrived, he knew nothing of the ground and requested permission to reconnoiter. Lee replied that Captain Johnston had already moved out to reconnoiter the ground. McLaws suggested that he join Johnston, but Longstreet, pacing nearby, refused to allow the Georgian to leave his division. Longstreet then pointed to the map and directed McLaws to place his division parallel to the Emmitsburg Road, but Lee voiced his disagreement. "No, General, I wish it placed just perpendicular to that," he insisted, "just the opposite" of the position designated by Longstreet. McLaws promptly reiterated his request to accompany Johnston, but Longstreet again forbade it. Lee said nothing more, and McLaws left the meeting to rejoin his command. "General Longstreet appeared as if he was irritated and annoyed," McLaws recalled, "but the cause I did not ask."[17]

Apparently, McLaws did conduct a little reconnaissance of his own while he awaited additional instruction and conditions convinced him that "my command could reach the point indicated by General Lee, in a half hour, without being seen. I then went back to the head of my column and sat on my horse and saw in the distance the enemy coming, hour after hour, on to

16 Floyd, *Commanders and Casualties*, 47-50.

17 McLaws, "Gettysburg," *SHSP*, 4: 68-69; Sorrel, *At the Right Hand of Longstreet*, 167. As noted previously, the Confederates were likely referring to the 1858 Adams County map which designated "Peach Orchard" as a specific landmark on the Emmitsburg Road.

the battle ground." Private McNeily of the 21st Mississippi later wrote, "We halted here an hour or more until the plan of battle was decided, whence we looked across the country a mile or so to Cemetery Ridge, where we could see outlines of the enemy's forces. It seemed, as it was, soon to prove, impregnable to a front attack."[18]

Around that time, Longstreet's Artillery Reserve began to arrive on the field. Colonel James Walton commanded the two attached battalions of 10 batteries. Walton was born in New Jersey, served in the Mexican War, and worked in New Orleans as a grocer before the Civil War. He was also a few months shy of his 50th birthday, and his most energetic days were likely behind him. Walton received orders from First Corps headquarters on the prior evening "to come on tonight" with his battalions under Colonel Edward Porter Alexander and Major Benjamin Eshleman. Due to ongoing delays from trains belonging to Edward Johnson's division, Walton's men did not start on the road until 2:30 a.m. and, after a relatively easy march, reached Gettysburg at sunrise. They halted in an open field off of the Chambersburg Pike, awaited further instructions, and perhaps tried to get some sleep.[19]

As the leader of one of the Artillery Reserve battalions under Walton, Colonel Edward Porter Alexander was highly regarded by Longstreet for his "unusual promptness, sagacity, and intelligence." The 28-year-old Georgian came from a wealthy family and graduated third in his West Point class of 1857. After graduation, he received his commission as an engineer, taught at West Point, and assisted in developing the "wig-wag" signal flag method used by both armies. In fact, Alexander became the first to use this signal flag system in combat at First Manassas in July 1861. He served as an engineer, signal officer, and chief of ordnance early in the war before joining Longstreet's artillery battalion in the fall of 1862. Alexander's artillery played an important part in Longstreet's successful defense of Marye's Heights at Fredericksburg.[20]

Alexander arrived at Gettysburg on the morning of July 2 with his battalion of six batteries. He reported to Lee and Longstreet and promptly received

18 McLaws, "Gettysburg," *SHSP*, 4: 69; McNeily, "Barksdale's Mississippi Brigade at Gettysburg," 233-234.

19 Krick, *Staff Officers in Gray*, 295; "Letter From Colonel J. B. Walton," *SHSP*, 5: 47-50; Sorrel, *At the Right Hand of Longstreet*, 77.

20 Longstreet, "Letter from General Longstreet," *SHSP*, 5: 52; Alexander, *Military Memoirs*, 3-4, 14-16, 30-32, 280, 309-311.

word that "we were to attack the enemy's left flank." He received instructions to take command of his own battalion, along with Cabell's and Major Mathis Henry's from Hood's Division. Major Eshleman's Battalion, more popularly known as the "Washington Artillery," remained in reserve.[21]

Alexander was advised to avoid exposing his movements to the enemy's signal station "on Round Top mountain." He must have been acutely aware of this danger due to his previous experience as a signal officer, yet having just arrived, Alexander knew nothing else of the situation. Nonetheless, he did not get the impression that "there was any unnecessary delay going on." Alexander was a young colonel undoubtedly hoping to impress his superior officers. Accordingly, he focused on completing his assignment "to reconnoiter the flank to be attacked, and choose my own positions and means of reaching them. This duty occupied me, according to the best of my recollection, one or two hours."[22]

Captain Johnston meanwhile completed his reconnaissance mission. As he recalled afterwards, his party traveled the same general route that Longstreet took later that afternoon and "got up on the slopes of Round Top, where I had a commanding view." When Johnston eventually turned back toward Confederate lines, several Union cavalry troopers rode slowly along the Emmitsburg Road and across his path, thus delaying his return. When he finally arrived on Seminary Ridge, Johnston found Lee was in conference with several subordinates. The captain reported his finding and sketched his route on Lee's map. Lee expressed surprise that Johnston had gotten so far and asked him to confirm that he had indeed reached Round Top. Longstreet and Hill left the meeting while Johnston and Lee continued to discuss the topography. Lee then instructed Johnston to join Longstreet, to which the engineer understood that he was to aid Longstreet "in any way I could." Johnston thought it about

21 Alexander, "Letter from General E. P. Alexander," *SHSP*, 4: 101-102. Alexander's *SHSP* letter estimated they reached the field "about 8 or 9 A.M." Also see Alexander, "The Great Charge and Artillery Fighting at Gettysburg," *Battles and Leaders*, 3: 358; Alexander, *Military Memoirs*, 390-391. Walton strongly denied post-war inferences that Alexander was serving as the de-facto commander of the First Corps artillery at Gettysburg. See "Letter From Colonel J. B. Walton," *SHSP*, 5: 47-53 including a reply from Longstreet. While acknowledging his high regard for Alexander, Longstreet told the senior Walton, "I beg to assure you that the idea of interfering with your prerogatives, or authority or fitness for your position, did not enter my mind. Your duties were such as to take you away from headquarters, and often render it difficult to find you just at the right moment, particularly when the entire corps was not together, as was the case on the 2d." See "Letter from General Longstreet," *SHSP*, 5: 52.

22 Alexander, "Letter From General E. P. Alexander," *SHSP*, 4: 101-102.

8:00 a.m. when his conference with Lee ended, and 9:00 a.m. when he joined Longstreet.[23]

Johnston's reconnaissance has confounded historians since 1863. Did he reach the summit of one of the Round Tops and accurately report what he saw? How did Johnston bypass John Buford's Federal cavalry along the Emmitsburg and Millerstown roads? How did he not see Sickles's Third Corps bivouacked in the lower ground north of Little Round Top? These questions were never fully resolved, but where Johnston actually went is less important than what he told Lee. Johnston did not know where the Federal left flank was, but he informed Lee where it was not. Meade's line appeared to end short of the imposing Round Tops. At this hour, Johnston's information was essentially accurate. However, several hours later, when Longstreet's attack finally commenced, the information proved outdated.[24]

With options for attack against the enemy right somewhat limited, it became apparent to Lee that his best opportunity was to strike the Federal left. The Confederate plan of attack for July 2 finally developed. Lee described the objectives in his July 31, 1863, report:

> The enemy held a high and commanding ridge, along which he had massed a large amount of artillery. General Ewell occupied the left of our line, General Hill the center, and General Longstreet the right. In front of General Longstreet the enemy held a position from which, if he could be driven, it was thought our artillery could be used to advantage in assailing the more elevated ground beyond, and thus enable us to reach the crest of the ridge. That officer was directed to endeavor to carry this position, while General Ewell attacked directly the high ground on the enemy's right, which had already been partially fortified. General Hill was instructed to threaten the center of the Federal line, in order to prevent re-enforcements being sent to either wing, and to avail himself of any opportunity that might present itself to attack.[25]

23 Samuel Johnston to Fitzhugh Lee, February 11, 1878; Johnston to Lafayette McLaws, June 27, 1892. Both copies on file at GNMP.

24 Hyde, "Did you get There?" *Gettysburg Magazine 29*, 86-91. Hyde speculated that Johnston reached Big Round Top around 5:30 a.m., and given the time of his trip, it was actually plausible that Johnston missed seeing or hearing Federal troops in that locale. Hyde also believed that Johnston could have easily slipped through Buford's cavalry line, which might have stretched 2700–2800 exhausted men for as long as nine miles. Pfanz, *Gettysburg: The Second Day,* 106-107, seems to have accepted Johnston reached Little Round Top but inexplicably "failed to detect" Federal troops in the area.

25 *OR,* 272/2: 308.

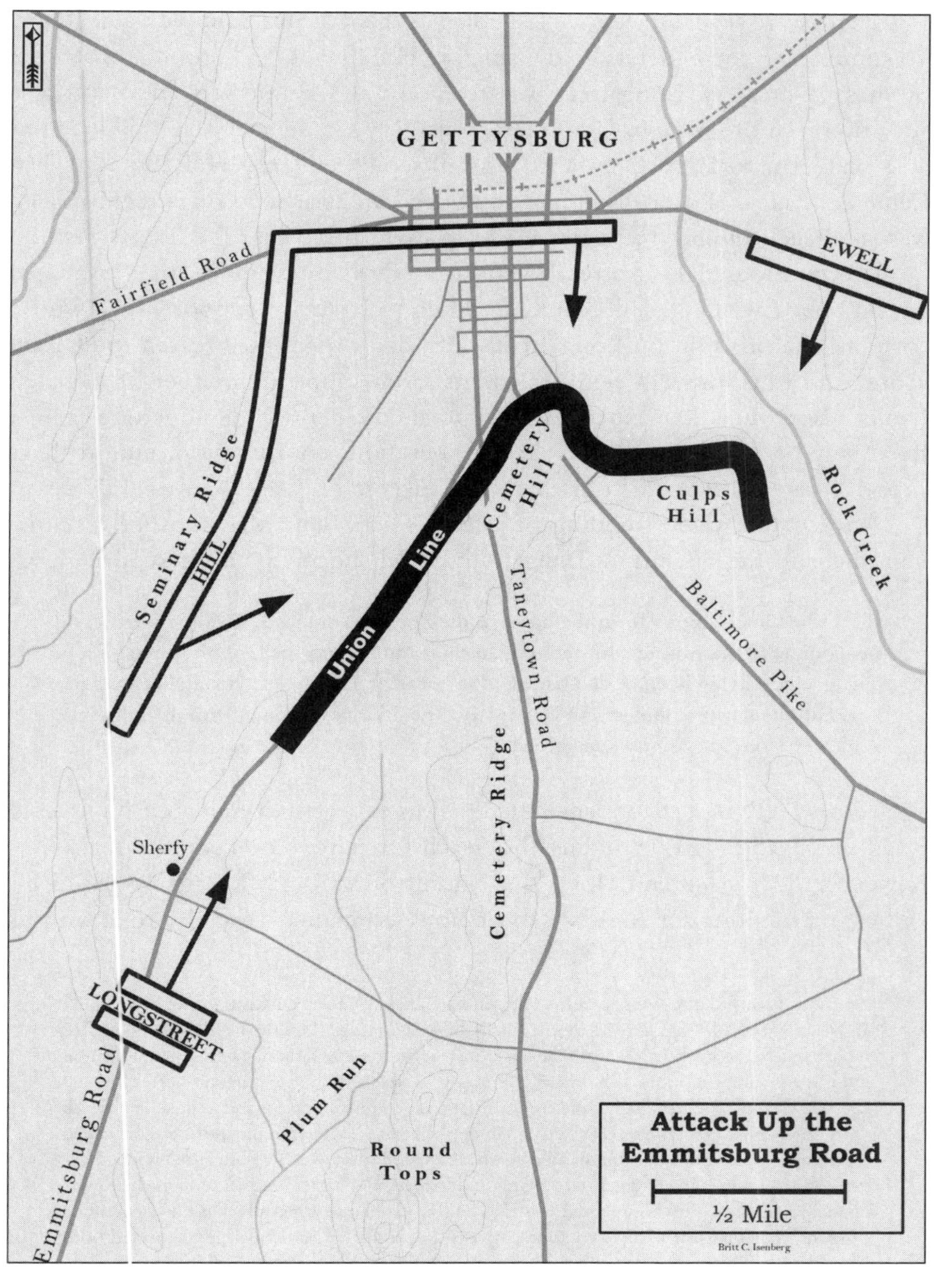

Representation of Lee's original attack plan based on an inaccurate understanding of the Union left flank.

There were several facets to Lee's plan as this was not a simple flank attack. To summarize, the Federals held Cemetery Hill; the "high" ground, protected by massed artillery. Longstreet was to attack the Union left and capture a specific piece of ground. Confederate artillery would then use this location as a platform to support infantry assaults on Cemetery Hill and northern Cemetery Ridge. The position Lee described, and directed Longstreet to carry, was the Peach Orchard and Emmitsburg Road ridge near the Sherfy farm.

Lee considered Longstreet's action on the Union left as the "principal attack," but Ewell and Hill would act in concert and in support. Hill, whose corps held a position on Longstreet's left, had orders to threaten the Union center and thus, prevent reinforcements from supporting either of Meade's flanks. Meanwhile, Lee expected Ewell to simultaneously demonstrate against the Army of the Potomac's right. Cooperation, coordination, and artillery support were all elements critical to the success of Lee's plan for July 2.[26]

An accurate understanding of Meade's left flank was another essential ingredient to the operation. Longstreet noted succinctly in his report:

> I received instructions from the commanding general to move, with the portion of my command that was up, around to gain the Emmitsburg road, on the enemy's left. The enemy, having been driven back by the corps of Lieutenant-Generals Ewell and A.P. Hill the day previous, had taken a strong position, extending from the hill at the cemetery along the Emmitsburg road.[27]

Longstreet's report confirmed that he was expected to gain the Emmitsburg Road on Meade's left, including the Peach Orchard. The Federals' main line, however, did not extend along the Emmitsburg Road. Lee likely based his earlier instructions for McLaws to deploy perpendicular to the road on this

26 Was Ewell to attack or merely "demonstrate" against the Federal right on Culp's Hill and Cemetery Hill? Lee's July 31 report stated, "Ewell attacked directly the high ground." Lee reported in January 1864, "General Ewell was instructed to make a simultaneous demonstration upon the enemy's right, to be converted into a real attack should opportunity offer." Ewell wrote, "Meantime orders had come from the general commanding for me to delay my attack until I heard General Longstreet's guns open on the right. . . . Early in the morning, I received a communication from the commanding general, the tenor of which was that he intended the main attack to be made by the First Corps, on our right, and wished me, as soon as their guns opened, to make a diversion in their favor, to be converted into a real attack if an opportunity offered." Whether intended as an attack or only a demonstration, Lee clearly expected both Ewell and Hill to be simultaneously active enough in order to prevent Meade from sending reinforcements against Longstreet. Battle students can judge for themselves whether Ewell and Hill were successful in that regard. *OR*, 27/2: 308, 318-319, 446.

27 *OR*, 27/2: 358. Longstreet's report indicated that he received these orders before Evander Law's brigade arrived, i.e. in the morning.

faulty assumption. As influential Southern historian Douglas Southall Freeman later asserted, "The major assumption of this plan was that the Federal line on Cemetery Ridge was short." This basic flaw disrupted much of Longstreet's attack when discovered later in the afternoon. However, the Peach Orchard remained a primary objective even after the Confederates realized the miscalculation. Any stated intention to capture Little Round Top was notably absent.[28]

Longstreet insisted that he did not receive his attack orders until 11:00 a.m. and intentionally delayed movement until after 12:00 p.m. to await the arrival of Brigadier General Evander Law's Brigade, still on the march toward Gettysburg. The ensuing outcome validated Longstreet's fear "that my force was too weak to venture to make an attack." Nevertheless, Law's Brigade arrived around noon and, after completing necessary preparations, Longstreet's two divisions and artillery began their march toward the Army of the Potomac's left flank. A long afternoon lay ahead of them.[29]

Longstreet's desire to wait for Law's Brigade was logical, but staff officer Moxley Sorrel saw something different in Lee's "Old Warhorse" at Gettysburg. Sorrel later offered his impressions:

> As Longstreet was not to be made willing and Lee refused to change or could not change, the former failed to conceal some anger. There was apparent apathy in his movements. They lacked the fire and point of his usual bearing on the battlefield. His plans may have been better than Lee's, but it was too late to alter them with the

28 Freeman, *Lee's Lieutenants*, 3: 118. To complicate this further, Lee's January 1864 report described the position of the Federal army in the afternoon, not when the morning plans were formulated. "The enemy occupied a strong position, with his right upon two commanding elevations adjacent to each other, one southeast and the other, known as Cemetery Hill, immediately south of the town, which lay at its base. His line extended thence upon the high ground along the Emmitsburg road, with a steep ridge in rear, which was also occupied." See *OR*, 27/2: 318. Freeman was correct that the Federal line was thought to be too short. Freeman also thought that Lee expected the Yankee left to end on northern Cemetery Ridge, but the "roll of the field" concealed troops in the low ground north of Little Round Top from Seminary Ridge. Many field interpretations at Gettysburg National Military Park adopt this scenario and propose that Lee thought the Federal left ended in the vicinity of the modern Pennsylvania State Memorial. This is a logical assumption and is supportable by the terrain, but it should be pointed out that neither Lee nor Longstreet's reports clearly support this description.

29 Longstreet, "Lee's Right Wing at Gettysburg," *Battles and Leaders*, 3: 340; *OR*, 27/2: 358. For insight regarding the timing of Lee's attack orders to Longstreet, his visit to Ewell, and whether or not Longstreet's lack of movement at this hour agitated the commanding general see, Longstreet, *From Manassas to Appomattox*, 363-365; Freeman, *Lee's Lieutenants*, 3: 114-115; Pfanz, *Gettysburg: The Second Day*, 111-113.

> troops ready to open fire on each other. Ewell on the left, A.P. Hill and Longstreet on the right, seemed never able to work together.[30]

Across the field, George Meade began his fifth day in command of the Army of the Potomac. The general busied himself by positioning troops along the ridges and fields south of Gettysburg. Having committed to Cemetery Hill, Meade and his lieutenants worked on strengthening their flanks and vital points that lay in between. By 8:00 a.m., Hancock's Second Corps and Major General George Sykes's Fifth Corps had arrived. This placed six of the army's seven infantry corps at Gettysburg. Major General John Sedgwick's large Sixth Corps was still on a forced march from Manchester, Maryland, and expected to arrive later in the afternoon.

Meade sent Slocum's Twelfth Corps to defend the right, at Culp's Hill. The battered Eleventh and First Corps filled in across Cemetery Hill and opposite the town. Hancock's Second Corps was behind Cemetery Hill's left and extended south along Cemetery Ridge for approximately one mile. Their position faced the Emmitsburg Road, but was posted several hundred yards east of it. Meade expected the Third Corps to continue the Cemetery Ridge line to Hancock's left, with Sykes's Fifth Corps in reserve. The Fifth Corps initially massed near Rock Creek on the Baltimore Pike to support the Twelfth Corps. "While thus situated," Sykes reported, "I was directed to support the Third Corps, General Sickles commanding, with a brigade, should it be required." The army's artillery reserve also arrived around 11:00 a.m. and parked near the Taneytown Road in the rear of Cemetery Hill.[31]

Meade's Gettysburg position began to resemble the shape of a horseshoe, although it was more commonly remembered as a fishhook. The line's curvature west from Culp's Hill to Cemetery Hill and then south along Cemetery Ridge gave Meade the benefit of interior lines, thus facilitating tactical troop movements and shortening lines of communications. Lee's smaller army held exterior lines and the Confederate general at an operational disadvantage. Simply put, Meade's 90,000-plus man army had more men to cover a smaller space than Lee's approximately 70,000 men. Meade also had natural defensive barriers to protect against the enemy's approach: Culp's Hill, Wolf's Hill, and

30 Sorrel, *At the Right Hand of Longstreet*, 167.

31 *OR*, 27/1: 115- 116, 592-593, 600; Hunt, "The Second Day at Gettysburg," *Battles and Leaders*, 3: 296; Meade, *Life and Letters*, 2: 63-64; Bigelow, *The Peach Orchard*, 51; Coddington, *The Gettysburg Campaign*, 332-333. Only two of Sykes's divisions, under Brigadier General James Barnes and Brigadier General Romeyn Ayres, were arriving near this hour. The third under Brigadier General Samuel Crawford did not reach Gettysburg for several more hours.

Rock Creek on the right; Cemetery Hill immediately south of the town; and the Round Tops further south on Cemetery Ridge.

General John Buford's cavalry division, including Lieutenant John Calef's artillery battery, remained on the Federal left during these early morning hours. Buford reported that his pickets extended "almost to Fairfield." Colonel Thomas Devin, one of Buford's brigade commanders, likewise noted that he was "engaged reconnoitering in rear of the enemy's right," indicating that his men patrolled along the Millerstown Road. The intersection near the Sherfy farm remained vital. The precise locations of Buford's individual regiments remain speculative, but the 6th New York Cavalry bivouacked in Sherfy's orchard and a detachment from the 9th New York Cavalry patrolled the Millerstown Road. Regardless of their exact positions, the reports from cavalry officers do not reflect the acquisition of any significant intelligence during the morning of July 2. Buford's men also missed Captain Johnston's party when it passed through the neighborhood.[32]

Brigadier General Henry Hunt, the Army of the Potomac's chief of artillery, remembered the morning as a "busy and in some respects an anxious one; it was believed that the whole Confederate army was assembled, that it was equal if not superior to our own in numbers, and that the battle would commence before our troops were up." Some demonstrations opposite the Federal right, along with the relatively short distance between Confederates in the town and Cemetery Hill, kept Meade's attention focused in that direction. He briefly entertained the idea of launching an offensive from the right, but both Slocum and Warren viewed the terrain unfavorably and advised against the idea. Meade postponed further offensive considerations until the enemy's intentions were more clearly developed.[33]

32 *OR*, 27/1: 914-915, 927-928, 939, 1032; 6th New York Cavalry battlefield monument inscription, GNMP; Murray, *E.P Alexander and the Artillery Action in the Peach Orchard*, 45; Wittenberg, *The Devil's to Pay*, 163-165. Although there were later accounts that the 9th New York discovered Longstreet's approach, no significant intelligence is reflected in the contemporary reports. See Pfanz, *Gettysburg: The Second Day*, 88-89, 485 (n. 53) for commentary.

33 Hyde, *The Union Generals Speak*, 106, 167; Hunt, "The Second Day at Gettysburg," *Battles and Leaders*, 3: 297. "Early in the morning it had been my intention," Meade later described, "as soon as the Sixth Corps arrived on the ground . . . to make a vigorous attack from our extreme right upon the enemy's left." The attack column would have included Slocum's Twelfth Corps, along with the Fifth and Sixth Corps. But Slocum "reported that the character of the ground in front was unfavorable to making an attack," and combined with the fact that the Sixth Corps would not arrive until early afternoon, Meade "abandoned my intention to make an attack from my right." General Warren likewise was ordered to reconnoiter the Union

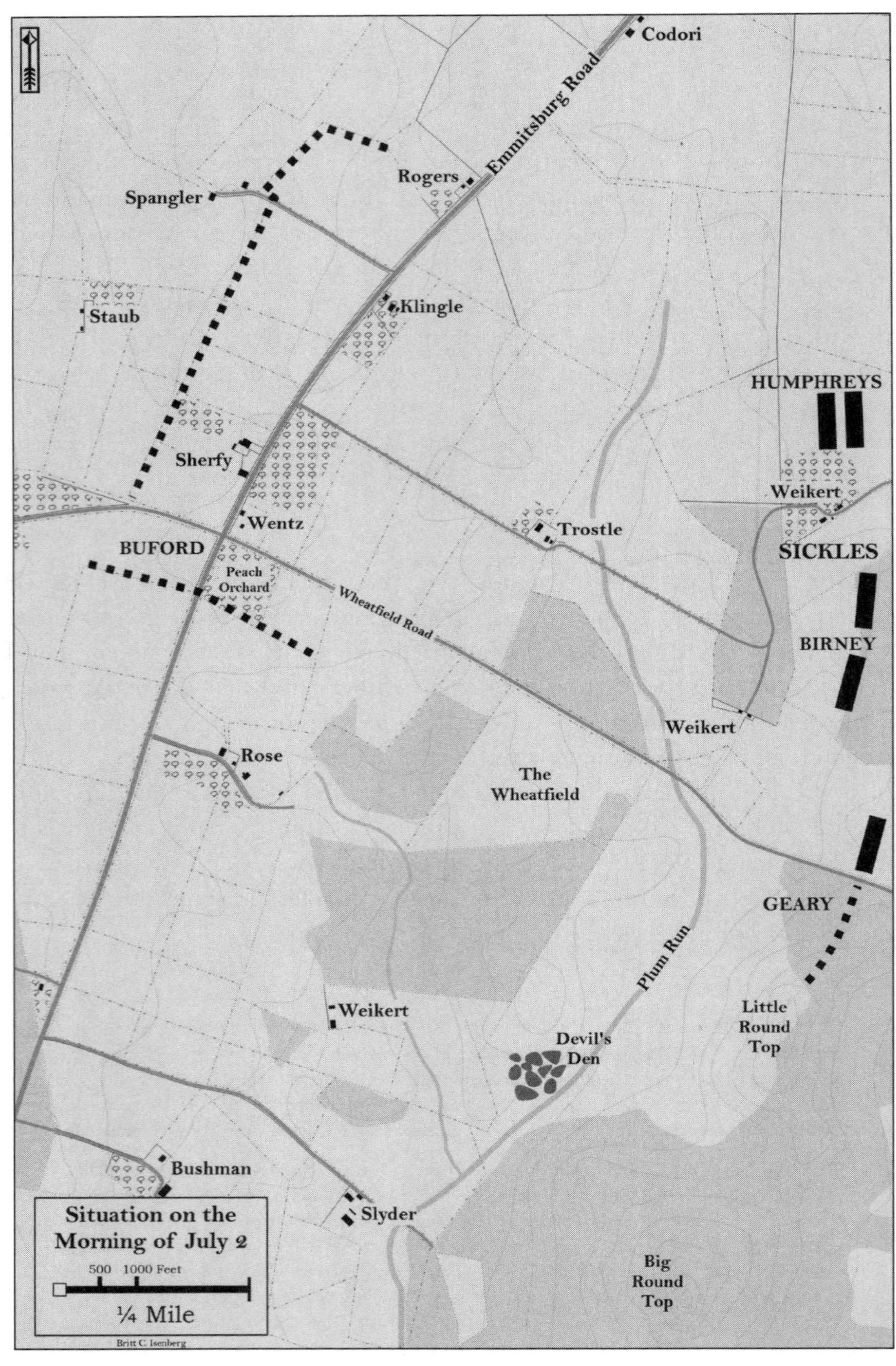
Codori
Emmitsburg Road
Rogers
Spangler
Klingle
Staub
HUMPHREYS
Sherfy
Weikert
Wentz
Trostle
BUFORD
SICKLES
Peach Orchard
Wheatfield Road
BIRNEY
Weikert
Rose
The Wheatfield
GEARY
Plum Run
Weikert
Little Round Top
Devil's Den
Bushman
Situation on the Morning of July 2
500 1000 Feet
¼ Mile
Slyder
Big Round Top
Britt C. Isenberg

Looking southwest from the area of Birney's encampment on the night of July 1 toward the Wheatfield Road. Note large rocks in foreground and wooded ridge in background that would have impeded artillery dispositions.

Photo by Authors

Sickles's Third Corps remained bivouacked near Cemetery Ridge, on low ground north of the Round Tops. The stone farmhouse of George Weikert, which still stands on the field today, acted as something of a divider between Birney's and Humphreys's divisions. Birney's two present brigades, one under Charles Graham and the other under Brigadier General J.H. Hobart Ward, were in the rocky and wooded fields south of Weikert's. Humphreys's brigades, commanded by General Joseph Carr and Colonel William Brewster, were north of Weikert's along open ground that sloped gently toward the west. Skirmishers stood along the Emmitsburg Road ridge several hundred yards in advance of the brigades. None of Sickles's regiments occupied Little Round Top to their left.[34]

right, but Warren also viewed the terrain unfavorably and "I advised General Meade not to attack in that direction."

34 Craft, *History of the 141st Regiment Pennsylvania Volunteers*, 117-118; Scott, *History of the One Hundred and Fifth Regiment of Pennsylvania Volunteers*, 82.

Sickles's staff officer Henry Tremain wrote that they "had simply gone into bivouac, pretty much in the gloom of the evening" of July 1 and "neither the batteries nor the infantry were occupying any special posts selected for defense or offense. That awaited the light, and was now to be done." Many of the men "were in large part reclining where they had spent the night; and their location proved to be on low ground, easily commanded by the land in front, and running off to the left."[35]

Upon examination of the field, the assembled officers concluded that the terrain along Birney's front was poor ground for the placement of troops and artillery. Major Thomas Rafferty of the 71st New York called the position "so faulty that it was impossible to occupy with any prospect of being able to hold it." This low ground "was quite springy and marshy, and was covered thickly with a growth of stunted bushes . . . and masked by the woods and the broken and rocky ground in our front, affording most excellent positions and covers for the rebels to take possession of without risk, and attack us with every advantage in their favor."[36]

Sickles's officers also noted that the Emmitsburg Road ridge dominated the position and thought that the Third Corps could not hold their section of the line if the Confederates placed artillery on that road. The Emmitsburg Road ridge ran parallel to Cemetery Ridge at an angle ranging between 1,100 – 1,400 yards distant and nearly 30 – 70 feet higher at some points. Early that morning, Captain George Randolph, chief of the Third Corps artillery brigade, placed two batteries along Birney's line "to the base of" Little Round Top. "The positions of both were low," Randolph reported, "unprotected, and commanded by the ridge along which runs the road from Emmitsburg to Gettysburg."[37]

Although the intervening Houck's Ridge and adjacent woodlots blocked direct observation of the Emmitsburg Road from Birney's immediate area, the ridge upon which the road ran became much more prominent along Humphreys's front. The flat elevation of the Peach Orchard was well within

35 Tremain, *Two Days of War*, 36-40, 42.

36 Rafferty, "Gettysburg," *Personal Recollections of the War of the Rebellion*, 6-8. Rafferty is sometimes referred to as either a captain (see Pfanz, *Gettysburg: The Second Day*, 348, 370) or a lieutenant colonel at Gettysburg. His service record indicates that he was promoted to major on December 1, 1862 to rank from July 31, 1862. He was promoted to lieutenant colonel on February 6, 1864 to rank from May 1, 1863. See New York Civil War Muster Roll Abstracts, 71st Infantry, accessed on fold3.com.

37 *OR*, 27/1: 581. Randolph identified the two batteries as his own (commanded by Lieutenant John Bucklyn) and Captain Judson Clark.

artillery range of Humphreys's morning bivouac. The largely open fields in between provided an unobstructed line of fire. Even Rafferty conceded, however, that the Emmitsburg Road "was overlooked and commanded by both the Round Tops."[38]

Elements of General Geary's Twelfth Corps division had remained around Little Round Top since directed there by Hancock during the previous evening. Several of the regiments in Colonel Charles Candy's brigade described being on or near the northern slope of the hill, but not on the summit itself. Colonel John Patrick of the 5th Ohio reported that they "occupied a hill covered with trees." The 147th Pennsylvania deployed as skirmishers "in our front across an open valley to a light strip of woods, and in front of that timber facing an open field, for the purpose of guarding against a flank movement of the enemy." Geary affirmed that his command departed the vicinity in order to rejoin the Twelfth Corps along the Union right at 5:00 a.m., "having been relieved by the Third Army Corps," in obedience to orders from Slocum.[39]

No Third Corps troops, however, reached the summit of Little Round Top as replacements for Geary. "At 7 a.m., under orders from Major-General Sickles," Birney reported, " I relieved Geary's division, and formed a line, resting its left on the Sugar Loaf Mountain [Little Round Top] and the right thrown in a direct line toward the cemetery, connecting on the right with the Second Division [Humphreys] of this corps." Birney added that a picket line remained "in the Emmitsburg road, with sharpshooters some 300 yards in advance." Birney's left likely rested at the foot of Little Round Top, and not on the summit itself. Accusations surfaced later that Geary had sent a staff officer to help guide Birney's men into position. The officer departed, however, after "his patience was exhausted" by Sickles's failure to relieve him. There is no record of Sickles personally making a morning visit to examine the hill for himself.[40]

38 Rafferty, "Gettysburg," *Personal Recollections of the War of the Rebellion*, 6-8. Also see Fasnacht, *Historical Sketch 99th Pennsylvania*, 8.

39 *OR*, 27/1: 825, 839. Battlefield monuments to Candy's 147th Pennsylvania, 5th Ohio, 7th Ohio, and 66th Ohio all describe holding positions near or on the northern slope of Little Round Top on July 1. The regimental history of the 141st Pennsylvania regiment also states that the 5th Ohio and 147th Pennsylvania occupied Little Round Top during the morning of the 2nd. See Craft, *History of the 141st Regiment Pennsylvania Volunteers*, 118.

40 *OR*, 27/1: 482; Meade, *Life and Letters*, 2: 354. Several months later, Birney testified before the Committee on the Conduct of the War that he was in position by 9:00 a.m. with his left "at and on Round Top". See Hyde, *The Union Generals Speak*, 150. Captain Meade later wrote,

At army headquarters, which was situated on the Taneytown Road at the farm of local widow Lydia Leister, Meade "seemed in excellent spirits, as if well pleased with affairs as they had proceeded." Sometime after 8:00 a.m., he exchanged pleasantries with his son, Captain George Meade who served on his staff, and ordered him to visit Sickles. Captain Meade received instructions "to indicate to [Sickles] where the general head-quarters were, to inquire of him if his troops were yet in position, and to ask him what he had to report."[41]

Captain Meade rode south down the Taneytown Road for about one half of a mile until he reached Third Corps headquarters located in a small woodlot on the west side of the road. Meade Jr. first encountered Captain Randolph, who informed him that Sickles was resting in a nearby tent. Randolph then entered the tent and soon returned to inform Captain Meade, "The Third Corps was not yet in position, [and] that General Sickles was in some doubt as to where he should go."[42]

Captain Meade was unable to provide Randolph or Sickles with any additional clarification. A more experienced staff officer might have asserted himself, but young Meade chose instead to return to the Leister house. He reported to his father, who told him "in a sharp, decisive way" to return and tell Sickles to form the Third Corps, "on the left of the Second Corps; that his right was to connect with the left of the Second Corps; that he was to prolong with his line the line of [Second] Corps, occupying the position that General Geary had held the night before." In hindsight, given the already contentious relationship between Meade and Sickles, the commanding general

---

"The corps, as thus placed, was, with the exception that Little Round Top was not occupied, posted comfortably to General Meade's instructions." Meade, *Life and Letters*, 2: 73.

41 Meade, *Life and Letters*, 2: 66. The exact details of Meade's original orders, the time they were delivered, and whether they were verbal or written, remain unclear. Captain Meade was unsure, so he presumably did not deliver the original, and he later wondered if Sickles had received his orders when General Meade arrived on Cemetery Hill the previous night. See George Meade Jr. to Alexander Webb, December 2, 1885, Alexander Webb Papers, Manuscripts and Archives, Yale University Library.

42 Meade, *Life and Letters*, 2: 66-67. Captain Meade presumed from the response that "previous instructions had evidently been sent and received." Meade's *Life and Letters* provided the best description of Sickles's morning headquarters. Captain Meade rode "for a distance of somewhere between a quarter and a half of a mile" when he came upon Sickles's headquarters "in a small patch of woods" on the west side of the Taneytown Road. The most logical candidate that fits the description is Patterson Woods which is about one-half mile from Meade's headquarters.

would have been better served to transmit the orders in writing or inspect the Third Corps position personally.[43]

Captain Meade returned quickly to Sickles's headquarters. Upon his arrival, he found the tents "about to be struck [and] the general just mounted," surrounded by several of his staff officers. This time, Meade Jr. spoke directly to Sickles, who replied, "his troops were then moving, and would be in position shortly, adding something as to General Geary's not having had any position, but being massed in the vicinity." Sickles then rode off in the "direction of the front." Before Meade Jr. departed, Randolph requested that General Hunt visit the Third Corps to review "some positions he had selected for artillery." The request was duly noted, and satisfied that Sickles apparently understood the instructions, Captain Meade returned once again to army headquarters.[44]

Around 9:00 a.m., the two remaining Third Corps brigades began to arrive from Emmitsburg. Under General Graham's direction, they departed Emmitsburg around daylight, leaving without breakfast, and officers had allowed only ten minute halts at the end of each hour for the men to make coffee. A member of the 2nd New Hampshire regiment described it as a

43 Ibid., 2: 67. As Sickles later told the Joint Committee on the Conduct of the War: "At a very early hour on Thursday morning [2 July] I received a notification that General Meade's headquarters had been established at Gettysburg, and I was directed by him to relieve a division of the Twelfth Corps, General Geary's division I think, which was massed a little to my left, and which had taken position there during the night. I did so, reporting, however, to General Meade that that division was not in position, but was merely massed in my vicinity; the tenor of his order seemed to indicate a supposition on his part that the division was in position." General Meade's own testimony before the committee countered: "I had sent instructions in the morning to General Sickles...directing him to form his corps in line of battle on the left of the 2d corps . . . and I had indicated to him in general terms, that his right was to rest upon General Hancock's left; and his left was to extend to the Round Top mountain, plainly visible, if it was practicable to occupy it." *CCW*, 297, 331.

44 Meade, *Life and Letters*, 2: 63-64, 67. General Sickles asserted that he was uncertain of where he was supposed to place his corps because Geary was allegedly "massed" in his vicinity and did not occupy a specific line. Sickles's critics, on the other hand, argue that he must have known Geary's position, and was only fabricating the claim that he was unsure of where to go. Most Gettysburg-pundits bias toward the assumption that Sickles was simply lying to cover-up his actions, but the differing times as reported by Geary (5:00 a.m. departure) and Birney (7:00 a.m. or 9:00 a.m. posting) offered a possible explanation for the discrepancy. The 141st Pennsylvania regimental history wrote, "Geary had moved about five o'clock in the morning, and Sickles did not receive his orders until an hour later, when being ignorant of the position Geary had held, and no officer being left to direct him, the order was imperfectly carried out." See Craft, *History of the 141st Regiment Pennsylvania Volunteers*, 118.

"weird" march. "The consciousness of impending battle had by some subtle influence taken possession of the minds of the men."[45]

Charles Graham was a 39-year-old native of New York City. He hailed from a family of attorneys and his father and brothers were prominent lawyers. His family might have expected Charles to follow in their footsteps but in 1841, at the age of 17, Graham enlisted in the U.S. Navy as a midshipman. He sailed across much of the world before resigning in 1848. He returned home and became a civil engineer in New York. The Graham's family status and connections to Tammany Hall linked them professionally and socially with Dan Sickles. Graham contributed engineering reports and designs for the development of New York's Central Park; a cause that Sickles championed. In addition, Graham's brother John was a member of the defense team that acquitted Congressman Sickles of murder in 1859.[46]

The relationship with Sickles enabled Charles Graham's appointment as chief construction engineer of the Brooklyn Naval Yard in 1857. Sickles faced accusations that he had disparaged the personal character of John McLeod Murphy, the position's incumbent. When Sickles did not adequately deny the accusation, Murphy burst into his room at Washington's Willard Hotel and assaulted the future general with a cowhide horsewhip. A spirited fistfight ensued in which both sides claimed victory, although Sickles suffered a discolored left eye during the altercation. The net result, however, was to Sickles and Graham's satisfaction. As a "consequence of his attack on Mr. Sickles,"

45 *OR*, 27/1: 519; Styple, *Our Noble Blood*, 116; Haynes, *A History of the Second Regiment*, 166-167; Smith, *A Famous Battery and Its Campaigns*, 100; Toombs, *New Jersey Troops*, 180; Charles Graham account, February 16, 1865, Participant Accounts File 5, GNMP. Historian Edwin Coddington took Graham and brigade commanders Burling and de Trobriand to task for not departing Emmitsburg immediately upon receiving their orders. He noted that Meade's orders did not allow for any departure delays. See Coddington, *The Gettysburg Campaign*, 335. However, no intentional delay occurred. Graham arrived with the departure orders during the night and in the darkness, time was required to bring the scattered command back together. Artillery Captain James Smith rationalized the departure time saying, "it required some time to withdraw the pickets."

46 *The Union Army*, VIII: 102-103; *List of Officers of the Navy of the United States and of the Marine Corps from 1775-1900*, 226; "Obituary. Charles K. Graham," *New York Times*, April 16, 1889; Homans, *Register of the Commissioned and Warrant Officers of the Navy*, 28, 46; *Brooklyn Daily Eagle*, January 9, 1898; Tagg, *The Generals of Gettysburg*, 67-69. A notice in the *New York Times*, March 14, 1855 states that Graham was admitted to the New York State Bar. For John Graham's role on the Sickles defense team, see Brandt, *The Congressman Who Got Away with Murder*, 153-155. Thanks to our friend David Malgee for sharing his extensive research on Charles Graham.

Brigadier General Charles Graham
David Malgee Collection

McLeod was dismissed a few days later. Graham received the appointment as his replacement.[47]

Hardship and tragedy frequently marred Graham's personal life. He was slight of build and plagued with ill health for much of his adult life. His first marriage ended in divorce, and he disowned his children from that union. In February 1861, his elderly mother burned to death in her home, when a heating grate set her dress on fire.[48]

When the Civil War began, Graham joined Sickles and volunteered his service to the Union cause. Sickles raised his Excelsior Brigade and Graham became the colonel of the brigade's 5th Excelsior regiment, later known as the 74th New York Volunteer Infantry. In April 1862, the Senate refused to confirm Sickles's nomination to brigadier general and Graham resigned in protest. However, Sickles did receive confirmation several weeks later, and Graham re-mustered into service as colonel of the 74th. Although Graham was away for only slightly more than one month, the episode underscored his close personal loyalty to Sickles.[49]

47 "The Attack of McLeod Murphy on Mr. Sickles," *New York Times*, May 9, 1857; *New York Times*, May 12, 1857; *Evening Star*, May 11, 1857. The *New York Tribune*, May 13, 1857 praised Sickles's refusal to engage Murphy in a duel. Although Graham is often cited as being "Chief Engineer" of the Brooklyn Navy Yard, a listing of officers in the *Brooklyn Evening Star*, January 22, 1861, listed Graham as Chief Engineer (Constructing), which was differentiated from Chief Engineer (Steam) held by another individual.

48 Charles K. Graham Service Record, NARA; "Lenora Graham's Suit," *The New York Sun*, January 25, 1880; *New York Times*, February 17, 1861.

49 Charles K. Graham Service Record, NARA. It is often stated that Graham resigned from the Navy Yard specifically to join the Army. However, the *New York Times*, March 29, 1861 reported that Graham had been dismissed from his position. Graham was no longer

Colonel Graham saw combat at the battle of Fair Oaks in the early summer of 1862. Unfortunately, the rigors of army life did not suit his delicate health. By late July, he came down with a case of severe dysentery and applied for leave of absence to recover. Examining surgeon Dr. Thomas Sim, who coincidentally amputated General Sickles's leg roughly one year later, noted that Graham was "very much reduced in strength and is frequently delirious. He has a highly nervous temperament." Graham returned to New York to recover and stayed on recruiting duty through September. He received medical permission to remain away from the regiment through early December 1862.[50]

In early 1863, despite his extended absences, Graham was among several officers promoted to brigadier general dated to November 29, 1862. General Graham capably led an all-Pennsylvania brigade at Chancellorsville in May 1863. His first test as a brigade commander was bloody. His command lost more than 700 men, the highest of any brigade in the Army of the Potomac that fought around the Chancellor house and the Hazel Grove salient. Graham's performance received praise from both his division commander, General Birney, and corps commander Sickles. Losses had been ghastly at Chancellorsville, but as Charles Graham and his men moved into Pennsylvania, they brought with them the invaluable combat experience.[51]

When Graham approached Gettysburg on the morning of July 2, for the second time in less than 24 hours, local citizens warned him that the enemy was "advancing in heavy force on my flank." As the column reached the Peach Orchard, artillery Captain James Smith noticed that nearby fences had been cleared away and "the pickets and skirmishers were uneasy and kept up a desultory fire, little puffs of thin blue smoke dotting the plain before us, indicating quite distinctly the respective lines of the two greatest armies on earth." The men turned off the Emmitsburg Road and into the fields on

---

at the Navy Yard when the war's opening shots were fired only days later. It is also often repeated that Graham caused nearly 400 Navy Yard workers to resign and join him in the 74th New York. The *New York Times*, July 9, 1873 (more than a decade later) reported, for example, "Over 400 of the men in his employ at the navy-yard, on hearing of his resolution immediately determined to follow his example, the result of which was that the 'Excelsior Guard' was organized, and Chas. K. Graham was elected Major."

50 Charles K. Graham Service Record, NARA; *New York Times*, September 24, 1862; *Philadelphia Inquirer*, October 25, 1862; *Evening Star*, November 28, 1862.

51 Charles K Graham Service Record, NARA; *The Union Army*, VIII: 102-103; *Dedication of the New York Auxiliary State Monument,* 147; *National Republican*, January 24, 1863. Some estimates placed Neill's brigade higher at 850 total losses, but they were engaged on the Fredericksburg front. See Sears, *Chancellorsville*, 480, 485.

their right, and continued on toward Cemetery Ridge. Once there, Graham reported to both Sickles and Birney.[52]

In Henry Tremain's words, daylight revealed the enemy's pickets "were discovered to be stronger and nearer to us than had been supposed; and at times they evinced no little activity." The 63rd Pennsylvania, posted along the Emmitsburg Road since the prior evening, remained in position with their left anchored on the Millerstown Road. Major John Danks reported that picket firing began early in the morning and was concentrated against the right of his line that stretched toward the Sherfy buildings. Sometime during the morning, the 63rd pushed forward (west) to a fence that ran in rear of the Sherfy house and parallel to the Emmitsburg Road. Between 11:15 a.m. and noon, several companies of the 105th Pennsylvania also joined the line in support of the 63rd, "which was keeping up a brisk fire on the skirmishers of the enemy." The 105th also reported the "fire from the enemy's sharpshooters was severe. One man was killed very soon after we got into position."[53]

Further to the right, a detachment of men from the 1st U.S. Sharpshooters and the 1st Massachusetts regiment extended the line. The morning's skirmishing kept tensions high on this part of the field. Men in both armies undoubtedly wondered what the day held in store for them and what their adversaries would do next.[54]

With their residence literally on the firing line, the Sherfys watched the escalating hostilities with both fascination and alarm. Continuing her obligations to bake bread and dish out the loaves to hungry soldiers, Mary's mother Catherine had a "thrilling experience" while standing near a fence. A Confederate ball passed through a fence board and into a fold of her dress before falling harmlessly to the ground nearby. By 10:30 a.m., with the danger increasing, a concerned Federal officer insisted that Joseph, Mary, and Catherine leave their home. The three refugees headed southeast

52 *OR*, 27/1: 519- 520, 522; *CCW*, 297; Charles Graham account, February 16, 1865, Participants File 5, GNMP; Haynes, *A History of the Second Regiment, New Hampshire Volunteer Infantry*, 167-168; Smith, *A Famous Battery and Its Campaigns*, 101; Humphreys, *Andrew Atkinson Humphreys*, 192; Coddington, *The Gettysburg Campaign*, 335-336; Craft, *History of the 141st Regiment Pennsylvania Volunteers*, 118; Styple, *Our Noble Blood*, 116. Several accounts, such as Captain Smith's and the 141st Pennsylvania's regimental history, timed their arrival around 9:00 a.m. Colonel Regis de Trobriand said he reported to Birney at 10:00 a.m.

53 Tremain, *Two Days of War*, 36-40; *OR*, 27/1: 498, 500; *Pennsylvania at Gettysburg*, 1: 387, 393; Scott, *History of the One Hundred and Fifth Regiment of Pennsylvania Volunteers*, 82; Georg, "The Sherfy Farm and the Battle of Gettysburg," 8; Fasnacht, *Historical Sketch 99th Pennsylvania*, 8-9.

54 *OR*, 27/1: 516, 543, 547; Ladd, *The Bachelder Papers*, 1: 193; Imhof, *Gettysburg Day Two*, 14-15.

toward the John Trostle farm to join the Sherfy children. They must surely have wondered how much of the home and farm would remain when they returned.[55]

As the morning continued, more and more of Sickles's Third Corps troops began to move forward from Cemetery Ridge. At about 9:30 a.m., Captain Judson Clark of the First New Jersey Battery B reported receiving orders from Captain Randolph to advance to "the front and left, and placed in line on the rise of ground midway between General Sickles' headquarters and the peach orchard, on the Emmitsburg road." It is unclear why Randolph ordered this movement, but from this position, Clark could support Union skirmishers along the Emmitsburg Road. His battery remained there into the afternoon and Clark's movement indicated that Third Corps leadership increasingly turned their attention toward the vicinity of the Peach Orchard.[56]

Around 11:00 a.m., Sickles rode to army headquarters to meet personally with Meade. Sickles later testified that the visit was motivated by "not having received any orders in reference to my position," and he claimed receiving "conclusive indications" of a pending enemy attack on his front. Unfortunately, as the corps commander recalled, "I found that my impression as to the intention of the enemy to attack in that direction was not concurred in at headquarters." Even worse, according to Sickles, "I was satisfied, from information which I received, that it was intended to retreat from Gettysburg." Meade had earlier ordered Chief of Staff Butterfield to familiarize himself with the surrounding road network, and to draft a potential retreat order as a contingency plan. Sickles, Butterfield, and those unfriendly to Meade, later used this order as proof of the new commander's reluctance to fight at Gettysburg. Sickles even alleged afterwards that his advance to the Peach Orchard was partially justified to bring on a battle when headquarters planned to retreat.[57]

55 Georg, "The Sherfy Farm and the Battle of Gettysburg," 8-9; Sherfy Family History, copy on file ALBG, GNMP.

56 *OR*, 27/1: 585. The reference to Sickles's headquarters likely alluded to his afternoon headquarters at the Trostle farm. Harry Pfanz assumed that someone in authority such as Birney perceived a special threat along the Emmitsburg Road at this early hour. See Pfanz, *Gettysburg: The Second Day*, 133. R.L. Murray suggested that Clark was positioned to support Berdan's mid-afternoon reconnaissance, which would also suggest that Clark's reported 9:30 a.m. time was in error. See Murray, *E.P. Alexander and the Artillery Action in the Peach Orchard*, 45.

57 *CCW*, 297-298; Meade, *Life and Letters*, 2: 70-71. Also see Hyde, *The Union Generals Speak*, 38-39; Downs, "His Left Was Worth a Glance," *Gettysburg Magazine 7*, 39; "Gen. Sickles Speaks Out," *New York Times*, August 14, 1886.

According to Meade, he again gave Sickles orders to assume Geary's previous position, extend Hancock's line, and place his left on Little Round Top. Meade later acknowledged that Sickles still expressed doubts over Geary's role, and the New Yorker requested a staff officer's assistance to oversee the posting of artillery. Sickles also inquired if he had discretion to post his command according to his best judgment. "Certainly," Meade replied, "within the limits of the general instructions I have given you; any ground within those limits you choose to occupy, I leave to you."[58]

Sickles suggested that either Meade or his chief of engineers, Gouverneur K. Warren, accompany him on an examination of the Union left. Meade denied those requests, and the generals agreed instead that Hunt, the chief of artillery, would go. Hunt had already examined the terrain for much of the morning and noted that Little Round Top offered a "natural termination of our lines." Yet, he pointed out that the "broken character of the ground in front of the southern half of our line was unfavorable to the use of artillery."[59] Hunt later recalled:

> General Meade sent for me and told me that General Sickles, who was there at the time, wished me to examine his line, or the line that he wanted me to occupy; and General Meade wished me to go with General Sickles and examine the line. I think he added that General Sickles had no good position for his artillery. At that time I did not know anything of the intentions of General Meade. . . .As we left the room I asked General Sickles what his idea was. He said he wished to throw forward his line from the position in which it was then placed, and where it was covered in its front by woods and rocks, with a view to cover the Emmitsburg road. . . .I [also] had learned that General Sickles had left his ammunition behind on that road, and I thought, among other things, he was naturally anxious to control that road until it should get in.[60]

Hunt and Sickles departed headquarters and rode "direct to the Peach Orchard," where the latter "pointed out the ridges . . . as his proposed line." Hunt acknowledged some benefits in the proposal. The Emmitsburg Road ridge

58 Meade, *Gettysburg*, 67; Hyde, *The Union Generals Speak*, 107.

59 Hyde, *The Union Generals Speak*, 41; Meade, *Life and Letters*, 2: 70-71; *CCW*, 298; *OR*, 27/1: 232.

60 Hyde, *The Union Generals Speak*, 305. Later, Hunt wrote more directly that, "General Meade told me that General Sickles, then with him, wished me to examine a new line." Whether or not Meade had a clear warning that Sickles intended to advance from Cemetery Ridge would depend on which of Hunt's versions is accurate. "The Second Day at Gettysburg," *Battles and Leaders*, 3: 301.

"commanded all the ground behind, as well as in front of them, and together constituted a favorable position for *the enemy* [original emphasis] to hold. This was one good reason for our taking possession of it." Significantly, however, a piece of terrain that the Emmitsburg Road ridge could not dominate was Little Round Top. At its peak, Little Round Top stood some 80 feet higher than the highest point in the Peach Orchard.[61]

The Emmitsburg Road ridge did not offer any geographical "anchors" to Sickles's proposed left flank. A Confederate attack "up the road" from the south could easily outflank any line posted on the road. In order to compensate, Sickles proposed refusing the Third Corps left wing to run southeast from the Peach Orchard in an attempt to connect with the Round Tops. Meanwhile, the right wing would front west along the Emmitsburg Road. This arrangement created an awkward right angle, or salient, at the Peach Orchard, leaving the point vulnerable to enemy attack from two directions.[62]

Hunt identified an additional flaw in Sickles's plan. The right of the proposed line was in front of and could not connect with the left of Second Corps. Thus, Sickles's line would require a portion of Hancock's command to advance and reconnect with the Third Corps. In fact, by being nearly three quarters of a mile in front of Meade's remaining army, Sickles's position would, in Hunt's words, "so greatly lengthen our line- which in any case must rest on Round Top, and connect with the left of the Second Corps- as to require a larger force than the Third Corps alone to hold it." Meade's intended Third Corps line on Cemetery Ridge measured approximately 1,600 yards in length. Although Sickles later claimed he lacked the manpower to adequately defend Meade's line, his own preferred position from flank to flank was nearly twice as long. Not only would Sickles need more men, but the distance between Sickles and Cemetery Ridge eliminated the advantages of Meade's interior lines. Any reinforcements sent to Sickles would have to cross this greater distance.[63]

Hunt declined to endorse the move without first ascertaining whether enemy troops occupied Pitzer's Woods, a narrow strip of woods about 600 yards west of the Emmitsburg Road, "as it would be difficult to occupy and

61 Hunt, "The Second Day at Gettysburg," *Battles and Leaders*, 3: 301.

62 Ibid. Regarding the salient, Hunt wrote, "It would, it is true, in our hands present a salient angle, which generally exposes both its sides to enfilade fires; but here the ridges were so high that each would serve as a 'traverse' for the other, and reduce that evil to a minimum."

63 Hyde, *The Union Generals Speak*, 305; Hunt, "The Second Day at Gettysburg," *Battles and Leaders*, 3: 301-302; Powell, "Advance to Disaster," *Gettysburg Magazine 28*, 40.

strengthen the angle if the enemy already held the wood in its front." Sickles agreed to send out a detachment to reconnoiter the woods. During their conversation, Hunt became increasingly concerned by the sound of artillery fire from the Union right. He decided to return to headquarters, but first headed toward the Round Tops, in order to "report its condition" to Meade. As Hunt was leaving, Sickles asked for permission to move his corps forward. "Not on my authority," Hunt countered, "I will report to General Meade for his instructions.'" According to Sickles's version of this exchange, the proposal "met with [Hunt's] approval" and "he said that I would undoubtedly receive" Meade's consent.[64]

In light of the subsequent events, it was unfortunate that Sickles or an aide did not accompany Hunt on his return to headquarters. Testifying before the Committee on the Conduct of the War in April 1864, Hunt asserted, "it was a very good line to occupy, provided it was necessary to watch our left flank and prevent a movement by the enemy, or from which to make an offensive demonstration; but one which exposed its own flank and the flank of the 2d corps."[65]

Writing years later for publication, Hunt acknowledged that as he rode back to Meade's headquarters, his perception of the situation began to change. He realized that the Peach Orchard was farther in advance of the main Union line than it had appeared during his meeting with Sickles. Hunt also recognized that Sickles's proposed left flank risked becoming entangled among the massive rocks in front of Little Round Top that were afterwards known as "Devil's Den." This position could be commanded by the higher Emmitsburg Road ridge to the front or Little Round Top to the rear. According to Hunt, all of these factors made it "not an eligible line to occupy, although it became of importance during the battle."[66]

Unfortunately, Hunt did not return to Sickles to share these objections, but instead continued toward army headquarters. Upon his arrival, Hunt

64 Hyde, *The Union Generals Speak*, 305-306; Hunt, "The Second Day at Gettysburg," *Battles and Leaders*, 3: 301-302; *CCW*, 298. Some have expressed skepticism that Major General Sickles would request the approval of the lower ranked Brigadier General Hunt, and this provides a measure of proof that Sickles manufactured an attempt to use Hunt's consent as an excuse to act. But, as illustrated by Hunt's July 3 debate with Major General Hancock over the authority of the artillery on Cemetery Ridge, Hunt viewed his own role as a direct representative of army headquarters. Sickles may have been more accepting of Hunt's authority in the matter than the fiery professional soldier Hancock was when he interacted with Hunt.

65 Hyde, *The Union Generals Speak*, 306.

66 Hunt, "The Second Day at Gettysburg," *Battles and Leaders*, 3: 301-302.

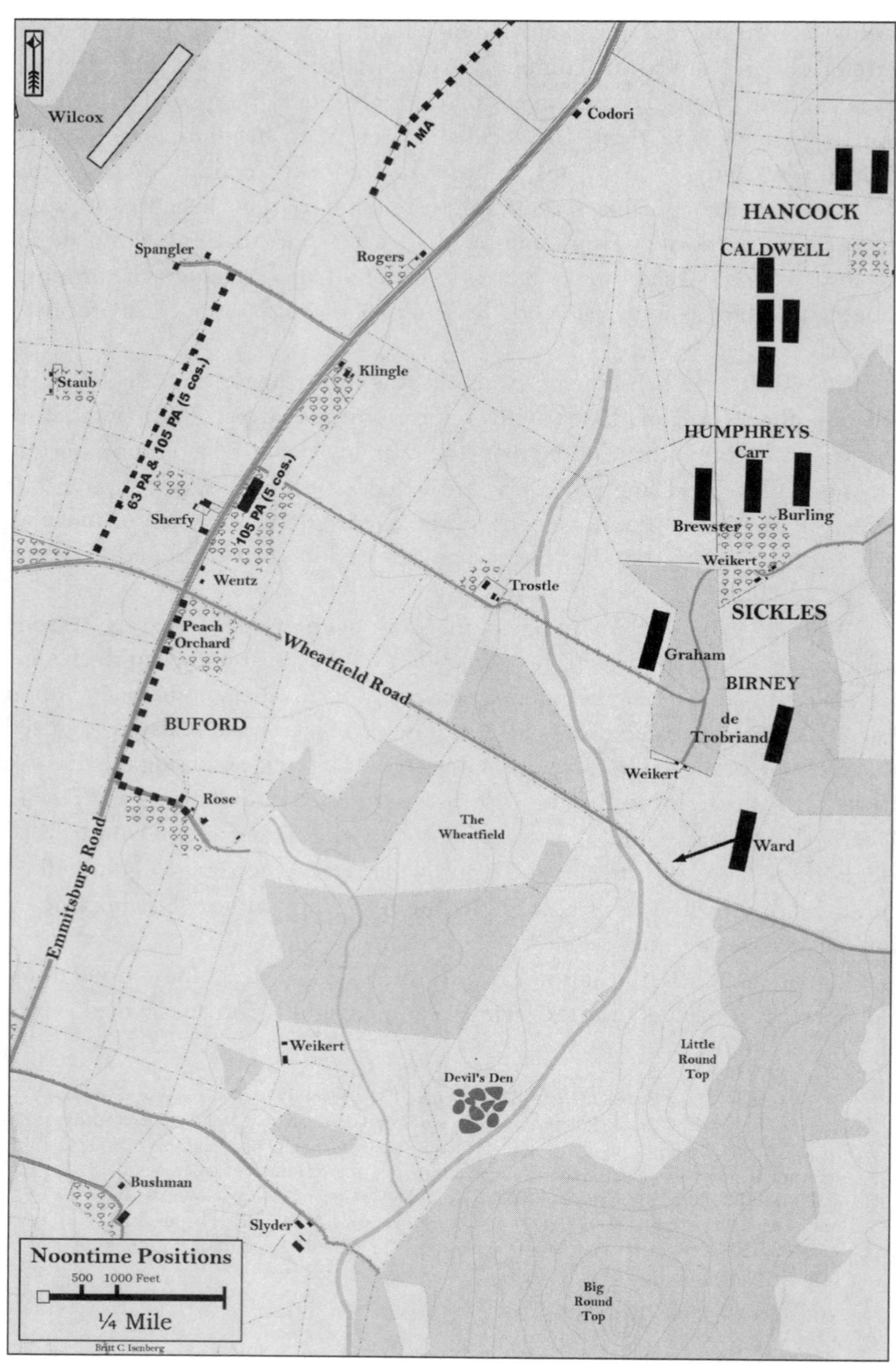
Wilcox
Codori
1 MA
HANCOCK
CALDWELL
Spangler
Rogers
Klingle
Staub
63 PA & 105 PA (5 cos.)
105 PA (5 cos.)
HUMPHREYS
Carr
Brewster
Burling
Sherfy
Weikert
Wentz
Trostle
SICKLES
Peach Orchard
Wheatfield Road
Graham
BIRNEY
BUFORD
de Trobriand
Weikert
Rose
The Wheatfield
Ward
Emmitsburg Road
Weikert
Little Round Top
Devil's Den
Bushman
Slyder
Noontime Positions
500 1000 Feet
¼ Mile
Big Round Top
Britt C. Isenberg

counseled Meade, "The proposed line was a good one in itself, that it offered favorable positions for artillery, but that its relations to other lines were such that I could not advise it." He suggested that Meade examine the position himself. Meade reportedly "nodded assent" and Hunt departed for Cemetery Hill.[67]

Whether or not Sickles violated orders intentionally, misunderstood them, or took too much discretion in executing them, remains an issue that Civil War historians have debated since 1863. The fact remains that Sickles considered the Peach Orchard and Emmitsburg Road ridge preferable to Meade's Cemetery Ridge line. A combination of factors influenced his reasoning.[68]

By the afternoon of July 2, the Confederates controlled the majority of roads into and out of Gettysburg. Meade's army retained clear access only to the Baltimore Pike and Taneytown Road. Federal skirmishers and cavalry occupied positions along the Emmitsburg Road, but with Confederates prowling the ridges and swales to the west, the road became a tenuous line of demarcation between the warring armies. The importance of the Emmitsburg Road had been apparent to the Third Corps since the men first marched into town. It functioned as their primary avenue of approach to Gettysburg, just as it had for the First and Eleventh Corps. The road also provided the army's remaining connection to Emmitsburg, an area that Meade originally considered of utmost importance. Even though the Third Corps infantry and artillery had united at Gettysburg, the supply and ammunition trains remained behind. "The arrival of Graham," wrote Henry Tremain, "left the highway to Emmitsburg unoccupied. Thus the corps trains would be at the enemy's mercy, unless the wagons had already been turned away to the east." The potential threat to their supplies and ammunition caused great uneasiness among Third Corps leadership. For them, the avenue of approach to Emmitsburg had to remain secure.[69]

Tremain's role as a courier on July 1, gave him an opportunity to consider the Millerstown Road and its intersection with the Emmitsburg Road near the left of the Federal picket line. The Millerstown road ran west toward Fairfield and east through the Peach Orchard, where it was known as the Wheatfield Road, and then to the northern base of Little Round Top and

67 Ibid., 3: 303; Meade, *Life and Letters*, 2: 74-75.

68 A full analysis of the so-called "Meade-Sickles Controversy" is beyond the scope of this work. Readers are encouraged to read Hessler, *Sickles at Gettysburg*, and Sauers, *Gettysburg: The Meade-Sickles Controversy*.

69 Tremain, *Two Days of War*, 48.

the Taneytown Road. Should the Confederates control this road, it would furnish them an avenue of approach toward the Federal left flank. Although this aspect remained unknown to both Union and Confederate commanders at this moment, Longstreet would, within a few hours, attempt to utilize the Millerstown Road for that very purpose.[70]

More importantly, however, the notion of enemy artillery occupying the high ground in the Peach Orchard, and thus dominating the low ground at Cemetery Ridge, became somewhat of an obsession among Sickles and his officers. Sickles later confessed "my anxiety to get out of the hole where I was & move up to the commanding ground." Henry Tremain thought it "easily perceived" that the Third Corps, "would be at the mercy of the occupants of the 'high ground' at the rear of the extreme left, as well as the possessors of the elevated land at the immediate front of the extreme left, i.e. the Peach Orchard." Years later, artillerist Captain Randolph wrote, "I have always been convinced that if the Rebels had occupied the Peach Orchard without a fight, they would easily have broken the part of the main line to which the 3d Corps was originally assigned."[71]

Many historians believe that Sickles was attempting to avoid a repeat of Hazel Grove at Chancellorsville. In later years, Sickles often cited the Chancellorsville defeat, but he did not name Hazel Grove as an influence on his movements at Gettysburg. Rather, he stated specifically a desire to avoid receiving an enemy flank attack motivated his move to higher "commanding" ground. Confederate artillerist Edward Porter Alexander, a beneficiary of the high ground at both battles, speculated this was the cause when he later wrote:

> [Sickles] unwisely ordered an advance of his whole corps to hold the ground about the Peach Orchard. He *probably* [emphasis added] had in mind the advantage given the Confederates at Chancellorsville in allowing them the occupation of the Hazel Grove plateau. But it was, nevertheless, bad tactics. It exchanged strong ground for weak, and gave the Confederates an opportunity not otherwise possible. They would be quite sure to crush the isolated 3d corps. If their attack was properly organized

70 Ibid., 40-42.

71 Tremain, *Two Days of War*, 43; Ladd, *Bachelder Papers*, 2: 666; Sauers, *Gettysburg: The Meade-Sickles Controversy*, 157. This ground today, immediately west of modern-day Sedgwick and Hancock avenues in Gettysburg National Military Park, retains these characteristics. A controlled burn of vegetation conducted by the National Park Service in 2016 once again revealed a rock strewn field beyond what is normally visible to the naked eye with typical vegetation growth.

> and conducted, it might become possible to rush and carry the Federal main line in the pursuit of the fugitives.[72]

In Little Round Top, Sickles had access to high ground along Cemetery Ridge; ground that he could have defended. The hill had limited room for artillery placements, but as an observation point and a natural barrier, the elevation would have alleviated Sickles's fears about an undetected Confederate force turning his flank. As noted, Sickles did not visit Little Round Top on the morning of July 2, and failed to assess its strengths and weaknesses. With his attention focused to the west and along the Emmitsburg Road, Sickles failed to consider opportunities or foresee contingencies that existed on other portions of the field.[73]

Not everyone agreed on the value of the Emmitsburg Road. Lieutenant Colonel Charles Morgan, Hancock's chief of staff, thought it "very unfortunate that General Sickles moved onto the field by way of Emmitsburg road for in riding along this Emmitsburg road one gets an exaggerated idea of the importance of the ridge on which the road lies, and underestimates the lesser ridge running from Cemetery Hill towards Round Top." Morgan considered Sickles's forward line as "a good one of itself," although both flanks were unprotected and "there can be no valid excuse for precipitating a battle in front of the general line."[74]

General Hunt, writing years later, thought the choice between Sickles and Meade's preferred lines "would depend on circumstances." The Cemetery Ridge position could be "made impregnable to a front attack. But, like that of Culp's Hill, it would be a purely defensive one." In contrast:

> The salient line proposed by General Sickles, although much longer, afforded excellent positions for our artillery; its occupation would cramp the movements of the enemy, bring us nearer his lines, and afford us facilities for taking the offensive. It was in my judgment tactically the better line of the two, provided it were strongly occupied, for it was the only one on the field from which we could have passed from the defensive to the offensive with a prospect of decisive results.[75]

72 Alexander, *Military Memoirs*, 392-393.

73 As the battle unfolded, the Army of the Potomac validated the limitations of this position as an artillery platform. The Federals placed only six guns on the summit and another battery on a lower shelf during the battle.

74 Ladd, *The Bachelder Papers*, 3: 1354. Morgan thought that Sickles's critics ultimately dealt "very tenderly" with him due to his "known bravery, and the terrible wound he received on the field. He committed a great blunder."

75 Hunt, "The Second Day at Gettysburg," *Battles and Leaders*, 3: 302 – 303.

Hunt acknowledged that a defensive battle was "just as likely, if not more likely, to win a victory than an offensive battle." Any tactical and artillery advantages of Sickles's proposed position were further mitigated by one glaring factor. Meade commanded the Army of the Potomac and did not want Sickles's Third Corps in the Peach Orchard or along the Emmitsburg Road. Despite several warnings, however, Meade apparently did not appreciate how close his troublesome subordinate actually was to moving his corps forward until it was too late.[76]

76 Ibid.

Chapter 3

Incomprehensible Movements

Colonel Edward Porter Alexander took several hours to complete his assigned reconnaissance of the proposed battleground. He then returned to collect his artillery battalion and guide his guns, men, and horses into position. Alexander was cautious when moving his guns to avoid exposing them to a Union signal station on Little Round Top, although his post-war accounts did not specify the route he took. The battalion came in sight of the signal station while moving on "the direct road" that led to Pitzer's Schoolhouse on Willoughby Run, a well-known landmark west of Seminary Ridge. "I turned out of the road before reaching the exposed part, and passing through some meadows a few hundred yards, regained the road without coming in sight," Alexander recalled. He continued to his destination undetected and it was early afternoon when he parked his batteries in the Willoughby Run valley to await the Confederate infantry's arrival.[1]

1 Alexander, "Letter From General E. P. Alexander," *SHSP*, 4: 101; *Military Memoirs*, 391-392; "The Great Charge and Artillery Fighting at Gettysburg," *Battles and Leaders*, 3: 359. Alexander's timings are problematic for some Gettysburg students. In his 1877 *Southern Historical Society Papers* letter, his reconnaissance occupied "according to the best of my recollection, one or two hours, when I rode back, and in person conducted my own battalion to the schoolhouse on Willoughby run." In *Battles and Leaders* (359), Alexander wrote that it took "about three hours" to reconnoiter and park his artillery. In *Military Memoirs* (392), he wrote that all was in readiness "by noon." Some historians have been troubled by the notion that Alexander's artillery sat unsupported along Willoughby Run for several hours, in close proximity to the subsequent Federal skirmishing in Pitzer's Woods, and in danger of Buford's still present cavalry. Yet Alexander clearly arrived ahead

Longstreet put his infantry column into motion sometime between 12:00 and 1:00 p.m. The objective was to reach Seminary Ridge and place his corps on the right of Major General Richard Anderson's division of A. P. Hill's Third Corps. General Joseph Kershaw's Brigade, in McLaws's Division, led the column. Kershaw's precise starting point is uncertain, but he began on or near Herr Ridge, a prominent ridgeline slightly more than one mile west of Seminary Ridge. One of Kershaw's post-war accounts suggested that he spent the morning about 500 yards from the Black Horse Tavern waiting to begin the march. If accurate, then the head of Longstreet's column needed to march over a distance of less than three miles to reach their destination. At a rate of two miles per hour, the march might have consumed 90 minutes. Longstreet's 14,000-man command, including supply wagons, occupied several miles of road space as they wound their way slowly along the narrow country roads.[2]

Longstreet's march did not go well. Concealment from the enemy's signal station was considered essential, as was the need for the troops to reach their destination quickly and avoid allowing Meade's army additional time to concentrate. Surely, Lee and Longstreet did not assume Johnston's early-morning intelligence would remain static for the entire day.

---

of Longstreet, so the question is how far in advance? An arrival closer to 1:00 p.m. rather than "by noon" would better address the above issues and still give Alexander time to go back and meet Longstreet's stalled column. It is also sometimes assumed that Alexander had charge of moving Cabell and Henry's battalions along with his own. But Alexander wrote in 1877 that he "rode back, and in person conducted my own battalion to the schoolhouse on Willoughby run." See *SHSP*, 4: 101. Alexander wrote in *Fighting for the Confederacy* (236) that he waited for the "infantry & Cabell's & Henry's battalions." Colonel Cabell wrote in 1877, "We moved with the infantry of Gen. McLaws' Division." See Cabell, "A Visit to the Battle-field of Gettysburg," VHS, 2. Ironically in his *OR*, Alexander wrote that his own "march into position was performed with these divisions" of Hood and McLaws. See *OR*, 27/2: 429.

2 Kershaw, "Kershaw's Brigade at Gettysburg," *Battles and Leaders*, 3: 331. General Kershaw described his brigade being halted "at the end of the lane leading to the Black Horse Tavern, situated some 500 yards to our right," which would have placed him near the war-time Adam Butt farm on Herr Ridge. Kershaw added, "We lay there awaiting orders until noon, or an hour later." Kershaw also wrote John Bachelder in 1876 that they moved "about one and a half o'clock" but cautioned, "I speak from memory." In the Bachelder version, Kershaw also said, "the head of the column having reached the mouth of a lane which the road then entered at Hoss' house." This would have placed Kershaw's head of column roughly an additional 0.6 miles further up Herr Ridge. See Ladd, *Bachelder Papers*, 1: 453. General McLaws's "recollection is that it was about 1 P.M" when put in motion. See McLaws, "Gettysburg," *SHSP*, 7: 69. J.S. McNeily wrote, "At eleven o'clock the battle order was delivered, and after waiting half an hour longer for one of Hood's brigades to come up, we moved off toward the right." See McNeily, "Barksdale's Mississippi Brigade," 234. NPS Ranger Karlton Smith estimated about 12:45 p.m. in his study. Smith, "To Consider Every Contingency," 108-109.

Captain Johnston's duty as a reconnoitering officer presumed that he knew how to guide Longstreet into position. Johnston later claimed, "no other instructions were given me," when Lee assigned him to join Longstreet. The captain "fully understood," however, that he was to assist the First Corps commander "in any way that I could." By Johnston's account, "we did not move off very promptly, nor was our march at all rapid. It did not strike me that Gen. Longstreet was in a hurry to get into position. It might have been that he thought hurry was unnecessary." According to McLaws, Johnston "came to me and said he was ordered to conduct me on the march." McLaws and Johnston then rode some distance ahead of Kershaw's Brigade.[3]

Longstreet understood clearly that Johnston was the guide. Yet, the general made the questionable choice to ride with Hood's Division near the middle of the column, rather than remain in front with McLaws. Whether or not he was irritated by pursuing Lee's plan of attack, Longstreet later justified his actions with an unconvincing explanation that he "was relieved for the time from the march."[4]

Longstreet's troops moved to the Black Horse Tavern Road, which passed by the stone tavern of the same name, along the west side of Herr Ridge. The ridge offered concealment from the prying eyes of Union signalmen on Little Round Top. After passing the tavern and crossing the Fairfield Road, McLaws and Captain Johnston soon led Longstreet's column to an elevation that rose to a height of about 40 feet. From this hill, McLaws observed Union signal flags "in rapid motion" roughly three miles away on Little Round Top. McLaws halted his division and rode with Johnston "rapidly around the neighborhood to see if there was any road by which we could go into position without being seen." Failing to locate any immediate alternatives, McLaws rejoined his command and met up with Longstreet, who had ventured forward to ascertain the cause of the delay.[5]

It was a hot afternoon and the delay added to a growing sense of frustration. Longstreet inquired, "What is the matter?" McLaws explained, "we can't go on

3 Samuel R. Johnston to Lafayette McLaws, June 27, 1892, S.R. Johnston MSS, transcribed copy on file GNMP; McLaws, "Gettysburg," *SHSP*: 7: 69.

4 *OR*, 27/2: 358; Longstreet, *From Manassas to Appomattox*, 366. Longstreet's report of July 27 stated, "Engineers, sent out by the commanding general and myself, guided us by a road which would have completely disclosed the move." Longstreet added in his memoirs (366), "General Lee rode with me a mile or more."

5 McLaws, "Gettysburg," *SHSP*, 7: 69; Longstreet, "Lee's Right Wing at Gettysburg," *Battles and Leaders*, 3: 340.

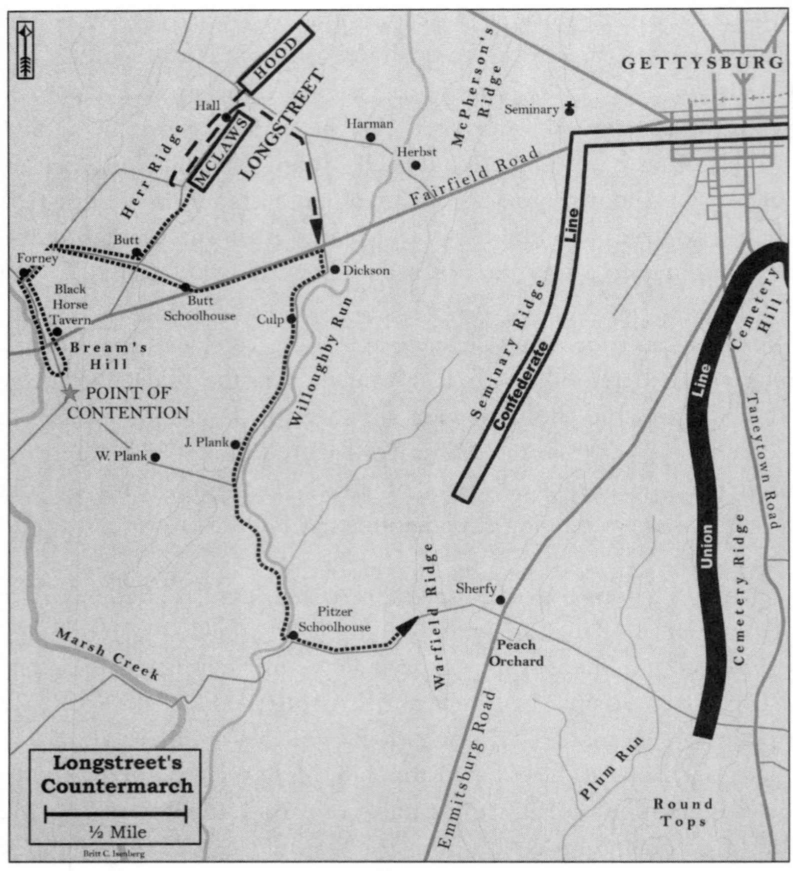

this route. . . without being seen by the enemy," and took his corps commander to the troublesome hill. When they reached the top, Longstreet surveyed the terrain and agreed. "Why this won't do. Is there no way to avoid it?" Captain Johnston offered no answers, but McLaws had reconnoitered the ground earlier that morning, despite Longstreet's request to the contrary. McLaws suggested an alternate route, but informed Longstreet that the only way to arrive was "by going back – by countermarching." Longstreet agreed, although Kershaw noticed that Longstreet and McLaws were "both manifesting considerable irritation."[6]

Colonel Alexander meanwhile became curious about the infantry's "non-arrival." He rode back and found the column halted at the hill. Alexander

6 McLaws, "Gettysburg", *SHSP*, 7: 69; Kershaw, "Kershaw's Brigade at Gettysburg," *Battles and Leaders*, 3: 331.

indicated the visible trail that his artillery had used to easily bypass the signal station, but the infantrymen would not follow it. "For some reason, which I cannot now recall," wrote Alexander, "they would not turn back and follow the tracks of my guns, and I remember a long and tiresome waiting; and at length there came an order to turn back and take another road around by 'Black Horse Tavern.'" Why Longstreet and McLaws were unable to follow Alexander's trail remains a mystery, but Longstreet's need for concealment took precedence over speed as his infantry retraced their steps back nearly to the starting point.[7]

Longstreet's difficulties were far from finished. General Hood's division had been following McLaws, but as the latter began to countermarch, the divisions became intermingled. Hood started to crowd into McLaws's rear and created some confusion. To solve the problem, Longstreet proposed that McLaws allow Hood to go first and consequently lead the attack. However, McLaws protested and refused to concede the honor. Longstreet consented and Hood remained in the rear. The countermarch required McLaws's infantry to essentially turn around and pass the head of Hood's waiting column. Nonetheless, this solution did not eliminate every problem. Colonel Cabell's artillery battalion, part of McLaws's command, found themselves cut off by Hood's men and had to await their passing before rejoining their division. Evander Law, one of Hood's brigade commanders, described the countermarch as one of "many vexatious delays" that plagued Longstreet's movements that day.[8]

Kershaw, whose brigade remained in the lead, described the situation as one in which his men "moved back to the place where we had rested during the morning, and thence by a country road to Willoughby Run, then dry, and down that to the school-house beyond Pitzer's." McLaws recalled, "very considerable difficulty, owing to the rough character of the country in places

7 Alexander, "Letter From General E. P. Alexander," *SHSP*, 4: 101-102; Alexander, *Military Memoirs*, 392; Alexander, *Fighting for the Confederacy*, 236-237. The question as to why the infantry did not follow Alexander's route has long puzzled and been debated by Gettysburg students, often disproportionately to its actual importance. Alexander's writings leave no doubt that his trail was visible but that there were reasons for not following it. In *Fighting for the Confederacy*, he wrote, "Of course I told the officers at the head of the column of the route my artillery had followed- which was easily seen- but there was no one with authority to vary the orders they were under." If accurate, then this means he did not speak to either Longstreet or McLaws. It is also typically assumed that McLaws stopped at the same hill that Alexander bypassed, although this is not explicitly stated in Alexander's accounts.

8 McLaws, "Gettysburg," *SHSP*, 7: 69; Law, "The Struggle for 'Round Top'," *Battles and Leaders*, 3: 320. Henry Cabell recalled that in this movement, "my battalion was cut off by Hood's Division and we were compelled to wait until his division passed." Cabell, "A Visit to the Battle-field of Gettysburg," VHS, 3.

and the fences and ditches we had to cross, the countermarch was effected, and my troops were moving easily forward along a road with fences on the side not giving room enough for a company front, making it necessary to break files to the rear." Evidently, Longstreet and his lieutenants did not solicit Captain Johnston's advice during this operation. Marching over unfamiliar ground, with no one to guide them, resulted in additional delays.[9]

Longstreet's post-war critics accused him of moving too slowly to the battlefield, arriving too late in the day, and thus contributing to the subsequent unfavorable outcome. The estimated hours of Longstreet's march were from 12:30 p.m. to 3:00 p.m. In total, the head of Longstreet's column travelled slightly more than five miles. The need to countermarch, or turn around and proceed to an alternate route, added approximately two and a half miles to the day's movements.[10]

The march was not at a particularly rapid pace, but it was not excessively slow, given the afternoon's heat and road conditions. Without the countermarch, Longstreet's infantry would have likely arrived opposite the Peach Orchard sometime before 2:00 p.m. The countermarch and the time lost waiting added at least one hour, and probably more, to the Confederate movements. This extra time allowed Meade to examine his left flank and begin deployment of infantry and artillery to support Sickles. Whether this was a deciding factor in the final outcome can never be conclusively proven, but the additional minutes worked in the Army of the Potomac's favor.[11]

9 Kershaw, "Kershaw's Brigade at Gettysburg," *Battles and Leaders*, 3: 332; McLaws, "Gettysburg," *SHSP*, 7: 69; McNeily, "Barksdale's Mississippi Brigade," 234. Also see Kershaw's description in Ladd, *Bachelder Papers*, 1: 454.

10 The countermarch's actual route is uncertain, but it is generally assumed here that the column backtracked from Blackhorse Tavern, worked their way some distance back up the western side of Herr Ridge, cut across to the Fairfield Road, and then continued to a road along the banks of Willoughby Run, where they marched to the Millerstown Road intersection. Using reasonable approximations for Longstreet's actual marching distances, including the countermarch, we estimate that the total actual march for Kershaw's head of column was about five and a quarter miles. Had they remained on the Black Horse Tavern Road and not turned around for an alternate route, then Kershaw's total marching distance would have been about two and three quarter miles. Thus, the countermarch added an incremental two and a half miles, plus the time lost waiting at the troublesome hill. These are estimates given the uncertainty of both the starting point and the actual route used.

11 Some pundits have proposed that Longstreet hit the Union left at "just the right time" thanks to Sickles's actions. That logic ignores the fact that a delayed Confederate attack gave the Sixth Corps time to arrive on the field, gave Meade the opportunity to inspect his own left, allowed for the Fifth Corps to better support the left, and bought additional time for Union artillery reserves to be called upon. Other than waiting for Law's arrival, these are

While Longstreet's men awkwardly navigated the roads through the back-country, Sickles responded to Hunt's warning about occupying the Emmitsburg Road, particularly "if the enemy already held the wood in its front." Sickles ordered Birney to send four companies of Colonel Hiram Berdan's elite 1st U.S. Sharpshooters, a total of approximately 100 men, plus an additional 210 infantrymen from the 3rd Maine regiment, to reconnoiter Pitzer's Woods on the west side of the Emmitsburg Road. Berdan described the mission as one "to feel the enemy, and to discover their movements, if possible."[12]

Berdan marched down the Emmitsburg road "some distance beyond our extreme left and deployed the sharpshooters in a line running nearly east and west." He then moved his men northward. Lieutenant Colonel Casper Trepp complained that every move the Sharpshooters made was within "plain view of the enemy," and as they marched, "the enemy must have seen every man from the time we reached the road until we entered the woods." Even worse, Colonel Moses Lakeman of the 3rd Maine halted on the Emmitsburg Road and gave the Confederates yet another opportunity to watch their deployment. "For this violation of rules of secret expeditions we paid dearly," grumbled Trepp.[13]

Berdan's reconnaissance party entered Pitzer's Woods from the south, and soon collided with Confederate skirmishers among the trees and undergrowth. "We soon came upon the enemy," Berdan reported, "and drove them sufficiently to discover three columns in motion in rear of the woods, changing direction, as it were, by the right flank." Their opponents were three Alabama regiments, the 8th, 10th, and 11th, in General Cadmus Wilcox's Brigade from Anderson's Division of Hill's Third Corps. General Anderson had ordered Wilcox to secure

---

several reasons why Lee and Longstreet could have benefitted from launching their attack one to two hours earlier in the day. It is, of course, all speculation since it did not happen.

12 Hunt, "The Second Day at Gettysburg," *Battles and Leaders*, 3: 302; OR, 27/1: 482, 515; Marcot, "Berdan Sharpshooters at Gettysburg," *Gettysburg Magazine 1*, 37. Birney (27/1: 482) reported the start time as 12:00 p.m., Berdan reported about 11:00 am (27/1: 515). Hunt takes credit for suggesting the reconnaissance in *Battles and Leaders*. His post-battle Official Report does not discuss the matter. Henry Tremain suggested that the reconnaissance was also influenced by the fear that the Confederates could use the Millerstown cross-road to hit the left of any Third Corps troops or trains who might be arriving from Emmitsburg. See Tremain, *Two Days of War*, 45-48.

13 *OR*, 27/1: 515-517. This would have initially put the command in Biesecker's Woods south of the Millerstown Road, although Birney's report stated that the group used a more direct route via the Millerstown Road to reach Warfield / Seminary Ridge. "They advanced from the peach orchard out the Millerstown road, and entered the woods in order to flank the enemy." See *OR*, 27/1: 482.

a position on the division's right. This effectively placed the Alabamians on the extreme right of the Confederate army as they awaited Longstreet's arrival. Wilcox refused his right flank to the south and southeast in the direction of the Peach Orchard and Pitzer's Woods. Like his Yankee counterparts, Wilcox was uncertain if the enemy already occupied these woods. He ordered the 10th Alabama into the woods, and directed the 11th to form in an open field on their left. As the regiments advanced behind a line of skirmishers, they collided with Berdan. Although this was unintended, Wilcox's movements gave the Northerners the misleading impression that a significant Confederate force was advancing toward the Emmitsburg Road.[14]

The U.S. Sharpshooters drew first blood. Wilcox's men advanced about 300 yards before receiving "a heavy volley of musketry on its right flank and rear from the enemy, concealed behind ledges of rock and trees in the woods on its right." The 3rd Maine had been initially behind the sharpshooters, but once the skirmish commenced, they moved to the front line and added more firepower. Colonel Lakeman led the 3rd Maine into position and "instantly formed my regiment under a heavy fire from the enemy, which we returned with a good will." The Maine men "labored under a decided disadvantage," however, because Trepp's sharpshooters had taken positions behind trees, thus leaving the 3rd Maine in open and exposed positions. "We attacked them vigorously on the flank," Berdan reported, "and from our having come upon them very unexpectedly, and getting close upon them, we were enabled to do great execution, and threw them for a time into confusion."[15]

The confusion that Berdan observed was probably within the 11th Alabama. The regiment took most of the initial fire and retreated several hundred yards toward a woodlot on Henry Spangler's farm. The 8th Alabama had already formed there in a lane near the wood's edge. As the gunfire became "very brisk," the sharpshooters rushed impetuously after the 11th Alabama and found themselves in an open field between the woodlots. Trepp's boys "drove the enemy about 300 yards, when he made a stand behind a rail fence." The 10th Alabama poured a return volley into the Federals, driving them back into the cover of Pitzer's Woods. Berdan acknowledged that his opponents "soon rallied, however, and attacked us, when, having accomplished the object of

14 *OR*, 27/1: 482, 515, 27/2: 613, 617; Marcot, "Berdan Sharpshooters at Gettysburg," *Gettysburg Magazine 1*, 37; Pfanz, *Gettysburg: The Second Day*, 98-99.

15 *OR*, 27/2: 617, 27/1: 507, 515.

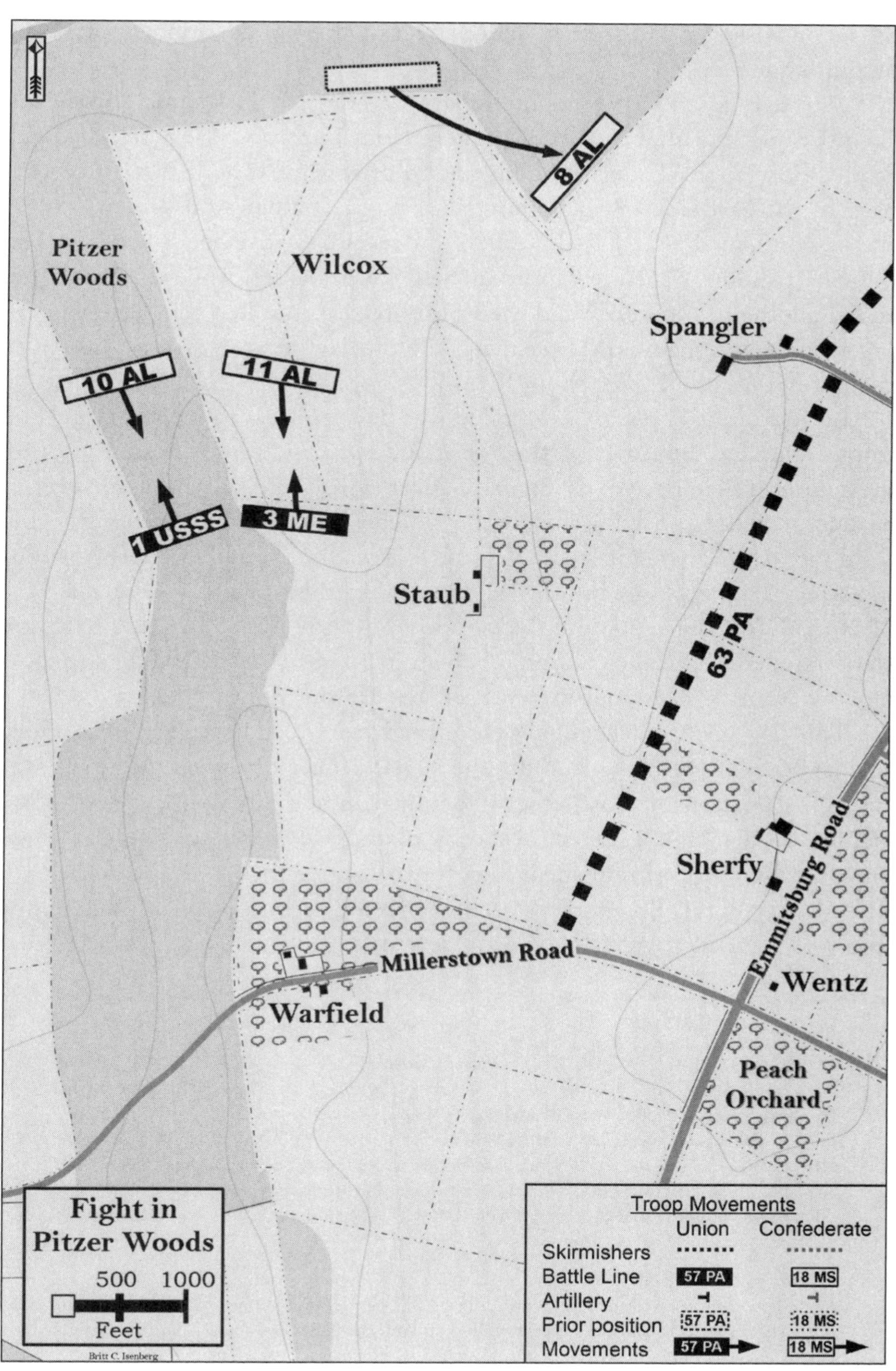

Pitzer Woods
Wilcox
8 AL
Spangler
10 AL
11 AL
1 USSS
3 ME
Staub
63 PA
Sherfy
Emmitsburg Road
Millerstown Road
Wentz
Warfield
Peach Orchard
Fight in Pitzer Woods
500 1000
Feet
Britt C. Isenberg
Troop Movements
Union
Confederate
Skirmishers
Battle Line
57 PA
18 MS
Artillery
Prior position
57 PA
18 MS
Movements
57 PA
18 MS

the reconnaissance, I withdrew under cover of the woods, bringing off most of our wounded."[16]

Wilcox boasted that a counter-charge by the 10th Alabama "broke the enemy's line, and they fled precipitately from the woods, leaving 20 or 25 dead and twice that number wounded and prisoners." The Union forces fell back to the east side of the Emmitsburg Road. Berdan's mission was over, and it confirmed that Rebel soldiers indeed infested Pitzer's Woods. The U.S. Sharpshooters suffered approximately 20 casualties, while the 3rd Maine added another 48 losses. Amid their hasty retreat, the Federals left some of the wounded on the field. These men were the day's first significant casualties in the fight for the Emmitsburg Road.[17]

Little Round Top's greatest value was as an observation point, and the troops manning the Army of the Potomac's signal station witnessed most of the action in Pitzer's Woods. Signal Officer Aaron Jerome sent a message to headquarters at 11:45 a.m. stating that Confederate skirmishers were advancing from the west. Ten minutes later, Jerome followed with another, more ominous message, "The rebels are in force, and our skirmishers give way. One mile west of Round Top signal station, the woods are full of them." At 1:30 p.m., the station added, "A heavy column of enemy's infantry, about 10,000 strong, is moving from opposite our extreme left toward our right."[18]

This last message seemingly confirmed fears that Lee planned to move against Meade's right flank. What the signal officer observed, however, was actually a portion of Longstreet's column countermarching away from the vicinity of Blackhorse Tavern, via a by-road on Herr Ridge. The signalmen on Little Round Top remained unaware that, after the Confederate column passed from sight, Longstreet's men changed direction again at Willoughby Run and headed toward the Union left. Ironically, the great efforts that

16 Ibid., 27/1: 515, 517.

17 Ibid., 27/1: 482, 507; 27/2: 617; Pfanz, *Gettysburg: The Second Day*, 100-101; Marcot, "Berdan Sharpshooters at Gettysburg," *Gettysburg Magazine 1*, 37. General Birney reported (27/1: 482) some 60 killed and wounded in the action. Colonel Lakeman (27/1: 507) admitted the 3rd Maine was "somewhat confused" in retreat and "I was obliged to leave my dead and seriously wounded on the field." One sharpshooter wrote home, "We had to fight there awhile as usual, which, of course, was absurd (a few skirmishers fighting a line of battle.) We have done so much of late that they expect wonders of us." See Murray, *Letters from Gettysburg*, 82.

18 *OR*, 27/3: 487- 488. The timing of this action creates problems with Alexander's assertion that he parked his artillery battalion in the valley of Willoughby Run at about 12:00 p.m. He might have only been 700-800 yards away during this fight, and possibly even behind Berdan's lines. However, if he arrived closer to 1:00 p.m. then the likelihood increases that he might have missed this fight, which he never described witnessing or even hearing.

Longstreet and McLaws undertook to avoid the signal station's detection did have some effect.

During this time, Sickles's anxiety was further intensified by the removal of Buford's cavalry screen from the army's left flank. The horsemen had witnessed the opening of Berdan's firefight and Colonel Thomas Devin, commander of Buford's Second Brigade, dismounted two squadrons to support the sharpshooters. Devin was not alone as artillery Lieutenant John Calef made dispositions to man his guns and "receive the enemy, who were driving our skirmishers rapidly." Before Buford's men could engage, however, they received orders to "collect all the trains in the vicinity of Taneytown and take them down to Westminster."[19]

Meade expected Major General Alfred Pleasonton, commander of the army's Cavalry Corps, to replace Buford along the Emmitsburg Road with additional troopers but none were forthcoming. Upon learning of Buford's departure, an "exceedingly annoyed" Meade notified Pleasonton at 12:50 p.m. that "the patrols and pickets upon the Emmitsburg road must be kept on as long as our troops are in position." Another hour passed before Pleasonton directed Brigadier General David M. Gregg, commanding the cavalry's Second Division, to bring forward replacements for Buford. As events unfolded, support from Gregg never materialized. As a result, Sickles was justifiably alarmed over the lack of a cavalry screen in his front.[20]

Colonel Berdan stated that it was about 2:00 p.m. when he returned to Cemetery Ridge and reported his findings to Birney, who in turn notified Sickles, "three columns of their forces were found marching to our left." It was a pivotal culmination of the morning's events. With Buford's withdrawal, Berdan's information provided the final straw for Sickles. Ironically, Henry Hunt had counseled against occupying the Emmitsburg Road if the Rebels

19 Ibid., 27/1: 939, 1032. Devin (27/1: 939) reported, "While I was engaged reconnoitering in rear of the enemy's right, our sharpshooters became engaged with a division of the enemy advancing to feel our lines in front of my position. I immediately dismounted and deployed two squadrons in support of Berdan's Sharpshooters (who were engaged in my front), and formed the brigade into line on the left of the First, with one section of Tidball's battery in position." Calef's report (27/1: 1032) added, "We had hardly got into position when an order came from General Buford for me to follow with my battery the First Brigade, of his division, and march with it to Taneytown, Md., for supplies and forage." Also see Wittenberg, "The Truth About the Withdrawal of Brig. Gen. John Buford's Cavalry," *Gettysburg Magazine 37*, 71-77 and Petruzzi, "John Buford at Gettysburg," *America's Civil War*, 37.

20 *OR*, 27/3: 490; Meade, *Life and Letters*, 2: 71. Buford's withdrawal, and Pleasonton's failure to replace him, has been the subject of much debate. For a summary, see Wittenberg, "*The Devil's to Pay: John Buford at Gettysburg, A History and Walking Tour.*"

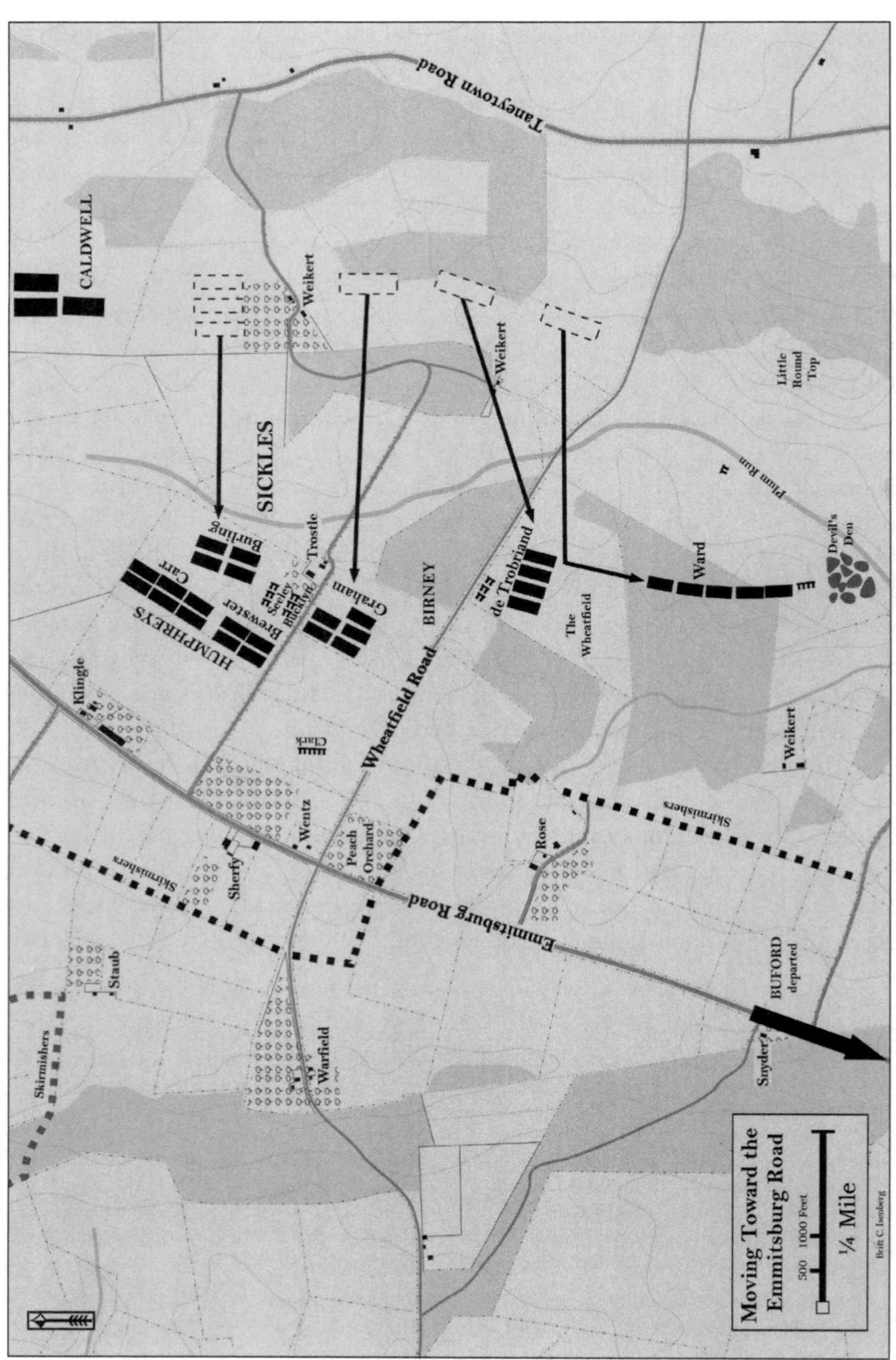
Moving Toward the Emmitsburg Road
500 1000 Feet
¼ Mile
Britt C. Isenberg
Taneytown Road
CALDWELL
Weikert
Weikert
Little Round Top
SICKLES
Burling
Carr
HUMPHREYS
Brewster
Seeley
Bucklyn
Trostle
Graham
BIRNEY
de Trobriand
Ward
Plum Run
Devil's Den
The Wheatfield
Wheatfield Road
Klingle
Clark
Wentz
Peach Orchard
Sherfy
Skirmishers
Skirmishers
Skirmishers
Rose
Weikert
Emmitsburg Road
Staub
Warfield
Snyder
BUFORD departed

occupied Pitzer's Woods. Sickles reacted to the Rebel presence at Pitzer's by pursuing the opposite of Hunt's advice. Sickles weighed the perceived lack of support from headquarters, and he believed he had confirmation that the enemy was moving toward his left flank. If Sickles wanted to prevent the Confederates from occupying the Emmitsburg Road ridge, then this was his final opportunity to act.[21]

Birney received orders from Sickles "to change my front to meet the attack." In order to do this, Birney advanced his left some 500 yards, and pivoted his right "so as to rest on the Emmitsburg road at the peach orchard." In front of Little Round Top, Ward's brigade became the left of Birney's so-called "line" holding a position on Houck's Ridge and along the large rock formations of Devil's Den. To Ward's right, and in the center of Birney's division, Colonel Regis de Trobriand's brigade took position near a non-descript wheat field on the George Rose farm. Graham's brigade became the division's right, and Birney posted them along the Emmitsburg Road near the Sherfy and Wentz properties.[22]

Graham's brigade consisted of six Pennsylvania infantry regiments totaling slightly more than 1,500 men. After advancing from the fields near Cemetery

21 *OR*, 27/1: 482, 514. Although Berdan had not actually discovered Longstreet's attack column, all that Sickles and his subordinates knew at this moment was that enemy troops were moving in their direction. They misinterpreted Berdan's intelligence to still arrive at the correct conclusion. Unfortunately the significance of Berdan's firefight, and the relevance to Sickles's actions, has been historically muddied by inflated post-war claims that Berdan had stumbled upon and delayed Longstreet's main attack. The sharpshooters' regimental history claimed that their mission had "stopped the advance of 30,000 foes. No greater display of heroism, no more self-sacrificing spirit of patriotism can be cited in the annals of war . . . surely, it may be fairly said to be a turning point in the Rebellion." Post-war speeches such as the one that James Longstreet gave at Gettysburg's 25th anniversary reunion only added to the fantastic tales. "The firing in question saved Sickles and the day. It caused me a loss of forty minutes, and could I have saved five of those minutes, the battle would have gone against Meade on the second day." Of course, any claims that Berdan directly delayed Longstreet are patently false. The sight of three Alabama regiments must have been disconcerting to Berdan's forces, but it is unlikely that they could have been mistaken for "30,000 foes." See Marcot, "Berdan Sharpshooters at Gettysburg," *Gettysburg Magazine 1*, 39. Harry Pfanz argued that the morning skirmishing should have left "no doubt that there were Confederates in Spangler's Woods. . . . Thus the only new information that Berdan's men could have provided was that the Confederates in some force were moving into the north end of Pitzer's Woods. Berdan might have assumed more and told a greater tale, but that is all his expedition uncovered and all he could rightly report. He could have seen nothing of Longstreet's corps, for it was out of his sight. His force might have delayed Wilcox's brigade in occupying its position on Anderson's right, but this was a meaningless achievement." See Pfanz, *Gettysburg: The Second Day*, 101-102. The point is that Berdan did tell more, and the Third Corps leadership did assume more. They assumed, correctly, that this confirmed Confederate movements toward their left.

22 *OR*, 27/1: 482-483.

Ridge, they formed a right angle that faced south and west at the intersection of the Wheatfield and Emmitsburg roads near the Wentz farm. The 141st and 68th Pennsylvania regiments faced south along a roughly 200 yard front on the north side of the Wheatfield Road. To the right of the 68th, and fronting west along the Emmitsburg Road for about 350 yards, the line extended north. From left to right, the alignment consisted of the 114th, 57th, and 105th Pennsylvania regiments. The 63rd Pennsylvania remained on the skirmish line west of the Emmitsburg Road beyond the Sherfy house. Several companies of the 105th Pennsylvania "Wildcats" supported the 63rd Pennsylvania. The main body of the 105th formed Graham's right and ended the brigade's formation at the farm lane leading to the Abraham Trostle residence. This lane, now modern United States Avenue, intersected the Emmitsburg Road between the Wentz and Daniel Klingle properties. The lane ran east from the Emmitsburg Road toward the Trostle farm and then to Cemetery Ridge beyond. Sickles established his headquarters at the Trostle farm, about 600 yards east of the Emmitsburg Road.[23]

It was not long before the commanders began to move their chess pieces around the field. During the earlier skirmishing, Birney ordered the 99th Pennsylvania from Ward's brigade to move in support of the 3rd Maine. Afterward, the 99th rejoined their brigade when Ward moved into position on Houck's Ridge.[24]

23 Busey and Martin, *Strengths and Losses*, 131; Floyd, *Commanders and Casualties*, 18; *OR*, 27/1: 504; Haynes, *A History of the Second Regiment*, 169-170 ; Craft, *History of the 141st Regiment Pennsylvania Volunteers*, 119; Scott, *History of the One Hundred and Fifth Regiment of Pennsylvania Volunteers*, 82; Imhof, *Gettysburg Day Two*, 10-15. The Daniel Klingle (alternately spelled Klingel) farm was about 400 yards north of the Sherfy house and on the opposite side of the Emmitsburg Road. The Klingles' location played a prominent part in the subsequent fighting. The house and a barn remain on the site today as part of Gettysburg National Military Park.

24 *OR*, 27/1: 513. Some interpretations have two other regiments from Ward's brigade, the 20th Indiana and 86th New York, joining the 99th PA along the Emmitsburg Road that morning. Major John Moore of the 99th (*OR*, 27/1: 513) reported being ordered by Birney, "to a position as support to the Third Maine Regiment, which was engaged in skirmishing with the enemy on the Emmitsburg road. This position I held for over an hour, when General Ward advanced the balance of the brigade, joined on my right, changed front, and moved farther to the left, as the enemy was massing his forces and moving on our left flank." Lieut. Col. Benjamin Higgins, 86th NY (*OR*, 27/1: 511), reported sending 35 men forward in the morning to demolish fences and walls to the Emmitsburg Road. This did not involve the entire regiment and they returned by 11:00 a.m. At noon, Higgins described advancing into the middle of a wheat field, which reads like the preliminary movements of the brigade to Houck's Ridge. Finally, Lt. Col. William Taylor of the 20th IN (*OR*, 27/1: 506) succinctly wrote, "On the morning of the 2d, the regiment was moved to the extreme left, to support the Ninety-ninth Pennsylvania and other troops then in the advance." Thus, it seems likely that the 99th Pennsylvania and perhaps the 20th Indiana were in the Peach Orchard vicinity

The 3rd Maine, however, was also from Ward's brigade and remained near the Peach Orchard upon their return from the firefight in Pitzer's Woods. This time, Birney deployed the 3rd Maine on Graham's left, in order to help cover a gap between the Peach Orchard and Wheatfield. Other examples of regiments being detached from their brigades occurred over the course of the afternoon. The net impact of these various separations proved detrimental to Third Corps command and control during the coming battle, caused confusion among the men, and disrupted the cohesion of the brigades themselves.[25]

General Humphreys's Second Division extended the Third Corps defenses north of the Trostle lane. Their move to the Emmitsburg Road occurred in stages. Humphreys spent much of the morning "massed" on Cemetery Ridge, with Birney on the left and Hancock's Second Corps on the right. Then at about noon, "or a little after, by direction of General Sickles," Humphreys later testified, "my division was formed some 400 or 500 yards in front of the position in which it had remained during the night." This was located "in a hollow" and "near the foot of the westerly slope" of Cemetery Ridge. Humphreys, an outsider in the Sickles-Birney-Graham clique, was the only

---

that morning. Their activities demonstrated the attention that Birney paid to this area, and also the piece-meal movements of regiments in brigades such as Ward's, but these regiments otherwise played no material role in the fight for the Peach Orchard.

25 The 3rd Maine deployment is often described as a skirmish line connecting with another skirmish line of the 3rd Michigan in front of the Wheatfield. See Pfanz, *Gettysburg: The Second Day*, 304; Laino, *Gettysburg Campaign Atlas*, 194; Imhof, *Gettysburg: Day Two*, 13. Colonel Moses Lakeman's OR does not describe a skirmish formation by the entire regiment. "I received an order from General Birney to take position in a peach orchard on the right of my previous one, and accordingly moved my regiment there and occupied it. Here I was enabled several times during the day to repulse the enemy's skirmishers (who seemed very anxious to drive us from it), and also to seriously harass the left flank of their advancing columns to the position which the other regiments of the brigade were holding, changing my front as circumstances required." See *OR*, 27/1: 507-508. The account in *Maine at Gettysburg* likewise does not indicate a skirmish line. "There to the left of Graham the regiment went into line of battle. . . . The regiment was posted behind the fence that bounded the Peach Orchard on the southwest side, its right resting along the east side of the Emmitsburg road." See *Maine at Gettysburg*, 130. The regiment's GNMP battlefield monument in the Peach Orchard simply states, "Fought here in the afternoon." Neither Birney (*OR*, 27/1: 483) nor Colonel Edwin Pierce of the 3rd Michigan (*OR*, 27/1: 524) who would have connected with Maine's left, describe the 3rd Maine as being in a skirmish line. John Bachelder wrote that the 3rd Maine "lay on the south side of the peach orchard, in front of a battery." In describing 3rd Michigan's actions, Bachelder noted that regiment's skirmish line "extended to the peach orchard, where it connected with that of the 3d Maine." This only implies that the 3rd Maine had a skirmish line, but does not say that the entire regiment was on the line as is often depicted. See Ladd, *Bachelder Papers*, 3: 1982-1983. The subsequent deployment of the 3rd Michigan will be discussed later in the narrative.

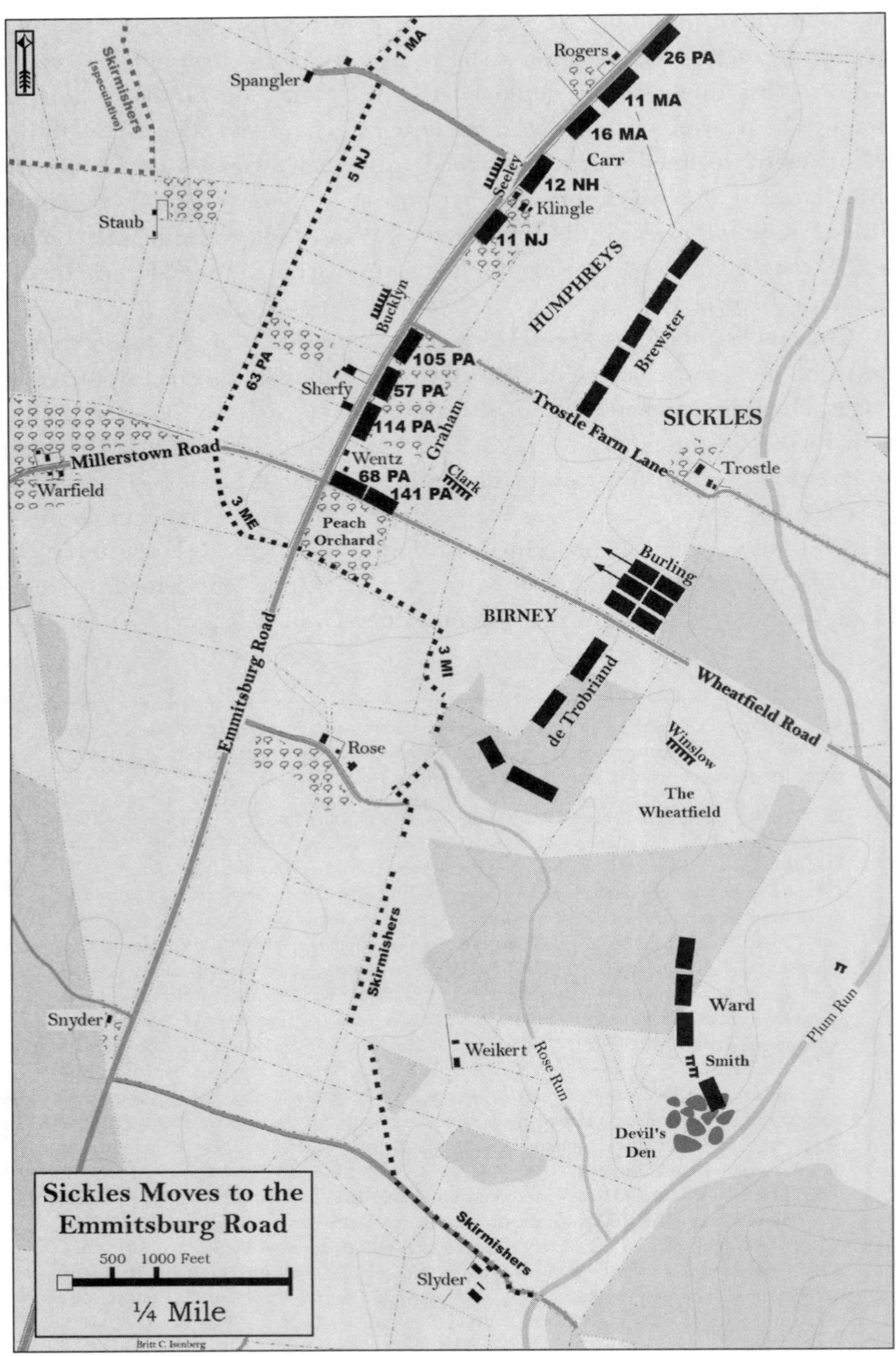
Sickles Moves to the Emmitsburg Road
500 1000 Feet
¼ Mile
Britt C. Isenberg
Skirmishers (speculative)
Spangler
1 MA
Rogers
26 PA
11 MA
16 MA
Carr
Seeley
12 NH
Klingle
11 NJ
5 NJ
Staub
HUMPHREYS
Brewster
Bucklyn
105 PA
57 PA
114 PA
Sherfy
63 PA
Graham
Trostle Farm Lane
SICKLES
Trostle
Millerstown Road
Warfield
Wentz
68 PA
141 PA
Clark
3 ME
Peach Orchard
Burling
BIRNEY
3 MI
de Trobriand
Wheatfield Road
Winslow
The Wheatfield
Emmitsburg Road
Rose
Skirmishers
Ward
Smith
Plum Run
Snyder
Weikert
Rose Run
Devil's Den
Skirmishers
Slyder

West Pointer in the group. He recalled specifically that Sickles never sent for him and he had "no knowledge" of Birney's position or intentions.[26]

Sometime after 1:00 p.m., the Excelsior Brigade's 73rd New York under Major Michael Burns moved in advance of the main body toward Daniel Klingle's farm along the Emmitsburg Road. Brigade commander Colonel William Brewster wrote that the New Yorkers marched "to the crest of the hill, about 250 yards in advance of the First Brigade [Carr's], with instructions that, should the enemy attempt to take it, to hold it at all hazards." A detachment of the 16th Massachusetts from General Carr's brigade later relieved them. This advance was likely intended to increase visibility to movements on the west side of the Emmitsburg Road ridge, where the 1st Massachusetts remained on the skirmish line. According to that regiment's Lieutenant Colonel Clark Baldwin, "troops could be seen moving into line of battle on the left as far as could be seen, which gave me plainly to understand that Gen. Sickles was preparing to defend his position or attack that of the enemy."[27]

Sickles soon detached Colonel George Burling's Third Brigade from Humphreys, and gave Birney operational control over these six regiments. Presumably, this was to strengthen the Third Corps left against an assault on that sector of the line, but Burling's departure left Humphreys with only Brewster and Carr's brigades, totaling about 3,500 infantrymen. Humphreys moved his remaining division forward so that his "first line ran along the Emmitsburg road a short distance behind the crest upon which that road lies." Although the loss of Burling diluted Humphreys's infantry strength, Lieutenant Francis Seeley's 4th US Artillery, Battery K, from the Third Corps Artillery Brigade, bolstered his defenses. Humphreys ordered Seeley to unlimber his six Napoleons on the right of Klingle's log house.[28]

26 *OR*, 27/1: 531; Hyde, *The Union Generals Speak*, 187-188; Humphreys, *Andrew Atkinson Humphreys: A Biography*, 192.

27 *OR*, 27/1: 543, 551, 558-559; Laino, *Gettysburg Campaign Atlas*, 168; Ladd, *The Bachelder Papers*, 1: 193. Brewster didn't specify the time that the 73rd New York was relieved, only that it occurred before 5:30 p.m. The reports of Carr and 16th Massachusetts's Captain Matthew Donovan suggest that it occurred around 4:00 p.m.

28 *OR*, 27/1: 532; Imhof, *Gettysburg Day Two*, 10-15; Hyde, *The Union Generals Speak*, 187-189; Busey and Martin, *Strengths and Losses*, 132. Humphreys reported that he "was directed" to move Burling's Brigade "to the rear of the right of General Birney's division, and make it subject to his order for support," meaning that these orders must have come from Sickles. Humphreys also estimated that it was about 4:00 p.m. when he moved his division toward the Emmitsburg Road. This seems too late in the day to be accurate, but illustrates the passage of several hours. Burling's brigade was initially massed in Trostle's Woods, "a piece of woods west

General Carr's brigade occupied Humphreys's front line along the Emmitsburg Road, with Colonel Brewster in reserve. Joseph Carr was a 34-year-old native of Albany, New York. As a youth, his immigrant family had limited means, and he received a public school education. He was considered energetic and "displayed a strong taste for the military" at an early age. In 1849, Carr joined the militia and advanced to the rank of colonel. At the same time, in civilian life, he established himself in business as a tobacconist.

After the Civil War started, Carr helped recruit the 2nd New York Volunteer Infantry and the men elected him lieutenant colonel of the regiment under the command of Colonel George L. Willard. However, Willard still held a commission in the regular army and was unable to command volunteers. The regiment held a new election and chose Carr as their colonel. He spent much of 1861 in camp training with his men, but also led the regiment at Big Bethel, Virginia, in June. By early 1862, some newspapers touted him as a "model colonel" and speculated that he was destined for promotion to brigadier general. He commanded a brigade during the Seven Days and Second Bull Run. At Chancellorsville, Carr temporarily assumed division command after General Hiram Berry fell mortally wounded, but he returned to brigade command during the army's reorganization prior to Gettysburg.

Although Carr received a promotion to brigadier general in September 1862, the Senate failed to act on it and his commission expired. The Senate did not confirm his re-nomination until 1864, with an effective date of March 1863. Thus, Carr's status as a brigadier general was in some doubt during the Gettysburg campaign. His large side-whiskers and thick moustache cut a physically distinctive appearance. The assertion that "a profane or objectionable word was never heard from his lips," along with his use of the phrase "coup de soleil" to describe sunstroke in his Gettysburg report, suggested that he possessed a somewhat sensitive persona. His resume was impressive, and this self-made son of Irish immigrants often won the praise of his superiors.[29]

---

of Little Round Top, and not far from the wheat field." Burling formed in massed columns, so they would be ready to move elsewhere when called upon, and awaited further instructions.

29 Carr biographical information: NARA Record Group 94, Letters Received by Commission Branch, C728, retrieved on fold3.com; *The Union Army*, VIII: 51-52; *New York State Bureau of Military Statistics, 3rd Annual Report of the Bureau of Military Statistics*, 49-61; "Our Newport News Correspondence," *New York Daily Herald*, January 17, 1862; *Dedication of the New York Auxiliary State Monument*, 148-149; *OR*,: 25/1: 445, 27/1: 542; "Gen. Joseph B. Carr Dead," *The New York Times*, February 25, 1895; Warner, *Generals in Blue*, 71-72; Tagg, *The Generals of*

Brigadier General Joseph Carr
LOC

However, Lieutenant Henry Blake of the brigade's 11th Massachusetts, who was witheringly critical of numerous general officers in his memoirs, relayed an allegation that has been generally accepted by historians as a reference to Carr:

> One general in the division, well known for his cowardice, marched through the populous districts with much ostentation at the head of his brigade, and shouted orders in a pompous tone of authority to attract the notice of the crowd; while the soldiers were saying, 'It is perfectly safe to be in front now;' 'There won't be any fighting while he leads the brigade,' and similar sentences. This officer had taught dancing schools of a low character before the war; and the members of some companies would 'call off' the various changes, - 'Right and left,' 'All promenade to the bar,' &c., whenever he rode by them, for the purpose of insulting him.[30]

Whether Carr was a dancer or a fighter, on the afternoon of July 2, his men held a position along the Emmitsburg Road, well in front of the rest of the Army of the Potomac. There was a gap between the left of Carr's brigade and the right of Graham's men, so Brewster's 71st and 72nd New York regiments moved into position in between these units. Since Hancock's command remained on Cemetery Ridge, about 500 yards to the rear of Sickles's advanced line, Carr's right regiment, the 26th Pennsylvania, did not

Gettysburg, 75-77. Some sources list him as 35 years old at Gettysburg, but his date of birth was August 16, 1828.

30 Blake, *Three Years in the Army of the Potomac*, 200-201. Henry N. Blake was 22 years old when he enlisted from Dorchester MA as a sergeant in 1861. He was promoted to lieutenant in 1862. He received promotion to captain in April 1864, however he was also under arrest awaiting court-martial. In June 1864, Captain Blake was listed as absent / wounded to date from May 12. He mustered out in June 1864 as a captain while absent. Blake referred to himself as a captain in his post-war memoirs, and he is often referred to by this rank in the Gettysburg literature, although he was still a lieutenant in 1863. Henry N. Blake, CMSR, NARA (accessed on www.fold3.com); Henry Nichols Blake, www.civilwardata.com.

connect with the left of the Second Corps. In military parlance, Humphreys's right flank was "in the air." The 74th New York moved to Carr's right, but Brewster's 70th and 120th New York remained in reserve behind the first line. In no way did these dispositions fulfill Meade's expectation that the Third Corps would extend Hancock's left along Cemetery Ridge to Little Round Top.[31]

From their location on Cemetery Ridge, Hancock's men knew nothing of General Sickles's intentions. Josiah Favill, an officer on Brigadier General Samuel Zook's staff, recorded, "we stood to arms, on observing Sickles begin to advance and maneuver; after making several incomprehensible movements, his troops marched forward from in front of Round Top, and immediately brought on the action." Lieutenant William Wilson of Brigadier General John Caldwell's staff offered, "Many were the criticisms made and opinions expressed as to the comparative merits of the line he was directed to take and the one he selected." General Hancock admittedly admired "the spectacle, but I did not know the object of it." Such displays of large troop movements typically captured the hearts of military men, and Hancock allegedly remarked that Sickles's advance was "beautiful to look at," but added, "gentlemen they will not be there long."[32]

Some of these criticisms undoubtedly took shape with the advantage of hindsight. Historians often ponder why Hancock and staff did not report Sickles's "incomprehensible movements" immediately to army headquarters. At that moment on July 2, however, no one in Meade's army, from the general's staff down to the company level, had a clear sightline across the entire field. As military men, they presumed that the Third Corps was carrying out orders, although the wisdom and nature of those orders may not have seemed evident.[33]

31 *OR*, 27/1: 558, 566; Imhof, *Gettysburg Day Two*, 14-15.

32 Ladd, *The Bachelder Papers*, 2: 1194; Hyde, *The Union Generals Speak*, 214; Favill, *Diary of a Young Army Officer*, 245. Lieutenant Frank Haskell pontificated that Sickles "supposed he was doing for the best; but he was neither born nor bred a soldier. But one can scarcely tell what may have been the motives of such a man,-- a politician, and some other things, exclusive of the Barton Key affair, - a man after show, and notoriety, and newspaper fame, and the adulation of the mob! O, there is a grave responsibility on those in whose hands are the lives of ten thousand men; and on those who put stars upon men's shoulders, too!" See Byrne and Weaver, *Haskell of Gettysburg*, 117.

33 Author Paul Bretzger examined a number of reasons why Sickles's advance could have gone unnoticed, or at least unreported. "Birney's half occurred behind the cover of trees, while Humphreys' movement was piecemeal and gradual until the last act, when it was too late to rectify." See Bretzger, *Observing Hancock at Gettysburg*, 81-90.

While Second Corps officers remained puzzled and critical, many Third Corps veterans viewed Sickles's actions more favorably. They saw their commander as a man of action who seized upon the needs of the moment. "General Sickles had one sterling quality of a good soldier—he was equal to an emergency," Major Thomas Rafferty argued, "and left as he now was to the exercise of his own judgment, he was prompt to act." Strategically, the new line forced "the enemy to develop his plan of attack, as our position there menaced any attempt he might make at turning our flank, and in fact compelled him to attack us, or suspend his movement and await our attack."[34]

Afterwards, there emerged a point of contention regarding authorization for Birney and Humphreys to call upon others for support. Birney maintained that Sickles "informed me that a division from the Second [Corps] and one from the Fifth Corps had been ordered to be in readiness to support me." Humphreys argued essentially the same, insisting that Sickles permitted him to "draw support, should I need it" from General Caldwell's Second Corps division. Humphreys also asserted that Sickles "authorized" him to draw from the army's Artillery Reserve "should I require more." Humphreys then sent Hancock a message to inquire whether Caldwell's division was ready to assist him.[35]

At headquarters, Meade recorded the initial arrival of his army's large Sixth Corps at 2:00 p.m. He then "immediately directed the Fifth Corps to move over to our extreme left," and placed the Sixth Corps in reserve for the right. Had Lee and Longstreet launched their assault at an earlier hour, the Sixth Corps would not have been on the field, and the Fifth Corps would not have been positioned to provide a timely defense of Meade's left. Whether this impacted the day's outcome remains speculative, but Confederate delays gave Meade's army more time to concentrate.[36]

Also, although Sickles's men had not yet spotted Longstreet's divisions moving to their left, the earlier encounter with Wilcox in Pitzer's Woods, and subsequent occupation of the Emmitsburg Road, eliminated any element of surprise that Lee hoped would offer the Confederates an advantage. Sickles

34 Rafferty, "Gettysburg," *Personal Recollections of the War of the Rebellion*, 7-8.

35 *OR*, 27/1: 483, 27/1: 532; Hyde, *The Union Generals Speak*, 187-189. Humphreys was afterwards "under the impression that I sent a request to [Hancock] to throw forward some troops between my right and his left."

36 *OR*, 27/1: 116; Hyde, *The Union Generals Speak*, 253-254. It is also worth remembering that Meade and the Union commanders incorrectly believed that they were outnumbered, and that the Sixth Corps presence was a necessity before taking any decisive action.

and his officers knew that an attack along their line was imminent. Longstreet had no way of knowing it, but continued attempts at concealment on his part were wasted efforts.[37]

Sometime around 3:00 p.m., Longstreet's two divisions approached the Millerstown Road and the western side of Warfield Ridge. The First Corps march into position took longer than expected and Longstreet certainly realized this fact. He rode up to Lafayette McLaws and asked, "How are you going in?" McLaws replied, "That will be determined when I can see what is in my front." Longstreet assured his subordinate, "There is nothing in your front; you will be entirely on the flank of the enemy." McLaws responded that he would continue until he arrived on the Union flank and "will face to the left and march on the enemy." Longstreet approved, "That suits me." He then rode away to attend to other duties.[38]

On July 7, McLaws summarized the battle plan in a letter to his wife:

> [W]e moved around Gettysburg towards the Emmitsburg road, to arrive at the Peach orchard, a small settlement with a very large Peach Orchard attached. The intention was to get in rear of the enemy who were supposed to be stationed principally in rear of Gettysburg or near of it. The report being that the enemy had but two regiments of infantry and one battery at the Peach orchard. On arriving at the vicinity of the Orchard, the enemy were discovered in greater force than was supposed.[39]

Longstreet likely intended for McLaws to deploy his division in the low ground immediately south of the Peach Orchard. From there, he would pivot

37 Sickles alluded to this in his 1905 introduction to Helen Longstreet's *Lee and Longstreet at High Tide*. Certainly they would not have acted upon Berdan's intelligence and then still have been surprised by the appearance of Rebel infantry. See Sickles, "Introduction," *Lee and Longstreet at High Tide*, 23-24. Likewise, Longstreet also suggested in *Battles and Leaders* that he abandoned secrecy because he believed it likely that he had been discovered near Black Horse Tavern by the Union signal station on Little Round Top. "It seemed there was doubt again about the men being concealed, when I stated that I could see the signal station, and there was no reason why they could not see us. It seemed to me useless, therefore, to delay the troops any longer with the idea of concealing the movement, and the two divisions advanced." If that is true, then one wonders why Longstreet countermarched his column at all. See Longstreet, "Lee's Right Wing at Gettysburg," *Battles and Leaders*, 3: 340.

38 McLaws, "Gettysburg," *SHSP*, 7: 69. The southern extension of Seminary Ridge is also referred to as Warfield Ridge. This is named after African-American James Warfield who lived on the south side of the Millerstown Road and about 500 yards west of the Emmitsburg Road. The Warfield house still stands today.

39 Oeffinger, *A Soldier's General*, 195-196. As noted previously, the 1858 Adams County map represented the Peach Orchard as a separately named location. McLaws's description suggests that the Confederates were using this map in their movements.

on the Emmitsburg Road and attack with Hood's Division to follow. But, Lee designed the attack based upon an erroneous supposition. The left flank of the Army of the Potomac did not rest on the Emmitsburg Road.

Commenting from the Federal perspective, Henry Hunt understood this when he explained that Lee apparently "mistook the few troops on the Peach Orchard ridge in the morning for our main line, and that by taking it and sweeping up the Emmitsburg road under cover of his batteries, he expected to 'roll up' our lines to Cemetery Hill."[40]

Adding to this fundamental flaw in the Confederate plan of attack, much had changed since Johnston's reconnaissance. Sickles now occupied the Emmitsburg Road. McLaws's column reached the western edge of Pitzer's Woods, and the Rebel general recalled, "one rapid glance showed them to be in force much greater than I had, and extending considerably beyond my right." McLaws rode forward to get a better look at the situation, "and the view presented astonished me, as the enemy was massed in my front, and extended to my right and left as far as I could see. . . . Thus was presented a state of affairs which was certainly not contemplated when the original plan or order of battle was given, and certainly was not known to General Longstreet a half hour previous."[41]

General Kershaw's brigade had remained in the lead throughout the march. As his command reached Pitzer's schoolhouse near the Millerstown Road, Longstreet directed him to advance the brigade, attack the enemy at the Peach Orchard, and "turn his flank." The corps commander expected Kershaw to cross the Emmitsburg Road, pivot north, and extend his brigade while keeping his left on the road as he swept the enemy out of their position. Kershaw began preparations for the attack and filed to the right (south) off of the Millerstown Road and behind a stone wall on Warfield Ridge. His main line formed for battle while his skirmishers engaged the enemy. However, Kershaw found the enemy "in superior force in the orchard, supported by artillery, with a main line of battle intrenched in the rear and extending to and upon the rocky mountain to his left far beyond the point at which his flank had supposed to rest." The capable South Carolinian knew that if he were to

40 Hunt, "The Second Day at Gettysburg," *Battles and Leaders*, 3: 300. Also see Cooksey, "Up the Emmitsburg Road," *Gettysburg Magazine 26*, 45-48, for an analysis of Longstreet's desire to "attack up the Emmitsburg Road." Cooksey proposed that the Confederates probably believed that the Union line ended along the Emmitsburg Road somewhere between the Rogers and Codori houses. In this scenario, the original Confederate plan called for McLaws to deploy in the low ground just south of the Peach Orchard before sweeping up the Emmitsburg Road.

41 McLaws, "Gettysburg," *SHSP*, 7: 69-71.

carry out his orders, and attack Sickles at the orchard, while keeping his left on the Emmitsburg Road, then he would expose his right and rear to other Yankee troops that stretched southeast toward the Round Tops. Kershaw communicated the situation to McLaws, and his men took cover behind the stone wall while awaiting further orders.[42]

Longstreet was apparently unaware of the current state of affairs. Since McLaws had discovered the Federals in greater force than expected, he deployed two brigades in his front: Kershaw on the right, south of the Millerstown Road, and William Barksdale's Brigade on Kershaw's left, north of the road. He placed Paul Semmes and William Wofford's brigades in the rear in order to give depth to the attack. These deployments consumed time, and Longstreet sent staff officer Major Osmund Latrobe to find out why McLaws had not attacked, since there was supposed to be no one in his front except for "a regiment of infantry and a battery of artillery.'"[43]

McLaws replied, presumably with growing irritation, that the Yankees were "in great force," supported by artillery, and their line "extended far to the right." Another message soon arrived from Longstreet repeating the orders. McLaws responded that the assault required careful preparation, and it was necessary for his own artillery to break up the enemy's before he ordered his infantry forward. McLaws requested that Longstreet "come to the front and see for himself."[44]

Instead of a visit from his corps commander, yet another order arrived "peremptorily" for McLaws "to charge, the officer representing that General Lee was with General Longstreet, and joined in the order." At that point, McLaws had no choice but to tell Longstreet "that in five minutes I would be under way." However, as McLaws prepared to initiate what he described as "a simultaneous move of the whole line," yet another courier arrived from Longstreet, this time with orders to "wait until Hood got into position."[45]

Although it took some time for him to do so, Longstreet became aware of the true tactical situation. This forced Longstreet to modify the original plan of attack. Without time to conduct a thorough reconnaissance, Longstreet

42 *OR*, 27/2: 367-368.

43 Oeffinger, *A Soldier's General*, 196; McLaws, "Gettysburg," *SHSP*, 7: 72; Pfanz, *Gettysburg: The Second Day*, 152-153.

44 McLaws, "Gettysburg," *SHSP*, 7: 72.

45 Ibid.; Oeffinger, *A Soldier's General*, 196. Longstreet omitted this exchange in his memoirs. See Longstreet, *From Manassas to Appomattox*, 366-367.

based his new orders on what was obviously visible from Warfield Ridge. The Southerners could see that the Union left extended farther than was expected, but they could not account for every Yankee regiment hidden behind woodlots or ridgelines on the field. As time slipped away, Longstreet ordered Hood's Division, still in position behind McLaws, to move to the Confederates' right. Lee later described Hood's revised objective as, "partially enveloping the enemy's left, which he was to drive in." Longstreet added that Hood's Division was "pressing upon" the Union's left, while McLaws was to do the same upon the enemy's "front." These revisions meant the Peach Orchard salient would be hit from two sides if Hood did his part to successfully "drive in" the enemy's left flank.[46]

Federal artillery soon uncovered Hood's initial movements. For much of the morning, Captain Judson Clark had unlimbered Battery B, 1st New Jersey Light Artillery in a position midway between Sickles's Trostle farm headquarters and the Peach Orchard. His battery consisted of six 10-pound Parrott rifles, and during the afternoon Clark spotted enemy infantry moving in column across the Emmitsburg Road. Clark estimated their distance at roughly 1,400 yards from his left and front, well within range of his rifled guns. Under Sickles's direction, Clark opened fire with six or seven rounds of shell and case shot before the column disappeared from view. At this stage, Sickles and Longstreet's forces were simply too close to each other to make further concealment possible.[47]

At around 3:00 p.m., with Clark's opening salvos likely reverberating on the horizon, Meade summoned his subordinates to headquarters for a meeting. Since skirmishing and artillery fire had increased along his front, Sickles requested that Meade excuse him from the meeting, "stating that the enemy were in great force in my front, and intimating that I would very soon be engaged, and that I was making my dispositions to meet the attack." While attending to battery dispositions, another courier from Meade arrived, this time carrying a "peremptory" order for Sickles to report to army headquarters at once.

46 *OR*, 27/2: 318, 358. Clark afterwards reported this encounter at 2:00 p.m. His time-estimate might have been off by an hour or so, but he otherwise described the movement of Hood's Division crossing the Emmitsburg Road in the vicinity of the present-day Texas State Memorial.

47 Ibid., 27/1: 585-586; Hanifen, *History of Battery B*, 68; Toombs, *New Jersey Troops*, 201. Clark's ability to fire directly to the west was obstructed by terrain and the Wentz buildings. This further supports that he was describing Hood's movements.

Sickles temporarily turned command over to Birney and rode to headquarters, "feeling assured that before I could return the engagement would open."[48]

As the corps commanders gathered at Meade's headquarters, Warren arrived with stunning news. "There seemed to be some doubt about whether he [Sickles] should occupy a line in front," the chief engineer later testified, "or the one on the ridge in the rear; and I am not sure but a report had come in from some of our officers that that position was not occupied. I know I had sent an officer there to ascertain and report." Warren confirmed what had been brewing all morning: Sickles's Third Corps was not where Meade expected them to be. In response, Meade ordered Fifth Corps commander George Sykes to immediately move his command over toward the left flank. Meade told Sykes that he would meet him there, and the commanding general was in the process of mounting a horse when Sickles arrived at headquarters.[49]

Warren's news and the sounds of increased firing terminated the meeting. Sickles had, by his own account, "hastened to headquarters with all speed, but before I got there the sound of the cannon announced that battle had opened." Meade met his difficult subordinate and announced, "You need not dismount, General. I hear the sound of cannon on your front. Return to your command. I will join you there at once." Sickles then turned on his horse and raced back toward his front lines, with Meade following a short distance behind.[50]

As Meade rode past the left of Hancock's Second Corps, he was "wholly unprepared to find it [Sickles' corps] advanced far beyond any possible construction of its being on the prolongation of the line of the Second Corps. Its lines were over half a mile out to the front, to the Emmitsburg Road, entirely disconnected with the rest of the army, and beyond supporting

48 *OR*, 27/3: 1086; Meade, *Life and Letters*, 2: 71-72; Hyde, *The Union Generals Speak*, 44. Meade did not mention this meeting in his report or later in his Congressional testimony, and other supporters such as Warren followed suit. See *OR*, 27/1: 116. Also at 3:00 p.m., Meade drafted a dispatch to General-in-Chief Henry Halleck in Washington, "I have today, up to this hour, awaited the attack of the enemy, I having a strong position for defensive. I am not determined, as yet, on attacking him till his position is more developed. He has been moving on both my flanks, apparently, but it is difficult to tell exactly his movements. I have delayed attacking, to allow the Sixth Corps and parts of other corps to reach this place and to rest the men." See *OR*, 27/1: 72.

49 Meade, *Life and Letters*, 2: 72-73; Hyde, *The Union Generals Speak*, 168; *OR*, 27/1: 592; Biddle, "General Meade at Gettysburg," *The Annals of the War*, 211.

50 Hyde, *The Union Generals Speak*, 44; Meade, *Life and Letters*, 2: 72-73; Sickles, "Further Recollections of Gettysburg," *North American Review*, 265-266; Tremain, *Two Days of War*, 60-61.

distance." Warren initially accompanied Meade but as they turned toward the Peach Orchard, he directed Warren to Little Round Top instead. "I wish you would ride over and if anything serious is going on, attend to it." Warren and several staff officers then rode rapidly toward the hill.[51]

Meade proceeded to the Peach Orchard, and arrived just after Sickles. The generals conducted their first meaningful conversation of the day. Needless to say, Meade was not pleased by what he saw:

> I told him [Sickles] it was not the position I had expected him to take; that he had advanced his line beyond the support of my army, and that I was very fearful he would be attacked and would lose the artillery, which he had put so far in front, before I could support it, or that if I undertook to support it I would have to abandon all the rest of the line which I had adopted- that is, I would have to fight the battle out there where he was.[52]

Meade assessed the new Third Corps line. He deemed the Emmitsburg Road ridge neutral ground. The Third Corps was beyond immediate support from the remainder of the army, and presumably any enemy troops that reached this sector would suffer from the same disadvantage. Therefore, in Meade's estimation, neither army could occupy or otherwise use the ridge to its advantage.[53]

Sickles "expressed regret" that he moved his corps to a position that did not meet with his commander's approval. He promptly offered to withdraw to the Cemetery Ridge line. However, with a Confederate attack imminent, Meade feared that the enemy "would not permit him to withdraw, and that there was no time for any further change or movement." As if Longstreet's artillerists sought to punctuate Meade's thoughts, before he "had finished that remark," Rebel batteries opened fire and the battle commenced. It was too late to withdraw the Third Corps. Meade would have to support Sickles's advanced front.[54]

51 Meade, *Life and Letters*, 2: 72-73; Trudeau, *Gettysburg: A Testing of Courage*, 320; Coddington, *The Gettysburg Campaign*, 388.

52 Hyde, *The Union Generals Speak*, 108.

53 Meade, *Life and Letters*, 2: 78-79; Biddle, "General Meade at Gettysburg," *The Annals of the War*, 211.

54 Hyde, *The Union Generals Speak*, 108. Meade similarly wrote in his report, "I was explaining to him that he was too far in advance, and discussing with him the propriety of withdrawing, when the enemy opened on him with several batteries in his front and on his flank, and immediately brought forward columns of infantry and made a most vigorous assault." *OR*, 27/1: 116.

"Second Day's Fight" Stereoview by Levi Mumper.
Author's Collection

Whether or not Sickles had any personal authority over supporting troops remained a point of debate among the participants. Meade told Sickles that he planned to move the Fifth Corps to the army's left. According to Sickles, Meade also pledged, "I could look to General Hancock for support on my right flank. I added that I should want considerable artillery; that the enemy were developing a strong force of artillery. He authorized me to send to General Hunt who commanded the reserve of the artillery, for as much artillery as I wanted." Sickles then confidently assured Meade "in my ability to hold the position; which I did."[55]

Given the mutual animosity between the generals, it seems unlikely that Meade would entrust Sickles with anything more than the Third Corps infantry. This lack of clarity, however, added to the afternoon's chaos when Sickles and

55 Hyde, *The Union Generals Speak*, 45. Also see Sickles, "Further Recollections of Gettysburg," *North American Review*, 266.

his staff later attempted to commandeer elements of the Fifth Corps away from their designated points.[56]

Artillery projectiles increasingly flew across the Peach Orchard as the conversation between Meade and Sickles drew to a close. The generals and their assembled staffs made inviting targets for the Confederate gunners. Apparently Meade's favorite horse, "Old Baldy," was unavailable when Meade needed to ride to the Peach Orchard, so he borrowed a mount from General Pleasonton. Rider and horse were unaccustomed to each other, and according to an amused Henry Tremain, Meade had some difficulty in keeping the beast from running. Fortunately for the Union war effort, Meade was uninjured, but his departure from the Peach Orchard marked the final time that he and Sickles met on the battlefield.[57]

Meanwhile, chief engineer Warren reached Little Round only to find his worst fears confirmed. Warren discovered that only a handful of signal officers occupied the hill with no infantry or artillery nearby to provide support. Standing near the summit, Warren's view to the west revealed Longstreet's developing battle line. Warren hurriedly sent a message to Meade urging the general "that we would at once have to occupy that place very strongly." Sykes's Fifth Corps was already en route to the Union left, but Meade feared they would not arrive in time to secure his flank. He ordered Humphreys to abandon the Emmitsburg Road and move at once toward Little Round Top.[58]

Humphreys received his orders and prepared his division to move at once. He also directed the courier to relay his concerns to Meade about vacating his current position along the Emmitsburg Road. Humphreys then decided to deliver the message personally to Meade. He presumed that Meade was in the Peach Orchard and rode in that direction. Before arriving, another of

56 Henry Tremain alleged in his memoirs, "just after the ball opened General Meade agreed with [Sickles] and promised him support." Unfortunately "the supports were not placed under his command and were not handled as intelligently as they would have been by one who knew the surroundings more perfectly." See Tremain, *Two Days of War*, 104.

57 Pfanz, *Gettysburg: The Second Day*, 142, 144; Tremain, *Two Days of War*, 63-65. According to Henry Tremain, one enemy "ball went high and harmlessly struck the ground. But the whizzing missile had frightened the charger of General Meade into an uncontrollable frenzy. He reared, he plunged. He could not be quieted. Nothing was possible to be done with such a beast except to let him run; and run he would, and run he did. The staff straggled after him; and so General Meade . . .was apparently ingloriously and involuntarily carried temporarily from the front."

58 Hyde, *The Union Generals Speak*, 168; Norton, *Attack and Defense of Little Round Top*, 309; Coddington, *The Gettysburg Campaign*, 388.

Meade's staff members intercepted Humphreys and notified him, "General Meade recalled his order [to deploy on Little Round Top] and that I should occupy the position General Sickles had directed me to take." Fifth Corps reinforcements were approaching Little Round Top and Meade no longer needed Humphreys to secure the hill.

Humphreys recalled, "In a second the division went about-face," as they returned to their prior position along the Emmitsburg Road. He boasted, "the whole thing was done with the precision of a careful exercise, the enemy's artillery giving effect to its picturesqueness." Those military men who watched the spectacle from Cemetery Ridge described it "as a beautiful sight." An aide soon arrived from Sickles instructing Humphreys to return to the Emmitsburg Road. This message presumably annoyed Humphreys and he responded that the shift was already underway. The whole incident probably consumed very little time, and overall, was of little importance. In the bigger picture, however, this was not the final time that troops marched in confusion along Sickles's front.[59]

59 Meade, *Life and Letters*, 2: 82-83; Woods, "Humphreys' Division's Flank March to Little Round Top," *Gettysburg Magazine 6*, 59-60; Humphreys, *Andrew Atkinson Humphreys: A Biography*, 193-194.

Chapter 4

Crush the Enemy's Line

After Sickles notified Captain George Randolph that he intended to "change his line," the Third Corps artillery chief responded by guiding Captain James Smith's 4th New York Independent Battery to the rocky Houck's Ridge. The large boulders at the southern end of this ridge, better known as Devil's Den, became the new left flank of the Third Corps. Artillery located along this platform had generally open fields of fire for about 1,100 yards west to the Emmitsburg Road. From a defensive perspective, the higher Little Round Top sat dominantly about 500 yards behind (east of) Houck's Ridge. The low ground of the Plum Run valley lay in between these two elevations. Attacking infantry could potentially exploit the gap between Devil's Den's left and the Round Tops. However, Randolph did not dwell on Houck's Ridge for long. After checking on Smith, he moved about 700 yards to the north, in the direction of the Peach Orchard, and supervised placement of Captain George Winslow's Battery D, 1st New York Light Artillery in the Wheatfield. This was not an ideal position for artillery, since wooded terrain blocked fields of fire to the west and south, but Winslow provided support for Colonel de Trobriand's nearby brigade. Despite an admittedly "sharp angle in our line," at the Peach Orchard, Captain Randolph considered the new deployment to be a "much more desirable one," than Cemetery Ridge.[1]

1 *OR*, 27/1: 581-582, 587; Smith, *A Famous Battery and Its Campaigns*, 101-102.

General Hunt meanwhile, determined that the artillery fire opposite Cemetery Hill was not of a serious nature, so he returned to the Peach Orchard, "knowing that its occupation would require large reinforcements of artillery." Hunt observed that the Third Corps infantry was already posted there when he arrived. He witnessed Meade and Sickles, "not far off, in conversation," and assumed erroneously that Meade consented to Sickles's movement. Hunt soon met up with Captain Randolph, who informed the general "that he had been ordered to place his batteries on the new line."[2]

The Army of the Potomac's artillery organization had a distinct advantage over that of their adversary. General Hunt had the authority to request more guns from Brigadier General Robert O. Tyler's Artillery Reserve. Lee's nominal chief of artillery, General William Pendleton, did not have the luxury of an army-wide reserve from which to draw additional guns. Hunt put this advantage to good use in defending the Peach Orchard. He requested two batteries from Tyler's reserve and then accompanied Randolph to station more artillery. Most of the Confederate batteries had already unlimbered along Warfield Ridge and soon opened, as Hunt reported, "a brisk fire."[3]

Randolph spotted a Confederate battery moving into place near a barn along the Millerstown Road, a site plainly visible from the Peach Orchard. From these guns, the Southerners "opened a smart artillery fire upon the troops massed in the open field." In response, Randolph ordered Judson Clark, whose battery was closest to the scene, to move slightly forward to "the foot of the next slope, near the peach orchard." General Sickles also instructed Clark, "Hold this position while you have a shot in your limbers or a man to work your guns." Captain Clark went to work immediately, issuing orders in what one artillerist recalled as a "clear, ringing voice that could be heard above the roar of battle." Clark moved from piece to piece and supervised the fire, type of projectile, and time of fuse. Eventually, when satisfied with his dispositions and alignments, Clark instructed his gunners to "Fire at will!" The enemy's return fire was also effective. Within moments of going into action, Thomas Post, a member of Clark's battery had his head "shot off."[4]

2 Hunt, "The Second Day at Gettysburg," *Battles and Leaders*, 3: 303-304. In his report, Hunt placed this meeting around 2:00 p.m. See *OR*, 27/1: 234.

3 *OR*, 27/1: 234- 235.

4 Ibid., 27/1: 582, 586; Hanifen, *History of Battery B*, 68-69; Murray, *E.P. Alexander and the Artillery Action in the Peach Orchard*, 46, 48. Battery member George Bonnell told John Bachelder in 1882 that Clark's battery was initially in the "corner of the Peach Orchard" and moved to the "rear and right flank" before they "blazed away." See Ladd, *The Bachelder*

Colonel Edward Porter Alexander
The Confederate General

Hunt and Randolph's desire to defend the Peach Orchard with artillery was well-founded. From the Confederate perspective, Robert E. Lee described the orchard and Emmitsburg Road ridge as "a position from which, if he [the enemy] could be driven, it was thought our artillery could be used to advantage" in assaulting Cemetery Hill beyond. Lee considered Longstreet's control of the Peach Orchard as essential in the larger strategic plan. As had occurred at Chancellorsville, the Confederates again expected their artillery to play a crucial role. Southern gunners were to unleash a destructive enfilade fire onto the Federal position and clear the way for the Confederate infantry to advance.[5]

The long, open slope of Warfield Ridge provided excellent fields of fire and ample space to unlimber Colonel E. P. Alexander's guns. Even more fortuitously, the opposing Federal commander had seemingly obliged by placing his troops into an awkward salient along the Emmitsburg Road. Surely an artillerist of Alexander's skill would take advantage of this error by pouring a converging fire toward the salient from the south and west. With any success,

Papers, 2: 843. The Battery history stated that after they earlier fired the opening rounds at Hood's infantry, they advanced to "within 50 yards of the Emmitsburg Road," but were then ordered by Randolph to engage in counter-battery fire, which resulted in a "right reverse" movement. See Hanifen, 68.

5 *OR*, 27/2: 308. In recounting the "great measure due" the Southern artillery for the Chancellorsville victory, Lee reported, "Every suitable position was taken with alacrity, and the operations of the infantry supported and assisted with a spirit and courage not second to their own. It bore a prominent part in the final assault which ended in driving the enemy from the field at Chancellorsville, silencing his batteries, and by a destructive enfilade fire upon his works opened the way for the advance of our troops." *OR*, 25/1: 803-804; Barnett, "Severest and Bloodiest Artillery Fight,*"* 65. Lee's description of Chancellorsville could easily apply to his intentions for July 2 at Gettysburg.

Confederate artillery would destroy Federal resistance and thereby compel enemy troops to retreat. If not withdrawn, the Union defenders might be so demoralized that Longstreet's infantry would sweep them from the field. If Alexander then rolled his guns into the captured orchard, and unleashed hell on Cemetery Ridge beyond, the tactical situation would resemble a replay of Hazel Grove.

In addition to his own reserve artillery battalion, two other units fell under Alexander's authority. These were McLaws's artillery battalion, led by Colonel Cabell, and Hood's battalion directed by Major Mathis Henry. This brought to 14 the number of batteries Alexander controlled. As befitted their roles, Cabell's battalion stood within mutual supporting distance of General McLaws's infantry, while Henry deployed further south, to the Confederate right in order to conform to Hood's movement in that direction. "It was about 3 p.m." recalled Alexander, "when Hood's division, in the advance, crossed the Emmitsburg Road about 1000 yards south of the Peach Orchard." Colonel Alexander also noted, "The enemy's artillery had opened upon us as soon as our approach was discovered, and we presently replied."[6]

Furthest to the Confederate right, Major Henry's battalion included Captain James Reilly's six-gun Rowan Artillery. Henry placed Reilly just east of the Emmitsburg Road, on an elevated position that provided line of sight to Devil's Den and the Round Tops. Captain Alexander Latham's five-gun battery, with only four guns engaged, held a position several hundred yards left of Reilly. Latham could reach Devil's Den and the Wheatfield, but his location also created the opportunity to fire up the Emmitsburg Road and strike Federal targets near the Peach Orchard; a distance of roughly 1,400 yards. Henry's other two batteries, eight guns under Captains William Bachman and Hugh Garden, did not deploy.[7]

6 Alexander, *Military Memoirs*, 394. It is curious that recollections from both sides generally recall the other as being the first to open fire. It seems probable that Clark fired the first shots at Hood's men and then Alexander replied in greater force.

7 *OR*, 27/2: 427. Latham was likely near the Bushman farm lane or possibly just west of the Emmitsburg Road. There is some lack of clarity on the number of guns in Reilly's Rowan Artillery. They have two War Department Tablets in Gettysburg National Military Park. The primary tablet says, "Two Napoleons, Two 10 Pounder Parrotts, ____ Rifles." Major Henry's brief report did not provide a number, "took position in the afternoon on the right of our line, and engaged the enemy's artillery with two batteries, Captains [James] Reilly and [A. C.] Latham." The matter is further complicated by the fact that one barrel burst and was later replaced by a captured 10 Pounder Parrott from Smith's battery. Evander Law told John Bachelder in 1886 that Reilly had six. See *Bachelder Papers*, 3: 1371. Among modern studies,

In fact, Confederate artillerists delayed or failed to deploy several batteries throughout the course of the afternoon. Strategically, Alexander perhaps held back some guns prior to their expected advance. Yet, tactically, this robbed the Southerners of potentially bringing to bear a superior number of guns when Federal resistance later proved surprisingly "obstinate."[8]

After having been cut off and delayed by Hood's Division during the countermarch, Colonel Cabell received orders to "hurry up," and he brought his guns onto the field at a full gallop. "It was a magnificent sight," Cabell remembered, "to see so much enthusiasm on entering a battlefield." Alexander showed Cabell where he wished the guns placed. Confederate skirmishers, already scrapping with their Federal counterparts, warned the artillerymen "don't go that way unless you want to be killed." As if to prove the point, enemy fire soon struck and wounded Cabell's horse. His artillery unlimbered several hundred yards to the left of Henry's guns and closer to the Federal position in the Peach Orchard. Cabell received further orders not to fire until Alexander's own battalion was also in position.[9]

Cabell's Battalion likely engaged with 14 guns. His batteries primarily unlimbered in the broad, flat and slightly elevated fields about 50-75 yards east of modern West Confederate Avenue. Cabell's batteries deployed from their right to left, or south to north as they extended from Henry's left, with Captain John Fraser's four-gun Pulaski Artillery fronting northeast toward the Peach Orchard. To Fraser's left was Captain Edward McCarthy's First Richmond Howitzers. McCarthy was initially in reserve, but within 30 minutes, two of the battery's four guns swung into action. On McCarthy's left, Captain Henry Carlton unlimbered two 10-pounder Parrotts. Next to him stood four more pieces of Captain Basil Manly's First North Carolina Artillery, Battery A and to Manly's

---

Busey and Martin, *Strengths and Losses* (177), Floyd, *Commanders and Casualties* (55), Pfanz, *Gettysburg: The Second Day* (160), Murray, *E.P. Alexander* (42), Laino, *Gettysburg Campaign Atlas* (448), Barnett, "Severest and Bloodiest Artillery Fight," (69) all accept six guns. It should be noted, however, that many of these sources cite each other or the inconclusive GNMP Tablet.

8 Murray, *E.P. Alexander and the Artillery Action in the Peach Orchard*, 41-44; Pfanz, *Gettysburg: The Second Day*, 160. Some have speculated that Henry did not have enough room to deploy his entire battalion, yet he reported on July 3, that he "engaged the enemy again in the same position with the whole battalion." Alexander wrote that Henry only engaged with ten guns. See *Military Memoirs*, 395. Latham's battery included a six-pounder and it is debatable whether the piece would have been effectively used in this action. See Barnett, "Severest and Bloodiest Artillery Fight," 80, n.35.

9 *OR*, 27/2: 375; Cabell, "A Visit to the Battle-field of Gettysburg," VHS, 3-4.

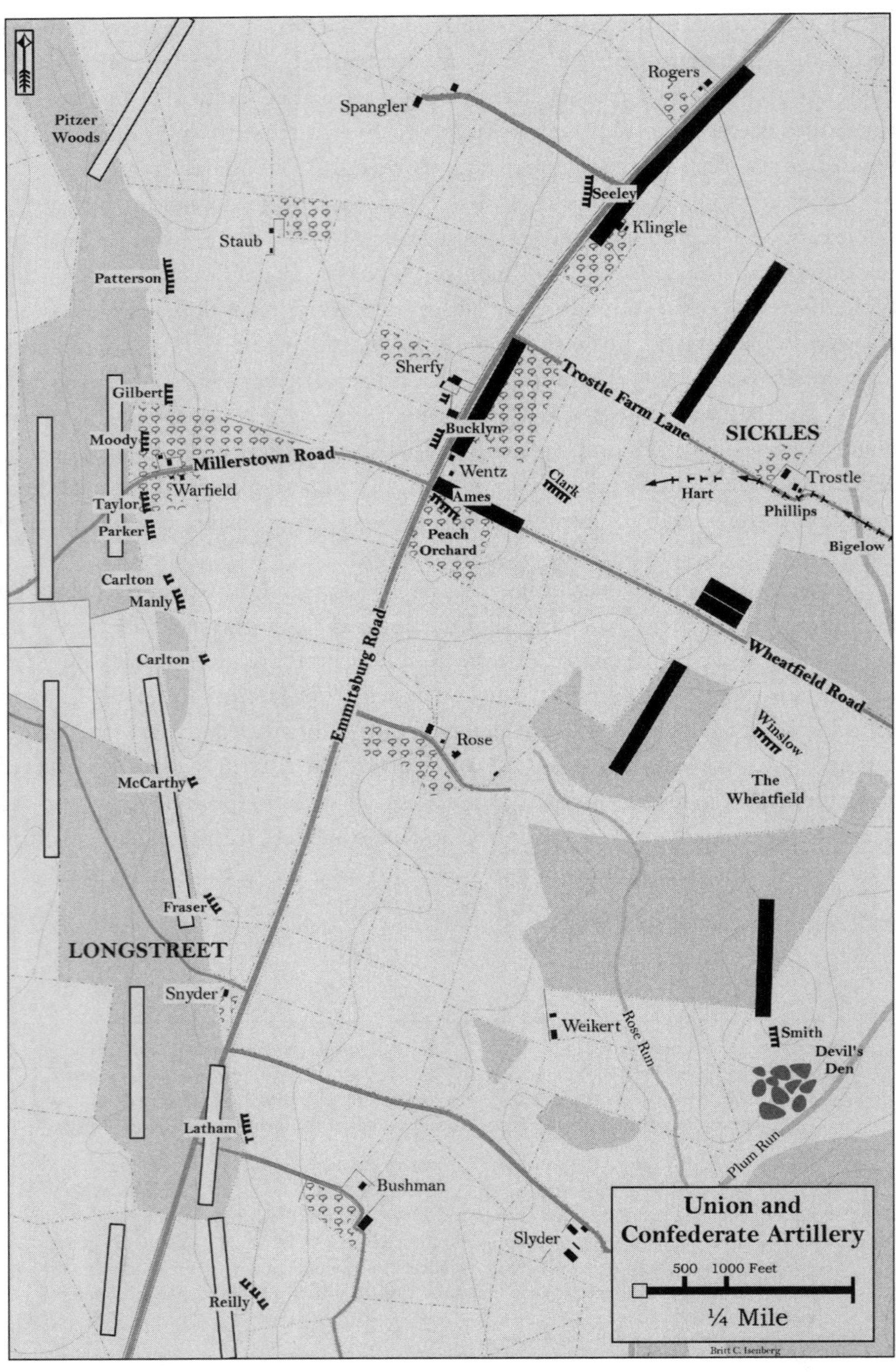

Pitzer Woods
Spangler
Rogers
Seeley
Klingle
Staub
Patterson
Sherfy
Trostle Farm Lane
Gilbert
Moody
Bucklyn
SICKLES
Millerstown Road
Wentz
Clark
Warfield
Ames
Hart
Trostle
Taylor
Phillips
Parker
Peach Orchard
Bigelow
Carlton
Manly
Carlton
Emmitsburg Road
Wheatfield Road
Winslow
Rose
McCarthy
The Wheatfield
Fraser
LONGSTREET
Snyder
Weikert
Rose Run
Smith
Devil's Den
Latham
Plum Run
Bushman
Slyder
Reilly
Union and Confederate Artillery
500
1000 Feet
¼ Mile
Britt C. Isenberg

left was another section from Carlton's battery. Carlton's left did not extend as far as the Millerstown Road.[10]

Captain Manly described his approach via the Millerstown Road. "The road on which we moved was perpendicular to the enemy's line, but it was supposed that their left did not extend to this point of intersection to which we were moving. My instructions were, if we gained this point, we would be on the enemy's left flank, and that I must form line on the left, and attempt to rake their line." This erroneous assumption was consistent with Longstreet's original expectations. However, after Manly discovered that the Federals held the Peach Orchard "with a large force of infantry and artillery," he moved his battery into line "by a right-oblique." Manly reported that the Federal guns "opened upon us immediately" and his battery replied in kind. He actively engaged the enemy at an estimated distance of 700 yards, "giving and receiving a very heavy fire for several hours."[11]

Captain Fraser's battery, on the right of Cabell's battalion, took a position north of the Phillip Snyder farm, "behind a loose rock fence" that ran along parts of the ridge. The battery was in place only a short time before it commenced firing. Fraser opened with all four of his guns on the Northern batteries that stood across the road to their far left-front. "The firing at first was rapid," wrote Lieutenant William Furlong, "but soon became slow and cautious, the gunners firing slow, evidently making each shot tell with effect on the enemy's batteries." Furlong acknowledged that the "enemy replied with spirit, their fire being incessant, severe, and well directed."[12]

10 According to Alexander, Cabell engaged with 18 guns but 14 seem like a more likely number. See Alexander, *Military Memoirs*, 394-395. The War Department tablets situated in Gettysburg National Military Park to denote the various battery positions are generally placed immediately next to modern West Confederate Avenue. This is for the convenience of visitors, but the batteries were not along the present-day avenue. There is no clear contemporary record of Cabell's alignment. The lineup reflected here is the same as the placement of the memorial tablets to Cabell's batteries in GNMP (N to S from Millerstown Road): Carlton's battery one section of two 10-lb Parrotts, Manly's battery of two Napoleons and two 3-inch Ordnance Rifles, Carlton's second section of two 10-lb Parrotts, McCarthy's battery of two Napoleons and two 3-inch Ordnance Rifles (only rifles engaged), and Fraser's battery of two 10-lb Parrotts and two 3-inch Ordnance Rifles. Most modern studies have followed this arrangement, including Laino, *Gettysburg Campaign Atlas*, 173; Pfanz, *Gettysburg: The Second Day*, 314; Desjardin, Friends of GNMP Second Day Map; Barnett, "Severest and Bloodiest Artillery Fight," 70; and Murray, E.P. Alexander and the Artillery Action in the Peach Orchard, 42-43. John Bachelder's Second Day Troop Position Map aligned Cabell differently as: Manly, McCarthy, Fraser, and Carlton.

11 *OR*, 27/2: 380.

12 Ibid., 27/2: 382. The description of Fraser's battery position "on the right of the battalion, behind a loose rock fence" originates with the battery's report written by Lt. Furlong on July 30,

Sergeant Anderson W. Reese, a member of Carlton's Troup Artillery, wrote that the Federals in the Peach Orchard were probably about 600 yards away "immediately in our front." Skirmishers fired aggressively at their counterparts across the lines as Reese's battery rolled into position. The Federal skirmishers made a "determined stand to hold" their line on the west side of the Emmitsburg Road, but the Rebels eventually drove them across the road and back into their main battle-line. Almost immediately after that, "our battalion opened fire upon the force in the peach orchard and field. The enemy's batteries (U.S. Regulars) responded promptly, and then the ball fairly opened."[13]

On the Federal side, Captain Nelson Ames's First New York Light, Battery G, was the first of Tyler's reserve to arrive in the Peach Orchard. Earlier that morning, Ames received instructions from Artillery Reserve headquarters to report to Sickles. This contradicts Sickles's later assertions that headquarters ignored his pleas for additional support. Ames followed orders and parked his guns near Trostle's large stone barn, a structure that provided a degree of protection. He remained there until about 3:00 p.m. when hostilities started to escalate. Randolph sent him forward about 700 yards to "take position in a thick peach orchard and engage the enemy's batteries."[14]

1863. The War Department tablet placed in Gettysburg National Military Park states, "took position here 3.30 P. M. and opened fire on Peach Orchard and the Union batteries east of it." Like other tablets, it is placed next to and on the east side of modern West Confederate Avenue, behind a reconstructed stone wall that runs the length of the avenue. The actual battery position was likely about 40 yards to the east and closer to the Snyder house. Little Round Top is visible to the right front, which is consistent with Cabell's assertion that they were "exposed ourselves to a flanking fire from the enemy's mountain batteries." See *OR*, 27/2: 375. The distance from the summit of Little Round Top to the Snyder house and points nearby is close to 1,700 yards. Devil's Den, where Smith's battery was located, is about 1,100 yards away. Also see Pfanz, *Gettysburg: The Second Day,* 528, n. 12 for a discussion.

13 Letter of Anderson W. Reese, *Southern Banner* (Athens, GA), August 8, 1863, Troup Artillery File, GNMP. This letter signed "A.W.R." has been misattributed by some to Private Andrew W. Reese. There was no Private Andrew W. Reese in the battery. Anderson Watkins Reese enlisted in the Confederate service in 1861 as a private. He was appointed Sergeant Major on May 11, 1863. Prior to the war, he was part owner and editor of the *Southern Banner* in Athens GA., to whom this was addressed. See Civil War Soldiers and Sailors Database, NPS.gov and Troup Artillery Roster, jackmasters.net/troup.

14 *OR*, 27/1: 900; Ames, *History of Battery G*, 62-63. In his *OR*, Ames reported receiving his initial orders at 11:00 a.m. In his battery history (62) Ames did not specify a time and described his park "in a small hollow near a large brick barn." The description and distance likely indicate the Trostle barn, near Sickles's headquarters. There is a dispatch in the *OR* correspondence timed at 12:50 p.m. from Chief of Staff Dan Butterfield for "Commanding Officer Artillery Reserve" to "send a battery to report to General Sickles on the left." See

With the opposing Southerners already unlimbered, Ames ran a gauntlet of artillery fire. His battery had to cross the large open field that lay between Trostle's farm lane and the Wheatfield Road. The ground rose gradually as they approached the Peach Orchard. One of the Confederate batteries had what Ames called "excellent range of my battery," and nearly all their shots struck within Ames's command. Fortunately for the men, the fire killed only two horses. "I was obliged to halt in plain sight of the enemy," Ames complained, "to clear away two fences which the supporting infantry had failed to throw down as they had been ordered to do."[15]

Upon reaching the Peach Orchard, Ames fronted his six guns to the southwest. He decided to personally remain with his less experienced center and left sections, but the orchard's foliage prevented him from seeing his right section. As the battery began firing at will, a sergeant from the right section raced up to Ames and yelled, "For God's sake, come and tell us where to place our guns; we have been running them up and down all over this field, no place is satisfactory to the lieutenant." An exasperated Ames hurried in that direction and threatened to send the lieutenant to the rear if he did not get to work. The warning was effective, and all three sections of the battery were soon in business.[16]

Visibility diminished quickly because smoke from the guns hung beneath the branches of the orchard's trees. The terrain, however, offered Ames the advantage of elevation, which he asserted, "made it possible for every one of our shots to take effect." The slight knoll upon which he unlimbered caused some Confederate shots to land in front of his battery and then rebound overhead. Ames kept his ammunition caissons closer than normal and "sheltered in the rear just where the ground began to descend." This proximity provided for more expedient resupply, but also increased the risk of an ammunition chest being blown sky high by an enemy projectile. Fortunately, this danger did not materialize.[17]

Lieutenant Colonel Freeman McGilvery, commander of the 1st Volunteer Artillery Brigade, received General Hunt's order for two additional batteries

---

OR, 27/3: 1086. This could be the order that brought Ames onto the field, with times later misremembered by Ames, or perhaps this 12:50 p.m. message was a response to the removal of Buford's cavalry.

15 *OR*, 27/1: 900; Ames, *History of Battery G*, 63.

16 Ames, *History of Battery G*, 64-65.

17 Ibid., 66-67; Murray, *E.P. Alexander and the Artillery Action in the Peach Orchard*, 52-53.

Lieutenant Colonel Freeman McGilvery
USAHEC

from the reserve. McGilvery selected Captain John Bigelow's 9th Massachusetts and Captain Charles Phillips's 5th Massachusetts batteries. McGilvery reported to Sickles, who directed the artilleryman to inspect the ground and place his guns accordingly. Accompanied by Bigelow, McGilvery made a brief reconnaissance under fire and decided these batteries would cover the ground between the Peach Orchard and the Wheatfield. In this sector, Graham and de Trobriand's infantry brigades lacked the manpower to fully connect with each other, thus leaving a gap between their positions. McGilvery's guns attempted to compensate for this weakness in the line. Bigelow also noted that the salient, formed by Graham's position at the Peach Orchard, would be difficult to defend. He explained that the position was vulnerable, "circled as it was (on both sides) by commanding ridges" and by enemy artillery "which concentrated their fire and enfiladed the two lines of the angle, with destructive effect."[18]

Bigelow brought his battery into action via Trostle's farm lane. He halted briefly at Sickles's headquarters and remembered, "a spirited military spectacle lay before us; General Sickles was standing beneath a tree close by, staff officers and orderlies coming and going in all directions." Approximately 700 yards away at the Peach Orchard, Bigelow observed, "white smoke was curling up from the rapid and crashing volleys" while "the enemy's shells were flying over or breaking around us."[19]

Bigelow moved his battery from the Trostle lane through a gateway and onto the fields toward the Wheatfield Road. Captain Ames had earlier run his battery through this field while under fire and Bigelow's men suffered from the same problem. As they crossed the field, Cabell's batteries had

18 Bigelow, *The Peach Orchard*, 11.

19 Ibid., 52.

a relatively clear view of them from the southwest. Not only was Bigelow unable to return fire while on the move, but the amount of time needed to unlimber and get the crews in position increased his vulnerability. One can imagine the feelings of these men – fear, excitement, anger - as their training kicked in and they systemically unlimbered their Napoleons while enemy projectiles fell all around them. "One man was killed and several wounded before we could fire a single gun," recalled a member of one of the gun crews. Bigelow placed his battery's left in the Wheatfield Road, but his right curved "about ten yards back from the road." The terrain inhibited the left section's field of fire, "being so far down as not to be able to sight their guns on anything." The section received orders to "limber to the rear; by the left flank, march!" and they went back into battery on the right of the line.[20]

Following Bigelow was Captain Phillips's 5th Massachusetts Artillery. Bigelow was already briskly engaged as Phillips came into action on his right. Phillips's left piece crashed over the remains of a rail fence and unlimbered "into battery right oblique." Almost immediately, Rebel gunners directed a shot at a guidon on the battery's right and killed two horses. Phillips exchanged fire with Confederate batteries for a lengthy period. He slowly controlled his rate of fire and sometimes stopped entirely to allow smoke to clear. The Confederate artillery remained partially hidden from view by the stone wall and the tree line that ran along Warfield Ridge. "Though no enemy could be seen on our immediate front," wrote Phillips, "the smoke of the enemy's guns could be seen over a rolling, open country."[21]

Captain Patrick Hart also arrived with his four-gun 15th New York Independent Battery. Hart told two versions of how he moved his guns into position. In his report, Hart wrote that he and McGilvery initially rode forward together and, after a brief consultation with Sickles, reconnoitered the ground. After McGilvery selected a position, Hart proceeded to move his battery there when General Hunt intercepted them. Hunt, then "ordered me to take a position on the left of the peach orchard." Hart obeyed "and came into battery as directed."[22]

20 Ibid.; Baker, *History of the Ninth Massachusetts Battery*, 57.

21 Ladd, *The Bachelder Papers*, 1: 166-167; Murray, *E.P. Alexander and the Artillery Action in the Peach Orchard*, 70, n. 35.

22 *OR*, 27/1: 887.

Years later, however, Hart described a more colorful exchange. In 1891, Hart told historian John Bachelder that he had orders from Hunt to report directly to Sickles. Hart claimed that he moved his battery to the rear of the infantry near the Wheatfield Road and then searched the field for Sickles. He noticed a party of officers under a large tree and hurried to meet them. Upon his arrival, Hart inquired of the group as to Sickles's whereabouts, but the officers refused to offer any information. As Hart prepared to return to his battery, Sickles stepped forward. The general "pointed over his shoulder and ordered me to go out there and you will find room enough to fight your Battery." It was as Hart rode forward to place his battery, in the position vaguely defined by Sickles, that Hunt intervened and posted the guns.[23]

General Hunt sandwiched Hart in between Phillips on the left, and Judson Clark's battery on the right. Attempting some last-minute inspiration, Hunt reminded Hart of the potential risks and rewards. "It will be a gold chain or a wooden leg for you," remarked Hunt. "Sacrifice everything before you give up that position." Hart then directed his fire "on one of the enemy's batteries, which was doing heavy execution on our line of battle. This battery was to my right and front, and distant about 900 yards. I used solid shot and shell with such effect that the enemy was compelled to withdraw their battery."[24]

Twenty-five years later, the monument to Hart's battery was placed on the north side of the Wheatfield Road. That position, however, would have made it impossible for Hart to fire effectively to his right and front. The intervening elevation of the Peach Orchard would have blocked his line of sight in those directions. Both sections of the battery were instead likely placed south of the Wheatfield Road and next to the eastern boundary of the Peach Orchard.[25]

According to the Lieutenant Edward M. Knox, the battery galloped into the orchard after Hunt pointed them in that direction shouting, "Go in there.

23 Ladd, *The Bachelder Papers*, 3: 1788.

24 *OR*, 27/1: 235, 887; Ladd, *The Bachelder Papers*, 3: 1788-1789.

25 John Bachelder's 4:00 p.m. July 2 map placed Hart in the Peach Orchard itself. It should also be noted that when the memorial was dedicated in 1888, it was placed on ground north of the Wheatfield Road that was owned by the Gettysburg Battlefield Memorial Association (GBMA). At the dedication, it was noted, "General Hunt . . . placed the battery at 4:30 p.m. in the Peach Orchard, with the four guns pointed south, from which position they opened on the enemy's artillery, using solid shot and shell with such good effect that one of the opposing batteries was forced to withdraw." See *New York at Gettysburg*, 3: 1328.

Rush!" As they went in, Hart turned to Knox and said, "Lieutenant, you fight the right section. I will look out for the left." Knox recalled that his speed and momentum "carried me fully 100 yards ahead of the artillery line on the left," meaning that his section was further forward than both Phillips and Bigelow's batteries.[26]

Sickles's headquarters at the Trostle farm was only several hundred yards behind the growing line of artillery along the Wheatfield Road. This meant that the corps commander was within range of Confederate over shots from Warfield Ridge. Excelsior brigade chaplain Joseph Twichell took cover behind the Trostle's large barn. He described the exchange of fire as "the most terrific artillery fire I ever witnessed. . . . It was awful. For half an hour it raged incessantly. Grape, canister, solid shot, and shell whizzed and shrieked and tore past us." Twichell watched as nearby trees and animals were torn apart by shell fragments. "Every moment I expected to be struck." Eventually the wounded started to come in. "One of our boys was brought to us with both legs gone."[27]

General Hunt estimated that it was approximately 3:30 p.m. when he detected more Confederate batteries rolling into position across the Emmitsburg Road. He sent to Tyler's artillery reserve yet again for more guns. Captain Smith's battery had not yet opened from Houck's Ridge above Devil's Den, so Hunt rode in that direction to determine the reason for the silence. Hunt arrived to find that Smith had "just opened fire," with four of his of his six guns in position along the rocky ridge. As General Hood's Confederate infantry emerged from the tree-line on the horizon, Hunt warned Smith that "he would probably lose his battery" in the ensuing assault.[28]

General Hunt then proceeded to the Wheatfield to examine Captain George Winslow's battery of six 12-pounders. From his vantage point, Winslow faced farmer Rose's woods and thus, was not yet engaged. By Hunt's order, Winslow threw a few rounds of solid shot in the enemy's direction. Winslow considered the enemy out of range and thought the fire likely ineffective. In

26 Beyer and Keydel, *Deeds of Valor*, 231.

27 Messent and Courtney, *Civil War Letters of Joseph Hopkins Twichell*, 248.

28 *OR*, 27/1: 235; Smith, *A Famous Battery and Its Campaigns*, 102; Hunt, "The Second Day at Gettysburg," *Battles and Leaders*, 3: 305. Hunt took opportunity in *Battles and Leaders* to complain that he had an insufficient staff for an officer of his responsibilities, thus making it "awkward" to perform such duties while also staying in contact with "every part" of the battlefield.

contrast, Bigelow, Phillips, and Hart were all "hotly engaged" at this point, so Hunt did not linger with Winslow for very long.[29]

As the hostilities intensified, Captain Randolph hurriedly added the remaining Third Corps batteries to the action. He posted his former battery, Lieutenant John Bucklyn's First Rhode Island, Battery E, along the Emmitsburg Road. The battery's Lieutenant Benjamin Freeborn reported that this movement occurred "under a heavy artillery fire from the enemy." Bucklyn's left and center sections took a position between the Wentz and Sherfy buildings, while the right rested in the Sherfys' garden between their house and barn. The battery commenced firing immediately. Although they claimed success in "silencing several of the enemy's guns" the salient in the orchard worked to their disadvantage. Their opponents "soon opened from different points, and, owing to the peculiar formation of the line, we were at times exposed to a heavy cross-fire."[30]

While the artillery remained busy, Colonel George Burling's infantry brigade waited nearby for their orders. The brigade, detached earlier from General Humphreys's division to support Birney, had massed in Trostle's Woods, about 700-800 yards southeast of the Peach Orchard. At roughly 3:45 p.m. Burling received orders to advance at the double quick toward the Emmitsburg Road. The men began to take fire from Confederate projectiles as they advanced, and after proceeding approximately 100 yards, Burling ordered them to return to the woods. A series of orders and counter-orders flew as thick as the artillery shells. Captain John Poland of Sickles's staff arrived and "in an excited manner" demanded to know why Burling had pulled back. Burling began to move forward again, when a message came from Birney ordering the brigade to instead move to the left.

Yet another courier arrived with instructions directing Burling to "detail two of my largest regiments" to report to General Graham. The colonel selected the 2nd New Hampshire and 7th New Jersey for the mission. The 7th New Jersey's Colonel Louis Francine reported to Graham and was placed in the field north of the Wheatfield Road as support for Clark's battery. Colonel Burling received additional orders throughout the afternoon progressively stripping him of the other regiments in his command. With his brigade scattered along Sickles's front, the orphaned Burling eventually reported back to General

29 *OR*, 27/1: 235, 587.

30 Ibid., 27/1: 589-590; Murray, *E.P. Alexander and the Artillery Action in the Peach Orchard*, 50; Pfanz, *Gettysburg: The Second Day*, 133.

Colonel Edward L. Bailey
USAHEC

Humphreys with no regiments of his own.[31]

Colonel Edward Bailey, a 21-year-old from Manchester, led the 2nd New Hampshire. Bailey had a common school education, no prior military experience, and worked as a post office clerk when the war started. The young man likely owed his original commission as 1st lieutenant to the influence of the town postmaster, who was the unit's first colonel before resigning in June 1861. The men of Company I elected Bailey captain and he saw action in nearly all early engagements in the Eastern Theater. By the time of Fredericksburg, he was a lieutenant colonel and earned a promotion to colonel in April 1863. The regiment was detached and missed Chancellorsville, but Bailey earned a reputation as a strict disciplinarian during the long, hot marches of mid-June. He ordered company officers court-martialed if more than three of their men were absent from the ranks. Despite his youth, the regiment's historian later characterized Bailey as "one of the bravest and most skillful" young officers in the army.[32]

The regiment advanced swiftly toward the Peach Orchard and General Graham. "If the movement was intended to develop the enemy's position by drawing his fire," wrote the regimental historian sarcastically, "it succeeded to perfection," as a barrage of shells greeted the men. The Rebel artillery fire left several soldiers wounded, and the regimental colors fell to the ground as the staff was broken into three pieces. After marching uphill at the double-quick, Graham placed the 2nd in support of Ames's battery near the northwest corner

31 *OR*, 27/1: 570-571, 578; Haynes, *A History of the Second Regiment*, 169-170; Toombs, *New Jersey Troops*, 205-206; Woods, "Humphreys' Division's Flank March to Little Round Top," *Gettysburg Magazine 6*, 60.

32 Haynes, *A History of the Second Regiment*, 286-287; Smith, "'We drop a comrade's tear': Colonel Edward Lyon Bailey and the Second New Hampshire Infantry at Gettysburg," *Papers of the 2006 Gettysburg National Military Park Seminar*, 101-106. At Fredericksburg, the 2nd New Hampshire primarily guarded pontoon bridges.

of the orchard, their left wing fronting south along the Wheatfield Road. The right wing, however, faced the Emmitsburg Road and received instructions to lie down. Company B, armed with Sharp's breechloaders, was detached as sharpshooters and began to move among the Wentz farm buildings.[33]

The Federals were not the only ones dealing with problems. The opening salvos from Smith's New York battery along Houck's Ridge exposed Colonel Cabell's Confederate batteries to a flanking fire from what he described as "mountain batteries." However, Cabell's position also gave his batteries a similar opportunity to enfilade the Union artillery aligned along the Emmitsburg Road. "The fire from our lines and from the enemy became incessant," reported Cabell, "rendering it necessary for us sometimes to pause and allow the smoke to clear away, in order to enable the gunners to take aim. During the same time, two guns were ordered to play upon the batteries on the stony mountain--I have reason to believe with great effect."[34]

"The Federal artillery was ready for us and in their usual full force and good practice," acknowledged Colonel Alexander. Sergeant Anderson Reese of Carlton's Troup Artillery affirmed, "The firing was the most rapid I have ever witnessed and the earth literally vibrated under the continuous roar. For about half an hour the fight raged without a moment's cessation" until the Confederate infantry finally advanced. "I have never seen guns better served, and right in the center of the battalion, working like beavers and covered with dust and smoke, were Carlton's brave boys."[35]

The ground along Cabell's front offered little protection for the battery crews. Alexander and Cabell both lamented the subsequent loss of men and horses. Sometime during the afternoon, Captain John Fraser of the Pulaski Artillery was mortally wounded by a shell, possibly fired from Ames's left section. The round also killed three other Southerners. As his men carried Fraser to the rear, another officer leapt from his horse to ascertain the identity of the dying soldier. Upon learning that it was Fraser, the officer's eyes welled with tears and he promptly kissed the dying artilleryman on the lips. Fraser was a close friend of Longstreet's staff officer Moxley Sorrel. Only a few days earlier, Sorrel kidded Fraser about his "very bad hat" and

33 Haynes, *A History of the Second Regiment*, 169-171, 185.

34 *OR*, 27/2: 375.

35 Alexander, "Artillery Fighting at Gettysburg," *Battles and Leaders*, 3: 359; Letter of Anderson W. Reese, *Southern Banner* (Athens, GA), August 8, 1863, Troup Artillery File, GNMP.

both men were pleased when the commissary supplied the captain with a new one. Sadly, according to Sorrel, the new hat now served as a pillow to Fraser's "shattered head." Fraser had only been a captain since April 30, but Cabell paid a fitting tribute in characterizing him as "an officer of great merit, brave, firm and heroic in action." Fraser died of his wounds on July 11. The losses in his battery were so great that his replacement, Lieutenant William Furlong, could subsequently muster only enough men to work two of their four pieces.[36]

Estimates of total losses in Cabell's battalion were 15 killed and 37 wounded, for a rate of 13.8%. Of these, Fraser's battery suffered the heaviest with 7 killed and 12 wounded (30.2%), followed by McCarthy's 3 killed and 10 wounded (14.4%). Not coincidentally, both batteries were next to each other on Cabell's extreme right. Fraser's casualty rate was second highest for any Southern battery in the battle, and their 30% loss rate was comparable to many storied infantry regiments.[37]

To assist the beleaguered Cabell, Colonel Alexander ordered 16 guns from his own battalion into position near Warfield's house. The battalion, commanded temporarily by Major Frank Huger, opened fire on the Peach Orchard from roughly 500 yards. Huger deployed the battalion to Carlton's left, starting with Captain William Parker's Richmond Battery of one 10-pounder Parrott and three 3-inch Rifles. One of Parker's artillerymen, John Hightower, fell off a limber as the guns moved into position. The rear wheels grievously crushed his leg and Hightower was out of action before the battery fired a single round. In his post-war writings, Alexander overestimated the number of pieces engaged under his total command. He put the number at 54, although 47 seems more likely. Regardless of the actual number, Alexander's intent was

36 Alexander, "Artillery Fighting at Gettysburg," *Battles and Leaders*, 3: 359; *OR*, 27/2: 375, 382; "Fought in Many Battles: Conflicts of the Pulaski Guards in the Civil War," Typescript from *Savannah Morning News*, June 13, 1898, Pulaski Artillery File, GNMP, original FSNMP; Sorrel, *At the Right Hand of Longstreet*, 182. The time at which Fraser was struck is unclear. In an account written 24 years later, Cabell said this shot came from Little Round Top and occurred as Sickles's troops were being driven from the Peach Orchard. Cabell, "A Visit to the Battle-field of Gettysburg, VHS, 5-6. Busey and Busey, *Confederate Casualties at Gettysburg*, 1: 541, said Fraser was struck with shrapnel to the head and thigh by a round from Ames's left gun just prior to the Confederate infantry advance.

37 Busey and Martin, *Strengths and Losses*, 270, 553. Unless noted otherwise, all loss estimates in this work come from Busey and Martin, or Steve Floyd's summarized *Commanders and Casualties*.

clear. "I hoped they would crush that part of the enemy's line in a very short time, but the fight was longer and hotter than I expected."[38]

As the time approached 4:00 p.m. Alexander's additional batteries roared into action. To Parker's left was Captain Osmond Taylor's Battery of four Napoleons. On the north side of the Millerstown Road stood Captain George Moody's four 24-pounder Howitzers of the Madison Light Artillery. Next to Moody was the Brooks South Carolina Artillery that consisted of four 12-pounder Howitzers. Lieutenant Stephen Gilbert commanded these guns, which were also referred to as Rhett's Battery in honor of their former commander. One artilleryman recalled, "Then commenced one of the most terrible fires of artillery I ever heard. Men and horses [were] falling on every hand." Alexander's final two batteries, under Captain Pichegru Woolfolk and Captain Tyler Jordan, remained temporarily in reserve. By progressively adding more batteries, the Confederate artillery threatened the Peach Orchard salient from two sides: the west and the south. Unfortunately for the Southerners, their officers did not exploit this advantage earlier in the action, and thus allowed the Northern batteries to deploy for a longer fight.[39]

Captain Taylor reported receiving orders to "to dislodge" the Federal batteries "if possible, from a commanding position which they held." He opened with spherical case from his Napoleons, but also added canister, which was unusual in counter-battery engagements. Canister would inflict damage on the enemy's personnel, rather than their guns, and demonstrated the relatively short distances between the opponents. While engaged here, Taylor lost "one of my best gunners," Corporal William Ray, who was killed while sighting one of the pieces. "He never spoke after receiving the shot, walked a few steps from his piece, and fell dead."[40]

The addition of Taylor's battery introduced one of the more curious human-interest stories to the afternoon's drama. Attached to the battery was

38 Alexander, "Artillery Fighting at Gettysburg," *Battles and Leaders*, 3: 359-360; Krick, *Parker's Virginia Battery*, 146. Alexander wrote that Huger had 18 guns instead of 16. R.L. Murray's excellent work, *E.P. Alexander and the Artillery Action in the Peach Orchard*, 75-77, estimated 41 cannon used in Alexander, Cabell, and Henry's battalions. The later deployment of Patterson's battery raised this total to 48, but a more practical estimate is 47. The authors address this issue later in this narrative.

39 The memorial tablets in Gettysburg National Military Park for all the above-named batteries indicate that they moved into position at 4:00 p.m. *OR*, 27/2: 429-430; Prince, "Brooks Artillery (Rhett's Battery) Unpublished History," n.p., Charleston Library Society.

40 *OR*, 27/2: 433.

Sergeant Henry Wentz, who returned to Gettysburg as a Confederate soldier and unlimbered his guns just a few hundred yards from his family home. Unfortunately, Wentz left no known account of his actions. This lack of a written record allowed a significant amount of misinformation regarding his fate to make its way into Gettysburg literature and lore.

While Wentz's service record indicated a professional dedication to the Confederate military, one can only imagine the mixed emotions the young man felt on the afternoon of July 2. Surely, he worried about his family's personal safety and the security of their modest holdings. One Northern account later claimed that Sergeant Wentz convinced his comrades to spare the family home from destruction. Although Wentz knew the local terrain, it remains unclear whether he provided reconnaissance information to his superior officers. Given the complexities of the day's maneuvers, it seems unlikely that the Confederate command would not have utilized his knowledge of the area. Perhaps this was another example of the poor communication that plagued Lee's operations on this day.[41]

The placement of Huger's batteries likely came at Longstreet's insistence. McLaws's infantry, specifically the front-line brigades of Kershaw and William Barksdale, were posted behind the Confederate guns, awaiting further orders. McLaws recalled that Longstreet pointed to a gap near the Millerstown Road in front of the division and asked, "Why is not a battery placed here?" McLaws protested and asserted, "it will draw the enemy's artillery right among my lines formed for the charge and will of itself be in the way of my charge, and tend to demoralize my men." Longstreet remained unmoved by the appeal and peremptorily ordered a battery placed in the gap. McLaws's prediction came true. These newly positioned Confederate batteries drew

41 McMillan, *Gettysburg Rebels*, 165-168; Barnett, "Severest and Bloodiest Artillery Fight," 72-73; Haynes, *A History of the Second Regiment*, 187. Wentz is listed as present for duty on the battery's muster roll from January 1862 until his capture at Sailor's Creek in April 1865. See Military Service Record for Henry Wentz, National Archives, (courtesy of Jim Clouse). Wentz was promoted to Orderly (sometimes noted as Ordnance) Sergeant on January 1, 1863. See Harry Pfanz to Joseph Gardner, October 8, 1959, GNMP; Milton E. Thompson to Lt. Robert Brake, September 13, 1966, GNMP. Some accounts erroneously reported that Sergeant Wentz commanded the battery and wrongly claimed that he was killed on his parent's farm. Clearly, records confirm that Wentz survived the battle. Harry Pfanz speculated that Wentz may have served the Confederates as a guide. See Pfanz, *Gettysburg: The Second Day*, 118, 533, n.96. Also see Tucker, *High Tide at Gettysburg*, 278. Author Tom McMillan identified at least one more member of the battery with probable Gettysburg connections. Sergeant Henry D. Wirt(s), who likely attended Pennsylvania (Gettysburg) College in the 1856-1857 school year and may be connected to a Henry D. Werts who appeared in the 1850 federal census in Straban Township, Adams County. See McMillan, 162-165.

Modern view of Ames's Battery with Warfield Ridge in background.
Photo by Authors

immediate Federal counter-battery fire onto the waiting infantrymen. McLaws described the effect as "cutting the limbs of the trees in abundance, which fell around my men, and the bursting shells and shot wounded or killed a number whilst in line formed for the advance, producing a natural feeling of uneasiness among them." McLaws mounted his horse and rode along his lines, directing his exposed men to lie down and "escape as much as possible from the shot and shell which were being rained around us from a very short range."[42]

McLaws later took Longstreet to task for this seeming indifference to the infantrymen's safety. Yet, the First Corps commander managed his exterior lines quite effectively. Longstreet recognized that the best way to use the position to his advantage, and turn the Peach Orchard salient to Sickles's disadvantage, was to hit the Union line from two sides. Huger could fire from the west while Cabell and Henry continued to strike from the south. Despite Alexander's

42 McLaws, "Gettysburg," *SHSP*, 7: 72-73. Whether McLaws's recollections were referring specifically to the placement of Moody or Rhett's guns is uncertain. See Barnett, "Bloodiest Artillery Fight I Ever Saw," 71.

skills as an artillerist, and his post-war proficiency as a commentator, he failed to identify this tactical opportunity.

This additional Southern firepower was a most unwelcome surprise to the Northern gunners. Before Captain Ames had time to "congratulate myself or men upon our success" thus far, one of the Confederate batteries fired upon his right from about 500 yards away, and another new battery opened upon his front. In response, Ames ordered his right section to turn their two pieces upon the flank battery, while his left and center sections directed their fire upon the battery in front. Ames considered it "as sharp an artillery fight as I ever witnessed."[43]

Ames and his men took notice when canister flew in their direction. The incensed lieutenant commanding the right section thought the occasion called for a response of canister in kind, but Ames decided to "show them what could be done with solid shot" in order to disable the Confederate pieces. The first two return shots were unsuccessful, but the third shot supposedly "struck under the barrel" of the target and "threw it nearly as high as the tops of the trees." Captain Ames suggested that his lieutenant "change his opinion about firing canister."[44]

It is uncertain which Rebel battery Ames targeted with his well-placed solid shot. Although Taylor reported firing canister, he did not indicate losing any pieces in such a manner. Lieutenant Gilbert, on the other hand, reported losing two howitzers from his Brooks Artillery and seems a likely candidate. Gilbert's battery suffered higher casualties, in fact, than any artillery unit in the Army of Northern Virginia during the battle. Modern analysis placed their casualties at 36 killed and wounded, although Alexander thought the number was 40, for an almost unheard-of artillery loss rate of 50.7%. Clearly Gilbert's battery took their share of return fire.[45]

Captain Ames was "soon pleased to see one piece of the flank battery dismounted, and the cannoneers of another either killed or wounded, when the other two pieces were taken from the field." Ames then refocused his attention upon the batteries in front, "but was obliged to fire very slowly, as my ammunition was getting exhausted, having but a few rounds of spherical case left, with a small supply of solid shot and canister." Since Ames was

43 *OR*, 27/1: 582, 900.

44 Ames, *Battery G*, 71-72.

45 Prince, "Brooks Artillery," n.p.; Alexander, *Military Memoirs*, 399; Alexander, *Fighting for the Confederacy*, 240; Busey and Martin, *Strengths and Losses*, 277, 549, 553. Alexander refers to the battery as "Fickling's" in reference to their later commander.

among the first batteries into action, his was also among the first to suffer from a depleted ammunition supply.[46]

Phillips and Hart's artillerymen also quickly noticed this increased threat on their extreme right. A rise of ground between their positions and the Emmitsburg Road, however, blocked their view in that direction. Yet, the rising terrain did not shield them from incoming fire. "We were most annoyed by a battery on our right," Phillips recalled, "hidden from us by the rising ground and the Peach orchard which enfiladed our line." Hart reported that the enemy "poured a tremendous cross-fire into me, killing three of my men and wounding five, also killing thirteen horses."[47]

The men and horses of Clark's Battery B, 1st New Jersey suffered terribly from enemy shot and shell exploding in their ranks. As two soldiers named Timm and Riley held a handspike, a Confederate shell plunged into the ground and detonated under their feet. The explosion threw the men some "twenty feet in the air." As they regained their senses, the men realized the extent of their injuries. Riley saw that the flesh from his right hip had been sheared to the bone and exclaimed, "By Jiminey, I didn't think they could touch me without taking a limb, and now, damn 'em, they have taken half the meat I did have." While Riley was understandably distracted, a lieutenant barked, "Riley, why the bloody hell don't you roll that gun by hand to the front?" To which Riley replied, "Lieutenant, if your hip was shot off like that, what the bloody hell would you do?" Riley was ordered to the hospital and departed "on one foot and two hands like a lame dog." Clark's remaining men shouted, "Take that for Riley!" as they subsequently returned fire.[48]

Meanwhile, the 2nd New Hampshire's Company B remained posted among the nearby Wentz buildings. Armed with Sharp's rifles, these men served as the regiment's skirmishers and sharpshooters. Confederate skirmishers and even some artillerists were in range, so the men of Company B opened fire and gave the enemy a "wicked reception." The remainder of the regiment was observing with great interest when the new Confederate batteries "completely enfiladed" their line. In order to secure shelter, the regiment's right wing changed front away from the Emmitsburg Road, so that the entire unit faced

46 *OR*, 27/1: 901.

47 *OR*, 27/1: 235, 887; Ladd, *The Bachelder Papers*, 1: 167, 2: 844; Murray, *E.P. Alexander and the Artillery Action in the Peach Orchard*, 65-67.

48 Hanifen, *History of Battery B*, 72, 74.

south along the Wheatfield Road. This probably offered slight protection, but the boys could do nothing more than lay in position. The regimental history remembered their "closely hugging the ground" as the afternoon hours slowly ticked away.[49]

In June 1863, the War Department issued an experimental and controversial "musket shell" bullet to the men of the 2nd New Hampshire. Shaped like a conventional Minie ball, the bullet contained an explosive charge as a filling along with a timed fuse. The bullet was intended to explode when it struck enemy troops or horses, increasing the projectile's lethality and the potential to induce panic. However, the bullet performed poorly in field tests. Not only did it fail to explode consistently, but it also lacked the accuracy and penetration ability of the conventional Minie ball. Some officers even questioned the morality of such a weapon. One such critic noted, "We think it is enough to shoot a man without afterwards blowing him up." Nevertheless, thousands of rounds of this controversial and experimental projectile remained in the hands of the 2nd New Hampshire at Gettysburg.[50]

The extent to which these "musket shells" affected the overall shooting accuracy of the 2nd New Hampshire is unclear, and there are no accounts of exploding bullets causing a panic in Longstreet's ranks. However, at least one New Hampshire soldier paid the ultimate price for carrying them. A Confederate artillery shell struck Corporal Thomas Bignall of Company C. "The cartridges [from his cartridge box] were driven into his body and fired," remembered a veteran, "and for nearly half a minute the devilish 'musket shells' issued at Washington were exploding into his quivering form." Bignall's death was "mercifully quick," but another shell fragment subsequently exploded the cartridge box of Sergeant James House. "The rapidity with which he tore off the infernal machine hanging by his side was astonishing, and he escaped with only a severe wound."[51]

John Barker of Company C was leaning against a small peach tree when a shell burst nearby and a fragment struck him in the head. The shell knocked him unconscious, but Barker awoke while his comrades were carrying him to the rear. The men suddenly dropped Barker to the ground and he did not learn the reason why until several months later. A Rebel shell had killed Charles Moore, the soldier carrying Barker's right

49 Haynes, *A History of the Second Regiment*, 170-172.

50 Thomas, *Round Ball to Rimfire*, 182-188.

51 Haynes, *A History of the Second Regiment*, 172.

leg. Barker began crawling toward the rear in search of a field hospital. While en route, he crawled to another soldier and asked for directions. The other man could not reply; he was dead. Barker was assisted eventually to a field hospital but did not receive treatment for his skull fracture until the following afternoon. Barker survived the wound. After several medical procedures, he was discharged in 1864 due to vertigo and "constant pain in the head." Moore's remains were recovered and his final resting place is in Gettysburg's National Cemetery.[52]

Most Northern participants agreed on the intensity of the enemy artillery fire. General Graham simply called it three hours of "terrible shelling." Much of his brigade remained lying down in the field across from Sherfy's house on the east side of the Emmitsburg Road. "We remained in this position nearly two hours," reported Colonel Andrew Tippin of the 68th Pennsylvania, on the left of Graham's line. Tippin's Pennsylvanians were "suffering severely from the destructive fire of the enemy's batteries posted on our left and front." On the brigade's far right, the 105th Pennsylvania "Wildcats" also considered the bombardment "very destructive" and suffered a "loss of some 12 men while in this position."[53]

A regiment's location could mean everything in determining life or death. The Emmitsburg Road ridge likely shielded some Federals positioned immediately beneath it on the eastern slope. Captain Edward Bowen, whose 114th Pennsylvania was then on the left of the line, admitted they were under "a most severe fire" for two and a half hours, "losing, however, but few men, the enemy's range being too high." To their right, a member of the 57th Pennsylvania recalled, "we were exposed to one of the hottest artillery fires we ever encountered." The Confederate batteries to the south and west "poured a regular stream of shells towards us, but fortunately most of them exploded after passing over us."[54]

Colonel Henry Madill commanded the nearby 141st Pennsylvania. Madill was a 34-year-old former lawyer from Bradford County, Pennsylvania, and another example of a local boy coming home for this battle. He was born in nearby Hunterstown, Pennsylvania, which was the scene of a spirited cavalry engagement on this same afternoon. In 1831, Henry's father accepted a job

52 Ibid., 172-174; Haynes, "Muster Out Roll of the Second New Hampshire," 13.

53 Charles Graham account, Participants File 5, GNMP; *OR*, 27/1: 498-499, 500, 504; Scott, *History of the One Hundred and Fifth Regiment of Pennsylvania Volunteers*, 82.

54 *OR*, 27/1: 502; *Pennsylvania at Gettysburg*, 1: 356.

in another township, moving the family when Madill was about two years old. Thus, it seems unlikely that Madill retained any strong local memories. Madill's regiment, raised from the state's northern counties, had much more pressing matters to occupy them on this day.[55]

Madill reported that his regiment received orders to lie down in an oat field less than 100 yards from the Emmitsburg Road. "At this point we sustained a severe fire from artillery for some time, the enemy having a good range." On the other hand, a sergeant in the 141st did not recall much damage from "their cursed iron hail" since "fortunately there was a slight rise of ground in our front" that protected the men.[56]

As the afternoon progressed, more guns were fed onto Sickles's forward line from the Army of the Potomac's Artillery Reserve. Two sections of Captain James Thompson's Independent Pennsylvania Light arrived in the Peach Orchard at some point in the late afternoon. There were conflicting accounts over whether Thompson reinforced or replaced Ames near the orchard's northwestern corner. The four 3-inch Rifles from Thompson's left and center sections might have squeezed in tightly next to Ames. However, several accounts indicated that these guns took Ames's position after the New York battery withdrew. In either scenario, Thompson's guns fronted south and continued the stand-off against Cabell's Confederate batteries. Colonel McGilvery fronted Thompson's right section to the west, and they opened fire on "rebel artillery posted in the woods, at canister range . . . the enfilade fire of which was inflicting serious damage through the whole line of my command." Thompson remarked that one of his rifles was "between Sherfy's stable and garden fence" and the other was in the Emmitsburg Road itself. Once Thompson deployed, McGilvery's entire reserve brigade was in action near the Peach Orchard adding substantial firepower to Sickles's Third Corps batteries.[57]

55 Craft, *History of the 141st Regiment Pennsylvania Volunteers*, V, 1-7; Heverly, *History of the Towandas*, 267; Lash, "A Pathetic Story," *Gettysburg Magazine 14,* 77. Colonel Madill was commissioned an officer in the 6th Pennsylvania Reserves (35th Pennsylvania Infantry Regiment) in June 1861. He was promoted to colonel and mustered out in August 1862. When the 141st was formed in late summer of 1862, Madill was commissioned an officer in the regiment and assumed command in September. See compiled *U.S. Civil War Soldier Records and Profiles, 1861-1865* and Craft, 13.

56 *OR*, 27/1: 504; Craft, *History of the 141st Regiment Pennsylvania Volunteers*, 121. Madill reported his position as "some 15 rods" from the road. A rod equals 5.5 yards and thus Madill's measurement would be 82.5 yards.

57 *OR*, 27/1: 235, 881, 890; *Pennsylvania at Gettysburg*, 2: 910; Murray, *E.P. Alexander and the Artillery Action in the Peach Orchard,* 67-68. Captain Ames reported that he was relieved

Several hundred yards north of the Peach Orchard, General Humphreys found himself equally occupied by enemy gunners. He placed Lieutenant Francis Seeley's 4th U.S. Artillery, Battery K on the right of Daniel Klingle's log house to bolster his defenses. The counter-battery action soon spread across this front when seven Confederate guns under the command of Captain George Patterson arrived and dropped trail about 800-900 yards west of Seeley. In response, Humphreys moved Seeley to the left of Klingle's house. Lieutenant John Turnbull's six Napoleons from the consolidated Batteries F & K, 3rd U.S. Artillery, then moved to occupy Seeley's original location. As Turnbull took up his new position, his guns drew heavy fire and Captain Dunbar Ransom was wounded while supervising the battery's placement. Seeley "immediately opened fire with solid shot and spherical case, and, after a rapid and well-directed fire, lasting about fifteen minutes, succeeded in silencing this battery and causing it to retire." Seeley and Turnbull combined to pummel Patterson, who withdrew having fired 170 rounds. Patterson's command suffered seven casualties and seven horses killed in this brief but spirited encounter.[58]

As the artillery duel raged, and many hours after Robert E. Lee formulated his initial attack plan, Longstreet's infantry finally neared readiness to launch their assault. Unfortunately, Longstreet's artillery under Colonel Alexander failed to overwhelm their Northern counterparts. As many as 47 Confederate cannon engaged the enemy up to this point,

---

"at 5.30 p.m. I was relieved by Battery I, Fifth U.S." See *OR*, 27/1: 901. As will be discussed later, this identification of Battery I (Watson's) is also debated. McGilvery reported that Thompson took position on Hart's right and did not mention anyone else. See *OR*, 27/1: 881. Thompson (27/1: 889) did not report anyone on his left or right. Captain Thompson said at the battery's monument dedication that he relieved Ames and took the position that Ames had formerly occupied. See *Pennsylvania at Gettysburg*, 2: 910. Bailey of the 2nd New Hampshire reported, "At 4.30 p.m. . . . about this time a battery and a section of Rodman pieces were substituted for those we were supporting." See *OR*, 27/1: 574. Clark's Battery B, 1st New Jersey history wrote, "At 5:30 Thompson relieved Ames." See Hanifen, *History of Battery B*, 70. The two batteries would have shared about 140 yards of space between the Emmitsburg Road and modern Birney Avenue if both occupied the ground at the same time.

58 *OR*, 27/1: 532, 590; 27/2: 636; Ladd, *The Bachelder Papers*, 1: 607; Murray, *E.P. Alexander and the Artillery Action in the Peach Orchard*, 68-69; Toombs, *New Jersey Troops*, 202; Laino, *Gettysburg Campaign Atlas*, 205. Patterson's six-gun battery was supplemented by one 12-lb. Howitzer of Captain Hugh Ross's battery. Both were attached to Major John Lane's "Sumter" Artillery Battalion. See Patterson's battery marker on West Confederate Avenue, GNMP.

but the Federals brought 56 guns into action and many of their batteries successfully unlimbered under fire.[59]

Although Union General Henry Hunt later complained, "the defects of our organization were made palpable at Gettysburg" due to the generally lower grade of artillery field officers, the action around the Peach Orchard was clearly a victory for the Union brigade and reserve system. Not only did Hunt successfully utilize his reserve, but subordinate officers brought in additional firepower with great effect. Alexander had nothing comparable to draw upon. Had the Federals not utilized their artillery reserve, then Longstreet's artillery would have outnumbered their opponents by nearly two to one. Whether Northern artillery defended the Emmitsburg Road in vain remained a separate question; one that was not yet answered at this point on the afternoon of July 2.[60]

The Southerners still held positions that allowed converging and enfilade fire on the Union salient, as well as a greater target density near the Sherfy farm and Wheatfield Road. Longstreet's late-stage placement of Alexander's battalion into a position directly west of the orchard proved most effective. Despite these apparent advantages, Confederates batteries such as Gilbert, Fraser, Moody, and Patterson suffered heavily. The concentrated and prolonged Confederate fire also telegraphed clearly that Meade's left was the target of Longstreet's attack. In that sense, Longstreet's infantry lost the element of surprise that Jackson had enjoyed at Chancellorsville.[61]

Colonel Alexander declared in later years, "I don't think there was ever in our war a hotter, harder, sharper artillery afternoon" than July 2 at Gettysburg. If he succeeded in any objective, it was in the casualties and demoralization that the artillery fire inflicted on the Union forces near the Peach Orchard. For example, the 105th Pennsylvania attributed at least 10-12 men lost due to artillery fire, or roughly 10% of their total battle casualties. Extrapolating a similar 10% of losses, as a statistical exercise, throughout all the Northern

59 Alexander's 47 summed as: Reilly (6), Latham (4 out of 5), Fraser (4), McCarthy (2 out of 4), Carlton (4), Manly (4), Parker (4), Taylor (4), Moody (4), Gilbert (4), and Patterson (7). The Federals' 56 summed as Smith (4 on Houck's Ridge), Clark (6), Ames (6), Bigelow (6), Phillips (6), Hart (4), Bucklyn (6), Thompson (6), Seeley (6), and Turnbull (6). For this count, Winslow (6) is omitted in the Wheatfield since his battery played a minimal role in this phase of the engagement. These totals agree with Murray, *E.P. Alexander and the Artillery Action in the Peach Orchard*, 42-43, 86, except we have deducted the 6-pounder from Latham's total to coincide with Alexander's assertion that Henry's battalion engaged with 10 guns.

60 *OR*, 27/1: 242.

61 Murray, *E.P. Alexander and the Artillery Action in the Peach Orchard*, 75-78.

regiments posted nearby, would create artillery casualties in excess of 120 men. The strength reductions combined with the effect of suffering under a blazing sun, and with minimal cover, undoubtedly impacted the Third Corps's ability to defend their ground. However, the Northern infantry and artillery still held their positions. General Longstreet would not capture the Peach Orchard without an infantry fight.[62]

62 Alexander, "The Great Charge and Artillery Fighting at Gettysburg," *Battles and Leaders*, 3: 359-360; Scott, *History of the One Hundred and Fifth Regiment of Pennsylvania Volunteers*, 82. In this hypothetical example, 10% of total losses for the regiments in Graham's brigade would sum to 74 casualties. Ten percent of the 2nd New Hampshire's total losses would be 19, the 3rd Maine would add 12, the 7th New Jersey would add another 11, along with 5 more from the 3rd Michigan, etc. Of course, the Confederate infantry on Warfield Ridge were not immune either to similar degradation from Northern cannon fire.

Chapter 5

Gain the Emmitsburg Road

The Confederates developed their plan of attack under a misconception regarding the strength, length, shape, and location of Meade's left flank. Sickles's occupation of the Emmitsburg Road was, for better or worse, unexpected to the Southerners. As a result, Longstreet could not "gain the Emmitsburg Road," turn the Union left flank there, and attack up the road toward Gettysburg. Although Sickles earned his share of criticism for his actions, he disrupted Lee and Longstreet's plans by advancing to the Emmitsburg Road. General Longstreet's aggravating afternoon continued, as he had to quickly develop an alternative strategy.[1]

1 *OR*, 27/2: 358. Emphasis is given to Longstreet's use of the phrase "gain" the Emmitsburg Road. Many Gettysburg students often emphasize only that he was to "attack up" the road. This minimizes the fact that Longstreet was also expected to gain a foothold on the road and at the Peach Orchard for his artillery. Gettysburg students also often speculate on how Longstreet's attack would have unfolded had Sickles remained in Meade's preferred position on Cemetery Ridge. Many historians, particularly those that are critical of Sickles's advanced position and the general's colorful personality, argue that Longstreet would have blindly attacked up the Emmitsburg Road and allowed properly posted Third Corps troops to rake the Confederate right and rear from Cemetery Ridge. This argument, however, ignores (a) the so-called attack "up the Emmitsburg Road" was based on a flawed understanding of where the Union left ended, and (b) the Confederates abandoned plans to have McLaws's Division attack up the road after they realized that the Federal line stretched south of the Peach Orchard toward the Round Tops. Why would Longstreet's attack have continued up the Emmitsburg Road into a non-existent flank, knowing that enemy forces were in his flank and rear? As the situation unfolded, he abandoned his plans in the face of both conditions. Of course, this is all speculation (the bane of historians) and we will never know how Longstreet's attack would have developed in any alternate scenario. Once Sickles moved forward into the Peach

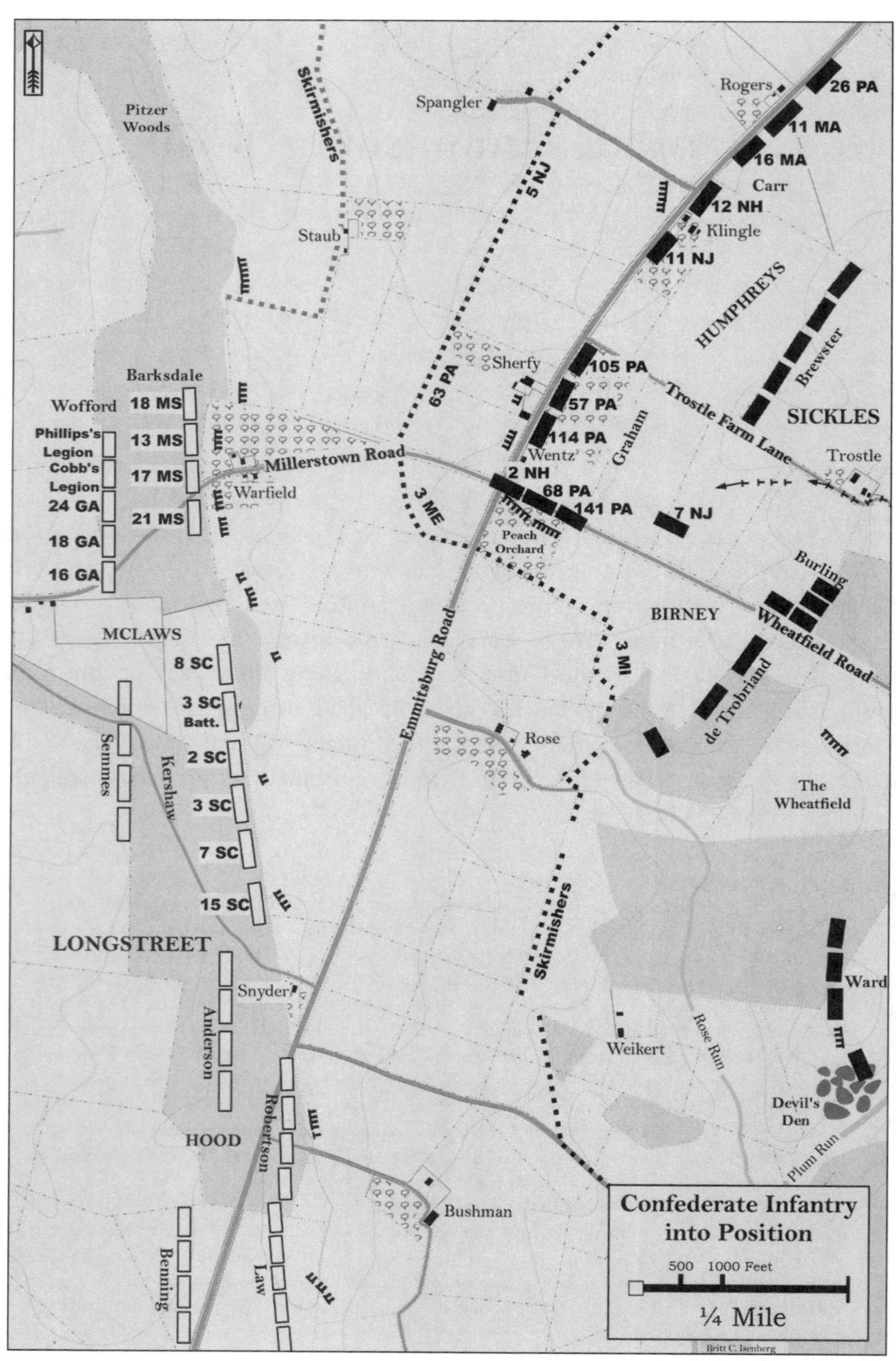
Pitzer Woods
Skirmishers
Spangler
Rogers
26 PA
11 MA
16 MA
Carr
5 NJ
12 NH
Klingle
Staub
11 NJ
HUMPHREYS
Brewster
Sherfy
105 PA
63 PA
57 PA
Trostle Farm Lane
SICKLES
Barksdale
Wofford
18 MS
Phillips's Legion
13 MS
114 PA
Graham
Cobb's Legion
17 MS
Millerstown Road
Wentz
Trostle
2 NH
Warfield
68 PA
24 GA
3 ME
141 PA
7 NJ
21 MS
Peach Orchard
18 GA
16 GA
Burling
BIRNEY
Wheatfield Road
MCLAWS
3 MI
8 SC
de Trobriand
Emmitsburg Road
3 SC
Batt.
Rose
Semmes
Kershaw
2 SC
The Wheatfield
3 SC
7 SC
Skirmishers
15 SC
LONGSTREET
Ward
Snyder
Anderson
Rose Run
Weikert
Devil's Den
Robertson
HOOD
Plum Run
Bushman
Confederate Infantry into Position
500 1000 Feet
¼ Mile
Benning
Law
Britt C. Isenberg

The most immediate modification meant that General John Bell Hood, and not General Lafayette McLaws, would lead the assault from Longstreet's right. Lee described this movement as "partially enveloping the enemy's left, which he [Hood] was to drive in." Longstreet added that Hood's Division was "pressing upon" the Federal left, while McLaws did the same upon the "front."[2] Regarding the dispositions themselves, Longstreet added:

> [A]s the line was deployed I rode along from left to right, examining the Federal position and putting my troops in the best position we could find. General Lee at the same time gave orders for the attack to be made by my right—following up the direction of the Emmitsburg road toward the Cemetery Ridge, holding Hood's left as well as could be toward the Emmitsburg road, McLaws to follow the movements of Hood, attacking at the Peach Orchard the Federal Third Corps, with a part of R.H. Anderson's following the movements of McLaws to guard his left flanks.[3]

Longstreet estimated that his troops were ready and their objectives identified by about 3:30 p.m. Despite the Sickles surprise, Longstreet and his men deployed for their alternate plan. A full reconnaissance of the enemy's new position was, of course, impossible. The officers would direct much of the First Corps actions based on what they could, and in some cases, could not see of the rolling, wooded, and rocky ground from Warfield Ridge.[4]

General Kershaw was waiting with his South Carolinians behind a stone wall on the ridge, when he received instructions to delay his attack until after Hood advanced. Kershaw saw Hood's troops moving "to gain the enemy's left flank, and I was directed to commence the attack so soon as General Hood became engaged, swinging around toward the peach orchard, and at the same time establishing connection with Hood, on my right, and co-operating

---

Orchard, his presence there disrupted the Confederate plans and caused significant on-the-field modifications. See Cooksey, "Up The Emmitsburg Road," *Gettysburg Magazine 26*, 45-48 for the best analysis of Longstreet's so-called desire to "attack up the Emmitsburg Road." Some historians have argued that Sickles, in his post-battle attempts to justify his actions, exaggerated the importance of the Peach Orchard in Lee's plans. As historian Richard Sauers wrote, "Many historians have fallen into the same trap and have repeated the same error of reasoning." See Sauers, *Gettysburg: The Meade-Sickles Controversy*, 155-156. However, numerous Confederate accounts support the theory that Lee intended to turn the Federal left at or near the Peach Orchard, and then use the orchard as an artillery platform. These accounts include Lee and Longstreet's official reports. Such a notion was not an invention of post-war posturing by Sickles or any other participant.

2 *OR*, 27/2: 318, 358.

3 Longstreet, "Lee's Right Wing at Gettysburg," *Battles and Leaders*, 3: 340-341.

4 Ibid.

with him." Kershaw understood that Hood would "sweep" the enemy's line northward and move "in a direction perpendicular to our then line of battle." Kershaw also understood that Barksdale's Brigade, on his left, was to "move with me and conform to my movement."[5]

In yet another Confederate breakdown, Hood's Division neither advanced promptly nor moved up the Emmitsburg Road as directed. "The instructions I received were to place my division across the Emmettsburg [sic] road," Hood later recalled, "form line of battle, and attack." Hood also sent several scouts ahead to establish the precise location of the Union Army's left flank. The scouts returned and advised Hood that the flank was "upon Round Top mountain." However, an opportunity existed for Hood's forces to pass around the hill, strike the enemy flank and rear, and capture the Union supply wagons parked nearby.[6]

Subsequent artillery fire from Smith's New York battery on Houck's Ridge helped to further define the position of the Federal lines. Hood's men observed that a "considerable body of troops was posted in front of their main line, between the Emmettsburg [sic] road and Round Top mountain. This force was in line of battle upon an eminence near a peach orchard."[7] Like Longstreet, McLaws, and Kershaw before him, Hood did not like what he saw:

> I found that in making the attack according to orders, viz: up the Emmettsburg road, I should have first to encounter and drive off this advanced line of battle; secondly, at the base and along the slope of the mountain, to confront immense boulders of stone . . . I found, moreover, that my division would be exposed to a heavy fire from the main line of the enemy, in position on the crest of the high range, of which Round Top was the extreme left, and, by reason of the concavity of the enemy's main line, that we would be subject to a destructive fire in flank and rear, as well as in front; and deemed it almost an impossibility to clamber along the boulders up this steep and rugged mountain, and, under this number of cross fires, put the enemy to flight.[8]

Hood relied on fresh intelligence provided by his own scouts, rather than outdated information from Lee, and accordingly, did not think the current plan had a chance of success. Instead, Hood proposed a flanking movement

5 *OR*, 27/2: 367.

6 Hood, "Letter from General John B. Hood," *SHSP*, 4: 148-149. Hood wrote the letter in 1875, more than a decade after the battle, and historians have noted some errors and inconsistencies in his recollection. Unfortunately, it remains Hood's best account of Gettysburg. The editors of the *Southern Historical Society Papers* reprinted the letter in 1877.

7 Ibid.

8 Ibid.

around the Round Tops. Longstreet must have felt genuinely conflicted at this moment. While he likely preferred such a maneuver, Hood's proposal stood clearly at odds with Lee's expectations. Several messages passed back and forth between Longstreet and Hood, but the plan of attack remained the same. Longstreet insisted, "General Lee's orders are to attack up the Emmettsburg [sic] road." Even with Sickles's flawed Peach Orchard salient clearly visible, Hood still thought the enemy's position seemed "so strong – I may say impregnable – that, independent of their flank fire, they could easily repel our attack by merely throwing and rolling stones down the mountain side as we approached."[9]

As the division prepared to advance, Longstreet arrived at Hood's position to discuss the situation. Hood again expressed his "regret at not being allowed to attack in flank around Round Top," but Longstreet insisted, "We must obey the orders of General Lee." Having argued his point unsuccessfully, Hood then rode forward to lead his men into battle.[10]

Hood's proposal had some merits, but it was not without significant problems, both operational and tactical. Such a movement would have stretched Lee's already over-extended lines. It also would have consumed more time, and given the lateness of the hour, leave little daylight for the men to execute such a massive attack. Hood would also have to conduct this redeployment under the watchful eye of an enemy who held a strong observation post on higher ground. Moreover, the Confederates had no way of knowing the true disposition of Union forces on the other side of the Round Tops, and Hood may have found his command trapped behind enemy lines."[11]

Some of Longstreet's post-war critics leveled accusations that his insistence on adhering to Lee's attack plan reflected his stubbornness. Some accused Longstreet of "sulking" and argued that he even persisted in order to "teach Lee a lesson." Longstreet was not sulking. He was a professional soldier acting as he felt his military duty required: to carry out his commanding officer's orders whether he personally agreed with them or not. Coincidently, the comportment that Longstreet demonstrated in this situation stood in direct contrast to the conduct displayed by his Union counterpart on the other side

9 Ibid. Also see McLaws, "Gettysburg," *SHSP*, 4: 71-72.

10 Hood, "Letter from General John B. Hood," *SHSP*, 4: 148-150.

11 Colonel Alexander considered it unlikely that Hood's proposal "would have accomplished much," noting that Lee's exterior line was already stretched to its limits. "Had our army been more united and able to follow up the move in force, it might have proved a successful one." See Alexander, *Military Memoirs*, 394.

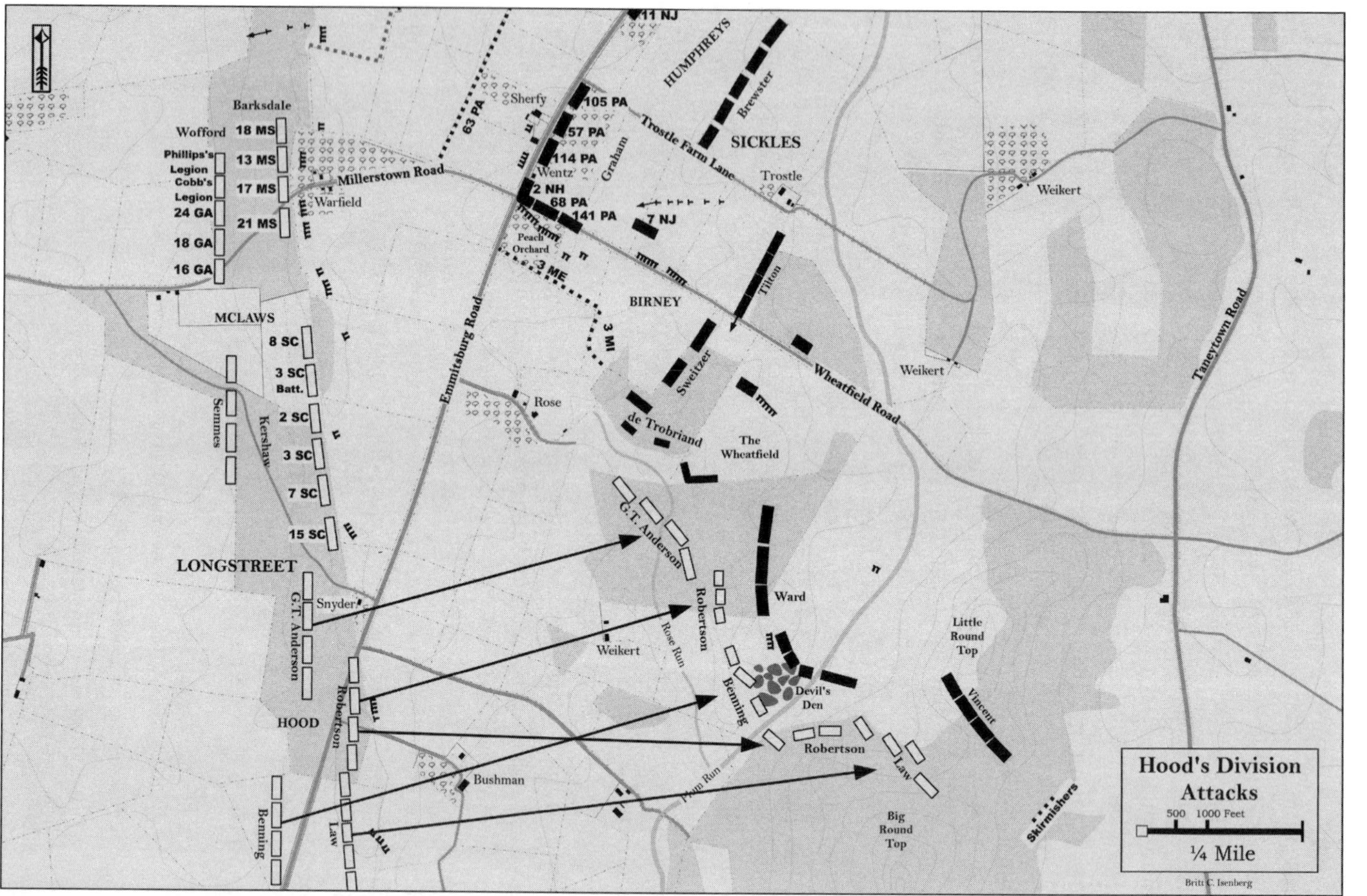
Hood's Division Attacks
500 1000 Feet
¼ Mile
Britt C. Isenberg
Taneytown Road
Wheatfield Road
Emmitsburg Road
Millerstown Road
Trostle Farm Lane
Weikert
Trostle
SICKLES
HUMPHREYS
Brewster
Tilton
Sweitzer
BIRNEY
de Trobriand
Graham
The Wheatfield
Ward
Devil's Den
Little Round Top
Vincent
Skirmishers
Big Round Top
Law
Robertson
Benning
Rose Run
Plum Run
G.T. Anderson
11 NJ
105 PA
57 PA
114 PA
141 PA
68 PA
2 NH
7 NJ
3 MI
3 ME
63 PA
Sherfy
Wentz
Peach Orchard
Rose
Bushman
Warfield
Snyder
Barksdale
18 MS
13 MS
17 MS
21 MS
Wofford
Phillips's Legion
Cobb's Legion
24 GA
18 GA
16 GA
MCLAWS
8 SC
3 SC Batt.
2 SC
3 SC
7 SC
15 SC
Kershaw
Semmes
LONGSTREET
HOOD

of the battlefield. In hindsight, some have criticized Longstreet for obeying his orders, while others have condemned Sickles for taking great liberties with his.[12]

Hood's Division stepped off sometime around 4:00 p.m. Brigadier General Evander Law's Brigade of Alabama regiments formed the division's right, while Brigadier General Jerome Robertson's Texas and Arkansas brigade was on the left. Following approximately 400 yards in the rear were two more brigades; one under Brigadier General Henry Benning and the other led by Brigadier General G. T. Anderson. Hood directed Benning to support Law, while Anderson was to reinforce Robertson. Almost immediately, Law's Brigade headed east toward the Round Tops instead of sweeping northward in the direction of the Peach Orchard. The rocky hills did not figure into the original Confederate plan of attack because according to the intelligence upon which Lee based the operation, the Federals did not occupy the area in force. However, with a considerably different situation confronting them, Hood's men instead committed imperfectly to a "partial envelopment" of Sickles's actual left flank.[13]

Brigadier General J. H. Hobart Ward's brigade, from Birney's division, opposed Hood on Houck's Ridge. With over 2,100 men in the ranks, Ward commanded the largest brigade in Meade's army. However, the detachment of the 3rd Maine and 1st U.S. Sharpshooters to points elsewhere, reduced Ward to six regiments and a total of approximately 1,650 men. General Ward also had earlier deployed Major Homer Stoughton's 2nd U.S. Sharpshooters as skirmishers near John Slyder's farm in front of Big Round Top. Ward reported that Stoughton "had scarcely obtained the position designated before the skirmishers of the enemy issued from a wood in front, followed by heavy lines of infantry." Stoughton's sharpshooters directed their fire toward Law's men and "did splendid execution, killing and wounding a great many." As a result, Law's Brigade advanced toward the U.S. Sharpshooters and pushed them back. In something of a cat-and-mouse pursuit, the retreating Federal

12 See Krick, "James Longstreet and the Second Day," *The Second Day at Gettysburg*, 75, for perhaps the most extreme manifestation of this scenario.

13 *OR*, 27/2: 318., Lee reported: "Longstreet was directed to place the divisions of McLaws and Hood on the right of Hill, partially enveloping the enemy's left, which he was to drive in." The Confederates abandoned the goal of driving in the Federal left by attacking "up" the Emmitsburg Road when that directive no longer made tactical or strategic sense. Also see Law, "The Struggle for 'Round Top," *Battles and Leaders*, 3: 323; Fox, *New York at Gettysburg*, 1: 45; Norton, *Attack and Defense of Little Round Top*, 255; Coddington, *The Gettysburg Campaign*, 386.

skirmishers drew Law's regiments closer to the Round Tops and further away from the Emmitsburg Road.[14]

Law's movements immediately created a gap between his left and the right of Robertson's Brigade. "I was ordered to keep my right well closed on Brigadier-General Law's left," Robertson reported, "and to let my left rest on the Emmitsburg pike." Robertson faced a dilemma. He advanced a short distance when he realized that his 1,700 men could not cover the widening gap with Law and also stay in contact with the road. Robertson understood "that the attack on our part was to be general, and that the force of General McLaws was to advance simultaneously with us on my immediate left, and seeing at once that a mountain held by the enemy in heavy force with artillery to the right of General Law's center was the key to the enemy's left, I abandoned the pike, and closed on General Law's left."[15]

Robertson's decision to follow Law was logical given the need to strike Meade's left, but it also ensured that subsequent assaults on the Peach Orchard occurred without Hood's Division. Their actions demonstrated that an attack "up" the Emmitsburg Road was impractical with Federal forces on and near the Round Tops. Adding to the problems on Longstreet's right, an artillery shell severely wounded General Hood early in the action and forced him from the field. The battery that fired this shot was unidentified. Given that Hood was likely in a line of fire from active batteries at the Peach Orchard and on the Wheatfield Road, one of them may have earned credit for the fateful shot. With Hood incapacitated, General Law assumed division command. While Law was a competent commander, this change further complicated coordination among Hood's four brigades and with McLaws's waiting division.[16]

14 *OR*, 27/1: 493, 515-516; Norton, *Attack and Defense of Little Round Top*, 256; Ladd, *The Bachelder Papers*, 2: 767; Adelman and Smith, *Devil's Den: A History and Guide*, 23-24. Coincidence or not, a movement toward the Round Tops was what Hood had favored. Was Law's departure away from the Emmitsburg Road an intentional "digression" by General Hood? See Trudeau, *Gettysburg: A Testing of Courage*, 321-324, 336-337 for a discussion.

15 *OR*, 27/2: 404. Also see Ladd, *Bachelder Papers*, 1: 36. Robertson elaborated in a post-war account, "My orders from Gen. Hood was to keep my left on the Emmitsburg road and in no event to leave it unless the exegency [sic] of the battle made it necessary or proper, in which case I was to use my judgment. A charge was started by Law's brigade on my right as I thought prematurely a full mile from the enemy's line of battle." See Ladd, *The Bachelder Papers*, 2: 860-861. The report of Colonel Van H. Manning, commanding the 3rd Arkansas, echoed this. See *OR*, 27/2: 407.

16 Hood, "Letter from General John B. Hood," *SHSP*, 4: 148-150; Law, "The Struggle for Round Top," *Battles and Leaders*, 3: 319. Numerous commentators have attributed Hood's early removal as a significant factor in the Confederate defeat. General Hood's departure certainly contributed to the numerous fractures in Confederate control as the attack advanced over

Colonel E.P. Alexander later acknowledged, with spectacular hindsight, "The management of the battle on the Confederate side during this afternoon was conspicuously bad. The fighting was superb." Some have characterized Longstreet's attack as *en echelon*, or a progressive assault that required each regiment to move only after the regiment on its right had advanced. Longstreet did not specify such a tactic in his report, although the Confederates essentially executed their attack in this manner at the brigade-level. In *Battles and Leaders*, he wrote only that Hood was supposed to hold his left to the Emmitsburg Road as best as possible and "McLaws was to follow the movements of Hood, attacking at the Peach Orchard." Only General Richard Anderson, commanding a division in A.P. Hill's Third Corps and positioned on McLaws's left, acknowledged orders to go "into action by brigades." This advance was to occur as soon as Longstreet's attack progressed far enough to connect with Anderson's right flank.[17]

In fact, the accounts of lower-levels officers in Longstreet's corps agree that they expected the assault to be "general," and that the other regiments would move with them. Robertson understood that McLaws was to advance "simultaneously" on his immediate left. However, the lack of coordinated execution between Longstreet's divisions exposed the left of Robertson's Brigade. Colonel Van H. Manning of the 3rd Arkansas, for example, complained of a lack of support on his left flank. Unfortunately for the Confederates, this type of misunderstanding occurred again when McLaws subsequently commenced his attack at the Peach Orchard.[18]

Despite their confusion over the nature of the attack, Hood's men pressed forward over the rocky terrain toward Devil's Den and the Round Tops. As Law and Robertson advanced, Captain Smith's four rifled Parrotts on Houck's Ridge "tore gap after gap throughout the ranks of the Confederate foe." General Robertson acknowledged, "For half a mile we were exposed to a

---

increasingly difficult terrain. Whether it was a deciding factor in the outcome will never be known. For treatment examples of Hood's wounding, see McNeily, "Barksdale's Mississippi Brigade," *Mississippi Historical Society*, 235; Coddington, *The Gettysburg Campaign*, 402; Trudeau, *Gettysburg: A Testing of Courage*, 323, 337; Pfanz, *Gettysburg: The Second Day*, 172-173.

17 Alexander, *Military Memoirs*, 393, 395; *OR*, 27/2: 358, 614; Longstreet, "Lee's Right Wing at Gettysburg," *Battles and Leaders*, 3: 341. General R.H. Anderson reported, "I received notice that Lieutenant-General Longstreet would occupy the ground on the right; that his line would be in a direction nearly at right angles with mine; that he would assault the extreme left of the enemy and drive him toward Gettysburg, and I was at the same time ordered to put the troops of my division into action by brigades as soon as those of General Longstreet's corps had progressed so far in their assault as to be connected with my right flank." See *OR*, 27/2: 614.

18 Ibid., 27/2: 404, 407.

heavy and destructive fire of canister, grape, and shell." Robertson observed no movements being made by Confederates on his left, so he sent a courier to Hood (who was already wounded) stating his men were "hard pressed" and needed reinforcements. Robertson's men reached the foot of Houck's Ridge, but they became pinned down by Federal fire.[19]

To throw the mass of one's forces upon an enemy's decisive point was one of Jomini's fundamental principles of war. However, Longstreet had only eight brigades at his disposal and was unable to concentrate his attack on any one point. His tactics might have differed if he had the additional manpower from General Pickett's Division at his disposal. The length of Sickles's line stretched Longstreet's 14,500 infantrymen across a front of roughly one and a quarter mile. As a result, Longstreet settled for an attacking depth of two brigades. While this depth gave Longstreet's attack some power, there was no reserve to exploit any potential success.[20]

In Hood's Division, Benning's Brigade was supposed to follow Law. However, confusion on the battlefield caused Benning to move to Robertson's assistance instead of supporting Law. Robertson's men remained stalled at the bottom of Houck's Ridge until Benning added roughly 1,400 fresh Georgians to their support. The Confederates combined their efforts and, after a fierce struggle, pushed Ward's brigade and Smith's battery off of Houck's Ridge. Sickles's left flank at Devil's Den proved to be indefensible against Longstreet's assault.[21]

Fortunately for General Meade, the Army of the Potomac's Fifth Corps reinforced Little Round Top before the Confederates capitalized on their success at Devil's Den. Although neither Lee nor Longstreet had ever designated the hill as an objective, the defense of Little Round Top by Colonel Strong Vincent's brigade later overshadowed all other combat on Gettysburg's second day. Colonel Vincent, aided by timely reinforcements from Brigadier General Stephen Weed's brigade, successfully prevented Alabama and Texas regiments in Law and Robertson's brigades from capturing the hill. To worsen matters for Longstreet's attacking force, Hazlett's Battery D, 5th United States Artillery, unlimbered on Little Round Top's summit and dropped shells on Benning's exhausted Rebels in Devil's Den. With no

19 Smith, *A Famous Battery and Its Campaigns*, 102-103; *OR*, 27/2: 404-405; Ladd, *The Bachelder Papers*, 1: 36-37.

20 Jomini, *The Art of War*, 63.

21 *OR*, 27/2: 408-409, 414-415, 422; Adelman and Smith, *Devil's Den*, 43-46; Busey and Martin, *Regimental Strengths and Losses*, 281.

Modern view of Peach Orchard with Round Tops
approximately one mile in the distance.
Photo by Authors

Confederate reinforcements available, the Union resistance and rocky terrain proved too much for Southern infantry to overcome. Meade's forces retained Little Round Top, while Longstreet's troops settled for the lower and less-significant Devil's Den.[22]

The military value of Little Round Top is often debated by historians. Whether or not it was the key to Meade's entire defense, the perception of that rocky hill's importance has eclipsed other second day objectives such as the Peach Orchard. Nevertheless, the defense of Little Round Top was a pivotal moment on July 2, since it contributed to the overall failure of

22 Law, "The Struggle for 'Round Top," *Battles and Leaders*, 3: 322; Ladd, *Bachelder Papers*, 1: 243-244, 465; *OR*, 27/1: 617; Norton, *Attack and Defense of Little Round Top*, 258-259. General Benning wrote that he "made my dispositions to hold the ground gained, which was all that I could do, as I was then much in advance of every other part of our line of battle, and the second line of the enemy on the mountain itself was in a position which seemed to me almost impregnable to any merely front attack even with fresh men. Indeed, to hold the ground we had appeared a difficult task. The shells of the enemy from the adjacent mountain were incessantly bursting along the summit of the peak, and every head that showed itself was the target for a Minie ball." See *OR*, 27/2: 415.

Longstreet's attack. The inability to "drive in" the Federal left kept McLaws's Division waiting in vain for Hood to come sweeping up the Emmitsburg Road.[23]

Yet, Hood's Division continued to fight. General G.T. Anderson's Brigade became the next to suffer from a lack of support as they advanced toward the Wheatfield. While Anderson's right regiments assisted in dislodging Ward's brigade from Houck's Ridge, their assault primarily slammed into Colonel de Trobriand's brigade in the Wheatfield. The Federals repulsed Anderson's first wave and his officers complained of lacking reinforcements. Captain George Hillyer's 9th Georgia found itself "having for nearly an hour and a half no support on its left, the advance of McLaws' division being for some reason thus long delayed." This exposed Anderson's Georgians to enfilade fire from Federal artillery at the Peach Orchard and Wheatfield Road; a distance of less than 1,000 yards. The Confederate infantry that attacked the Wheatfield paid a heavy price for the inability of their own artillery to dislodge the enemy from the Peach Orchard.[24]

General McLaws's infantrymen continued to remain idle. According to McLaws, "I was directed not to assault until General Hood was in position." Since Hood had gone further to the right and unexpectedly found the enemy "very strongly posted on two rocky hills," McLaws was ordered to wait in readiness. Hood's Division was ultimately unsuccessful in dislodging the Yankees, but it must have appeared that his fighting men gained enough ground to finally order McLaws's brigades into action.[25]

Approximately one hour after Hood opened the battle, Kershaw finally received the signal to initiate McLaws's participation in the attack. Cabell's

23 Since Benning's brigade successfully but erroneously advanced on Devil's Den, Longstreet's attack on Little Round Top lacked the depth necessary to follow-up initial repulses. This forced Law's regiments, such as William Oates's 15th Alabama, to repeatedly and unsuccessfully strike the same positions.

24 *OR*, 27/2: 396-397, 399, 403. B.H. Gee of the 59th Georgia offered a succinct explanation for Anderson's first repulse, "The men were completely exhausted when they made it, having double-quicked a distance of some 400 yards, under a severe shelling and a scorching sun."

25 Oeffinger, *A Soldier's General*, 196. In an 1878 paper, McLaws claimed that the delay occurred simply because, "I was waiting General Longstreet's will [sic] . . . Hood had been in the meanwhile moving towards the enemy's left, but he never did go far enough to envelop the left, not even partially. It was said at the time, on the field, that he would have done so, but his guides and scouts, who had been around to the enemy's left in the morning, had gotten confused on their return with the division and missed carrying the head of the column far enough to the right, and it became heavily engaged before Hood intended it, and being pressed on his left sent to me for assistance, and the charge of my division was ordered." See McLaws, "Gettysburg," *SHSP*, 7: 73.

Looking east from the Longstreet Observation Tower showing the general route of Kershaw's attack.

Photo by Authors

artillery paused and then three guns fired in rapid succession, thus indicating that Kershaw "was to move without further orders." Kershaw's men clambered over the stone wall in their front, reformed their ranks, and then moved forward with all field and staff officers advancing dismounted.[26]

26 Kershaw, "Kershaw's Brigade at Gettysburg," *Battles and Leaders*, 3: 334; Alexander, *Military Memoirs*, 395. Alexander wrote that Hood's second line attacked before McLaws started his first. Historian Edwin Coddington thought that a one hour estimate seemed "excessive," but given the amount of time needed for Law, Robertson, Benning, and Anderson to advance and in some cases make repeated attacks, one hour is probably not too far off of the mark. See Coddington, *The Gettysburg Campaign*, 403, 749 (n.104). According to Kershaw, Longstreet accompanied them on foot as far as the Emmitsburg Road. One might question the accuracy as this would have put the corps commander perilously close to Yankee skirmishers and artillery, as well as leaving him out of communication with the remainder of his command. Kershaw, "Kershaw's Brigade at Gettysburg," *Battles and Leaders*, 3: 334. Kershaw also acknowledged in 1882 that the passage of time might challenge the reliability of post-war accounts. "Official reports are the best data, but even these are not always reliable, indeed are mostly not. I believe mine is accurate." See Ladd, *Bachelder Papers*, 2: 901. General Law, commanding for the wounded Hood, wrote that after having "seen nothing of McLaws' division, which was to have extended our left and to have moved to the attack at the same time," rode back and urged Kershaw to begin the attack. See Law, "The Struggle for 'Round Top," *Battles and Leaders*, 3: 325.

It was readily apparent by then, that Hood was not sweeping down the enemy's line perpendicular to McLaws's line of battle. In order to connect with Hood's left, Kershaw's attack would have to advance in a west to east direction. To compound matters, Kershaw understood "that Barksdale would move with me and conform to my movement." However, as he neared the Emmitsburg Road, Kershaw heard Barksdale's drums beat assembly and knew, only then, "that I should have no immediate support on my left."[27]

Some commentators later blamed the day's communication lapses on the fact that Hood was wounded early in the fight. Yet, that does not explain why similar misunderstandings occurred in McLaws's Division. Edward Porter Alexander thought the delay in sending McLaws forward was a result of "some unaccountable lack of appreciation of the situation." In Kershaw's case, he added, it was "especially unfortunate" because "advancing Kershaw without advancing Barksdale would expose Kershaw to enfilade by the troops whom Barksdale would easily drive off. Few battlefields can furnish examples of worse tactics." In other words, the South Carolinians reached the Emmitsburg Road with only enemy troops and artillery on their immediate left. Thus, Longstreet's attack lacked the synergy and proper timing needed between his brigades to maximize Confederate combat strength.[28]

General Kershaw appreciated the need to eliminate the Federals at the Peach Orchard and the artillery along the Wheatfield Road. The 41-year-old lawyer, who McLaws described as "a very cool, judicious and gallant gentleman," endeavored to pivot perpendicular to the Emmitsburg Road and strike the Peach Orchard with his left regiments. Kershaw later explained his attempt succinctly, "The directions were 'to dress to the right [toward Hood] and wheel to the left [toward the orchard].'" Major Robert Maffett of the 3rd South Carolina confirmed, "Our orders from General Kershaw were to gradually swing round to the left until nearly facing an orchard, from which the enemy were pouring a deadly fire of artillery."[29]

Kershaw, however, had more than just the Peach Orchard to occupy his attention. Slightly more than 500 yards from his brigade's center stood George Rose's stone house and barn. A "stony hill, covered with heavy timber and thick undergrowth," lay behind the Rose buildings. Rose's large wheat field

27 *OR*, 27/2: 367; Kershaw, "Kershaw's Brigade at Gettysburg," *Battles and Leaders*, 3: 334.

28 Alexander, *Military Memoirs*, 397.

29 Ladd, *Bachelder Papers*, 1: 455; *OR*, 27/2: 372; McLaws, "Gettysburg," *SHSP*: 7: 70; Wyckoff, "Kershaw's Brigade at Gettysburg," *Gettysburg Magazine 5*, 35.

Brigadier General Joseph Kershaw
National Archives

also stretched behind the house, and Union infantry commanded by Colonel Regis de Trobriand, along with Winslow's battery, defended this terrain. Kershaw decided to "move upon the stony hill, so as to strike it with my center, and thus attack the orchard on its left rear." As his troops swept across the fields, they quickly found that fences and artillery fire "rendered it difficult to retain the line in good order." There was scant cover to shield the attackers from deadly projectiles or screen their advance. Every movement was made in the open, in full view of the Union troops posted near the orchard.[30]

Kershaw's South Carolinians struggled against Northern skirmishers, including those from Colonel Byron Root Pierce's 3rd Michigan regiment. This unit served as part of de Trobriand's brigade that was engaged in the Wheatfield. Concern likely remained high over gaps in the Union line between the Wheatfield and the Peach Orchard, especially as Confederate pressure mounted. Colonel de Trobriand was ordered to detach a regiment to support that sector, and he sent Pierce's men. Colonel Pierce was wounded and the command fell to his brother Lieutenant Colonel Edwin Pierce. One company was soon "detached to support a portion of General Graham's line on our right" near the Sherfy house, but the majority of the 3rd Michigan moved to

30 *OR*, 27/2: 367-368, 372; Kershaw, "Kershaw's Brigade at Gettysburg," *Battles and Leaders*, 3: 332-334. From Kershaw's Warfield Ridge starting position, an intervening ridge and woods blocked the view of the Wheatfield, the base of the Rose Farm, Houck's Ridge, and Devil's Den. See Cooksey, "Around the Flank: Longstreet's July 2 Attack at Gettysburg," *Gettysburg Magazine 29*, 100-102. Cooksey challenged the notion that Longstreet moved Hood's Division further to McLaws's right because Longstreet could see a well-extended Federal line. Instead, Cooksey wondered if Hood moved because of what Longstreet could not see. In this scenario, Longstreet's attack was delayed until the Confederates could develop the enemy line and determine the disposition of Federal troops that lay hidden behind the ridge.

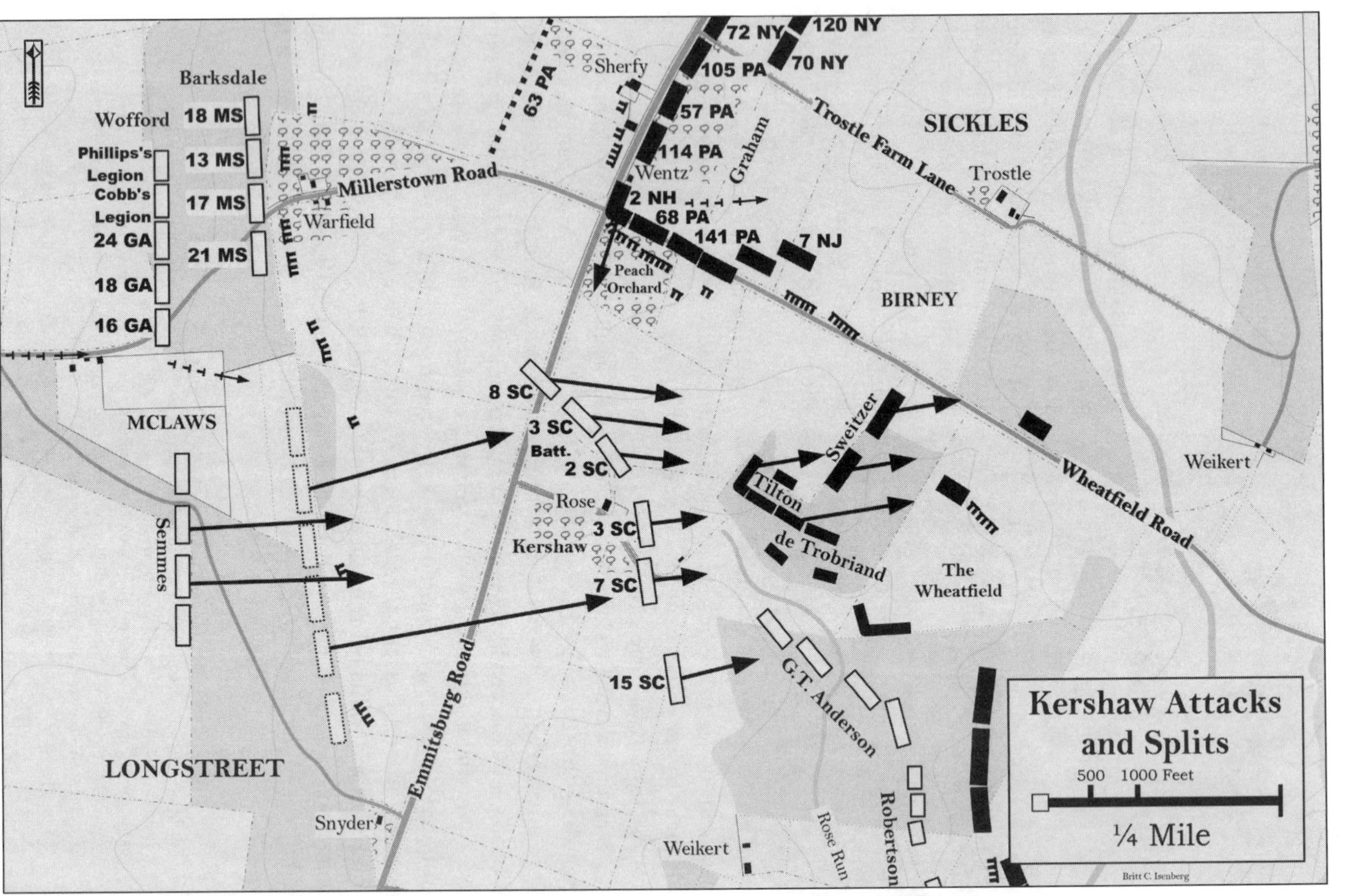
Kershaw Attacks and Splits
500 1000 Feet
1/4 Mile
Britt C. Isenberg
Barksdale
Wofford
18 MS
Phillips's Legion
13 MS
Cobb's Legion
17 MS
24 GA
21 MS
18 GA
16 GA
Millerstown Road
Warfield
63 PA
Sherfy
72 NY
120 NY
105 PA
70 NY
57 PA
114 PA
Wentz
Graham
2 NH
68 PA
141 PA
7 NJ
Peach Orchard
Trostle Farm Lane
SICKLES
Trostle
BIRNEY
MCLAWS
8 SC
3 SC
Batt.
2 SC
Rose
3 SC
Kershaw
7 SC
Semmes
Sweitzer
Tilton
de Trobriand
The Wheatfield
Wheatfield Road
Weikert
15 SC
G.T. Anderson
LONGSTREET
Emmitsburg Road
Snyder
Weikert
Rose Run
Robertson

what the lieutenant colonel described as "the left of the peach orchard, of which the enemy held a portion." He reported deploying three of his companies as skirmishers to challenge the enemy in that location and the Michigan men probably connected with skirmishers from the 3rd Maine. Pierce wrote that he "drove the enemy's skirmishers back," but then likely fell back toward the orchard as Kershaw's main body approached the Rose farm in greater numbers. Although the 3rd Michigan provided valuable service, their deployment added another regiment to the increasing jumble of Northern mixed-commands defending the Peach Orchard.[31]

Kershaw's attack had its own share of problems. His brigade operated essentially as a left wing and a right wing, and accordingly, he ordered his three left regiments (the 2nd and 8th South Carolina regiments, and the 3rd battalion) to wheel left and "attack the batteries in rear of the Peach Orchard." They headed for the Wheatfield Road artillery line. Meanwhile, he directed his two right regiments (3rd and 7th South Carolina) to "occupy the stony hill and wood." Major Maffett recalled that his 3rd South Carolina "moved forward under a galling fire of grape, shell, and canister."[32]

Private John Coxe of the 2nd South Carolina recalled "Well, just as our left struck the depression in the ground every Federal cannon let fly at us with grape." He continued, painting a vivid description of the action: "O

31 *OR*, 27/1: 524. As with the 3rd Maine, the skirmish strength and positions of the 3rd Michigan are problematic. Some studies assume that the entire regiment was placed on the skirmish line. Colonel de Trobriand reported in *OR*, 27/1: 520, "Our skirmishers soon after having been hardly pressed, and the fire becoming more brisk, I was ordered to detach a regiment to their support, and while our artillery was opening fire I sent the Third Regiment Michigan Volunteers, which, under the command of Col. Byron R. Pierce, proceeded forward to a peach orchard close to the road to Emmitsburg, and, deploying rapidly, checked any farther advance of the rebel skirmishers on that point." Lt. Colonel Pierce reported (*OR*, 27/1: 524) that his brother was "ordered to deploy his regiment as skirmishers. He moved his regiment by the right flank to the left of the peach orchard, of which the enemy held a portion, where he deployed Companies I, F, and K, deploying forward on the right of Company F. We drove the enemy's skirmishers back." Colonel de Trobriand told John Bachelder in 1869 that the regiment was deployed as "skirmishers on my right connecting with the peach orchard." See Ladd, *Bachelder Papers*, 1: 374. Bachelder, however, wrote that four companies "were on the skirmish line extending from the peach orchard to the Rose house. The reserve lay in the peach orchard to the right front of Clark's N. Jersey battery." See Ladd, *Bachelder Papers*, 3: 1981. Pierce's report identified Company A as the company detached to support Graham's right. See Colonel Bailey's 2nd New Hampshire *OR*, 27/1: 574 who reported that the 3rd Maine was "withdrawn from our front to our rear" before the Confederate infantry attacked, and see prior discussion regarding the placement of the 3rd Maine. Some accounts indicate that the "Twin Thirds" were next to each other, although Pierce reported that his right rested "in front of the orchard, near the road."

32 *OR*, 27/2: 372; Kershaw, "Kershaw's Brigade at Gettysburg," *Battles and Leaders*, 3: 334-336.

the awful deathly surging sounds of those little black balls as they flew by us, through us, between our legs, and over us! Many, of course, were struck down." Captain Robert Pulliam, also in the 2nd South Carolina, was among the numerous casualties. Pulliam suffered a wound to the head and died the next day. Despite the ghastly casualties, officers ordered the men to advance at the double-quick, and as Coxe recalled, "we were mad and fully determined to take and silence those batteries at once." The regiment got so close to the enemy guns that they could see "bewildered" expressions on the faces of the Union artillerymen. A round of canister passed between Private Coxe's legs and miraculously left the private unharmed. "But just then," Coxe declared, many years later, "–and, ah me! To think of it makes my blood curdle even now, nearly fifty years afterwards- the insane order was given to 'right flank.'"[33]

Kershaw's two right regiments began to overlap each other as they approached the Stony Hill. He "ordered the 7th to move by the right flank to uncover the 3d Regiment." Unfortunately "some unauthorized person" passed the same order along Kershaw's left wing and so they too moved "by the right flank." As a result, Kershaw's left wing veered to their right and away from the Wheatfield Road batteries. Union artillery responded quickly to the snafu and blasted the exposed left of Kershaw's South Carolina brigade. "Hundreds of the bravest and best men of Carolina fell," Kershaw remembered, "victims of this fatal blunder." It was, he concluded, "a terrible mistake which cost so dearly."[34]

Another member of the 2nd South Carolina remembered those horrific moments: "We were in ten minutes or less time, terribly butchered. I saw half a dozen at a time knocked up and flung to the ground like trifles. There were familiar forms and faces with parts of their heads shot away, legs shattered, arms tore off." Private William Preston Miller of the 3rd South Carolina Battalion was one of many who went down. "A ball hit him in the head and it sounded like a drum beat," recalled a comrade.[35]

"Of course no one ever knew who gave the order," opined Private Coxe, "or any reason why it was given. General Kershaw denied being responsible for it, but somebody must have been." Apparently Kershaw did not take

33 Coxe, "The Battle of Gettysburg," Confederate Veteran, Vol. XXI, 9: 434; Busey and Busey, *Confederate Casualties*, 3: 125; McNeily,"Barksdale's Mississippi Brigade," *Mississippi Historical Society*, 246.

34 *OR*, 27/2: 368; Kershaw, "Kershaw's Brigade at Gettysburg," *Battles and Leaders*, 3: 335-336.

35 Wyckoff, *History of the Second South Carolina Infantry*, 191; Davis, *History of the 3rd South Carolina Volunteer Infantry Battalion*, 140, 422; Busey and Busey, *Confederate Casualties*, 3: 1305.

responsibility for the deadly mistake. He blamed Colonel John D. Kennedy, the commander of the 2nd South Carolina. "His failure to understand that he should have carried out my order to take the battery," Kershaw complained in 1882, "without regard to the movements of the rest of the brigade was a fatal disaster to my movements as well as to his regt. He let go when he had his hands on the battery, so to speak." Notwithstanding Kershaw's allegations, Colonel Kennedy served with distinction throughout the war. He survived wounds to the hand and hip at Gettysburg. Not only was Kennedy wounded six times during the course of the war, but he was also reportedly struck another 15 times by spent bullets.[36]

"I gave them canister and solid shot with such good effect that I am sure that several hundred were put hors de combat in a short space of time," reported Colonel McGilvery. "The column was broken--part fled in the direction from whence it came; part pushed on into the woods on our left; the remainder endeavored to shelter themselves in masses around the house and barn." Captain Hart directed his battery's "fire with shrapnel on this column to good effect. I then changed to canister, repulsing the attack made on my battery."[37]

Captain John Bigelow's 9th Massachusetts battery joined in the target practice. Visibility must have been poor due to the smoke and dust, because Bigelow hesitated to fire thinking the Rebels at his front might be retreating Union forces. He became convinced otherwise when one of the battle flags unfurled enough to reveal a Southern cross. Bigelow opened on them with spherical case and promptly witnessed the confusion in Kershaw's ranks. "My battery had a fine enfilading fire on their line, and used double-shotted canister with such good effect, that, with the other batteries on its right, it succeeded in breaking the enemy's battle formation." The Confederates managed to gain Rose's woods in their front and on Bigelow's left "as a confused crowd."[38]

Captain Ames's battery, meanwhile, was running low on ammunition and withdrew from the Peach Orchard. The captain initially hesitated because the

36 Coxe, "The Battle of Gettysburg," *Confederate Veteran*, Vol. XXI, 9: 434; Ladd, *Bachelder Papers*, 2: 900; *OR*, 27/2: 368, Busey and Busey, *Confederate Casualties*, 3: 1283. Kennedy's post-war accomplishments included his election to U.S. Congress in 1865, although he then refused to take the Oath of Allegiance to the United States. In the 1880s, Kennedy served as lieutenant governor of South Carolina and consul general to Shanghai, China.

37 *OR*, 27/1: 881-882, 887, 901.

38 Ladd, *Bachelder Papers*, 1: 172.

Confederates were "so close that it would have meant the loss of our guns had we attempted to limber up at that time and retreat." Ames recalled that the Confederate officers "yelled hoarsely and coarsely, 'surrender you Yankee ____ ____.'" The artillerymen agreed to first push back the enemy with a "stream of fire and death." Only after the Southerners were checked in their advance did the battery then retire by sections toward Sickles's headquarters at the Trostle farm.[39]

Afterwards, there was confusion in regard to which battery replaced Ames: Thompson's battery or Lieutenant Malbone Watson's Battery I, Fifth U.S. Artillery. Although their arrival time is debated, Thompson's battery definitely went into action in the Peach Orchard; Watson's battery is less likely to have done so. Yet, Henry Hunt, George Randolph, and Ames all reported that Watson was the replacement. Hunt later acknowledged, however, to historian John Bachelder that his report was likely mistaken on this topic. Ames's battery paused briefly at the Trostle farm after they fell back from the Peach Orchard. It is likely that Watson relieved Ames at the Trostle farm, and never reached the Peach Orchard. This scenario would partially vindicate the after-action reports.[40]

The Federal infantry near the Peach Orchard also played a substantial role in repulsing Kershaw's attack. The men of the 2nd New Hampshire were still hugging earth around the Wentz property, and eager to get into action, when Colonel Bailey requested permission from General Graham to "charge." Graham replied, "Yes, for God's sakes, go forward!" At this moment, a nearby

39 *OR*, 27/1: 901; Ames, *History of Battery G*, 73-74. Ames reported, "After having been engaged for two and a half hours, at 5.30 p.m. I was relieved by Battery I, Fifth U.S." Also see Imhof, *Gettysburg: Day Two*, 89-92; Woods, *Ebb and Flow of Battle*, 314-315; Pfanz, *Gettysburg: The Second Day*, 317.

40 *OR*, 27/1: 236, 583-584, 660, 901; Ladd, *Bachelder Papers*, 1: 228; Imhof, *Gettysburg: Day Two*, 147; Pfanz, *Gettysburg: The Second Day*, 317. The assumption that Watson relieved Ames at the Trostle farm agrees with Woods, "Defending Watson's Battery," *Gettysburg Magazine* 9, 40-47. In an alternate scenario, Watson was waiting near the Trostle farm for orders and was ordered to the front by Sickles or an aide, but before Watson could reach the orchard, the position was collapsing and the other batteries were in retreat. Watson's battlefield tablet, which many consider to be inaccurately located due to the post-war development of modern United States Avenue, states that the battery arrived on the field about 4: 30 and first took position north of Little Round Top. "[At] 5: 30 moved to the front at the Peach Orchard." As discussed previously, Thompson did end up in the Peach Orchard and appears to have been in position for at least an hour before the position collapsed. If Ames's reported 5: 30 departure time is accurate, then his replacement would likely have been in position for less than one hour when the orchard fell, thus making Thompson problematic as the replacement. See Murray, *E.P. Alexander and the Artillery Action in the Peach Orchard*, 97-98 for a discussion on Thompson.

artillery lieutenant, possibly from Thompson's battery, began to spike his guns, thus "indicating that he considered them as good as lost." Bailey's regiment dashed from the Wheatfield Road through the Peach Orchard, and took a new position along a rail fence at the orchard's southern end. They had the advantage of elevation and poured a hot fire on Kershaw's beleaguered men, who remained on lower ground, several hundred yards to the front and left of the Federals.[41]

The 2nd New Hampshire's "charge" to the south end of Sherfy's orchard set events in motion that had momentous consequences on this part of the field. Within a few moments, the 68th Pennsylvania came in on Bailey's right, and the 3rd Maine took position on the left. The regiments fronted south toward Kershaw, except for the 68th Pennsylvania. They faced west toward Warfield Ridge. As a result, the 2nd New Hampshire and 68th Pennsylvania formed a right angle along the Emmitsburg Road. "Many regiments fought in a peach orchard at Gettysburg," recalled Private Martin Haynes of the 2nd New Hampshire, "but the three enumerated . . . were the only ones who formed a line in 'the' peach orchard that day."[42]

The men of Colonel Henry Madill's 141st Pennsylvania regiment could take exception to that claim. Madill supported Clark's battery but received orders to "the front of the Peach Orchard," and advanced in between the Third Maine on his right and the Third Michigan on his left. The 141st regimental history asserted, perhaps with some dramatic license, that Madill's men sprung up from concealment in the sunken Wheatfield Road and "delivered a murderous fire" into the faces of the South Carolinians who were rushing the Federal batteries. The "appalled" Confederates beat a hasty retreat, and the Pennsylvanians cleared the fence in their front "with a bound" as they pushed their foe back beyond the south side of the Peach Orchard. Sergeant John Bloodgood added that they "poured out a tempest of leaden hail" upon which the South Carolinians "reeled, and staggered like drunken men, then scattered and ran in every direction."[43]

The Union Army's new line ran along the southern edge of the Peach Orchard and consisted of the 3rd Michigan, 141st Pennsylvania, 3rd Maine, 2nd New Hampshire, and the 68th Pennsylvania (from left to right). At full

41 Haynes, *History of the Second Regiment*, 175-176.

42 Ibid., 178; Woods, *Ebb and Flow of Battle*, 269, 273.

43 *OR*, 27/1: 504; Craft, *History of the 141st Regiment Pennsylvania Volunteers*, 120; Lash, "A Pathetic Story," *Gettysburg Magazine 14*, 93.

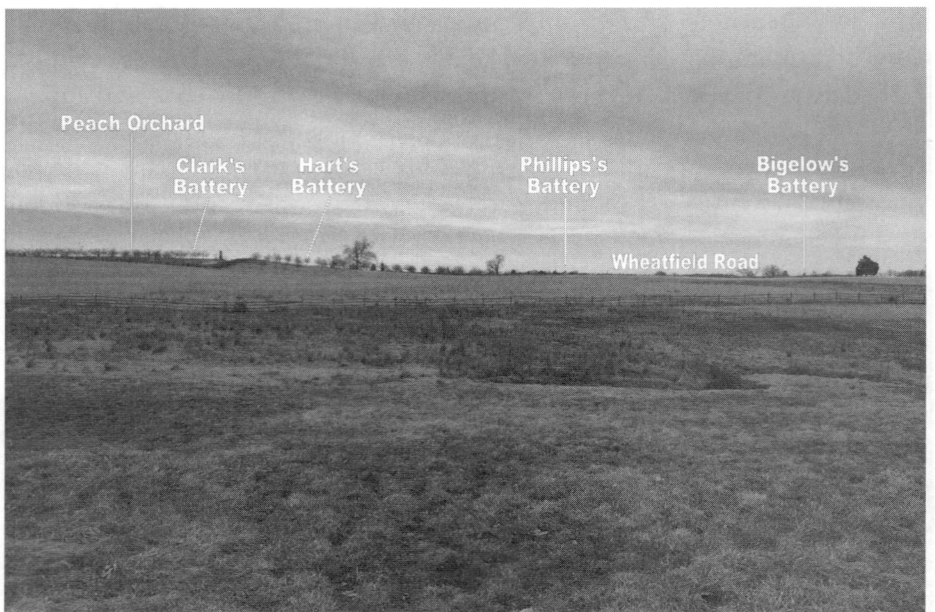

Looking north and uphill toward the Peach Orchard and Wheatfield Road from the position of Kershaw's Brigade near the Rose farm buildings.
Photo by Authors

strength, these units mustered a total of about 1,330 men. However, the day's exertions had already reduced the number of effective soldiers in the ranks. All of the regiments fronted south, except for the 68th Pennsylvania that still faced west along the Emmitsburg Road. In leaving the Wheatfield Road, the regiments extended Graham's defensive perimeter along the Emmitsburg Road by an additional 150 yards. Graham was already stretched thin and needed support from other nearby brigades. The question remained as to who would fill the gap along the Emmitsburg Road.[44]

William Loring of the 141st Pennsylvania beheld the magnificent view from the southern edge of the Peach Orchard. Longstreet's massive, yet flawed attack had surged across the Union front from Warfield Ridge and toward the Wheatfield, Devil's Den, and Little Round Top. "At this time we had a fine view of the left of our line," wrote Loring, "and watched the advancing and receding lines of the blue and gray as they struggled for the mastery at our

44 *OR*, 27/1: 499, 504, 574; Haynes, *History of the Second Regiment*, 177 -178; Craft, *History of the 141st Regiment Pennsylvania Volunteers*, 121; Busey and Martin, *Regimental Strengths and Losses*, 131-133.

left. Over that rugged ground we watched the surging lines, and could see the telling effect of volley after volley. It was a picture never to be effaced from memory."[45]

The martial splendor of the scene proved temporary. While Cabell's batteries had paused long enough to allow Kershaw's Brigade to pass, they soon resumed their bombardment of the Peach Orchard. "Then came the storm," noted Private Haynes of the 2nd New Hampshire. The new Federal position, on the military crest of the orchard, exposed Union troops to renewed Confederate artillery fire. "Every Rebel gun was let loose, until the Peach Orchard seemed to be almost moving in the windage of hurtling metal," Haynes recalled.[46]

From Kershaw's perspective, the Yankees held the high ground, and the Northern artillery rained destructive fire down toward the Rose farm. The observant Private Coxe, of the 2nd South Carolina wrote, "Why, in a few moments the whole brigade was jumbled up in a space less than a regiment behind a rocky, heavily wooded bluff with the right flank in the air . . . with our left flank disconnected and wholly unsupported for a mile or more. We were truly 'in a box,' liable to be captured or annihilated at any moment."[47]

Although Kershaw's attack stalled, it had accomplished at least one objective. His brigade's advance toward the Wheatfield and the Stony Hill forced the withdrawal of Fifth Corps reinforcements from Brigadier General James Barnes's division. This created considerable alarm among Third Corps officers including Birney and de Trobriand, and later led to some memorable post-battle accusations and recriminations.[48]

Kershaw's men directed return fire uphill to discourage Union defenders at the Peach Orchard from moving forward. But Kershaw's left regiments were "roughly handled" by the Union forces and remained hunkered down in the fields and among Rose's structures. Federal batteries continued to shell them, and Captain Hart's Napoleons "made a veritable shambles of the Rose grounds." After the battle, the area they targeted "was found covered with dead South Carolinians." Private Coxe watched many of his comrades fall,

45 Loring, "The 141st Pa. at the Battle," *Fighting Them Over*, 309.

46 Haynes, *History of the Second Regiment*, 178 -179.

47 Coxe, "The Battle of Gettysburg," Confederate Veteran, Vol. XXI, 9: 434. Also in McNeily,"Barksdale's Mississippi Brigade," *Mississippi Historical Society*, 246.

48 For additional discussion on the departure of Barnes's regiments from Stony Hill, and the post-battle debate, see Hessler, *Sickles at Gettysburg*, 186–188, 283, 287–288.

"but our 'spunk' was up to white heat, and we didn't care, but made up our minds to die right there to the last man if necessary."[49]

Among the day's casualties was Captain George Marshall McDowell of the 2nd South Carolina. While on the march to Gettysburg, the 25-year-old Citadel graduate was placed under arrest for refusing to obey an order. He returned to the ranks before the battle and, on July 2, suffered a mortal wound. In his dying breath, McDowell left a message for his mother: "I died with my sword drawn in defense of my country." Despite his death at Gettysburg, Confederate authorities court-martialed McDowell posthumously two weeks later due to the earlier arrest. The court "privately reprimanded" the deceased captain, but the ruling was considered lenient given his service. Military justice was duly served.[50]

As Kershaw's men struggled, they anxiously awaited Barksdale's assistance. Adding to their predicament, a Federal force moved across the Wheatfield and threatened their right flank. Kershaw hastened to locate General Semmes, whose brigade was somewhere in his right rear. Semmes's men soon came up and joined the fight in the Wheatfield, thus assisting Kershaw's beleaguered brigade. After the passage of perhaps 30 minutes, recollected Private Coxe, "the thunder and roar of the Federal cannon and musketry in our front suddenly stopped, and the next moment we heard a tremendous Rebel cheer, followed by an awful crash of small arms." General Barksdale's attack had finally commenced.[51]

49 *OR*, 27/1: 132-133; 27/2: 368; Haynes, *History of the Second Regiment*, 178; De Trobriand, *Four Years with the Army of the Potomac*, 497-498; Imhof, *Gettysburg Day Two*, 101-102; Coxe, "The Battle of Gettysburg," *Confederate Veteran XXI*, 9: 434.

50 Wyckoff, *History of the Second South Carolina Infantry*, 190, 530-531; Busey and Busey, *Confederate Casualties*, 3: 1289.

51 Ladd, *Bachelder Papers*, 1: 475; Kershaw, "Kershaw's Brigade at Gettysburg," *Battles and Leaders*, 3: 336; Coxe, "The Battle of Gettysburg," *Confederate Veteran XXI*, 9: 434.

Chapter 6

Let Me Charge

William Barksdale.

Life had taken the 41-year-old brigadier general far from his birthplace in Rutherford County, Tennessee. Barksdale's origins did not suggest a military future. He attended the University of Nashville before he moved to Columbus, Mississippi. While there, he studied law and was admitted to the bar in 1839. He did not maintain a law career, but instead pursued journalism as editor of a newspaper. He also became involved in local politics and was generally respected as a prominent voice in his community.

None of this background had any relevance to leading men in combat. However, he enlisted with a Mississippi regiment when war with Mexico broke out. Captain Barksdale was a staff officer, but he honed organizational skills that later proved valuable. More importantly, even though he was not a line officer, he made an indelible impression by favoring the front during battle. Barksdale was not afraid to fight.

After Mexico, Barksdale returned to Mississippi and politics. He campaigned for Congress as "Captain Barksdale," and won election to the U.S. House of Representatives for the term that began in March 1853. Barksdale positioned himself as a States' Rights Democrat who maintained that states had the right to secede peacefully if oppressed by the federal government. As tensions escalated, he became known as a "fire-eater," one of a group of prominent pro-slavery Southern leaders who urged their states to form a new nation.[1]

Congressman Barksdale served four consecutive two-year terms that ran up to the eve of the Civil War. In 1857, another Democrat attorney with even less military experience joined him in the House of Representatives: Daniel E. Sickles from New York. Barksdale is often portrayed as being elderly during the Civil War. However, he was actually two years younger than Sickles, the former born in 1821 and the latter in 1819. The men served on the House Committee on Foreign Affairs, where they voted together on many issues including the appropriation of funds to negotiate the purchase of Cuba.[2]

Barksdale was in the middle of many volatile incidents of the pre-war Congress, as national discourse increasingly disintegrated into violence. In 1856, he reportedly stood by Representative Preston Brooks when the South Carolinian viciously caned abolitionist Senator Charles Sumner on the Senate floor. Two years later, in February 1858, Barksdale was again involved in a fight that broke out between pro and anti-slavery politicians on the House floor. South Carolina Democrat Laurence Keitt, who the House previously censured for supporting Brooks in the Sumner assault, attacked Pennsylvania Republican Galusha Grow. Barksdale grabbed ahold of Grow, although some accounts suggested he was only trying to separate the two political pugilists. As others joined in the ensuing melee, one representative seized Barksdale by the head. The wig that Barksdale wore to cover his thinning hair came off. After Barksdale threw a wild punch that missed its target, he excitedly put his wig on backwards. The fight was not as celebrated in the annals of history as the Brooks-Sumner bout, but as one contemporary newspaper reported, "The scene must have been a rich one, especially Barksdale with his wig on wrong side foremost."[3]

Not surprisingly, Barksdale resigned his congressional seat in January 1861, when Mississippi seceded from the Union. He emphasized that he

1 McKee, "William Barksdale and the Congressional Election of 1853," *Journal of Mississippi History*, 129-158; "Col. R. Davis and Captain Barksdale," *Southern Standard*, June 11, 1853; Tagg, *The Generals of Gettysburg*, 218-220.

2 "Sickles and Barksdale on Foreign Affairs Committee," *Detroit Free Press*, December 10, 1858; *Hartford Courant*, January 15, 1859.

3 "The Late Fight in the House," *Semi-Weekly Standard*, February 13, 1858; "Who Killed Cock Robin?" *Buffalo Morning Express*, February 28, 1858; "More Southern Bullying," *Lewisburg Chronicle*, February 12, 1858.

Congressional Portrait of William Barksdale
LOC

never "desired a dissolution of this Union," but secession seemed the only alternative to living under a Republican-controlled government. Barksdale was confident of Southern success in their bid for independence and elaborated on his views:

> In the event of its dissolution, I shall have no fears for the South. With a territory larger than all of Europe; with our cotton now swelling up in value to more than two hundred million dollars; with our rice, and sugar, and tobacco; with a people united in feeling and sentiment, she has within her own borders all the elements of a splendid republic. If, then, we are to have no peace; if these aggressions are still to be continued; if this sectional warfare is never to cease, the South, with the strong arms and brave hearts of her gallant sons, will build up her own eternal destiny.[4]

Barksdale's congressional years may forever be known for the wigless farce on the House floor, but his Civil War combat career proved considerably more successful. In the spring of 1861, he received an appointment as colonel of the 13th Mississippi Volunteer Infantry. The regiment saw action at First Manassas, Ball's Bluff, and in the Seven Days Battles. He assumed brigade command after Brigadier General Richard Griffith suffered a mortal wound at Savage's Station, and in August 1862, Barksdale received a promotion to brigadier general. The command became known as "Barksdale's Mississippi Brigade" and they saw action during the 1862 Maryland campaign. Most notably, the brigade contested Federal attempts to cross the Rappahannock

4 "The Mississippi Delegation in Congress," *Harper's Weekly*, February 2, 1861. Accessed at http://www.sonofthesouth.net/leefoundation/civil-war-feb-1861/mississippi-delegation-biographies.htm.

at Fredericksburg, and mounted a strong defense in the face of superior numbers at "Second Fredericksburg," during the Chancellorsville campaign.[5]

Barksdale was not the model Confederate general in terms of aesthetics, and he must have appeared older than his years by the summer of 1863. Private J.S. McNeily of the 21st Mississippi remembered him as:

> [A] large, rather heavily built man of a blond complexion, with thin light hair. He was not a graceful horseman, though his forward, impetuous bearing, especially in battle, overshadowed and more than made up for such deficiencies. He had a very thirst for battlefield glory, to lead his brigade in the charge. Of the comfort of his men he was most considerate, would tolerate no neglect or denial of their rights, or imposition on them from anyone.[6]

It remains unknown as to whether Barksdale had the time or inclination on July 2, 1863, to reminisce about his old Foreign Affairs committee colleague Dan Sickles, whose command stood just across the field. Barksdale and his Mississippians, like those Confederates who attacked before and after them, simply awaited their opportunity as the hours passed and artillery shells continued to burst around them.

Colonel Alexander needed assistance to move some heavy 24-pounders from Moody's battery into line along Barksdale's front. Barksdale gave permission to call for volunteers from among his men. Alexander later wrote, "In a minute I had eight good fellows, of whom, alas! We buried two that night, and sent to the hospital three others mortally or severely wounded."[7]

Fire from the Federal batteries remained hot right up until the last minute. Alexander was "annoyed" by the enemy's "obstinacy" and finally decided to call in his last reserve. He sent for his two remaining batteries, under captains Pichegru Woolfolk and Tyler Jordan. These batteries did not unlimber, however, because Barksdale's Brigade advanced just as they arrived.[8]

5 For biographical information on Barksdale: Evans, *Confederate Military History*, Volume IX, 239, 256; Pfanz, *Gettysburg: The Second Day*, 318; Tagg, *The Generals of Gettysburg*, 218-220; Winschel, "Their Supreme Moment," *Gettysburg Magazine 1*, 71.

6 McNeily, "Barksdale's Mississippi Brigade at Gettysburg," 236.

7 Alexander, "The Great Charge and Artillery Fighting at Gettysburg," *Battles and Leaders*, 3: 360. Alexander wrote that Moody also had two 12-pounders. See Alexander, *Military Memoirs*, 399. Jennings Wise copied Alexander's text almost verbatim and therefore made the same claim. See Wise, *The Long Arm of Lee*, 645. Moody's NPS tablet only references four 24 –pounder Howitzers.

8 *OR*, 27/2: 429-430; Alexander, "The Great Charge and Artillery Fighting at Gettysburg," *Battles and Leaders*, 3: 360; *Military Memoirs*, 399; Wise, *The Long Arm of Lee*, 645.

Moody and Woolfolk likely did not have the opportunity to contemplate their proximity to one another. On July 1, the two officers had quarreled over the order of march. Such an issue was not insignificant since one could spend a long day eating the other's dust. The Maine-born and Harvard-educated Moody challenged the Virginian Woolfolk to a duel. They agreed upon terms and decided to settle their differences on the morning of July 2 with rifled muskets at ten paces. The battle intervened and the duel never materialized. Both men survived Gettysburg and the war. Moody was a lawyer and later murdered by a man he "had abused in the courthouse that day." Woolfolk met his end in 1870 when he was among dozens killed by the collapse of a crowded upper-level courtroom floor in the Richmond Capitol building. As Colonel Alexander noted dryly in his memoirs, "So the two men never met again after their quarrel."[9]

Being subjected to enemy artillery fire produced a "natural feeling of uneasiness" among the men, recalled General McLaws. James Booth of the 21st Mississippi elaborated on that sentiment: "I remember vividly the effects of the first shot that came from the battery in our front," he wrote, adding that the fire "called forth General Barksdale's request to General Longstreet to allow him to order in his brigade and take the battery." The artillery barrage became personal for Booth when a "shell exploded in the ranks of my company, near me." The attack could not begin soon enough for these Mississippians, but protocol and orders forced them to wait. Private McNeily called this the "severest of all tests on troops, to receive fire without returning it," yet the Confederates sustained it "unflinchingly." All of this, however, only increased Barksdale's impatience to get his men into action. "Never was a body of soldiers fuller of the spirit of fight," added McNeily, "and the confidence of victory."[10]

General McLaws mounted his horse and rode among his troops, directing them to lie down and avoid the "shot and shell which were being rained around us from a very short range." Barksdale pleaded with McLaws, "General, let me go; General, let me charge!" However, McLaws was still waiting for Longstreet's permission and thought incorrectly that the enemy was threatening their own

9 United States Census of 1860, Port Gibson, Claiborne County, Mississippi, house number 160; Warren, *History of the Harvard Law School and Early Legal Conditions in America*, Volume III, 25; Booth, *Records of Louisiana Confederate Soldiers and Louisiana Confederate Commands,* Volume III, Book 1, 1023; Alexander, *Fighting for the Confederacy*, 230-231. The 1870 incident that claimed Woolfolk's life is sometimes referred to as the "Capitol Disaster." See *Harper's Weekly*, Vol. XIV, No. 698, May 14, 1870.

10 McLaws, "Gettysburg," *SHSP*, 7: 72-73; McNeily, "Barksdale's Mississippi Brigade," 235, 238.

advance. McLaws instructed Barksdale "to wait and let the enemy come half way and then we would meet on more equal terms."[11]

When Longstreet arrived, he found McLaws "ready for his opportunity, and Barksdale chafing in his wait for the order to seize the battery in his front." Barksdale pressed his case directly to Longstreet, "I wish you would let me go in, General. I would take that battery in five minutes." Longstreet responded, "Wait a little, we are all going in presently." A soldier in the 13th Mississippi observed Longstreet, McLaws, Barksdale, and other officers studying the field with their glasses. As the moment finally neared, Longstreet instructed a detachment from the 17th Mississippi to clear a fence that obstructed the field in their front.[12]

Longstreet did not specify afterwards what finally prompted his decision to unleash Barksdale's Brigade. Nor did Longstreet acknowledge the delay as part of an en echelon strategy of attack. He was clearly aware that Hood's Division had made no progress in attacking up the Emmitsburg Road to strike the Peach Orchard in flank. He was also presumably aware that Kershaw had started without Barksdale's immediate movement. Longstreet implied in his memoirs that responsibility for the delay fell partially on McLaws. "After additional caution to hold his ranks closed," recalled the corps commander, "McLaws ordered Barksdale in." McLaws acknowledged that both Barksdale and Wofford's brigades found themselves stalled by getting badly "mixed up with the batteries which had been placed among their lines, and were temporarily delayed in extricating themselves therefrom." Kershaw later cited McLaws as blaming the sluggishness on "some confusion" caused by the Federal artillery fire that resulted in several casualties. Whatever the actual cause of the delay, it was no wonder that Colonel Alexander added this to his litany of post-war complaints. He explained, "There were thus four partial attacks of two brigades each [in McLaws and Hood's division], requiring at least an hour and a half to be gotten into action; where one advance by the eight brigades would have won a quicker victory with far less loss."[13]

11 McLaws, "Gettysburg," *SHSP*, 7: 72-73.

12 Longstreet, *From Manassas to Appomattox*, 370; McLaws, "Gettysburg," *SHSP*, 7: 72-73; Winschel, "Their Supreme Moment: Barksdale's Brigade at Gettysburg," *Gettysburg Magazine 1*, 74; Gottfried, *Brigades of Gettysburg*, 412.

13 Longstreet, *From Manassas to Appomattox*, 370; McLaws, "Gettysburg," *SHSP*, 7: 73; Ladd, *The Bachelder Papers*, 2: 902; Alexander, *Military Memoirs*, 395. Alan Brunelle, a student of the battle, hypothesized that a combination of two factors may have contributed to Barksdale's delay. First, a rise in the intervening ground prevented Barksdale from seeing Kershaw begin his advance. Second, the position of Alexander / Huger's battalion, located between

Barksdale's route of attack. Looking east from his starting position on Warfield Ridge toward the Sherfy farm.
Photo by Authors

Once Longstreet finally authorized the advance, McLaws sent his aide-de-camp, Lieutenant Gazaway Bugg "G.B." Lamar, to carry the directive to Barksdale. Lamar found Barksdale "anxious" and "eager" to attack, and "when I carried him the order to advance his face was radiant with joy." Lamar "witnessed many charges marked in every way by unflinching gallantry . . . but I never saw anything to equal the dash and heroism of the Mississippians."[14]

Confederate battery commanders received instructions to temporarily cease firing. According to Private McNeily, "every man in the brigade knew that 'our turn' had come at last. The scenes and events as they moved thereafter were charged with intensely dramatic and never to be forgotten incidence [sic]. General Barksdale's appearance, riding rapidly along in rear of the line, was

Barksdale and Cabell's guns, prevented Barksdale from hearing the signal shots that initiated Kershaw's movements.

14 McLaws, "Gettysburg," *SHSP*, 7: 74. McLaws referred to Lamar as a captain in his post-war writings. However, Lamar was a First Lieutenant to date from January 3, 1863. See Krick, *Staff Officers in Gray*, 196.

the signal to the respective regimental commanders to get alert." As the final order reached the men, they understood that the Federal "lines before you must be broken and the enemy must be driven from the field." Every officer received instructions to "animate his men by his personal presence on the front line." When Colonel Benjamin Grubb "B.G." Humphreys of the 21st Mississippi shouted, "Attention!" the call rang "like an electric shock" and "brought every man of his regiment up standing."[15]

As the time approached 6:00 p.m., the 1,600 Mississippians unleashed their peculiar Rebel yell and sprang forward. The rank and file stripped off their excess clothing and equipment. Officers were encouraged to dismount and advance on foot, primarily due to the difficulty in replacing horses.[16]

The heavyset Barksdale remained mounted and advanced at the front of his old regiment, the 13th Mississippi. "As this was destined to be my last sight of him," wrote Private McNeily, "impressions of his appearance are indelible. Stamped on his face, and in his bearing, as he rode by, was determination to 'do or die'." Barksdale's Brigade moved along a front that measured approximately 350 yards wide.[17]

The 420-odd men of Humphreys's 21st Mississippi formed on the right, and south of the Millerstown Road. Colonel Humphreys was 54 years old at the time of Gettysburg, somewhat older than many other regimental commanders. The Mississippi native attended school in Kentucky and New Jersey before entering West Point in 1825. His Academy career was most notable for his being among 19 cadets expelled following the "eggnog riot" of 1826. During this infamous incident, several drunken cadets assaulted officers with clubs and weaponry on Christmas Eve. After his expulsion, Humphreys returned to Mississippi where he became a planter, practiced law, and entered politics. An opponent of secession, he nevertheless raised a company of the 21st Mississippi and, by May 1861, received a commission as captain. Promoted to colonel of

15 McNeily, "Barksdale's Mississippi Brigade," 235; B.G. Humphreys Manuscript, 11; Winschel, "Their Supreme Moment: Barksdale's Brigade at Gettysburg," *Gettysburg Magazine 1*, 74. Benjamin Grubb Humphreys was not related to Union General Humphreys in Sickles's corps.

16 Gerald, "The Battle of Gettysburg," *Waco Daily Times Herald*, July 3, 1913, transcript in Brake Collection, USAHEC; Busey and Martin, *Regimental Strengths and Losses*, 267; Floyd, *Commanders and Casualties*, 48.

17 McNeily, "Barksdale's Mississippi Brigade," 236; Winschel, "Their Supreme Moment: Barksdale's Brigade at Gettysburg," *Gettysburg Magazine 1*, 74. It is challenging to measure the front of Barksdale's Brigade with precision. The distance from the modern day intersection of Emmitsburg Road and Birney Avenue to the Sherfy house is about 415 yards. These points might approximate where Barksdale's right and left struck.

Colonel Benjamin G. Humphreys,
21st Mississippi
LOC

the regiment by November of that year, he still led the unit at Gettysburg.[18]

Proceeding from Barksdale's right (south) to left (north), Humphreys's 21st Mississippi was followed in line by the 17th, 13th, and finally the 18th regiment on the brigade's left. Colonel Humphreys recalled receiving "general instructions 'to swing to the left.'" Steadily, the brigade moved forward over the open field and were "greeted by a deadly volley" of enemy projectiles.[19]

Major George Gerald of the 18th Mississippi, only 242 men-strong, remembered shouts of, "Dress to the colors and forward to the foe!" reverberating above the din of the battle. Joseph Lloyd of the 13th Mississippi recalled, "Our colonel stepped briskly a little further to the front. 'Attention. Fix Bayonets. Forward March. Double Quick March. Charge bayonets,' and the great battle was raging. Oh, that horrible dream. Did we hear shot, shell, and canister; see men falling all around us and still live through it?"[20]

According to Private McNeily of the 21st Mississippi, "Next came the ringing command- 'Double quick, charge,' and at top speed, yelling at the top of their voices, without firing a shot, the brigade sped swiftly across the field

18 Warner, *Generals in Gray*, 145. Another cadet, future Confederate President Jefferson Davis, purportedly took a leading role in the drinking but was not expelled because he did not participate in the riot. For more on Davis and the West Point eggnog riot, see Davis, *Jefferson Davis: The Man and His Hour*, 35-36.

19 B.G. Humphreys Manuscript, 11-12; McNeily, "Barksdale's Mississippi Brigade," 235; Busey and Martin, *Regimental Strengths and Losses*, 267.

20 Gerald, "The Battle of Gettysburg," *Waco Daily Times Herald*, July 3, 1913, Brake Collection, USAHEC; McNeily, "Barksdale's Mississippi Brigade," 239; Floyd, *Commanders and Casualties*, 49; Soldiers and Sailors DB, NPS.gov.

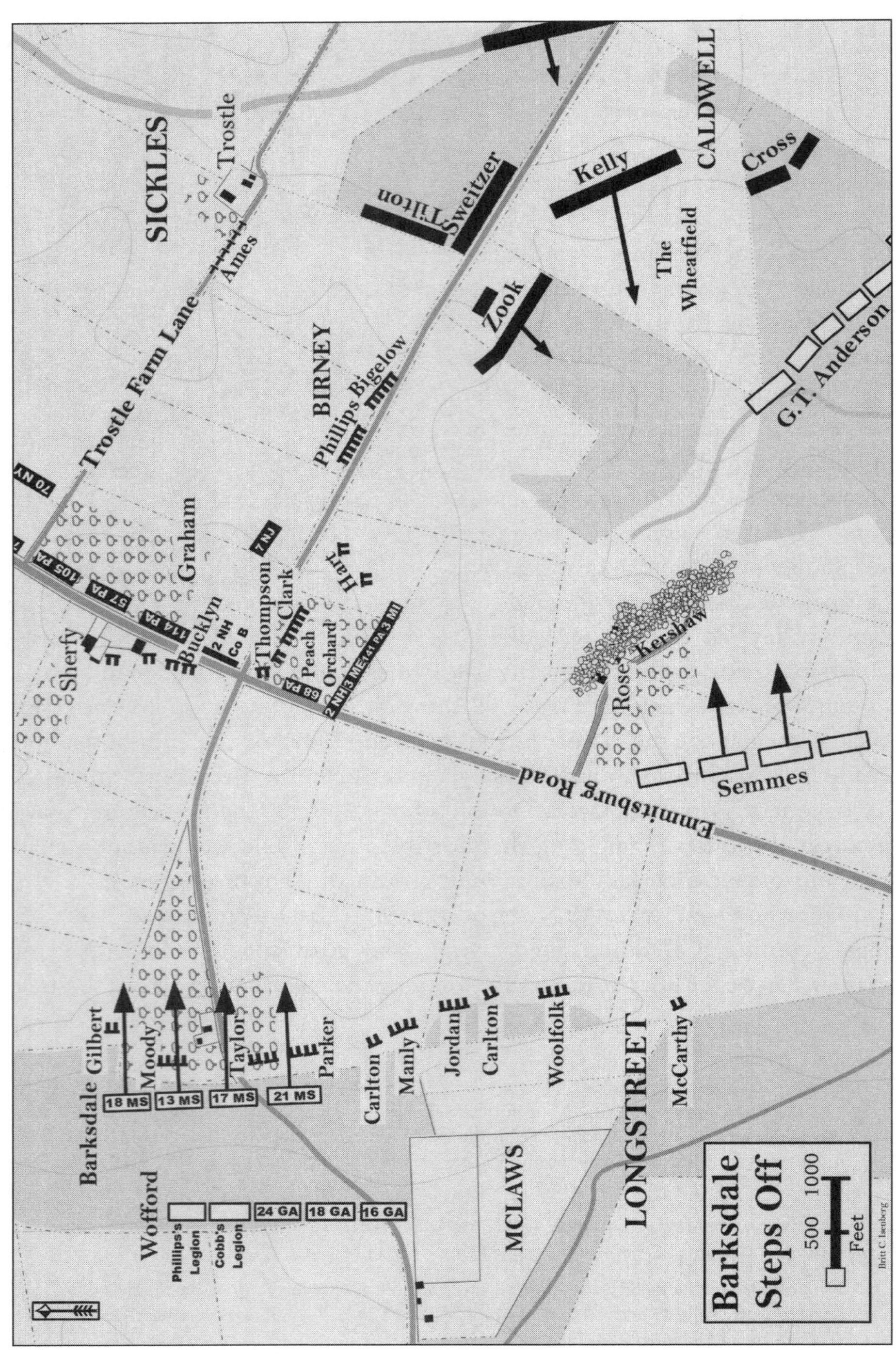
Barksdale Steps Off
500
1000
Feet
Britt C. Isenberg
SICKLES
Trostle
Ames
Trostle Farm Lane
BIRNEY
Phillips
Bigelow
Tilton
Sweitzer
Kelly
CALDWELL
Cross
The Wheatfield
Zook
G.T. Anderson
70 NY
105 PA
57 PA
114 PA
Graham
Sherfy
Bucklyn
2 NH
Co B
Thompson
Clark
7 NJ
Hart
Peach Orchard
68 PA
2 NH
3 ME
141 PA
3 MI
Rose
Kershaw
Semmes
Emmitsburg Road
Barksdale
Gilbert
Moody
Taylor
Parker
18 MS
13 MS
17 MS
21 MS
Carlton
Manly
Jordan
Carlton
Woolfolk
LONGSTREET
McCarthy
Wofford
Phillips's Legion
Cobb's Legion
24 GA
18 GA
16 GA
MCLAWS

and literally rushed the goal. Our men began to drop as soon as they came to attention, and were well peppered in covering the distance to the enemy."[21]

Observing the action from a safer distance was George Clark of the 11th Alabama, in General Wilcox's nearby brigade. As Wilcox's men awaited orders to advance, they watched the Mississippians' attack unfold. Clark offered what may be the classic description of Barksdale's charge:

> As Longstreet's brigades came into action the roar of the cannon was accompanied by the rattle of the musketry, mingled with the yells of our boys as they moved forward on the run, and the scene was grand and terrific. As the fire and the clamor approached the Alabama Brigade, Barksdale threw forward his Mississippians in an unbroken line in the most magnificent charge I witnessed during the war, and led by the gallant Barksdale, who seemed to be fifty yards in front of his brave boys. The scene was grand beyond description.[22]

Of course, romantic hyperbole such as the "most magnificent charge" often flowed from Southern pens. The awaiting Yankee infantry had already spent hours under artillery fire on a hot afternoon and considered nothing "grand" about Barksdale's attack.

Barksdale's men had one distinct advantage over their counterparts in Longstreet's previous attacking brigades. They only had to cover about 600 yards, the shortest distance of any Confederate brigade yet to attack on July 2. Barksdale's charge was a frontal assault; typically this would be a disadvantage for the attacking force. However, since they hit the Peach Orchard head-on and directly from the west, their left flank was not exposed, as had been the case with Kershaw's South Carolinians. As a result, the Mississippians were on top of the Peach Orchard's defenders in a matter of minutes.

Yankee skirmishers were certainly not going to stop the Confederate onslaught. The 63rd Pennsylvania was withdrawn from west of the Emmitsburg Road due to low ammunition prior to Barksdale's charge. They were relieved by the 5th New Jersey, from Burling's brigade, and the men covered parts of both Birney and Humphreys's divisional fronts. Colonel William Sewell of the 5th stated in his report that his left "became engaged first, and immediately after was entirely driven in by the giving way of some regiments of the First Division to my left."[23]

21 McNeily, "Barksdale's Mississippi Brigade," 236.

22 Clark, "Wilcox's Alabama Brigade at Gettysburg," *Confederate Veteran*, XVII: 229.

23 *OR*, 27/1: 498, 577; *Pennsylvania at Gettysburg*, 1: 387. According to Major John Danks of the 63rd Pennsylvania, it was between 4:00 and 5:00 p.m. when his company commanders

The Confederates moved quickly to take advantage of the rise in ground that they had taken from the 5th New Jersey. Sewell noted "the enemy placing a battery where my left had rested. I now had a direct musketry fire and a battery of artillery on my flank." Sewell withstood a withering fire on his left and held his forward position while vainly hoping for support from behind him.[24]

Company A of the 3rd Michigan was earlier detached to support Graham and advanced to an area near the Sherfy house. According to the regiment's Lieutenant Colonel Pierce, his men held "their position until overpowered by a superior force." Confederate Anderson Reese of the Troup artillery watched with delight as the Federal skirmishers "were driven back across the road upon their supports."[25]

"I saw him [Barksdale] as far as the eye could follow," remembered McLaws's staff officer G.B. Lamar, "still ahead of his men, leading them on." Lamar noticed a picket fence that stood in front of Barksdale's line. The captain was "anxious to see how they would get over it and around it. When they reached it, the fence disappeared as if by magic, and the slaughter of the 'red breeched Zouaves' [114th Pennsylvania] on the other side was terrible!"[26]

Barksdale's three left regiments advanced primarily on the north side of the Wheatfield Road. They were slightly "swinging to the left" with the

---

began to report that their ammunition was nearly spent. A courier was sent to notify General Birney, and sometime around 5: 30, the 63rd was replaced by a regiment from Humphreys's division. Kathleen Georg wrote that the 63rd retired "before overwhelming numbers," but this is not clear from Danks's report, his monument dedication speech, or reports from the 5th New Jersey. Georg, "The Sherfy Farm and the Battle of Gettysburg," 14.

24 *OR*, 27/1: 577. Danks was uncertain who replaced him, remembering only a "regiment wearing a white patch," but it was the 5th New Jersey. General Humphreys reported: "Colonel Sewell, commanding the Fifth New Jersey Volunteers, of my Third Brigade, reported to me at this time and relieved the pickets of General Graham's brigade (on my left), some of which extended over a part of my front." *OR*, 27/1: 532. Toombs, *New Jersey Troops*, 206, likewise said Humphreys ordered the 5th to replace the 63rd on picket duty. This arrangement is not reflected in the 5th's own report filed by Captain Henry H. Woolsey, *OR*, 27/1: 575-576. However, an addendum submitted by Colonel William Sewell "adds the following corrections to the report of Captain Woolsey, who was mistaken as regards the duty which the regiment was intended to perform: My orders were to report to General Graham, for the purpose of relieving the Sixty-third Pennsylvania, on picket. My right rested at a white house, my left extending to a large barn on the Emmitsburg road, thus covering the front of the Second Division; Seeley's battery a few paces in the rear of my center, and two brigades of the Second Division on the slope of the hill." *OR*, 27/1: 576-577.

25 *OR*, 27/1: 524; Letter of Anderson W. Reese, *Southern Banner*, August 8, 1863, Troup Artillery File, GNMP. Regarding the timing of the picket withdrawal, Reese, writing only weeks later, said that the Yankee skirmishers fell back prior to the opening of the Confederate artillery fire, which is at odds with Sewell's version.

26 McLaws, "Gettysburg," *SHSP*, 7: 74.

17th Mississippi headed toward the large gap between the 68th and 114th Pennsylvania regiments. Colonel B.G. Humphreys meanwhile directed his 21st Mississippi toward the southern end of the Peach Orchard and Colonel Andrew Tippin's 68th Pennsylvania. Like the remainder of Graham's brigade, Tippin's Pennsylvanians had withstood Confederate artillery fire for several hours. Additionally, the 68th's Private Lewis Schaeffer recorded that they had received no rations for two days.[27]

As noted previously, Tippin's Pennsylvanians fronted west along the Emmitsburg Road, while the 2nd New Hampshire held a position in their left rear and fronted to the south. The connection between the 2nd New Hampshire's right (facing south) and the 68th Pennsylvania's left (facing west) was particularly tenuous. Since the regiments formed a right angle, they were the true salient in Sickles's overstretched line. To the 2nd New Hampshire's left, the defensive line continued with the 3rd Maine, 141st Pennsylvania, and 3rd Michigan. These regiments were from four different brigades – Burling, Ward, Graham, and de Trobriand's. In fact, no two regiments from the same brigade were next to each other. Coordination among the individual units was clearly going to be an issue in a crisis.[28]

Colonel Andrew Tippin of the 68th Pennsylvania was a 40-year-old veteran of the Mexican War, where he had twice been brevetted for gallantry in battle. He was a man of many personal accomplishments. Earlier in life, Tippin had learned printing and once co-owned a newspaper. After returning home from Mexico, he was elected clerk of the courts for Montgomery County. He departed that office in 1852, was a conductor on the state railroad, and then in 1857 was appointed as a First Assistant U.S. Marshal. Tippin was later remembered as possessing "in an unusual degree the noblest elements of manhood-earnest, active, gifted with rare qualities of head and heart, and above all characterized by a degree of uprightness in all his dealings with his fellow-men which commanded the confidence and respect not only of those who enjoyed his intimate acquaintance and friendship but of the community at large."[29]

27 Diary of Lewis Schaeffer, West Virginia and Regional History Center.

28 B.G. Humphreys Manuscript, 12; Craft, *History of the 141st Regiment Pennsylvania Volunteers*, 120-121; OR, 27/1: 498-499; 504-505, 508, 574; Haynes, *A History of the Second Regiment*, 170-171, 177-178; Imhof, *Gettysburg Day Two*, 110.

29 Bates, *History of Pennsylvania Volunteers*, 2: 673; "Death of a Gallant Soldier," *Montgomery Ledger*, February 8, 1870.

Colonel Andrew H. Tippin
Pottstown Historical Society

His regiment hailed from Philadelphia and neighboring counties. After the Mexican War, a group of local veterans, who served under General Winfield Scott, formed a fraternal organization called the "Scott Legion." Upon the outbreak of the Civil War, the members raised a regiment for national service. This unit was designated the 20th Pennsylvania Volunteers, and they had a three-month term of enlistment. The men elected Tippin as their major. At the end of the unit's relatively uneventful service, Tippin reorganized the regiment for a three-year term as the 68th Pennsylvania. He was commissioned colonel of the new regiment.[30]

The 68th saw combat at Fredericksburg and Chancellorsville. Following the defeat at Chancellorsville, division commander Birney's report included Tippin among a number of officers who were "distinguished for their gallantry." However, Birney added that Tippin was one of two colonels who "left their commands without permission and went to the rear" during the fighting. Fortunately, "the excuse made by Colonel Tippin was well supported and satisfactory," so Birney appeared to not hold the indiscretion against him. Tippin conceded in his own report that he had been "completely prostrated" and forced to "retire to the rear for medical treatment."[31]

30 Bates, *History of Pennsylvania Volunteers*, 1: 185-186; 2: 673.

31 *OR*, 25/1: 410, 420. Tippin's Chancellorsville report reads: "All this time the battle had been raging furiously all over the field. My men were now suffering greatly from exhaustion and lack of sustenance, having been engaged some four hours without intermission and had nothing to eat as yet. Many dropped from complete exhaustion, and with great difficulty some got within the lines. I myself, having lost my horse the day previous, and being on foot nearly all of both days, was completely prostrated, and compelled to deliver the command over to Major Winslow, and retire to the rear for medical treatment."

Colonel Tippin's Pennsylvanians were in a dangerous situation on the late afternoon of July 2. "We had been in this position but a short time," Tippin reported, "when significant movements on the part of the enemy made it evident we were about to be attacked." As Barksdale's men approached, Tippin ordered the 68th to "reserve their fire until reaching a certain point." Once the Confederates were within range, Tippin proclaimed, "a destructive fire was opened, the enemy halting and dropping behind a fence." Briefly staggered by this volley, the 21st Mississippi paused and likely waited for the 17th Mississippi to close up on their left.[32]

The Federals initially "stood firm and continued a furious fire," wrote Confederate Colonel Humphreys, "killing many of our brave boys, but the brigade moved steadily on." Humphreys praised the courage of his command noting that the men never wavered, "and when within three hundred yards commenced firing, still advancing." The exchange was "terrible, but never doubtful," as the Mississippians unleashed their Rebel yell and charged.[33]

When the unrelenting Confederate fire killed the color sergeant of the 68th Pennsylvania, Corporal James McLarnon grabbed the flag from the hands of the dying man as he fell, to prevent the colors from touching the ground. McLarnon then held the flag high for his comrades to see and waved it to encourage them to continue the fight. For his efforts, courage, and patriotism, McLarnon earned a promotion to sergeant. He survived the battle and the war and returned to Gettysburg for the dedication of the regimental monument in 1889. "It was a terrible afternoon in that orchard," Private Alfred Craighead recalled, "and we were all anxious for reinforcements to come up, as we were being decimated by their artillery." However, the 68th Pennsylvania was already "greatly weakened by its losses, and exhausted by frequent maneuverings, outflanked and vastly outnumbered, [the regiment] was compelled to yield, but not in disorder, retiring slowly and contesting the ground inch by inch."[34]

Colonel Tippin expressed alarm by what he described as the enemy's "re-enforcements, and heavy masses of his infantry coming down on our right." No Union regiment had been sent into line to plug the gap between the 68th's right and the 114th Pennsylvania's left. Not only did Tippin face the 21st Mississippi, a regiment hell-bent on delivering a deadly attack, but he

32 *OR*, 27/1: 499.

33 B.G. Humphreys Manuscript, 12.

34 *Pennsylvania at Gettysburg*, 1: 393, 397-398.

View north along the Emmitsburg Road showing the area of the gap in the Third Corps line. The monument in the foreground is the original to the 68th Pennsylvania. Ames's 1st New York Battery G is on top of the hill.

Photo by Authors

could see most of Barksdale's Brigade and perhaps the initial movements of Wofford's Brigade. Certainly, heat, fatigue, and demoralization had an effect on the Pennsylvanians. "I ordered my command to fall back to the position in the rear of the batteries," Tippin reported, "which was done in good order."[35]

As an isolated movement by one regiment, Tippin's decision to fall back toward the Union batteries was justifiable. However, the withdrawal set in motion an irrevocable chain reaction among neighboring regiments. Tippin's retreat emboldened the 21st Mississippi, since it removed their immediate opposition and appeared to Colonel Humphreys that he "broke the first line." The 68th's withdrawal further widened the troublesome gap in Union defenses along the Emmitsburg Road. In fact, this left the Emmitsburg Road on the south side of the Wheatfield Road undefended by infantry. To further compound the problem, Tippin's departure exposed the 2nd New Hampshire and the other

35 *OR*, 27/1: 499.

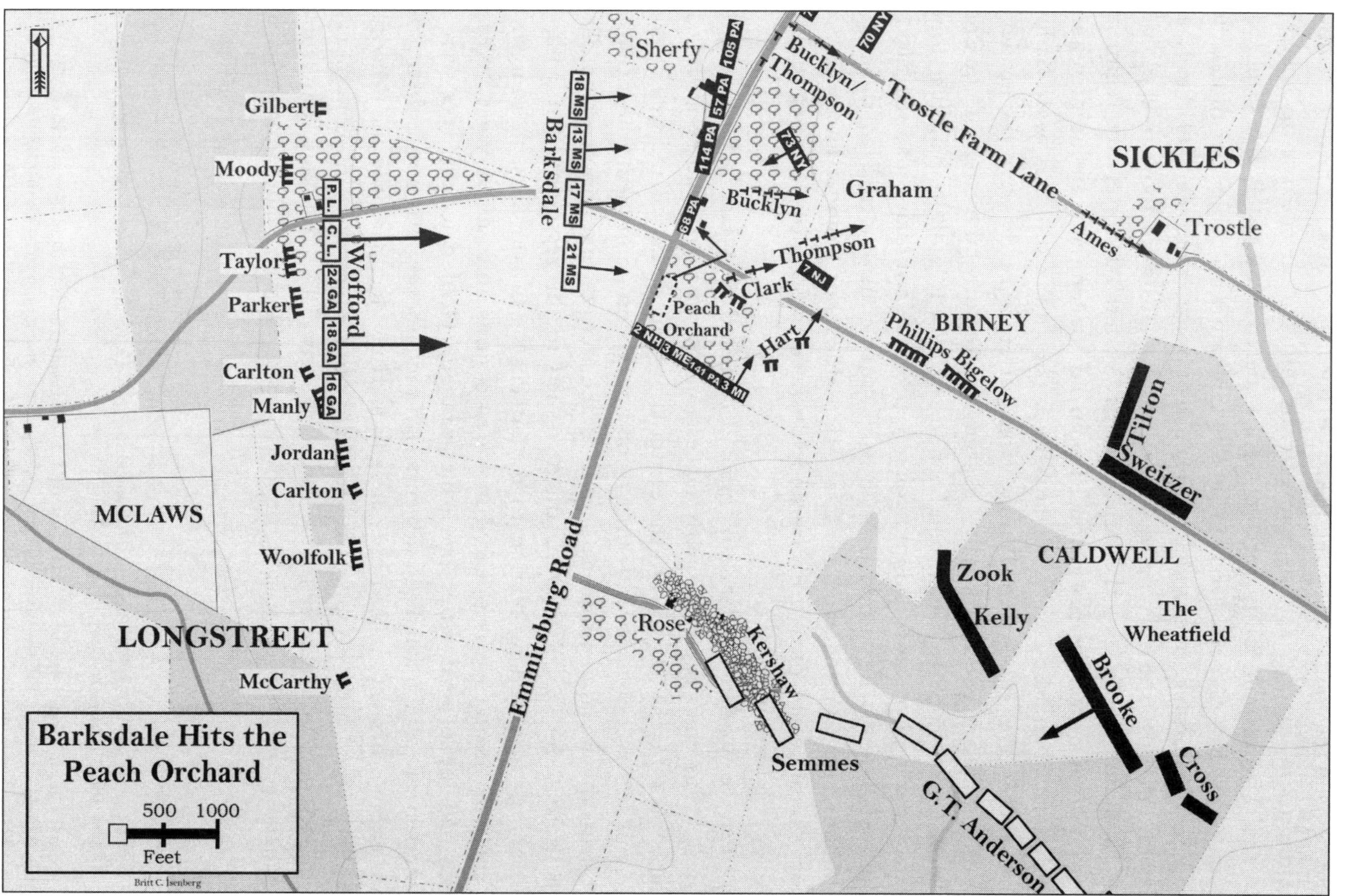
Barksdale Hits the Peach Orchard
500 1000
Feet
Britt C. Isenberg
Gilbert
Moody
Taylor
Parker
Carlton
Manly
Jordan
Carlton
Woolfolk
McCarthy
MCLAWS
LONGSTREET
P. L.
C. L.
24 GA
18 GA
16 GA
Wofford
18 MS
13 MS
17 MS
21 MS
Barksdale
Sherfy
105 PA
57 PA
114 PA
68 PA
Bucklyn/
Thompson
70 NY
73 NY
Bucklyn
Thompson
7 NJ
Clark
Peach
Orchard
2 NH
3 ME
141 PA
3 MI
Hart
Trostle Farm Lane
SICKLES
Graham
Ames
Trostle
BIRNEY
Phillips
Bigelow
Tilton
Sweitzer
Emmitsburg Road
Rose
Kershaw
Semmes
G.T. Anderson
Zook
Kelly
CALDWELL
The
Wheatfield
Brooke
Cross

regiments in the south end of the Peach Orchard. The Mississippians were now behind them. Tippin's actions inadvertently initiated the collapse of Sickles's salient. The responsibility for the tactical defense of the Peach Orchard, however, fell to General Graham. It was Graham who earlier permitted the 2nd New Hampshire to charge into the current position and then failed to send any infantry into the opening that the Mississippians were about to exploit.[36]

With no one directing the Peach Orchard's overall defense, each regiment was left to their own devices. Colonel Tippin did not communicate his intentions to the officers of the 2nd New Hampshire. The 2nd's Colonel Edward Bailey acknowledged that the 68th Pennsylvania suffered greatly from the artillery barrage that preceded Barksdale's charge. The regimental history of the 2nd claimed that the 68th "which had been losing heavily, withdrew up the slope before the impact came, and immediately after, the 3rd Maine also fell back." Colonel Bailey's men opened up a brief but "constant fire" to the right oblique. This again slowed the 21st Mississippi, but Colonel Humphreys's boys continued to press forward and advanced close enough to get behind Bailey's right flank.[37]

Private Wyman Holden, a member of the 2nd New Hampshire, did not consider his unit's fire particularly successful. "When their infantry advanced, the constant crowding toward the center kept their ranks full and well closed up, our fire making apparently little or no impression upon them," he insisted. Perhaps this was the unfortunate result of the ineffective experimental musket shells that the U.S. War Department issued to the regiment. The rolling terrain also offered protection to the attackers as, from time to time, the Rebels momentarily disappeared into depressions and out of view. "When they had approached within point-blank range," Holden added, "they were a compact mass of humanity, and, although the shooting was good, there was not enough of it. Our thin line, already fearfully decimated by the dreadful artillery, could offer no successful resistance to such overwhelming numbers, and, lacking reinforcements, were forced to retire." The 2nd New Hampshire changed front and withdrew through the Peach Orchard. They stopped near

36 Ibid., 27/1: 498-499; Bigelow, *The Peach Orchard*, 11-12; Ladd, *Bachelder Papers*, 1: 480-481; Gottfried, *Brigades of Gettysburg*, 413; Imhof, *Gettysburg Day Two*, 143.

37 *OR*, 27/1: 574; Haynes, *A History of the Second Regiment*, 179-180; Ladd, *Bachelder Papers*, 2: 846-847. Colonel Bailey insisted that the 3rd Maine's retreat coincided with that of the 68th Pennsylvania and before his own. See *OR*, 27/1: 574 and *Bachelder Papers*, 2: 846.

Colonel Moses B. Lakeman after the war wearing his colonel's frock coat and proudly displaying his Kearny Cross along with other veteran's medals.
Author's Collection

the halfway point and again delivered a "sharp fire" toward the Mississippians before continuing back toward the Wheatfield Road.[38]

The 3rd Maine also abandoned their position on the left of the 2nd New Hampshire. Although some accounts blamed them for doing so prematurely, they had already undergone a particularly grueling day, even before Barksdale attacked. Several hours earlier, the regiment assisted Berdan's sharpshooters in flushing Wilcox's Rebels out of Pitzer's Woods. Later, while in the Peach Orchard, the regiment sustained Confederate artillery fire, fought enemy skirmishers, and harassed Kershaw's left flank. Now the Southerners "came forward again with a force much greater than before." Seeing his regiment's rear and avenues of escape threatened, Colonel Moses Lakeman changed his front toward the Emmitsburg Road. As they turned away from Kershaw to confront Barksdale, the 3rd Maine received what was described as a "withering fire" and an "enfilading volley" that caused the color Company K to melt away.[39]

"I then saw a large force marching round to cut me off," reported Lakeman, "and ordered my regiment to retire, and while doing so we received a most distressing fire, which threw my command into much confusion, and mixing them up with a portion of the First Brigade, which was also falling back." Lakeman offered no excuses for his retreat, and given their long day's service, none were necessary. His unit started the day with 210 men and lost 113 between Pitzer's Woods and the Peach Orchard. The fighting at the Peach

38 Haynes, *A History of the Second Regiment*, 179-180, 187.

39 *Maine at Gettysburg*, 131-132; *OR*, 27/1: 508.

Orchard, later described as "wrapped in a vortex of fire," may have claimed 50 of those lives, lost in "a short time, measured by minutes."[40]

The 141st Pennsylvania was in line to the left of the 3rd Maine. Colonel Henry Madill complained that regiments on either side of him abandoned their position. "The Third Maine, after exchanging a few shots with the enemy at this point, withdrew. Colonel Pierce's regiment (Third Michigan) withdrew about the same time, or a few minutes before. I found myself alone, with a small regiment of about 180 men." Madill held this position for a "short time" longer, before he too ordered a withdrawal in the general direction taken by Tippin's 68th Pennsylvania and toward the Wentz buildings.[41]

To Madill's left, the ranks of the 3rd Michigan from Colonel de Trobriand's brigade were already reduced by Company A's detachment near the Sherfy house. De Trobriand personally ordered the regiment to retreat: "Third Michigan, change front to right. I give ze order tree or four times. Change quick, or you all be gobbled up; don't you see you are flanked? Ze whole rebel army is in your rear." The regiment's Lieutenant Colonel Edwin Pierce reported, rather nonchalantly, "The most of General Graham's force having retired, we held our position until about 7 p.m., when the left had retired so far that we were in danger of being flanked. We retired in good order, and assisted in bringing off a portion of two batteries." The 3rd Michigan's estimated casualty rate of 18.9% was considerably lower than their neighbors. This seemingly supported Madill's accusations that the Wolverines' departure had been among the earliest or the least hazardous. Nonetheless, their retreat contributed to the mass exodus of infantry from the southern boundary of the Peach Orchard. This withdrawal of five Federal regiments was even more remarkable because only one Confederate regiment, the 21st Mississippi, directly opposed them.[42]

With Union infantry support crumbling, and no guiding hand to rally them, the Peach Orchard's artillery hastened to get out. The right section of Captain Thompson's battery, two guns that fronted west along the Emmitsburg Road, found themselves swept "out of position like a whirlwind." Thompson had been in position for about one hour when he stated, "The enemy advanced

40 *OR*, 27/1: 508 *Maine at Gettysburg*, 131-132; Busey and Martin, *Regimental Strengths and Losses*, 131. In ibid., the authors estimate the 3rd Maine casualties at 122 out of 210 engaged for a rate of 58.1%.

41 *OR*, 27/1: 505; Craft, *History of the 141st Regiment Pennsylvania Volunteers*, 121-122; Lash, "A Pathetic Story," *Gettysburg Magazine* 14, 95.

42 *Michigan at Gettysburg*, 76; *OR*, 27/1: 524; Busey and Martin, *Regimental Strengths and Losses*, 132.

and drove back our infantry supports, capturing one of the two guns facing west, but our infantry, rallying, recaptured it." Sergeant William Loring of the 141st Pennsylvania affirmed that an unnamed captured Federal battery was retaken in a "charge" by their regiment. Thompson limbered up his pieces and retired about 300 yards, where he temporarily reunited his entire battery. However, after firing "a few rounds," things got too hot in this new position and he discovered that "our infantry was again falling back."[43]

Barksdale's pursuing infantrymen directed their fire at the horses in Thompson's battery, killing a few and resulting in "the enemy again capturing a gun and one caisson." As the battery fell back under a galling fire, Private Casper Carlisle assisted Captain Thompson in disengaging four dead horses from one of the guns. With another horse fatally wounded, Carlisle personally led the gun off of the field toward the Trostle farm. The young private saved the piece from an artilleryman's ultimate humiliation: capture by the enemy.[44]

Captain Thompson was so impressed that in his report he urged for a "medal be granted him [Carlisle] for his conduct on this occasion and subsequent good conduct on the 3d instant." Unfortunately, Carlisle received no commendation. After the war, he returned to the Pittsburgh area where he worked as a laborer, and not surprisingly, as a teamster. Carlisle was also an active member of a local GAR post. A veterans reunion in 1888 prompted his comrades to lobby for his long-deserved recognition. Finally, in 1892, the United States awarded Carlisle the Medal of Honor. Unfortunately, his receipt of the nation's highest military honor did not prevent him from dying penniless, in "exhaustion" and obscurity, in 1908. Sadly, his grave remained neglected and forgotten until re-discovered by historians in the 1990s. In 1998, a Civil War enthusiast paid for a new headstone, which was dedicated in a long-overdue ceremony.[45]

Meanwhile, utter confusion reigned among the troops around the Peach Orchard. The Confederates were "advancing in heavy force" when Captain

43 *OR*, 27/1: 889; *Pennsylvania at Gettysburg*, 2: 910; Georg, "The Sherfy Farm and the Battle of Gettysburg," 17; Pfanz, *Gettysburg: The Second Day*, 339; Loring, "Gettysburg. The 141st Pa. at the Battle," *Fighting Them Over*, 309.

44 *OR*, 27/1: 890; James Thompson to Ezra Carman, October 3, 1898, Page 3, Museum Collections, *GNMP*; Hanna, *Gettysburg Medal of Honor Recipients*, 51.

45 *OR*, 27/1: 890; Hanna, *Gettysburg Medal of Honor Recipients*, 52; Rodgers, "Medal of Honor winners from Greene County never stopped leading," *Pittsburgh Post-Gazette*, June 30, 2013; "Artillery Hero of Gettysburg's Peach Orchard Gets New Gravestone," *Gettysburg Times*, December 14, 1998. Carlisle was 67 years old when he died on April 29, 1908. Cause of death listed as "exhaustion" with "epileptic mania" as a contributing factor.

Patrick Hart fired the last round of canister from his 15th New York battery. Moments earlier, Hart sent to the rear for two of his caissons, but word quickly reached him "that they were not where I left them. I sent another messenger to bring them up. When they were convenient to me, they were again ordered to the rear." With only a few rounds of solid shot remaining, Hart limbered up and retired about one mile. He later expressed resentment toward Colonel McGilvery for leaving him without adequate ammunition.[46]

Hart had previously ordered Second Lieutenant Edward Knox to command his right section, which stood about 100 yards in front of the left section. Perhaps with some dramatic license, Lieutenant Knox remembered:

> The Confederates thought they had my guns and made a dash for them. As they came, I let go both pieces with double canister, and as I did so, I yelled to my boys to lay down and pretend that they were done for. And thus, not heeding us, the 'Johnnies' swept through my section to meet a charge from the support in our rear. . . .Then, repulsed and driven back, they came back more rapidly than they came in. After they had again passed over us, we got up and with our prolonges and the assistance of the infantry boys, hauled our guns back.[47]

Knox was wounded in action but escaped with his guns. He survived another wound on July 3, and Hart officially praised Knox's "gallant conduct." In 1892, Knox was awarded a Congressional Medal of Honor for holding "his ground with the battery after the other batteries had fallen back until compelled to draw his piece off by hand." All while being "severely wounded."[48]

The Federal batteries on the north side of the Wheatfield Road were also under heavy pressure. Lieutenant John Bucklyn's Battery E, 1st Rhode Island Light Artillery, faced west along the Emmitsburg Road. Bucklyn's battery performed well, but three of Barksdale's four regiments were sweeping toward

46 *OR*, 27/1: 887; Ladd, *The Bachelder Papers*, 3: 1797; Imhof, *Gettysburg Day Two*, 151, 155-156. In later years, Captain Hart harbored a grudge against both McGilvery and Captain Phillips. Hart told John Bachelder in 1891, "I hear [sic] solemnly declare that I did not at anytime during the Battle of Gettysburg receive any orders from Col. McGilvray [sic] and that he through ignorance and prejudice left my guns without ammunition . . . in regard to Capt. Phillips and his officers . . . I requested General Hunt to try those officers by a drum head court martial. The reply he [Hunt] gave me was the man who fights and runs away will live to fight another day." But Hart's 1891 account contradicts his own report which stated that he received orders from McGilvery on several occasions throughout the day. See *OR*, 27/1: 887 and Ladd, *The Bachelder Papers*, 3: 1797.

47 Beyer and Keydel, *Deeds of Valor*, 231. Knox erroneously identified the 72nd New York Infantry "I think" as the Federal regiment that led the charge from his rear.

48 Ibid., *OR*, 27/1: 888.

them. Captain Randolph had once commanded this battery, and he was particularly concerned over its fate. The Federal infantry's various maneuvers at the south end of the Peach Orchard gave Randolph the impression that Bucklyn's infantry support had been withdrawn "and the subsequent repulse of our troops in that position made its [Bucklyn's] withdrawal a matter not only of prudence but of necessity."[49]

The 114th Pennsylvania was behind Bucklyn's battery position. The regiment was conspicuous for their distinctive uniforms of baggy red pantaloons, short blue Zouave jacket, and red fez. Randolph approached Captain Edward Bowen of the 114th, and asked the Pennsylvanians to buy time for Bucklyn to extricate his guns. Captain Bowen reported that Randolph "ordered us to advance, saying, 'If you want to save my battery, move forward. I cannot find the general. I give the order on my own responsibility.'" Bowen's men then rushed through the battery, which promptly limbered up and went to the rear, while the 114th dashed crossed the Emmitsburg Road.[50]

Before Bucklyn's battery escaped, a German immigrant named Corporal Ernest Simpson approached the lieutenant and requested permission to command a gun. Barksdale's Mississippians were already within a few yards and delivered a round of heavy musketry into the artillerymen. Bucklyn replied that "we would probably be killed," but evidently, Simpson wanted to die. He had left his home in Germany because his parents opposed his love affair. Simpson attempted to commit suicide in London, and enlisted in Bucklyn's battery after arriving in America "with the expectation of being killed." Simpson told Bucklyn that the lieutenant was his only friend in America. Bucklyn consented to Simpson's request "and in a few minutes his head was shot off." The star-crossed immigrant was buried on the south side of Sherfy's

49 OR, 27/1: 584, 590; Imhof, *Gettysburg Day Two*, 136-137; Murray, *E.P. Alexander and the Artillery Action in the Peach Orchard*, 42-43.

50 *OR*, 27/1: 502-503, 584; *Pennsylvania at Gettysburg*, 2: 610-611, Haggerty, *Collis' Zouaves*, 22. The story later became more dramatic in that Randolph was credited with shouting, "You boys saved this battery once before at Fredericksburg, and if you will do it again, move forward!" Lieutenant Benjamin Freeborn, who took command of the battery after Bucklyn was wounded, also complained that the fighting on the battery's left was so "severe" that "our supports were either sent to that point or some other, as for twenty minutes before we left the battery was without any support, and nothing in front but a few sharpshooters." See *OR*, 27/1: 590. Individual variations of dress existed within the 114th Pennsylvania regiment. Consult Haggerty, *Collis' Zouaves*, 139-164.

Looking north toward Bucklyn's position. Sherfy farm on the far side of the Emmitsburg Road and the Wentz foundation in the foreground. The area to the right of the road saw the day's bloodiest action in the fight for control of the Peach Orchard.

Photo by Authors

farm after the battle, but he was later removed to the Rhode Island plot in Gettysburg's National Cemetery.[51]

Enemy case shot ripped through Lieutenant Bucklyn's shoulder as he attempted to free a caisson from its dead and maimed horses. "My battery is torn and my brave boys have gone," Bucklyn later bitterly lamented, "never to return. Curse the rebels." For their service on the Emmitsburg Road, Bucklyn's battery paid a higher price than any in the Third Corps: 30 casualties out of 108 men (27.8%) with 40 horses lost.[52]

Picket fire had earlier prevented Graham's pioneers from removing all of the fences bordering the Emmitsburg Road. This forced the 114th's right to climb a fence while the left's advance was unobstructed. The disparity

51 Lewis, *History of Battery E*, 210-211; Coco, *Killed In Action – Union*, 82-83; *OR*, 27/1: 590. Simpson is sometimes referred to as a private, however he was promoted to corporal as of January 1862. See Lewis, *History of Battery E*, 493.

52 *OR*, 27/1: 584, 590; Ladd, *The Bachelder Papers*, 1: 72-73; Busey and Martin, *Regimental Strengths and Losses*, 247.

required the regiment to pause and realign after they crossed the road. The commander of the 114th, Lieutenant Colonel Frederico Cavada, asked one of his soldiers to observe the enemy's movements from between the Sherfy buildings and determine their rate of advance. The sergeant assigned to the task came back swiftly with the reply, "You bet your life they are coming!"[53]

Captain Randolph meanwhile requested another of Graham's regiments, the 57th Pennsylvania, to join the 114th on the west side of the road. The 57th crossed the Emmitsburg Road, took advantage of the cover afforded by the Sherfy buildings and trees, and opened fire. A detail of 15 men from the 57th, moving ahead of the regiment, entered Sherfy's house and fired at Barksdale's men from the house's west windows.[54]

Captain Bowen of the 114th Pennsylvania saw "the enemy advancing in force" and promptly ordered the 114th's right wing to move behind the Sherfy house. Raising his voice above the din of fire, one Zouave shouted, "Give it to them boys, we have them on our own ground!" Bowen then attempted to form a line with the 57th Pennsylvania. "I was but partially successful, as the enemy had already advanced so quickly and in such force as to gain the road," he reported. A sharp firefight ensued between the Pennsylvania and Mississippi regiments. Barksdale's 13th and 17th Mississippi reached a rail fence about 100 yards away and poured "a murderous fire" on the 114th's flank, throwing "the left wing of the regiment on to the right in much confusion."[55]

The 105th Pennsylvania "Wildcats," another of Graham's regiments, had their front blocked by the movements of the 57th Pennsylvania. To compensate for this, the Wildcats charged across the Emmitsburg Road and took position to the right of the 57th. "Having gained this position," wrote the 105th's Colonel Calvin Craig, "the fire from the enemy being very severe, we immediately opened fire." With these actions, three of Graham's Pennsylvania regiments found themselves deployed on the west side of the road and engaged in close combat with an equal number of Barksdale's units.[56]

A short time earlier, General Graham had urgently appealed to Sickles for reinforcements. Sickles sent staff officer Captain Tremain to locate General Humphreys and direct him to send one more regiment to assist Graham. At that

53 Hagerty, *Collis' Zouaves*, 242.

54 *OR*, 27/1: 497; *History of the Fifty-Seventh Regiment Pennsylvania Veteran Volunteer Infantry*, 91.

55 Hagerty, *Collis' Zouaves*, 242; *OR*, 27/1: 503.

56 *OR*, 27/1: 497, 500, 503; *Pennsylvania at Gettysburg*, 1: 356, 2: 607; Georg, "The Sherfy Farm and the Battle of Gettysburg," 19; Gottfried, *Brigades at Gettysburg*, 192.

moment, things were considerably less active along Humphreys's front. Seeley and Turnbull's batteries actively engaged the Confederates near the Klingle house, but the infantry hostilities in Humphreys's sector were thus far limited to demonstrations and picket fire. Shortly after the 5th New Jersey manned the Federal picket line, Tremain located Humphreys and delivered the urgent request. However, the general had little time to ponder this order. "At this moment," Humphreys reported that the colonel of the 5th New Jersey "sent me word that the enemy was driving in my pickets, and was about advancing in two lines to the attack."[57]

Since much of Burling's brigade was already cannibalized to support Birney's division, Humphreys had a dwindling selection of available regiments to send to Graham. Despite his own pending problems, Humphreys dispatched the 73rd New York from Colonel William Brewster's Excelsior Brigade. Humphreys also ordered an aide to find General Hancock, "with the request that he would send a brigade, if possible, to my support." Tremain led the 73rd New York, under Major Michael Burns, into their new position. They moved through a storm of bullets and shells, and Tremain placed the regiment into line of battle in the field north of the Wheatfield Road and facing the Emmitsburg Road. (This was near the location of the 73rd New York's present-day regimental monument.) The position Tremain selected was a poor one for the situation; Burns's regiment faced threats from Barksdale on their front and left. In addition, Graham's units along the Emmitsburg Road held a position in front of the 73rd and blocked the regiment's fields of fire. Tremain was uncertain if the Excelsiors should stay there, so he went to Graham and asked for additional instructions. Graham told Tremain to leave the New Yorkers where they were and he would direct them further. As Tremain departed for Sickles's headquarters, Graham exclaimed, "We're giving them hell!" Unfortunately for Tremain, "The regiment, it seems, was driven from this position shortly after I had posted it. . . . It was like dropping a peanut in a stone crusher."[58]

According to the 73rd's Lieutenant Frank Moran, "we were hurried at double-quick to a point directly in rear" of the Sherfy barn where the 114th Pennsylvania was already fighting and "bravely disputing the ground with the

57 *OR*, 27/1: 532-533; Tremain, *Two Days of War*, 79-81; Imhof, *Gettysburg Day Two*, 141-142. At the 73rd New York monument dedication, Tremain said that their detachment occurred at 5:00 p.m. See *New York at Gettysburg*, 2: 605. Colonel Brewster reported that the 73rd was sent to Graham's support around 5: 30. See *OR*, 27/1: 559.

58 *OR*, 27/1: 532-533, 559; *New York at Gettysburg*, 2: 605-606; Tremain, *Two Days of War*, 79-81; Moran, "A Fire Zouave," *National Tribune*, November 6, 1890; Hawthorne, *Gettysburg: Stories of Men and Monuments*, 77.

Mississippi Brigade." Barksdale's men soon "came swarming up the slope, yelling like devils." The New Yorkers took an early volley, but for "a few impatient minutes, our regiments were unable to return a shot." The 114th was still crowding in their front "about forty yards ahead of us, so that it was impossible to fire upon the enemy without shooting our friends in the back altogether, we stood in a shower of bullets from [the] front and a merciless storm of bursting shells from Longstreet's batteries on our left." The incoming rounds were spewing slivers of hot metal throughout the ranks. As Tremain recalled, "It did not seem possible for a horse to live on the crest."[59]

While fighting escalated against Barksdale's left regiments near the Sherfy buildings, the Federal units that retreated from the south end of the Peach Orchard reformed temporarily near the Wentz property. Their actual positions during this particular phase of the action remain uncertain, primarily because the units were disorganized and fighting individually against both the 17th and 21st Mississippi. The important point is that the Northerners made one last attempt to stop the rout as the action moved north of the Wheatfield Road.

As the 68th Pennsylvania fell back from the Peach Orchard, Graham halted Tippin and ordered him to immediately "engage the enemy coming down on our right flank." Graham was subsequently wounded in the hip by a shell fragment, and then by a musket ball that tore through his shoulders. The general also had his horse shot from beneath him. Graham relinquished brigade command temporarily to Tippin and began walking to the rear. Tippin reported that he received orders to "take command and fight on. I supposed him [Graham] able to get to the rear, as, after dismounting, he walked with apparently little difficulty." The 68th then advanced again to the Emmitsburg Road, and with the Wheatfield Road to their immediate left, confronted the enemy advancing from the west, likely squaring off against the 17th Mississippi. Unfortunately, Tippin and his men again were unable to stand their ground. "We held the position as long as it was possible to hold it. The artillery having retired and the ranks very much decimated by the fire of the enemy, who were pushing forward in heavy masses, I ordered the command to retire in order, which was done."[60]

59 Ladd, *The Bachelder Papers*, 1: 225, 2: 773, *New York at Gettysburg*, 2: 605; Gottfried, *Brigades of Gettysburg*, 220-221.

60 *OR*, 27/1: 499; Charles Graham account, Participants Accounts File 5, GNMP; *Soldiers' and Sailors' Half-Dime Tales*, 117; Craft, *History of the 141st Regiment Pennsylvania Volunteers*, 122-123, 137; Smith, "We drop a comrade's tear," 112.

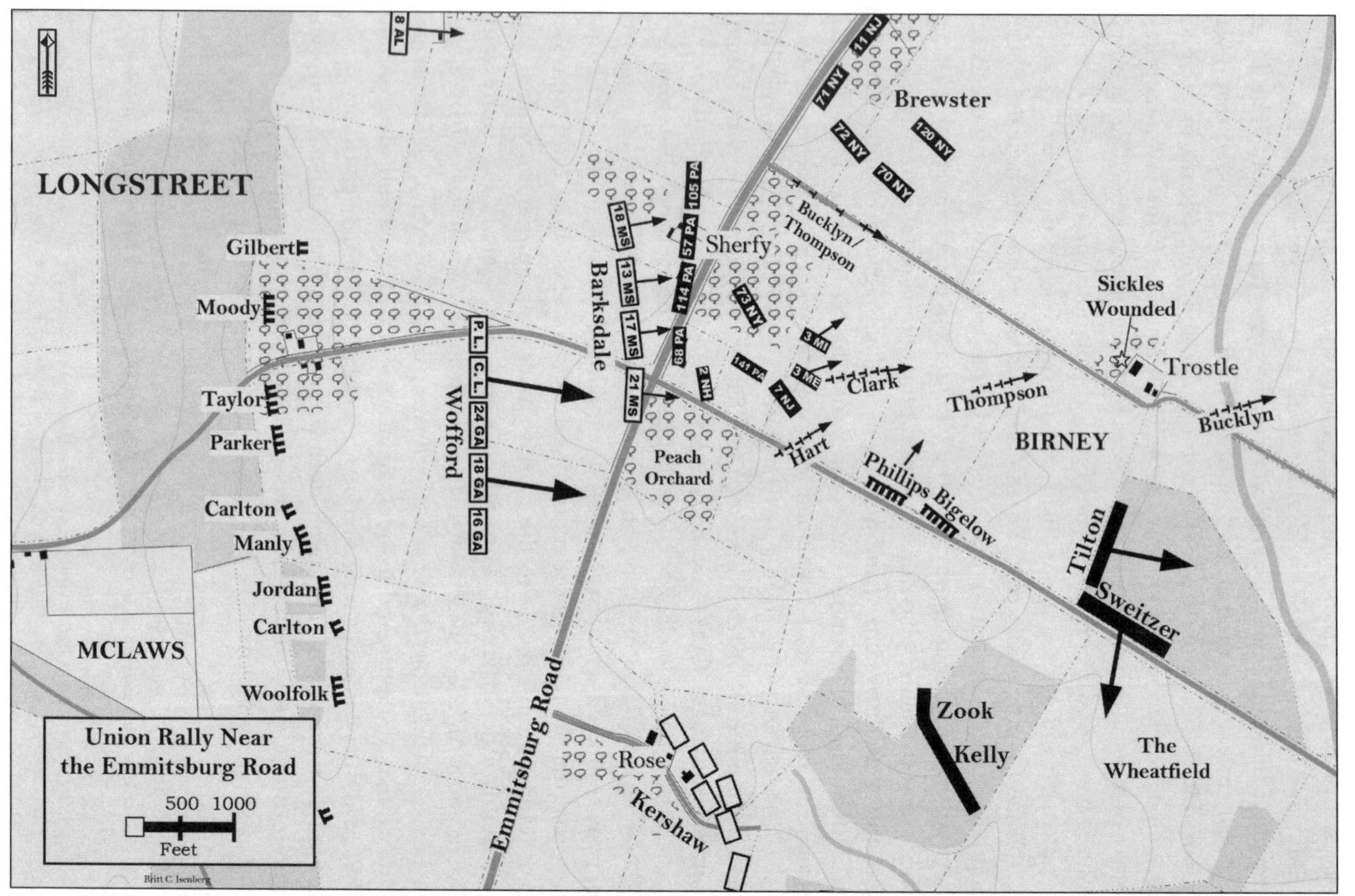
Union Rally Near the Emmitsburg Road
500 1000
Feet
Britt C. Isenberg
LONGSTREET
MCLAWS
BIRNEY
Emmitsburg Road
Trostle
Bucklyn
Sickles Wounded
Tilton
Sweitzer
The Wheatfield
Thompson
Brewster
120 NY
70 NY
72 NY
71 NY
11 NJ
Bucklyn/ Thompson
Clark
3 MI
3 ME
Phillips
Bigelow
Zook
Kelly
Hart
7 NJ
141 PA
73 NY
2 NH
Sherfy
105 PA
57 PA
114 PA
68 PA
Peach Orchard
18 MS
13 MS
17 MS
21 MS
Barksdale
P. L.
C. L.
24 GA
18 GA
16 GA
Wofford
8 AL
Rose
Kershaw
Gilbert
Moody
Taylor
Parker
Carlton
Manly
Jordan
Carlton
Woolfolk

Captain Bigelow, of the 9th Massachusetts Battery, later criticized Tippin's brief tenure in brigade command. "It does not appear that he (Col. Tippin) took active charge of the brigade at this critical time," Bigelow asserted, "when the enemy were closing in on the Peach Orchard. None of the reports of the officers commanding the different regiments of the brigade, when they retired, nor of the batteries, make any reference to Col. Tippin, but each seems to have been left to their own resources." Bigelow praised the fighting abilities of the various Northern regiments, but they all retreated "when each thought best. There was no commanding officer to collect them and form a second line; nor use them to cover the long gap in the lines, between the Round Tops and the left of the 2nd Corps, which they were leaving open."[61]

Bigelow's assessment was accurate, although he could have expanded his criticism to include Birney and Graham's leadership. Tippin received orders to take command of the brigade, and from his experience, the colonel knew what that entailed. Yet, he focused solely on his individual regiment. Nonetheless, no other Union officer took the initiative to organize a rally or attempted to conduct an orderly withdrawal. By comparison, Barksdale's men were well-led and increasingly motivated by the sight of retreating Yankees.

Colonel Madill's 141st Pennsylvania was not ready to abandon the fight. They fell in behind the 68th Pennsylvania, as Tippin's men engaged the Confederates near the Sherfy barn. Sergeant Loring remembered this position as "on the Emmitsburg Road at the right of the orchard contesting its possession." However, the 68th's withdrawal left an exasperated Madill to report, "I was thus left alone on the hill" near the Wentz buildings. He insisted that his regiment alone "held [the Confederates] in check for twenty minutes or upward, but being overpowered by the large numbers of the enemy, I was compelled to retire, which I reluctantly did." The regimental history of the 141st claimed, in contrast to those around them, that the regiment stood "immovable as the granite rocks about them."[62]

As more Mississippians rushed past the Sherfy buildings in the wake of the retreating 68th Pennsylvania, Sergeant George Kilmer of the 141st Pennsylvania's Company C described, "a yell as though all Pandemonium had

61 Bigelow, *The Peach Orchard*, 12.

62 *OR*, 27/1: 505; Loring, "The 141st Pa. at the Battle," *Fighting Them Over*, 309; Craft, *History of the 141st Regiment Pennsylvania Volunteers*, 122-123. Their regimental history claimed that the 141st was the last of Graham's regiments to retreat as the enemy "rush upon the devoted band [of the 141st] at the Wentz house. The 114th [Pennsylvania] break and run. Before our men can get into position, every regiment in the brigade except the 68th has been retired, and that soon follows the others."

broken loose." Captain John Clark of Company E asked Madill, "Hadn't we better get out of this?" Madill dismissed the idea and insisted, "I have had no orders to get out!" The colonel paused briefly to look "with pride upon the little band of heroes, [and] exclaimed enthusiastically, 'If I had my old regiment back again, I could whip all of them!'" The smoke and confusion of battle rendered some Pennsylvanians unable to distinguish retreating friends from attacking foes. Major Israel Spalding mistook Southern attackers for friendly troops and ordered his men to hold their fire. When his men finally identified a Confederate battleflag in the breeze, a private yelled out, "They are rebels, major!" and both sides opened fire.[63]

A single volley from Barksdale's men took down as many as 30 Pennsylvanians. The 141st eventually crumbled and retreated under the weight of additional volleys. Private John Stockholm picked up the state flag after one of the color bearers fell. "Just as I raised it," Stockholm recalled, "while it was gathering in my hands, a musket ball cut about half of the staff away, made a line of holes the length of the flag and went through my hat rim." As they fell back, a corporal was shot down while carrying the United States flag. Stockholm was behind him and caught the flag. Colonel Madill saw Stockholm coming, took the flag out of his hand, and carried it safely from the field. Sergeant Loring recalled Captain Clark making a valiant but futile attempt to plant the colors and rally the regiment. Loring was shot in the thigh and left on the field, but he dryly noted afterwards that his wound created "a foundation for a pension." As Madill finally trudged to the rear, General Sickles met him. The Third Corps commander thundered, "Colonel! For God's sake can't you hold on?" A teary-eyed Madill could only stammer, "Where are my men?"[64]

Madill had good reason to be concerned for his men. He reported 151 casualties out of 209 engaged. The regimental history claimed that only 19 men returned unscathed, although a handful more undoubtedly made their way back into the ranks throughout the night. Modern estimates place Madill's total losses at 149, including 25 killed. As a result, the 141st Pennsylvania's 71.3% casualty rate holds the dubious distinction of the highest casualty rate

63 Craft, *History of the 141st Regiment Pennsylvania Volunteers*, 122; Lash, "A Pathetic Story," *Gettysburg Magazine 14,* 95-96.

64 *OR*, 27/1: 505; Craft, *History of the 141st Regiment Pennsylvania Volunteers*, 122-123; Lash, "A Pathetic Story," *Gettysburg Magazine 14*, 96; Loring, "The 141st Pa. at the Battle," *Fighting Them Over*, 309.

in Graham's brigade at the Peach Orchard, and the 10th highest of all Union infantry regiments at the battle of Gettysburg.[65]

During their withdrawal from the Peach Orchard, Colonel Bailey's 2nd New Hampshire made "two changes of front to rear on my left company." Such a maneuver was difficult under fire and in close proximity to the enemy, but it spoke highly of the regiment's discipline. The last of these moves found the 2nd on the crest of the hill near the Wentz house. They halted and unleashed a volley into the Confederates who were only 20 yards away. However, this latest position was also untenable so Bailey moved again. The regiment reformed under the eastern slope of the Emmitsburg Road ridge, and stood parallel to the road. Bailey described this formation as "the apex of the echelon," with the 3rd Maine positioned in their left rear and the 68th Pennsylvania briefly in the right rear. The 2nd New Hampshire maintained a steady fire against Barksdale's men, who Bailey believed "must have suffered frightfully." Private Martin Haynes described the action as "a few moments of very close and very ugly work."[66]

During this last stand, Bailey ordered his company captains to correct the regiment's alignment. After adjusting his line, an excited Captain Henry Metcalf of Company F, "with a twinkle of satisfaction lighting his eye," shouted to Bailey, "How does that line suit you, Colonel?" Bailey replied, "Excellent! Excellent!" Metcalf was immediately shot in the head and killed. After the battle, his body was found among the "regimental line plainly marked by our dead."[67]

Captain Joseph Hubbard of Company B also suffered a rifle-shot wound to the forehead. The wound initially appeared to be non-fatal because Hubbard "regained his feet and wandered aimlessly about for some time" as the Confederate infantry rushed by him. Hubbard survived for about two hours before succumbing to his wound. He was a Freemason and wore an emblem

65 Busey and Martin's totals for the 141st were: 149 casualties out of 209 total men (71.3%), including 25 killed, 103 wounded, and 21 MIA. Although the 68th and 114th had higher numeric casualties, they were also larger regiments, thus giving Madill the highest loss rate. The 68th suffered 152 casualties out of 320 engaged (47.5%), while the 114th's totals were 155 out of 259 (59.8%). See Busey and Martin, *Regimental Strengths and Losses*, 131, 392.

66 *OR*, 27/1: 498-499; Ladd, *The Bachelder Papers*, 2: 846-847; Haynes, *A History of the Second Regiment*, 179; Smith, "We drop a comrade's tear," 112-113; Laino, *Gettysburg Campaign Atlas*, 228; Lash, "A Pathetic Story," *Gettysburg Magazine 14*, 92, 95. For an alternate alignment, author James Woods placed the 3rd Maine well to the right and rear of the 2nd New Hampshire during this encounter. See Woods, *Ebb and Flow of Battle*, 355.

67 Haynes, *A History of the Second Regiment*, 180.

of the order. Accordingly, fellow Freemasons in the Confederate ranks ensured that his grave was marked properly, thus allowing subsequent identification and recovery of the captain's remains.[68]

Bailey saw what appeared to be "overwhelming numbers" of Southern soldiers charging toward his position. Fearing that his left would soon be flanked, "and knowing our efforts must prove futile against such fearful odds, I gave the order to retire, which was done quite rapidly, yet coolly, and without excitement as they went." Of the roughly 354 men of the 2nd New Hampshire, as many as 193, (54.5%) fell as casualties. Seven commissioned officers were killed or mortally wounded; only three of 24 officers escaped unharmed. The regiment had sustained incoming artillery rounds, fought while detached from their own brigade, and made several difficult maneuvers while under fire. The regimental history asserted that their final retreat was made "in perfect order," but it is pointless to debate whether they or any other Northern regiment were the last to abandon this part of the field. These regiments received no direction from high-ranking officers and the men grudgingly retreated within minutes of each other.[69]

As the Confederates began to overwhelm Union infantry support, Northern batteries near the Wheatfield Road had little choice but to limber up and fall back. While "doing great execution," Captain Judson Clark's New Jersey battery fired canister at the Rebels, but the situation disintegrated rapidly. Clark realized, "our infantry on both sides had fallen back, as had also several batteries, when, having no supports, I deemed it best to retire, which I did." The approaching Mississippians shot one of Clark's lead horses, but a portion of the 68th Pennsylvania hit Barksdale's 21st Mississippi with a volley that bought Clark some escape time. A Rebel shouted, "Halt you Yankee sons of bitches, we want those guns!" Corporal Samuel Ennis, of Clark's Battery, replied, "Go to Hell, we want to use them yet awhile!" Men and horses fell as they raced away from the Peach Orchard under a blistering fire. One blast of Confederate canister wounded four of Clark's men and killed ten horses, forcing the men to abandon a caisson. The battery eventually reached Trostle's lane and then continued on to the artillery park beyond the Taneytown Road.

68 Ibid., 182; Coco, *Killed in Action: Union*, 68-69.

69 *OR*, 271: 574; Floyd, *Commanders and Casualties*, 21; Haynes, *A History of the Second Regiment*, 181-182.

Clark's battery fired over 1,300 rounds during this afternoon, suffered 20 casualties, and lost 22 horses.[70]

To Clark's left, Captain Phillips and his 5th Massachusetts battery had been too pre-occupied to notice the trouble brewing. "Fighting was going on all this time on our right, but we were too busy to pay much attention to it until I happened to see our infantry falling back in the Peach orchard and a skirmish line coming in, in front of the right of our line of batteries." Phillips saw Hart's battery retreat and noticed much confusion and "retreating stragglers on our right." The enemy had "got through the Peach orchard," he recalled, "and were coming in our direction though not in very good order." Phillips directed his right guns (not section) under Lieutenant Frederick Lull to retire to a small knoll about half way to the Trostle house. Once there, they were to wait until the rest of the battery withdrew. Phillips intended for his other guns to "fire retiring by section," but Colonel McGilvery arrived and ordered the entire battery to fall back immediately. Phillips felt that had he been allowed to retreat, as originally planned, he would have minimized much of the enemy fire that he and Bigelow subsequently faced.[71]

Phillips's battery had gone into position that day with the right section on the left end of the line. Lieutenant Henry Scott commanded that section and was the last to retreat. Scott recalled, "As the muzzle of the gun passed me a shot went through my face and I was out of the fight. I threw my hand up, thinking my face was gone. The blood flew and I was gone." The lieutenant was assisted off of the field. Captain Phillips wrote that the bullet went through both of Scott's cheeks, "breaking off the roof of his mouth. . . . Fortunately it missed his eyes and teeth, and he will easily recover." Henry Scott, in fact, did recover and lived until 1907.[72]

The lead driver of the left piece, who wore an armor vest, also suffered a shrapnel wound and his horses were all shot and killed. As a result, the men of the battery pulled the guns from the field themselves. Phillips threw a prolonge from the left piece over his shoulder. The artillerymen afterwards marveled that "every felly and spoke was hit but one spoke" on this particular cannon. Corporal Jonas Shackley thought, "The left side of the piece looked

70 Hanifen, *History of Battery B, First New Jersey Artillery*, 76; *OR*, 27/1: 586; Busey and Martin, *Regimental Strengths and Losses*, 247.

71 Ladd, *The Bachelder Papers*, 1: 167-168. Phillips also said it was about this time that Thompson's Battery, "got out of the way losing one gun." See *History of the 5th Mass. Battery*, 627.

72 *History of the 5th Massachusetts Battery*, 624, 631, 633; "Recent Deaths - Henry D. Scott", *Newport Mercury*, March 30, 1907.

as if you had dipped your fingers in black lead, and then marked the side of the piece with them." During the retreat and ensuing pursuit, Captain Phillips also endeavored to lead a wounded comrade to the rear on a horse. His efforts proved unsuccessful. A cannon ball killed both the man and horse, but miraculously caused no harm to Phillips. "On the whole," the captain later remarked, "the old iron flew round pretty lively."[73]

The 7th New Jersey had been positioned behind Clark's battery, but found themselves disrupted by a retreating Federal battery that ran through their ranks. This created what the 7th's Major Frederick Cooper called, "considerable confusion for a time, but through the exertions of the officers the line was reformed." The 21st Mississippi threatened the 7th's left from the direction of the Wheatfield Road, so Colonel Louis Francine threw forward the regiment's right and opened fire.[74]

The 2nd New Hampshire had not yet retired and was in danger of being overwhelmed. Ironically, these regiments had been detached earlier from Burling's brigade, but they received one final opportunity to fight together. Colonel Francine ordered a charge at the double-quick, and with "hearty Yankee cheers," to check the Mississippians. The charge of the 7th New Jersey brought them alongside the 2nd New Hampshire's line "which stood like a wall." The New Jersey boys quickly realized, however, that any further advance meant "certain annihilation" and they fell back along with the other nearby Federal units. The 7th New Jersey rallied briefly near the Trostle farm lane until their right flank found itself in danger of being overwhelmed by enemy forces. The remaining officers promptly pulled the regiment off the field.[75]

73 *History of the 5th Massachusetts Battery*, 636, 639, 643; Phillips Obituary, *The Salem Gazette*, April 4, 1876. There were seven fellies and fourteen spokes in total.

74 *OR*, 27/1: 578. Some studies suggest that this was Clark's battery that rode through the 7th New Jersey's ranks. However, Major Frederick Cooper wrote in his report that this occurred "when the enemy made a vigorous charge upon a battery on our left, which compelled the battery to retire. In falling back, the battery broke through our ranks." The report does not name specific batteries but implies that this battery was different than the one they were supporting (i.e. Clark's). See Woods, *Ebb and Flow of Battle*, 346, who proposed that this was instead Bucklyn's battery. Paul Lader, in his study of the 7th New Jersey, proposed that it was either Clark's or Phillips's battery (or perhaps only a section.) See Lader, "The 7th New Jersey in the Gettysburg Campaign," *Gettysburg Magazine 16*, 60 (n.70.) Although not described in the regiment's report, it was afterwards written that the regiment became separated with the four right companies ending up in Trostle's lane. See Toombs, *New Jersey Troops*, 223. Lader, "The 7th New Jersey in the Gettysburg Campaign," *Gettysburg Magazine 16*, 60, was skeptical that almost half the regiment was forced out of action and yet not noted in the regiment's report.

75 *OR*, 27/1: 578; Toombs, *New Jersey Troops*, 223-224; Lader, "The 7th New Jersey in the Gettysburg Campaign," *Gettysburg Magazine 16*, 61.

Of the 275 men in the 7th New Jersey, 114 (41.5%) fell as casualties. Half of the regiment's officers were killed or wounded, including Colonel Francine who suffered a wound to the thigh. The injury was serious and the 26-year-old colonel was transported to a hospital in Philadelphia. Unfortunately, Francine's condition deteriorated and he died on July 16. The spot where Francine fell mortally wounded is purportedly marked by the regiment's monument in Gettysburg National Military Park.[76]

Having broken what appeared to be the Federals' "first line" with his 21st Mississippi, Colonel B.G. Humphreys wrote, "The second line essayed some resistance but gave way. The third did no better. Soon the plain before us was a moving mass of retreating Yankees."[77]

General Graham was among the many wounded Northerners headed to the rear. Graham was dismounted and walking, but he borrowed a lieutenant's horse in order to return to the field and "endeavor to collect the remnant of my troops." Graham spotted a regiment drawing closer, "which I took at first for one of my own but which on approaching within 150 yards of me I discovered to belong to the enemy." Graham attempted to flee. "As soon as the discovery was made, I turned my horse, drove my spurs into the flanks, at the same time throwing myself forward on his neck to present as little surface as possible."[78]

The Confederates called on Graham to surrender, but when the general took flight astride his horse, the Rebels fired a volley in his direction. "Fifty or more voices were heard 'shoot down that horse' and down came the horse pierced by a dozen balls," recalled Colonel Humphreys. The shooting of Graham's horse, as Private McNeily of the 21st Mississippi wrote, "pitched the General over his head, leaving him in a dazed state of mind." A Rebel soldier approached the vanquished New Yorker and demanded, "Major, give me that 'ere hat-band," an apparent reference to the general's gold cord. Graham replied indignantly that he "was no major, and would surrender only to an officer," so the Southern "brute" jerked the cord from the general's hat and then moved onward. The loss of blood left Graham too weak to rise, and he pleaded for the Southerners to give his wounded men water. Captain William Dudley, of the 21st Mississippi, arrived and offered to share water from his

76 Floyd, *Commanders and Casualties*, 21; Lader, "The 7th New Jersey in the Gettysburg Campaign," *Gettysburg Magazine 16*, 61, 63.

77 B.G. Humphreys Manuscript, 12.

78 Charles Graham account, February 16, 1865, GNMP; *Soldiers' and Sailors' Half-Dime Tales,* 117.

own canteen. Before departing, Dudley asked Graham for some memento by which to remember the general. Graham took off his sword-belt, which a shell fragment had struck earlier in the day and quite possibly saved his life by blunting the impact. In a reciprocal act of chivalry, Graham handed it to Dudley.[79]

At his headquarters several hundred yards from the Peach Orchard, General Sickles knew that his position was in danger. The Confederates had driven the Third Corps left flank from Houck's Ridge, which was not visible from his headquarters, and the center of Sickles's line was collapsing at the Peach Orchard. Sickles spent the majority of the afternoon at the Trostle farm and kept staff officers busy delivering orders. Sometime around 6:00 p.m. the area became, as Captain Randolph later described, "too hot for a corps headquarters; not so much from fire directed at that point as on account of high shots coming over the crest on both sides and centering there."[80]

Intervening ridges blocked the sight lines from lower ground near the Trostle house and farm lane. However, the higher elevation surrounding the barn provided a better view toward the Emmitsburg Road. As General Sickles later elaborated, "I rode around through the low ground below the house and up to this knoll [near the barn]. I had hardly reached it when the shot struck me."[81]

A Confederate projectile struck the general in the right leg without injuring his horse. "I never knew I was hit," Sickles claimed, until he touched his leg and found his hand dripping with blood. Since he was "conscious of approaching weakness," Sickles slid off his horse and called for a surgeon to treat him. "They found that the knee had been smashed, probably by a

79 B.G. Humphreys Manuscript, 14; McNeily, "Barksdale's Mississippi Brigade at Gettysburg," 237; Charles Graham account, February 16, 1865, GNMP; *Soldiers' and Sailors' Half-Dime Tales*, 117-118. Dudley is likely a reference to William H. Dudley of Company "G". See Soldiers and Sailors Database, NPS and *The Roster of Confederate Soldiers*, 5: 154.

80 Ladd, *The Bachelder Papers*, 1: 240.

81 Sickles interview, undated 1882 newspaper, J. Howard Wert Scrapbook, ACHS. Sickles said in 1884 that the incident occurred between 5:30 and 6:00, as "the last memorandum in my field book was made at 5:38 p.m." See "Seventy Five Years Ago," news clipping, Box B-36, Misc. Info- Gen. Daniel Sickles, GNMP. Randolph told John Bachelder in 1886 that it was "towards 5 or 6 o'clock." David Birney reported that it occurred "at 6 o'clock." See *OR*, 27/1. The *New York Times* reported under a July 14 byline that Sickles's wound occurred "about" 6 o'clock. See "Affairs at Gettysburgh," *New York Times*, July 18, 1863.

piece of shell, and that the leg had been broken above and also below the knee."[82]

Sickles was losing blood rapidly as he dismounted, and a soldier bound the general's leg with a strap from his saddle. A small detachment of men stood on guard as all awaited the appearance of a doctor or an ambulance. Staff officer Captain Tremain arrived and found Sickles, "reclining with apparent suffering against the wall of the barn." Someone improvised a field tourniquet and applied it to the general's leg. Sickles ordered in a clear voice, "tell General Birney he must take command." Birney soon arrived and assumed command of the Third Corps. With multiple pressing emergencies, Birney did not linger for long; he promptly went toward General Humphreys's front.[83]

"I had no sooner been wounded," Sickles recalled, "then the conflict became more terrific than ever." The number of retreating Third Corps troops streaming past the Trostle farm increased as the Emmitsburg Road line crumbled. Later accounts emphasized Sickles's calm and cool demeanor, but Captain Randolph remembered the situation differently. "Meanwhile our line had been broken about the Peach Orchard and our infantry and artillery came pouring by in rapid retreat. Sickles' only thought seemed to be fear of being taken prisoner. He repeatedly urged us not to allow him to be taken."[84]

A nearby private offered the wounded general a drink from his canteen "filled with stimulants," and placed a small cigar in Sickles's mouth. An ambulance finally appeared and Tremain thought the conveyance "would be shattered by shot and shell before the patient could be placed in it." Tremain and a chaplain climbed into the ambulance with Sickles. The chaplain, Tremain recalled, tended to Sickles by continuing to administer "stimulants by the wholesale. Doubtless this was all that kept him alive."[85]

82 Ladd, *The Bachelder Papers*, 1: 240; Tremain, *Two Days of War*, 89; *Dedication of the New York Auxiliary State Monument*, 112-113.

83 Sickles interview, undated 1882 newspaper, J. Howard Wert Scrapbook, ACHS; Ladd, *The Bachelder Papers*, 1: 240; Tremain, *Two Days of War*, 88-89. General Birney reported, "At 6 o'clock I found Major-General Sickles seriously wounded, and, at his request, took command of the troops." General Ward assumed command of Birney's division. See *OR*, 27/1: 483, 494.

84 Sickles interview, 1882 undated newspaper, J. Howard Wert Scrapbook, ACHS; Ladd, *The Bachelder Papers*, 1: 239-240.

85 *Two Days of War*, 89-90, 105. The image of General Sickles being borne from the field calmly smoking his cigar is one of the most iconic images of Gettysburg's second day. It also became the heart of his 1897 Medal of Honor citation: that he continued to "encourage his

Sickles's decision to occupy the Peach Orchard resulted in an inglorious personal departure from the battlefield. He was grievously wounded, heavilysedated, and under a steady stream of Confederate artillery fire. Dan Sickles never again led troops in combat after his leg was amputated that evening. However, the battle for the Emmitsburg Road continued after his departure.

troops after being himself severely wounded." Neither Henry Tremain nor George Randolph made note of Sickles using the moment as a grand exercise in motivating his men. For a discussion on whether the event occurred and how it has been treated in the Gettysburg historiography, see co-author James Hessler's *Sickles at Gettysburg*, 206-212.

Chapter 7

We Are Going to Have a Fight

General Barksdale's left regiments began to force Federal opposition away from the Sherfy buildings. Major George Gerald of the 18th Mississippi called out that the Sherfy barn was "occupied by the enemy and must be taken." Gerald then led his men to the structure. "They followed me with a rush, and I forced the door open, and within less than two minutes we had killed, wounded or captured every man in the barn." Dense smoke filled the barn and the men could barely distinguish friend from foe, much less anything else that lay within. Soon, the action moved away from the building as the Mississippians continued to drive the Yankees back. General Barksdale led from the front and encouraged his men by shouting, "Forward, men, forward!"[1]

Outside the barn, "murderous fire" from the 13th and 17th Mississippi created confusion within the ranks of the 114th Pennsylvania. Captain Bowen noted that the enemy was "already on our left and in our rear" as the Federal regiments on his left were "swept away." Fearful of being surrounded, as "only one avenue of escape was open to us, and that was up the Emmitsburg road," the 114th poured one last volley into Barksdale's men before attempting to rally. The Zouaves failed to do so, however, because the enemy was advancing too rapidly. Bowen briefly succeeded

1 Gerald, "The Battle of Gettysburg," *Waco Daily Times Herald*, July 3, 1913, transcript in Brake Collection, USAHEC; B.G. Humphreys Manuscript, Mississippi Department of Archives and History, 12.

View of Sherfy house from east side of Emmitsburg Road. Monuments to 114th PA on left and 57th PA on right show relative positions of the regiments during the fighting.
GNMP

"in rallying a number around the colors, and brought them off, but, in doing so, got separated from the brigade."[2]

A short distance up the Emmitsburg Road, Captain Adolfo Cavada of General Humphreys's staff watched anxiously as events transpired near the Sherfy buildings. His brother Frederico commanded the 114th Pennsylvania and was lost somewhere in the turbulence of battle. The Cavada brothers had a unique background; their Spanish father and American mother raised them in Cuba before relocating to Philadelphia after their father died in 1838. "While standing by Seely's battery," Adolfo later wrote, "I looked towards the left to ascertain the condition of things and try to make out the Zouaves, in whom I felt a particular interest at that moment. The enemy's fire slackened for a moment, then came a rebel 'cheer' sounding like a continuous yelp, nearer and nearer it came, the 'red legs' (Zouaves) jumped to their feet, volley upon volley rained into them and another regiment formed alongside of it." He noted apprehensively, "The fire was bravely returned but the enemy's

2 OR, 27/1: 503; *Pennsylvania at Gettysburg*, 2: 605-606, 612; Imhof, *Gettysburg Day Two*, 143, 146; Gottfried, *Brigades of Gettysburg*, 192; Winschel, "Their Supreme Moment: Barksdale's Brigade at Gettysburg," *Gettysburg Magazine 1*, 74.

columns were upon them before they could fall back. All was confusion on that side."[3]

During the retreat, Captain Bowen and Sergeant Major Alexander Givin spotted Frederico resting near the Wentz house. Bowen asked if he was wounded, but Cavada indicated that he was only "utterly exhausted." Captain Bowen begged Cavada to keep moving, since the enemy was advancing rapidly and only a few yards away. Cavada could simply go no further and Bowen left him behind. Givin later explained, "There was no time to parley." The Confederates took Cavada prisoner and he spent several months in Richmond's Libby Prison. Meanwhile, some of the 114th's wounded sought refuge in the Sherfy barn. Their decision later had tragic consequences.[4]

The retreat of the 114th Pennsylvania exposed the left of the 57th Pennsylvania. Although the 57th held a position that utilized the Sherfy house and outbuildings for cover, Captain Alanson Nelson reported the regiment was soon overwhelmed and fell back. Sergeant E.C. Strouss, situated near one of Sherfy's large cherry trees, thought they could have "beaten back the enemy, but . . . we learned that the enemy had broken through the angle at the peach orchard, and were swarming up the road in our rear. It was evident that if we remained at the house, we would all be captured, so we were obliged to fall back." A squad from the 57th continued to snipe at the Confederates from inside the Sherfy buildings, and some Pennsylvanians were in what was described as "an old cellar" that may have been the foundation of an earlier structure.[5]

Nelson told Colonel Peter Sides, the commander of the 57th, that they must retrieve the men inside the Sherfy buildings before the regiment retired. Sides declined to wait and told Nelson that he could stay behind if he so desired. Nelson gathered a small party and "made the rounds of the

3 Adolfo Cavada Diary, Participant Accounts: V-5, Library & Research Center, *GNMP*; Stoudt, "The Cavada Brothers: Two Soldiers, Two Wars," Blog of Gettysburg National Military Park, https://npsgnmp.wordpress.com/2012/05/10/the-cavada-brothers-two-soldiers-two-wars/.

4 *OR*, 27/1: 503; *Pennsylvania at Gettysburg*, 2: 605-606, 612; Hagerty, *Collis' Zouaves*, 243; Imhof, *Gettysburg Day Two*, 143, 146; Stoudt, "The Cavada Brothers: Two Soldiers, Two Wars," Blog of Gettysburg National Military Park. It has been suggested that Bowen misidentified the Wentz farm and that Cavada was actually captured near the Klingle farm. This might better explain Cavada's physical exhaustion. See Georg, "The Sherfy Farm and the Battle of Gettysburg," 22. However, based on the location of the regiment's collapse and the proximity of the pressing Confederates, the Wentz property seems more likely. Sergeant Major Givin's name is alternately spelled as "Given" in some accounts.

5 *OR*, 27/1: 497; *Pennsylvania at Gettysburg*, 1: 356; Georg, "The Sherfy Farm and the Battle of Gettysburg," 19-21; Gottfried, *Brigades of Gettysburg*, 192-193.

South-facing wall of Sherfy house. Nelson looked out these windows and saw the garden full of Confederates. Note bullet damage on wall.

Photo by Authors

outbuildings and got the men started to the rear." They then raced into the main house, where the noise was so deafening that Nelson had to shout directly into the men's ears. "I ran up the stairs and from one room to the other, and started them to the rear as fast as I could get them to understand what I wanted of them. I then started downstairs to notify those in the lower part of the house."

Fearing his own capture, Nelson looked out a window toward "the left, where the enemy first broke through our lines" and was horrified to see the Confederates advancing through Sherfy's yard, less than 50 feet away. When the Rebels demanded his surrender, Nelson instead bolted from the house, jumped a fence in the yard and sprinted to catch up with the remainder of his regiment. Not everyone was so lucky or fleet-footed. Those men that did not receive the message to withdraw "kept on firing from the windows after the rest of the men fell back." Sergeant Strouss lamented that they could not make many of the men "understand the situation" and they were unable to reach many others, particularly those on the first floor of the house and in the open cellar. More than 50 men from the regiment fell into the hands of Barksdale's Mississippians as prisoners of war. A significant number of them eventually died in Southern prisons.[6]

The 105th Pennsylvania was the last of Graham's regiments near the Sherfy house. Colonel Calvin Craig had positioned his "Wildcats" on the right of the 57th, but after a short time he saw the men from both the 57th and 114th regiments "cluster in groups" behind the house and out-buildings. This indicated that cohesion and discipline within these units had broken down. Only a "few moments later" the 114th Pennsylvania "fell to the rear" and the 57th "very soon followed," lamented Craig, "leaving my left flank entirely unprotected." The Mississippians took advantage of this, advanced across the Emmitsburg Road in front of Sherfy's house, and opened fire upon the 105th's left flank. "Seeing this," Craig reported, "I ordered my regiment to retire slowly a short distance."[7]

The fight between the Mississippians and Pennsylvanians occurred at very close range. At times their lines nearly intermingled. Private Samuel Fulmer of the 105th was shot through the right leg as he retreated with his comrades. He next saw an enemy soldier thrusting a bayonet toward him. A Confederate lieutenant precipitously intervened, however, and slashed the gun out of the would-be killer's hands with a saber. This intervention saved Fulmer's life.[8]

Barksdale's men poured a "most murderous fire" into the 105th's flank and rear as the regiment retreated. Although men fell like "grass before the scythe," post-battle accounts declared that the regiment conducted the retro-movement "in good order." One man heard Colonel Craig shouting along the rapidly disintegrating line, "Boys, stand by the flag until the last man is killed, and then I will take it out!" Craig had at least three horses shot from under him and was wounded in the ankle. The Mississippians clamped down upon the regiment's left flank, held by Company A. In the melee, Private Cassius

6 *History of the Fifty-Seventh Regiment,* 93; *OR,* 27/1: 497; *Pennsylvania at Gettysburg,* 1: 356; Georg, "The Sherfy Farm and the Battle of Gettysburg," 19-22; Floyd, *Commanders and Casualties,* 18. Forty-four of the prisoners reportedly died in Southern prisons. See *Pennsylvania at Gettysburg,* 2: 357.

7 *OR,* 27/1: 500-501.

8 "The Wild Cats: Some Random Sketches of the 105th Pennsylvania," *The National Tribune,* January 26, 1888.

McCrea stripped the guidon flag from its staff to prevent the colors from falling into enemy hands. McCrea stuffed the precious fabric into his jacket and saved the flag, while barely escaping capture. Colonel Craig later reflected that his Wildcats "never fought better than at Gettysburg, and had all done as well as this regiment, our loss would have not been so great. We rallied some eight or ten times after the balance of the brigade had left us, and the boys fought like demons. Their battle-cry was 'Pennsylvania'."[9]

As General Graham's defenses collapsed, the burden of stopping Barksdale next fell upon the 73rd New York. General Humphreys had presumed that the 73rd would support Graham, but Humphreys complained that Graham "gave way" quickly and left the 73rd "exposed alone to the enemy." One benefit of the 114th's retreat was that the 73rd now had a clear front, and they hit Barksdale with at least one volley that caused the Southerners to fall "in scores among the dead and wounded Pennsylvanians." The New Yorkers charged briefly to the west side of the Emmitsburg Road, but this coincided with the collapse of Graham's regiments on their left and the 73rd's flank became vulnerable. The 73rd's Lieutenant Moran claimed that the Mississippians:

> Staggered under our fresh fire, but waved their flags, cheered and returned our volley, seeing their supports close at hand. Their advance, however, was checked at the barn, as our men continued to load and fire with rapidity and coolness, but our thin line in the left could be seen melting away through the smoke and our wounded in hundreds went streaming back over the Emmitsburg road, and rider less horses went dashing among them in bewilderment and fright.[10]

Realizing that the Southerners had outflanked their left, the 73rd New York hastily fell back and ignored the pleas of an officer to save his artillery. Moran recalled, "The smoke grew thicker each minute and the sound of exploding shells was deafening. Officers and men were falling every minute and on every side." It was impossible to hear spoken orders. The 73rd's Major Burns shouted himself hoarse in a futile attempt to maintain control.[11]

9 OR, 27/1: 500-501; "June 30," *Robert I. Boyington's Army Life Journal (1861-1863)*, http://www.robert-ford.ws/105%20PA%20Intro.htm; Scott, *History of Jefferson County,* 676; Sauers, *Advance the Colors!*, 352-353; Scott, *History of the One Hundred and Fifth Regiment*, 83, 156. The flag that McCrea carried is in the collection of Gettysburg National Military Park.

10 Ladd, *Bachelder Papers*, 2: 773.

11 Ibid.; Georg, "The Sherfy Farm and the Battle of Gettysburg," 24.

A Confederate shell burst near Moran's head, and the lieutenant described the sensation as "something like hot sand entered my left eye." The shell also took down several other soldiers and a nearby horse. "It was as if I had been struck by lightning, and I fell as unconscious as if my head had been taken off from my shoulders by the blade of the guillotine." The horse fell and partially covered Moran's face. He might have suffocated beneath the poor animal, but Moran's new sword-belt drew the attention of a passing Confederate officer and he dragged the New Yorker out from under the horse. The Mississippian assisted Moran in getting under the shade of the Sherfys' large cherry trees on the north side of the house. Moran was dazed and recalled that he "could scarcely realize that I was in the enemy's hands." An ankle wound filled his shoe with blood. After the 73rd retreated, he remained with scores of disabled men in the unenviable position "between the fire of friends and foes, the field being open and affording no shelter whatever. In this sorry plight I waited in a tornado of bullets and shells." Within a few moments Barksdale's 13th Mississippi "came over me cheering and firing."[12]

Colonel James Carter led the 13th Mississippi. The 30-year-old farmer had commanded the regiment since June 1862. As Carter's men swept across the Emmitsburg Road, he was shot through the body four times and killed. He reportedly fell on the Emmitsburg Road, but the men carried him back to Barksdale's field hospital, located on the John Crawford farm. Carter's body lay buried there until his remains were disinterred and removed to Richmond in 1872.[13]

The commander of the 17th Mississippi also became a casualty. Colonel William Dunbar Holder was a 37-year-old Tennessee native, a planter, and a former U.S. Marshal who had led the regiment since April 1862. At Gettysburg, Holder suffered a wound to the lower body, and reportedly held in his own entrails while one of the men led him back to the hospital. Holder somehow survived his horrific wound. Despite their tactical success in breaking the Union defenses at the Peach Orchard, Barksdale's officers and men continued to fall from

12 Moran, "A Fire Zouave," *National Tribune*, November 6, 1890; Ladd, *The Bachelder Papers*, 2: 773-774.

13 Busey and Busey, *Confederate Casualties at Gettysburg*, 685; B.G. Humphreys Manuscript, Mississippi Department of Archives and History, 15-16. Colonel Humphreys wrote, "Col. Carter was killed and left on the turnpike."

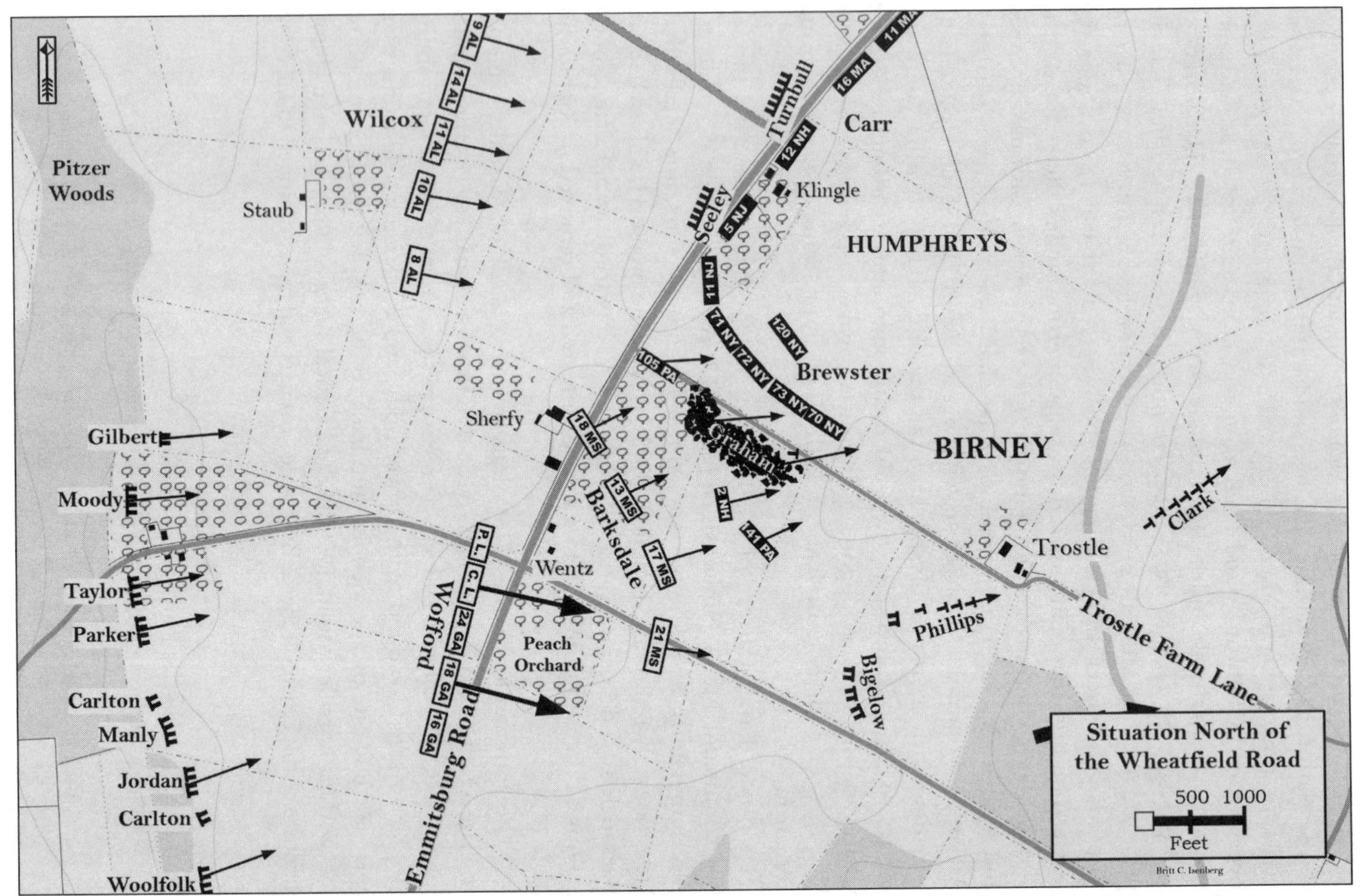

Pitzer Woods
Wilcox
9 AL
14 AL
11 AL
10 AL
8 AL
Staub
Turnbull
Carr
16 MA
11 MA
12 NH
Klingle
Seeley
5 NJ
11 NJ
HUMPHREYS
71 NY
72 NY
73 NY
70 NY
120 NY
Brewster
105 PA
Sherfy
18 MS
Graham
BIRNEY
Gilbert
Moody
13 MS
Barksdale
2 NH
141 PA
17 MS
Wentz
Trostle
Clark
Taylor
Parker
P. L.
C. L.
24 GA
18 GA
16 GA
Wofford
Peach Orchard
21 MS
Phillips
Trostle Farm Lane
Bigelow
Carlton
Manly
Jordan
Carlton
Woolfolk
Emmitsburg Road
Situation North of the Wheatfield Road
500 1000
Feet
Britt C. Isenberg

Brigadier General William Wofford
LOC

enemy projectiles and exhaustion as they advanced.[14]

With the Federal infantry and batteries in flight, Longstreet brought forward Wofford's Brigade to support Barksdale. Brigadier General William Tatum Wofford was 39 years old and bald-headed. The Georgia native came from a line of Revolutionary War veterans, and like so many other officers on the field at Gettysburg, he was a lawyer in antebellum civilian life. Wofford also served as a captain of Georgia mounted volunteers in the Mexican War. Afterwards, he entered state politics and voted against Georgia's secession from the Union. Wofford began the Civil War as colonel of the 18th Georgia, and was promoted to brigadier general in January 1863. He was experienced, well-regarded, and even "loved" by his men. However, the 21st Mississippi's B.G. Humphreys wrote of Wofford after the war, "We all know that he was too prone to go forward."[15]

As they began their advance, the 24th Georgia briefly became entangled among the guns of Parker's battery. Wofford rode over and urged his men forward by waving his hat. Captain Parker shouted at Wofford in response, "Hurrah for you of the bald-head!" Other artillerists took up to heartily cheering the Georgians as they passed. Parker later wrote, "Oh he was a grand sight, and my heart is full now while I write of it."[16]

The sight of Wofford's nearly 1,600 screaming Georgians likely did nothing to strengthen the resolve of the Union defenders. Briefly riding in front of the Confederate brigade was none other than General Longstreet

14 Busey and Busey, *Confederate Casualties at Gettysburg*, 705; Henley, "On the Way to Gettysburg," GNMP.

15 Warner, *Generals in Gray*, 343-344; Smith, *One of the Most Daring of Men*, 1, 19-20, 65, 75.

16 Smith, *One of the Most Daring of Men*, 85.

himself. Longstreet explained in his memoirs that he did so in order "to urge the troops to their reserve power in the precious moments." Regardless of whether Longstreet intended to inspire the troops or closely supervise Wofford, he urged the boisterous Georgians as they advanced, "Cheer less, men, and fight more." The Georgians soon came under enemy artillery fire, however, and Colonel Goode Bryan of the 16th Georgia remembered one shell alone causing 30 casualties.[17]

Given the lack of coordination between Confederate brigades all afternoon, it is not surprising that there was no apparent synchronization between Wofford and Barksdale's movements. Barksdale's three left regiments wheeled generally to their left, toward the Trostle lane and the fields beyond. However, instead of moving directly behind these regiments, and adding weight to Barksdale's main attack, Wofford moved astride the Wheatfield Road. This placed Wofford's Georgians in potential support of only one of Barksdale's regiments, the 21st Mississippi, and several hundred yards away from the majority of Barksdale's men.[18]

In his memoirs, Longstreet addressed his reasons for not directing Wofford behind Barksdale. By this point in the struggle, Union Brigadier General John Caldwell's Second Corps division had pushed Confederate forces out of the Wheatfield. Portions of Brigadier General Romeyn Ayres's Fifth Corps division were also beginning to surge across the Plum Run valley toward the northern terminus of Houck's Ridge. Longstreet asserted that by moving Wofford's men along the Wheatfield Road he could strike these Union forces in the right flank, drive toward Little Round Top, and supposedly "lift our desperate fighters to the summit." Whether Longstreet's strategy was reasonable or not, and not a justification for his memoirs, it deprived Barksdale of extra strength as the Mississippians continued their own thrust toward Cemetery Ridge.[19]

17 Longstreet, *From Manassas to Appomattox*, 372; Smith, *One of the Most Daring of Men*, 85-86; Fremantle, *Three Months in the Southern States*, 261.

18 McNeily, "Barksdale's Mississippi Brigade," 246. McNeily disputed any assertions that Kershaw or Wofford helped Barksdale clear the orchard, writing that Kershaw's left assisted with "only long range fire." He further added that Graham's men had been swept out by the time Wofford arrived. "When Wofford reached there, Alexander's batteries occupied Peach Orchard hill." Wofford instead "swung away to the right" and connected with Kershaw's left to clear the Wheatfield.

19 Longstreet, *From Manassas to Appomattox*, 372; Alexander, *Military Memoirs*, 399; Wert, *General James Longstreet*, 275-76; Imhof, *Gettysburg Day Two*, 150, 153. Author John Imhof considered "one of the most important, yet least discussed controversies" of the battle to be "why did Longstreet divert Wofford's men from their role as support for Barksdale? Longstreet seems to have ignored this question in the post-war period." See Imhof, 150.

When Colonel Humphreys advanced his 21st Mississippi roughly 100 yards beyond the Peach Orchard, he could "see to our left some Federal lines moving to the rear hurriedly but in good order . . . [and] some guns at the foot of the slope, to my right firing rapidly on Kershaw's line." These guns were from Captain Bigelow's 9th Massachusetts Battery, which was still along the Wheatfield Road and had not yet joined the mass withdrawal of other Federal forces in the vicinity. The Napoleons were too tempting for Humphreys to pass up, so he "immediately wheeled the 21st Regt. away from the [Barksdale's] brigade and to the right."[20]

Colonel McGilvery's orders to "limber up and get out" reached Bigelow after Phillips's withdrawal. Bigelow observed that there were no longer any Northern troops near the Peach Orchard. Instead, lines of gray stretched across the field approximately 200 yards to his right "as far as could be seen." To Bigelow's left front, a "swarm of sharpshooters" from Kershaw's brigade also threatened the artillerymen. Bigelow requested and received permission from McGilvery to retire firing "by prolonge" due to the danger. This method allowed the battery to retire approximately 400 yards toward the Trostle farm while continuing to fire; lobbing solid shot toward Colonel Humphreys and canister at Kershaw.[21]

Although Barksdale and Wofford's assaults had launched later than expected, their presence nevertheless succeeded in relieving pressure on Kershaw's brigade. While hunkered down near the Rose farm, the South Carolinians heard "a tremendous Rebel cheer," and the increasing crash of small arms. One of Kershaw's officers shouted, "That's help for us! Spring up the bluff, boys!" Kershaw's men were initially unsure of who was saving them, but "an officer galloped from the right of the advancing line and ordered us to join his right and go forward. And that officer was Brig. Gen. William T. Wofford." Private John Coxe of the 2nd South Carolina wrote, "Both Longstreet and McLaws knew Wofford well, and that in a 'tight pinch' he could be relied on for succor. Hence on that day they decided to hold his splendid brigade in reserve for a probable emergency. And, indeed, the trying emergency had come."[22]

20 Ladd, *Bachelder Papers*, 1: 480-481.

21 Bigelow, *The Peach Orchard*, 16-18; *OR*, 27/1: 882. Bigelow described this as attaching rope "one end to the pintless of the limbers, [and] the other end to the guns trails."

22 Coxe, "The Battle of Gettysburg," *Confederate Veteran XXI*, 9: 434-435. Coxe added, "From his position in reserve on the pike Wofford plainly saw the death struggle of Kershaw's men,

From his vantage point, Kershaw watched, "Wofford riding at the head of his fine brigade, then coming in, his left being in the Peach Orchard, which was then clear of the enemy. His movement was such as to strike the stony hill on the left, and thus turn the flank of the troops that had driven us from that position." Since Wofford was moving east toward Cemetery Ridge, Kershaw's left wing joined Wofford's right in advancing toward the Wheatfield's "Stony Hill." Here, they forced portions of two outflanked Federal brigades from Caldwell's division off of the hill. The collapse of the Union's Peach Orchard defenses reinvigorated the Confederate attack and made the Wheatfield untenable for Northern forces.[23]

The time had also arrived for Brigadier General Cadmus Wilcox's 1,700-man Alabama brigade, in General R. H. Anderson's division of Hill's Third Corps, to begin their own advance. Cadmus M. Wilcox was born in 1824 in North Carolina, but raised in Tennessee where his family moved when he was a toddler. He attended the United States Military Academy and graduated in 1846, ranked 54 out of 59 in his class and behind more storied classmates such as George B. McClellan and Thomas J. "Stonewall" Jackson. After graduation, Wilcox received a commission in the 4th U.S. Infantry and was sent to Mexico. He received a brevet promotion to first lieutenant for gallant and meritorious conduct at Chapultepec. His low academic ranking did not prevent a return to West Point in 1852 as an instructor of military tactics. In 1859, he authored *Rifles and Rifle Practice*, a manual that became a standard West Point textbook.

Wilcox resigned his U.S. Army captaincy upon Tennessee's secession. He was originally commissioned a captain of artillery for the Confederacy, but quickly made colonel of the 9th Alabama Infantry. By October 1861, he was a brigadier general and saw action at Williamsburg, Seven Pines, and Gaines' Mill. Wilcox had six enemy bullets pierce his clothing during heavy combat at Glendale, but he survived the battle unscathed. His nervous excitement when going into action led to his men dubbing him, "Old Billy

---

cut off as they were and fighting against such frightful odds, and it was said at the time that he asked McLaws for permission to go to our relief as many as three times before it was granted."

23 Kershaw, "Kershaw's Brigade at Gettysburg," *Battles and Leaders of the Civil War*, 3: 336-337; *OR*, 27/1: 386; Jorgensen, *Gettysburg's Bloody Wheatfield*, 108-112; Imhof, *Gettysburg Day Two*, 173. Colonel Patrick Kelly, commanding Caldwell's Second "Irish" Brigade, "found the enemy forming line faced to our right along the edge of the wood. Finding myself in this very disagreeable position, I ordered the brigade to fall back, firing." See *OR*, 27/1: 386. The Confederates' success in the Wheatfield was further aided by the brigades under generals Paul Semmes and G.T. Anderson.

Brigadier General Cadmus Wilcox
LOC

Fixin." His attire also created a less than dashing impression, as he favored a short jacket and straw hat, which was not exactly regulation for a brigadier general. Historian Douglas Southall Freeman described Wilcox as "off duty, genial and informal, on duty precise and insistent on precision."

Wilcox temporarily led a small division under Longstreet at Second Manassas. However, Longstreet soon promoted his old friend George Pickett to command a new division, and the experienced Wilcox felt slighted. He asked for a transfer, but the request was denied and Wilcox remained with the Army of Northern Virginia. Wilcox performed well at Chancellorsville, where he blocked the advance of General Sedgwick's Union Sixth Corps toward Lee's rear. Nonetheless, he was passed over again for promotion during the reorganization prior to Gettysburg. At just shy of 40 years old, Lee referred to Wilcox as "one of the oldest brigadiers" in the army. "Old Billy Fixin" was a career military man, but he likely remained disgruntled with his own station when his men stepped off on July 2.[24]

After repulsing Berdan's reconnaissance in Pitzer's Woods several hours earlier, Wilcox's Brigade waited to go forward on Barksdale's left. Captain George Clark of the 11th Alabama remembered a most oppressive afternoon. "The sun was fiercely hot and there was no shade or other protection for the men. Here they sweated, sweltered, and swore." Wilcox reported that prior to the attack, McLaws's Division formed at "right angles" to his own brigade.

24 Wilcox biographical information: Evans, *Confederate Military History*, X: 342; Hall, *Military Records of General Officers of the Confederate States of America*, 66; Freeman, *Lee's Lieutenants*, 3: 109, 202-203; Tagg, *The Generals of Gettysburg*, 310 – 311.

This made sense if a portion of Wilcox's line was still refused after the action in Pitzer's Woods.[25]

The reports of Hill, Anderson, and Wilcox all agree on their role in conjunction with Longstreet's July 2 assault. "General Longstreet was to attack the left flank of the enemy," Hill reported, "and sweep down his line, and I was ordered to co-operate with him with such of my brigades from the right as could join in with his troops in the attack." Unlike Longstreet's own commanders, Hill specifically referred to their attack as unfolding "en echelon." General Anderson added that McLaws's movements were to "regulate" his own division's actions. Wilcox reported that his instructions "were to advance when the troops on my right should advance, and to report this to the division commander [Anderson], in order that the other brigades should advance in proper time."[26]

Yet, there were post-battle disagreements. Some of Longstreet's writings implied that Wilcox's inability to cover McLaws's left was a contributing factor in the defeat. Wilcox rebutted in 1878, "Nothing was ever said or ordered of an echelon movement of which my brigade was to be the directing brigade, or that I was to guard McLaws' flank."[27]

Wilcox joined in the attack perhaps 20 minutes after Barksdale stepped off from Warfield Ridge. In order to avoid overlapping Barksdale, Wilcox shifted his brigade further to the left than anticipated, but moved "as rapidly as the nature of the ground with its opposing obstacles (stone and plank fences) would admit. Having gained 400 or 500 yards to the left by this flank movement, my command faced by the right flank, and advanced." The intervening field between Wilcox and the Emmitsburg Road was relatively open and "rising slightly" toward the road. Since Longstreet's forces had failed to drive in the Federal left, Wilcox launched a frontal attack against General Humphreys's

25 Clark, *A Backward Glance*, 36; *OR*, 27/2: 617.

26 *OR*, 27/2: 608, 614, 618; Winschel, "Their Supreme Moment," *Gettysburg Magazine 1*, 74.

27 *OR*, 27/2: 358-359; Wilcox, "General C.M. Wilcox on the Battle of Gettysburg," *SHSP*, 6: 98. In his report, Longstreet maintained, "a strong force met the brigades of Major-General Anderson's division, which were co-operating upon my left, drove one of them back, and, checking the support of the other, caused my left to be somewhat exposed and outflanked." Wilcox insisted, "The orders given me during the day were to advance when the troops on my right moved forward; and I may add now that these orders were repeated three times during the day. Nothing was ever said or ordered of an echelon movement of which my brigade was to be the directing brigade, or that I was to guard McLaws' flank. . . . Had there been such an order as the echelon movement, it would have been impossible of execution, as the lines of battle held by Anderson's and McLaws' divisions were nearly, if not quite at right angles to each other, and my brigade was on the right of the former."

division. Although this is not what the Confederate leadership had originally hoped for, Wilcox's threat prevented Humphreys from sending additional reinforcements to the Peach Orchard's defense. Once Barksdale finished disposing of Graham's troops, the Mississippians and Wilcox combined to pressure Humphreys on both his left and front. Whether it was intentional or providential, this provided one of the afternoon's few examples where Confederate infantry successfully struck the Third Corps line simultaneously from two sides.[28]

"The breeze blowing from the southward carried the heavy sulfurous smoke in clouds along the ground," wrote Humphreys's staff officer Captain Cavada, "at times concealing everything from my view. Our skirmishers now began a lively popping, the first drops of a thunder shower that was to break upon us." Reports of heavy enemy troops massing in Humphreys's front indicated that an attack was imminent. Humphreys's skirmish line fell back as Wilcox's Alabamians approached the Emmitsburg Road. While Federal accounts suggested that they struck the Rebels with well-directed fire, Wilcox's report did not indicate that the skirmishers gave him any significant trouble.[29]

General Humphreys aggressively considered throwing his own left forward to meet this threat. But shortly after detaching the 73rd New York to help Graham, Humphreys received orders from General Birney, who had taken Third Corps command after Sickles's was wounded. Birney ordered Humphreys to throw back his left and somehow connect with Birney's own

28 *OR*, 27/2: 618. George Clark wrote, "Our brigade commander during the morning took occasion to explain to the officers the general plan of the battle, in so far as our immediate front was concerned, stating that the movement forward would be by echelon, beginning with the right of Longstreet's Corps and extending to the left as each brigade came into action; and that, owing to our situation, the Alabama Brigade at the proper time would move by the left flank rapidly, so as to give Barksdale's Mississippi Brigade, which would be on our immediate right, room to move forward in proper line. . . . The order was then given our brigade to move rapidly by the left flank, and the movement was made at full speed until space was cleared sufficient for the Mississippians, and then with right face the brigade moved forward to the assault." See Clark, "Wilcox's Alabama Brigade at Gettysburg," *Confederate Veteran,* Vol. XVII, 229.

29 Adolfo Cavada Diary, Participant Accounts: V-5, Library & Research Center, *GNMP; OR*, 27/1: 533, 576; 27/2: 618; Ladd, *The Bachelder Papers*, 1: 193; Toombs, *New Jersey Troops*, 230; Imhof, *Gettysburg Day Two*, 141, 146. The skirmish line likely included remnants of the 5th New Jersey, 1st U.S. Sharpshooters, and the 1st Massachusetts. There have been questions over the 5th New Jersey's actual position; their battlefield monument is on the west side of the Emmitsburg Road, roughly across the street from Turnbull's battery. The 5th's monument states: "The regiment first held the skirmish line 400 yds. to the front and left of this spot and afterwards took position in line of battle here."

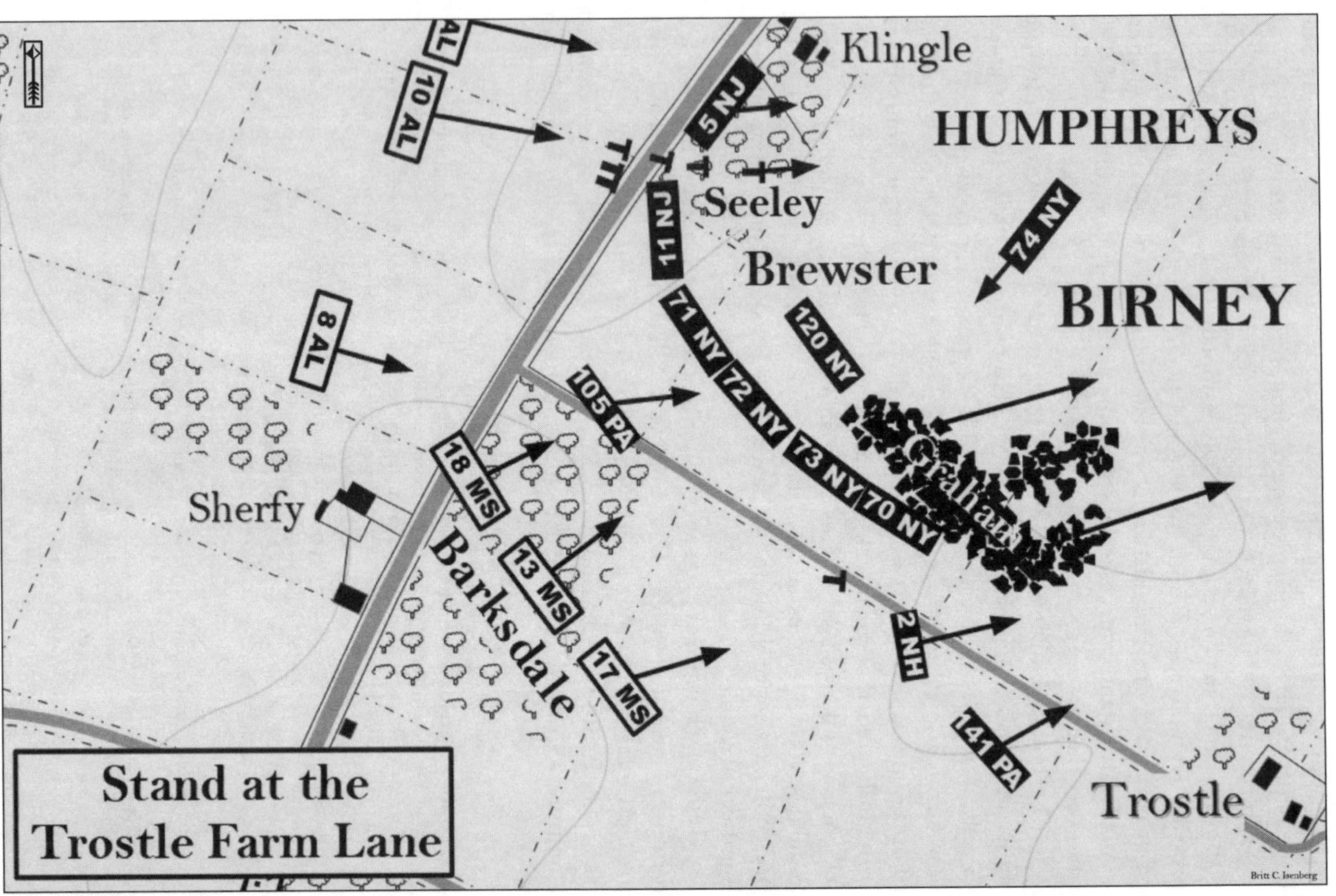
Klingle
HUMPHREYS
Seeley
Brewster
BIRNEY
Graham
Sherfy
Barksdale
Trostle
10 AL
8 AL
5 NJ
11 NJ
71 NY
72 NY
73 NY
70 NY
120 NY
74 NY
105 PA
18 MS
13 MS
17 MS
2 NH
141 PA
Stand at the
Trostle Farm Lane
Britt C. Isenberg

tattered division, to "form a line oblique to and in rear" of the existing line. Birney was then supposed to complete the line to "the Round Top ridge." Humphreys did his part while under a heavy fire from Confederate artillery and infantry, but the rest of Birney's troops "passed to the rear and did not wait to swing back with my div." Humphreys bitterly characterized Birney's order as "bosh." Barksdale, in overrunning Graham, threatened to outflank Humphreys's left.[30]

Graham's 57th, 105th, and 114th Pennsylvania regiments were in flight from the Sherfy buildings as Humphreys began to swing back his left. Colonel Craig and his 105th Pennsylvania rallied briefly near the intersection of the Emmitsburg Road and Trostle lane. Fronting south, the 105th, joined temporarily by a small remnant of the 57th Pennsylvania, formed a line along the lane. Craig's men "again opened fire, and checked the advancing rebels for a few minutes." Since the Northerners were badly outnumbered, however, and with "both flanks being entirely unprotected," Craig ordered his regiment to retire slowly and form a new line "a short distance" to the rear.[31]

The Wildcats' Lieutenant Robert Boyington found himself caught up in this whirlwind. As the regiment moved to form a "new line, a Minnie ball struck my left leg, just above the knee, crashing through flesh and bone. . . . So hard it struck, I thought it was a cannon ball, but looking, after I fell, I saw my leg still there."[32]

Federal batteries under lieutenants Seeley and Turnbull directed their fire at the attacking Rebel infantry. Seeley later declared that he was "under a heavy musketry fire" as well as artillery fire from some enemy batteries "which completely enfiladed our battery front doing much damage." After the retiring Third Corps infantry "had cleared our path- [we] opened with good effect on the enemy." Sergeant Charles Woolhiser of the nearby 120th New York wrote that Seeley's Napoleons were "charged with grape and canister and the Capt. was waiting until the Rebs were close to them and then 'Give 'em hell.'" General Humphreys reported, "The firing of Seeley's

30 *OR*, 27/1: 533; Ladd, *Bachelder Papers*, 1: 225-226; De Trobriand, *Four Years with the Army of the Potomac*, 503.

31 *OR*, 27/1: 501; Georg, "The Sherfy Farm and the Battle of Gettysburg," 22; Imhof, *Gettysburg Day Two*, 151, 156. The 57th Pennsylvania's participation may not have been very substantial, since their brief report does not even mention the episode. See *OR*, 27/1: 497.

32 "June 30," Robert I. Boyington's Army Life Journal (1861-1863), http://www.robert-ford.ws/105%20PA%20Intro.htm.

battery was splendid, and excited my admiration, as well as that of every officer who beheld it."[33]

A shell exploded above Wilcox and his staff as they neared the Federal line. A fragment severed the bridle reins of Wilcox's horse and another killed one of his couriers. During the march into Pennsylvania, Wilcox had rebuked a young wagon driver for stealing chickens against orders. Wilcox assigned the lad to a regiment as punishment, reasoning that if he was old enough to forage then he was old enough to fight. It was at this moment of confusion that the youngster reappeared to present Wilcox with 16 Federal prisoners. "Here are your chickens, sir."[34]

The Southerners pressed forward. Lieutenant Seeley was severely wounded by a rifle musket shot in the upper right thigh. He remained briefly in command until:

> Orders came to change the position of the battery to what point I cannot now recollect- when being very weak and faint from loss of blood, and unable to mount my horse, I was carried to the rear- by two infantry soldiers. While being so carried over the ground- on an open plain & between the orchard and the heights in the rear, I observed that the ground was completely scoured by the projectiles from the Confederate Arty.; shells were screaming through the air and bursting in every direction![35]

A short distance away, "in the midst of the tornado," Seeley spied General Humphreys, "I think, bareheaded, and unattended . . . endeavoring to rally (with only partial success, I judge) the retreating infantry of the 3rd Corps. I believe it to be almost an impossibility to rally the most staid veterans under such a fire of artillery as our troops were then exposed to."[36]

Lieutenant Robert James took command of the six Napoleons after Seeley's untimely departure and fired "a few rounds of canister, which,

33 "U.S.A. Jarvis General Hospital Baltimore, MD. Aug. 1, 1863," Diary of Charles Parmer Woolhiser, Boyle Family Collection; *OR*, 27/1: 532.

34 Wilcox, "Annotations on Official Report, July 17, 1863," Wilcox Papers, LOC; Freeman, *Lee's Lieutenants*, 3: 203. Lee's General Order Number 73, issued on June 23, 1863, prohibited Confederate soldiers from stealing property during the campaign into Pennsylvania.

35 Ladd, *The Bachelder Papers*, 1: 607-608.

36 Ibid.; *OR*, 27/1: 533. Seeley assured John Bachelder, "I have been informed by the officers of the battery that it did good service in its second position, and was finally extricated without any assistance from the infantry." Bachelder's Map [2] N-18, places Seeley's second position south and slightly east of the Nicholas Codori farm, suggesting that the battery was retiring diagonally toward Cemetery Ridge.

although creating great havoc in their ranks, did not check their advance." The Confederates continued to press toward his position and forced James to retire in order to save his guns. The battery retreated a short distance when they moved approximately 400 yards by the right flank and unlimbered again. Their renewed objective was to enfilade the Southern line. Scarcely had his guns gone into position when James reported, "the enemy appeared on my right flank and in rear, deployed as skirmishers, and not more than some 30 yards distant." James did not have time to fire and stated, "It was with the utmost difficulty I succeeded in moving by the left flank and retiring to the rear." The men of the nearby 5th New Jersey considered Seeley's safety to be "our especial care," and also fell back with the artillerymen. "The regiment was collected around the pieces of the battery," reported Captain Henry Woolsey, "and it and the battery commenced firing in retreat."[37]

A few yards to the north along the Emmitsburg Road, Lieutenant Turnbull's 3rd U.S. Artillery Batteries F & K, consisting of six Napoleons, tore furiously into yet another Confederate threat advancing on Wilcox's left. These Confederates were the small Florida infantry brigade of roughly 700 men from Anderson's Division. Colonel David Lang of the 8th Florida commanded the brigade at Gettysburg because Brigadier General Edward Perry was absent due to illness. "At 6 p.m., General Wilcox having begun to advance," Lang reported, "I moved forward, being met at the crest of the first hill with a murderous fire of grape, canister, and musketry."[38]

General Humphreys had long considered himself a soldier who relished leading men in combat. Now, he found himself under attack from Wilcox and Lang's brigades from the west, while most of Barksdale's men swept in from the south. The earlier cannibalization of Burling's brigade and the 73rd New York compounded Humphreys's problems and left him with roughly 3,200 effectives. With Graham driven from the field, Humphreys's left flank was in the air, and "being the only troops on the field, the enemy's whole attention was directed to my division, which was forced back slowly, firing as they receded." Humphreys positioned

37 *OR*, 27/1: 553-554, 575-577, 591. Captain Phillips wrote that as his 5th Massachusetts battery retreated from the field "what bothered us most was a battery on our right which we could not see, and which was throwing case shot at us very carelessly, and every minute a shower of bullets would come in, whoosh, - just like a heavy shower of hailstones." This might have been a reference to either Seeley or Turnbull's batteries. See *History of the 5th Massachusetts Battery*, 636.

38 *OR*, 27/2: 631.

Colonel William Brewster's Excelsior Brigade facing south to confront the onrushing Barksdale. Meanwhile, most of General Carr's brigade awaited the onslaught of Wilcox and Lang.[39]

Colonel Brewster was a Connecticut-born revenue agent prior to the war. He had no formal military training, a disturbing pattern in the upper echelons of the Third Corps, and had been absent during several prior engagements including Chancellorsville. Brewster was present at Gettysburg, perhaps to his chagrin, and reported afterwards, "The enemy advanced upon us in great force, pouring into us a most terrific fire of artillery and musketry, both upon our front and left flank." The Excelsiors returned fire "with great effect, and for some time held the enemy in check," but with no support on their left, "we were obliged to fall back, which was done in good order, but with terrible loss of both officers and men."[40]

The Excelsior Brigade's exact regimental positions remain uncertain. None were specifically described in post-battle accounts. Perhaps the 70th, 71st, 72nd, and 73rd New York were in a line just north of the Trostle lane with the 120th New York in reserve. The 74th New York had earlier been detached to Carr's right and was the last to arrive on the scene. Remnants of Graham's units, such as the 57th and 105th Pennsylvania, might have intermingled as part of their brief rally in this sector.[41]

Barksdale's 13th, 17th, and 18th Mississippi regiments charged this line. Some historians presume that the Excelsiors broke without much of a fight, in part because of after-action accusations made by others on the field. Their losses suggest otherwise. The 70th New York suffered 117 casualties, a rate of 40.6% that included only four men missing. The 71st and 72nd both sustained a 37.4% casualty rate. Perhaps the 72nd New York struggled the most to maintain its cohesion, since they claimed the highest number of missing /captured in the brigade at 28 men. The 74th New York had the lowest loss rate of the brigade at 33.5%. The 120th New York lost 203 men and had the highest casualty rate of 53.0%. These were losses comparable to or higher than many of the most esteemed units in either army. For example, Brewster's overall 42.4% casualty rate was considerably higher than Strong Vincent's 26.3% brigade losses suffered on Little Round Top, or the 32.4%

39 Ibid., 27/1: 533.

40 Tagg, *The Generals of Gettysburg*, 77-78; *OR*, 27/1: 559.

41 Laino, *Gettysburg Campaign Atlas*, 230; *OR*, 27/1: 558-559.

incurred by the celebrated 20th Maine. Clearly, the Excelsior Brigade was in the thick of the fighting.[42]

One of the Excelsior soldiers along this line was Corporal John Tomney of the 70th New York. Tomney was a Chinese immigrant who arrived in the United States shortly before the war began. In May 1861, he enlisted in New York City. Despite the cultural differences, Tomney gained a reputation as "being bright, smart, and honest." He soon became a favorite of the men in the regiment and according to a New York newspaper, "was at once the butt and the wit of the whole regiment." His comrades also considered him "one of the bravest soldiers" in the brigade. Unfortunately, Tomney "was struck by a shell which tore off both legs at the thighs, and he shortly bled to death" for his adopted country.[43]

Colonel John Austin, commander of the 72nd New York, was another Excelsior with an unusual background. He had something peculiar in common with General Sickles. Both men were politically active New Yorkers who had been tried for murder. In 1842, Austin was a principal promoter in a brutal 119-round prize-fight that resulted in the death of one of the participants. The organizers, including Austin and future prizefighting champion "Yankee" Sullivan, were indicted for manslaughter. Austin was already no stranger to the law. He ran a popular porter-house, where prize-fighting exhibitions were frequently held, and authorities had previously prosecuted him for selling alcohol without a license.[44]

Austin also cofounded the "Empire Club," an organization established in opposition to the New York mayor's prohibition on firecrackers and gunpowder. His activities brought Austin into the orbit of Tammany Hall politicians such as Dan Sickles. In 1848, while serving as president of the Empire Club, Austin got into a fight with one Timothy O'Shea. Austin suffered a cut from either glass or a knife, and as a result, he drew a revolver and shot O'Shea dead. Police arrested Austin but a jury acquitted him due to a lack of motive. According to

42 Busey and Martin, *Regimental Strengths and Losses*, 132; Floyd, *Commanders and Casualties*, 20-21, 24.

43 Busey, *These Honored Dead*, 120; *New York Times*, July 12, 1863. Tomney's name was reported in the *Times* as "John Tommy."

44 "John S. Austin," *The Buffalo Daily Republic*, October 5, 1848; *New York Times*, July 12, 1863; "Shocking Affray," *The Louisville Daily Courier*, October 7, 1848; "The Last Item In The Case of Shea," *Brooklyn Evening Star*, March13, 1849; "The Prize Fight Murder in New York," *Baltimore Sun*, September 17, 1842; "The Prize Fight Trials," *Baltimore Sun*, November 24, 1842; "Prize Fighting," *Cabinet* (Schenectady, NY), September 20, 1842.

Left to right standing: Colonel William Brewster and Colonel John S. Austin, with Brigadier General John H.H Ward seated.
LOC

the New York press, Austin's "friendly terms with the Police Officers" also helped him win the acquittal.[45]

Nonetheless, violence seemed to follow Austin everywhere. In December 1852, he instigated a riot at Tammany Hall when he interrupted a meeting of the Democratic General Committee. Sickles was in attendance as one of several politicos engaged in a heated debate. Austin, who was described in the press as a "somewhat notorious character," was asked to leave the meeting since he was not a member. Austin then allegedly gave some sort of signal, upon which a mob "well primed with drink" burst into the meeting room. "It would not take much to punch his head," Austin exclaimed as he shook his fist at the committee chairman. In the ensuing melee, the chairman was mortally wounded by flying fists and chairs. "The scene was frightful," reported the New York press. Austin was sentenced to three months in the penitentiary for leading the riot.[46]

Other misadventures followed, but none of this precluded military service when Dan Sickles needed men to enlist in the Excelsior Brigade at the war's outset. Despite being 49 years old at time of enlistment in 1861, Austin became captain of Third Excelsior's (72nd New York) Company K. He also served as the brigade quartermaster under Sickles. Austin had extended absences for

45 "Shocking Affray," *New York Evening Post*, September 29, 1848; Barram, *72nd New York Infantry*, Kindle edition "Chapter 10: Gettysburg." Many thanks to the late Donald K. Cody and Rich Landwehrle for sharing their research on the colorful John Austin.

46 "The Row in Tammany Hall," *Weekly Herald* (New York), December 4, 1852; "New York Morals and Politics," *Daily Missouri Republican* (St. Louis), December 13, 1852; "Riot in Tammany Hall," *Times-Picayune* (New Orleans), December 12, 1852; "Sentence of the Tammany Hall Rioters," *Republic* (Washington DC), July 20, 1853.

recruiting duty and health issues, but still received a promotion to Lieutenant Colonel in October 1862. In June 1863, Austin was scheduled for court-martial by General Carr due to his "alleged leave of absence," but the urgencies of the upcoming campaign prevented that from occurring. Austin led the regiment at Gettysburg because the previous commander, Colonel William O. Stevens, was killed at Chancellorsville.[47]

In his Gettysburg report, Austin acknowledged that his regiment withstood "a most terrific fire of shot and shell, when we were pressed so hard on the left flank that we were obliged to fall back." He thought this was done "in as good order as the circumstances would permit." Austin did not personally supervise the withdrawal, however, because he was wounded "in the arm and side." He turned command over to Lieutenant Colonel John Leonard, "who fought the regiment after I left." Austin commended Leonard and other officers who were "indefatigable in their exertions to rally the men, who were still hard pressed and obliged to fall slowly back to the crest of the hill from which the brigade started in the morning."[48]

Captain Adolfo Cavada from Humphreys's staff also tried to rally the Excelsior Brigade. While three Rebel battle flags were only yards away, Cavada vowed that the New Yorkers maintained a "spirited" fire. He admitted later that both the 71st and 72nd New York eventually broke, partially because portions of Graham's command fled toward them in disorder. Just as Cavada thought he saw the enemy waver and hesitate, his horse was struck and killed. The animal fell and pinned the captain's leg to the ground. Cavada barely freed himself, but as the Northern troops fell back firing, this "placed me between their fire & the Rebels, who fired as they advanced." Adolfo escaped and survived the war, as did his brother Frederico who published a sketchbook of his experiences in Libby Prison. Both men returned to their native Cuba and were killed in 1871 while fighting for independence from Spain.[49]

47 Brown, *History of the 3rd Regiment*, 12, 96, 113, 149, 181; Barram, *72nd New York Infantry*, Kindle edition "Chapter 10: Gettysburg". Austin's gravestone in Brooklyn's Green-Wood Cemetery lists his birth year as 1812, which made him 49 in June 1861. Barram in his recent regimental history indicates that Austin was 44 years old. Austin survived the war but died in May 1865.

48 *OR*, 27/1: 566; Busey and Busey, *Union Casualties at Gettysburg*, 474.

49 Adolfo Cavada Diary, Participant Accounts: V-5, Library & Research Center, GNMP; Stoudt, "The Cavada Brothers: Two Soldiers, Two Wars," Blog of Gettysburg National Military Park.

Yelling Mississippians were everywhere and flushed with success as they pushed their opponents down the slope from the Emmitsburg Road ridge. Colonel Thomas Holt's 74th New York was ordered from the right of Humphreys's line, probably to support the Excelsior Brigade's left. Since the 74th arrived as the brigade's other regiments turned rearward, many of their comrades tumbled through their line and temporarily masked their ability to fire on the advancing Mississippians. Surely some men stopped running to join their comrades, and for a few moments the remaining Excelsiors "commenced a direct fire," but this stand was short-lived.[50]

Major Thomas Rafferty of the 71st New York was an Irish immigrant and successful businessman in New York City, where he specialized in selling "superior white beaver hats" during the 1850s.[51] After the war, he offered his perspective on the struggle of the Excelsior Brigade:

> Humphreys could not hold his men, for as soon as they found themselves assailed both in front and flank they broke and retreated. The confusion was but momentary, for although disrupted and somewhat in disorder, they had a soldier for a leader; they were soldiers themselves and almost immediately rallied. They understood the matter as well as their officers. They knew that the position could not now be held, and they seemed to have simultaneously made up their minds that they were going back to a position they could hold, and back they did, but fighting, not disorderly.[52]

A volley from the 120th New York temporarily stalled Barksdale's drive, but the Confederates soon overwhelmed their adversaries. "The enemy at last broke the first line, and we advanced to meet him," reported the 120th's Captain Abraham Lockwood. "The regiment soon became hotly engaged, and held its position without flinching until it was flanked." The 120th's Charles Woolhiser claimed that in the 15 minutes since Seeley's battery departed from their front, "one half or our Regt. was either killed or wounded. Myself among them." He had been struck and "at the first sting of the bullet in my leg I took no notice of it, but when I went to step on my foot I went down. Using my gun for a crutch, I started for a brick house nearby."[53]

50 *OR*, 51/1: 203.

51 Parry, "Rafferty: Thomas Rafferty (1822-1888) and Susan McCoun Rafferty (1824-1900)," 3.

52 Rafferty, "Gettysburg," *Personal Recollections of the War of the Rebellion*, 26-27.

53 *OR*, 27/1: 568; "U.S.A. Jarvis General Hospital Baltimore, MD. Aug. 1, 1863," Diary of Charles Parmer Woolhiser, Boyle Family Collection.

Post-war view of the Emmitsburg Road, looking south. The Klingle house is on left and the Rogers property is on right. Wilcox and Lang attacked from right to left.
GNMP

Colonel Brewster fell in among their file closers while General Humphreys and the 120th's commander, Lieutenant Colonel Cornelius Westbrook, rode back and forth behind the line. Such attention suggests that the 120th might have been the Federals' last hope, and the final butcher's bill proves that they paid a ghastly price. As noted previously, the 120th New York suffered the highest casualty rate in the Excelsior Brigade, including the largest number of killed and wounded.[54]

Meanwhile to Brewster's immediate right, the 11th New Jersey in Carr's brigade held an unenviable assignment. They spent the earlier hours posted near the Klingle house on the Emmitsburg Road. There, they hugged the ground during the preliminary artillery bombardment when the "air seemed thick with flying missiles." The regiment was led by Colonel Robert McAllister, a 50-year-old Pennsylvania native who Sickles later praised "as good an officer as New Jersey sent to the war, and that is saying a great deal." McAllister described the artillery fire as "no ordinary kind. It was very brisk and extremely fierce."[55]

As Humphreys swung back his left, the 11th acted as what has been described as the "joint" between the division's left (the Excelsiors) and right (the remainder of Carr's brigade), pivoting behind Klingle's house and somewhat perpendicular to the Emmitsburg Road. According to the regiment's adjutant, Lieutenant John Schoonover, this order came from Carr "to change front by bringing our left to the rear" in order to meet Barksdale's charge. This unfortunately left the regiment vulnerable to crossfire from Wilcox.[56]

It was almost a relief when the men were given the opportunity to stand and meet the enemy infantry. McAllister ordered his soldiers to "fire by rank, rear rank first, so as to be enabled to hold in check the enemy after the first fire." An aide cautioned the colonel "to be careful and not fire on our own men," but in a few moments the pickets came rushing in, followed closely by Rebel infantry. McAllister ordered, "Fire!" before he fell severely wounded.

54 Pfanz, *Gettysburg: The Second Day*, 349. In this estimate, missing and captured are excluded from casualty totals. Busey and Martin estimated that the 120th lost 186 killed and wounded out of 383 engaged for 48.6%. The 70th New York lost 113 killed + wounded out of 288 engaged (39.2%). The 71st lost 78 K+W out of 243 (32.0%), while the 72nd suffered 86 / 305 for 28.2%. The 73rd was 154 / 349 = 44.1% and the 74th was 86/266 = 32.3%. See Busey and Martin, *Regimental Strengths and Losses*, 132.

55 Marbaker, *History of the Eleventh New Jersey*, 97; Robertson, *Civil War Letters of General Robert McAllister*, 5-6, 332.

56 Imhof, *Gettysburg Day Two*, 161; Marbaker, *History of the Eleventh New Jersey*, 98-99; *OR*, 27/1: 553. Colonel Robert McAllister described in his report, "I was ordered to change my front by throwing back my left. This done, we lay down awaiting the enemy." The 11th New Jersey's battlefield monument is just south of the Klingle house and states, "this stone marks the spot reached by the right of the regiment. The left extending towards the south-east. The position was held under a severe fire."

He was struck by a Minie ball in his left leg and a piece of shell in his right foot. McAllister was carried to the rear and survived his wounds.[57]

As the enemy appeared in the 11th New Jersey's front, Major Philip J. Kearny, a cousin of the famed major general who was killed in 1862, shouted excitedly, "I tell you we are going to have a fight!" No sooner had those words been uttered when a Confederate bullet tore through his knee, "and he spun like a top to the rear, landing at least ten feet" from Schoonover. Kearny was also carried to the rear, but he died on August 9. As an epitaph, Colonel McAllister considered Kearny "among the bravest officers I have ever seen." Schoonover hastened to tell McAllister of Kearny's departure, only to learn that the colonel had already been wounded and sent to the rear.[58]

This elevated Captain Luther Martin, the senior remaining officer, to command. However, Martin was soon struck in the foot, and while making his way rearward, was mortally wounded. Captain Andrew Ackerman was next in the chain, but he was killed just as Schoonover informed him that the regiment was his to command. Captain William Lloyd then briefly took charge until he, too, was wounded. Finally, in the confusion, Lieutenant Schoonover took over. "The fire of the enemy was at this time perfectly terrific," he reported, "men were falling on every side. It seemed as if but a few minutes could elapse before the entire line would be shot down, yet the galling fire was returned with equal vigor." All of these events probably unfolded over no more than 30 minutes when the "sadly thinned and somewhat disorganized" 11th New Jersey fell back. The 275-man regiment suffered an estimated 55.6% casualties, the second highest in Humphreys's division, including Schoonover who was wounded twice during his brief time in command. "With one half of the officers and men killed and wounded," wrote McAllister, "with a heavy flank and front fire, the wonder is how the regiment held together even as long as it did."[59]

According to the regimental historian of the 11th New Jersey, an officer thought to be Barksdale was quite conspicuous on a white horse and wearing a red fez, probably taken from one of the Pennsylvania Zouaves. Accordingly,

57 *OR*, 27/1: 553.

58 Marbaker, *History of the Eleventh New Jersey*, 98-99, 352; *OR*, 27/1: 553-554; Robertson, *The Civil War Letters of General Robert McAllister*, 309; "Claim For Mother's Pension," Eliza G. Kearny, Box 32656, Civil War Pension Files, NARA.

59 *OR*, 27/1: 554; Marbaker, *History of the Eleventh New Jersey*, 99; Floyd, *Commanders and Casualties*, 20; Robertson, *Civil War Letters of General Robert McAllister*, 334. Schoonover survived the battle and the war.

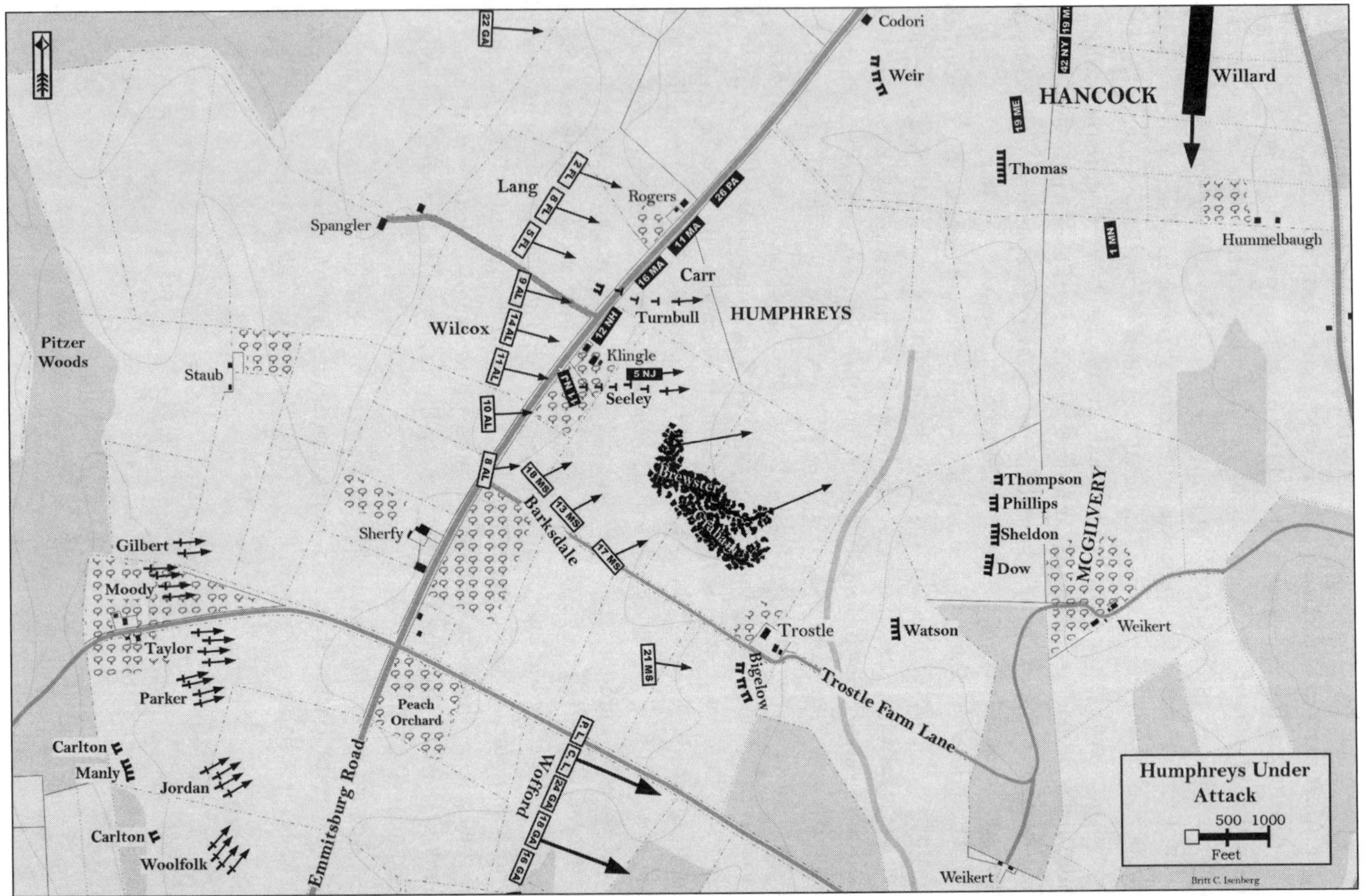
Humphreys Under Attack
500 1000
Feet
Britt C. Isenberg
Codori
Weir
Willard
HANCOCK
42 NY
19 ME
Thomas
1 MN
Hummelbaugh
Lang
2 FL
8 FL
5 FL
Rogers
26 PA
11 MA
16 MA
Spangler
Carr
Turnbull
HUMPHREYS
9 AL
14 AL
11 AL
10 AL
12 NH
Wilcox
Klingle
5 NJ
11 NJ
Seeley
Pitzer Woods
Staub
Brewster
8 AL
18 MS
13 MS
17 MS
Barksdale
Thompson
Phillips
Sheldon
Dow
McGILVERY
Gilbert
Sherfy
Moody
Taylor
Parker
Trostle
Watson
Weikert
21 MS
Bigelow
Trostle Farm Lane
Peach Orchard
Carlton
Manly
Jordan
Carlton
Woolfolk
Emmitsburg Road
Wofford
P. L.
C. L.
24 GA
18 GA
16 GA
Weikert

Carr ordered his men to shoot down this brave officer. Company H on the regiment's left unleashed their full fire and dropped this fez-wearing Rebel. The man's body was carried to Carr's headquarters after the fighting ceased for the day. Cause of death was five bullets. Of course, this was not General Barksdale, but it made for an interesting yarn in the regimental history.[60]

With the exception of the 11th New Jersey's rough patch, Carr's brigade angered some of the Excelsiors by appearing relatively inactive. This perception was inaccurate, since the Emmitsburg Road ridge blocked the view of Wilcox and Lang's approaching assaults. Both Confederate General Wilcox and Yankee General Humphreys disputed the notion that Wilcox had advanced behind Barksdale's left rear, and thus struck Humphreys well after Barksdale did. In 1877, Humphreys emphatically told Wilcox, "I am positive" that the attack "was nearly simultaneous with that on my left -- perhaps, owing to swinging back my left, preceding it a little."[61]

After scattering Humphreys's skirmishers, Wilcox's Alabamians advanced to the Emmitsburg Road. "A brisk musketry fight for a few minutes followed," reported Wilcox, "when the enemy gave way; not, however, till all save two pieces of a battery that was in the road had been removed. These fell into our hands, the horses having been killed." Wilcox's command crossed the road and began to descend the slope on the eastern side.[62]

Colonel Lang's brigade of Floridians was a small one, but they were welcome support to Wilcox. Lang was initially met with artillery fire from Lieutenant Turnbull's battery. The 5th Florida, on Lang's right, suffered terribly. One lieutenant was struck by a blast of canister which tore "a gaping hole in his breast and he sank to the ground." Lang continued forward at the double-quick and drove the Federals back beyond their guns. The Southerners opened "a galling fire," and as Lang reported, "thickly strewing the ground with their killed and wounded. This threw them into confusion, when we charged them, with a yell, and they broke and fled in confusion into the woods and breastworks beyond." Lang added afterwards, "I do not remember having seen anywhere before, the dead lying thicker than where the Yankee infantry attempted to make a stand in our front."[63]

60 Marbaker, *History of the Eleventh New Jersey*, 98.

61 Wilcox, "General C.M. Wilcox on the Battle of Gettysburg," *SHSP*, 6: 99; Pfanz, *Gettysburg: The Second Day*, 349.

62 *OR*, 27/2: 618.

63 Ibid., 27/2: 631; Dempsey, "The Florida Brigade at Gettysburg," *Blue & Gray*, 22-23.

General Carr sent one of his staff officers to the commander of the 12th New Hampshire with orders to retreat. The regiment held a position in the left-center of the brigade line near the Klingle house. Through the horrendous noise, the regiment's Captain John Langley was instructed to shout the retreat orders in the ears of "every company commander, and let them watch the motion of your sword as the signal for its execution." Enemy fire cut down Color-Sergeant William Howe. As he fell with the flag in his hand, a large swath of the colors tore away from the banner. Private Albert Bacheler refused to allow a piece of the national colors to fall into the enemy's hands and quickly retrieved the cloth from Howe's tight grip. The larger portion of the flag was borne from the field by Corporal John Davis. Captain Asa Bartlett remembered the ordeal, "with screeches and yells, mingling with the volleys of musketry, they press on against a storm of canister and Minie balls that is lining the opposite side of the highway with their wounded and dead; for they are now face to face with men, who, though less sanguine of success, are no less brave and determined."[64]

Lieutenant Turnbull's six Napoleons continued to fire until their ammunition was nearly exhausted. The gunners inflicted many casualties in the Southern ranks, but they found themselves in the same predicament as their infantry comrades. Like other Northern batteries on the field, Turnbull attempted to retire firing by prolong. The Confederates, however, got close enough to kill as many as 45 horses, compelling the artillerymen to abandon four pieces. The 115-man battery suffered 24 total casualties. The infantrymen of the nearby 16th Massachusetts, retreating with 81 casualties of their own including their wounded commanding officer, likely assisted the battery's right section in escaping.[65]

The 11th Massachusetts occupied Carr's right-center. They spent much of the day along the Emmitsburg Road. The Peter Rogers farm buildings, in their front on the west side of the road, provided some shelter. The "lady who lived in the cottage," a likely reference to the Rogers' niece Josephine Miller, was baking bread. According to the unit's Lieutenant Henry Blake, she also sold chickens to the hungry men. The balls from Confederate artillery had

64 Bartlett, *History of the Twelfth New Hampshire*, 123; Pfanz, *Gettysburg: The Second Day*, 369.

65 *OR*, 27/1: 533, 551; Ladd, *Bachelder Papers*, 1: 230-231,284, 3: 1975-1976; Floyd, *Commanders and Casualties*, 20, 44. The GNMP battlefield marker for Turnbull's battery states, "Moved to a position on the right of a log house on the Emmitsburg road with General A. A. Humphreys' Division Third Corps. Engaged here but was compelled to retire with the loss of 45 horses killed and 4 guns which were afterwards recaptured."

earlier swept through the residence and struck her bake oven, much to the chagrin of a male occupant whom Blake described as "trembling with fear for hours in his place of refuge." The woman refused to leave the house, but she finally heeded the demands of an officer who ordered her into the cellar.[66]

The Confederate infantry advance riddled the Rogers house with bullets. A kitten, "mewing piteously," ran from it and jumped on one soldier's shoulder. Before the men of the 11th could return fire, orders came from what Lieutenant Blake called "some stupid general" (presumably Carr in the chain of command) to "about-face" and abandon the road. The "stars and bars of treason," as Blake termed them, became visible as Confederate officers urged their men to load, fire, and press forward. Along came another order "from a blockhead, termed upon the muster-roll a brigadier-general," for the 11th Massachusetts to withhold their fire for fear of hitting their own men. Blake excused this error on the grounds that the general was too far in the rear to clearly see the state of affairs. Although this gave the Confederates an early advantage, the regiment quickly disregarded the order and their return fire temporarily checked the Southerners. Another mass of Confederate infantry appeared on the right of the Rogers house, and as the 11th Massachusetts took enfilade fire, at times from three different positions, they fell back under Minie balls and artillery fire, saturating "the plain with their blood."[67]

After Lieutenant Colonel Clark Baldwin brought his 1st Massachusetts in from the skirmish line, he prepared the men to reform in rear of the main battle line as support. A staff officer instructed him instead to move in front of the 26th Pennsylvania, the regiment on the right of Carr's line. The order surprised Baldwin so much that he thought he must have misunderstood it. "Still thinking it was wrong," recalled Baldwin, "I asked who gave the order, and was told it came from Gen. Carr . . . knowing no military rule for such a move I could not understand it, but formed my regt. in obedience to the order." At this moment, Lang's Floridians "appeared on the rise of ground in our front and poured a terrible volley into our ranks." Baldwin was among 23 wounded in this "killing fire." The fighting became "furious" and Baldwin's men were "obliged to give way before much superior odds; but fell back in good order to the crest of a hill in our rear." To add to the confusion, the presence of the 1st Massachusetts inhibited the ability of the 26th Pennsylvania to return

66 Blake, *Three Years in the Army of the Potomac*, 206-208; "A Heroine of the Battle," *Gettysburg Compiler*, January 25, 1911; Smith, *Farms at Gettysburg*, 17-19.

67 Blake, *Three Years in the Army of the Potomac*, 208-210.

View toward Emmitsburg Road from near Plum Run showing the route of Humphreys's retreat toward the camera. The Sherfy buildings can be seen on the Emmitsburg Road ridge to the left and the Klingle buildings to the right.
Photo by Authors

fire. The 26th's Major Robert Bodine had "never seen such desperation on the part of the rebels" and the Pennsylvanians too, were eventually overwhelmed with a 58.4% casualty rate.[68]

Astonishingly, General Carr claimed that he still held the upper hand on the Rebels. In a prime example of an officer writing an official report to embellish his performance, Carr reported, "I could and would have maintained my position but for an order received direct from Major-General Birney, commanding the corps, to fall back to the crest of the hill in my rear." Carr further insisted, "At that time I have no doubt that I could have charged on the rebels and driven them in confusion, for my line was still perfect and unbroken, and my troops in the proper spirit for the performance of such a task."[69]

68 Ladd, *The Bachelder Papers*, 1: 193-194; Dempsey, "The Florida Brigade at Gettysburg," *Blue & Gray*, 22; Floyd, *Commanders and Casualties*, 20.

69 *OR*, 27/1: 543.

As Carr was riding along his line, his horse was struck by enemy fire and fell onto the general. Carr worked himself out from underneath the carcass, but his leg was seriously injured. With his line in full retreat, he hobbled back toward Cemetery Ridge. Carr's enthusiasm for his position was thoroughly unwarranted, and he admitted as much in later years. In reality, Humphreys's broken and disorganized division had no choice but to retreat. Barksdale, Wilcox, and Lang's assaults forced them to abandon the Emmitsburg Road, and in doing so, ended the Third Corps occupation of Sickles's advanced line.[70]

According to General Humphreys, "the fire that we went through was hotter in artillery and as destructive as at Fredericksburg. It was for a time positively terrific; the troops on my left retired, leaving me to catch it, my left flank being turned all the time; I had to retire." Humphreys complied with Birney's orders to fall back to Cemetery Ridge, but did so "very slowly, continuing the contest with the enemy, whose fire of artillery and infantry was destructive in the extreme." Humphreys refused to retreat "at double quick before the enemy," so the general and his staff prevented the movement from turning into an utter rout. "Twenty times did I bring my men to a halt & face about" to return fire on the Confederates, "forcing the men to do it." Lieutenant Jesse Bowman Young of Humphreys's staff admired his superior's cool and collected efforts. Young thought the general was "without a superior on the field of battle, full of fire, and yet in absolute equipoise."[71]

Not surprisingly, the veterans later debated whether or not the retreat was an orderly withdrawal or a total panic. Given the large numbers of men and animals involved, it was undoubtedly a mixture of both. Lieutenant Colonel Baldwin of the 1st Massachusetts thought the division did as well as could be expected under the circumstances. "For a short time the fighting was furious, but the enemy's three lines of battle proving too much for our one, we were obliged to give way before much superior odds; but fell back in good order." On the other hand, the 73rd New York's Felix Brannigan confided to his father, "all organization ceased and the corps [was] now a rabble." The 72nd New York's regimental history admitted only that Humphreys's division,

70 Styple, *Generals in Bronze*, 95; Murray, *Letters from Gettysburg*, 87. Years later, Carr acknowledged to sculptor James Kelly that his men were actually demoralized by the Rebels pouring around his flank. See Styple, 95.

71 *OR*, 27/1: 533; Humphreys, *Andrew Atkinson Humphreys*, 198-199; Hyde, *The Union Generals Speak*, 191; Young, *The Battle of Gettysburg*, 257.

"changed front and rallied three times, but was compelled to fall back to the second line."[72]

Major Rafferty of the 71st New York thought they fell back "fighting." The men would, Rafferty wrote, "fire at the enemy, walk to the rear, loading as they went, then turn, take deliberate aim and fire again, and so on, but slowly and deliberately, and so deliberately that the enemy kept at a very respectable distance." Rafferty acknowledged that heavy fire of both enemy musketry and artillery continued to kill and wound "our poor fellows very rapidly; and yet the coolness and self-possession of our men under it was most remarkable." One incident that stuck with Rafferty long afterward was that of a young private who struggled with a speech impediment. Brigade commander Brewster's horse had been killed and he was walking to the rear with Rafferty, who was leading his own horse. The private presented Rafferty with a "handsome bridle in his hand all covered with blood." The private had unbuckled the bridle from Brewster's fallen horse. "M-m-major, don't you want a b-b-bridle?" Rafferty was impressed by such coolness under fire, but "Poor fellow, in less than two minutes afterward he was struck with a grapeshot and killed!"[73]

To make matters even worse for the beleaguered Humphreys, the Emmitsburg Road deployment had placed his right flank in the air, leaving it exposed and vulnerable. Another Confederate brigade, under Brigadier General Ambrose R. Wright, advanced on Lang's left and threatened to cut off Humphreys's potential escape in that direction. Fortunately, two regiments from Hancock's Second Corps, the 19th Massachusetts and the 42nd New York, were "judiciously posted" in Humphreys's rear to help cover the retreat.[74]

Also in his rear, albeit further to the 42nd New York's right, stood another Second Corps regiment, the 19th Maine. Many of Humphreys's men fled diagonally toward the 19th Maine. Unlike the stoic fighting recollections of Third Corps men, some Maine veterans remembered fleeing Excelsiors crying out, "Run boys, we're whipped, the day is lost." By at least one account, Humphreys approached the 19th Maine's commander, Colonel Francis Heath, and ordered him to stop the running Excelsiors with their bayonets. Colonel Heath, serving under Hancock, declined to submit to Humphreys's authority.

72 Ladd, *The Bachelder Papers*, 1: 193-194; Felix Brannigan to father, undated, original in LOC, copy in ALBG files, GNMP; Brown, *History of the Third Regiment*, 104.

73 Rafferty, "Gettysburg," *Personal Recollections of the War of the Rebellion*, 26-27.

74 Imhof, *Gettysburg Day Two*, 166, 171-178; *OR*, 27/1: 533.

An outraged Humphreys attempted to go over the colonel's head and direct the Maine regiment himself, but Heath and his men held firm. "Let your troops form in the rear and we will take care of the enemy in front."[75]

As the Confederate line emerged from the smoke, a tall color-bearer was observed at a distance of about 50 yards away. Colonel Heath ordered the men to "Drop that color bearer," and the regiment "poured in its first volley" which caused the enemy line to stagger.[76]

First Lieutenant Gulian Weir's Battery C, 5th United States Artillery, held a position on a slight rise southeast of the Nicholas Codori buildings. Weir was in ill health at Gettysburg, suffering from a chronic "ulcerated throat," and the increasing number of Federal soldiers who raced past and through the battery made his assignment even more difficult. Weir was afterwards critical of the Union infantry posted along the Emmitsburg Road. The enemy advanced toward his battery and "met with no opposition whatever from our infantry, who were posted on my right and front." This account suggests that most, if not all of his guns faced to the south. Weir first employed his six 12-pounders with solid shot and spherical case, and then fired canister as the Confederate attack moved closer. The battery quickly ran out of canister, so Weir began to limber up and retire. However, he spotted additional Union infantry forming in his left rear, so he came into battery again. Weir was optimistic because the Rebel force "seemed to be small and much scattered." To his dismay, enemy troops were on top of the guns quickly, so Weir ordered them back yet again. His horse was shot from under him, and as he rose, a spent ball hit him and "everything seemed to be very much confused." Weir was able to get off the field, but several of his guns temporarily remained behind. "I left that field in sorrow," he later wrote, "for I thought that half of the battery was on its way south."[77]

75 *OR*, 27/1: 422, 533; Meade, *Life and Letters*, 2: 88-89; Humphreys, *Andrew Atkinson Humphreys*, 198-199; Coddington, *The Gettysburg Campaign*, 413-414, 755 n.22; Gottfried, *Brigades of Gettysburg*, 221; Tucker, *High Tide at Gettysburg*, 285; Imhof, *Gettysburg Day Two*, 157, 179; Hyde, *The Union Generals Speak*, 191.

76 *Maine at Gettysburg*, 293.

77 *OR*, 27/1: 880; Ladd, *Bachelder Papers*, 2: 1152-1154. In addition to being in poor health, Weir was clearly troubled by Gettysburg. He wrote to General Hancock in 1880, "My mouth has been closed for 15 years on the battle (both days for different reasons). . . . I felt bad to think that this [his battery's temporary abandonment] had taken place over my guns in my absence. I wrongfully blamed myself . . . I did not care to talk much about the 2d day- except to own up when charged with running away." In his official report, Weir stated that three guns were left on the field. In his correspondence to Hancock he elaborated, "When I was running up the hill on my retreat, I looked behind me, and saw three (3) guns remaining on

Humphreys rightfully complained that "they had taken away my reserve brigade to support others, and a large part of my second line I had to bring to my front line and part of it went to others. The troops that were to support me were sent to others." He thought that it took half an hour to reach Cemetery Ridge. Once there, General Hancock directed the remnants of Humphreys's command to reform near the position vacated by Caldwell's Second Corps division, sent earlier to the Wheatfield. Ironically, this was near the same ground that Humphreys would have occupied had Sickles not advanced to the Emmitsburg Road. All that remained of Humphreys's proud division were the fragments of his shattered regiments. The division suffered approximately 2,092 casualties out of 4,924 engaged, a rate of 42.5%. This was the third highest numerical total for any division in the Army of the Potomac. Birney's division was right behind them with the fourth largest total (2,011), and Graham sustained the highest casualty rate (48.8%) of the three brigades in the First Division. The enormous losses in both Third Corps divisions provided clear testimonials to the intensity of the fighting, the difficulties of defending Sickles's position, and the success of Barksdale, Wilcox, and Lang.[78]

---

the field- the others were going off the middle (entire) section (platoon) where I had my position, of the battery had suffered most- It is not likely that both of these guns and one belonging to the right section, were those I saw. Everything else was going back. The left section must have been intact, so I made my report accordingly." Lieutenant Jacob Roemer, who took charge of the left section on the field afterwards gave Weir the impression that he (Roemer) had removed five guns. "My impression all along has been that I had three guns with me that night, but it must have been one (1) gun." See Ladd, *Bachelder Papers*, 2: 1152.

78 Humphreys, *Andrew Atkinson Humphreys*, 198-199; *OR*, 27/1: 533; Hyde, *The Union Generals Speak*, 191; Busey and Martin, *Regimental Strengths and Losses*, 462-463. By Busey and Martin's estimates, Wadsworth and Doubleday / Rowley's First Corps divisions both suffered higher numeric losses. On a percentage basis, Humphreys and Birney were further down the list, ranked 7th (42.5%) and 8th (39.5%) respectively among Union divisions. See Busey and Martin, 462-463.

CHAPTER 8

I Wish I Were Already Dead

Confederate artillerist Colonel Edward Porter Alexander observed the battle from Warfield Ridge as McLaws's Division drove the Union regiments out of the Peach Orchard in confusion. Alexander believed, or at least so he later wrote, that "the war was nearly over." He had six batteries limbered up and "charged in line across the plain and went into action again at the position the enemy had deserted." The opportunity to achieve one of the afternoon's primary objectives, placing Southern artillery in the Peach Orchard, was within Alexander's grasp. However, Alexander could not directly see much of Cemetery Ridge from Warfield Ridge. The Federal retreat from the Peach Orchard and Emmitsburg Road likely appeared to represent the collapse of the Army of the Potomac's left flank.[1]

Alexander later recalled "no more inspiriting moment during the war than that of the charge of these six batteries. An artillerist's heaven is to follow the routed enemy, after a tough resistance, and throw shells and canister into his disorganized and fleeing masses." His excited men ran a "general race and scramble to get there first." They did not move forward in a regular line, but rather the "pieces and caissons went at a gallop, some cannoneers mounted, and some running by the sides."[2]

1 Alexander, "The Great Charge and Artillery Fighting at Gettysburg," *Battles and Leaders,* 3: 360.

2 Ibid.

Although the ground over which they advanced was gently undulating, remnants of fences remained as obstacles. Major James Dearing, the head of artillery in General Pickett's Division, had come forward to observe the action. Dearing crossed paths with a group of Yankee prisoners being prodded to the rear. He demanded that they remove some rails from the path of the advancing artillery. According to Alexander, "Never was an order executed with more alacrity. Every prisoner seemed to seize a rail, and the fence disappeared as if by magic." Colonel Cabell, commanding McLaws's Division artillery, called this movement "one of the most exciting and heroic actions" of the war.[3]

Captain Osmond Taylor's Virginia battery was among those that dashed across the field and unlimbered near the Sherfy and Wentz properties. Sergeant Henry Wentz must have been conflicted by his assignment; he literally went into action within a stone's throw of his parent's home.[4]

The Federal artillery had stubbornly held their ground earlier that afternoon, and Alexander had but one thought on his mind. "Now we would have our revenge, and make them sorry they had stayed so long." However, upon reaching the Peach Orchard, the young officer was disappointed by what he saw. From that position, Cemetery Ridge and additional Union reinforcements were clearly visible in the distance. "We had only a moderately good time with Sickles's retreating corps after all. They fell back upon fresh troops in what seemed a strong position extending along the ridge north of Round Top. . . . Our infantry lines had become disjointed in the advance, and the fighting became a number of isolated combats between brigades." Despite his displeasure, Alexander established his position in the orchard and along the Emmitsburg Road ridge. "The artillery took part wherever it could," he later explained, "firing at everything in sight, and a sort of pell-mell fighting

3 Alexander, *Military Memoirs*, 399; Wise, *Long Arm of Lee*, 648; Cabell, "A Visit to the Battle-Field of Gettysburg," 4. Southern artillery historian Jennings Cropper Wise later waxed about the entire episode, "Perhaps no more superb feat of artillery drill on the battlefield was ever witnessed than this rapid change of position. . . . For 500 yards the foaming horses dashed forward, under whip and spur, the guns in perfect alignment, and the carriages fairly bounding over the fields." See Wise, *Long Arm of Lee*, 648.

4 McMillan, *Gettysburg Rebels*, 173-174, 309, n.41. To add another twist to the Wentz story, Henry may have owned property that he was passing through or fighting on. Tom McMillan presented deed evidence that John had sold and conveyed land to Henry in February 1850. William Frassanito, *Early Photography*, 249, acknowledged this deed, "but this evidence is not supported by local tax records." The GNMP *Survey Report for Restoration and Rehabilitation of Historic Structures* (dated 1957), Record of Conveyance, 9, has John Wentz owning two acres as of 1836 and transferring that to daughter Susan, by will, in 1870. See Wentz file, GNMP, copy on file with ALBG.

lasted until darkness covered the field and the fuses of the flying shells looked like little meteors in the air."[5]

Although the Confederates occupied Sickles's former position, many Third Corps wounded remained suffering on the field. As the Southerners overran the orchard, a shot struck Corporal Josiah Bosworth of the 141st Pennsylvania in the right leg below the knee. Unable to retreat with the rest of his regiment, Bosworth stumbled over a stone wall and collapsed. "In a short time the enemy came over the wall where I lay. I asked one of them for a drink of water; he gave it to me, but while I was drinking he was loading his gun. He said he hated our men, then went off about eight rods and shot at me, but I happened to lay down so he did not hit me." Bosworth spent the next 48 hours on the field with no food or water, but he survived.[6]

Such behavior by the enemy might be what prompted the actions of Private Samuel Fulmer from the 105th Pennsylvania. Earlier that afternoon, he suffered a severe wound from a Minie ball in the right leg and narrowly escaped being thrust-through by a Mississippi bayonet. Fulmer feared that he might be captured and subjected to similar treatment, so he crawled into the Sherfy bake oven and hid until the fighting was over.[7]

Wounded and taken prisoner, Lieutenant Frank Moran of the 73rd New York was deeply moved by the many injured horses that littered the field. "As I was assisted to the rear," Moran recalled, "the field from the Emmitsburg road, to the field south of Sherfy's was strewn with killed and wounded Confederates, and a sad number of our own men. The poor horses had fared badly, they lay in all directions and many of the poor maimed beasts, - those

5 Alexander, "The Great Charge and Artillery Fighting at Gettysburg," *Battles and Leaders*, 3: 360.

6 Craft, *History of the 141st Regiment,* 128; Bradsby, *History of Bradford County*, 652-653. The 141st regimental historian complained about similar brutality. "Several instances similar to this are related where our men were shot at in cold blood." Bosworth mustered out in 1865, and returned to his farm in Bradford County, Pennsylvania, where he raised a family and was active in his local G.A.R. Post. The regimental history referred to this specific incident as happening to Sergeant J.A. Bosworth of Company B. However, Corporal Josiah A. Bosworth was promoted from corporal to sergeant on December 5, 1863. See Craft, 161. Also see Pension Record of Josiah A. Bosworth, NARA, accessed on Fold3.com. Busey, *Union Casualties at Gettysburg*, 948, misidentified the corporal as Joshua A. Bosworth.

7 "Some Random Sketches of the 105th Pennsylvania," *The National Tribune*, January 1902. Also see Busey, *Union Casualties at Gettysburg*, 902.

ungazetted heroes, - gave us a helpless appealing look as we passed them that would painfully touch the stoutest heart."[8]

Moran's guards escorted him past Sherfy's barn, "where the Confederates lay dead in great numbers, as well as on the slope in front, which the Mississippi Brigade had advanced. Many of the wounded, friend and foe, had sought shelter in the barn and as I passed I could hear the groaning of the wounded within. Shot, shell and bullets had riddled the boards from the ground to the roof." After passing the barn, Moran noticed Longstreet, "riding unattended to the front, a shell from our side struck a pile of rails between us and sent them into the air." Longstreet spotted the wounded New Yorker and "politely bowed in passing" before he turned his horse and attention toward the Confederates' right.[9]

Moran also saw Lieutenant George Dennen of the 73rd New York among the wounded. Dennen's twin brother Tom had been killed on May 2 at Chancellorsville, and George became increasingly despondent after his brother's death. Before the march into Pennsylvania, Moran complimented Dennen on his promotion to second lieutenant and the appearance of his new officer's attire. "I shall not wear it long," Dennen replied. "I shall follow Tom, and be killed in the next battle." George Dennen was struck in the left leg during the fighting on July 2. Surgeons amputated the leg, but he died on July 11, fulfilling the premonition of joining his twin brother. Dennen was later buried in Gettysburg's National Cemetery.[10]

On their own merits, the Confederate assaults had been smashing successes. The attacks dislodged Federal forces from the Peach Orchard and Emmitsburg Road, and Southern artillery was rolling into those positions. The day might be considered a Confederate victory if it ended there. The fighting, however, was not over. Both armies – one seemingly in retreat and the other flushed with success – pressed on toward Cemetery Ridge.

The Northern batteries that withdrew from the Wheatfield Road toward the Trostle farm lane had created a chaotic traffic jam in front of Trostle's

8 Ladd, *Bachelder Papers*, 2: 774.

9 Ibid.; Georg, "The Sherfy Farm and the Battle of Gettysburg," 25. At the dedication of the 73rd New York monument, Henry Tremain related, "Brave young Lieutenant Moran, who fell here [near the 73rd monument], told me that when he recovered consciousness Longstreet slowly passed him, riding alone up the by-road, as it then was, with his eyes anxiously looking towards Round Top Mountain." See *New York at Gettysburg*, 2: 606.

10 "A Fire Zouave," *The National Tribune*, November 13, 1890; Busey, *Union Casualties at Gettysburg*, 481.

Dead horses of Bigelow's battery in the Trostle barnyard.
LOC

house, but for the most part, escaped intact. Captain John Bigelow's 9th Massachusetts Battery was the last one. The wounded General Sickles had already been removed and his staff abandoned Third Corps headquarters. For Bigelow, "no friendly supports, of any kind, were in sight; but Johnnie Rebs in great numbers. Bullets were coming into our midst from many directions and a Confederate battery added to our difficulties."

Bigelow was preparing to make a rush "for high ground in the rear" when Colonel Freeman McGilvery arrived on the scene carrying new orders. Not only had Sickles's advance of the Third Corps opened a gap on Cemetery Ridge between the left of Hancock's Second Corps and Little Round Top, but this gap widened when General Caldwell's division went into action in the Wheatfield. To worsen matters, the retreating Third Corps troops failed to rally and plug this hole. If Barksdale and Wilcox's infantrymen reached this gap

Private John Norwood hiding behind his rock near the Trostle buildings. Sketches by Private Richard Holland.
GNMP

in force, the possibility still existed for the Confederates to turn Meade's left-center on Cemetery Ridge. "The crisis of the engagement had now arrived. I gave Captain Bigelow orders to hold his position as long as possible at all hazards, in order to give me time to form a new line of artillery," wrote McGilvery. A "surprised and disappointed" Bigelow ordered his four remaining pieces to fire double canister at the pursuing Confederates, who soon appeared over the crest in their front.[11]

Colonel B.G. Humphreys's 21st Mississippi, still well-separated from Barksdale's remaining brigade, threatened Bigelow's battery. The Union artillerymen and horses began to drop under enemy fire. At the number five gun, every man was struck down except for 24-year-old Private John K. Norwood. He soon collapsed near the trail of the gun when a bullet passed through his lungs and lodged near his spine. Within seconds "the enemy were on the gun and limber, and a color bearer mounted the limber and waved his flag." Luckily, one of Norwood's comrades saw him fall, and after allowing the Confederates to pass by, assisted Norwood to the shelter of a large tree and boulder approximately 50 yards away. Norwood survived and received a discharge for disability in 1864. He returned to Gettysburg in 1883, and again the following year, to assist in determining the location of the battery's monument. He identified the boulder that had offered

11 Bigelow, *The Peach Orchard*, 16-19, 22, 55-58, 60; Ladd, *The Bachelder Papers*, 1: 168; OR, 27/1: 882, 897. Bigelow's two left pieces were "crowded among boulders" and not in position to render effective service, so were ordered to the rear. One piece went through a gateway into Trostle's farm lane and promptly overturned where it was "righted amid a shower of bullets." The other piece was driven in desperation "over the stone wall" near the lane.

him protection so many years earlier. This visit inspired his comrade Richard Holland, one of three artists in the 9th Massachusetts Battery, to sketch the location and preserve the story for posterity.[12]

Two Confederate bullets seriously wounded Bigelow, but he remained with his men. "The air was alive with missiles" hurled from Alexander's batteries near the Emmitsburg Road. Finally, Bigelow spotted McGilvery forming a new artillery line in the rear. Estimating that he had delayed the Rebel infantry for at least 30 minutes, Bigelow ordered his guns to fall back. Bugler Charles Reed led the wounded captain off the field through friendly fire from McGilvery's fledgling artillery line.[13]

McGilvery formed his guns near the banks of Plum Run, about 400 yards to the rear, and ironically in front of the ground that Sickles had earlier abandoned as inadequate for artillery. According to McGilvery's report, his patchwork command included Watson's battery, three of Phillips's guns, two guns from Thompson's battery, Lieutenant Edwin Dow's 6th Maine Light Artillery, and an unnamed volunteer battery that likely was Lieutenant Albert Sheldon's Battery B, 1st New York Light Artillery. These individually disorganized units were rallied together into a formidable force. As dusk approached, Phillips remembered, "The rebel batteries had by this time moved up to the Peach Orchard and opened a very heavy fire on us."[14]

As the 21st Mississippi pushed through the abandoned Trostle farm, Colonel Humphreys spotted Watson's battery unlimbering on the left of McGilvery's line. A quick charge by the Confederates captured these guns before they fired. Humphreys ordered his Mississippians to turn the pieces toward the Union lines. However, they discovered that Watson's men had carried off their tools and friction primers, giving Humphreys a hollow and short-lived victory.[15]

12 Baker, *History of the Ninth Massachusetts Battery*, 75; Heiser, "'The Enemy Were on the Gun and Limber...' Gunner John Norwood's Narrow Escape at Gettysburg." *The Blog of Gettysburg National Military Park*, 5 Apr. 2017, npsgnmp.wordpress.com/2017/03/10/the-enemy-were-on-the-gun-and-limber-gunner-john-norwoods-narrow-escape-at-gettysburg/.

13 Bigelow, *The Peach Orchard*, 18-19, 22, 57-58, 60.

14 Ibid., 22-26; Ladd, *The Bachelder Papers*, 1: 168-169; *OR*, 27/1: 882-883, 897. Captain Phillips only had three guns because his battery became separated in their efforts to extricate the caissons and guns beyond the Trostle farm. As it turned out, Captain Patrick Hart superintended the removal of three of Phillips's guns and took them with his own battery. See Appleton, *History of the Fifth Massachusetts Battery*, 627.

15 Bigelow, *The Peach Orchard*, 22-26; Ladd, *The Bachelder Papers*, 1: 169, 481; *OR*, 27/1: 883; Winschel, "Their Supreme Moment," *Gettysburg Magazine 1*, 76. Organized resistance from

Further to the right on McGilvery's line, the Yankee colonel spotted Rebel sharpshooters parallel to his front along the low bushy ground of Plum Run. The Northerners opened fire on them with canister. Captain Phillips also exchanged rounds with a Confederate battery in the Peach Orchard. Lieutenant Dow claimed, "we paid no attention" to Alexander's artillery although they admittedly "had gotten our exact range, and gave us a warm greeting." Dow instead focused on the nearby enemy infantry and reported firing 27 rounds of canister. Although McGilvery's performance was effective, the unnamed volunteer battery soon withdrew from the line, Thompson ran out of ammunition and was sent back, and Watson's battery was captured. Phillips and Dow appear to have handled the lion's share of firing from McGilvery's gunline.[16]

While Colonel Humphreys and his lone regiment wrestled with Watson's guns, General Barksdale thrust the remainder of his brigade forward. Barksdale and Humphreys were separated by about 300 yards and too far apart to support each other. The three regiments under Barksdale's supervision had initially moved on a path somewhat parallel to the Emmitsburg Road. After passing the Trostle farm, the Mississippians wheeled slightly right (east) toward Cemetery Ridge. As Humphreys later reminisced, Barksdale's "fiery mettle flamed high." Yet, after charging more than three-quarters of a mile and overcoming multiple waves of Federal resistance, a stunning accomplishment, Barksdale's formations simply broke down. Although the Mississippians were nearly "faint from exhaustion" in the late afternoon heat, Barksdale refused requests from his officers to stop and reform. "'No, we've got them whipped and can drive them across the Susquehanna!" he thundered. "Crowd them! Move forward your regiments!" He urged his men forward through the low scrub and bushes that lined Plum Run. "Brave Mississippians, one more charge and the day is ours!" The men responded with cheers and followed their general toward Cemetery Ridge.[17]

Fortunately for the Union cause, the Confederates approached the Second Corps front, and General Winfield Scott Hancock vigorously defended his

---

Third Corps infantry was conspicuously absent. Bigelow later blamed this on Colonel Tippin's inability to reform Graham's brigade following their rout in the Peach Orchard.

16 Dow's Abstract Report for Ammunition expenditure "In Action at Gettysburg, PA," author's collection; Bigelow, *The Peach Orchard*, 22-26; *OR*, 27/1: 882-883; Ladd, *Bachelder Papers*, 1: 169; *Maine at Gettysburg*, 327.

17 B.G. Humphreys Manuscript, 15-16; Winschel, "Their Supreme Moment," *Gettysburg Magazine 1*, 74-76; Pfanz, *Gettysburg: The Second Day*, 348-349; Gottfried, *Brigades of Gettysburg*, 221-222.

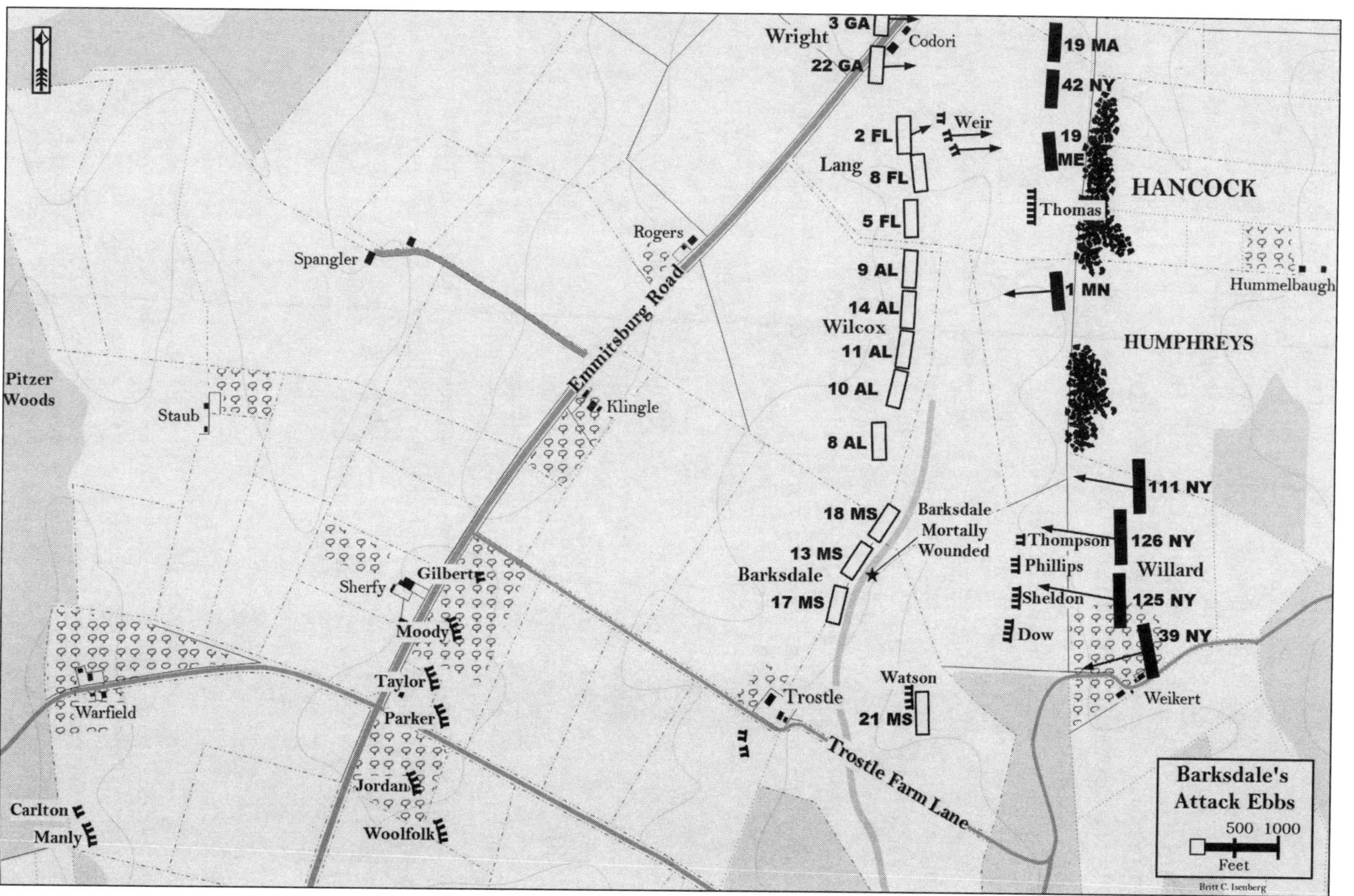
3 GA
Wright
Codori
22 GA
19 MA
42 NY
2 FL
Weir
19
ME
Lang
8 FL
HANCOCK
Thomas
5 FL
Rogers
Spangler
9 AL
1 MN
Hummelbaugh
14 AL
Wilcox
11 AL
HUMPHREYS
Emmitsburg Road
Pitzer
Woods
10 AL
Klingle
Staub
8 AL
111 NY
18 MS
Barksdale
Mortally
Wounded
Thompson
126 NY
13 MS
Barksdale
Phillips
Willard
Gilbert
Sherfy
17 MS
Sheldon
125 NY
Moody
Dow
39 NY
Taylor
Watson
Trostle
Weikert
Warfield
Parker
21 MS
Trostle Farm Lane
Jordan
Carlton
Manly
Woolfolk
Barksdale's
Attack Ebbs
500 1000
Feet
Britt C. Isenberg

position. Upon learning of Sickles's wounding, Meade directed Hancock to assume command of the remaining Third Corps in addition to his own Second Corps. As General Humphreys's battered division fell back, Hancock directed him "to form his command on the ground from which General Caldwell had moved to the support of the Third Corps." Humphreys carried out the orders to the best extent possible given the disorganized condition of the men.[18]

Hancock also ordered in Colonel George Willard's brigade from the northern end of Cemetery Ridge to help stop Barksdale. Just before putting Willard into action, Hancock "encountered General Birney, who informed me that his troops had all been driven to the rear." Birney then departed to collect his command. Hancock later claimed that Birney acknowledged the Third Corps "had gone to pieces." Hancock saw Third Corps soldiers fleeing ahead of the advancing Rebels but had little time to dwell on it since enemy fire was "commencing to fall among us." He stated that since the Third Corps was "all gone as a force," he "never really exercised any command" over it. Most of the corps remained "scattered, and could not be collected then. That was the end of it as a corps for that day."[19]

Colonel George L. Willard was a 35-year-old veteran of the Mexican War. He received a citation for gallantry at Chapultepec and held a captain's rank in the Regular Army when the Civil War broke out. Willard's career held great promise, but he and his men entered the Gettysburg campaign under a cloud. During the 1862 Maryland campaign, the brigade's regiments - the 39th, 111th, 125th (then commanded by Willard), and 126th New York - were among the Federal garrison that surrendered Harper's Ferry. Ironically, Barksdale's Mississippians participated in that capture. The New Yorkers were paroled afterwards, and some earned the derisive nickname "Harper's Ferry Cowards" within the Union Army. In late June 1863, Willard received command of the brigade and they were assigned to hard-hitting Brigadier General Alexander Hays's division in the Second Corps.[20]

18 *OR*, 27/1: 370-371.

19 Ibid.; Ladd, *The Bachelder Papers*, 2: 1134, 3: 1356; Hancock, *Reminiscences of Winfield S. Hancock*, 196; Campbell, "Remember Harper's Ferry," *Gettysburg Magazine 7*, 64-65; Hyde, *The Union Generals Speak*, 216.

20 Campbell, "Remember Harper's Ferry," *Gettysburg Magazine 7*, 51-59; *Dedication of the New York State Auxiliary Monument*, 138-139. The brigade was assigned to General Hays in early 1863. When Hays was promoted to division command in June, Willard received the brigade as senior colonel.

The late afternoon of July 2 offered Willard's men an opportunity to prove themselves in combat. Amid deafening noise, General Hancock ordered Willard's brigade to halt just north of the George Weikert farm and form a line of battle. To their front, Cemetery Ridge descended gradually to the west into a swale approximately 400 yards away and overgrown with thick bushes, old stumps, and rough boulders. Willard placed the 125th New York on his left and the 126th New York on his right, with the 39th and 111th New York in the rear to protect the flanks. Upon their approach, Barksdale's men commenced firing immediately. As if the "storm of missiles from Minie balls and bursting shells" were not enough, the New Yorkers also had to manage the continued flight of the Third Corps soldiers who were "pouring through the gap to the rear, closely pursued by a line of rebel infantry who were firing rapidly." Willard's officers complained that it was "difficult to keep a line in the face of these squads of flying men," and not even a series of "blistering curses" from Hancock stopped the stampede. "The enemy had driven back the Excelsior Brig.," one member of the 126th wrote, "and the men were running back before the enemy as if they were but a line of skirmishers."[21]

The smoke of battle hung in the low ground along Plum Run and mingled with the growing dusk to limit visibility. On the ridge along the Emmitsburg Road, approximately 800-900 yards to the west, Alexander's artillery enjoyed an elevation advantage of some 60 feet over their Union counterparts. From this platform, Confederate gunners poured their fire into the Union lines. McGilvery's artillery returned fire from the lower ground near Willard's position. The infantry numbers at this moment favored the Federals. Willard's four fresh regiments, at full strength, mustered approximately 1,500 men. In contrast, Barksdale's three exhausted regiments could not have exceeded 1,000 men by this stage of the contest. Nonetheless, Willard's men initially hesitated amidst the confusion and fading sunlight. They fired an opening volley into the smoke-filled swale but heard the cry of "Firing on your own men!" Willard and his officers promptly shouted, "Cease Firing!" Willard had earlier ordered his men to fix bayonets, and while the New Yorkers awkwardly tried to reload, the Mississippians seized the advantage and blasted a volley of their own into the enemy line.[22]

21 Ladd, *Bachelder Papers*, 1: 339; Campbell, "Remember Harper's Ferry," *Gettysburg Magazine 7*, 64-67; Hancock, *Reminiscences of Winfield S. Hancock*, 196.

22 Campbell, "Remember Harper's Ferry," *Gettysburg Magazine 7*, 67; Busey and Martin, *Regimental Strengths and Losses*, 44, 180. Busey and Martin's modern analysis put Willard's brigade

No longer doubting who stood opposite them, Colonel Willard ordered the 125th and 126th New York forward. Colonel James Bull of the 126th reported that Willard's order was "to charge two rebel batteries, supported by infantry, posted on the hill in front." An initial cry of "Remember Harper's Ferry!" swelled into hundreds of shouts as Willard's brigade raced down slope from Cemetery Ridge toward the lower ground along Plum Run. Despite the "bullets whizzing by our ears" and "rough rugged ground," Willard's men gained momentum as they ran toward the swale. Bull declared that Barksdale's Mississippians, "in considerable force were found in this underbrush. They fired upon the brigade as it advanced, which fire was returned by a portion of the brigade without halting. Many fell in the charge through the woods." Willard's earlier decision to fix bayonets now worked in favor of the Northerners. "Our brigade was a large one and, despite its losses," remembered one veteran, "presented a long line of bright bayonets. As we neared the rebel lines their fire slackened and they began to give back. I have never seen soldiers who would stand and receive a bayonet charge." The Mississippians' wavering inspired Willard's men to press forward. For the first time, Barksdale faced a full-fledged counter-attack. Throughout the afternoon, Barksdale had successfully pushed his men to the limits of their endurance. With daylight fading, and no troops within supporting distance, the "magnificent charge" of the Mississippians began to falter.[23]

"As many absurd statements have been made about the killing of Gen. Barksdale," Captain Charles Richardson, of the 126th New York, later observed, "I will here state what can be proved beyond question if need be." According to Richardson:

> Gen. Barksdale was trying to hold his men, cheering them and swearing, directly in front of the left of the 126th near the right of the 125th who both saw and heard him as they emerged from the bushes and immediately several from both regiments fired at him and he fell hit by several bullets, and a corporal in my company which was next to the left passed over his body while advancing up the hill.[24]

---

strength at 1,508 engaged. The three regiments under Barksdale's immediate supervision were estimated, at full strength, at 1,191.

23 *OR*, 27/1: 472; Campbell, "Remember Harper's Ferry," *Gettysburg Magazine 7*, 68-71; Murray, *Letters from Gettysburg*, 71.

24 Ladd, *Bachelder Papers*, 1: 340; Campbell, "Remember Harper's Ferry," *Gettysburg Magazine 7*, 68-69.

One of General Barksdale's Masonic cuff links and a bullet that was removed from him by Assistant Surgeon Alfred Hamilton.

Photo by Authors courtesy of GNMP

Private Joseph Lloyd of the 13th Mississippi recalled that just after Barksdale ordered, "Forward through the bushes!" his men heard the general "make a sound." Several soldiers rushed to Barksdale's side and helped him dismount from his horse. Although his men began to carry Barksdale from the field, they left him behind in the ensuing confusion of retreat. Private Lloyd was likewise wounded and abandoned. To his right, Lloyd heard a "weak hail," and turned to see his general lying grievously wounded on the ground. Lloyd attempted to give Barksdale some water but discovered that a bullet hole had emptied his canteen. Lloyd then attempted to comfort Barksdale. "I took his last message to his brigade and left him," he later reflected, "with the promise to sent [sic] the litter bearers. I know that I was the last on that part of the field and the last man that saw General Barksdale."[25]

Meanwhile, Hancock noticed that Wilcox's approach threatened Willard's right flank, and he directed Colonel Clinton MacDougall's 111th New York "to charge the rebel advance, which had broken through our lines on the right." The 111th secured Willard's right, but the New Yorkers were increasingly burdened by rounding up Confederate prisoners, who "threw down their arms and lay down in ranks." The majority of Willard's brigade

25 Lloyd's account reprinted in McNeily, "Barksdale's Mississippi Brigade at Gettysburg," 239. Lloyd was wounded in the left forearm and his arm was subsequently amputated. He was captured afterwards and exchanged in September 1863. He was discharged due to his Gettysburg disability. See Busey and Busey, *Confederate Casualties*, 691.

continued through the swale and ascended toward the Emmitsburg Road beyond. Colonel Bull of the 126th reported, "The brigade advanced at a 'charge bayonets' up the hill mentioned, and within a few minutes recaptured part of a battery previously taken from us." These repatriated guns were probably from Turnbull's battery. The 111th's Captain Aaron Seeley recalled being "met by a terrible storm of grape and canister." The Emmitsburg Road ridge, from the Peach Orchard to the Daniel Klingle house, seemed "alive with Confederates" and their artillery rained fire into the Union ranks. "The boys were falling all around me and appealing to me for help," one lieutenant recalled, "but I could only give them words of encouragement, and charge on." The brigade advanced several hundred yards before Willard realized the situation was untenable.[26]

Colonel Bull reported that Willard, "finding his brigade unable to stand so severe a fire, ordered the regiments to retire, which was done in good order down the hill and through the underbrush." Willard's first action in brigade-command had been a smashing success. He prevented Barksdale and part of Wilcox's Brigade from reaching a beckoning gap in the Union defenses. Willard had little time to savor his victory or dwell on thoughts of Harper's Ferry and vindication. While riding at the head of his brigade, as they crossed over Plum Run back toward Cemetery Ridge, an artillery projectile struck Willard in the head. The colonel was killed instantly and fell from his horse. One soldier recalled that the shell "carried away part of his face and head." Some of his horrified men quickly carried his "terribly mangled" body to the rear in order to avoid causing demoralization in the ranks. Unfortunately, George Willard's sacrifice is frequently overshadowed by other July 2 episodes, including Barksdale's mortal wounding. The loss of Willard was noteworthy and even the often-critical General Hancock praised him as "one of the best officers of his age and rank." General Hays, their division commander, declared, "The Harper's Ferry boys wiped out Harper's Ferry."[27]

Colonel B.G. Humphreys's 21st Mississippi still held Watson's captured battery and threatened the other remaining guns on McGilvery's artillery

26 *OR*, 27/1: 472, 474-476; Campbell, "Remember Harper's Ferry," *Gettysburg Magazine 7*, 71; Pfanz, *Gettysburg: The Second Day*, 406; Gottfried, *Brigades of Gettysburg*, 178.

27 *OR*, 27/1: 482-483; *New York at Gettysburg*, 2: 887; Campbell, "Remember Harper's Ferry," *Gettysburg Magazine 7*, 73; Murray, *Letters from Gettysburg*, 71; Gottfried, *Brigades of Gettysburg*, 181. Not only has Barksdale's story overshadowed Willard's, but as historian Eric Campbell noted, Willard's performance has even been overshadowed by another Union counter-attack, that of the 1st Minnesota which occurred only a few hundred feet away from him.

line. Birney sent an aide, Captain John Fassett, to help reform Andrew Humphreys's division on Cemetery Ridge. Fassett ran into the battery's Second Lieutenant Samuel Peeples, who warned him, "Those troops you have just been reforming on the ridge will not stay there a minute if the rebs can serve those guns." Fassett invoked Birney's authority and ordered Willard's 39th New York, also known as the "Garibaldi Guard," to retake Watson's battery. Major Hugo Hillebrandt, the commander of the 39th refused Fassett's order and insisted that his regiment was under Hancock's authority. The quick-thinking Fassett replied, "Then I order you to take those guns, by order of General Hancock!" That directive satisfied Hillebrandt, who then ordered the 39th "forward, cheering as they went, and driving the Mississippians from the guns." Fassett received a Congressional Medal of Honor in 1894 for recapturing Watson's battery.[28]

Colonel Humphreys saw that his isolated 21st Mississippi "had advanced too far to the front for safety." He observed that Barksdale, on his left, and Kershaw, to his right, had been checked in their progress and were falling back toward the Peach Orchard. Federal reinforcements were also arriving on his left, and Humphreys realized, "I saw my safety was in a hurried retreat. I abandoned the 5 guns [Watson] on the slope and retreated to the 4 Napoleon guns [Bigelow], where I met orders to continue the retreat." Barksdale's threat to Cemetery Ridge was finished.[29]

After putting Willard into action, Hancock rode north and detected Wilcox's Brigade also moving toward Cemetery Ridge. The nearest regiment was another in Hancock's own Second Corps, the 1st Minnesota. Commanded

28 Bigelow, *The Peach Orchard*, 22-26; Ladd, *Bachelder Papers*, 3: 1868-1869; *OR*, 27/1: 660; Campbell, "Remember Harper's Ferry," *Gettysburg Magazine 7*, 70; Pfanz, *Gettysburg: The Second Day*, 408-409; Beyer, *Deeds of Valor*, 240-242. There was later a dispute within the brigade as to whether the 39th New York deserved credit for re-capturing Watson's guns. Colonel Bull assumed command of the brigade following Willard and Eliakim Sherrill's deaths. Bull reported, "During this march the Thirty-ninth New York Volunteers, by order of Colonel Willard, were detached, and ordered about a third of a mile from the point where the residue of the brigade advanced in line of battle. The commanding officer of this regiment claims that, in obedience to such order, at the point designated, he charged on a line of rebel skirmishers, drove them in, and retook four pieces of artillery with caissons belonging to Battery I, Fifth U.S. Artillery, which had been captured by the enemy. The commanders of the other regiments of the brigade claim that at least two of these guns and caissons were captured in the advance of the brigade. I am unable to settle the conflict of statement from my personal knowledge, nor am I able to state whether any regiment of this brigade is the one referred to in this circular from my knowledge, or from evidence before me which I deem conclusive." See *OR*, 27/1: 474 and the report of Captain Aaron Seeley of the 111th New York, *OR*, 27/1: 476.

29 Ladd, *Bachelder Papers*, 1: 481; B.G. Humphreys Manuscript, 16.

by Colonel William Colvill, the regiment had supported Lieutenant Evan Thomas's Battery C, 4th Artillery, in harassing Wilcox's attack. According to Colvill, his regiment "arrived at this position just about the time Sickles' troops, broken and disorganized, passed the ridge in retreat, and many of them, to the number of thousands passed between our files." Wilcox came almost immediately behind Sickles's fleeing men, and Hancock exclaimed, "My God! Are these all the men we have here?" The general then ordered Colvill to "Advance Colonel, and take those colors!" Colvill pushed his lone regiment forward at the double-quick, and they rushed down the slope toward Wilcox's much larger battle-line. Colvill received a "galling fire" from the Confederates, but his Minnesotans returned fire into the Rebels "very faces, which broke up their line completely." The 1st Minnesota's Captain Henry Coates reported, "Although we inflicted severe punishment upon the enemy, and stopped his advance, we there lost in killed and wounded more than two-thirds of our men and officers who were engaged." The 1st Minnesota's sacrifice helped stop Wilcox, but roughly 215 of the estimated 262 men who made the audacious charge suffered casualties.[30]

General Wilcox found himself well beyond support and from the vantage point of the exhausted Alabamians, Cemetery Ridge appeared as a "stronghold of the enemy." Wilcox dispatched an aide to division commander General Richard H. Anderson with a request for assistance, but none came. "This struggle at the foot of the hill on which were the enemy's batteries," reported Wilcox, "though so unequal, was continued for some thirty minutes. With a second supporting line, the heights could have been carried. Without support on either my right or left, my men were withdrawn, to prevent their entire destruction or capture."[31]

Wilcox's assessment that he fought alone for 30 minutes might have been an exaggeration. Yet, the essence of his comment was accurate. His was among the many disjointed Southern brigades that were far from their starting point and fighting fresh Yankee reinforcements.

Lang's Florida brigade reached "the foot of the heights" immediately to the left of Wilcox. Lang ordered his men to halt and reorganize. The

30 *OR*, 27/1: 371, 425; Ladd, *Bachelder Papers*, 1: 256-257, 2: 1135; Hancock, *Reminisces of Winfield S. Hancock*, 199-200; Imhof, *Gettysburg Day Two*, 193, 197; Hill, Throll, and Johnson, "On This Spot..." Gettysburg Magazine 32, 96-97. As with every other topic in this genre, the precise strength and losses of the 1st Minnesota can be debated. The totals provided in the text are traditionally accepted for July 2 but are uncertain. The relevant point is that the regiment suffered heavy casualties.

31 *OR*, 27/2: 618; Wilcox, "General C.M. Wilcox on the Battle of Gettysburg," *SHSP*, 6: 103.

colonel hoped to reignite what remained of the Confederate momentum but noticed "a heavy column was thrown against Wilcox." The Floridians held their ground for a moment, but they found themselves under increasing close-quarter pressure from Federals along Cemetery Ridge. In his report, Lang acknowledged, "a heavy fire of musketry was poured upon my brigade from the woods 50 yards immediately in front, which was gallantly met and handsomely replied to by my men." He then learned that Wilcox's troops were in retreat and "discovered that the enemy had passed me more than 100 yards, and were attempting to surround me." Unsupported and isolated, Lang's small command also fell back and left this part of the field to the Northerners.[32]

During this chaotic encounter, "the entire Color-guard of the Eighth [Florida] were killed or wounded, and their colors left on the field," in what Lang acknowledged was a "confused order of the retreat." Scores of Southerners were captured. Sergeant Thomas Horan of the Excelsiors' 72nd New York picked up the 8th Florida's colors. Horan's bravery attracted the personal attention of General Humphreys, and in 1898, the sergeant received a Congressional Medal of Honor for his actions.[33]

The sudden reversal "was irresistible, and glorious" to the Federal soldiers who had been without hope only moments earlier. Hancock's defenders unleashed a furious counter-attack along their lines. Humphreys rallied the fragments of his own division and, along with Hancock's men, the rejuvenated soldiers charged. Officers and enlisted men alike advanced with a yell and moved defiantly across the fields that they abandoned only moments before. Humphreys ordered Colonel Brewster to retake several Federal guns that were in the enemy's possession.

32 *OR*, 27/2: 631-632; Fleming, *Memoir of Captain C. Seton Fleming*, 81. The version of Lang's report reprinted in Fleming is dated July 19 and differs significantly from Lang's official report dated July 29.

33 *OR*, 27/2: 632; Fleming, *Memoir of Captain C. Seton Fleming*, 82. The 72nd's Colonel Austin did not name Horan in his report, but noted the captured prize was "one battle-flag belonging to the Eighth Florida Regiment," along with "a large number of prisoners. See *OR*, 27/1: 566. The Excelsiors' Colonel Brewster wrote that a charge took "the colors of the Eighth Florida Regiment, and bringing in as prisoners the major of that regiment and some 30 of his men. The colors were taken by Sergt. Thomas Hogan [sic], Third Excelsior, who by his bravery attracted the personal attention of the general commanding the division." See *OR*, 27/1: 559. Also Teague, *Gettysburg by the Numbers*, 62; http://www.cmohs.org/recipient-detail/644/horan-thomas.php.

Brewster "made a charge at the head of about 150 men," from his Excelsior Brigade.[34]

Colonel Craig of the 105th Pennsylvania "saw General Humphreys, and formed line with some of his troops." The Pennsylvanians joined in the surge and moved forward "steadily until we had regained nearly all the ground we had lost." Craig reported that his men assisted the Excelsiors in drawing off three pieces of artillery, at least one of which they identified as belonging to Weir's Battery C, 5th United States Artillery. These guns and an estimated 92 Southern prisoners were turned over to Captain Carswell McClellan of Humphreys's staff.[35]

This action was one final measure of revenge for the battered Third Corps. The Northerners almost reached the Emmitsburg Road before officers called a halt and attempted to restore organization to the mixed regiments. The Confederates offered little resistance, largely because they found themselves as unorganized and exhausted as their newly liberated pursuers. Humphreys bragged, "Our troops got back close to the line I had occupied." This was not accurate, since Longstreet and E.P. Alexander still held the Peach Orchard and the Emmitsburg Road ridge south of the Klingle farm. By exacting token retribution against the Confederates, however, Humphreys ended the day for the Third Corps on a somewhat uplifting note.[36]

By this point in the late afternoon, the decisive moments had passed from Longstreet's front to that of A.P. Hill's. On Lang's left, yet another of General Richard Anderson's brigades, this one under Brigadier General Ambrose R. Wright, smashed into the center of the Union line on Cemetery Ridge. In an increasingly familiar scenario, Wright's men advanced unsupported and suffered a repulse by more of Hancock's fresh troops. The next Confederate brigade

34 *OR*, 27/1: 533, 559; Felix Brannigan to his father, unknown date, 73rd New York File, *ALBG* Library, original in LOC.

35 *OR*, 27/1: 501; 51/1: 204. The GNMP battery tablet for Weir's Battery C, 5th U.S. Artillery states, "Three of the guns were captured by the Confederates and drawn off to the Emmitsburg Road but were recaptured by the 13th Vermont and another regiment." Francis Randall of the 13th Vermont wrote in his Official Report that he was "told" that his regiment recaptured guns that belonged to Weir. See *OR*, 27/1: 352. It seems likely that the Vermonters overran the guns in their own charge, and the New Yorkers and Pennsylvanians followed up their efforts by securing the pieces. Overall, Longstreet's men temporarily captured more than a dozen guns on July 2, but only four were taken from the field: one 3-inch ordnance rifle from Thompson's Battery and three 10-pounder Parrots from Smith's Battery.

36 *OR*, 27/1: 371, 422, 434, 534, 804-806; *New York at Gettysburg*, 2: 606-607; Humphreys, Andrew *Atkinson Humphreys*, 198-199; Brown, *History of the Third Regiment, Excelsior Brigade*, 105.

in line, that of Brigadier General Carnot Posey, advanced only part way across the field while Brigadier General William Mahone's Brigade failed to move at all. This provided a fitting example of how Lee's offense had gone awry. Having failed to drive in the Federal left, and without time or opportunity to convert the Emmitsburg Road ridge into an impregnable artillery platform, the Confederate attacks deteriorated into a series of uncoordinated frontal assaults.[37]

In contrast to Robert E. Lee's detached command style on this afternoon, General Meade found himself right in the thick of the action. While on Cemetery Ridge, accompanied by only a few members of his staff, Meade spotted a battle-line of Rebels heading straight for him. He "straightened himself in his stirrups" and braced for the collision. However, the arrival of two divisions in Major General John Newton's First Corps broke the tension of the moment. The Army of the Potomac's commander reportedly advanced briefly with the First Corps skirmish line, giving the solidly unspectacular command, "Come on, gentlemen." In the best spirit of the old army, Newton offered Meade a flask just as a Confederate shell dropped in front of them and showered the generals with dirt. An aide remarked that things seemed desperate, but Meade replied, "Yes, but it is all right now, it is all right now."[38]

Meanwhile, the ramifications of the Peach Orchard fight extended well beyond Meade's left flank. As Hancock continued to close the gaps in his line, Meade pulled the majority of the Twelfth Corps off Culp's Hill and ordered them to reinforce the line along Cemetery Ridge. Twelfth Corps commander Slocum sent his First Division, temporarily commanded by Brigadier General Thomas Ruger, along with two brigades from Geary's Second Division, toward the Union left. Ruger's men arrived on Cemetery Ridge, but Geary's brigades accidentally marched too far south on the Baltimore Pike and out of the fight. Ruger's division helped stabilize Hancock and McGilvery's lines but played no significant combat role.[39]

37 *OR*, 27/2: 608, 614, 621, 623-624; 27/1: 422; Swinton, *Campaigns of the Army of the Potomac*, 352; Imhof, Gettysburg Day Two, 197-198, 201-203.

38 The Confederates in this action were probably from Wright's Georgia brigade or perhaps the remnants of Lang's Floridians before they retreated. Meade, *Life and Letters*, 2: 88-89; Cleaves, *Meade of Gettysburg*, 152-154. Newton replaced the KIA Major General John Reynolds as First Corps commander.

39 *OR*, 27/1: 371, 759.

In hindsight, Meade pulled more troops than necessary from Culp's Hill. The Federals repulsed Longstreet's attacks without any material help from Ruger and Geary. Only one Union brigade, under command of Brigadier General George Greene, remained on Culp's Hill. This nearly proved fatal to Meade's right flank later that evening when portions of Ewell's Confederate Second Corps finally launched an infantry assault on the position. The attack failed due in large part to Greene's defensive efforts and oncoming darkness, which slowed the movements of Ewell's subordinates. The need to reinforce the Union left nearly lost their right, and the after-effects of Sickles's move to the Peach Orchard reverberated on Culp's Hill as both sides battled for control of the strategic position well into July 3.[40]

The Army of the Potomac's superior numbers and position allowed Meade to shift reinforcements against Longstreet's increasingly disjointed attack. South of the Wheatfield Road, portions of Kershaw's Brigade had joined others to drive the Federals from the Wheatfield. The Confederates advanced toward the Plum Run valley, with the northern slope of Little Round Top in their sights. Wofford's brigade was on the left of this ragged Confederate line and his Georgians briefly captured Lieutenant Aaron Walcott's Massachusetts Light, 3d Battery (C); guns that had been earlier posted in the valley by one of Sickles's staff officers. Wofford's men had no time to use or savor their trophies. Brigadier General Samuel Crawford, commanding the Third Division of the Union Fifth Corps, along with Colonel David Nevin's Sixth Corps brigade, counterattacked and drove the Confederates back. These Union reinforcements secured Cemetery Ridge north of Little Round Top, as well as the Plum Run valley to the immediate west of that hill.[41]

After obliterating Sickles's advanced line and suffering his own heavy casualties in the process, Longstreet watched the arrival of ever-increasing Federal reinforcements. The Confederate general had no hopes of additional support. "While Meade's lines were growing my men were dropping," Longstreet complained bitterly in his memoirs, adding, "we had no others to call to their

40 *OR*, 27/1: 371, 759, 770, 778, 804; Cleaves, *Meade of Gettysburg*, 154; Ladd, *Bachelder Papers*, 2: 1135; Imhof, *Gettysburg Day Two*, 190-193, 206, 224. For a discussion on exactly how many men Meade intended to detach from Culp's Hill, see *Pfanz, Culp's Hill and Cemetery Hill*, 194-195.

41 *OR*, 27/1: 593, 654, 657, 662, 685; Meade, *Life and Letters*, 2: 87-88; *Pennsylvania at Gettysburg*, 1: 224-226; Ladd, *The Bachelder Papers*, 2: 1198; Jorgensen, *Gettysburg's Bloody Wheatfield*, 124-125, 129. In addition to Kershaw and Wofford's brigades, the Confederate offensive on this part of the field also included portions of the brigades under generals Henry Benning, G.T. Anderson, and the mortally wounded Paul Semmes.

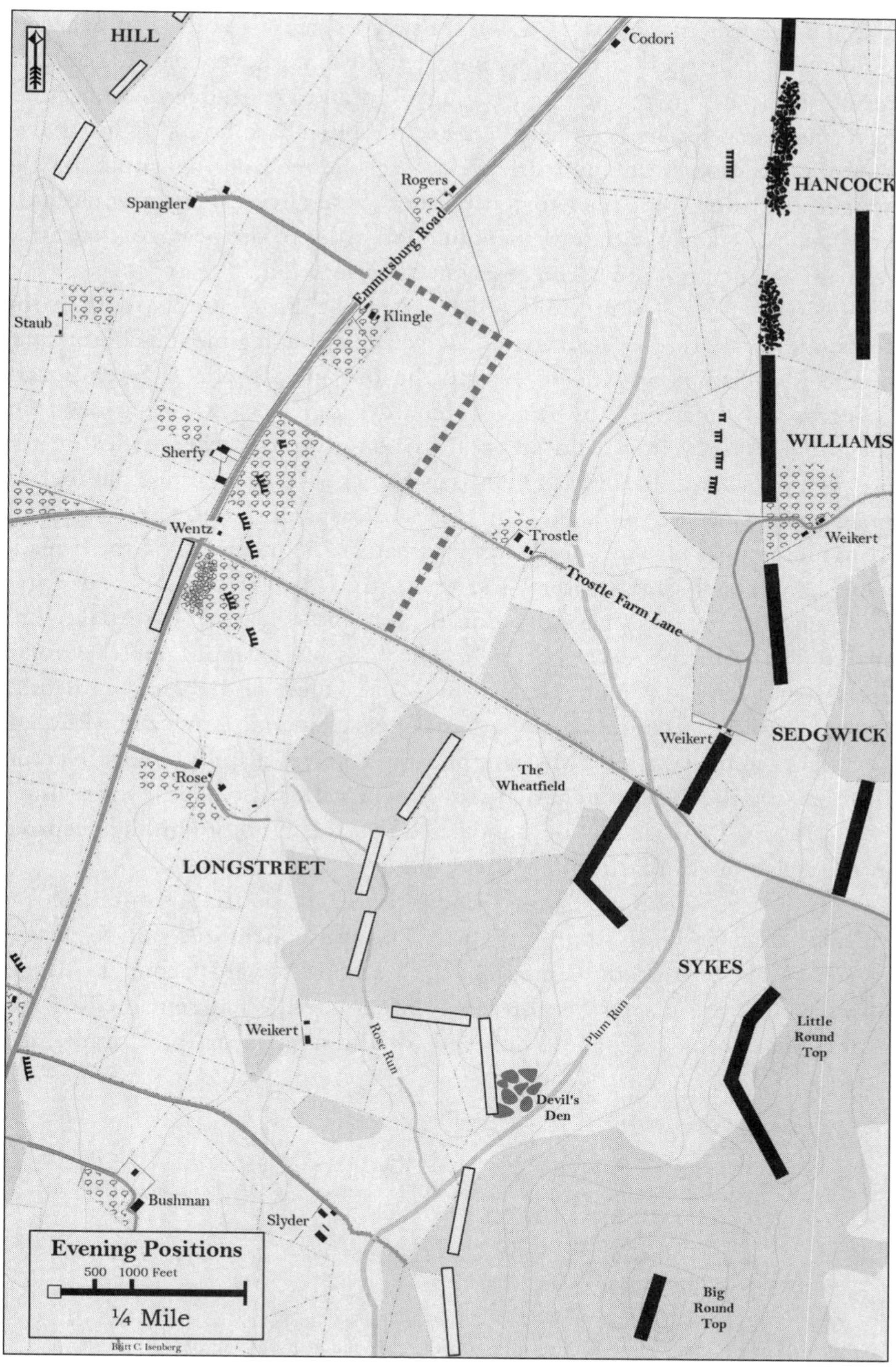
HILL
Codori
Rogers
HANCOCK
Spangler
Emmitsburg Road
Staub
Klingle
WILLIAMS
Sherfy
Wentz
Trostle
Weikert
Trostle Farm Lane
Weikert
SEDGWICK
Rose
The Wheatfield
LONGSTREET
SYKES
Weikert
Rose Run
Plum Run
Little Round Top
Devil's Den
Bushman
Slyder
Evening Positions
500 1000 Feet
¼ Mile
Big Round Top
Britt C. Isenberg

aid, and the weight against us was too heavy to carry." As the sun began to set below the western horizon, "with it went down the severe battle. I ordered recall of the troops to the line of Plum Run and Devil's Den." Longstreet never hesitated to characterize July 2 as "the best three hours' fighting ever done by any troops on any battle field." Yet, he realized the futility of the situation. "To urge my men forward under these circumstances would have been madness, and I withdrew them in good order to the peach orchard that we had taken from the Federals early in the afternoon."[42]

Colonel B. G. Humphreys fell back to the Peach Orchard with the remainder of Barksdale's survivors. He was the only regimental commander in the Mississippi brigade to escape the day unscathed. The temporary "success" of smashing the Peach Orchard came at a staggering cost. Of the roughly 1,619 men who stepped off only hours earlier, an estimated 804 (49.7%) were casualties. The Mississippians lost the largest number of men, and sustained the highest percentage casualties, among all attacking Confederate brigades on July 2. Approximately 156 members of the brigade were killed, including Colonel Carter of the 13th Mississippi. All three Mississippi regiments that moved on the left and center of Barksdale's line suffered casualties in excess of 50%. The 17th Mississippi fared the worst. They lost 57.7% of their strength, 64 were killed, and their commander Colonel Holder was among several officers wounded. Ironically, although Colonel Humphreys's 21st Mississippi often receives disproportionate credit for breaking the Peach Orchard, his regiment suffered the least with "only" 32.8% losses. The casualty totals indicated that the heaviest fighting occurred in the fields north of the Wheatfield Road.[43]

The charge of Barksdale's Brigade is often justifiably portrayed as "magnificent" in Gettysburg literature. The subsequent decision to pursue Sickles's men beyond the Emmitsburg Road and toward Cemetery Ridge, however, proved disastrous for the Confederates. What remained of the proud Mississippi brigade bivouacked for the night near the Emmitsburg Road.[44]

42 *OR*, 27/2: 358-359; Longstreet, "Lee's Right Wing at Gettysburg," *Battles and Leaders*, 3: 341; Longstreet, *From Manassas to Appomattox*, 373; Longstreet, "General Longstreet's Second Paper on Gettysburg," *SHSP*, 5: 258, 261.

43 Busey and Martin, *Regimental Strengths and Losses*, 267; Floyd, *Commanders and Casualties*, 48-49. Wright's Brigade was a close second in % loss at 49.3%.

44 As an example, Trudeau's *Gettysburg: A Testing of Courage* (368) opined, "William Barksdale was not to be denied. His men drove forward, a living definition of unstoppable. Overwhelmed

Wofford's Georgians bivouacked that night to the right of the Mississippians. Wofford's boys fared better than Barksdale's with only 22.7% casualties and an estimated 48 killed. Wofford and all his regimental commanders survived the day. Although Wofford's advance provided psychological benefits to the Confederate attack, the numbers confirmed that Barksdale had cleared most of the Peach Orchard resistance before them. It is unknown if Wofford's failure to follow Barksdale toward Cemetery Ridge impacted the day's outcome. Certainly, Wofford's losses would have been higher if he had.[45]

Since General Barksdale was missing and feared to be dead, Colonel Humphreys took command of the brigade. He learned that Captain Isaac Stamps of Company E, 21st Mississippi, was among the mortally wounded, having been shot through the bowels early in the assault. Captain Stamps was the nephew of Confederate President Jefferson Davis and was married to Humphreys's daughter Mary. During his last furlough in the spring, Stamps had confided in his wife that he would soon fall in battle. He extracted a promise that she would retrieve his body and bury it at the family home.

Humphreys did his best to comfort his suffering son-in-law, as they sprawled upon the ground near the now-wrecked Peach Orchard. They undoubtedly talked about Mary, who was in Richmond with President and Mrs. Davis awaiting news from Pennsylvania. Humphreys said his goodbyes to Isaac. The captain was then removed to Barksdale's field hospital on the John Crawford farm along Marsh Creek. He died there the next day. Varina Davis consoled Mary when they learned of Isaac's death, but the young widow kept her promise. Mary made the arduous and sad journey to Gettysburg in the late fall, located her husband's grave, and brought him home for reburial.[46]

As darkness fell on July 2, Confederate artillery on the high ground near the Peach Orchard continued to fire rounds toward Cemetery Ridge. A veteran of Parker's battery, which unlimbered nearby, vividly recalled how "the shadows of coming night are falling around us, the flames leap out from our guns in lovely contrast." A comrade shouted, "Oh! Captain, this

---

Federal units began to scramble out of their way, batteries limbering to their rear, regiments falling back in hasty disorder." Although Trudeau's assessment is justified, Gettysburg historians (other than acknowledging Barksdale's subsequent death) seldom consider the total cost of the decision to push the brigade beyond the Emmitsburg Road.

45 B.G. Humphreys Manuscript, 18; Busey and Martin, *Strengths and Losses*, 269.

46 Winschel, "To Assuage the Grief," *Gettysburg Magazine 7*, 77-82; Coco, *Confederates KIA at Gettysburg*, 84-87; B.G. Humphreys Manuscript, 18.

Dusk settles across the Peach Orchard.
Photo by Authors

is beautiful!" Nevertheless, the threat of a Federal counterattack kept many Southern men on high alert throughout the night. Major George Gerald of the 18th Mississippi bivouacked at the Peach Orchard but did not get a wink of sleep. "The moon was about full, and everything around us was nearly as bright as day, and I feared a night attack similar to the one made at Chancellorsville." During the evening, Kershaw received orders to move his South Carolinians from the vicinity of the Wheatfield to the Peach Orchard. Although Kershaw's South Carolinians suffered 30.6% casualties, their losses were less than Barksdale's and they further strengthened the Southerners' presence near the orchard.[47]

47 Wise, *The Long Arm of Lee*, 650; Figg, *Where Men Only Dare to Go*, 138-141; Gerald, "Gettysburg," *Waco Daily-Times Herald*, July 3, 1913, Brake Collection, USAHEC; *OR*, 27/2: 370, 372. Kershaw's Brigade lost only one regimental commander. Colonel William DeSaussure of the 15th South Carolina was mortally wounded. As noted, Colonel Kennedy of the 2nd South Carolina survived his wound. See Floyd, *Commanders and Casualties*, 47-48.

Despite Gerald's fears, both sides were badly disorganized and wary of undertaking any operations in the darkness beyond bringing in the wounded. Colonel E.P. Alexander recounted the grisly work in detail:

> There were many of the enemy's [wounded] within our lines beside all of our own. Most of our own dead, too, were promptly buried; but the enemy's dead were left where they lay. Then our poor horses needed to be taken off somewhere & watered & brought back & fed, the crippled ones killed, & harness taken from the dead, & fresh ones scuffled for with the quartermasters. . . . By one o'clock I had everything in shape for the morning, & nothing more to do but to try & get a little sleep myself. What with deep dust & blood, & filth of all kinds, the trampled & wrecked Peach Orchard was a very unattractive place.[48]

Some of the Confederate artillerists did, however, aid wounded Union soldiers near the Emmitsburg Road. Sergeant E. S. Duffey of Parker's battery recalled that they "gave a number of wounded Yankees water" to ease their suffering. Another battery member had a long conversation with a dying Pennsylvanian, who inquired, "Why did you all come over here?" The Southerner curtly replied, "We have come to give your people a taste of what we have had to suffer." The Yankee gave the Rebel his name and messages to forward to his loved ones. The Southerner later fulfilled his opponent's final wishes and passed on the messages.[49]

At least one other young man in blue, who was also behind Confederate lines, surely would have appreciated such a gesture. Private Thomas Murray Watson of the 105th Pennsylvania had been shot through the back and lung as the regiment was retreating from the Emmitsburg Road. The 23-year-old remained on the field until the following night, but was eventually sent to a field hospital. Watson lamented the loss of his Bible, which had been left on the field. He lingered for several weeks but succumbed to his wounds on July 29. His mother travelled to Gettysburg to tend to her son and, upon his death, transported his body home to Apollo, Pennsylvania. The grieving mother transformed his final experiences into poetry, which she published in the local newspaper. "Lying beneath a stranger's eye . . . the battlefield

48 Gallagher, *Fighting for the Confederacy*, 243-244.

49 George T. Fleming, "Diary of 'Reb' (Sergeant E. S. Duffey) Soldier of Battle of Gettysburg," *Pittsburgh Post Gazette*, July 4, 1913; Figg, *Where Men Only Dare to Go*, 140-141.

it was my bed . . . I took the Bible Father gave me, And laid it underneath my head."[50]

On the opposite side of the field, General Birney's Third Corps assembled in the fields near the Taneytown Road. The melodies of battle echoed across the night as the Confederate assaults on the Union right continued. Except for the moans of the wounded and sporadic shots across picket lines, the bloodletting had subsided on the Union left. Ammunition resupply wagons arrived, the soldiers lit campfires, and some men attempted to eat. "We were still ignorant of the day's results," recalled Colonel Regis de Trobriand, whose own brigade had escaped from the hell of farmer Rose's wheat field, "but we well knew what it had cost us. There remained only to find out how many of the missing would rejoin us during the night." Birney was uncertain at that moment of the battle's outcome, the fate of the army, and the future of his country. He surveyed the small number of men who surrounded him and confessed, "I wish I were already dead."[51]

The individual Third Corps regiments attempted to regroup along Cemetery Ridge into some semblance of order. While nearly three quarters of the 141st Pennsylvania were dead, wounded, or unaccounted for that evening, casualties among the regiment's companies B, G, and K were particularly catastrophic. These companies had been on the left "in closest contact with the enemy while retiring from the Peach Orchard." Private Joel Molyneux served as the orderly to Captain James Darling, the acting assistant adjutant general to Graham, and was with the brigade staff during the fighting. When he finally returned to his comrades of the 141st, Molyneux inquired about his own Company K. Private Charles Webster, who was resting nearby, "raised upon his elbow and said, 'Here is Company K.'" Webster was the only member of the company accounted for that night.[52]

The historian of the 12th New Hampshire, in Carr's Brigade, said there were so many men missing from the ranks that when Humphreys's division finally reformed, "it looked like a line of color guards, so thick were the battle-flags

50 Hadden Family Collection, Thomas Murray Watson Papers; Busey, *Union Casualties at Gettysburg*, 2, 902.

51 Craft, *History of the 141st Pennsylvania*, 124-125; De Trobriand, *Four Years with the Army of the Potomac*, 505-506. According to de Trobriand, General Birney's gloom lifted when his brother Fitz-Hugh Birney arrived with news of Hancock and Crawford's success in stopping the Confederate assaults.

52 "Three Companies Annihilated," *The Bradford Star*, April 14, 1898; Craft, *History of the One Hundred Forty-First Regiment*, 128.

in proportion to the number of men." The moonlit scenes were ineffaceable as some Federals picked their way through the wreckage searching for lost comrades. A member of the 120th New York recalled, "The low moans of the wounded, as they broke upon the chilly air, guided us in our search." The party located Lieutenant William Cockburn of the 120th's Company H, and the rescuer never forgot "his calm demeanor as he lay upon the damp earth, patiently waiting his turn to be cared for. While his young life was ebbing away, he was as composed as he could have been sitting by his mother's fireside." Cockburn's comrades took the 28-year-old lieutenant to the rear where he received medical attention, but died on July 22 at a hospital in Harrisburg, Pennsylvania.[53]

Similar search and recovery efforts occurred throughout the evening. One Pennsylvanian bemoaned to the mother of a missing friend that they "hunted the battlefield all over and we could not hear nor find anything of him." A member of the 114th Pennsylvania recalled, "the 2d of July was a day of horror. To and from our hospital the ambulances heaped with the wounded were running all day; some of the men were dead when delivered to the surgeons, and others were more dead than alive."[54]

Captain William Henry Chester of Humphreys's staff had been shot through the back while trying to rally the Union line just before sunset. The bullet entered near his spine before exiting his abdomen, and he lay upon the field barely clinging to life as darkness descended. A small search party located him late that night near a large boulder. "His horse and orderly both lay dead beside him, and across his legs lay a Confederate soldier, whom he had killed with his revolver whilst in the act of plundering him of his watch." Chester was "tenderly conveyed to the hospital on Rock Creek," but died on July 5. His epitaph in the newspapers stated succinctly, "He died as he lived, a faithful defender of the Flag of the Union. Peace be to his ashes."[55]

53 Bartlett, *History of the Twelfth Regiment New Hampshire Volunteers*, 129; Gates, *The Ulster Guard*, 460.

54 Joseph B. Brown to Matilda Crandall, July 29, 1863, Crandall Family Papers, USAHEC; Rauscher, *Music on the March*, 94. Captain James Bates, the Chief Ambulance Officer for the Fifth Corps, reported that his team of 81 ambulances recovered 1,300 wounded "from 4 p. m. July 2 to 4 a. m. July 3." Although Bates is the only corps ambulance chief to file a report, it seems likely that similar efforts were made by Hancock's Second and Sickles's Third Corps ambulances on the south end of the battlefield. See *OR*, 27/1: 597.

55 "Obituary: The Death of Captain Wm. H. Chester," *New York Herald*, July 18, 1863; also in the *Flushing Journal*; Busey, *These Honored Dead*, 125; Luther W. Minnigh, *Gettysburg What They Did Here*, 128.

Site of the field hospital where Barksdale was treated at the Hummelbaugh house. Barksdale was initially buried in the yard before being disinterred and taken back to Mississippi.
Photo by Authors

General Graham was not with his men; he remained a prisoner of the Confederates. Major John Fairfax of Longstreet's staff had the troublesome assignment of leading Yankee prisoners behind the Confederate lines. Fairfax had perhaps as many as 1,000 prisoners under his immediate care. By evening, he was reportedly in "bad humor." According to Confederate artillerist William Owen, Graham requested the name of the general who led the charge against his brigade. Upon learning that it was Longstreet (the praise was curiously not directed at Barksdale), Graham responded, "Our generals do not do that sort of thing."[56]

56 Owen, *In Camp and Battle with the Washington Artillery*, 246; Fremantle, *Three Months in the Southern States*, 261; Charles Graham account, February 16, 1865, Gettysburg Participants Accounts File 5, GNMP. Among the Federal infantry, estimated missing /captured in Graham's brigade alone was 165. Among other nearby regiments, the 3rd Maine's estimate was 45, the 3rd Michigan was seven, and the 2nd New Hampshire was 36. See Busey and Martin, *Regimental Strengths and Losses*, 131-133.

A Confederate soldier named Fisher had personal custody of Graham. Fisher's assignment was to deliver the general to Longstreet. Graham had a tickler of good brandy and Fisher, coincidentally, happened to love brandy. "Graham's hospitality unbalanced Fisher," according to Colonel Humphreys, "and when they reached Longstreet, Fisher was too drunk for explanation and Graham had to introduce himself." Graham was also in a debilitated state from his own wounds and the brandy certainly did not help. This likely contributed to otherwise improbable innuendo that Graham had been drunk throughout the day.[57]

Charles Graham had followed Sickles from their pre-war days together in New York City to Gettysburg's Peach Orchard. He faced the sobering reality of life as a prisoner of war. In addition, he faced the inglorious distinction of being the highest-ranking Union officer to remain captured at the battle of Gettysburg.[58]

Sometime late that night, Northern soldiers found General Barksdale suffering on the field. They brought him to a Union field hospital at the Jacob Hummelbaugh farm along the Taneytown Road. The Hummelbaugh family had earlier abandoned their home in haste, even leaving a partially eaten meal on the table. The Hummelbaughs' small farmhouse was already filled to capacity with wounded, so Barksdale was placed on blankets in the yard.[59]

57 B.G. Humphreys Manuscript, 14. Arthur Fremantle wrote, in an apparent reference to Graham, that among the Yankee prisoners was "a general, whom I heard one of his men accusing of having been 'so G-d d----d drunk that he had turned his guns upon his own men.'" Fremantle acknowledged however that the source of the story was "not worthy of much credit." See Fremantle, *Three Months in the Southern States*, 261-262. *Soldiers' and Sailors' Half-Dime Tales* (118) recounted, "Graham was dragged into the rebel lines, staggering, as might be supposed, from his weakness, which led to the almost brutal judgment of the English rebel sympathizer and eye-witness, Colonel _______ , 'That the loyal officer in command, who was captured on the 2d P.M. was apparently drunk.'"

58 Union Brigadier General Francis Barlow was wounded on July 1 and captured but recovered by the Federal forces after the Confederates withdrew from Gettysburg.

59 Winschel, "Their Supreme Moment," *Gettysburg Magazine 1*, 77; Muffly, *The Story of our Regiment*, 172. The identity of the soldiers who found Barksdale on the field is open for debate. David Parker of the 14th Vermont claimed that after dark the regiment's colonel asked for volunteers to locate and recover Barksdale. Four Union soldiers searched the field until about 11:00 p.m. when a wounded "young lad" who was lying nearby directed the rescuers to Barksdale. The general was "bleeding inwardly and suffering very much." Parker placed Barksdale's head in his lap and attempted to spoon feed him coffee. The 240-pound Confederate told his captors that they would need a stretcher and more men to carry him back to the lines, so Parker remained with Barksdale while the others went for assistance. Barksdale bragged that he had continued to lead his men despite three wounds, and had parting words for his wife and sons, "tell them all that I died like a brave man. That I led my men fearlessly in the fight." See Winschel, "Their Supreme Moment," *Gettysburg Magazine 1*,

Alfred Hamilton, the assistant surgeon of the 148th Pennsylvania, examined Barksdale and recorded his impressions of the wounds and of the warrior:

> I attended General Barksdale of Mississippi. He was shot through the left breast from behind, and the left leg was broken by two missiles. He was brought by some staff orderly to my temporary hospital. I gave him what I had to relieve him. He asked several times whether I considered his wound necessarily mortal. I told him I did. He desired peace, but only upon terms that would recognize the Confederacy. He was large, corpulent, refined in appearance, bald, and his general physical and mental makeup indicated firmness, endurance, vigor, quick perception and ability to succeed whether as politician, civilian, or warrior . . . He asked about our strength and was answered that heavy re-enforcements were coming. . . . He said that Lee would show us a trick before morning; that before we knew it Ewell would be thundering in our rear.[60]

Barksdale did not live to see any more "tricks" from Lee. He died during the early morning hours of July 3. Lieutenant Colonel Charles Morgan, of General Hancock's staff, wrote, "I was told at the time that he said, probably in the delirium attending his last moments, 'Tell my wife I fought like hell.'" George G. Benedict of the 12th Vermont saw the body that morning and recognized Barksdale from his days in Congress. Benedict noted a hole in the general's chest and that both legs were bandaged and bloody. "He had fought without the wig which Speaker Grow once knocked off in the Hall of Representatives, and his bald head and broad face, with open unblinking eyes, lay uncovered in the sunshine. There he lay alone, without a comrade to brush the flies from his corpse." William Barksdale was buried under a tree in the yard, until friends recovered his body and returned him to his beloved Mississippi in early 1867.[61]

76-77. John Bachelder credited Barksdale's rescue to James Hooper of the 1st Massachusetts and a "Birch Herkizemer" of the 26th Pennsylvania. According to Bachelder, Barksdale was "very abusive to the men who carried him." See Ladd, *Bachelder Papers*, 3: 1976.

60 Muffly, *The Story of our Regiment*, 173.

61 Ladd, *Bachelder Papers*, 3: 1357, 1977; Benedict, *Army Life in Virginia*, 170; The *Adams Sentinel* of January 15, 1867, reported the body was en route home and had passed through Lynchburg, VA, on January 5. Courtesy of GNMP.

Chapter 9

The Ground Secured by Longstreet

The battle for the Peach Orchard was over, but Joseph Sherfy's property still had a significant role to play as Robert E. Lee planned his operations for July 3. If July 2 proved that Sickles and his Third Corps were unable to defend the Emmitsburg Road line, then the question of the third day was whether Lee and Longstreet could capitalize on it. In fact, the disastrous July 3 assault known as "Pickett's Charge" occurred partially because of the prior day's results in the Peach Orchard.

"In front of General Longstreet the enemy held a position from which," Lee asserted in his July 31 report, "if he could be driven, it was thought our artillery could be used to advantage in assailing the more elevated ground beyond, and thus enable us to reach the crest of the ridge." In assessing the results of the second day, Lee added, "After a severe struggle, Longstreet succeeded in getting possession of and holding the desired ground. Ewell also carried some of the strong positions which he assailed [lower Culp's Hill], and the result was such as to lead to the belief that he would ultimately be able to dislodge the enemy. . . . These partial successes determined me to continue the assault next day."[1]

There is no doubt that Sickles's advance to the Peach Orchard and Emmitsburg Road influenced combat along the road on July 2, as well as in connected areas such as the Wheatfield and Devil's Den. Lee and Sickles both desired the orchard's elevation as an artillery platform. Longstreet

1 *OR*, 27/2: 308.

may not have agreed, but he committed his corps and fought tenaciously to gain the position. Meade did not want to occupy the ground either, but he scrambled to mount a defense that closed the gaps Sickles's advance had created. This included shifting Union troops from lower Culp's Hill.

While some may argue that Lee's declaration of "partial successes" indicated an attempt to put the best face possible on a July 2 defeat, the subsequent events of July 3 demonstrated clearly that Lee felt confident enough to continue the battle. Whether or not his assessment was accurate, the ground gained in and around the Peach Orchard was a lynchpin of Lee's July 3 plans. General Lee elaborated in his January 1864 report:

> The result of this [second] day's operations induced the belief that, with proper concert of action, and with the increased support that the positions gained on the [Confederate] right would enable the artillery to render the assaulting columns, we should ultimately succeed, and it was accordingly determined to continue the attack. The general plan was unchanged. Longstreet, re-enforced by Pickett's three brigades, which arrived near the battle-field during the afternoon of the 2d, was ordered to attack the next morning, and General Ewell was directed to assail the enemy's right at the same time.[2]

Unlike Meade, who met with all his key subordinates on the evening of July 2, Lee did not summon his corps commanders together that night. This proved unfortunate, given the lack of coordination that plagued the Confederate efforts on the second day of battle. Longstreet sent a dispatch via courier to army headquarters, more than two miles away, but declared later that Lee "did not give or send me orders for the morning of the third day." Thus, Longstreet maintained, "in the absence of orders, I had scouting parties out during the night in search of a way by which we might strike the enemy's left, and push it down towards his centre."[3]

Colonel E.P. Alexander made his way to Longstreet's bivouac during the night. Alexander received instructions "that we would renew the attack early in the morning. That Pickett's division would arrive and would assault the enemy's line. My impression is the exact point for it was not designated, but I was told it would be to our left of the Peach Orchard." Longstreet directed Alexander to select a position for the Washington Artillery, the distinguished Louisiana battalion that he expected to arrive at dawn. On the other end of

2 Ibid., 27/2: 320.

3 Longstreet, *From Manassas to Appomattox*, 385.

the field, General Richard Ewell reported, "I was ordered to renew my attack at daylight Friday morning."[4]

Chief of Confederate artillery William N. Pendleton remained in communication with General Lee. Regarding the second day's results, Pendleton reported, "On the left and in the center, nothing gained; on the right, batteries and lines well advanced." Lee and Pendleton expected these advanced batteries to play a crucial role in the renewed attack. "By the direction of the commanding general," Pendleton added, "the artillery along our entire line was to be prepared for opening, as early as possible on the morning of the 3d, a concentrated and destructive fire, consequent upon which a general advance was to be made." In reference to the guns that Alexander commanded near the Peach Orchard, "the right, especially, was, if practicable, to sweep the enemy from his stronghold on that flank."[5]

Alexander began aligning his batteries at about 3:00 a.m., and Major Eshleman's Washington Artillery soon joined him. At daylight, Alexander discovered to his chagrin that Federal artillery on Cemetery Hill could enfilade about 20 of his guns. "It scared me awfully," he recalled, "for did they discover the chance I had given to them to enfilade us, they would surely rake us awfully before we could get out." Alexander corrected his mistake before the enemy seized on the opportunity, although the Yankee artillery took occasional "pot-shots" at his batteries. The Confederates generally resisted returning their fire in order to conserve ammunition, even though Union shelling struck down a number of their artillerymen and horses. Alexander was grateful that the sporadic fire did not escalate because his advanced Emmitsburg Road position lacked available cover to shield his men and materiel. It became apparent to Major Eshleman that in order to protect his guns against an enfilade fire, "the left of my line had better be thrown a little to the rear." Thus, as the Confederate batteries extended from south to north, the left of the Emmitsburg Road artillery line bent back toward Seminary Ridge. The defects of the Emmitsburg Road as an artillery platform became increasingly apparent with the light of day.[6]

4 Gallagher, *Fighting for the Confederacy*, 244; *OR*, 27/2: 447. Also see Alexander, "The Great Charge and Artillery Fighting at Gettysburg," *Battles and Leaders*, 3: 360-361.

5 *OR*, 27/2: 351-352.

6 Alexander, "Artillery Fighting at Gettysburg," *Battles and Leaders*, 3: 361; Gallagher, *Fighting for the Confederacy*, 244-245; *OR*, 27/2: 434. None of this seemed to concern General Pendleton, who paid a visit to the Peach Orchard, "I found much (by Colonel Alexander's energy) already accomplished on the right." *OR*, 27/2: 352.

Hindsight often influenced Colonel Alexander's post-war reminiscences, but his assessments remained accurate in many cases. "All the vicinity of the Peach Orchard, anyhow, was very unfavorable ground for us, generally sloping toward the enemy," he recalled. The open ridgeline, "exposed all our movements" to the enemy's view and artillery fire. Perhaps it was the darkness, on the evening of July 2, that prevented the Confederates from grasping the weakness of the terrain they occupied, but this became evident on the morning of July 3. While the Confederates had succeeded in moving closer to their foe, the gains of July 2 did not necessarily translate to a strategic or tactical advantage.[7]

Meanwhile, Longstreet reported that during the morning, "arrangements were made for renewing the attack by my right, with a view to pass around the hill occupied by the enemy on his left, and to gain it by flank and reverse attack." Shortly after Longstreet issued orders to execute this movement, Lee arrived with a change of plans. Longstreet's preparations became meaningless due to developments elsewhere on the battlefield.[8]

In the early morning hours of July 3, the Army of the Potomac's Twelfth Corps stole the initiative from the Confederates. Around 4:30 a.m., before Longstreet was ready to move, the Federals opened fire on Ewell's troops at Culp's Hill. Lee realized that uncoordinated efforts had failed on July 2, and accordingly, he called a halt to Longstreet's operations. The two generals instead searched for a viable alternative.[9]

After examining the enemy's position on Cemetery Ridge, Lee decided to attack Meade's left center. Lee selected infantry from Major General George Pickett's Division, of Longstreet's First Corps, and parts of two divisions under Brigadier General Johnston Pettigrew and Major General Isaac Trimble from A.P. Hill's Third Corps. General Wilcox and Colonel Lang's battered brigades were assigned to protect Pickett's right flank. The total number of Confederate soldiers engaged in the assault approximated 12,500 infantrymen.

7 Gallagher, *Fighting for the Confederacy*, 244-245.

8 *OR*, 27/2: 359.

9 Lee implied in his own report that Longstreet bore some responsibility for this. "General Longstreet's dispositions were not completed as early as was expected, but before notice could be sent to General Ewell, General Johnson had already become engaged, and it was too late to recall him." See *OR*, 27/2: 320. In his memoirs, Longstreet argued that since he had received no orders, Lee's proclamation that he was not ready "as early as was expected" was "disingenuous." See Longstreet, *From Manassas to Appomattox*, 385-386.

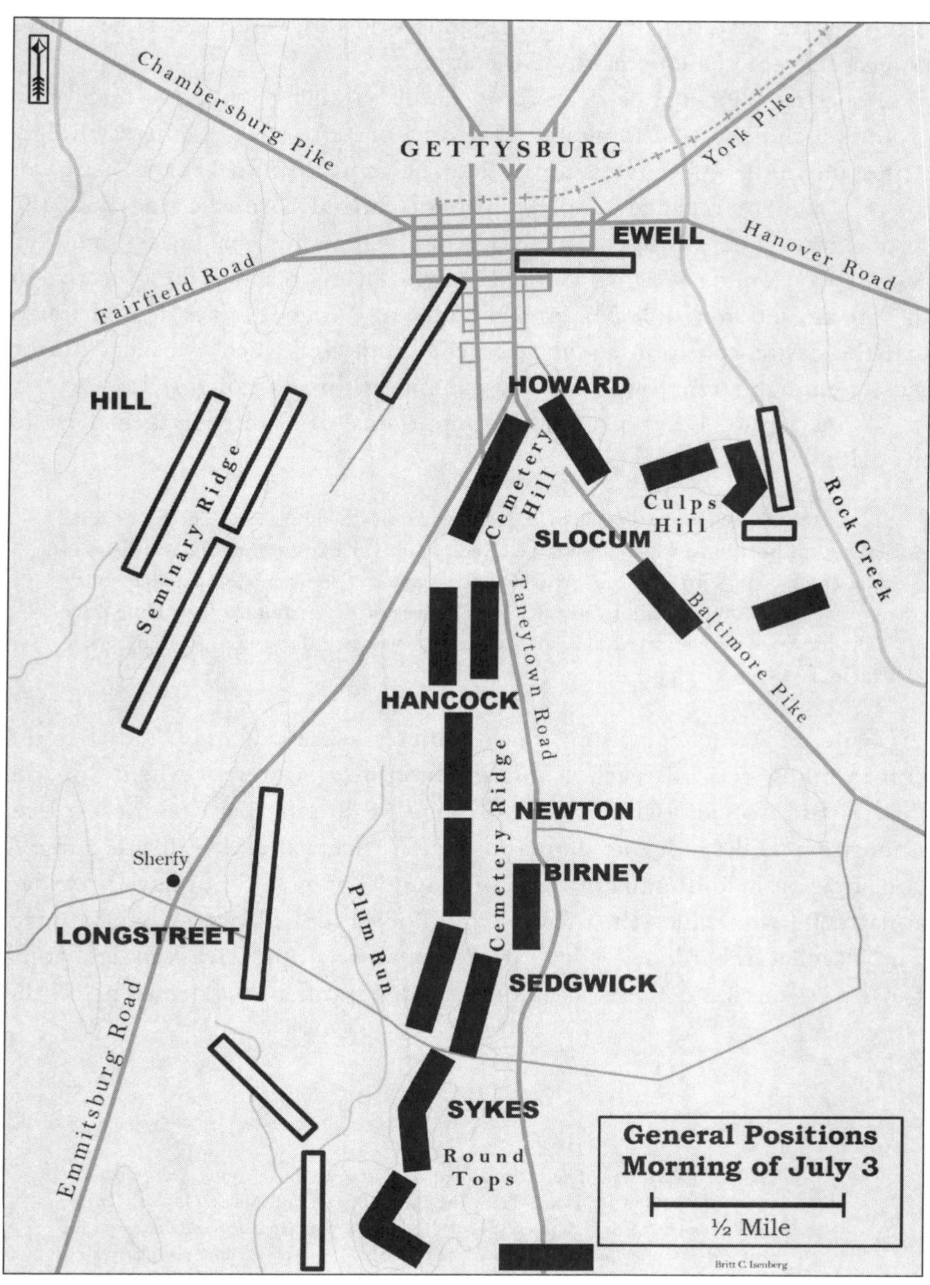

Chambersburg Pike
GETTYSBURG
York Pike
EWELL
Hanover Road
Fairfield Road
HOWARD
HILL
Seminary Ridge
Cemetery Hill
Culps Hill
SLOCUM
Rock Creek
Taneytown Road
Baltimore Pike
HANCOCK
Cemetery Ridge
NEWTON
Sherfy
BIRNEY
Plum Run
LONGSTREET
SEDGWICK
Emmitsburg Road
SYKES
Round Tops
General Positions
Morning of July 3
½ Mile
Britt C. Isenberg

Although the majority of the participating brigades were from Hill's corps, Longstreet received command of the attack.[10]

Longstreet's infantry needed to cross nearly one mile of open and undulating ground, including the Emmitsburg Road, in order to strike Cemetery Ridge. Although the Confederates controlled the road near the Peach Orchard, the thoroughfare remained under control of Federal skirmishers north of the Codori farm. Lee was likely encouraged in his decision-making by the brief success of General Wright's Georgians, who nearly reached the objective in the late afternoon of July 2 before withdrawing. Wright's attack demonstrated that the desired position could be reached, but could Lee's weakened army muster enough strength to hold and exploit any breakthroughs?[11]

In his report, Lee explained the importance of Confederate artillery to his plan:

> A careful examination was made of the ground secured by Longstreet, and his batteries placed in positions, which, it was believed, would enable them to silence those of the enemy. Hill's artillery and part of Ewell's was ordered to open simultaneously, and the assaulting column to advance under cover of the combined fire of the three. The batteries were directed to be pushed forward as the infantry progressed, protect their flanks, and support their attacks closely.[12]

Colonel Armistead Long, Lee's military secretary, indicated that the commanding general reached this decision at a conference held "on the field in front of and within cannon-range of Round Top." Generals Lee, Longstreet, Hill, Heth, and numerous staff officers attended this meeting. A consultation held literally in front of Round Top would not have provided a platform from which the officers could observe their proposed objective. The Peach Orchard, however, offered a more impressive vantage point for the assembled officers. One of the most momentous decisions of the

10 *OR*, 27/2: 320, 359, 632. The divisions led by Pettigrew and Trimble were normally commanded by Major General Henry Heth (wounded July 1) and Major General Dorsey Pender (mortally wounded on July 2) respectively. The proper name for the charge is the "Pickett-Pettigrew-Trimble Charge," but "Pickett's Charge" is generally more popularly used.

11 *OR*, 27/2: 624. Historians have debated how and when Lee learned of Wright's perceived success, but it is logical to assume Lee was aware of it. See Cooksey, "The Plan for Pickett's Charge," *Gettysburg Magazine 22*, 69-70 for a discussion.

12 *OR*, 27/2: 320.

battle, to proceed with Pickett's Charge, was likely made near the Peach Orchard.[13]

Longstreet expressed his reservations about the proposal. His right flank, held by what remained of Hood and McLaws's divisions, remained vulnerable. These troops were subsequently removed from participation in the main attack. Despite Longstreet's misgivings, Lee considered success attainable in large part because of the captured ground along the Emmitsburg Road ridge. Lee ordered his "Old War Horse" to begin preparations for the assault.[14]

At 6:00 am, British military observer Arthur Fremantle and Lieutenant Colonel Peyton Manning of Longstreet's staff rode over the ground that the Confederates captured the previous evening. "The dead were being buried," Fremantle recalled, "but great numbers were still lying about; also many mortally wounded, for whom nothing could be done." The casualties of the 114th Pennsylvania were notably visible. "Amongst the latter were a number of Yankees dressed in bad imitations of the Zouave costume. They opened their glazed eyes as I rode past in a painfully imploring manner."[15]

The two men met up with Lee and Longstreet's staff near the Peach Orchard as "they were reconnoitering and making preparations for renewing the attack. As we formed a pretty large party, we often drew upon ourselves the attention of the hostile sharpshooters, and were two or three times favored with a shell." Unfortunately, one of the Union Army's shells struck the Sherfy barn and set it on fire. "The building was filled with wounded," Fremantle wrote, "principally Yankees, who, I am afraid, must have perished miserably in the flames."[16]

13 Long, *Memoirs of Robert E. Lee*, 287-288; Fremantle, *Three Months in the Southern States*, 262; Owen, *In Camp and Battle with the Washington Artillery*, 247. It is outside the scope of this work to provide all the details involved in planning Lee's July 3 assault. For additional details, see Hessler, Motts & Stanley, *Pickett's Charge at Gettysburg*, 2-12.

14 Longstreet, "General James Longstreet's Account of the Campaign and Battle," *SHSP*, 5: 68; *From Manassas to Appomattox*, 387; Long, *Memoirs of R.E. Lee*, 288. Lee acknowledged, "General Longstreet was delayed by a force occupying the high, rocky hills on the enemy's extreme left, from which his troops could be attacked in reverse as they advanced. His operations had been embarrassed the day previous by the same cause, and he now deemed it necessary to defend his flank and rear with the divisions of Hood and McLaws. He was, therefore, re-enforced by Heth's division and two brigades of Pender's, to the command of which Major-General Trimble was assigned." *OR*, 27/2: 320.

15 Fremantle, *Three Months in the Southern States*, 262. The 114th suffered 155 casualties (9 killed, 86 wounded, and 60 missing / captured) out of 259 engaged for a rate of 59.8%. Floyd, *Commanders and Casualties*, 18.

16 Fremantle, *Three Months in the Southern States*, 262.

Confederate artilleryman Andrew Barker shouted, "The wounded! The wounded!" Barker was aware that a number of Northerners were among the barn's occupants. Captain William Parker ordered his battery to cease firing, but by the time they "went to rescue of these unfortunates . . . some of them burnt to death." The 114th Pennsylvania's gaudy Zouave uniforms were later identified among the charred remains in the Sherfys' barn.[17]

Lee spent a fair amount of time in the Sherfys' neighborhood. "Early in the morning General Lee came around," Alexander recalled, "and I was then told that we were to assault Cemetery Hill, which lay rather to our left." Lee approached Major Gerald of the 18th Mississippi and asked the major to identify the troops that were nearby. "It is what is left of Barksdale's brigade," Gerald replied, and he informed Lee of Barksdale's presumed death. Lee was likely assessing his available strength on this part of the field. He could not have been pleased by the results.[18]

General McLaws seemed to be excluded from the morning's planning sessions and occupied himself by examining what remained of his division. After the war he recalled, "I was not notified that it was in contemplation even to make any further attack by either Hood's or my division, nor was I informed that it was the intention to assault the enemy's centre with Pickett's division, with the assistance of troops from other corps." Clearly, with all that was going on around him, McLaws felt slighted, "I was not told to be ready to assist, should the assault be successful, nor instructed what to do should the assault fail and the enemy advance."[19]

17 Figg, *Where Men Only Dare to Go*, 142-143; Select Committee Relative to the Soldiers' National Cemetery, *Report of the Select Committee*, 32. Frank Rauscher of the 114th Pennsylvania also commented on the use of the Sherfy barn as a place of refuge by his comrades, see Rauscher, *Music on the March*, 92. According to the report of the "Select Committee" for Gettysburg's Soldiers' National Cemetery, graves 12-14 in Row F hold the "burned" remains of three of these Zouaves. There are four more buried on either side, but without that descriptive annotation in the report. Interestingly, historian John Bachelder met a Confederate officer (whom he did not identify) after the war, "who assured him that he was personally in the barn immediately before it was burned and that such was not the case." Bachelder, *Gettysburg: What to See, and How to See It*, 81. See also: Cole and Frampton, *Lincoln and the Human Interest Stories of the Gettysburg National Cemetery*, 52.

18 Alexander, "Artillery Fighting at Gettysburg," *Battles and Leaders*, 3: 360-362; Alexander, *Military Memoirs*, 420; Gerald, "The Battle of Gettysburg," *Waco Daily Times-Herald*, July 3, 1913, Box 7, Brake Collection, USAHEC. It was shortly after Pendleton's departure that Alexander "conversed with both Gen. Lee & Longstreet, & most of their staff officers, & got more exact ideas of where Pickett was to direct his march." Gallagher, *Fighting for the Confederacy*, 253.

19 McLaws, "Gettysburg," *SHSP*, 7: 79.

At daylight, McLaws ordered Colonel Humphreys to deploy Barksdale's men as skirmishers and "to drive the Yankee pickets until they would go no further, and then hold them there." McLaws also cautioned the colonel to seek cover where available "as he expected to open all his artillery over our heads and would doubtless be responded to by the enemy's batteries." The Federal skirmishers yielded when pressed and fell back to within a short distance of Cemetery Ridge. "Thus Barksdale's brigade spent the day with only desultory skirmishing," Humphreys later wrote, "exposed to the heat of the July sun, the dangers of premature explosions and sharpshooters, and in the midst of wounded and dying Federals [who had fallen the day before] . . . From this line I could see the hurried preparations going on in our line on the ridge to our rear, and in the Federal lines on the mountains in front. I waited in painful suspense for the terrible conflict."[20]

By 10:00 a.m., Pickett's divisional artillery under Major James Dearing was also on the field and under Alexander's supervision. The colonel described "what was virtually one battery, so disposed as to fire on Cemetery Hill and the batteries south of it," aligned along a roughly 1,500-yard front. There were probably as many as 73 cannons deployed under Alexander during the afternoon of July 3. Nine guns under captains Alexander Latham and Hugh Garden were located south of the Wheatfield Road around the Peach Orchard. Four more batteries of 16 guns extended north of the Wheatfield Road and passed the Sherfy buildings to Trostle's farm lane. Eight additional batteries of 24 pieces continued the line along the Emmitsburg Road to the Rogers farm. This last group included Taylor's battery and Sergeant Henry Wentz. Also engaged was Captain Robert Stribling's Fauquier Artillery, which included Private Frank Hoffman, another local boy, in the ranks. After that, the remaining 24 guns in Alexander's line angled away from the road toward the northeast corner of Spangler's woods.[21]

"There was one single advantage conferred by our exterior lines," wrote Alexander, "and but one, in exchange for many disadvantages. They gave us

20 Humphreys, "Benj. Grubb Humphreys Manuscript," Mississippi Department of Archives and History, 21-22; Gerald, "The Battle of Gettysburg," *Waco Daily Times-Herald*, July 3, 1913, Box 7, Brake Collection, USAHEC; McNeily, "Barksdale's Brigade at Gettysburg," 252.

21 Alexander, "Artillery Fighting at Gettysburg," *Battles and Leaders*, 3: 360-362; Alexander, *Military Memoirs*, 420. See Hessler, Motts & Stanley, *Pickett's Charge at Gettysburg*, 63-66 for overall Confederate battery positions. Our principal source for battery placements was John Bachelder's July 3 "Troop Position Map," with adjustments made in the "Engaged Confederate Artillery" appendix (278-280.) For Frank Hoffman's story see Hessler, Motts & Stanley, *Pickett's Charge at Gettysburg*, 61-62 and McMillan, *Gettysburg Rebels*, 179-182.

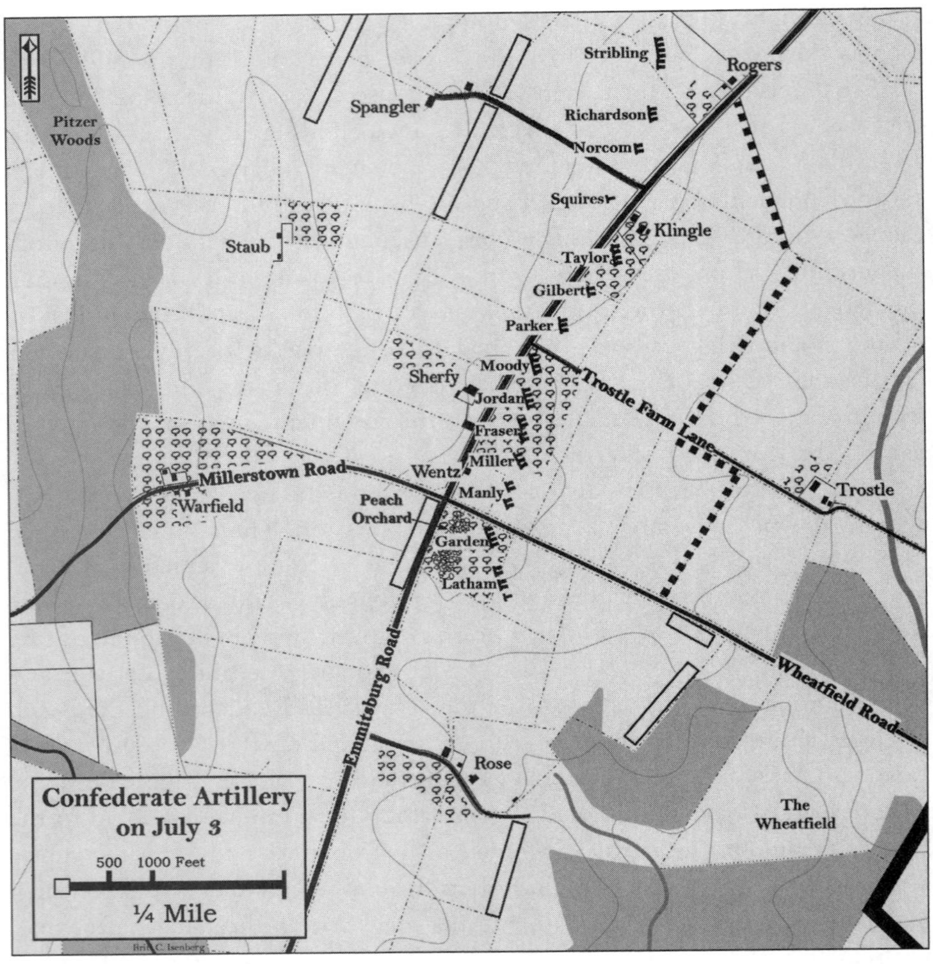

the opportunity to select positions for our guns which could enfilade the opposing lines of the enemy." The Confederates also needed to complement the Emmitsburg Road batteries with converging fire from Hill's Third Corps batteries to the west of Cemetery Ridge, and from Ewell's Second Corps guns to the north and northeast.[22]

The silencing of the Federal artillery would determine whether Longstreet's attacking infantry reached the Emmitsburg Road in formation. The artillery's

22 Alexander, *Military Memoirs*, 417. The combined Confederate artillery engaged on July 3 likely totaled nearly 160 pieces. See Hessler, Motts & Stanley, *Pickett's Charge at Gettysburg*, 66, 278-280.

Looking north toward Cemetery Hill from the edge of the Peach Orchard. Confederate artillery had the ability to enfilade the key to the Union position on July 3.
Photo by Authors

success was what Lee needed and hoped for when planning the assault. The ground gained along the Emmitsburg Road on July 2 seemingly made Confederate victory more likely on July 3. Longstreet remained skeptical but knew that he did not have the discretion to call off the attack.

"It had been arranged that when the infantry column was ready," asserted Alexander, "General Longstreet should order two guns fired by the Washington Artillery. On that signal all our guns were to open on Cemetery Hill and the ridge extending toward Round Top, which was covered with batteries. I was to observe the fire and give Pickett the order to charge." Longstreet addressed the order to Colonel Walton: "Let the batteries open. Order great care and precision in firing. When the batteries at the Peach Orchard cannot be used against the point we intend to attack, let them open on the enemy's on the rocky hill." It was after 1:00 p.m. when the message to open fire passed to Captain Merritt Miller's Louisiana Battery, posted perhaps 100 yards north of the Peach Orchard.[23]

23 Alexander, "Artillery Fighting at Gettysburg," *Battles and Leaders*, 3: 362; Longstreet, *From Manassas to Appomattox*, 390. From his home on West Middle Street in the town of Gettysburg, Professor Michael Jacobs of Pennsylvania College recorded the opening salvos

There was a flash, a puff of smoke, and a subsequent roar from the Washington Artillery. "Two guns in quick succession were fired from Captain Miller's battery," Major Eshleman later reported, "and were immediately followed by all the battalions along the line opening simultaneously upon the enemy behind his works." The second gun's friction primer failed to ignite, but nevertheless a cloud of smoke quickly enveloped the Sherfy farm. The Union guns on Cemetery Hill and Cemetery Ridge responded vigorously, and a terrific artillery duel soon ensued.[24]

Confederate Colonel Henry Cabell remembered the spectacle, "the like of which was never equaled, which cannot be described in words, and can only be appreciated by those who witnessed it." As Cabell rode up and down his battalion's line, he observed, "There were two loud explosions for every gun fired, one when emerging from the gun and the other when the shell exploded. The sky seemed full of missiles and the continuous explosions made music of its own exceeding in sublimity and loudness the lightning and thunder bolts of Heaven."[25]

Cabell assumed that the Rebel artillery must have been "far more effective" than that of their opponents, who were "doubled up and back on themselves by the two days previous fights." His assessment proved wrong. Although the Peach Orchard and Emmitsburg Road were indeed elevated over portions of Cemetery Ridge, Federal artillery held even higher ground at Cemetery Hill and Little Round Top. Confederate dominance of those points was impossible. Worse still for Longstreet, the advanced position of the Confederate guns near the Emmitsburg Road forced most of his infantry to lie in wait behind the artillery. Overshoots from Yankee artillery frequently landed among the massed ranks of Longstreet's foot-soldiers. This created an undetermined

---

of Alexander's guns. "At seven minutes past 1 P. M., the awful and portentous silence was broken." See Jacobs, *The Rebel Invasion of Maryland & Pennsylvania & Battle of Gettysburg*, 41. William Miller Owen thought it was 1:30 p.m. when the order to commence arrived. Quoted in Alexander, "Artillery Fighting at Gettysburg," *Battles and Leaders*, 3: 362.

24 *OR*, 27/2: 434-435; Wise, *The Long Arm of Lee*, 677; Alexander, "Artillery Fighting at Gettysburg," *Battles and Leaders*, 3: 362. The marker for Miller's battery at Gettysburg National Military Park states that the battery was in position 100 yards north of the Peach Orchard. A note in the William Storrick Collection, Box 1, A-D, Artillery at Gettysburg Folder, ACHS, states that Miller's battery position was "275 feet at right angles from the centre of the Emmitsburg Road at a point near John [sic] Sherfy's barn. 570 feet north-easterly from the centre of the Wheatfield Road near the 68th Pa. monument. 445 feet from the iron marker U.S. marker [sic.] Said marker being 350 feet S.E. of the 105th Pa. monument. Authority of Lieut. Hero. General Alexander marks this position 40 feet in advance, 6 A.M. to 1 P.M. July 3rd, 1863."

25 Cabell, "A Visit to the Battle-Field of Gettysburg," 7.

number of casualties and demoralization among the troops. "We suffered considerable loss before we moved," confirmed Captain John Holmes Smith of the 11th Virginia regiment.[26]

On Cemetery Ridge, the remainder of Sickles's Third Corps was still under Birney's command. Sickles had departed Gettysburg earlier that morning, bound for Washington D.C. and a lengthy period of recuperation from the amputation of his right leg. The soldiers of the Third Corps held a position on a wooded knoll east of George Weikert's house. Ironically, many were in nearly the same location where they bivouacked on the morning of July 2. This caused Second Corps staff officer Frank Haskell to quip sarcastically that had they simply stayed there, "instead of moving out to the front, we should have many more men today, and should not have been upon the brink of disaster yesterday." [27]

General John Newton recalled that when he asked Birney to more actively support the nearby First Corp, Birney replied, "he would rather be excused, as his men had a good deal of hard work and were exhausted . . . so they went into the woods which was rather thick and had coffee." Private Lewis Schaeffer of the 68th Pennsylvania recorded in his field diary, "It is dreadful to look at our brigade this morning." Many of the "happy fellows who were anxious for the fight yesterday are now hushed in death or lay frightfully wounded."[28]

The 68th Pennsylvania's unfortunate Colonel Andrew Tippin, still temporarily in command of Graham's brigade, turned in a questionable performance on July 3. Captain Edward Bowen of the 114th Pennsylvania complained that Tippin received orders to move the brigade further to the right, but "whether it was that the brave Colonel didn't know the right from the left, or just which way it was he was ordered to go, or whether it was that his soldierly instinct led him to lead the brigade towards the enemy . . . we were in the midst of a most severe shower of flying missiles of all sorts and kinds." Colonel Tippin was removed from command sometime during the day. The colonel reported only that he "was relieved of the command" that evening, but Private Schaeffer confided in his diary, "Our colonel was

26 Ibid.; Smith, "John Holmes Smith's Account," 32: 190. The captain estimated his company's losses at 10 out of 29 men before the charge even began.

27 Craft, *History of the 141st Regiment Pennsylvania Volunteers*, 125; Scott, *History of the One Hundred and Fifth Regiment of Pennsylvania Volunteers*, 83; Byrne and Weaver, *Haskell of Gettysburg*, 140.

28 Diary of Lewis Schaeffer, West Virginia and Regional History Center; Styple, *Generals in Bronze*, 77-78.

put under arrest for being drunk." The 141st Pennsylvania's Colonel Madill assumed temporary brigade command.[29]

Tippin returned to his regiment and appeared to suffer from no long-term disciplinary repercussions. Apart from being captured in October 1863 and held in Libby Prison until March of the following year, he served with distinction through the end of the war. Colonel Tippin died at 47 years old in 1870 of "chronic diarrhea," a malady he endured since the Mexican War.[30]

Lieutenant Colonel Freeman McGilvery's artillery lineup remained in front of the powerless Third Corps. In a repeat of his July 2 performance, McGilvery effectively used the terrain that Sickles and his officers had earlier considered indefensible. On the morning of July 3, McGilvery determined the whereabouts of his batteries and "brought them into line on the low ground on our left center, fronting the woods and elevated position occupied by the enemy along the Gettysburg and Emmitsburg road, a point at which it was plain to be seen they were massing artillery in great force." According to McGilvery's post-battle report, he commanded 39 guns, but his was not a static line as some batteries moved in and out during the day. Several of the batteries had seen action in and around the Peach Orchard on the prior day, including those under captains Ames, Hart, Phillips, and Thompson. Also nearby stood two guns each in Lt. Turnbull's 3rd U.S. and Captain Bigelow's 9th Massachusetts (now under Lieutenant Richard Milton) batteries, although both likely departed the area by early afternoon. Captain Judson Clark's First New Jersey Light Artillery also unlimbered in proximity but was unengaged.[31]

29 Diary of Lewis Schaeffer, West Virginia and Regional History Center; *OR*, 27/1: 499; Craft, *History of 141st PA*, 125; Scott, *History of the One Hundred and Fifth Regiment of Pennsylvania Volunteers*, 83; Gottfried, *Brigades of Gettysburg*, 193; Dyer, *A Compendium of the War of the Rebellion*, 1: 295.

30 "Death of a Gallant Soldier," *Montgomery Ledger*, February 8, 1870. Colonel Tippin was captured October 14, 1863 at Auburn, Virginia, during the Bristoe Station Campaign and paroled on March 14, 1864. He returned to his regiment on June 19, 1864. See Hunt, *Colonels in Blue*, 166. Tippin spent much of the final year of the war commanding the Army of the Potomac's Provost Guard Headquarters Reserves. The 68th Pennsylvania was one of the attached regiments. Tippin and the 68th were assigned to an Independent Brigade, which also included the 114th Pennsylvania, during the Appomattox Campaign. See *OR*, 42/3: 874, 901, 46/1: 574, 51/1: 242 as examples.

31 OR, 27/1: 586, 883; Cooksey, "The Union Artillery at Gettysburg on July 3," 76; Laino, *Gettysburg Campaign Atlas*, 318-319. As a result of the various movements, there is not complete historical agreement on the exact alignment during the cannonade or during the Confederate assault. See Laino, *Gettysburg Campaign Atlas*, 384, n. 13, for a discussion.

"To attempt to describe the fearful artillery duel of this day reveals the poverty of language and the impossibility of clear narrative," remembered Captain Ames. "There was one continuous roar from nearly three hundred pieces [sic] of artillery. The consequences of this action was that men and horses and gun carriages were being blown to pieces in every direction."[32]

Regardless of the exact number of field pieces engaged, Lee's massive artillery cannonade had little impact on McGilvery's portion of the field. "This [Confederate] fire was very rapid and inaccurate," McGilvery reported, "most of the projectiles passing from 20 to 100 feet over our lines." For those shots that did not pass overhead, McGilvery "had a slight earthwork thrown up" in front of his guns "which proved sufficient to resist all the projectiles which struck it."[33]

Control of the Emmitsburg Road brought Alexander's batteries closer to their targets, but this did not necessarily improve the accuracy of their fire. General Hunt observed a considerable portion of the action from a location behind McGilvery. Although he called the scene "indescribably grand," Hunt thought the demonstration to be more visually stimulating than effective. "In fact, the fire was more dangerous behind the ridge than on its crest. . . . Most of the enemy's projectiles passed overhead, the effect being to sweep all the open ground in our rear, which was of little benefit to the Confederates – a mere waste of ammunition."[34]

Contrary to Hunt's recollections, some Federal batteries posted further north on Cemetery Ridge suffered considerable damage and losses. A heavy concentration of Confederate fire struck areas later designated as "The Angle" and the "Copse of Trees." It was an exaggeration for Hunt to portray the July 3 Confederate artillery barrage as a wasting of ammunition, but the results showed that the attack was insufficient to turn the outcome in Lee's favor. Sickles's earlier fears of Confederate artillery dominating Cemetery Ridge from the Peach Orchard proved unwarranted. Chancellorsville's Hazel Grove did not repeat itself.

32 Ames, *Battery G*, 77.

33 *OR*, 27/1: 883-884. In his post-battle writings, General Hunt varyingly estimated the overall number of Federal guns that participated in the great cannonade as being between 75 and 80. Although historians will likely never know the precise number, since the Army of the Potomac's artillery commander did not know, a comprehensive modern study placed the number at 78 total cannons engaged during the cannonade (from Little Round Top to Cemetery Hill.) See Cooksey, "The Union Artillery at Gettysburg," 89-90.

34 Hunt, "The Third Day at Gettysburg," *Battles and Leaders*, 3: 372-373.

Longstreet and Alexander did not expect the cannonade to be of a lengthy duration. Such an endeavor required a large expenditure of ammunition and therefore endangered key components of Lee's plan: the advance of the artillery to support the infantry and provide protection of the flanks. Longstreet left it to Alexander's judgment to determine when the enemy's batteries were "silenced or crippled" enough to allow the advance of Pickett, Pettigrew, and Trimble. At one point, Longstreet even notified the young colonel, "If the artillery fire does not have the effect to drive off the enemy or greatly demoralize him, so as to make our efforts pretty certain, I would prefer that you should not advise General Pickett to make the charge." Alexander had originally determined to "give Pickett the order to advance within fifteen or twenty minutes after it began," but could not find the opportunity as it "seemed madness to launch infantry into that fire, with nearly three-quarters of a mile to go at midday under a July sun."[35]

It was General Hunt, rather than an overwhelming convergence of Alexander's artillery fire, who brought the matter to a head. At around 2: 30 p.m., finding his own ammunition running low and realizing the problems inherent in bringing up more caissons and limbers while under fire, Hunt "directed that the fire should be gradually stopped, which was done, and the enemy soon slackened his fire also."[36]

Instructions from Longstreet had forced Alexander to look for such a moment, and he hoped that the reduced fire represented a withdrawal of Union batteries from Cemetery Ridge. Quickly, Alexander sent a note to Pickett, urging him to advance. Pickett then approached Longstreet, who reluctantly granted permission to begin the attack.[37]

Hunt later confirmed that the Confederates ceased fire "under the mistaken impression that he had silenced our guns." The Union artillery commander recalled, "almost immediately his [Confederate] infantry came out of the woods and formed for the assault." While the Southerners began to mass

35 Alexander, "Artillery Fighting at Gettysburg," *Battles and Leaders*, 3: 362- 364; Longstreet, "Lee's Right Wing at Gettysburg," *Battles and Leaders*, 3: 345.

36 *OR*, 27/1: 239. Generals Meade, Warren, and Major Thomas Osborn, commanding Eleventh Corps artillery, also claimed to come to the same conclusions about ordering a cease-fire. See Hessler, Motts, and Stanley, *Pickett's Charge at Gettysburg,* 169-170 for a discussion.

37 Longstreet, "Lee's Right Wing at Gettysburg," 3: 345. For Alexander's perspective on this, see Alexander, *Military Memoirs*, 423; Alexander, "Artillery Fighting at Gettysburg," 3: 364-365; Gallagher, *Fighting for the Confederacy*, 258-259.

for the attack, Hunt paused and proclaimed that the enemy's ranks appeared "magnificent, and excited our admiration."[38]

As the time approached 3:00 p.m., and the Confederate infantry fell into attack formation, Longstreet paid a visit to Alexander. The artillerist told the general that he feared "our artillery ammunition might not hold out." Longstreet replied, "Stop Pickett immediately and replenish your ammunition," but Alexander explained that it would take too long to resupply and there was very little remaining anyways. "I don't want to make this attack," Longstreet confessed to his subordinate. "I would stop it now but that General Lee ordered it and expects it to go on. I don't see how it can succeed." Alexander listened, "but did not dare offer a word. The battle was lost if we stopped."[39]

Both men were correct. The battle was lost. "Meanwhile, the infantry had no sooner debouched on the plain," recalled Alexander, "than all the enemy's line, which had been nearly silent, broke out again with all its batteries." Longstreet and Alexander had gambled in assuming that the Union artillery had withdrawn from Cemetery Ridge. Instead, "a storm of shell began bursting over and among our infantry."[40]

The Yankee fire did not subside as the Southern infantry moved forward. Lieutenant Colonel Rawley Martin of the 53rd Virginia estimated that the enemy batteries opened from about 1,100 yards, "hissing, screaming shells break in their front, rear, on their flanks, all about them." After crossing about half of the field, Joseph Cabell of the 38th Virginia described his regiment being "subjected to a severe enfilading fire from the right" and "until nearly to their works, grape and canister were poured onto us from the right and front."[41]

General Pickett's location, while his men made their futile attack, later became a controversy among veterans and historians. Accounts in various post-battle recollections ranged from placing Pickett near the Nicholas Codori farm to his hiding among a limestone ledge of rocks behind the Confederate lines. Pickett remained mounted and in motion during the charge, thus making

38 Hunt, "The Third Day at Gettysburg," *Battles and Leaders*, 3: 374.

39 Longstreet, "Lee's Right Wing at Gettysburg," *Battles and Leaders*, 3: 343-345; Alexander, "Artillery Fighting at Gettysburg," *Battles and Leaders*, 3: 365.

40 Alexander, "Artillery Fighting at Gettysburg," *Battles and Leaders*, 3: 365.

41 Martin, "Rawley Martin's Account," *SHSP*, 32: 186; OR, Supplement, Part I, Reports, Vol. 5, Serial 5, 332.

several scenarios possible for his whereabouts. Some accounts placed Pickett near the Sherfy farm during and after the attack. Major John Cheves Haskell in Henry's Artillery Battalion and Colonel David Aiken of Kershaw's 7th South Carolina, posted near the intersection of the Emmitsburg and Wheatfield Roads, both claimed to have encountered Pickett and staff. Aiken accused Pickett of being drunk, while Haskell claimed that the general and his staff appeared "in great confusion" during the close of the assault.[42]

Was George Pickett at the Peach Orchard during Pickett's Charge? The orchard's elevation provided an excellent point of observation, but intervening smoke and obstacles would have obscured the view. The distance from the Peach Orchard to the penetration point of "The Angle" on Cemetery Ridge measured roughly 1,800 yards. Communication and coordination with the men engaged in the attack would have been nearly impossible at that distance. Given the importance that Lee, Longstreet, and the artillerists placed on the Peach Orchard, it is likely that this was one of many stops that Pickett made during that fateful afternoon. However, it would have been negligent for Pickett to spend any significant amount of time there during the attack itself; demonstrating again, the limitations of this position.

Due to shortages in ammunition, Alexander was unable to find enough guns to advance with the infantry attack. He rode "to the end of [the] line in the Peach Orchard" to round up cannons that had enough remaining ammunition, ideally those with more than 18 rounds each, to follow Pickett. Alexander estimated that he found somewhere between 15 and 18 candidates. Unfortunately, nine short-range howitzers promised from A.P. Hill's corps artillery were nowhere to be found. General Pendleton had moved them to the rear for their protection.[43]

The situation forced Longstreet to find other means for safeguarding his flanks. General Kemper's Brigade formed the right of Pickett's Division and found itself exposed to Union flanking fire as they crossed the Emmitsburg Road. Pickett sent staff officer Captain Robert Bright to Longstreet with a message requesting reinforcements. Bright found Longstreet sitting on a fence

42 Harrison, *Nothing but Glory*, 132-133, 162 n. 14. Also see Hessler, Motts, and Stanley, *Pickett's Charge at Gettysburg*, 148-151. Pickett's role as a division commander did not call for him to ride across the field in front of his men, and he did not. However, both generals Pettigrew and Trimble had comparable roles, were conspicuous with their men, and were both wounded. In comparison, it was noted by some observers that neither Pickett nor any of his staff officers were killed or wounded, and accounts of their whereabouts were lacking.

43 *OR*, 27/2: 320; Alexander, *Military Memoirs*, 419-420; "Artillery Fighting at Gettysburg," 3: 363; Gallagher, *Fighting for the Confederacy*, 261-262.

and in ill humor. British military observer Arthur Fremantle was also present, and he told Longstreet, "I wouldn't have missed this for anything." Longstreet laughed and replied, "The devil you wouldn't! I would like to have missed it very much; we've attacked and been repulsed. Look there!" After commenting, "The charge is over," Longstreet then instructed Bright to "ride to General Pickett, and tell him what you have heard me say to Colonel Fremantle." As Bright started off, Longstreet called out to him again. "Tell General Pickett that Wilcox's Brigade is in that peach orchard [pointing], and he can order him to his assistance."[44]

General Wilcox's Brigade lost perhaps as many as 570 men fighting over much of the same ground on July 2. During the July 3 assault, Wilcox received orders to "move in rear" of Pickett's right flank, "to protect it from any force that might attempt to move against it." Wilcox's tattered command had been positioned to support Alexander's guns since before sunrise. They stood about 200 yards from the Emmitsburg Road and 40 yards behind the batteries. Colonel Lang's Florida Brigade was again posted to Wilcox's left and had orders to conform to "Billy Fixin's" movements.[45]

According to Wilcox, "the advance had not been made more than twenty or thirty minutes," when orders arrived through three separate couriers "to advance to the support of Pickett's division." Captain Bright was reportedly the last of the three to reach Wilcox, who raised his hands in exasperation and replied, "I know. I know." As Wilcox's Alabamians moved forward, Lang's small command joined the advance. All knew full well what awaited them, particularly considering their experience on July 2. "There were ominous shakings of the heads among the boys as to the wisdom of the move," George Clark recalled, "and expressions were heard on all sides to the effect that 'Old Billy Fixin' (the Brigadier's nickname), was not satisfied with having lost half his brigade the day before." Pickett and Pettigrew's main assault had already crossed the Emmitsburg Road. Pickett's Division made a left oblique after doing so. Due to smoke, terrain, and poor communication the Virginians were nowhere in sight.[46]

44 Rollins, *Pickett's Charge: Eyewitness Accounts*, 142; Alexander, *Military Memoirs*, 432; Fremantle, *Three Months in the Southern States*, 265-266. Bright added in his post-war account, "Some have claimed that Wilcox was put in the charge at its commencement . . . but this is a mistake."

45 *OR*, 27/2: 359, 619, 632.

46 *OR*, 27/2: 320, 360, 619-620; Rollins, *Pickett's Charge: Eyewitness Accounts*, 142; Clark, *A Glance Backward*, 38-39; Dempsey, "Florida Brigade at Gettysburg," 26. Colonel Lang curiously reported that his order to advance came "soon after General Pickett's troops retired behind

As Wilcox's men came in view of the Emmitsburg Road, Federal artillery poured a concentrated fire into their ranks, from the front and the flanks. Wilcox characterized the fire as "more than on the evening previous. Not a man of the division that I was ordered to support could I see; but as my orders were to go to their support, on my men went down the slope until they came near the hill upon which were the enemy's batteries and entrenchments." Alexander described the scene as "at once both absurd and tragic." The Southern artillerist observed, "There was no longer anything to support, and with the keenest pity at the useless waste of life, I saw them advance."[47]

McGilvery's artillery exacted a terrible toll on the Confederates when they crossed the Emmitsburg Road. "My men falling all around me with brains blown out," recalled a lieutenant in Lang's 5th Florida, "arms off and wounded in every description." McGilvery admitted, "The execution of the fire must have been terrible, as it was over a level plain, and the effect was plain to be seen. In a few minutes, instead of a well-ordered line of battle, there were broken and confused masses, and fugitives fleeing in every direction."[48]

Despite the mounting casualties, Wilcox and Lang's commands lurched toward the same ground from which they had been repulsed on the previous day. They advanced to within 300 yards under "a shower of such missiles" that "plow[ed] their deadly paths through our ranks." Wilcox spurred his horse back toward the Emmitsburg Road to seek support from the Confederate artillery, but there "were none near that had ammunition" to aid his floundering assault. Wilcox ordered his men to fall back. His brigade's losses for the entire battle were estimated at 778 out of 1,726 engaged (45.1%), and he reported 204 of those casualties on July 3.[49]

Brigadier General George Stannard's infantry brigade of Vermonters held a position to the right of McGilvery's guns. Stannard's men had just finished

---

our position." One wonders if the increasing number of walking wounded and stragglers were so numerous that Lang mistakenly assumed Pickett's entire division had retired. See *OR*, 27/2: 632. It is beyond the scope of this narrative to fully dissect the performance of Pickett, Pettigrew, and Trimble's divisions. See Hessler, Motts & Stanley, *Pickett's Charge at Gettysburg* for a more detailed analysis.

47 *OR*, 27/2: 620; Alexander, "The Great Charge and Artillery Fighting at Gettysburg," 3: 366-367.

48 Dempsey, "Florida Brigade at Gettysburg," 26; *OR*, 27/1: 884.

49 *OR*, 27/1: 349, 883-884, 889, 27/2: 620, 632; Fleming, *Memoir of Captain C. Seton Fleming*, 82; Clark, *A Glance Backward*, 40; Busey and Martin, *Strengths and Losses*, 308.

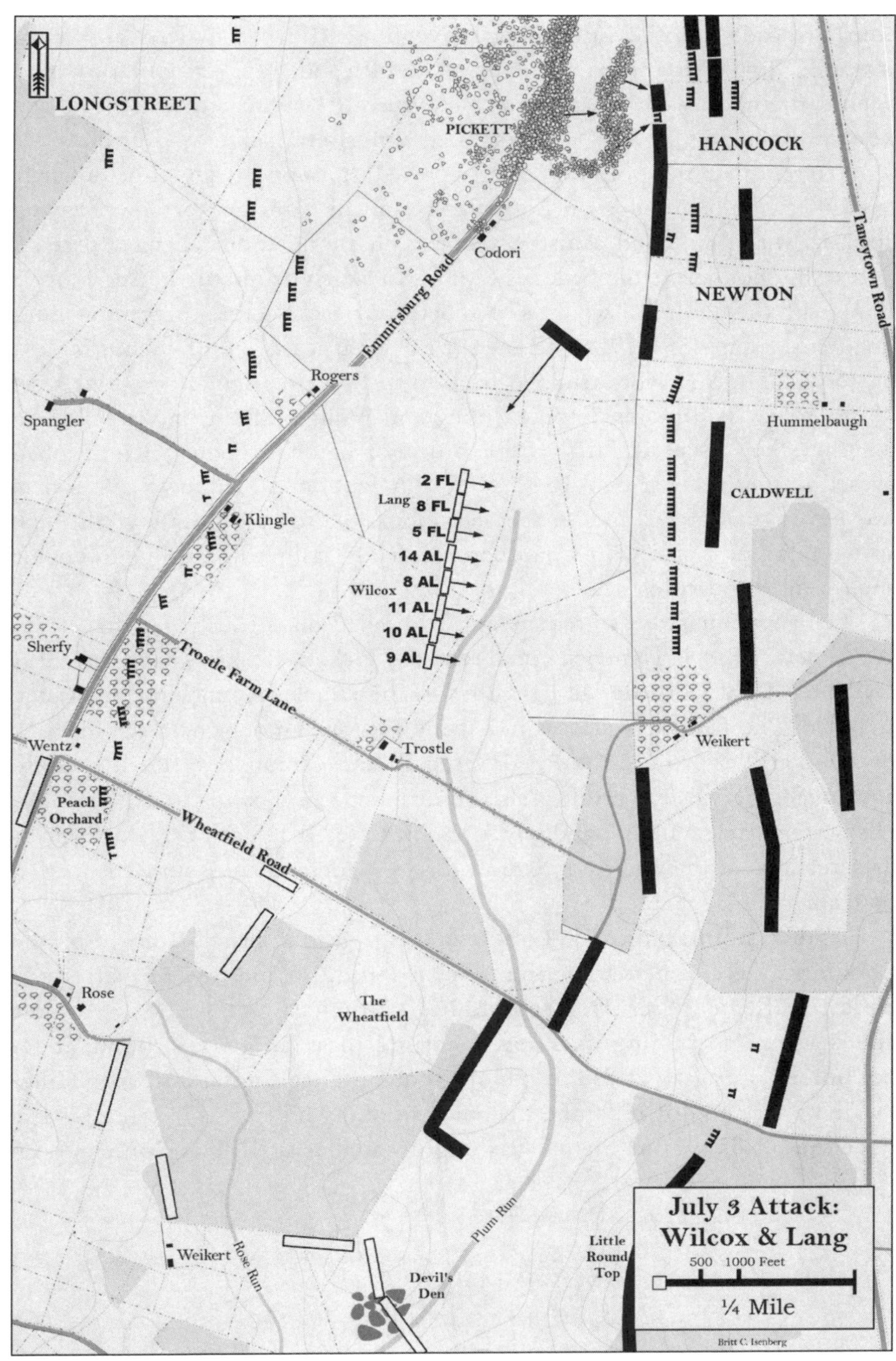
LONGSTREET
PICKETT
HANCOCK
Codori
Emmitsburg Road
NEWTON
Taneytown Road
Rogers
Spangler
Hummelbaugh
2 FL
Lang 8 FL
5 FL
14 AL
Wilcox 8 AL
11 AL
10 AL
9 AL
CALDWELL
Klingle
Sherfy
Trostle Farm Lane
Trostle
Weikert
Wentz
Peach Orchard
Wheatfield Road
Rose
The Wheatfield
Weikert
Rose Run
Plum Run
Devil's Den
Little Round Top
July 3 Attack: Wilcox & Lang
500 1000 Feet
¼ Mile
Britt C. Isenberg

pouring deadly gunfire into Kemper's right flank when Wilcox and Lang appeared. Two of Stannard's regiments, the 14th and 16th Vermont, promptly opened fire upon Lang's men. The volleys further "decimated" the Floridians who, in Stannard's words, "were scooped almost en masse into our lines."[50]

"To remain in this position," Lang reported, "unsupported by either infantry or artillery, with infantry on both flanks and in front and artillery playing upon us with grape and canister, was certain annihilation." Lang ordered a retreat, but not before the Federals captured a large portion of the 2nd Florida along with their colors. Two days of repetitive attacks across the Emmitsburg Road cost Lang 455 of his 742 men (61.3%), at least 150 of whom he lost on July 3. The survivors trudged back to near their original positions west of the road. As captains Seton Fleming and William McCaslin were retiring together, they discussed "the terrible ordeal of battle through which they had passed during the last two days." McCaslin cautioned Fleming that survival was never guaranteed, and "it seemed impossible to pass in safety" through so many battles. The words had barely left McCaslin's lips when an enemy shell went through his head. [51]

Lee and Longstreet's great assault had failed disastrously. Further north on Cemetery Ridge, Hancock's men repulsed Pickett, Pettigrew, and Trimble's divisions. Total Confederate casualties in the attack may have been as high as 6,400. The Federals' success had many authors, among them the inability of Lee's artillery to use the Peach Orchard and Emmitsburg Road ridge to advantage. McGilvery's artillery also contributed significantly to the outcome. His performance on July 2 and July 3 demonstrated that Sickles and his officers underestimated the ability of Union forces to defend the southern portion of Cemetery Ridge.[52]

As his infantry retired, Longstreet's attention turned quickly to the possibility of an enemy counterattack. "I rode to the line of batteries," he later reflected, "resolved to hold it until the last gun was lost." Enemy shells were "screaming over my head and ploughing the ground under my horse." Longstreet found his old acquaintance Captain Merritt Miller "walking up and down behind his guns, smoking his pipe, directing his fire over the heads of our men." Washington artillerist William Miller Owen

50 *OR*, 27/1: 349-350; Ladd, *Bachelder Papers*, 1: 56, 62.

51 *OR*, 27/2: 633; Busey and Martin, Strengths and Losses, 307; Dempsey, "Florida Brigade at Gettysburg," 40; Fleming, *A Memoir of Captain C. Seton Fleming*, 79-80.

52 Alexander, *Military Memoirs*, 427-431; Hessler, Motts & Stanley, *Pickett's Charge at Gettysburg*, 256.

recalled, "Our boys worked their guns splendidly today, and my leather bottles were passed around and received with pleasure." Luckily for the Confederates, the Union Army's counterattack never materialized. The uncertainty of those hours prompted Royall Figg of Parker's Battery to reminisce afterwards, "We expected every moment that all the Federal artillery in our front would concentrate upon us; but, to our surprise, they did not."[53]

Lee seemed to be everywhere as he encouraged his men throughout the fading hours of the late afternoon. Alexander described a solitary Lee sitting near him, undoubtedly, to help rally fugitives in the event of an enemy attack. The general provided words of encouragement to nearly every man who passed him. Arthur Fremantle noticed Lee comforting his men with words such as, "All this will come right in the end: we'll talk it over afterwards; but, in the meantime, all good men must rally." Lee explained to Fremantle, "This has been a sad day for us, Colonel- a sad day; but we can't expect to always gain victories." General Wilcox was in tears as he returned from his foray across the Emmitsburg Road. Lee assured him, "Never mind, General, all this has been MY fault- it is I that have lost this fight, and you must help me out of it in the best way you can." Sometime that evening, Lee approached Major George Gerald in Barksdale's Brigade near the Peach Orchard. Gerald articulated what had become obvious to so many Southern soldiers, "General, this has been a sad day for us." To which Lee replied, "Yes, but I take the whole responsibility upon myself."[54]

Colonel B.G. Humphreys insisted that Lee "gave every comfort and encouragement to the fugitives that kind words could bestow on their wounded hearts. He magnanimously assumed all the responsibility of the defeat, assuring the officers and men that as the fight was his, his was all the fault and blame." For his part, Humphreys continued in command of Barksdale's old brigade and later received a promotion to brigadier general as of August 1863. In 1865, he became Mississippi's first elected post-war governor. However, he was forcibly removed from office in 1868 when Radical Republicans in Congress

53 Longstreet, *From Manassas to Appomattox*, 395; Owen, *In Camp and Battle with the Washington Artillery*, 253; *OR*, 27/2: 435-436; Figg, *Where Men Only Dare to Go*, 150.

54 Alexander, *Military Memoirs*, 425; Fremantle, *Three Months in the Southern States*, 268-269; G. B. Gerald, "The Battle of Gettysburg," *Waco Daily Times-Herald*, July 3, 1913, Box 7, Brake Collection, USAHEC.

rejected the President's Reconstruction plan. Benjamin G. Humphreys then retired from public life and died on his plantation in 1882.[55]

Except for minor skirmishing, the most significant tactical operations around the Peach Orchard came to an end following Pickett's Charge. Longstreet began moving his infantry and artillery back toward Seminary Ridge after it became apparent that the Federals would not launch a full-scale counterattack. "Little by little," wrote Colonel Alexander, "we got some guns to the rear to replenish and refit . . . and some we held boldly in advanced positions all along the line." The Federal artillery "generally let us alone," a fact that the young colonel acknowledged gratefully. "Night came very slowly, but came at last; and about 10[p.m.] the last gun was withdrawn to Willoughby Run, whence we had moved to the attack the afternoon before." Alexander later estimated that Longstreet's First Corps artillery fired approximately 9,000 rounds during the entire battle, much of which was expended at the Peach Orchard and along the Emmitsburg Road. [56]

There was one last round to fire before that final withdrawal. Sergeant Edward Duffey of Parker's Battery had survived two days of the worst fighting imaginable and was undoubtedly pleased to see the onset of darkness on July 3. He asserted that his section was the last of Alexander's Battalion to leave the line just north of the Peach Orchard. It was shortly after 7:00 p.m. when his crew limbered up and began rolling south along the Emmitsburg Road toward the orchard. As they approached the intersection with the Wheatfield / Millerstown Road, Duffey was surprised to encounter Lee and Longstreet conversing in the roadway. Longstreet approached the sergeant and inquired curtly about the gun's available ammunition. Sergeant Duffey replied that only a few rounds of canister remained. Longstreet ordered Duffey to elevate the barrel and "go and fire down the roadway." Duffey sighted his gun down the Wheatfield Road and fired at enemy skirmishers that were in view.[57]

55 Humphreys, "Benj. Grubb Humphreys Manuscript," 23-24; Warner, *Generals in Gray*, 145-146; *Confederate Military History*, IX: 259.

56 Longstreet, "Lee's Right Wing at Gettysburg," *Battles and Leaders*, 3: 347-349; Gallagher, *Fighting for the Confederacy*, 266; Alexander, "Artillery Fighting at Gettysburg," *Battles and Leaders*, 3: 367; *Military Memoirs*, 426, 434. Later in the afternoon of July 3, Brigadier General Judson Kilpatrick's cavalry initiated a mounted assault against Longstreet's right, but the Confederates repulsed the attack.

57 George T. Fleming, "Diary of 'Reb' (Sergeant E. S. Duffey) Soldier of Battle of Gettysburg," *Pittsburgh Post Gazette*, July 4, 1913; Evans, "The Last Shot at Gettysburg," *Confederate Veteran,* Vol. XXXIII, No. 12, 450-451.

The Federal skirmishers advancing toward the Peach Orchard belonged to Sixth Corps troops in Colonel David Nevin's brigade. They were supporting a reconnaissance made against Longstreet's right-front by portions of the Fifth Corps under Brigadier General Samuel Crawford. The 139th Pennsylvania, under Lieutenant Colonel William Moody, advanced on the right of this reconnaissance, and they were likely the recipients of Sergeant Duffey's canister. The Pennsylvanians pushed the Rebel picket line back and reported recapturing one Napoleon and three caissons that Bigelow's 9th Massachusetts Battery had lost on July 2. It is unclear how effective Duffey's lone gun was against the men of the 139th, and the clash was brief, but the sergeant later insisted, "The fourth gun of Parker's battery of Huger's battalion fired the last gun at Gettysburg on this day, July 3, 1863" from the Peach Orchard.[58]

58 *OR,* 27/1: 654, 685, 688; Nicholson, *Pennsylvania at Gettysburg*, 679-680; Fleming, "Diary of 'Reb' (Sergeant E. S. Duffey) Soldier of Battle of Gettysburg," *Pittsburgh Post Gazette*, July 4, 1913; Evans, "The Last Shot at Gettysburg," Vol. XXXIII, No. 12, 451.

Chapter 10

The Wreck of Battle

The United States turned 87 years old on the morning of July 4, 1863. The nation's tenuous existence was still very much in question, despite the outcome at Gettysburg. It is unlikely that local citizens pondered such weighty issues at that moment. John and Mary Wentz awoke that morning in the cramped dirt basement of their small home. Perhaps the story is apocryphal, but as it was later told, Mr. Wentz noticed a piece of paper pinned to his lapel. On it were the simple words, "Good-bye and God bless you!" If nothing else, the Wentzes received evidence that their son survived the battle. Just as quickly as he had returned to Gettysburg, Henry Wentz departed again.[1]

General Lee conceded that the battle was over and consolidated his reduced lines into a defensive posture on Seminary Ridge. He also initiated plans for a general retreat. "Owing to the strength of the enemy's position," Lee reported, "and the reduction of our ammunition, a renewal of the engagement could not be hazarded, and the difficulty of procuring supplies rendered it impossible to continue longer where we were." Lee pulled Ewell's Second Corps back from opposite Culp's Hill to a position on Oak Ridge, the northern extension of Seminary Ridge. The disposition of General Hill's Third Corps remained relatively unchanged. Longstreet's

1 Storrick, *Gettysburg, The Place, The Battle, The Outcome*, 52-53; Clouse, "Whatever Happened to Henry Wentz?" 7-8; Coco, *War Stories*, 30-31; Frassanito, *Early Photography at Gettysburg*, 249-250.

First Corps, and the Confederate batteries that held the Peach Orchard since the evening of July 2, redeployed along Warfield Ridge. Longstreet still held Lee's right flank.[2]

In the morning hours, Major James Dearing's Battalion took position on the right end of the army's line along Pitzer's Woods, just west of the Peach Orchard. Kershaw's Brigade posted a picket line on the Emmitsburg Road. Union pickets also attempted "to develop their position" from the opposite side of the field. There was considerable skirmishing, which instilled reasonable confidence that an attack seemed possible. On the nearby Rose farm, members of the Pennsylvania Reserves noted that Confederate pickets "called to us to come and get our wounded who lay between the two lines." Although Dearing did not report the incident, some of his guns fired several rounds over the Peach Orchard toward the Yankees on the Rose farm. These projectiles ricocheted harmlessly across the field. According to the Pennsylvanians, "these were the last shots fired at Gettysburg."[3]

The skirmish lines of both armies continued their tedious work throughout the day, "but the whole affair was spiritless." Just after noon, rain set in and fell in "blinding sheets." This certainly did not help Lee's preparations for retreat. It was not until late afternoon that the long Confederates trains began to slog westward toward South Mountain. The infantry followed at night.[4]

The Army of Northern Virginia needed to shed the burden of guarding thousands of prisoners on the return trip home. Some of Lee's officers offered parole to a large number of Yankee captives before the retreat got underway. General Charles Graham, still held by the Rebels as he recovered from his injuries, learned of this and convinced many captured Union soldiers to reject such offers. His premise was, "they would be recaptured by Meade before the rebels could get them across the Potomac." Graham's powers of persuasion were admirable if ultimately inaccurate. He remained in captivity

2 *OR*, 27/2: 309. Longstreet reported, "After night [July 3], I received orders to make all the needful arrangements for our retreat. The orders for preparation were given, and the work was begun before daylight on the 4th." See *OR*, 27/2: 360-361.

3 Ibid., 27/1: 655, 27/2: 372-373, 389; Nicholson, *Pennsylvania at Gettysburg*, 120-121; Fremantle, *Three Months in the Southern States*, 272.

4 Imboden, "The Confederate Retreat from Gettysburg," *Battles and Leaders*, 3: 422-423; *OR*, 27/1: 655-656.

Modern view of the south side of the rebuilt Sherfy barn.
Photo by Authors

and his prominence attracted the attention of newspapers in both the North and South, who soon reported on his status.[5]

On the morning of July 5, General Meade's army began to probe the abandoned Confederate positions. The men of the 20th Maine, who had fought on Little Round Top, advanced with their brigade "over the battle field, across the Emmetsburg [sic] pike, and went into line upon the ground occupied on the 3rd by batteries of the enemy." On their way toward the Peach Orchard, Major Ellis Spear recalled that the ground remained "strewn with muskets, haversacks, soldiers' caps, dead horses and dead men." They found no enemy forces and erected breastworks around the Sherfy farm buildings. The men destroyed most of the Sherfys' remaining fences in building their fortifications.[6]

5 *The Star and Enterprise* (Newville, PA), August 13, 1863; *Detroit Free Press*, July 8, 1863; *Daily State Journal* (Raleigh, NC), July 16, 1863.

6 Gallagher, *Fighting for the Confederacy*, 267; Longstreet, *Manassas to Appomattox*, 427; Spear, *The Civil War Recollections of General Ellis Spear*, 40; *OR*, 27/1: 632; William T. Livermore Letter

The burned Sherfy barn provided a memorable sight for all who ventured past the Peach Orchard. Spear examined the conspicuous "small barn which had hay upon the floor, and was burned down to the hay." The major noticed, "On the charred surface lay half burned bodies, evidently of wounded men placed there and too much hurt to move. There they were half burned and ghostly." He detected the body of an officer just outside the barn, whom he identified as a Confederate by his boots. The corpse's "head and shoulders, towards the fire, had been scorched to a shapeless mass." The "damp hot July air" added a "penetrating deadly smell" to the gruesome scene. William Livermore of the 20th Maine identified the Zouaves of the 114th Pennsylvania, known for their "red Breeches as we call them," scattered around the farmyard. "There were as many as 30 or 40 lay dead there . . . 3 days in hot July weather. And I wish I never could see another such sight."[7]

The 20th Maine's commander, Colonel Joshua Chamberlain, was uncharacteristically hesitant to share his observations. "There lay the remnants too terrible to describe of officers and men - rebel and union - half burned or with roasted heads . . . a number of them being shot through the head still breathing after twenty-four hours. We tried to do something for them but they were past all human wants or human aid. I hold back rather than attempt to describe this scene."[8]

General Meade ordered Sedgwick's Sixth Corps "forward to determine the position of the enemy." They also passed the Sherfy property. Assistant Surgeon George Stevens of the 77th New York recalled the scene near the barn as "more than usually hideous." Stevens added:

> Blackened ruins marked the spot where, on the morning of the third, stood a large barn. It had been used as a hospital. It had taken fire from the shells of the hostile batteries, and had quickly burned to the ground. Those of the wounded not able to help themselves were destroyed by the flames, which in a moment spread through the straw and dry material of the building. The crisped and blackened limbs, heads and other portions of bodies lying half consumed among the heaps of ruins and ashes, made up one of the most ghastly pictures ever witnessed, even on the field of battle.[9]

---

to "Brother Charles", July 6, 1863, in VF V6-ME20, Library & Research Center, GNMP. See also, Coco, *A Strange and Blighted Land*, 50; *Maine at Gettysburg*, 278; Copy of the Claims of Joseph Sherfy, National Archives, RG 92, Records of the Quartermaster General, on file at GNMP, Library Box B-5.

7 Spear, *The Civil War Recollections of General Ellis Spear*, 40; William T. Livermore Letter to "Brother Charles," July 6, 1863, in VF V6-ME20, Library & Research Center, GNMP.

8 Desjardin, *Stand Firm Ye Boys from Maine*, 102.

9 *OR*, 27/1: 663, 666, 669, 672, 674; Stevens, *Three Years in the Sixth Corps*, 254-255.

Private George Pickup of the 2nd New Hampshire.

Kendra Debany Collection. Photo by Lynn Heller

A detail of men from the 16th Michigan buried Southern soldiers around the Wentz house. The men dug a trench in the family's garden. As the work progressed, Adjutant Rufus Jacklin noticed an elderly man and woman approaching. It was John and Mary Wentz. He watched as they busied themselves gathering branches from a tree before retiring into their home, which Jacklin described as "literally perforated by shot and shell." Jacklin had a brief conversation with the couple before resuming his grisly task of hauling dead bodies from the field to the trench.[10]

10 Clouse, "Whatever Happened to Henry Wentz?" 8-10; Wentz Obituary, *Martinsburg Statesmen*, December 14, 1875; Storrick, *Gettysburg: The Place, The Battle, The Outcome*, 52-53. Adjutant Jacklin claimed papers were found upon the body of a Confederate artillery officer "indicating the same name as the family." He then purportedly received confirmation from John and Mary that this was their son. Such accounts have spawned much confusion over the years about the fate of Henry Wentz. Whoever the Confederate artillery officer was, it was certainly not Henry Wentz, who survived the battle.

John and Mary Wentz continued with their simple way of life after the armies departed from their small farm. John passed away in 1870, and Mary died in the following year. It remains uncertain how frequently Henry Wentz returned to Gettysburg after the war. He probably reappeared in March 1872, in order to sell family property. In 1875, Henry died in Martinsburg at 47 years old.[11]

The 2nd New Hampshire's Colonel Edward Bailey and his orderly rode to the Peach Orchard, where they identified the bodies of several dead officers. "I went over the field before the men were buried," wrote Private John Henry Burrill of the 2nd, "and such a sight I never wish to see again. The men had turned black, their eyes swollen out of their heads and they were twice their natural size. The stench of the field was awful. Dead men were thick you may well believe."[12]

Bailey's regiment, along with the remainder of Burling's brigade, spent the next several days in bivouac and on light picket duty. They departed Gettysburg during the early morning hours of July 7 and continued fighting the war. Bailey mustered out in June 1864 and went home to New Hampshire. Despite achieving regimental command at a young age and being wounded three times, he never received promotion to general. In 1867, he reenlisted and served in the infantry out West. Bailey struggled in his new assignment with disciplinary issues and alcohol. He was court-martialed five times on charges ranging from embezzlement, neglect of duty, and writing bad checks. In 1893, the army dismissed Bailey from the service for "conduct unbecoming an officer and a gentleman." His various transgressions included failure to repay a debt to a fellow officer, entering a house without permission, "beckoning" to a married woman with his hand, and cavorting with a prostitute in a saloon while dressed in uniform. Bailey returned to New Hampshire, and despite the inglorious end to his military career, attended many veteran reunions. In 1903, President Theodore Roosevelt vetoed a Senate bill to place Bailey on the retired list due to the sheer volume of disciplinary actions against him. Bailey died in 1930 at the age of 88.[13]

While the two armies prepared for their departures from Gettysburg, the wounded received care in field hospitals established throughout the area. Private

11 McMillan, *Gettysburg Rebels*, 210-211.

12 Haynes, *History of the 2nd Regiment*, 180; John Henry Burrill letter, July 13, 1863, John Henry Burrill Papers, USAHEC.

13 Haynes, *History of the 2nd Regiment*, 188 – 190; Smith, "We Drop a Comrade's Tear," 117-118; *Presidential Vetoes, 1789-1988*, Senate Library, 190; *Congressional Record-Senate 1903*, 3000.

George Pickup was just one of the 2nd New Hampshire's 137 wounded men. Pickup was from England, but lived in New Hampshire where he enlisted at the outset of the war. In June 1862, Pickup was captured and held in Richmond for 73 days before being exchanged. At Gettysburg, he suffered a minor foot wound and eventually recovered.[14]

Lieutenant Charles Vickery's injuries were considerably more serious. Vickery was shot in the back, and then stripped and robbed by the Confederates "with their customary dexterity." On July 3, canister fire struck him again while he lay in a barn. Vickery died on July 10.[15]

Harriet Patience Dame, a 48-year-old native of Concord, was among those caring for the wounded at the 2nd New Hampshire's field hospital. Although she had no formal training as a nurse, early in the war she opened her home to the regiment's sick, and subsequently volunteered to accompany the 2nd to the front. Dame became a hospital matron and established a reputation as one who "roughed it" with the soldiers in the field. Prior to Gettysburg, she was captured twice by the Confederates but released. On one occasion, Stonewall Jackson reportedly met with her and secured her freedom. At Gettysburg, surrounded by "such a multitude of her old boys, wounded and dying, as would have appalled any but the stoutest heart," Dame performed some of her finest work. She was unable to save Vickery, but she aided countless others. The soldiers remembered her afterwards as "the bravest, the sweetest and best beloved" of the regiment.[16]

In addition to Harriet Dame, women actively supported at least two other Peach Orchard regiments. Anna (or "Annie") Etheridge was a nurse in the 3rd Michigan. The young woman, no more than 24 years of age, had already acquired a reputation on several battlefields. In 1862, Anna received the Kearny Cross for bravery, as she often rode fearlessly to the front to assist wounded soldiers. Not surprisingly, Northern soldiers observed Anna actively supervising transportation of the wounded during the fighting on July 2.[17]

14 George Pickup's National Archives and Pension Records courtesy of Kendra Debany. Also see Busey, *Union Casualties*, 336. Pickup lived until 1917.

15 Haynes, *History of the Second Regiment*, 183.

16 Ibid., 183, 296-297, 300-302. Harriet Dame survived the war. She died in 1900 at the age of 85. In 1901, the New Hampshire State Legislature commissioned an artist to paint her portrait. They also directed that the painting be displayed in the New Hampshire State House. It hangs there to this day.

17 Mulholland, *Story of the 116th Regiment Pennsylvania Volunteers*, 124; Moore, *Women of the War*, 513-518; "A Heroine," *Buffalo Commercial Advertiser*, February 23, 1863. Available sources

Marie Brose Tepe Leonard, also known as "Marie Tepe," was another Kearny Cross recipient who took action near the Peach Orchard. She was attached to the 114th Pennsylvania as a vivandiere, and shared many of the same dangers as the soldiers. Her duties included carrying water or whiskey to the men on the front lines. Marie was wounded at the battle of Fredericksburg and still carried the bullet in her ankle. A member of the 63rd Pennsylvania thought "my kind lady friend Zuave [sic] Mary" looked odd in her uniform, "but it cannot be denied that Mary is as brave and fearless as any soldier in the old Kearny Division. She is kind and tender hearted withal [sic], and has received many a 'God bless you' from the poor bleeding soldier on the Battle field and in the hospital." Marie received an extra 25 cents for each day that she worked in the field hospitals, and likely served in that capacity at Gettysburg. As with other women and noncombatants, Marie's movements were recorded in less detail than those of the soldiers. However, she had at least two Gettysburg experiences that differed from Harriet Dame and Anna Etheridge. Marie was photographed after the battle on Cemetery Hill, and then had her portrait taken at the Tyson Brothers studio in Gettysburg before departing the area.[18]

Joseph Sherfy and his oldest son Raphael returned home on Sunday, July 5, 1863. The barn was their biggest loss, but the previously bountiful orchards and crops were also decimated. The total estimated loss in fruit trees was $180. Damage to the mature Peach Orchard was not documented, but at least 80 trees in the younger lot were "destroyed by being pulled out & broken off." Their hog stable had also been consumed by flames. At least two of their hogs, 20 chickens, one cow and three calves were killed during the battle. The brick walls on the northwest, west, and south sides of the house were badly scarred by bullet and shell damage. Most of the fencing was destroyed; a dead Confederate soldier hung from one of the few remaining sections. The soldier had been shot while climbing the fence. His legs were still on a railing and his face was in the mud. There were at least 17 dead Southerners in "a forward state of decomposition" in a nearby field. The Emmitsburg

---

alternately list Etheridge's birth year as 1839 and 1844. Etheridge died in 1913 and is buried in Arlington National Cemetery.

18 Frassanito, *Early Photography at Gettysburg*, 140; Hagerty, *Collis' Zouaves*, 94, 319-320; Robert M. Morton to parents, August 1863, courtesy of Ronn Palm Museum of Civil War Images; Cozzens, *Fearless French Mary*, http://www.historynet.com/fearless-french-mary.htm. Vivandieres were often attached to regiments as a combination of sutler, canteen keeper, nurse, cook, seamstress, and laundress. Robert Morton, 63rd Pennsylvania, wrote in private correspondence that Marie was immersed in both battles at Chancellorsville and Gettysburg. Sadly, Marie's later years were filled with hardship. In 1901, she took her own life.

Artillery projectile embedded in one of the Sherfys' cherry trees.
GNMP

Road artillery positions were identified by "heaps" of dead horses. Such was the sad state of affairs.[19]

As they entered the house, Joseph and Raphael Sherfy were greeted by the sound of the "eight-day clock" ticking away in the sitting room. The Sherfys surveyed their once proud home. Four feather beds were "soaked with blood and bloody clothes and filth of every description was strewn over the house." After taking count, more than 180 Minie balls had struck the residence. In one way, however, the Sherfys still had much to be thankful for. No one from their family was buried in any of the fresh graves outside. Joseph and his son immediately went to work in making the grounds more presentable for the remainder of the family's eventual return.[20]

Not every Union survivor was engaged productively at field hospitals or in burial details. Major Michael Burns of the Excelsior Brigade's 73rd New York spent the evening of July 5 in town. For uncertain reasons, the "grossly intoxicated" Irishman visited the home of civilian Mary Wade, whose daughter Mary Virginia (popularly remembered as "Jennie" Wade) was killed two days earlier. Reverend Walter Alexander from the U.S. Christian Commission was also in the home, perhaps comforting the grieving mother. An altercation

19 Copy of the Claims of Joseph Sherfy, National Archives, RG 92, Records of the Quartermaster General, on file at GNMP, Library Box B-5. As will be discussed later, the Sherfys' total damage claim was $2,466.75. After the barn's $1,000 value, the next highest total was $395 in sundry / household articles. Sherfy oddly did not state the exact damage to his mature Peach Orchard, except that $180.00 in total damage occurred to "fruit trees" and at $1 per tree, 80 trees were destroyed in the younger orchard. This suggests that 100 trees were destroyed in the mature orchard. Also see Sherfey, *The Sherfey Family in the United States*, 207, transcribed copy, Sherfy file, GNMP; Coco, *A Strange and Blighted Land*, 38.

20 Strouss, *History of the Fifty-Seventh Pennsylvania Veteran Volunteers*, 95-96; Coco, *A Strange and Blighted Land*, 42; "Newlyweds in the Grove," *Asbury Park Press*, June 17, 1914; Minnigh, *Gettysburg What They Did Here*, 150. At least 33 bullet scars are still visible on the southern and western sides of the house.

erupted between the two men. Major Burns struck Alexander with his sword, and then put a pistol to the reverend's head, "threatening to blow out his brains." One might speculate that Burns was drinking to escape from the battle's trauma. However, this appears to have been typical behavior since Burns was brought up on misconduct charges at least three times during his military career. Such conduct did not prevent future promotions in the Army of the Potomac. Burns mustered out as a lieutenant colonel in June 1865.[21]

Mary Sherfy and the remainder of the family returned home within a day or two of Joseph and Raphael. By July 9, a correspondent from the New York *Herald* recorded little improvement in conditions on the Sherfy property. "In every place it is strewn with the wreck of battle," the *Herald* reported. The Peach Orchard left the impression of desperate fighting. "Artillery shot had ploughed through the ground in every direction, and the trees did not by any means escape the fury of the storm." Confederate artillery refuse remained strewn everywhere. Fifteen dead horses were "swollen to an enormous size. As yet the citizens have made no attempt to bury the putrefying horses." The correspondent empathized with the Sherfys' plight. "I fear the battle has made sad havoc with their property." Nevertheless, the family had safely reunited and began the process of rebuilding amid an uncertain future.[22]

The Army of Northern Virginia's future also remained in doubt as they departed Gettysburg. Heavy rains and bad roads impeded their march, and Longstreet acknowledged his "exhausted men and animals were not in condition for rapid movement." Encounters with local civilians sometimes tested his patience. During one stop, a number of women approached Longstreet to complain that his soldiers were killing their fattest hogs and best cows. The general shook his head and replied, "Yes, madam, it's very sad – very sad; and this sort of thing has been going on in Virginia more than two years – very sad." Fremantle marveled at Longstreet's "iron endurance" which seemed to require neither food nor sleep. For over 10 days after the battle, Longstreet

21 U.S. Christian Commission, *Second Annual Report 1863*, 74-75. As a result of the assault, the U.S. Christian Commission reported that they "did not accomplish quite as much here as we should" in the Third Corps field hospital. The report further added that Alexander was "quietly attending to his duties" when he was attacked by "an intoxicated major." Credit was also given to General Birney who "promptly arrested" the major. Also see Coco, *Bloodstained Field II*, 83-84; Raus, *Generation on the March*, 72-73; Small, *Jennie Wade Story*, 39, 80 (n. 62.)

22 Copy of the Claims of Joseph Sherfy, National Archives, RG 92, Records of the Quartermaster General, on file at GNMP, Library Box B-5; Thomas W. Knox, "The Battle Field at Gettysburg," *New York Herald*, July 9, 1863; Sherfey, *The Sherfey Family in the United States*, 207, transcribed copy, Sherfy file, GNMP.

tirelessly led his men out of Pennsylvania, through Maryland, and back across the Potomac River with the remainder of Lee's army.[23]

Gettysburg created friction, however, between Longstreet and one of his subordinate division commanders. Writing to his wife on July 7, General McLaws complained bitterly about the Peach Orchard assault. "In place of there being but two regiments of infantry and one battery, the enemy were in very great force, very strongly posted and aided by very numerous arty. I think the attack was unnecessary and the whole plan of battle a very bad one." Likely still smarting from Longstreet's close supervision on July 2, McLaws blamed his old friend and classmate for much of the debacle:

> Genl Longstreet is to blame for not reconnoitering the ground and for persisting in ordering the assault when his errors were discovered. During the engagement he was very excited [,] giving contrary orders to everyone, and was exceedingly overbearing. I consider him a humbug- a man of small capacity, very obstinate, not at all chivalrous, exceedingly conceited, and totally selfish. If I can it is my intention to get away from his command.[24]

Although Gettysburg was a frustrating battle for Longstreet, McLaws's criticisms were largely unwarranted. In reassessing Longstreet's July 2 performance, his greatest error was likely his over-reliance on Captain Johnston's reconnaissance and guidance. Johnston's intelligence became increasingly stale with each passing hour, yet Longstreet conducted no additional reconnaissance of the Union left flank. Although many circumstances were beyond Longstreet's control, notably Sickles's advance to the Emmitsburg Road, the careful attention to detail that characterized the First Corps commander at Second Manassas seemed lacking on July 2. Contrary to McLaws's criticisms, however, Longstreet's persistence "in ordering the assault when his errors were discovered," occurred because Lee ordered and expected an attack. Longstreet did not have the option of cancelling the assault. He modified the plan of attack, particularly Hood's movements, to adapt to Sickles's actions but this proved unsuccessful.

23 *OR*, 27/2: 361; Longstreet, *Manassas to Appomattox*, 427-428; Fremantle, *Three Months in the Southern States*, 273, 279-280.

24 Oeffinger, *A Soldier's General*, 197. McLaws, who seems to have possessed a sensitive personality, also resented an event that allegedly occurred following the repulse of Pickett's Charge. In an 1896 essay, he recalled that he had resisted being pulled back to Warfield Ridge on the afternoon of July 3, but Moxley Sorrel issued a direct order from Longstreet to do so. However, once Federal skirmishers reoccupied the abandoned ground, Sorrel reappeared and requested McLaws to re-take the position he had just abandoned. When McLaws challenged the conflicting orders, Sorrel allegedly replied that Longstreet "now denies that he gave the order for this command to retire." See Oeffinger, *A Soldier's General*, 58.

Gettysburg was not Longstreet's finest battle, but his mistakes only combined with other Confederate errors, as well as actions by the enemy, to determine the outcome. Once the July 2 attack launched, Longstreet's men characteristically hit their opponents hard. Despite many complications, Longstreet's assault appeared to succeed when Sickles's defensive position at the Peach Orchard collapsed. Better coordination among Longstreet's brigades might have made a difference on July 2, but the Union still had superior numbers and a stronger position on Cemetery Ridge.

In September 1863, Longstreet and his corps were detached from the Army of Northern Virginia and sent to Tennessee to support Lieutenant General Braxton Bragg. The assignment started well for Longstreet and he enjoyed success on the offensive at the battle of Chickamauga. There, on September 20, Longstreet stacked eight of his brigades in a deep column and directed them against a narrow Federal front. Ironically, many of his men were the same soldiers that attacked the Union left on July 2. Although Longstreet was inadvertently assisted by a Federal mistake that removed some of the opposition from his front, his powerful thrust poured through a gap in the Union lines and contributed greatly to a Confederate victory. The situation and terrain differed from Gettysburg, but Chickamauga demonstrated that Longstreet could still manage large-scale assaults.[25]

Later that winter, Longstreet's independent campaign failed against Federal forces near Knoxville. Longstreet relieved McLaws of command after an unsuccessful assault on Fort Sanders resulted in a lopsided Confederate defeat. Afterwards, the capable General Kershaw received command of the division, and McLaws was reassigned to the defenses of Savannah, Georgia. While McLaws's animosity began on July 2 at Gettysburg, the Knoxville campaign permanently embittered him against Longstreet.[26]

25 For details on Longstreet at Chickamauga, see Wert, *General James Longstreet*, 310-318; Knudsen, *General James Longstreet: The Confederacy's Most Modern Soldier*, 59-62; Furqueron, "The Bull of the Woods," 119-124.

26 Fort Sanders is also sometimes referred to as Fort Loudon, but it was named after Brig. General William P. Sanders, who was mortally wounded in a skirmish on November 18, 1863. In the disastrous defeat, Longstreet's forces lost nearly 800 men against less than 100 Union casualties. After the campaign, Longstreet requested the court-martial of generals Jerome Robertson and Evander Law. However, it was McLaws, and not Longstreet, who requested his own court-martial in order to clear his name. The court found McLaws not guilty on two specifications, but guilty on the charge of "failing in the details of his attack to make arrangements essential to success." A review by the adjutant general noted "irregularities" in the board's proceedings and ordered McLaws returned to his command. Ironically, given that he had expressed his desire to go elsewhere, McLaws lobbied hard to get his old division back.

Meanwhile, Dan Sickles arrived in Washington D.C. on July 5 to begin the painful recovery from amputation of his right leg. Among the general's first visitors was President Lincoln, who inquired on Sickles's health, but was also eager to obtain first-hand news from the field. The President thoroughly quizzed Sickles on the recent battle. Although criticism of Sickles's advance to the Peach Orchard was not yet in the public domain, one of his attending staff officers later commented that the general "certainly got his side of the story of Gettysburg well into the President's mind and heart that Sunday afternoon; and this doubtless stood him in good stead afterward." Lincoln visited the general on numerous occasions, and as Sickles slowly regained his strength over the following weeks, the New Yorker undoubtedly portrayed himself as one of the principal architects of the Union Army's victory.[27]

Sickles and the other Third Corps officers also remained worried over the fate of General Graham; last seen in a bloody heap at the Peach Orchard. On July 6, the *Philadelphia Inquirer* reported inaccurately that Graham was mortally wounded. The story undoubtedly upset the general's wife and friends. Sickles sent a terse message to Meade, "Where is Brig. Gen. C. K. Graham [?] Is he a prisoner [?] What is the state of his health [?]" On July 10, they received confirmation that Graham was alive and a prisoner of the Confederates.[28]

By the end of July, the Confederates had incarcerated Graham at the infamous Libby Prison in Richmond. Despite the prison's notorious reputation, the general later acknowledged receiving "remarkably good treatment" from an assistant surgeon posted there. The Federal Commissioner of Exchange, Brigadier General Sullivan Meredith, attempted to negotiate a prisoner exchange with his Confederate counterpart, Colonel Robert Ould. A significant amount of correspondence on the subject passed between the two governments. Charles Graham's brother John also appealed directly to Ould. Their interaction on this matter was particularly ironic. Ould was the United States Attorney who unsuccessfully prosecuted Congressman Sickles for murder in 1859,

---

Longstreet, however, clearly wanted someone else in the role and prevented McLaws's return until the job was given to Kershaw. See Oeffinger, *A Soldier's General*, 41-46, 56.

27 Rusling, *Men and Things I Saw in Civil War Days*, 13-14; Rusling, *Lincoln and Sickles*, n.p.; "Major General Daniel E. Sickles," *National Republican*, July 6, 1863; Tremain, *Two Days of War*, 99-100. For more details on this meeting and its impact see Hessler, *Sickles at Gettysburg*, 235-238; Peatman, "General Sickles, President Lincoln, and the Aftermath of the Battle of Gettysburg," *Gettysburg Magazine 28*, 117-123.

28 Tremain, *Two Days of War*, 105; *The Philadelphia Inquirer*, July 6, 1863; D.E. Sickles to Major General Meade, July 6, 1863, courtesy of the National Civil War Museum, Harrisburg, PA. Thanks to Wayne Motts for providing access.

General Sickles with his staff after Gettysburg.
LOC

while John Graham was a member of the defense team. After some tense communications, the two governments agreed to exchange General Graham for Confederate General James Kemper, who was seriously wounded during Pickett's Charge and captured afterwards. Kemper's wound was far more severe than Graham's, causing the Rebel to joke that the "Confederacy was being swindled by giving a sound man in exchange for an utterly useless one." Nevertheless, the governments agreed to swap the two generals and the Confederates released Graham in September 1863.[29]

Graham's influential friends threw lavish receptions for him upon his return to New York. He also briefed government officials on intelligence that he

29 *OR*, Series II, Vol.6 (Serial 119): 239, 266, 284-285, 315. During their correspondence, Ould replied to John Graham, "I have a very pleasing recollection of the time when we met. We were in contest, but it was without the horrors that attend this. . . . If your brother is not released it will not be any fault on this side." Also see *New York Herald*, September 25 and 29, 1863; *The Times-Picayune* (New Orleans, LA), July 29, 1863.

had gathered while in Richmond, including estimations of Longstreet's troop strength in Tennessee. In late September, Graham met up with Sickles, who was also recuperating in New York, and the men revisited their old haunts such as the Brooklyn Navy Yard. Although newspapers repeatedly reported Graham's wounds as less than serious, he recuperated for several months before receiving an assignment to the Naval Brigade with the Army of the James. As Graham's military career continued elsewhere, Sickles lost a longtime friend and partisan within the Army of the Potomac.[30]

In October 1863, after a recuperation of only three months, Sickles attempted to rejoin the Army of the Potomac. The general travelled from New York to the army's encampment in Virginia, where his Third Corps officers and men greeted him enthusiastically. Nevertheless, Meade declined Sickles's request to resume corps command. The reason, Sickles later explained, was on "account of his doubts as to my physical ability to meet the exigencies of the position of a corps commander." At least, that was the excuse Meade used. In all likelihood, their personal history also worked heavily against Sickles's reinstatement. After reviewing his Third Corps one final time, a disheartened Sickles reluctantly departed from the camp.[31]

Although Sickles no longer had a role with the Army of the Potomac, the events of the previous 90 days did not shake the confidence of his most loyal supporters. "We have great faith here in him," General Birney wrote privately. "His conduct at Gettysburg in firing on the enemy as he was massing in our front was disapproved by Meade's do nothing wait until you can't help it policy but was approved by all of this Corps. Sickles will I think command this army and in time be President. I have great confidence in him and his management." Birney's prediction of a "President Sickles" never materialized. However, the unsubstantiated theory that political aspirations motivated Sickles's advance to the Peach Orchard still creeps occasionally into Gettysburg historical interpretation.[32]

30 *New York Herald*, September 24 and 29, 1863; *Pittsburgh Daily Commercial*, September 29, 1863; Charles Graham account, February 16, 1865, Participant Accounts File 5, GNMP; *Dedication of the New York Auxiliary State Monument*, 146-147; Swanberg, *Sickles the Incredible*, 230, 405 (n. 31); Warner, *Generals in Blue*, 179; Tagg, *The Generals of Gettysburg*, 69. Graham was brevetted major general of volunteers in March 1865.

31 *CCW*, 303-304. The Third Corps enthusiasm for Sickles's return was also enhanced by their disregard for his replacement, General William H. French. See Styple, *Our Noble Blood*, 130-132, 136, 140; De Trobriand, *Four Years With the Army of the Potomac*, 545-546; Messent and Courtney, *Civil War Letters of Joseph Hopkins Twichell*, 269-270.

32 David Birney to George Gross, October 28, 1863, Birney Papers, USAHEC. For an example of the notion that politics motivated Sickles at Gettysburg, see Noah Andre Trudeau's *Gettysburg: A Testing of Courage*, 367. "Whether one of his [Sickles's] possible prizes might

Despite his lack of professional military training, Sickles based his actions at Gettysburg on what he believed was in the best interest of his command. The advance to the Peach Orchard left hundreds of men from his corps dead or wounded in the fields around the Emmitsburg Road. Yet, a reciprocal admiration emerged between Sickles and many survivors. In the battle's immediate aftermath, however, Sickles's career and reputation depended upon a favorable interpretation of his command decisions.

In October 1863, Meade submitted his official report on the Gettysburg campaign. His criticism of Sickles was fairly moderate considering the cost incurred by the Third Corps. Meade reported that Sickles, "not fully apprehending the instructions in regard to the position to be occupied," had placed his corps roughly "half a mile or three-quarters of a mile in front of the line of the Second Corps, on the prolongation of which it was designed his corps should rest." Despite this, the Third Corps sustained themselves "most heroically" from a vigorous assault.[33] General-in-Chief Henry Halleck's report was more critical of Sickles's performance:

> General Sickles, misinterpreting his orders, instead of placing the Third Corps on the prolongation of the Second, had moved it nearly three-quarters of a mile in advance an error which nearly proved fatal in the battle. The enemy attacked this corps on the 2d with great fury, and it was likely to be utterly annihilated, when the Fifth Corps moved up on the left, and enabled it to reform behind the line it was originally ordered to hold.[34]

Halleck accused Sickles directly of misinterpreting his orders. Meade, meanwhile, came under fire for failing to thwart Lee's retreat to Virginia. This politically charged atmosphere in Washington D.C. culminated in testimony by several officers before the Joint Congressional Committee on the Conduct of the War. The Committee began their investigation of Meade and the Gettysburg campaign in the spring of 1864. Meade, Sickles, Birney, and Humphreys were among those officers who testified, and the investigation became a significant

---

be a place in the White House would depend to a great extent on how well his luck held today. If he could maintain his position even to a tactical draw, his cunning and connections would let him weave his tale of near disaster into a glowing paean of victory." While Sickles was certainly ambitious, how he would have translated the Peach Orchard – win, lose, or draw – into occupation of the White House is unclear. The authors have observed this theory perpetuated by others.

33 *OR*, 27/1: 116.

34 Ibid., 27/1: 16.

forum for political partisans in the Army of the Potomac. Sickles may have been less likely to engage in a public war of words with Meade had the army commander allowed him to return to command the Third Corps. By refusing to do so, Meade unwittingly opened himself up to attacks from Sickles and his supporters.[35]

The Committee called Sickles as one of its first witnesses and the New Yorker actively supported their agenda to remove Meade from command. Sickles's testimony was far-reaching in its criticism of Meade, and also addressed Halleck's censure of his advance to the Emmitsburg Road:

> It [the advanced position] was not through any misinterpretation of orders. It was either a good line or a bad one, and, whichever it was, I took it on my own responsibility, except so far as I have already stated, that it was approved of in general terms by General Hunt. . . . I took up that line because it enabled me to hold commanding ground, which, if the enemy had been allowed to take - as they would have taken it if I had not occupied it in force - would have rendered our position on the left untenable; and, in my judgment, would have turned the fortunes of the day hopelessly against us.[36]

While Sickles's testimony appeared to accept responsibility for his actions, he also undermined his own narrative with bold falsehoods. "Fortunately, my left had succeeded in getting into position on Round Top and along the commanding ridge to which I have referred; and those positions were firmly held by the Third Corps." Such a misstatement indicates that even Sickles likely realized his error in leaving Little Round Top unoccupied. Although the hill had not originally figured into Lee's plan of attack, Little Round Top increasingly played a key role in the interpretation of July 2 at Gettysburg. As a result, the significance of other terrain features such as the Peach Orchard diminished due to an increased focus on Little Round Top.[37]

35 It is beyond our scope to provide a full analysis of the so-called "Meade Sickles Controversy" or the Joint Committee testimony. For a recent detailed interpretation, see Hessler, *Sickles at Gettysburg*, 235-299. The Joint Committee was a "committee of inquiry into the general conduct of the war," created early in the war to investigate the Union's difficulty in achieving battlefield victories. The committee consisted of three senators and four representatives, and was controlled by "Radical" Republicans who favored a merciless punishment of the South. They were also skeptical of West Point graduates and their commitment to the war effort. Since Southern Democrats had led the charge to secession, the committee's Republicans increasingly linked Union battlefield defeats with the presence of Democrats in the Northern army's leadership and distrusted West Point as a breeding ground of allegedly traitorous Democrat generals. See Tap, *Over Lincoln's Shoulder*, 18-24; Hyde, *The Union Generals Speak*, X, 2-5; Sauers, *Gettysburg: The Meade Sickles Controversy*, 50.

36 *CCW*, 298. Also see Hyde, *The Union Generals Speak*, 42-43.

37 Hyde, *The Union Generals Speak*, 44-45. In another example, Sickles claimed that he had told Meade at the Peach Orchard, "I could not, with one corps, hold so extended a line

The question of whether Sickles truly understood the tactical or strategic value of Little Round Top, and why he preferred the Peach Orchard, remains perplexing to Gettysburg historians. There is no evidence that Sickles ever went to Little Round Top's summit on the morning of July 2. As a result, there is no indication that he assessed the advantages offered by that high ground.[38]

Little Round Top's primary military value was as an observation point for studying enemy movements and as a signal station for communications with other Union positions. The limited Federal artillery on Little Round did assist in repulsing Longstreet's attacks on July 2 – 3. However, modern analysis has questioned the long-held belief that Confederate artillery could have successfully used the summit to fire north and dislodge Meade's army from Cemetery Ridge. In comparison, the Peach Orchard proved inadequate for Northern defense on July 2 and for Southern artillery on the following day. Sickles shouldered the blame for failure to comply with the intent of Meade's orders. He overextended Union interior lines and in doing so created the chaos that resulted in a patchwork defense of the left flank.[39]

On July 2, when Meade learned of Sickles's advance, he immediately directed troops to occupy Little Round Top. This demonstrated that Meade considered the hill an important component of his overall Cemetery Ridge defense. In his report dated October 1863, Meade referred to Round Top only as a "very prominent ridge." During his March 1864 committee testimony, however, the general greatly elevated the significance of Little Round Top, characterizing it as, "the key-point of my whole position." Meade insisted, "If they [the Confederates] had succeeded in occupying that, it would have prevented me from holding any of the ground which I subsequently held to the last." Whether Meade purposely increased Little Round Top's importance during his

---

against the rebel army; but that, if supported, the line could be held; and, in my judgment, it was a strong line, and the best one." The committee did not bother to challenge him on this point. If he knew his line was too extended, and could only be saved by support from others, then why did he advance in the first place? Such lack of scrutiny offers some proof that the committee was treating Sickles lightly as a part of their broader agenda to discredit Meade.

38 The closest acknowledgment that Little Round Top was occupied by Third Corps leadership remains General Birney's report that his division was "resting its left on the Sugar Loaf Mountain" that morning. *OR*, 27/1: 482.

39 See Adelman, *The Myth of Little Round Top*, for a summary of Little Round Top's evolving importance and an assessment of the hill's military value. However, there is irony in the continued criticism of Sickles's failure to defend Little Round Top while modern revisionism also attempts to diminish the hill's importance. The authors agree that Cemetery Hill, and not Little Round Top, was the key to the Union Army's overall defensive position. See Harman, *Cemetery Hill: The General Plan was Unchanged* for an analysis of Cemetery Hill's value.

testimony is open to conjecture. Nevertheless, his apparent reassessment of Little Round Top amplified the severity of Sickles's failure to occupy the hill.[40]

In response to Meade's testimony, the New York *Herald* printed a letter penned under the pseudonym of "Historicus." The author claimed to be an "impartial" eyewitness to the July 2 engagement. In this version of events, Sickles realized the importance of occupying the elevated Emmitsburg Road ridge "and to extend his lines to the commanding eminence known as the Round Top. . . . Unless this were done, the left and rear of our army would be in the greatest danger." According to Historicus, Sickles's advanced position represented the most effective defense of Little Round Top, because otherwise Longstreet "would have had easy work in cutting up our left wing." In order to "prevent this disaster, Sickles waited no longer for orders from General Meade," but proactively advanced his men to hold the Emmitsburg Road crest and "cover the threatened rear of the army." Historicus further portrayed Meade as a timid commander who "had decided upon a retreat," and by implication, did not deserve credit for the victory. In fact, the account provided by Historicus perpetuated several inaccuracies. It was impossible, for example, to defend the Army of the Potomac's rear from the Peach Orchard. This sort of illogic and mudslinging directed more scrutiny toward the perceived military merits of Little Round Top and away from the Emmitsburg Road. Meade originally testified that he was of the "opinion that General Sickles did what he thought was for the best." However, the escalating "false and perverted statements," convinced him that Sickles was acting on behalf of a broader agenda to discredit and remove him from command.[41]

Fortunately, Meade was not alone in this fight. General Humphreys was among several Union officers who testified in Meade's support. Humphreys had been a staunch Meade ally before Gettysburg, and his time served under Sickles in the Third Corps likely strengthened that bond. Shortly after the battle, in an obvious reference to Sickles, Humphreys wrote privately of "my mortification at seeing men over me and commanding me who should have been far below me." Five days after Gettysburg, Humphreys accepted a role

40 *OR*, 27/1: 116; *CCW*, 332-333; Hyde, *The Union Generals Speak*, 108-109. Meade referred to "Round Top" or "Round Top Ridge" and did not differentiate between Big Round Top and Little Round Top. This was common in the battle's immediate aftermath.

41 Historicus reprinted in *OR*, 27/1: 128-136; Meade, *Life and Letters*, 2: 178-180. Historicus submitted two letters to the *Herald*. His true identity has unnecessarily mystified historians and Gettysburg students. Whether or not Sickles wielded the pen that wrote the actual letters, the expressed words were clearly his. See Hessler, *Sickles at Gettysburg*, 281-287, 296; Sauers, *Gettysburg: The Meade Sickles Controversy*, 58-62.

as Meade's chief of staff and he appeared before the committee on March 21, 1864. Since Humphreys was now free of the Third Corps, he detailed mistakes such as his own circuitous arrival at Gettysburg on July 1 and the collapse of Birney's line on July 2. Humphreys asserted that Sickles erred in moving too far in advance of Meade's main battle line. The fact that the Confederates had crushed Sickles's position, and yet failed to capture Cemetery Ridge, "undoubtedly" proved the sagacity of Meade's judgment.[42]

Meade ultimately survived efforts to remove him from command and remained at the helm of the Army of the Potomac for the remainder of the war. In March 1864, he reorganized the army into three corps, and in doing so, dismantled Sickles's Third Corps. Birney assumed command of a division that consolidated many of the old Third Corps regiments and became part of Hancock's Second Corps. Meade took some satisfaction in overseeing the demise of Sickles's old command and the end of what he referred to as "the smashed up Third Corps."[43]

Although the Third Corps's death occurred in a series of paper shuffles and personality conflicts, the 4,211 total casualties incurred at Gettysburg accelerated their fall. The end came as a heavy blow to many of Sickles's officers and men. The Third Corps may have been deficient in military training at the upper levels of command, but Sickles's tenure had created a fighting spirit among the troops. To Colonel Regis de Trobriand, these men would always be remembered as "the veterans of Sickles." After the war, the veterans looked back on their corps as "first in attack, last in retreat, third - only in name."[44]

42 Humphreys, *Andrew Atkinson Humphreys*, 202, 329; *CCW*, 388-389, 393-395, 397-398; Hyde, *The Union Generals Speak*, 182-193, 195-202; Tagg, *The Generals of Gettysburg*, 75. Much of the committee agenda and testimony centered on whether Meade had acted aggressively enough in pursuing Lee's army after Gettysburg and at Williamsport. The committee tried to get Humphreys to admit, after having fought a defensive battle, that the Army of the Potomac should have been fresher than Lee's army and better equipped to prevent the Confederate escape. Humphreys did admit, "We should have attacked them as soon as possible" at Williamsport, but generally thought that the later examination of Lee's line proved that "we should have suffered very severely." Humphreys served with the Army of the Potomac through the remainder of the war, and in November 1864 he assumed command of the Second Corps. In 1883, he died of natural causes at the age of 73.

43 Meade, *Life and Letters*, 2: 189-190; Davis, *Life of David Bell Birney*, 211; De Trobriand, *Four Years with the Army of the Potomac*, 564, 567; *OR*, 27/1: 104-105; Jordan, *Winfield Scott Hancock*, 107-108. Earlier, the Eleventh and Twelfth Corps were shipped to Tennessee. Meade's consolidation reduced the Army of the Potomac into three corps. The Second Corps remained under Hancock, and the Sixth Corps under John Sedgwick, while Gouverneur Warren took command of the Fifth Corps. Hancock sent Birney the Third Corps colors to keep as their "proper custodian."

44 De Trobriand, *Four Years with the Army of the Potomac*, 517-518; "Third Army Corps Union," *New York Times*, May 6, 1871.

Maj. Gen. Winfield Scott Hancock
LOC

Perhaps none shifted their allegiances as promptly as David Birney, one of Sickles's most outwardly loyal supporters. He quickly accepted life under Hancock, and distanced himself from Sickles in the process. Yet, Birney had to awkwardly grovel to prove his loyalty. In early April 1864, Hancock helped his new subordinate gain an audience with Meade. Despite the fact that the two Philadelphians had been hostile to each other since Fredericksburg, Meade claimed that during this meeting, Birney "disclaimed ever having entertained unfriendly feelings towards me, or being a partisan of Sickles, and expressed the hope that he would be permitted to serve under me."[45]

Birney remained with the army and served with distinction through Grant's 1864 Overland campaign, but did not live to see the end of the war. He died of illness on October 18, 1864, at his home in Philadelphia. Somewhat surprisingly, Birney earned Meade's professional respect during their final year together. "General Birney is undoubtedly a loss to the army," Meade confided to his wife. "He was a very good soldier, and very energetic in the performance of his duties. During the last campaign he had quite distinguished himself." Although the two men had settled their professional differences, the commanding general confessed, "I never liked him personally, because I did

45 David Birney to George Gross, April 5 and 18, 1864, Birney Papers, USAHEC; Meade, *Life and Letters*, 2: 189-190; George Meade to Margaret Meade, April 11 and 18, 1864, George Meade Collection, HSP. Meade outwardly claimed that he was unaware of any hard feelings with Birney other than what he had read of Birney's own Congressional Committee testimony in the newspapers. This was disingenuous, since Meade was privately telling his wife, "I don't consider him a reliable man & think the less I have to do with him the better. There is always an issue . . . between us about Fredericksburg." After their meeting, Birney wrote friends, "I am again on very pleasant terms with Gen. Meade." Birney described a "quite pleasant" meeting in which he supposedly offered to resign, but Meade "assured me of his high regard" and asked that he remain. Clearly each man had different perceptions of their conversation or Birney was putting the best face possible on it.

not consider him a reliable person." Given their acrimonious history together, Meade's praise was a testimonial to Birney's abilities on the battlefield.[46]

Although Meade remained in command of the army and Sickles never returned to the field, their supporters continued to argue the merits of their respective cases. The general consensus among Civil War historians asserts that Sickles's advance to the Peach Orchard and Emmitsburg Road was a critical blunder, one that nearly lost the battle for the Army of the Potomac. The simple fact that the Federals lost the position while suffering heavy casualties seems to validate this viewpoint, although the steady supply of reinforcements directed to Meade's left flank prevented the Army of the Potomac from courting a full-blown defeat.

The fact also remains that Longstreet suffered heavy losses fighting for what proved to be meaningless positions. The ultimate objective of the Confederates was Cemetery Hill, but Longstreet wasted considerable manpower against Sickles's advance line, specifically the majority of the 4,700 casualties in McLaws and Hood's divisions. On the afternoon of July 2, as the first shots of the battle for the Peach Orchard echoed across the Sherfy farm, Meade warned Sickles that the Peach Orchard was "neutral ground" and could not be used to advantage by either army. Sickles, Lee, Longstreet, and thousands of other men learned the truth of this assessment. It took two of the bloodiest days of the war to prove George Meade correct. Longstreet and Sickles fought for ground that was not key terrain; neither army gained an advantage from the Emmitsburg Road. In the final assessment, neither side was helped by Sickles's advance to the Peach Orchard.[47]

Many factors influenced Sickles's decision to advance, most notably his belief that the "commanding ground" along the Emmitsburg Road was preferable to the rocky and wooded low-ground north of Little Round Top. Other influences included Sickles and Meade's inability to effectively work together,

46 Davis, *Life of David Bell Birney*, 274-279; De Trobriand, *Four Years with the Army of the Potomac*, 654; Warner, *Generals in Blue*, 34-35; George Meade to Margaret Meade, October 19, 1864, George Meade Collection, HSP; Meade, *Life and Letters*, 2: 235. Meade's quote, "I never liked him personally," was stricken from the published *Life and Letters*.

47 Numerous examples abound of history's negative judgment of Sickles's advance. See Coddington, *The Gettysburg Campaign*, 445-447; Pfanz, *Gettysburg, The Second Day*, 425; Powell, "Advance to Disaster: Sickles, Longstreet, and July 2nd, 1863," *Gettysburg Magazine 28*, 40-48. Hessler, *Sickles at Gettysburg*, 389-406, summarized a large number of historians' opinions on Sickles. Gettysburg students often debate the merits of Sickles's advance through any number of "what-if" scenarios that typically assume Sickles stayed on Cemetery Ridge and then debate hypothetical outcomes. In reality, these debates are unnecessary. The actual outcome and casualties adequately portray the results of Sickles's advance.

Buford's cavalry removal, and the specter of the recent Chancellorsville defeat. Hindsight was not one of the elements available to Sickles and his officers on July 2. In spite of the battlefield casualties that his actions created, Sickles's historical reputation has been damaged the most by his post-battle attacks against Meade. Sickles would likely enjoy a better standing among historians had he gone away quietly after Gettysburg. For a man like Sickles, however, such a course of action was unimaginable.

The battle for the Peach Orchard and Emmitsburg Road was a soldier's fight. Barksdale's inspirational example led his Mississippians across the road. Their combat abilities carried the brigade until exhaustion and Yankee reinforcements broke their cohesion. Three of Barksdale's four regimental commanders and one half of the Mississippi brigade fell killed or wounded. Nearby, scores of Kershaw's South Carolinians fell due to lack of support and a miscarriage of orders. The less-heralded sacrifices in brigades led by Wilcox and Lang were even more futile. These soldiers fought over the same ground for two consecutive days with no decisive result except the loss of life.

From a defensive perspective, Federal command and control was severely impaired at the division and brigade-levels. This was due to a mixture of poor positioning, a lack of coordination, erratic communication, and the natural chaos of battle. As the Northern regiments and batteries disintegrated under the weight of the Confederate attack, the officers and men displayed both the best and the worst aspects of leadership. Men like Edward Bailey, Henry Madill, Calvin Craig, Freeman McGilvery, Nelson Ames, George Willard, and many others fought to keep the actions of superiors from bringing disaster to the army. Their resistance helped check Longstreet's attack and afforded Meade the time needed to send reinforcements to the south end of the battlefield.

The Peach Orchard witnessed some of the most intense artillery and infantry fighting at Gettysburg. At least 5,000 men fought near the Sherfys' immediate property and almost 2,300 became casualties. Many more fell further north along the Emmitsburg Road and in adjoining actions. The sad irony is that commanders on both sides misjudged the military value of the Sherfys' ground as an artillery platform. This miscalculation arose primarily from their inability to properly reconnoiter and assess the terrain. Meade correctly understood the small plot of peach trees and the surrounding Emmitsburg Road ridge as neutral ground. Its occupation by General Sickles set in motion a chain of events that sacrificed his Third Corps, forced Meade to maneuver men across all parts of the field, weakened Longstreet's attack, encouraged Lee to continue fighting on July 3, and cost thousands of men in both armies. At the battle of Gettysburg, no other single terrain feature can claim such far-reaching impacts as the Peach Orchard. [48]

48 These totals sum Federal strengths (3,439) and losses (1,474) from Graham's entire brigade, 2nd New Hampshire, 3rd Michigan, 3rd Maine, 73rd New York, 7th New Jersey, and the batteries under Clark, Hart, Thompson, Ames, and Bucklyn. On the Confederate side, Barksdale's 1,615 men with 789 losses were the primary brigade to fight on the Sherfys' property. Both sides then total 5,054 men with 2,263 losses.

Chapter 11

Sherfy's Peach Orchard Immortal

The civilians inherited the task of rebuilding Gettysburg. The dead of both armies primarily remained buried on the fields where they fell. By the fall of 1863, the exhumation of Union soldiers for reburial in the new National Cemetery was underway. The burial crews worked their way slowly across the battlefield and collected any evidence available to assist in properly identifying the bodies.[1]

A pocket-book, a small bill, and 50 cents were among the items found on the body of Private Alonzo Hemstreat of the 105th Pennsylvania. With nothing to indicate his native state, he was mistakenly buried in the New York plot. Private William Crowl of the 141st Pennsylvania was identified by a needle case and pencil. The identity of Corporal Joseph Wentworth of the 12th New Hampshire was determined by a letter. Such was the macabre work carried out across the farms that sprawled along the Emmitsburg Road. Of course, none of these efforts impacted the Confederate dead, who remained buried unless exhumed accidentally.[2]

1 "There was not a grave permitted to be opened or a body searched unless I was present," reported supervisor Samuel Weaver. *Report of the Select Committee relative to the Soldiers' National Cemetery together with the accompanying documents as reported to the House of Representatives of the Commonwealth of Pennsylvania, March 31, 1864*, 39.

2 Ibid., 41, 44-46, 52. Samuel Weaver confidently noted in his report, "I firmly believe that there has not been a single mistake made in the removal of the soldiers to the cemetery by taking the body of a rebel for a Union soldier." Confederate dead were exhumed in the early 1870s and sent to cemeteries in the South, the most notable being Richmond's

During these months, S.G. Elliott & Company of Philadelphia drafted a map to denote the gravesites of Union and Confederate soldiers, along with dead horses, on the battlefield. It was an impressive undertaking, although not completely accurate. At least four mass graves, containing more than 25 Northern dead, were recorded surrounding the Sherfy house and barn. At least five Confederate corpses also lay buried nearby. Across from the house, on the east side of the Emmitsburg Road, numerous burials stretched east from the road toward the site of Sickles's headquarters at the Trostle farm. Several clusters of graves were in the immediate vicinity of the Wentz property, including at least 20 Confederate dead and one Union grouping of six. Recorded burials were much lighter in the Peach Orchard south of the Wheatfield Road; where some six Union and nine Confederates lay at rest. In total, the map indicated more than 100 corpses between the Sherfy, Wentz, Trostle, and Klingle properties. The burial concentrations suggested that the most lethal combat occurred in the fields north of the Wheatfield Road, and not in the Sherfys' mature Peach Orchard south of the road.[3]

The Sherfys and their neighbors never returned completely to their pre-battle livelihoods. Tourists replaced soldiers marching up and down the Emmitsburg Road. These visitors sometimes trampled crops and, as with tourists of any era, they did not always have the best interests of locals at heart. One such visitor was Henry Turrell, a Union veteran who attended the 1864 Dedication Day ceremonies. As Turrell travelled along the Emmitsburg Road, he stopped at the Peter Rogers house and requested some flowers from the yard. Rogers declined the request, but Turrell proceeded to help himself. The two men exchanged words and the encounter escalated with Rogers grabbing an axe. Turrell was armed, however, and shot Rogers in the abdomen. Turrell was arrested and taken to jail in Gettysburg. He then attempted an unsuccessful

---

Hollywood Cemetery. Coco, *A Strange and Blighted Land*, 94, stated that 40 Confederates "were said to be interred and never recovered" from a mass grave beneath the Peach Orchard.

3 "Elliott's Map of the Battlefield of Gettysburg," S. G. Elliott & Co. of Philadelphia, published in 1864, LOC. Although students of the battle consider the actual numbers of recorded graves on the "Elliott Map" to be inflated, the concentrations of burials represented where large numbers of bodies had been brought together for interment. It stands to reason that decaying corpses were generally not moved over extensive distances for burial. A very heavy concentration of graves surrounded the Rose farm and Wheatfield, but the mature Peach Orchard was surprisingly light on burials.

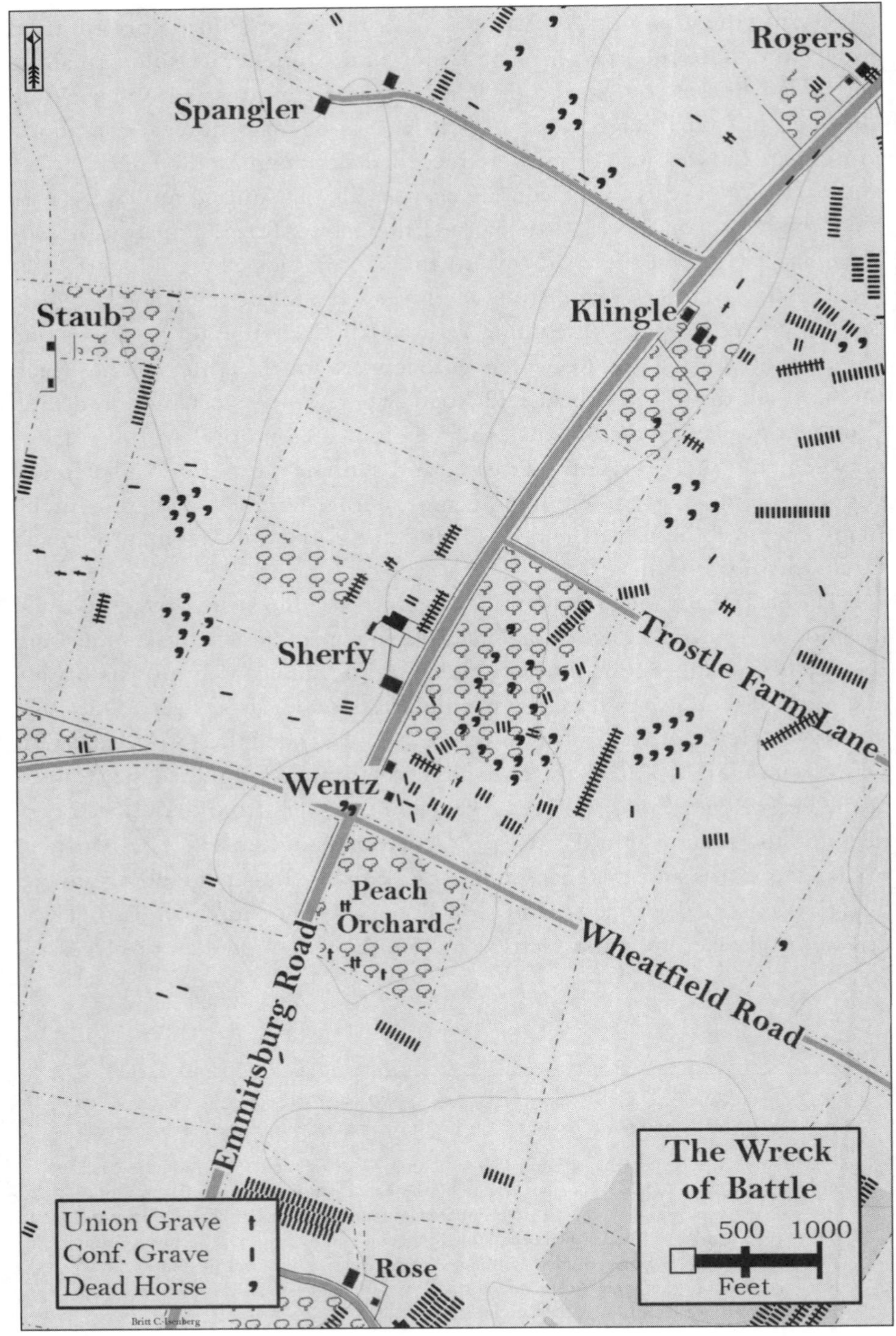
Rogers
Spangler
Staub
Klingle
Sherfy
Trostle Farm Lane
Wentz
Peach Orchard
Emmitsburg Road
Wheatfield Road
Rose
The Wreck of Battle
500 1000
Feet
Union Grave
Conf. Grave
Dead Horse
Britt C. Isenberg

jailbreak. Fortunately, Rogers survived his wound, but such news from the neighborhood surely disconcerted the Sherfys.[4]

The Sherfy family repaired their home and replanted their orchards, but it took time to recoup their losses. Reverend Sherfy had an entrepreneurial spirit and was willing to try almost any means necessary to support his family. He used his orchard's battlefield fame as a promotional tool in marketing his peaches to visitors and locals alike. He promoted the "budded, high-flavored, and cultivated" fruit as coming "right from the trees on the Battle Ground at Gettysburg." Sherfy also sold his peaches by mail order and advertised in larger nearby markets such as Baltimore.[5]

The Sherfys rebuilt their barn that was destroyed during the battle. Unfortunately, the family suffered another setback on July 4, 1866. The replacement structure burned down in a fire believed to have been set accidentally by chicken thieves. The fire destroyed the uninsured barn and some equipment, with the estimated value of the losses totaling $1,500. The family succeeded in getting their horses and cattle out safely, but Raphael Sherfy was temporarily overcome by the intense heat. A local news report described Reverend Sherfy as "one of the most inoffensive citizens" and assured readers, "he has the sympathies of the entire community."[6]

From 1868 to 1883, the Sherfys continued efforts to secure government compensation for their $2,466 war-damage claim. Agents investigated their affidavits, verified the family's loyalty, and reviewed damage details. Unfortunately, the Federal government did not accept responsibility for destruction caused by Confederate armies. Although the investigation dragged on for years, the agent inspecting the Sherfys' claim decided that Southern forces were more likely responsible for the losses. On October 17, 1883, the United States government denied the Sherfys' compensation request.[7]

4 *Adams Sentinel & General Advertiser*, November 22, November 29, 1864. The veteran may have been Henry Turrell of Company A, 14th United States Infantry, who therefore would have served at Gettysburg.

5 By 1865, consumers could purchase a dozen quart cans at $4.50 and gallon cans at $12.00. *The Baltimore Sun*, September 14-16, 1865.

6 "Barn Burnt," *Adams Sentinel*, July 10, 1866.

7 Sherfy Damage Claims, GNMP. Agent James W. Nightingale inspected the claim and filed his affidavit on August 31, 1881: "It does not appear from the claimants statement, that the United States Army took or used any of his property. The circumstances was such at the time that it was impossible to tell which side did the most damage, the rebels were as likely to have taken it all, as the Union troops, and in my opinion more so." On September 28, 1883, a report of no payments was issued to Reverend Sherfy, before being disallowed in October.

View of Peach Orchard ca. 1880.
GNMP

The family got back on their feet through their own persistence and without government help. By 1870, Joseph Sherfy's farm had a value of $5,000 and his personal estate was valued at $1,300. Eldest son Raphael returned to teaching and inspired his three sisters, Otelia, Mary and Annie, to teach. The income likely supplemented their parents' finances, and this was important since agricultural production was subject to nature's constraints. Peach trees have relatively short lives and by 1878 the majority of the wartime Peach Orchard had died. The Sherfys added new trees and the orchard's fame increased the public's demand for their peaches. The Sherfy name became synonymous with agricultural success throughout the region.[8]

8 United States Census of 1870, house number 85; Bachelder, *Gettysburg: What to See, and How to See It*, 82. For instance, in February of 1873 Reverend Sherfy reported to the local paper that "the peach buds are nearly all frozen" due to a local cold spell. The story of the frozen buds was closed with the remark, "It is hoped that other localities have escaped the severity of the winter better, but a failure of Sherfy's peaches heretofore has proven a sure index of a failure throughout the county." See "The Peach Buds," *The York Daily*, February 14, 1873. In 1880, Reverend Sherfy made the local newspapers again for his flock of six sheep. They were sheared in the spring for a combined "80 pounds of wool – the heaviest flees being 17 1/2." The story closed by simply saying, "Hard to beat." See *The York Daily*, June 18, 1880.

Raphael Sherfy married Ellen Rebert in 1871. The following year, they purchased nearly 40 acres along the Taneytown Road just east of Little Round Top and planted an orchard of their own. Raphael had a large circle of friends and was highly regarded in the community. In 1877, Adams County Democrats selected him as a Representative Delegate to the State Convention. His political career was short-lived, however, largely due to his other budding passions. He frequently delivered horticultural programs for organizations throughout the region and became well known for his expertise.[9]

The year 1882 started with great promise for the Sherfys. In addition to his speaking engagements, Raphael became the secretary for the Gettysburg-Harrisburg Railway. By then, Raphael and Ellen's family included four little girls. In September, they welcomed a son and named him Raphael.[10]

Only weeks after the birth of Raphael Jr., Reverend Joseph Sherfy became ill with typhoid and malarial fever. He died at home on October 2 at the age of 70. He was laid to rest a few days later in the yard of the German Baptist Brethren "Pfoutz" church along Marsh Creek, west of Gettysburg. "Thus has gone out another leading light in this community," mourned an obituary in the Gettysburg *Compiler*. "Rev. Sherfy was a close observer and an honest thinker, a practical, useful man." The *Compiler's* epitaph expressed the sentiments of the community. "All who have in any way been associated with him will miss him – long, long miss him."[11]

Tragically, within a few weeks of his father's death, Raphael Sr. also contracted malarial-typhoid fever. On November 18, he succumbed to the illness at only 39 years of age. The *Compiler* eulogized him as a "useful and respected citizen." The Sherfy family laid him to rest atop Cemetery Hill in Gettysburg's Evergreen Cemetery. Although she was left to raise their children

9 Bradsby, *History of Adams County*, 403; 1872 Cumberland Township Tax Records, Leonard Bricker and Raphael Sherfy, ACHS; Lake, *Atlas of Adams Co., Pennsylvania*, 43; "State Politics," *The Times* (Philadelphia), May 19, 1877; *York Daily*, June 14, 1883; *Reading Times*, January 22, 1883; "Household Farm and Garden," *The Democratic Chronicle*, March 10, 1882. In addition to his orchards, Raphael possessed a great interest in beekeeping. Students of the battle would know the property acquired by Raphael and Ellen as the Leonard Bricker property.

10 "Railroad Meeting," *The York Daily*, May 23, 1882; United States Draft Registration Cards 1942, Serial Number 83, Raphael Sherfy.

11 "Death of Rev. Joseph Sherfy," Gettysburg *Compiler*, October 4, 1882; Gettysburg *Compiler*, October 11, 1882. A transcription of the Sherfy family history erroneously lists his date of death as October 4. However, contemporary news accounts and his gravestone report the date of death as October 2.

alone, his widow Ellen also remained in the fruit business for a number of years after his death.[12]

While the Sherfys moved on, the battle's veterans took increased interest in commemorating the regiments and batteries that fought near the Peach Orchard. In August 1869, the survivors of Thompson's battery became the first to officially mark their position in the Peach Orchard. By the late 1870s, increased veterans' involvement in preservation led to more monument placements across the battlefield, including in the Peach Orchard and Emmitsburg Road sector. In October 1885, Phillips's 5th Massachusetts and Bigelow's 9th Massachusetts Battery monuments were dedicated along the Wheatfield Road. Although not in the Peach Orchard proper, these became the first monuments formally erected in the vicinity. These somber ceremonies allowed survivors to reflect on the battle's outcome, lost comrades, and their own pending mortality. Corporal Thomas Chase of the 5th Massachusetts Battery described his experience: "I visited the Cemetery at Gettysburg alone at five a.m., and stood by the graves of two of our Battery who fell there, and my thoughts went back to the day I saw them fall. There they sleep, in those acres of graves and monuments."[13]

New York passed legislation in 1886 to establish a Monuments Commission for the Battlefield of Gettysburg. Dan Sickles received an appointment as the commission's chairman. For nearly the remainder of his life, Sickles undertook a mission to appropriate funds and place monuments to all New York regiments, batteries, and ranking commanders on the battlefield. These new monuments required dedication speeches in front of aging but enthusiastic

12 *Gettysburg Compiler*, November 23, 1882, October 26, 1886; Sherfy, *The Sherfy Family in the United States*, 195-197; Bradsby, *History of Adams County*, 403. Also see "100 Years Ago," *Gettysburg Times*, November 23, 1982. Although Raphael Sherfy did not live to see his children grow, he would have likely been proud as a lifelong believer in education to know that his only son became the first family member to graduate from college. After graduating from Strayer Business College in Lancaster, Pennsylvania, Raphael Jr. continued to George Washington University and obtained his doctoral degree in dental surgery. He spent his professional life practicing in Washington D.C. See "Dr. Raphael Sherfy," *The Evening Sun* (Hanover, PA), June 20, 1950.

13 Vanderslice, *Gettysburg: A History of the Gettysburg Battle-field Memorial Association*, 199-204, 210-211, 216-217; "Hampton's Battery at Gettysburg," *Pittsburgh Weekly Gazette*, August 30, 1869; Appleton, *History of the Fifth Massachusetts Battery*, 676, 680; Baker, *History of the Ninth Mass. Battery*, 209; Platt, *This is Holy Ground,* 8. In August 1883, Massachusetts appropriated $5,000 to purchase the ground upon which their units fought, along with an additional $500 per unit to erect a monument on-site. Among the other monuments dedicated at that time was the 11th Massachusetts Volunteer Infantry from Carr's brigade further north along the Emmitsburg Road.

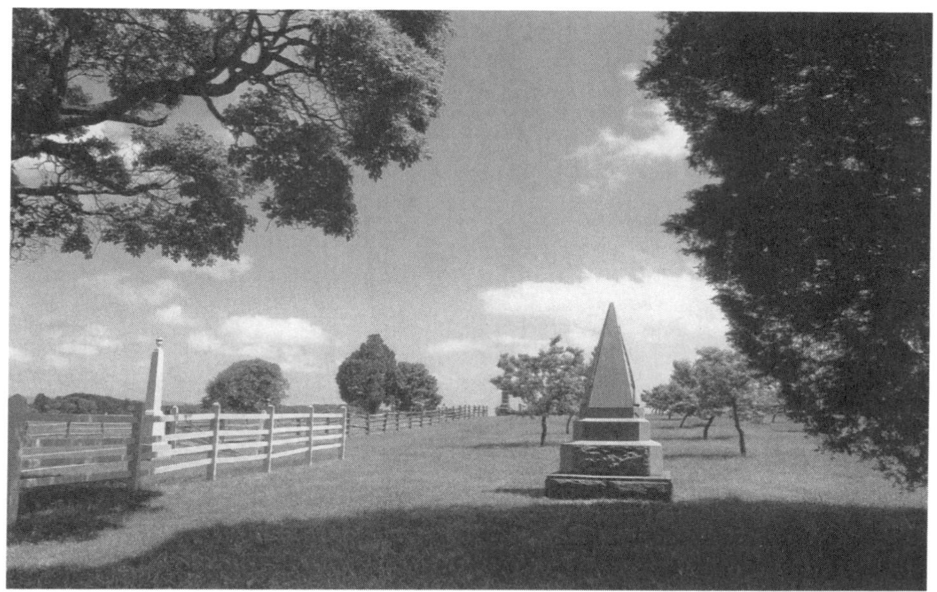

The "bloody angle of the second day." Monuments to the 2nd New Hampshire and 68th Pennsylvania.
Courtesy of Licensed Battlefield Guide Steve Slaughter

veterans, along with ever-present newsmen. Sickles's role secured his place as a prominent fixture at battlefield reunions, where he was always ready to defend his controversial move to the Peach Orchard.[14]

A large Third Corps reunion took place in Gettysburg during the early days of July 1886. The attendees included Henry Tremain, Charles Graham, George Randolph, Joseph Carr, and Thomas Rafferty. On July 2, Sickles and Graham observed the dedication of the 2nd New Hampshire's monument in the Peach Orchard. The address by regimental historian Martin Haynes recalled how "the old Second fought the greatest of its many battles, and helped to render Sherfy's peach orchard immortal." Rationalizing their inability to hold the Peach Orchard quickly became a lasting theme in the dedicatory addresses of Third Corps veterans. "Not that they were surrounded, demoralized, and shot down like sheep," Haynes recalled, "but in every instance in square, stand-up fight of line to line, face to face with the enemy." The 2nd's position

14 *New York at Gettysburg*, 1: 1-6 The New York Monuments Commission's formal responsibilities included securing appropriations, charting a battlefield map, overseeing the creation of a detailed history of the battle, and selecting and supervising the creation of new monuments.

had been the "bloody angle" of the second day, and if the regiment's charge into the orchard had been "dashing and plucky," their subsequent retreat was "an exhibition of consummate, nervy discipline." The memories of the veterans increasingly transformed the Peach Orchard fight into one that was lost against overwhelming odds and not due to any lack of fighting ability.[15]

Sickles was the keynote speaker at the 1886 reunion and used the occasion to "explain and vindicate his movement in bringing on the engagement of the second day." His remarks did not disappoint the partisan audience. Pandemonium erupted in the auditorium when Sickles took to the stage, "on one leg and two crutches, a towering figure in a major general's uniform . . . once more at the head of his old Third Corps." Sickles promptly launched into a lengthy criticism of George Meade, who "knew nothing of Gettysburg." Sickles insisted that he had repeatedly attempted to direct Meade's attention to the left flank and occupy "the Round Tops, the key of our position, and the elevated ridge extending to the Emmitsburg Road." Sickles even dramatically "appealed to Heaven" for confirmation that he received no orders from Meade and therefore was not guilty of disobedience. "So help me God!" he exclaimed to thunderous applause. He also proposed a progressive idea that officers from both armies should return to Gettysburg in order to examine and discuss operations together. Although Southerners were not yet revisiting the battlefield in large numbers, both James Longstreet and Lafayette McLaws were reportedly open to the suggestion.[16]

Sickles's 1886 speech generated such publicity that even the long-dead George Meade responded. Prior to his demise in 1872, Meade had corresponded with Gettysburg veteran and Medal of Honor recipient George G. Benedict. In order to defend Meade's reputation from these latest attacks, Benedict published their correspondence in the Philadelphia *Weekly Press*. "Sickles's movement practically destroyed his own corps, the Third," Meade wrote, "caused a loss of 50 per cent in the Fifth Corps, and very heavily damaged the Second Corps . . . producing 66 per cent of the loss of the whole battle." In assessing the outcome, Meade astutely observed, "and with what result- driving us back to the position he was ordered to hold originally." Meade argued that these crippling losses prevented him "from having the audacity in the offense that I might otherwise have had." By Meade's reasoning, Sickles was to blame

15 "Third Corps Reunion," Undated newspaper clipping, GNMP Vertical Files; Haynes, *A History of the Second Regiment*, 306-309. Our thanks to Alan Brunelle for sharing his insights on the "Gallant Second" New Hampshire throughout this project.

16 "A New Sensation," *Gettysburg Compiler*, July 6, 1886.

for the Army of the Potomac's inability to destroy Lee's army. "If this is an advantage - to be so crippled in battle without attaining an object - I must confess I cannot see it."[17]

Lafayette McLaws joined the fray and rejected the notion that Sickles had caused the Union victory on July 2. In the Philadelphia *Weekly Press*, McLaws pointed out that Sickles's command was driven from the advanced position it held on July 2, and that the Confederates occupied the same ground until ordered to retire on July 3. If this outcome was a triumph for Sickles, then McLaws sarcastically quipped, "the word 'victory' must mean something in the more modern vernacular which is not given to it in the dictionaries."[18]

After the war, McLaws lived in Georgia where he became active in business and received political appointments. He also wrote papers and lectured publicly about his wartime experiences. Although McLaws tempered his criticisms of Longstreet's actions at Gettysburg, he never completely forgave his former commander for being removed during the Knoxville campaign. Lafayette McLaws died in 1897 at 76 years old.[19]

James Longstreet was motivated to support Sickles's arguments. While Sickles and veterans of the Army of the Potomac revisited Gettysburg during the 1870s and 1880s, these post-war years remained complicated for Lee's "Old War Horse." Longstreet angered many Southern Democrats, and former Confederate colleagues, by cooperating openly with the governing Republican Party during Reconstruction. Following Lee's death in 1870, former Confederate generals Jubal Early and William Pendleton exploited these political grievances by publicly criticizing Longstreet's military record. Their goal was to deflect criticism of Gettysburg away from Lee and toward the increasingly unpopular Longstreet. Beginning in 1877, Early and a lengthy list of former Southern leaders brought the dispute to the pages of the *Southern Historical Society Papers*. Although they supposedly assessed the "causes of the defeat" at Gettysburg, Longstreet's recent actions negatively biased most of the participants. Not surprisingly, most contributors were critical of his battle performance. Debates over the fighting on the second day typically focused on whether Lee expected Longstreet to attack at sunrise on July 2. Although

17 Meade, *Life and Letters*, 2: 350-351, 354. At the time of this writing, the National Park Service utilizes quotations from this letter in its wayside interpretive exhibit at the Peach Orchard.

18 McLaws, "The Federal Disaster on the Left," Philadelphia *Weekly Press*, August 4, 1886.

19 Oeffinger, *A Soldier's General*, 56-60.

allegations of impropriety on Longstreet's part were false, the general defended himself against accusations of tardiness and disobedience of orders for the remainder of his life.[20]

Longstreet attempted to communicate his side of the story in print. Publishing reminiscences from aging veterans boosted newspaper and magazine circulation during the post-war era, and Longstreet became a prolific contributor to series such as *The Century* magazine's "War Series." From 1884 to 1887, many surviving leaders from both sides of the late unpleasantness assailed each other on paper rather than on battlefields. Longstreet's Gettysburg-related contributions highlighted Lee's insistence on attacking and abandonment of "our original plans" to fight on the defensive. Regarding the ground gained at the Peach Orchard on July 2, Longstreet told his readers, "General Lee pronounced it a success . . . but we had accomplished little toward victorious results. Our success of the first day had led us into battle on the 2d, and the battle on the 2d was to lead us into the terrible and hopeless slaughter on the 3d." While there was some truth in such analysis, Longstreet's prose typically inflamed his Southern critics and their response was predictably negative.[21]

The upshot of efforts to vilify Longstreet in the South was that he became a popular figure in the North. His well-publicized Republican affiliations illustrated perhaps the preeminent example of a reconstructed Confederate leader. Consequently, the Northern press often covered Longstreet's travels around the country.

In July 1888, Longstreet and Sickles both returned to Gettysburg for the 25th anniversary. In a scene that would be repeated for years to come, the citizens of Gettysburg welcomed throngs of veterans, newsmen, and visitors to the town. "Gettysburg is a beautiful place," observed the *New York Sun*, "but most of the people are mighty queer." The reporter believed that the

20 See "Causes Of The Defeat Of General Lee's Army At The Battle Of Gettysburg -- Opinions Of Leading Confederate Soldiers," in *Southern Historical Society Papers*, Vol. IV, 1877. Among Longstreet's perceived sins during this period, in 1866, he contributed criticism of Robert E. Lee to William Swinton's *Campaigns of the Army of the Potomac*. See Swinton, 338-341. In 1867, Longstreet then publicly proposed that the vanquished Southern Democrats cooperate with the victorious Northern Republicans during Reconstruction. He followed up his words by becoming a member of the Republican Party and accepted political appointments in Louisiana. Jubal Early replied with an 1872 address at Washington and Lee University, in which he accused Longstreet of failing to attack as supposedly ordered "at dawn" on July 2, and that the Round Tops "could have been taken in the morning without a struggle." See Early, "The Campaigns of Gen. Robert E. Lee," *Lee the Soldier*, 60. For the best analysis of Longstreet's actions during this period, see Piston, *Lee's Tarnished Lieutenant*, 96, 105-120.

21 Longstreet, "Lee's Right Wing at Gettysburg," *Battles and Leaders*, 3: 339-342. The *Century* magazine articles were later re-printed as *Battles and Leaders of the Civil War*.

battle had created a "depressing effect" from which the locals never recovered. "Ask a sarcastic visitor what the people do for a living," the *Sun* continued, "and he will answer: 'Nothing. They live on people who come here. They sell pretend relics and poor photographs.'" Yet, despite the lack of cosmopolitan accommodations and the need to take carriages everywhere, the dissatisfied reporter from New York acknowledged that visitors came because "the sentiment which attracts is more powerful than the feeling of disgust created at the meanness of the people of the place."[22]

The veterans, however, were there to see the field and reminisce with each other. This anniversary, more than any other, emphasized the parallels between two aging warriors. Longstreet was an old soldier struggling in the world of politics. Sickles was a consummate politician who found renewed celebrity as a war veteran. Both men had their share of supporters and detractors, but it was Longstreet who emerged as the star attraction during the 1888 visit. News reporters eagerly followed his movements and one characterized him as "the man of all others who is never permitted to spend a moment alone is a tall soldierly-looking man with white hair and flowing gray whiskers." Many took notice of Longstreet's visibly failing health, and the passage of time had caused him to accept the battle's outcome. "There is evidence in its plan and conduct that the hand of God was with the cause of the Federal and against that of the Confederate army."[23]

Curious newsmen monitored Sickles and Longstreet's interactions with great interest. The sight of former enemies touring amiably across fields once strewn with their dead made an indelible impression upon all who witnessed the reunion. "It was a thrilling ride for old white-headed Longstreet," one Northern scribe editorialized about their battlefield tour. Their contingent included Joseph Carr, Dan Butterfield, and Henry Slocum. Longstreet and Sickles accomplished something that neither man did in July 1863: they reached the summit of Little Round Top. The 146th New York's monument dedication was in progress nearby, "but as soon as word passed that Longstreet was on the hill one-half of the spectators left their places and scampered to the spot where the famous group was." They found Sickles sitting on a rock resting

22 "On Gettysburg's Field," *New York Sun*, July 1, 1888.

23 "It's Again a Tented Field," *New York Times*, July 1, 1888; Undated newspaper article, Folder #190, Battle of Gettysburg: 25th Anniversary, ACHS; Wert Scrapbook, #34, Vol. 3, p. 146; *Gettysburg Star and Sentinel*, July 17, 1888.

Joshua Chamberlain, Henry Slocum, Longstreet, Sickles, Joseph Carr and other veterans at the 25th battle anniversary.
GNMP

the stump of his leg and Longstreet standing at his side. The crowd eagerly rushed Longstreet to catch his hand and gave him an enthusiastic reception.[24]

While continuing across the battlefield, Sickles turned to Longstreet and said, "General, there has been a great deal of controversy about the position I took; its precipitating your attack and causing a great loss of life to the Union army." In view of Meade's disapproval of the advanced Third Corps line, Sickles asked Longstreet, "Which position would you have preferred to attack me in?" Longstreet took the cue without missing a beat. "Why, on the continuation of Hancock's lines, by all means. It would have enabled me to

24 "It's Again a Tented Field," *New York Times*, July 1, 1888; "The Second Day's Fight: Interesting Ceremonies on the Gettysburg Battlefield," *The Sun* (New York), July 3, 1888; *New York World*, July 4, 1888.

obtain a much better view of your line and give me more open field in which to work." Longstreet continued, "I was thoroughly acquainted with Hancock's position, but had to go at you in the Peach Orchard without exactly knowing what I was meeting."[25]

This exchange established a public alliance between Sickles and Longstreet. For the remainder of their lives, each man stood ready to defend the other's war-record when called upon. Longstreet's life almost ended, however, on the return trip home. On July 12, he survived a deadly train accident that claimed nine lives and became known as the "Wreck at the Fat Nancy."[26]

Among other veterans, Charles Graham also remained a Third Corps loyalist and Sickles confidant. Graham served as president of the Third Army Corps Union fraternal organization, and presided over many reunions. In the 1870s, he replaced General George B. McClellan as chief engineer of the New York City Department of Docks, and also received an appointment as port surveyor for New York. In 1879, Graham collected a disability pension from the effects of his injuries sustained at Gettysburg. Personal scandal touched Graham in 1880 when a New York actress, who was likely his estranged daughter, filed a slander suit against him after he called her a "bastard."[27]

Graham joined Sickles and Carr on the New York Board of Commissioners for Gettysburg Monuments. Graham also served as engineer of that organization. He put his professional skills to good use by surveying and mapping the battlefield for proposed New York monuments sites. As result, Graham returned to Gettysburg frequently with other Third Corps leaders. One of their priorities was marking the site of Sickles's wounding. During a July 1886 visit, an old soldier approached the commissioners and promised to identify the exact location for them. The man kept disappearing and the frustrated commissioners eventually realized that he was vanishing in order

25 Undated newspaper article, Folder #190, Battle of Gettysburg: 25th Anniversary, ACHS; Wert Scrapbook, #34, Vol. 3, p. 146, ACHS. The *New York Times* of July 2, 1888, reported that although "everybody" visited Little Round Top, the Peach Orchard, and Culp's Hill, it was East Cemetery Hill at which visitors typically spent the most amount of time.

26 "The Virginia Midland Wreck," *Baltimore Sun*, July 13, 1888; Swain, "Wreck at the Fat Nancy," *Historical Marker Database*, https://www.hmdb.org/Marker.asp?Marker=41517. The "Fat Nancy" was the nickname of a trestle that collapsed when the train carrying Longstreet passed over it.

27 "Third Army Corps Union," *New York Times*, May 6, 1871; "The Dock Commissioners," *New York Times*, July 9, 1873; "C.K. Graham Appointed Surveyor of the Port," *Brooklyn Eagle*, July 21, 1878; "Charles K. Graham: Invalid Claim for Pension (No. 304.126), National Archives; "Leonora Graham's Suit," *The Sun*, January 25, 1880. Thanks again to David Malgee for sharing his research on Charles Graham.

Generals Carr, Sickles, and Graham at the site of Sickles's wounding. October 1886.
GNMP

to get intoxicated. Graham showed himself as a master of bad puns by responding, "It is topography that we want in this matter, not toper-graphy!"[28]

In October of that year, Sickles, Graham, and Carr were among a large group of commissioners who posed for photographs at the wounding site. Although he remained active professionally, Graham's health was delicate throughout his life. Less than three years later, in April 1889, he died of pneumonia at 64 years old.[29]

28 *Brooklyn Daily Eagle*, February 17, 1887; *The Sun*, February 18, 1887; *New York Times*, December 7, 1887; *New York Tribune*, July 18, 1886. During an October 5, 1886, commissioners' meeting at Sickles's home in New York, Graham exhibited his survey of the field. General Carr was also in attendance and suggested that a large monument be placed over the graves of New York's unidentified Gettysburg dead. ""On the Gettysburg Field," *New York Times*, October 6, 1886; New *Brooklyn Daily Eagle*, October 6, 1886.

29 *Gettysburg Compiler*, November 2, 1886; *New York at Gettysburg*, 1416; "Died: Graham," *New York Times*, April 18, 1889. Thanks to Gettysburg Licensed Battlefield Guide Fred Hawthorne for determining the date of the widely reproduced Sickles wounding site photographs. These almost certainly were taken during an October 26-27, 1886 visit by the commissioners to mark positions.

The years brought more Gettysburg reunions, reconciliation, and the passing of old soldiers. Henry Cabell, former commander of McLaws's artillery battalion, attended the 1887 anniversary reunion. During the evening of July 4, he received an invitation to meet Henry Hunt. Both officers had played crucial roles in the attack and defense of the Peach Orchard. The two artillerymen discussed the battle long into the night. Both commented on, what Cabell described as, "the present happy reunion and of the entire restoration of peace and good will between the survivors of that memorable battle. It was the most pleasant incident of my visit." Hunt and Cabell both died in 1889, less than two years after this meeting, and within 11 days of each other.[30]

The increasing number of memorials in the Peach Orchard, and on the surrounding battleground, created opportunities for veterans to express their grief, hope, and to search for meaning. Medal of Honor recipient Edward Knox, of Hart's 15th New York Battery, imparted this idea simply but eloquently in an 1888 gathering. "I greet you; I respect you; I love you all; and I will hold you in my heart until the end." In spite of the ongoing tensions between Meade and Sickles partisans, and other disagreements that naturally occurred when old men came together, the numerous dedication ceremonies deepened the camaraderie among these former warriors.[31]

The 105th Pennsylvania "Wildcats" initially dedicated their monument on July 2, 1888, across the Emmitsburg Road from the Sherfy house. They held another dedication on September 11, 1889, during "Pennsylvania Day" at Gettysburg, when many other Keystone State regiments commemorated the exploits of their individual units. Lieutenant Colonel Levi Bird Duff, who served on General Birney's staff at Gettysburg, spoke to his comrades and predicted, "In times yet to come and long after we have passed away, many pilgrims will visit this battlefield. They will pause before this stone & when they read the list of battles & turn to the other face & read the number of the killed & wounded they will be filled with admiration at the heroism the loyalty & devotion of the 105 regiment." In reflecting on the deeds of his comrades,

30 Cabell, "A Visit to the Battle-Field of Gettysburg," Cabell Family Papers, VHS, 16. The 1887 reunion was noted for the attendance of numerous members of General George Pickett's Division. News accounts confirm that General Hunt was also present. See "Shoulder to Shoulder," *The Baltimore Sun*, July 4, 1887. Henry Cabell died January 31, 1889. Henry Hunt passed away on February 11, 1889.

31 *New York at Gettysburg*, 3: 1327.

The 105th Pennsylvania monument before the bronze Wildcat replaced the original "calf."
B.J. and Kathleen Pino Collection

Duff offered, "There can be no more eloquent eulogy of the dead."[32]

The ceremony went off without a hitch except for one detail. Sergeant Joseph Gray, a veteran Wildcat, delivered what he considered to be a few appropriate remarks. He told his comrades, "the only imperfection" on the monument was "the carved wildcat's head, which looks more like that of a young calf." A Pittsburgh newspaper assured readers that the image "will be remedied, however, by a bronze plate being sunk over a head bearing a correct likeness of the wildcat." Eventually, the veterans replaced the offending wildcat head with a more suitable version that remains in place today.[33]

The 68th Pennsylvania dedicated two monuments in the Peach Orchard vicinity. Former Private Alfred Craighead delivered the 1888 address for their larger monument along the Wheatfield Road. Craighead referred to this as "the most elevated part of the field, but not sufficiently so to be of any advantage in defense, it was a conspicuous mark for artillery for long range around, and open to the charge of infantry. . . . As this was the key to the whole position it was necessary to hold it all hazard, and the only alternative was to stand and be shot down without the opportunity to reply." After 25 years of reflection, Craighead remembered, "it was a terrible afternoon in

32 Helmreich, *To Petersburg with the Army of the Potomac*, 220. Levi Bird Duff's original collection of letters is preserved at Allegheny College in Meadville, Pennsylvania. The 141st Pennsylvania monument was dedicated in the Peach Orchard on "Pennsylvania Day" in September 1889. Numerous monuments were also commemorated across the battlefield on this occasion. One newspaper commented, "The crowd today was something awful. The streets were filled with people last night who were unable to find quarters and they came in by thousands today. . . .The whole affair has been rather poorly managed." See "Pennsylvania Day," *The Scranton Republican*, September 12, 1889.

33 "Granite Lasts and so do the Memories of the Battlefield of Gettysburg: The Peach Orchard," *The Pittsburgh Dispatch*, September 12, 1889.

that orchard, and we all were anxious for reinforcements to come up, as were being decimated by their artillery."[34]

Former Sergeant Major Alexander Givin continued the theme of stubborn Union resistance during the dedication ceremony for the statue atop the 114th Pennsylvania monument, held in November 1888. He noted that the Zouave statue was "looking to our left which is being driven back. . . . Men of the One hundred and fourteenth stood as this man stands, contesting the ground inch by inch." Givin recalled the gruesome memory of the burned Sherfy barn, "That sickening sight that met your gaze as you advanced to where the old barn stood, to find it in ashes, and the charred remains of many of your companions."[35]

Not everyone received a formal dedication ceremony. There was no such observance for Captain Nelson Ames's battery monument in 1893. "But thirteen of the survivors of the battery were present," Ames wrote afterwards, "and we dedicated the noble monument in silence and in tears. No one wanted to make a speech, and none was made. Our meeting was like the meeting of a family, and formalities seemed out of place." Instead of a formal service, Ames and the others "dedicated the monument with our tears, prayed for our dead comrades and for each other, and indulged ourselves in loving each other and the flag under which we fought so long and so faithfully." Ames restlessly moved across the country in the decades after the war. He pursued many business ventures including oil, cattle, and lumber, before settling in Iowa and entering local politics. There, he served as justice of the peace and mayor of his small town. Ames died in 1907 of illness brought on by wartime

34 *Pennsylvania at Gettysburg*, 1: 389, 393. In elaborating on the site of the Wheatfield Road monument, Craighead added, "This spot marks the left of our regiment, the right extended to and rested north of this point to where you will see a flank stone marker standing . . . we advanced from here into that peach orchard beyond, and formed an angle, which we have marked by a white marble shaft; in that orchard we engaged the enemy in heavy musketry firing." The regiment's other monument is a white marble shaft placed by the veterans on the southwest boundary of the Peach Orchard, where the regiment formed a salient with the 2nd New Hampshire along the Emmitsburg Road.

35 Ibid., 2: 609-612, 619. Lieutenant Colonel Edward Bowen praised General Meade's services, a rarity in many of these Third Corps speeches. "He deserves at the hands of his countrymen a monument worthy of his military skill, his bravery, and his patriotism and commensurate in its beauty, and durability with the important service he rendered." Meade's equestrian monument was dedicated on Cemetery Ridge in 1896.

Veterans gather in the Peach Orchard after the dedication of the 141st Pennsylvania monument. September 1889.
Jeff Kawalis

wounds. His obituary claimed, "He has really not known a day of perfect health since the memorable battle of Gettysburg."[36]

Despite their fraternal camaraderie, arguments among veterans often spilled over into the pages of newspapers. Their memories did not always align with the version of events generated by friends or former foes. Although actions such as Little Round Top and Pickett's Charge garnered more coverage, disagreements also existed over what had occurred in the Peach Orchard. During the battle, the fighting had been confusing and chaotic. Union veterans had to reconcile themselves with memories of being overrun. The fact that

36 *New York at Gettysburg*, 3: 1236; "Death Ends Life of Noted War Veteran," *Times-Republican* (Marshalltown, Iowa), March 1907. According to his obituary, Ames was struck in the head by a shell fragment during the close of fighting on July 2. The resulting concussion jammed him between the spokes of an artillery carriage "twisting the little man out of shape and breaking several ribs. He never regained his once perfect physique since that day, and has always suffered from the effects of his wounds." However, Ames authored the battery history and did not record such an incident. In 1868, he filed and received a disability pension as an "invalid." His widow also received a pension on his behalf after his death.

there were really two orchards, one on each side of the Wheatfield Road, only added to the confusion and conflicting accounts. Since artillery had moved in and out of the action, the identities and positions of these batteries became a source of contention.

Private William Quay of the 68th Pennsylvania took Captain Patrick Hart to task for the latter's post-war assertions that his battery was "in" the Peach Orchard. Quay cited Hart's own report and insisted that he was actually on "the left" of the orchard. Such an argument might seem trivial, but this represented the level of accuracy and detail to which the veterans often held one another. Quay held no ill-will toward Hart, however, and promised the captain "the best bunk there is in the tent" if he desired a trip to Quay's home in Meadville, Pennsylvania. George Marshall of Thompson's battery marveled that so many batteries claimed to be in the Peach Orchard. "I have concluded our battery had better make a claim or we will be crowded out," he quipped. Private A. Randolph of the 16th Pennsylvania Cavalry, who did not fight at the Peach Orchard, offered his perspective. Randolph thought it best "to give the old soldiers a rest about the batteries that fought in the Peach Orchard at Gettysburg." The veterans often continued to squabble, both in print and at reunions, until the last of them answered the final roll call. These types of debates still continue today among Gettysburg scholars and students alike.[37]

Sickles, Longstreet, Edward Porter Alexander, and several other old officers received a lively battlefield tour in April 1893. They travelled over much of the field in open carriages and Longstreet listened attentively despite being nearly deaf. The tour bypassed the Peach Orchard, however, in favor of spending extended time on Little Round Top. Confederate artillerist Alexander had never been on Little Round Top before, and after examining the vistas it afforded exclaimed, "By George! How grand! What a position!" Their guide shouted the battle's details into Longstreet's ear, while Sickles lagged behind to examine a New York monument. "Hurry up Sickles," cried out General Oliver Howard, "This concerns you!" Sickles sat down on a nearby rock and replied, "Fire ahead." The guide then explained to Longstreet that Sickles's advance prevented the Confederates from getting around the Union position. Sickles interrupted and added that Longstreet would have otherwise gained Little Round Top and "had the key to the situation." The New Yorker asked

37 Quay, "Still in Error," *Fighting Them Over*, 306-307; "Another Peach Orchard Battery at Gettysburg," *National Tribune*, February 5, 1891, 3; "What Troops Fought in the Peach Orchard," *The Pittsburg Daily Headlight*, October 2, 1891; *The National Tribune*, February 26, 1891, 3.

Portrait of James Longstreet. Taken in Gettysburg on April 29, 1893.
ACHS

for confirmation, to which Longstreet smiled and agreed, "That is what I was trying to do."[38]

The battle's 30th anniversary in July 1893 was designated as "New York Day." The dedication of the Excelsior Brigade monument occurred in the fields once farmed by the Sherfys and Wentzes. The memorial's design consisted of five columns supporting a dome. Atop the dome sits a bronze eagle and an empty pedestal rests between the five columns. "Within the inclosure [sic] formed by the five columns it is understood that a bronze bust of Gen. Sickles will be placed when he passes away," reported the *New York Times*. The statue honoring General Sickles was never completed, however, and the pedestal remains empty to this day.[39]

Henry Tremain, who remained among Sickles's most devoted supporters, spoke at the Excelsior Brigade dedication. The July 2 battle, Tremain declared, had been fought for control of the Emmitsburg Road. Without Sickles's advance, "yonder Round Top Mountain might have been gained by the enemy without firing a gun." While such an outcome was unlikely, given the large number of reinforcements that Meade had on Cemetery Ridge, Tremain added on a more accurate note, "we have assembled here to dedicate to the memory of our dead who fell on this field this beautiful monument, which stands like a temple of fame on the front line of the second day's contest." Sickles spoke briefly and praised his old brigade's "heroism and never-faltering courage."

38 "Making War History," *The Times* (Philadelphia), May 1, 1893. The group paused to have their portrait taken near East Cemetery Hill. Longstreet also stopped by William Tipton's Gettysburg photography studio on April 29 to have his individual portrait taken. A Tipton descendant donated the Longstreet image, with the date penciled on the back, to the Adams County Historical Society in 2018. Thanks to ACHS historian Tim Smith for sharing this information.

39 *New York at Gettysburg*, 2: 575, 698; "At Their Memorial Temple," *New York Times*, July 3, 1893. The memorial's corner stone had been laid with a brief ceremony during the 1888 anniversary.

General Carr then presented Sickles with a gold medal as "a testimonial of the affection and loyalty" of the Third Corps veterans. Sickles was so overcome that he could only muster a brief promise to "preserve the medal as a priceless treasure and wear it near his heart as long as he lived." Sickles's veterans often displayed genuine emotion at these events, even if historical accuracy was not their forte.[40]

Tremain spoke again in 1897 at the dedication of the Excelsiors' 73rd New York monument. This memorial was located east of the Emmitsburg Road, opposite the Sherfy barnyard, near where Tremain personally led the regiment into action on July 2. He emphasized that foremost in Sickles's mind was the protection of the Emmitsburg Road and this led to the decision to move the Third Corps forward. Tremain insisted, "It became essential to decide if the Emmitsburg Road, by which we had marched was to be held or abandoned. . . . In the absence of explicit orders to abandon it, military necessity and good discipline required it should be held." Once again, Tremain displayed a flexible grasp on truthfulness. In essence, he argued that Sickles's advance to the road was justified by Meade's failure to order its abandonment.[41]

The surviving Sherfy family members frequently hosted the returning veterans. A solid shot wedged in one of their large cherry trees on the north side of the house was a popular attraction. Sometimes the Sherfys provided guests with their famous fruit and told stories. In 1888, Mary Sherfy explained to Sergeant Ellis Strouss of the 57th Pennsylvania that the family found a limber chest filled with ammunition during their initial cleanup along the Emmitsburg Road. The Sherfy men "were afraid to handle the ammunition," so they instead dug a hole and buried the chest beside the road. She told Strouss that the burial "had not been disturbed since."[42]

40 *New York at Gettysburg*, 2: 584-586, 593, 596-597; "At Their Memorial Temple," *New York Times*, July 3, 1893. In addition to the large brigade monument, a tablet was placed christening the nearby field as "Excelsior Field." Five small markers were placed in the meadow extending to the Trostle Lane (modern United States Avenue), supposedly denoting the position of each regiment in the brigade. These markers are inaccurate and do not represent where the Excelsior regiments fought, which was actually north of the lane. This serves as a reminder to visitors that monuments were sometimes placed based on available land, visibility, and other factors. Not every monument is accurately positioned on the battlefield.

41 *New York at Gettysburg*, 2: 599, 603, 605.

42 *OR*, 27/1: 590, 27/2: 434; Strouss, *History of the Fifty-Seventh Pennsylvania Veteran Volunteers*, 96. Mrs. Sherfy told the visiting veteran that this chest belonged to Bucklyn's Battery. While the battery's official report of Lieutenant Benjamin Freeborn admitted that the Rhode Islanders left one caisson on the field during their retreat, making this a possibility, it seems improbable that the Confederate artillery, which was in position along the roadway during

Mrs. Sherfy also collected images of the men that once fought across her property. Private Ivester Dean wrote to her in 1891, promising to send a photograph of himself. He hoped she would place his image on her walls, alongside those of his comrades from Company K, 63rd Pennsylvania. Mary Sherfy was 87 years old when she died in 1904. Her obituary remembered "her gentle manners, her kindness and goodness of her life."[43]

On other occasions, it was the veterans who entertained their hosts with stories of the battle. A Sherfy family member later recorded one such account. Purportedly, Second Lieutenant Harry E. Rulon of Company B, 114th Pennsylvania, saw the enemy upon him, "threw his sword into the wall, to prevent its capture by Conf. – ran into the house & jumped out a window." Unfortunately, he was "pierced by seven waiting bayonets & killed. After the battle many swords & Bayonets were taken from the Wall." Whatever the identity of this unlucky Zouave, if the event even occurred, it was not Rulon. The lieutenant was initially reported as missing in action, but he returned to the ranks and lived until 1925. Like many good stories, perhaps there was some truth at the root and a different Zouave met such a gruesome end.[44]

The repeated processions across the battlefield began to take a toll upon the landscape. In the early 1890s, the construction of the Gettysburg Electric Railway exacerbated this problem. One of the company's trolley lines extended from Washington Street in Gettysburg, through town and south along the Emmitsburg Road to the Peach Orchard, where it turned east before looping around the Wheatfield and toward Little Round Top. Many veterans, including

---

the preceding days, would not have stumbled across this chest and put it to good use. More likely, the discarded limber chest belonged to one of Alexander's Confederate guns. This limber chest also could have been hauled in with Thompson's lost 3-inch Ordnance Rifle by Richardson's battery on July 3.

43 Ivester H. Dean to Mrs. Mary Sherfy, March 4, 1891, Sherfy Family File, ACHS; "Mary H. Sherfy," *Gettysburg Compiler*, March 30, 1904. Although Dean's name is on the Pennsylvania State Monument with the 63rd PA and he claimed that he fought in an "open cellar" on the property, he is listed in muster out rolls for the 105th Pennsylvania (after their consolidation with the 63rd Pennsylvania) as having enlisted in February of 1864. His comrades whose portraits were on display at the Sherfy house included Captain George Chalmers, Sergeant John Woods and First Sergeant Robert Stanford, all of whom are listed on the Pennsylvania State Monument at Gettysburg.

44 Human Interest stories of the battle of Gettysburg file, Transcribed by Timothy H. Smith, ACHS; Busey and Busey, *Union Casualties at Gettysburg*, 2: 921. Harry E. Rulon is buried at Westminster Cemetery in Bala Cynwyd, Montgomery County, Pennsylvania.

View toward Clark's Battery monument and Round Tops in background. Peach Orchard is to the far right. Prior to construction of Sickles Avenue.
GNMP

Dan Sickles, opposed the trolley line and argued that it destroyed the historic landscape on the south end of the battlefield.[45]

As for the Peach Orchard itself, any remaining wartime trees had died by this time period. A newspaper account from May 1885 noted that only a few recently planted saplings marked the site. Another newspaper reported in August 1895: "The trees gradually died until a few years ago not over half a dozen were left. Branches were cut from these by visitors and all but one was destroyed. That lone tree, a mere skeleton of what it once had been, stood there until the early part of the present summer when workingmen engaged in laying out a new road through the battlefield chopped it down."[46]

The workmen were likely contractors hired by the War Department to construct Sickles Avenue. The avenue's lengthy route extended over much of the Third Corps advanced battle line. A 900-yard segment ran through the fields on the east side of the Emmitsburg Road and north of the Wheatfield Road. The avenue improved access to the Peach Orchard and surrounding

45 Platt, *This is Holy Ground,* 17-21.

46 "The Peach Orchard," *The News* (Frederick, MD), May 4, 1885; "The Gettysburg Battlefield," *The Philadelphia Times*, October 13, 1887; *The North Platte Semi-Weekly Tribune*, August 27, 1895.

vicinity, but altered historically significant ground in the process. By the mid-1890s, veterans erected more than two dozen monuments in the general area, but there was nothing left to see of the original orchard.[47]

In a way, the Peach Orchard still lived even after the battlefield's trees had disappeared. In 1897, Corporal Frederick Cole planted a peach pit from Gettysburg's orchard at his home in Macedonia, Pennsylvania. Cole was among a handful of men from the 141st Pennsylvania who escaped the battle unharmed, and he chose to commemorate the Peach Orchard at his home. Undoubtedly, an unrecorded number of other veterans did the same. The wood from Peach Orchard trees also turned up as souvenirs ranging from decorative canes to gavels. These items sometimes took on the significance of a rare religious artifact.[48]

The greatest relics, however, remained the surviving heroes of the battle. Sickles and Longstreet, when health permitted, frequently travelled together to reunions. During one memorable encounter in Atlanta, on St. Patrick's Day in 1892, the two aged warriors walked back to their respective hotels after a late night of heavy drinking. "Old fellow," Sickles asked, "I hope you are sorry for shooting off my leg at Gettysburg. I suppose I will have to forgive you for it someday." An inebriated Longstreet retorted, "Forgive me? You ought to thank me for leaving you one leg to stand on."[49]

Sickles revisited Gettysburg repeatedly, due in part to his role with the New York Monuments Commission and because of his popularity as a speaker. He also returned to Congress from 1893-1895, and introduced the legislation that established Gettysburg National Military Park in 1895. Locals anticipated a return visit from both Longstreet and Sickles in May 1899 for Memorial Day. Unfortunately, Longstreet's deteriorating health prevented him from making the journey. He was instead represented by his son, Lieutenant James Longstreet of the United States Army. Still, there was no concealing the disappointment among those who attended, with one newspaper reporting, "The ceremonies went on very much as if the play of 'Hamlet' was acted

47 "Locating a New Avenue at Gettysburg," *National Republican*, October 2, 1884; *Annual Reports of the Gettysburg National Military Park Commission to the Secretary of War 1893-1904*, 21, 29. Sickles Avenue was reported as finished in the October 21, 1896 report.

48 *The Bradford Star*, September 9, 1897; "Souvenirs for the President," *The St. Louis Republic*, October 12, 1902; *Altoona Tribune*, September 1, 1906. Frederick Cole was wounded severely in the hip during the initial assaults against Petersburg in June 1864 and transferred to the Veteran Reserve Corps before mustering out of Federal service in August 1865.

49 Sickles, "Introduction," *Lee and Longstreet at High Tide*, 19.

without Hamlet in the dramatis personae." Consequently, the interest of the day centered on Sickles, who was just months shy of his 80th birthday. As usual, the old general did not disappoint.[50]

"I am sorry that Longstreet is not here," Sickles told the audience, "I would have been glad to say something about his assault and the impression he made upon me; things that he would have been glad to hear." Sickles remained unwilling to admit regret over his move to the Peach Orchard. He declared that he was often asked what he would do if given the opportunity to refight July 2 again. "I would do tomorrow under the conditions and circumstances that then existed exactly what I did on July 2." In reflecting upon more than three decades of controversy, Sickles insisted, "I have heard all the criticisms and read all the histories and after hearing and reading all I would say to them I would do what I did and accept the verdict of history on my acts. It was a mighty good fight both made and I am satisfied with my part in it."[51]

Upwards of 10,000 people heard the New Yorker speak at the National Cemetery. Understanding that Pennsylvanians comprised much of the audience, he focused astutely on the valor of their fight from the Peach Orchard to Cemetery Ridge. He praised the recapture of seven artillery pieces and highlighted the performance of the 105th Pennsylvania. "Scarcely had Sickles ceased speaking when an old soldier who just arrived came up to take him by the hand. 'What was your regiment he asked?' 'The One Hundred and Fifth Pennsylvania,' was the answer. 'Did you help in the capture of these guns?' 'I did, indeed.' If the scene had been arranged as a stage effect it could not have been more convincing." The elderly general, leaning on his crutch, was once again the talk of the town.[52]

In the fall of 1902, Longstreet received another invitation to Gettysburg for the dedication of Henry Slocum's equestrian monument. Longstreet declined again for health reasons, and instead sent Sickles a letter of regret. Longstreet took one more opportunity to reflect upon their battle of almost 40 years earlier:

> I believe it is now conceded that the advanced position at the Peach-Orchard, taken by your corps and under your orders, saved that battle-field to the Union cause. It

50 "Longstreet and Sickles to Meet at Gettysburg," *The Philadelphia Times*, May 28, 1899; "Flowers on Our Soldiers' Tombs," *The Philadelphia Times*, May 31, 1899; *Gettysburg Compiler*, June 6, 1899.

51 *Gettysburg Compiler*, June 6, 1899.

52 "Flowers on Our Soldiers' Tombs," *The Philadelphia Times*, May 31, 1899.

> was the sorest and saddest reflection of my life for many years; but, to-day, I can say, with sincerest emotion, that it was and is the best that could have come to us all, North and South; and I hope that the nation, reunited, may always enjoy the honor and glory brought to it by the grand work.[53]

In early January 1904, Longstreet took ill and died in Georgia. He was only days away from his 83rd birthday. Longstreet apparently went to his grave defending Sickles's move to the Peach Orchard. But did he express that viewpoint for public consumption or did he truly believe it? From Longstreet's perspective, Sickles's advance movements had clearly disrupted Confederate strategy. Longstreet had little time or opportunity to reconnoiter the revised Federal position, and Sickles's troops blocked his avenues of approach to Cemetery Ridge. Perhaps, Longstreet felt obligated in his later years to support his former opponent, but the Georgian remained consistent in his post-war corroboration of Sickles's version of events.

Later that same year, Longstreet's second wife Helen published a defense of her husband's war record in a book titled, *Lee and Longstreet at High Tide.* Since Longstreet had openly supported Sickles's controversial actions, this became the New Yorker's opportunity to return the favor. Sickles contributed a lengthy introduction to Helen's book, and not surprisingly, revisited the one event that truly connected the two men: the battle of Gettysburg.[54]

"Longstreet was unjustly blamed for not attacking earlier in the day at Gettysburg," Sickles believed. "I can answer that criticism, as I know more about the matter than the critics." Employing a rather ambiguous analysis, Sickles maintained that a morning attack would have brought Longstreet in contact with "five thousand sabers" of Buford's cavalry, the Fifth Corps, and Caldwell's division of the Second Corps. "On the other hand, if Lee had waited an hour later I would have been on Cemetery Ridge, in compliance with General Meade's orders, and Longstreet could have marched, unresisted, from Seminary Ridge to the foot of Round Top, and might, perhaps, have unlimbered his guns on the summit." Sickles's arguments were often compelling, even when riddled with inaccuracies and scenarios that remained impossible to prove.[55]

53 Longstreet, *Lee and Longstreet at High Tide*, 15-16. The Henry Slocum equestrian monument was dedicated on September 19, 1902. See Harrison, *The Location of Monuments, Markers and Tablets*, 41.

54 Longstreet, *Lee and Longstreet at High Tide*, 7-17; Wert, *General James Longstreet*, 425-426.

55 Longstreet, *Lee and Longstreet at High Tide*, 21-22. Likewise, Sickles's historical critics typically assail his Gettysburg performance with similar "what-if" scenarios that are equally impossible to prove.

As the old soldiers fought for their place in historical memory, the ground upon which they made history came under threat. The danger of losing the land to private development cast an ominous cloud over portions of the battlefield. Private owners still held much of the acreage around the Peach Orchard. The government's first serious effort at obtaining the Peach Orchard began in early 1905. Colonel John P. Nicholson, chairman of the Gettysburg National Park Commission, offered up to $100 per acre to the owner, Dr. Howard Diehl. However, Diehl refused to make a deal and insisted that the land's historic value justified a higher price. Diehl demanded $400 an acre. In the spring of 1905, Nicholson initiated condemnation proceedings. By June 30, Diehl's land had successfully transferred to Gettysburg National Military Park. The federal government now guaranteed protection of the ground where Sherfy's orchard stood from future development. From 1905 to 1910, the War Department acquired more than fifty acres around the site of the famed Peach Orchard.[56]

Meanwhile, Sickles remained in the public spotlight well past the age of 90. By 1912, he was financially bankrupt and embroiled in a messy public squabble with his second wife and adult children. To compound Sickles's problems, a state audit of the New York Monument Commission's books discovered more than $28,000 unaccounted for. Chairman Sickles was in serious legal trouble as New York attempted unsuccessfully to recover the missing money. Longstreet's widow Helen was among those who wired words of support to Sickles. He avoided jail time but was removed as chairman of the commission. All of these events were reported enthusiastically by the New York newspapers and led up to the battle's 50th anniversary in 1913.[57]

In July, when the anniversary arrived, there were many faces missing from previous reunions. Still, attendance by veterans remained high and the ceremonies, highlighted by the appearance of President Woodrow Wilson,

56 "Jury to View Peach Orchard," *Gettysburg Compiler*, February 22, 1905; "After Peach Orchard," *Harrisburg Star Independent*, February 24, 1905; "Uncle Sam Takes 150 Acres," *Gettysburg Compiler*, March 29, 1905; "Appeals Taken," *Gettysburg Compiler*, May 3, 1905; *Annual Reports of the Secretary of War*, 1905-1910. The government acquired 11 acres of battlefield land from Diehl, which included four acres at the Peach Orchard. A jury listened to appraisals from the government whose witnesses estimated the value of the 11 acres somewhere between $1,050 and $1,500. They also heard from a private individual who placed the value at $2,300. The jury awarded $1,900 for the 11 acres.

57 For a more detailed account of this colorful period in General Sickles's life, see Hessler, *Sickles at Gettysburg*, 369-381.

were impressive. A massive encampment was open from June 29 through July 6 along the Emmitsburg Road.

Despite his legal troubles in New York, Sickles attended and garnered much attention. Helen Longstreet also attended and "walked a mile through the broiling sun" to meet with Sickles near his reunion headquarters at the Rogers house site. She had drafted a letter on behalf of Confederate veterans defending the honor of General Sickles during his recent scandals. A newspaper reported that as Helen read the letter aloud, "General Sickles leaned back in his chair, closed his eyes, and looked back to meeting Longstreet." Those who were gathered listened attentively and watched as, "Tears flowed down Sickles cheeks, now tanned by his ninety-third summer, and his old followers doffed their hats and mingled their tears with those of their old leader, wetting the ground upon which long ago had been soaked by their blood."[58]

While the elderly veterans struggled with the emotional impact of this gathering, thousands of people walked across the ground that once held the Peach Orchard. A newsman bemoaned the way in which visitors "thoughtlessly and recklessly run over" historic properties south of town. "Mrs. Sherfey [sic], a plain Dunkard woman, was much sought after by visitors," although the family reportedly "abandoned the neighborhood entirely, the celebrated peach orchard being one of their leavings." Regardless of whichever family member met with the news reporter, since Mary Sherfy had died years earlier, the irony remains that the battle's impact ultimately helped destroy the Sherfy family farm.[59]

Former First Sergeant Harry Hall of the 114th Pennsylvania was another attendee at the reunion. Hall was the regiment's national color-bearer 50 years earlier and he wore his old Zouave uniform to the event. Hall's purpose was not only to honor his comrades, but also to search for a friend who disappeared in the maelstrom of battle on July 2, 1863. Corporal Michael Cannon carried the state color on that day and Hall lost track of him during the regiment's retreat. Cannon was severely wounded but survived and brought the flag off

58 "Sidelights of Gettysburg Reunion," *The News* (Newport, PA), July 10, 1913; "Thaw to Sickles," *Gettysburg Times*, July 4, 1913; "Penrose Mixing in Camp," *The Pittsburgh Post*, July 4, 1913; "Son and Grandsons of Gen. Longstreet," *Atlanta Constitution*, June 30, 1913. Longstreet's son, Major Robert Lee Longstreet, also attended. He said that his father and Sickles had predicted 30 years earlier that such a momentous reunion would occur.

59 "After 50 Years," Newspaper Clipping, July 19 1913, GNMP file 11-61. Of the remaining Sherfy members, Otelia Sherfy Hereter died in 1939, Mary Sherfy Myers died in 1931, Anna Sherfy Brumbaugh died in 1935, John L. Sherfy died in 1934, and Ernest Sherfy died in 1925. Sherfy Family History, GNMP file.

Stuckey's as it once existed at the northwest intersection of the Emmitsburg and Millerstown Roads.
GNMP

with the help of Sergeant Benjamin Baylitts. Unfortunately, Hall never found his friend. Although Cannon survived the battle, he died 11 years before the reunion.[60]

As late as 1907, Sickles still held out hope for an equestrian statue on the battlefield. "If at some future time it may be the pleasure of the State of New York to place some memorial of myself on that battlefield," he instructed John T. Nicholson, "I should prefer to have it on the high ground at or near the Peach Orchard." In July 1913, Sickles toured the Gettysburg battlefield with his devoted Chaplain Joseph Twichell. The minister expressed surprise that there was still no statue of the general on the field. Sickles supposedly replied that the whole damned battlefield was his monument. Perhaps the story is apocryphal, but if it did not happen that way then it should have. The general whose battlefield actions guaranteed the Peach Orchard's lasting fame,

60 "Zouave Uniform," *Gettysburg Times*, July 3, 1913; Busey and Busey, *Union Casualties at Gettysburg*, 2: 921; NARA, Record Group 15, T289, Michael Cannon. Corporal Cannon died in 1892 and is buried at the Dayton National Cemetery in Ohio.

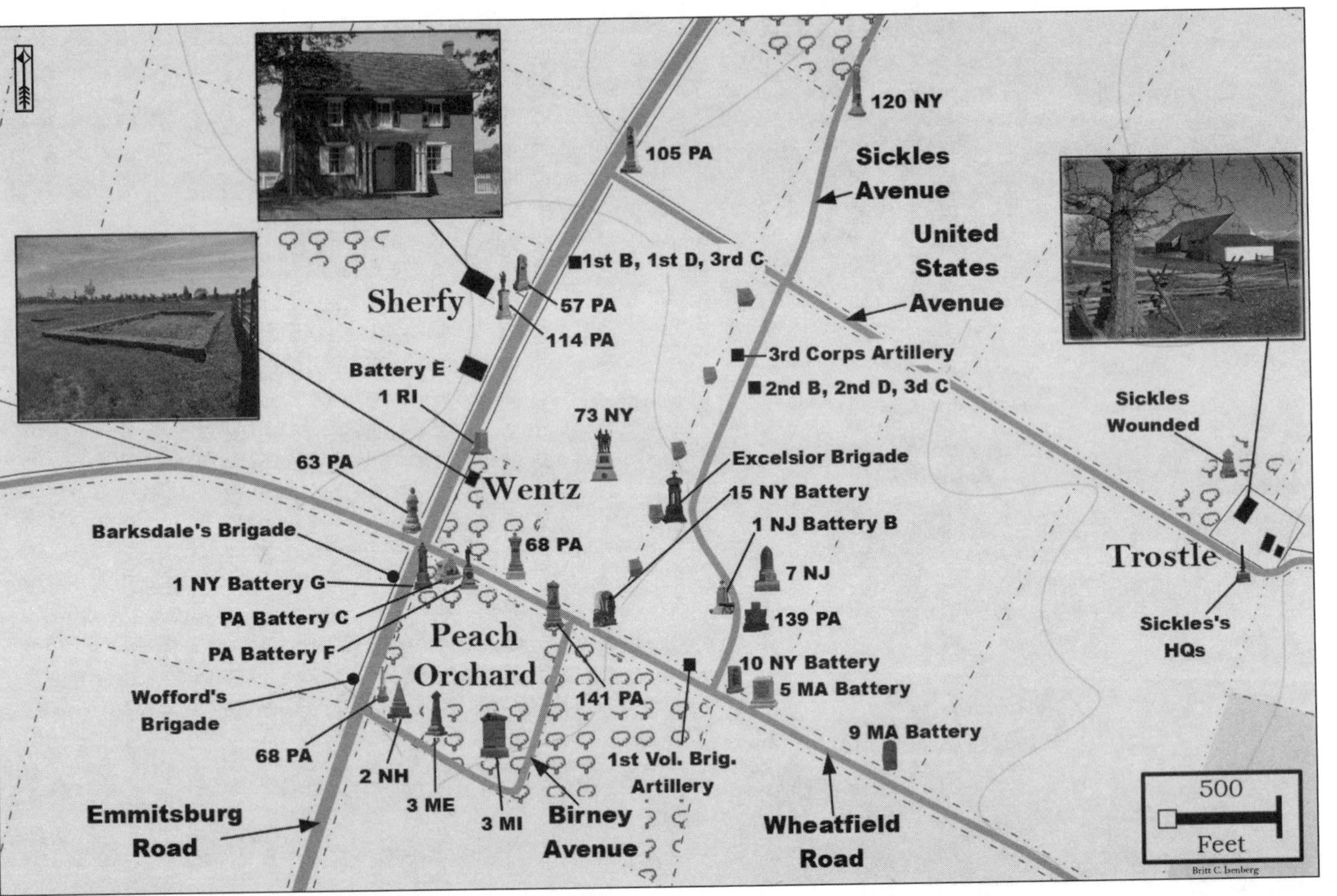
120 NY
105 PA
Sickles Avenue
United States Avenue
1st B, 1st D, 3rd C
Sherfy
57 PA
114 PA
3rd Corps Artillery
2nd B, 2nd D, 3d C
Battery E
1 RI
73 NY
Sickles Wounded
63 PA
Wentz
Excelsior Brigade
15 NY Battery
1 NJ Battery B
Barksdale's Brigade
68 PA
7 NJ
Trostle
1 NY Battery G
PA Battery C
139 PA
Sickles's HQs
PA Battery F
Peach Orchard
10 NY Battery
5 MA Battery
Wofford's Brigade
141 PA
9 MA Battery
68 PA
2 NH
3 ME
3 MI
1st Vol. Brig. Artillery
Birney Avenue
Emmitsburg Road
Wheatfield Road
500 Feet
Britt C. Isenberg

Twilight on the Sherfy farm.
Photo by Authors

and also generated a lifetime of controversy, died in May 1914 at his home in New York City. Although Gettysburg hosted anniversary celebrations in subsequent years, never again would so many men who fought in the bloodiest battle of the American Civil War reunite on this battlefield.[61]

Commercial development, rather than agriculture, best typified the Peach Orchard in the immediate post-veterans era. The acquisition of a farm off the Millerstown Road in 1950, by soon-to-be President and Mrs. Dwight Eisenhower, spurred the opening of several motels and commercial ventures along the nearby Emmitsburg Road. Perhaps the most notable of these was the Stuckey's chain "pecan shoppe" that opened in 1955. Although Stuckey's advertised itself as "at the Peach Orchard," the restaurant actually stood at the northwest corner of the Millerstown and Emmitsburg roads, which was not really any more palatable to battlefield preservationists. Customers ate candy, tropical jellies, and marmalades on the site where the 63rd Pennsylvania skirmished and Barksdale's men charged.[62]

61 *Dedication of the New York Auxiliary State Monument*, 114-115. For commentary on Sickles's alleged "whole damn battlefield is my monument," see Hessler, *Sickles at Gettysburg*, 381, 458 (n. 59).

62 Platt, *This is Holy Ground*, 58; "Stuckey's to Open Saturday," *Gettysburg Times*, August 20, 1955; "Pecan Shoppe Grand Opening" (advertisement), *Gettysburg Times*, August 19, 1955.

The presence of commercial ventures on hallowed ground did not go unnoticed by Gettysburg tourists. In 1971, one appalled visitor described their recent visit: "Across the road from the entrance to the Peach Orchard – where a series of monuments recall how the Army of the Potomac's Third Corps tried vainly to stop a larger Southern force here on the second day of the battle – we have a Stuckey's. You know it is a Stuckey's because the Coca-Cola sign, which is adjacent to the establishment's Texaco sign, tells you so."[63]

Stuckey's operated on this site for almost two decades until the federal government acquired the property in late 1972. The neighboring "Twin Kiss Snack Bar" was also obtained the following year and demolished in one of Gettysburg National Military Park's many attempts to restore the field "to its 1863 appearance." Likewise, the National Park Service removed non-historic residential structures from the Wentz property site in the early 1960s. All that remains there today is a marker and house's foundation outline, giving many visitors the false impression that an empty field stood at the Wentz location in 1863.[64]

The 1990s and early 21st century brought renewed focus on restoring the Gettysburg battlefield to its 1863 appearance. In 2005, then Gettysburg National Military Park Superintendent John Latschar began efforts to fully rehabilitate the orchard. Latschar requested funding assistance from Richard J. Sawhill, a longtime member of the Friends of Gettysburg. Latschar provided Sawhill with the total cost of the project and the number of trees he hoped to plant in the new Peach Orchard. Sawhill then contacted "everyone I had ever taken to Gettysburg," and asked each person to fund the cost of one tree. Sawhill received contributions from 34 states and completed the funding project in less than two weeks. Latschar designated Sawhill's group "The Peach Orchard Brigade," and by 2008, their generosity enabled the National Park Service to plant 133 Messina peach trees.[65]

Other preservation efforts during this era included razing private non-historic homes and burying modern power lines that stood along the Emmitsburg Road ridge. The Gettysburg Foundation currently maintains the Sherfy house and post-war barn. For visitors to the battlefield, these efforts improve the

63 "Finds Many Commercial Areas Here," *Gettysburg Times*, August 5, 1971.

64 "The Twin Kiss Snack Bar," *Gettysburg Times*, April 18, 1974; "Park Service Will Remove Wentz House," *Gettysburg Times*, April 29, 1960; McMillan, *Gettysburg Rebels*, 227-228.

65 "Spotlight on Members: Dick Sawhill," *Gettysburg Foundation*, Vol.24, Issue 3, 6; "Revived Orchard," *Gettysburg Times*, April 18, 2008.

understanding, interpretation, and appreciation of the events that transpired in and around Sherfy's Peach Orchard.[66]

The story of the Peach Orchard is typically interpreted through a military lens, and one that is not always well focused. The never-ending debate over whether Dan Sickles's advance helped or hurt the Union cause often overshadows Robert E. Lee's stated intentions to occupy the ground around the Sherfy farm. The impact that Sickles's movements had on James Longstreet's attack often rests on conjecture and unsolvable what-if scenarios, rather than on an analysis of what actually happened. Moreover, the influence that the Peach Orchard and Emmitsburg Road had on Pickett's Charge is often ignored. Finally, the historical emphasis placed on other battle actions, such as Little Round Top, has further neglected the significance of the Peach Orchard and overlooked the stories of the men who fought there.

Civilians, such as the Joseph Sherfy family, are typically ignored in the military-centric narratives. The Sherfys' story began with the desire to build a home and a better life. Due to the battle, however, they persevered in the aftermath of a catastrophic event. They returned home and rebuilt their farm, only to eventually lose their Peach Orchard to tourism and commercialization. Fortunately, preservation took root and eventually saved their home and land for future generations. Gettysburg's Peach Orchard stands as a living memorial not only to the men that sacrificed their lives amid the broken branches of battle, but to a family whose name is now synonymous with the history of Gettysburg.

66 "Gettysburg battlefield attempts to turn back the clock," *Miami Herald*, June 24, 2013; Gettysburg National Military Park, "Replanting More Missing Orchards and Woods at Gettysburg," 2.

Appendix: Select Order of Battle

(Engaged near the Peach Orchard)

Union Army of the Potomac
Maj. Gen. George G. Meade
93,921 men (3,155 k, 14,531 w, 5,369 m/c = 23,055 or 24.5%)

Third Corps
Maj. Gen. Daniel E. Sickles (w), Maj. Gen. David B. Birney
10,674 men (593 k, 3,029 w, 589 m/c = 4,211 or 39.5%)

1st Division
Maj. Gen. David B. Birney, Brig. Gen. J. H. Hobart Ward (w)
5,094 men (271 k, 1,384 w, 356 m/c = 2,011 or 39.5%)

1st Brigade
Brig. Gen. Charles K. Graham (w/c),
Col. Andrew H. Tippin, Col. Henry J. Madill
1,516 men (67 k, 508 w, 165 m/c = 740 or 48.8%)

57th Pennsylvania (8 companies)
Col. Peter Sides (w), Capt. Alanson H. Nelson
207 men (11 k, 46 w, 58 m/c = 115 or 55.6%)

63rd Pennsylvania
Maj. John A. Danks
246 men (1 k, 29 w, 4 m/c = 34 or 13.8%)

68th Pennsylvania
Col. Andrew H. Tippin, Capt. Milton S. Davis
320 men (13 k, 126 w, 13 m/c = 152 or 47.5%)

105th Pennsylvania
Col. Calvin A. Craig
274 men (8 k, 115 w, 9 m/c = 132 or 48.2%)

114th Pennsylvania
Lt. Col. Frederico F. Cavada (c),
Capt. Edward R. Bowen
259 men (9 k, 86 w, 60 m/c = 155 or 59.8%)

141st Pennsylvania
Col. Henry J. Madill
209 men (25 k, 103 w, 21 m/c = 149 or 71.3%)

Other 1st Division Units
3rd Maine (2nd Brigade)
Col. Moses B. Lakeman
210 men (18 k, 59 w, 45 m/c = 122 or 58.1%)

1st United States Sharpshooters
(8 companies, 2nd Brigade)
Col. Hiram Berdan, Lt. Col. Casper Trepp
312 men (5 k, 23 w, 45 m/c = 15 or 25.4%)

2nd Division
Brig. Gen. Andrew A. Humphreys
4,924 men (314 k, 1,562 w, 216 m/c = 2,092 or 42.5%)

1st Brigade
Brig. Gen. Joseph B. Carr
1,718 men (121 k, 604 w, 65 m/c = 790 or 46%)

1st Massachusetts
Lt. Col. Clark B. Baldwin (w)
321 men (16 k, 83 w, 21 m/c = 120 or 37.4%)

11th Massachusetts
Lt. Col. Porter D. Tripp
286 men (23 k, 96 w, 10 m/c = 129 or 45.1%)

16th Massachusetts

Lt. Col. Waldo Merriam (w), Capt. Matthew Donovan
245 men (15 k, 53 w, 13 m/c = 81 or 33.1%)

12th New Hampshire

Capt. John F. Langley
224 men (20 k, 70 w, 2 m/c = 92 or 41.1%)

11th New Jersey

Col. Robert McAllister (w),
Capt. Luther Martin (k),
Capt. Andrew Ackerman (k),
Capt. William H. Lloyd (w),
Lt. John Schoonover (w), Capt. Samuel T. Sleeper
275 men (23 k, 96 w, 10 m/c = 153 or 55.6%)

26th Pennsylvania

Maj. Robert L. Bodine
365 men (30 k, 176 w, 7 m/c = 213 or 58.4%)

Note: The 84th Pennsylvania of the same brigade was not present during the battle. The regiment was guarding the 3rd Corps trains to the rear. The regiment does however have a monument on Cemetery Ridge to commemorate their service through the entire war.

2nd Brigade

Col. William R. Brewster
1,837 men (132 k, 573 w, 73 m/c = 778 or 42.4%)

70th New York

Col. J. Egbert Farnum
288 men (20 k, 93 w, 4 m/c = 117 or 40.6%)

71st New York

Col. Henry L. Potter (w)
243 men (10 k, 68 w, 13 m/c = 91 or 37.4%)

72nd New York

Col. John S. Austin (w),
Lt. Col. John Leonard
305 men (7 k, 79 w, 28 m/c = 114 or 37.4%)

73rd New York
Maj. Michael W. Burns
349 men (51 k, 103 w, 8 m/c = 162 or 46.4%)

74th New York
Lt. Col. Thomas Holt
266 men (12 k, 74 w, 3 m/c = 89 or 33.5%)

120th New York
Lt. Col. Cornelius D. Westbrook (w),
Maj. John R. Tappen
383 men (32 k, 154 w, 17 m/c = 203 or 53%)

Other 2nd Division Units:

2nd New Hampshire (3rd Brigade)
Col. Edward L. Bailey (w)
354 men (20 k, 137 w, 36 m/c = 193 or 54.5%)

5th New Jersey (3rd Brigade)
Col. William J. Sewell (w),
Capt. Thomas C. Godfrey,
Capt. Henry H. Woolsey (w)
206 men (13 k, 65 w, 16 m/c = 94 or 45.6%)

7th New Jersey (3rd Brigade)
Col. Louis R. Francine (mw),
Maj. Frederick Cooper
275 men (15 k, 86 w, 13 m/c = 114 or 41.5%)

Third Corps Artillery Brigade
Capt. George E. Randolph (w),
Capt. Judson A. Clark
596 men (8 k, 81 w, 17 m/c = 106 or 17.8%)

1st New Jersey Light Artillery, Battery B
Capt. Judson A. Clark, Lt. Robert Sims
Six 10 pdr Parrotts
131 men (1 k, 16 w, 3 m/c = 20 or 15.3%)

1st Rhode Island Light Artillery, Battery E
Lt. John K. Bucklyn (w),
Lt. Benjamin Freeborn (w)
Six Napoleons: 108 men
(3 k, 26 w, 1 m/c = 30 or 27.8%)

4th United States Artillery, Battery K
Lt. Francis W. Seeley (w),
Lt. Robert James
Six Napoleons: 113 men
(2 k, 19 w, 4 m/c = 25 or 22.1%)

Artillery Reserve
Brig. Gen. Robert O. Tyler

3rd United States Artillery,
Battery F & K (1st Regular Brigade)
Lt. John G. Turnbull
Six Napoleons: 115 men
(9 k, 14 w, 1 m/c = 24 or 20.9%)

1st New York Light Artillery,
Battery G (4th Volunteer Brigade)
Capt. Nelson Ames
Six Napoleons: 84 men (7 w = 7 or 8.3%)

1st Volunteer Brigade
Lt. Col. Freeman McGilvery
385 men (17 k, 71 w, 5 m/c = 93 or 24.2%)

5th Massachusetts,
Battery E
Capt. Charles A. Phillips
Six 3-inch Rifles
104 men (4 k, 17 w = 21 or 20.2%)
NOTE: 10th New York Battery attached

9th Massachusetts Battery
Capt. John Bigelow (w),
Lt. Richard Milton
Six Napoleons: 104 men (8 k, 18 w, 2 m/c = 28 or 26.9%)

15th New York Independent Battery
Capt. Patrick Hart (w)
Four Napoleons:
70 men (3 k, 13 w = 16 or 22.9%)

Pennsylvania Independent Batteries C & F
Capt. James Thompson
Six 3-inch Rifles: 105 men
(2 k, 23 w, 3 m/c = 28 or 26.7%)

Confederate Army of Northern Virginia
Gen. Robert E. Lee
71,699 men (4,708 k, 12,693 w, 5,830 m/c = 23,231 or 32.4%)

Longstreet's Corps
Lt. Gen. James Longstreet
20,941 men (1,617 k, 4,205 w, 1,843 m/c = 7,665 or 36.6%)

McLaws's Division
Maj. Gen. Lafayette McLaws
7,160 men (478 k, 1,391 w, 458 m/c = 2,327 or 32.5%)

Kershaw's Brigade
Brig. Gen. Joseph B. Kershaw
2,185 men (179 k, 439 w, 51 m/c = 669 or 30.6%)

2nd South Carolina
Col. John D. Kennedy (w), Lt. Col. Franklin Gaillard
412 men (53 k, 100 w, 17 m/c = 170 or 41.3%)

3rd South Carolina
Maj. Robert Maffett, Col. James D. Nance
407 men (22 k, 59 w, 6 m/c = 87 or 21.4%)

3rd South Carolina Battalion
Lt. Col. William G. Rice
203 men (14 k, 31 w, 3 m/c = 48 or 23.6%)

7th South Carolina
Col. Wyatt Aiken
408 men (29 k, 79 w, 7 m/c = 115 or 28.2%)

8th South Carolina
Col. John W. Henagan
300 men (31 k, 74 w = 105 or 35.0%)

15th South Carolina
Col. William DeSaussure (mw), Maj. William M. Gist
449 men (30 k, 96 w, 18 m/c = 144 or 32.1%)

Barksdale's Brigade
Brig. Gen. William Barksdale (mw)
1,619 men (156 k, 470 w,
178 m/c = 804 or 49.7%)

13th Mississippi
Col. James W. Carter (k),
Lt. Col. Kennon McElroy (w),
Maj. John M. Bradley (mw),
Lt. Absalom H. Farrar (w/c)
481 men (39 k, 171 w, 33 m/c = 243 or 50.5%)

17th Mississippi
Col. William D. Holder (w),
Lt. Col. John C. Fiser (w),
Maj. Andrew J. Pulliam (w),
Maj. Richard E. Jones (k),
Capt. Gwen R. Cherry
468 men (64 k, 108 w, 98 m/c = 270 or 57.7%)

18th Mississippi
Col. Thomas M. Griffin (w),
Lt. Col. William H. Luse (c),
Maj. George B. Gerald
242 men (20 k, 81 w, 36 m/c = 137 or 56.6%)

21st Mississippi
Col. Benjamin Humphreys
424 men (18 k, 110 w, 11 m/c = 139 or 32.8%)

Wofford's Brigade
Brig. Gen. William T. Wofford
1,632 men (48 k, 184 w, 138 m/c = 370 or 22.7%)

16th Georgia
Col. Goode Bryan
303 men (20 k, 41 w, 43 m/c = 104 or 34.3%)

18th Georgia
Lt. Col. Solon Z. Ruff
303 men (3 k, 16 w, 17 m/c = 36 or 11.9%)

24th Georgia
Col. Robert McMillan
303 men (10 k, 29 w, 46 m/c = 85 or 28.1%)

Cobb's Georgia Legion
Lt. Col. Luther J. Glenn
213 men (6 k, 16 w = 22 or 10.3%)

Phillips Georgia Legion
Lt. Col. Elihu Sandy Barclay
273 men (6 k, 41 w, 19 m/c = 66 or 24.2%)

3rd Georgia Battalion
(Sharpshooters)
Lt. Col. Nathan L. Hutchins
233 men (3 k, 3 w, 7 m/c = 13 or 5.6%)

Cabell's Artillery Battalion
Col. Henry C. Cabell
378 men (15 k, 37 w = 52 or 13.8%)

1st North Carolina Artillery (Manly's Battery)
Capt. Basil C. Manly
Two Napoleons, two 3-inch Rifles:
131 men (3 k, 10 w = 13 or 9.9%)

Pulaski (Georgia) **Artillery** (Fraser's Battery)
Capt. John C. Fraser (mw),
Lt. William J. Furlong
Two 3-inch Rifles, two 10 pdr
Parrotts: 63 men (7 k, 12 w = 19 or 30.2%)

1st Richmond (Virginia):
Howitzers (McCarthy's Battery)
Capt. Edward S. McCarthy (w),
Lt. Robert M. Anderson
Two Napoleons, two 3-inch Rifles:
90 men (3 k, 10 w = 13 or 14.4%)

Troup County (Georgia):
Artillery (Carlton's Battery)
Capt. Henry H. Carlton (w), Lt. C.W. Motes
Two 12 pdr Howitzer, two 10 pdr
Parrott: 90 men (2 k, 5 w = 7 or 7.8%)

Dearing's Artillery Battalion
Maj. James Dearing
420 men (9 k, 12 w, 4 m/c = 25 or 6.0%)

Fauquier (Virginia) **Artillery** (Stribling's Battery)
Capt. Robert M. Stribling
Four Napoleons, two 10 pdr Parrotts:
135 men (1 k, 4 w = 5 or 3.7%)

Richmond Hampden (Virginia)
Artillery (Caskie's Battery)
Capt. William H. Caskie
Two Napoleons, One 3-inch Rifle,
One 10 pdr Parrott:
90 men (3 w, 1 m/c = 4 or 4.4%)

Richmond Fayette (Virginia)
Artillery (Macon's Battery)
Capt. Miles C. Macon
Two Napoleons, two 10 pdr
Parrotts: 90 men (3 k, 1 w,
1 m/c = 5 or 3.7%)

Lynchburg (Virginia) **Artillery**
(Blount's Battery)
Capt. Joseph G. Blount
Four Napoleons:
96 men (5 k, 3 w, 2 m/c = 10 or 3.7%)

Longstreet's Corps Artillery Reserve
Col. James B. Walton
918 men (30 k, 122 w, 17 m/c = 169 or 18.4%)

Alexander's Artillery Battalion
Col. Edward P. Alexander
576 men (22 k, 111 w, 6 m/c = 139 or 24.1%)

Ashland (Virginia)
Artillery (Woolfolk's Battery)
Capt. Pichegru Woolfolk, Jr. (w),
Lt. James Woolfolk
Two Napoleons, two 20 pdr Parrotts:
103 men (3 k, 24 w, 1m/c = 28 or 27.2%)

Bedford (Virginia)
Artillery (Jordan's Battery)
Capt. Tyler C. Jordan
Four 3-inch Rifles:
78 men (1 k, 7 w, 1m/c = 9 or 11.5%)

Brooks (South Carolina)
Artillery (Gilbert's Battery)
Lt. Stephen C. Gilbert
Four 12 pdr Howitzers:
71 men (7 k, 29 w = 36 or 50.7%)

Madison (Louisiana)
Light Artillery (Moody's Battery)
Capt. George V. Moody
Four 24 pdr Howitzers:
135 men (4 k, 29 w = 33 or 24.4%)

Richmond (Virginia)
Battery (Parker's Battery)
Capt. William W. Parker
Three 3-inch Rifles
One 10 pdr Parrott: 90 men
(3 k, 14 w, 1m/c = 18 or 20.0%)

Bath (Virginia)
Artillery (Taylor's Battery)
Capt. Osmond B. Taylor
Four Napoleons: 90 men
(4 k, 8 w, 1m/c = 13 or 14.4%)

Washington (Louisiana) Artillery Battalion
Maj. Benjamin Franklin Eshleman
338 men (8 k, 11 w, 11 m/c = 30 or 8.9%)

1st Company (Squires's Battery):
Capt. Charles W. Squires
One Napoleon
77 men (1 k, 3 m/c = 4 or 5.2%)

2nd Company (Richardson's Battery):
Capt. John B. Richardson
Two Napoleons, One 12 pdr
Howitzer: 80 men
(2 k, 3 w, 1 m/c = 6 or 7.5%)

3rd Company (Miller's Battery)
Capt. Merritt B. Miller
Three Napoleons
92 men (6 w, 4 m/c = 10 or 12.5%)

4th Company (Norcom's Battery)
Capt. Joe Norcom (w),
Lt. Henry A. Battles
Two Napoleons, One 12 pdr
Howitzer: 80 men
(6 w, 4m/c = 10 or 12.5%)

Hill's Corps
Lt. Gen. Ambrose P. Hill
21,948 men (1,724 k, 4,683 w,
2,088 m/c = 8,495 or 38.7%)

Anderson's Division
Maj. Gen. Richard H. Anderson
7,136 men (381 k, 1,180 w, 624 m/c = 2,185 or 30.6%)

Wilcox's Brigade
Brig. Gen. Cadmus M. Wilcox
1,726 men (78 k, 443 w, 257 m/c = 778 or 45.1%)

8th Alabama
Lt. Col. Hilary A. Herbert
477 men (40 k, 146 w,
80 m/c = 266 or 55.8%)

9th Alabama
Capt. Joseph H. King (w),
Capt. John N. Chisholm (w/c),
Capt. Gaines C. Smith (w/c),
Capt. M.G. May (w)
306 men (8 k, 32 w, 76 m/c = 116 or 37.9%)

10th Alabama
Col. William H. Forney (w/c),
Lt. Col. James E. Shelley
311 men (15 k, 89 w = 104+ or 33.4%)

11th Alabama
Col. John C.C. Sanders (w),
Lt. Col. George E. Tayloe
311 men (7 k, 68 w = 75+ or 24.1%)

14th Alabama
Col. Lucius Pinckard (w/c),
Lt. Col. James A. Broome
316 men (8 k, 40 w = 48+ or 15.2%)

Perry's Brigade
Col. David Lang
742 men (80 k, 228 w,
14 m/c = 455 or 61.3%)

2nd Florida
Maj. Walter R. Moore (w/c),
Capt. William D. Ballatine (w/c),
Capt. Alexander Mosely (w/c),
Capt. C. Seton Fleming
242 men (24 k, 71 w,
11 m/c = 106+ or 43.8%)

5th Florida
Capt. Richmond N. Gardner (w),
Capt. John S. Cochran (mw),
Capt. Council A. Bryan,
Capt. John W. Hollyman
321 men (39 k, 77 w,
13 m/c = 129+ or 40.2%)

8th Florida
Lt. Col. William Baya
176 men (17 k, 80 w,
11 m/c = 108+ or 61.4%)

Lane's Artillery Battalion
Maj. John Lane
384 men (3 k, 35 w,
4 m/c = 42 or 10.9%)

Sumter (Georgia) **Artillery,**
Company B (Patterson's Battery)
Capt. George M. Patterson
Four 12 pdr Howitzers,
Two Napoleons: 124 men
(2 k, 6 w, 1 m/c = 9 or 7.3%)

Bibliography

Archival Sources and Manuscripts

Adams County Historical Society (ACHS), Gettysburg, PA

Civilian Accounts – Aftermath of the Battle

County Tax Records

Human Interest stories of the battle of Gettysburg File

Sherfy Family File

Wentz Family Files

William Storrick Collection

Eleanor S. Brockenbrough Library, The Museum of the Confederacy, Richmond, VA

Moody Family Collection

Centre County Library and Historical Museum, Bellefonte, PA

John B. Linn Diary

Charleston Library Society, Charleston, SC

Albert Happoldt Prince Unpublished History of Brooks Artillery (Rhett's Battery)

Clarion County PA Historical Society

Calvin Augustus Craig Collection

State Archives of Florida

Council A. Bryan Papers

Gettysburg National Military Park (GNMP), Gettysburg, PA

Association of Licensed Battlefield Guides (ALBG) Library

Farm Family Files

Henry Wentz File

Library

Richard Holland Sketches of Norwood Rock

Museum Collections

105th Pennsylvania Company A Flag

Dr. Alfred Hamilton Artifacts

James Thompson Papers

Journal of Doctor John W.C. O'Neal, M.D.

Participant Accounts Files

Adolfo Cavada

Charles Graham

Regimental Files

Historical Society of Pennsylvania, Philadelphia, PA

George Meade Collection

Library of Congress (LOC), Washington, DC

Daniel E. Sickles Papers, Manuscripts Division

Louis T. Wigfall Papers, Manuscripts Division

Cadmus Wilcox Papers, Manuscripts Division

Prints and Photographs Division

Louisiana National Guard Archives

Souvenir Book of the Washington Artillery of New Orleans, 1894, Washington Artillery Collection Box 7, 2000.024.090, New Orleans, Louisiana

Mississippi Department of Archives and History, Archives and Library Division, Jackson, MS

Benj. Grubb Humphreys Manuscript

National Archives and Records Administration (NARA), Washington, DC

Annual Reports of the Secretary of War

Compiled Military Service Records (CMSR) and Pension Records

Official Military Personnel Files

National Civil War Museum, Harrisburg, PA

D.E. Sickles to Major General Meade, July 6, 1863

Pennsylvania Historical and Museum Commission, Harrisburg, PA

Civil War Muster Rolls

Soldier Personnel Records

Pottstown Historical Society, Pottstown, PA

Andrew Tippin

Rhode Island Historical Society, Providence, RI

Soldiers and Sailors Historical Society Records, MSS 723 (John K. Bucklyn)

South Carolina Library, University of South Carolina, Columbia, SC

David Wyatt Aiken Collection

United States Army History and Education Center (USAHEC), Carlisle, PA

David B. Birney Papers

Robert L. Brake Collection

John Henry Burrill Papers

Crandall Family Papers

Philip Rockwell Papers

Virginia Historical Society, Richmond, VA

Cabell Family Papers, 1774-1941 (Mss1 C1118 a)

West Virginia and Regional History Collection, West Virginia University Libraries, Morgantown, WV

Diary of Lewis Schaeffer (a&m collection 1540)

Yale University Library, Manuscripts and Archives, New Haven, CT

Alexander Stewart Webb Papers

Private Collections

Boyle Family Collection: Charles P. Woolhiser Diary

The Joseph Bucklin Society: John K. Bucklyn Papers

Kenneth Burkett Private Collection

Kendra Debany Private Collection

Erik Dorr, Gettysburg Museum of History

Ellen Gonsalves: Madison Light Artillery Research Notes

Hadden Family Collection: Thomas Murray Watson Papers

Charles T. Joyce Private Collection

David Malgee Private Collection: Charles K. Graham Research Notes

Ronn Palm Museum of Civil War Images

William John Parry: Unpublished Family History of Thomas Rafferty and Susan McCoun Rafferty

B.J. and Kathleen Pino Collection

Official Documents, Reports, and Government Papers

Annual Reports of the Gettysburg National Military Park Commission 1893-1904.Washington: Government Printing Office, 1905

Documents of the U.S. Sanitary Commission, Vol. II, Numbers 61 to 95, 1866.

Congressional Record – Senate. Washington: U.S. Government Printing Office, 1903.

General Orders of the War Department, Embracing the Years 1861, 1862, & 1863 (Two Volumes). New York: Derby & Miller, 1864.

Georg, Kathleen. "The Sherfy Farm and the Battle of Gettysburg." Environmental & Interpretive Planning, Research & Curatorial Division, Gettysburg National Military Park, January 1977.

Heitman, Francis B. *Historical Register and Dictionary of the United States Army: From its organization September 29, 1789, To March 2, 1903.* Washington: Government Printing Office, 1903.

New York Bureau of Military Statistics. *3rd Annual Report of the Bureau of Military Statistics.* Albany, NY: The Bureau, 1866.

Presidential Vetoes, 1789-1988. Compiled by the Senate Library. Washington: U.S. Government Printing Office, 1992.

Report of the Joint Committee on the Conduct of the War, Washington: Government Printing Office, 1865.

United States Census, for the Years: 1820, 1860, 1870, 1880, 1900, 1910.

The War of the Rebellion: A Compilation of the Official Records of the Union and Confederate Armies, Washington: Government Printing Office, 1880-1901.

Books, Magazines, Maps, and Pamphlets

Acken, J. Gregory, editor. *Service with the Signal Corps: Memoir of Captain Louis R. Fortescue.* Knoxville: The University of Tennessee Press, 2015.

Adelman, Garry. *The Myth of Little Round Top.* Gettysburg: Thomas Publications, 2003.

———. "The Third Brigade, Third Division, Sixth Corps at Gettysburg." *Gettysburg Magazine*, No. 11 (July 1994): 91-101.

Agassiz, George R., editor. *Meade's Headquarters 1861-1865: Letters of Colonel Theodore Lyman from The Wilderness to Appomattox.* Boston, MA: The Atlantic Monthly Press, 1922.

Alexander, E. Porter. "The Great Charge and Artillery Fighting at Gettysburg." *Battles and Leaders of the Civil War*, 3: 357-368.

———. "Letter from General E. P. Alexander, March 17th, 1877." *Southern Historical Society Papers*, 4: 97-110.

———. *Military Memoirs of a Confederate: A Critical Narrative.* New York: Charles Scribner's Sons, 1907.

Ames, Nelson. *History of Battery G, First Regiment N.Y. Light Artillery.* Wolcott, NY: Benedum Books, 2000. Reprint of the 1900 edition.

Andrews, J. Cutler. "The Press Reports the Battle of Gettysburg." *Pennsylvania History: A Journal of Mid-Atlantic Studies* 31, No. 2 (April 1964): 176-98.

The Annals of the War Written by Leading Participants North and South. Originally Published in The Philadelphia Weekly Times. Philadelphia: The Times Publishing Company, 1879.

Appleton, Nathan, Henry D. Scott, John F. Murray, Thomas E. Chase, and George L. Newton. *History of the Fifth Massachusetts Battery.* Boston: Luther E. Cowles, 1902.

Association of Licensed Battlefield Guides. *Monuments, Markers, & Tablets Location Guide.* Gettysburg, PA: 2018.

Bachelder, John B. *Gettysburg: What to See, and How to See It.* Boston: John B. Bachelder, 1878.

———. *Position of Troops, Second Day's Battle*. New York: Office of the Chief of Engineers, U.S. Army, 1876.

Baker, Levi W. *History of the Ninth Mass. Battery*. South Framingham, MA: Lakeview Press, 1888.

Bandy, Ken and Florence Freeland, editors. *The Gettysburg Papers, Two Volumes in One*. Dayton, OH: Morningside Bookshop, 1986.

Barnett, Bert. "'The Severest and Bloodiest Artillery Fight I Ever Saw:' Colonel E. P. Alexander and the First Corps Artillery Assail the Peach Orchard, July 2, 1863." *Gettysburg Seminar Papers, Programs of the Seventh Annual Gettysburg Seminar*, National Park Service (1999): 61-82.

Barram, Rick. *The 72nd New York Infantry in the Civil War: A History and Roster*. Jefferson, NC: McFarland & Company Inc., 2014. Kindle edition.

Bartlett, Asa W. *History of the Twelfth Regiment New Hampshire Volunteers in the War of the Rebellion*. Concord, NH: Ira C. Evans, Printer, 1897.

Bates, Samuel P. *History of Pennsylvania Volunteer Regiments, 1861-1865*. Harrisburg, PA: B. Singerly, State Printer, 1871.

Beidler, Peter G. *Army of the Potomac: The Civil War Letters of William Cross Hazelton of the Eighth Illinois Cavalry Regiment*. Seattle, WA: Coffeetown Press, 2013.

Benedict, George G. *Army Life in Virginia*. Burlington, VT: Free Press Association, 1895.

———. *Vermont in the Civil War* (2 Volumes). Burlington, VT: Free Press Association, 1886.

Bennett, Gerald R. *Days of "Uncertainty and Dread": The Ordeal Endured by the Citizens at Gettysburg*. Harrisburg, PA: Gettysburg Foundation, 1994.

Bernard, George S., editor. *War Talks of Confederate Veterans*. Petersburg, VA: Fenn & Owen Publishers, 1892.

Besley, William B., Hillman Allyn Hall, Gilbert Guion Wood. *History of the Sixth New York Cavalry (Second Ira Harris Guard)*. Worcester, MA: The Blanchard Press, 1908.

Biddle, James C. "General Meade at Gettysburg." *The Annals of the War Written by Leading Participants North and South*. Dayton, OH: Morningside House, 205-219.

Bigelow, John. *The Peach Orchard*. Baltimore, MD: Butternut & Blue, 1984. Reprint of the 1910 edition.

Birkhimer, William E. *Historical Sketch of the Organization, Administration, Material and Tactics of the Artillery, United States Army*. Washington, DC: James J. Chapman, 1884.

Blake, Henry N. *Three Years in the Army of the Potomac*. Boston: Lee and Shepard, 1865.

Blight, David W. *When This Cruel War Is Over: The Civil War Letters of Charles Harvey Brewster*. Amherst, MA: The University of Massachusetts Press, 1992.

Booth, Andrew B., Comp. *Records of Louisiana Confederate Soldiers and Louisiana Confederate Commands*. Volume III. - Book 1. New Orleans: 1920.

Bowden, Scott, and Bill Ward. *Last Chance for Victory: Robert E. Lee and the Gettysburg Campaign*. Da Capo Press, 2001.

Bradsby, Henry C. *History of Adams County* (Part III of History of Cumberland and Adams Counties). Chicago: Warner, Beers & Co., 1886.

———. *History of Bradford County, Pennsylvania, with Biographical Sketches.* Chicago: S.B. Nelson & Co., 1891.

Brandt, Nat. *The Congressman Who Got Away with Murder.* New York: Syracuse University Press, 1991.

Bretzger, Paul E. *Observing Hancock at Gettysburg: The General's Leadership through Eyewitness Accounts.* Jefferson, NC: McFarland & Company, 2016.

Broadhead, Sarah M. *The Diary of a Lady of Gettysburg, Pennsylvania, from June 15 to July 15, 1863.* Hershey, PA: Gary T. Hawbaker, 1863.

Brown, Henry Le Fevre. *History of the Third Regiment Excelsior Brigade 72nd New York Volunteer Infantry 1861-1865.* Jamestown, NY: Journal Printing Co., 1902.

Brown, Kent Masterson. *Retreat from Gettysburg: Lee, Logistics, and the Pennsylvania Campaign.* Chapel Hill, NC: The University of North Carolina Press, 2005.

Buehler, Fannie J. *Recollections of the Rebel Invasion and One Woman's Experience during the Battle of Gettysburg.* Hershey, PA: Gary T. Hawbaker, 1900. Reprint of the 1896 edition.

Burns, James A. "The 12th New Hampshire Regiment at Gettysburg and Beyond." *Gettysburg Magazine,* No. 20 (June 1999): 113-120.

Busey, John W. *These Honored Dead: The Union Casualties at Gettysburg.* Hightstown, NJ: Longstreet House, 1988.

———, and Travis W. Busey. *Confederate Casualties at Gettysburg: A Comprehensive Record.* McFarland & Company, Inc., 2016.

———. *Union Casualties at Gettysburg: A Comprehensive Record* (Three Volumes). Jefferson, North Carolina and London: McFarland & Company, Inc., 2011. Reprint of the 1977 edition.

———, and David G. Martin. *Regimental Strengths and Losses at Gettysburg.* Hightstown, NJ: Longstreet House, 1994. Reprint of the 1982 edition.

Byer, Walter F., and Oscar F. Keydel, compilers. *Deeds of Valor: How America's Heroes Won the Congressional Medal of Honor.* Stamford, CT: Longmeadow Press in association with Platinum Press, Inc. Reprint of the 1903 edition.

Byrne, Frank L. and Andrew T. Weaver, editors. *Haskell of Gettysburg: His Life and Civil War Papers.* Kent, OH: The Kent State University Press, 1989.

Callahan, Edward W., editor. *List of Officers of the Navy of the United States and of the Marine Corps from 1775 to 1900.* New York: L. R. Hamersly & Co., 1901.

Campbell, Eric A. *"A Grand Terrible Dramma" From Gettysburg to Petersburg: The Civil War Letters of Charles Wellington Reed.* New York: Fordham University Press, 2000.

———. "Baptism of Fire: The Ninth Massachusetts Battery at Gettysburg, July 2, 1863." *Gettysburg Magazine,* No. 5 (July 1991): 47-78.

———. "The Key to the Entire Situation: The Peach Orchard, July 2, 1863." *Papers of the 2006 Gettysburg National Military Park Seminar.* National Park Service (2008): 101-121.

———. "'Remember Harper's Ferry': The Degradation, Humiliation, and Redemption of Col. George L. Willard's Brigade." *Gettysburg Magazine*, No. 7 (July 1992): 51-74.

———. "'Sacrificed to the bad management…of others.': Richard H. Anderson's Division at the Battle of Gettysburg." *Gettysburg Seminar Papers, Programs of the Seventh Annual Gettysburg Seminar.* National Park Service (1999): 103-135.

Carmichael, Peter S. "Never Heard Before on the American Continent." *Gettysburg Magazine*, No. 10 (January 1994): 107-111.

Carter, Robert Goldthwaite. *Four Brothers in Blue or Sunshine and Shadows of the War of the Rebellion.* Washington: Press of Gibson Bros., 1913.

Casey, Powell A. *An Outline of the Civil War Campaigns and Engagements of the Washington Artillery of New Orleans.* Baton Rouge, LA: Claitor's Publishing Division, 1986.

Cheney, Newel. *History of the Ninth Regiment New York Volunteer Cavalry, War of 1861 to 1865.* Jamestown, NY: Martin Merz & Son, 1901.

Clark, George. *A Glance Backward: Or Some Events in the Past History of My Life.* Houston: Rein & Sons Company, 1914.

Cleaves, Freeman. *Meade of Gettysburg.* Norman, OK: University of Oklahoma Press, 1960.

Clouse, Jim. "Whatever Happened to Henry Wentz?" *The Battlefield Dispatch.* Association of Licensed Battlefield Guides (October 1998): 6-10.

Coco, Gregory A. *Confederates Killed in Action at Gettysburg.* Gettysburg, PA: Thomas Publications, 2001.

———. *Killed In Action: Eyewitness Accounts of the Last Moments of 100 Union Soldiers Who Died at Gettysburg.* Gettysburg, PA: Thomas Publications, 1992.

———. *My Gettysburg Battle Experiences: By Captain George Hillyer, 9th Georgia Infantry, C.S.A.* Gettysburg, PA: Thomas Publications, 2005.

———. *A Strange and Blighted Land: Gettysburg: The Aftermath of a Battle.* Gettysburg, PA: Thomas Publications, 1995.

———. *A Vast Sea Of Misery: A History and Guide to the Union and Confederate Field Hospitals at Gettysburg, July 1-November 20, 1863.* Gettysburg, PA: Thomas Publications, 1988.

———. *War Stories: A Collection of 150 Little Known Human Interest Accounts of the Campaign and Battle of Gettysburg.* Gettysburg, PA: Thomas Publications, 1992.

———. *Wasted Valor: The Confederate Dead at Gettysburg.* Gettysburg, PA: Thomas Publications, 1990.

Coddington, Edwin B. *The Gettysburg Campaign: A Study in Command.* New York: Simon & Schuster, 1968.

Cole, James, and Rev. Roy E. Frampton. *Lincoln and the Human Interest Stories of the Gettysburg National Cemetery.* Hanover, PA: The Sheridan Press: 1995.

Colston, Capt. F. M. "Gettysburg As I Saw It." *Confederate Veteran* (Vol. V, No. 11): 551-553.

Cooksey, Paul Clark. "Around the Flank: Longstreet's July 2 Attack at Gettysburg." *Gettysburg Magazine,* No.29 (July 2003): 94-105.

———. "Forcing the Issue: Brig. Gen. Henry Hunt at Gettysburg on July 3, 1863." *Gettysburg Magazine,* No.30 (January 2004): 77-88.

———. "The Plan for Pickett's Charge." *Gettysburg Magazine,* No.22 (January 2000): 66-79.

———. "The Union Artillery at Gettysburg on July 3." *Gettysburg Magazine,* No.38 (July 2008): 72-90.

———. "Up the Emmitsburg Road: Gen. Robert E. Lee's Plan for the Attack on July 2nd on the Union Left Flank." *Gettysburg Magazine,* No. 26 (January 2002): 45-52.

Coxe, John. "The Battle of Gettysburg." *Confederate Veteran* (Vo. XXI, No. 9): 433-436.

Craft, David. *History of the One Hundred Forty-First Regiment, Pennsylvania Volunteers.* Towanda, PA: Reporter-Journal Printing Company, 1885.

Crocker, James Francis. *Gettysburg- Pickett's Charge, Address by James F. Crocker, November 7, 1894.* Portsmouth, VA: W.A. Fiske, 1906.

Crotty, D. G. *Four Years Campaigning in the Army of the Potomac.* Grand Rapids, MI: Dygert Bros & Co., 1874.

Culp, Edward C. *The 25th Ohio Vet. Vol. Infantry in the War for the Union.* Topeka, KS: Geo. W. Crane & Co., 1885.

Cutrer, Thomas W., editor. *Longstreet's Aide: The Civil War Letters of Major Thomas J. Goree.* Charlottesville, VA: University Press of Virginia, 1995.

Davis, O. Wilson. *Sketch of Frederic Fernandez Cavada, A Native of Cuba.* Philadelphia: James B. Chandler, 1871.

Davis, William C. *Jefferson Davis: The Man and His Hour.* New York: Harper Collins, 1991.

Deane, Frank Putnam, editor. *"My Dear Wife...." The Civil War Letters of David Brett 9th Massachusetts Battery, Union Cannoneer.* Pioneer Press, 1964.

Dempsey, Stuart R. "The Florida Brigade at Gettysburg." *Blue & Gray,* XXVII (#4, 2010): 6-40.

Dickert, D. Augustus. *History of Kershaw's Brigade with Complete Roll of Companies, Biographical Sketches, Incidents, Anecdotes, etc.* Newberry, SC: Elbert H. Aull Company, 1899.

DiNardo, R.L. "James Longstreet, the Modern Soldier." *James Longstreet: The Man, the Soldier, the Controversy,* 31-51.

———; and Albert A. Nofi, editors. *James Longstreet: The Man, the Soldier, the Controversy.* Conshohocken, PA: Combined Publishing, 1998.

Downs, David B. "'His Left was Worth a Glance': Meade and the Union Left on July 2, 1863." *Gettysburg Magazine*, No. 7 (July 1992): 29-40.

Dreese, Michael. *Never Desert the Old Flag: 50 Stories of Union Battle Flags and Color-Bearers at Gettysburg.* Gettysburg, PA: Thomas Publications, 2002.

————. "'Say Goodbye to All' Battlefield Premonitions," *The Gettysburg Experience* (May 2006): 51-52.

————. *This Flag Never Goes Down: 40 Stories of Confederate Battle Flags and Color-Bearers at Gettysburg.* Gettysburg, PA: Thomas Publications, 2004.

Durkin, Joseph T. editor. *John Dooley Confederate Soldier: His War Journal.* University of Notre Dame Press, 1963.

Dyer, Frederick H. *A Compendium of the War of the Rebellion Compiled and Arranged from Official Records of the Federal and Confederate Armies.* Des Moines, IA: Dyer Pub. Co., 1908.

Eckenrode, H.J. and Bryan Conrad. *James Longstreet: Lee's War Horse.* Chapel Hill, NC: University of North Carolina Press, 1986. Reprint of the 1936 edition.

Elliott, S. G. "Elliott's Map of the Battlefield at Gettysburg Pennsylvania." Map. Philadelphia: F. Bourgum & Co., 1864.

Elmore, Thomas L. "The Florida Brigade at Gettysburg." *Gettysburg Magazine*, No. 15 (1996): 45-59.

————. "Torrid Heat and Blinding Rain: A Meteorological and Astronomical Chronology of the Gettysburg Campaign." *Gettysburg Magazine*, No. 13 (July 1995): 7-21.

Evans, Clement A., editor. *Confederate Military History* (12 Volumes). Atlanta, GA: Confederate Publishing Company, 1899.

Evans, W. McR. "The Last Shot At Gettysburg." *Confederate Veteran* (Vol. XXXIII, No. 12): 450-451.

Evans, Willis F. *History of Berkeley County, West Virginia.* Martinsburg, WV: Willis F. Evans, 1928.

Everson, Guy R. and Edward W. Simpson, Jr. *Far, Far From Home: The Wartime Letters of Dick and Tally Simpson, 3rd South Carolina Volunteers.* Oxford University Press, 1994.

Fasnacht, C. H. *Historical Sketch, by C. H. Fasnacht, and Oration, by E. K. Martin, Esq., Delivered at Dedication of the 99th Pennsylvania Monument, Gettysburg, PA, July 2, 1886.* Lancaster, PA: Examiner Steam Book and Job Print, 1886.

Fatout, Paul, editor. *Letters of a Civil War Surgeon.* West Lafayette, IN: Purdue University Press, 1996.

Favill, Josiah Marshall. *Diary of a Young Army Officer.* Baltimore, MD: Butternut & Blue, 2000. Reprint of the 1909 edition.

Figg, Royall W. *Where Men Only Dare To Go: Or The Story Of A Boy Company, C.S.A.* Baton Rouge, LA: Louisiana State University Press, 2008. Reprint of the 1885 edition.

Fleming, Francis P. *A Memoir of Captain C. Seton Fleming, C.S.A.* Alexandria, VA: Stonewall House, 1985. Reprint of the 1884 edition.

Floyd, Steven A. *Commanders and Casualties at the Battle of Gettysburg: The Comprehensive Order of Battle.* Gettysburg, PA: Gettysburg Publishing.

Fornieri, Joseph R., editor. *The Language of Liberty: The Political Speeches and Writings of Abraham Lincoln.* Washington, DC: Regnery Publishing, 2009.

Fox, William F. *Regimental Losses in the American Civil War, 1861-1865: A Treatise on the Extent and Nature of the Mortuary Losses in the Union Regiments, With Full and Exhaustive Statistics Compiled From the Official Records on File in the State Military Bureaus and at Washington.* Albany, NY: Brandow Printing Company, 1889.

Frassanito, William A. *Early Photography at Gettysburg.* Gettysburg, PA: Thomas Publications, 1995.

Frederick, Gilbert. *The Story of A Regiment Being a Record of the Military Services of the Fifty-Seventh New York State Volunteer Infantry in the War of the Rebellion 1861-1865.* Chicago: The Fifty-Seventh Veteran Association, 1895.

Freeman, Douglas S. *Lee's Lieutenants: A Study in Command.* New York: Charles Scribner's Sons, 1942.

Fremantle, Arthur James Lyon. *Three Months in the Southern States: April-June, 1863.* New York: John Bradburn, 1864.

Furqueron, James R. "The Bull of the Woods: James Longstreet and the Confederate Left at Chickamauga." *James Longstreet: The Man, the Soldier, the Controversy,* 99 – 164.

Gallagher, Gary, editor. *Fighting for the Confederacy: The Personal Recollections of General Edward Porter Alexander.* Chapel Hill, NC: The University of North Carolina Press, 1998.

————. *Lee: The Soldier.* Lincoln, NE: University of Nebraska Press, 1996.

————. *The Second Day at Gettysburg: Essays on Confederate and Union Leadership.* Kent, OH: Kent State University Press, 1993.

————. *The Third Day at Gettysburg & Beyond.* Chapel Hill, NC: The University of North Carolina Press, 1998.

Gambone, A. M. *Hancock at Gettysburg . . . and beyond.* Baltimore, MD: Butternut & Blue, 2002.

Gates, Theodore B. *The Ulster Guard and the War of the Rebellion.* New York: Benjamin H. Tyrrel, 1879.

Gerald, G. B. "The Battle of Gettysburg." *Waco Daily Times-Herald,* July 3, 1913.

Gettysburg National Military Park. "Replanting More Missing Orchards and Woods at Gettysburg." *The Gettysburg Quarterly,* Vol.17, No. 2 (Summer 2010): 2.

Gottfried, Bradley M. *Brigades of Gettysburg.* Cambridge, MA: Da Capo Press, 2002.

Gracey, Rev. S. L. *Annals of the Sixth Pennsylvania Cavalry.* Pennsylvania: E.H. Butler & Company, 1868.

Gudmestad, Nancie W. *The Shriver's Story: Eyewitnesses to the Battle of Gettysburg.* Gettysburg, PA: The Shriver House Museum, 2008.

Hadden, R. Lee. "The Granite Glory: The 19th Maine at Gettysburg." *Gettysburg Magazine,* No. 13 (July 1995): 50-63.

Hagerty, Edward J. *Collis' Zouaves: The 114th Pennsylvania Volunteers in the Civil War.* Baton Rouge, LA: Louisiana State University Press, 1997

Haines, Douglas Craig. "'Lights Mingled with Shadows': Lt. Gen. Richard S. Ewell – July 1, 1863." *Gettysburg Magazine,* No. 45 (July 2011): 40-60.

Hall, Charles B., *Military Records of General Officers of the Confederate States of America*. Austin, TX: The Steck Company, 1898.

Hall, Hillman A., editor. *History of the Sixth New York Cavalry*. Worcester, MA: The Blanchard Press, 1908.

Hancock, Almira. *Reminiscences of Winfield Scott Hancock*. Gaithersburg, MD: Olde Soldier Books. Reprint of the 1887 edition.

Hanifen, Michael. *History of Battery B, First New Jersey Artillery*. Providence, RI: Snow and Fordham, 1894.

Hanna, Charles. *Gettysburg Medal of Honor Recipients*. Springville, UT: Bonneville Books, 2010.

Hard, Abner. *History of the Eighth Regiment Cavalry Illinois Volunteers, During the Great Rebellion*. Aurora, IL: 1868.

Harman, Troy D. *Cemetery Hill: The General Plan was Unchanged*. Baltimore, MD: Butternut & Blue, 2001.

Harrison, Kathleen Georg. *The Location of the Monuments, Markers, and Tablets on Gettysburg Battlefield*. Gettysburg National Military Park.

————. *Nothing But Glory*. Gettysburg, PA: Thomas Publications, 2001.

Hartwig, D. Scott. "The Army of Northern Virginia and the Gettysburg Campaign – 'We came here with the best army the Confederacy ever carried into the field'." *Papers of the 2010 Gettysburg National Military Park Seminar*. National Park Service (2012): 40-65.

————. "The Betrayal of George Meade." *America's Civil War*, Vol. 29, No. 1 (March 2016): 14-16.

————. "'I Have Never Been in a Hotter Place': Brigade Command at Gettysburg." *Gettysburg Magazine*, No. 25 (January 2002): 61-74.

Hawthorne, Frederick. *Gettysburg: Stories of Men and Monuments*. Gettysburg, PA: Association of Licensed Battlefield Guides, 1988.

Haynes, Martin. *A History of the Second Regiment, New Hampshire Volunteer Infantry in the War of the Rebellion*. Lakeport, NH: 1896.

————. *Muster Out Roll of the Second New Hampshire Regiment in the War of the Rebellion*. Lakeport, NH: Privately Printed, 1917.

Hays, Gilbert Adams. *Under the Red Patch: Story of the Sixty Third Regiment Pennsylvania Volunteers*. Pittsburgh, PA: Sixty-Third Pennsylvania Volunteers Regimental Association, 1908.

Heiser, John. "Action on the Emmitsburg Road: Gettysburg, Pennsylvania July 2, 1863." *Gettysburg Magazine*, No. 1 (July 1989): 79-85.

Helmreich, Jonathan, editor. *To Petersburg with the Army of the Potomac: The Civil War Letters of Levi Bird Duff, 105th Pennsylvania Volunteers*. Jefferson, NC: McFarland & Company, 2009.

Hess, Earl J. *Pickett's Charge: The Last Attack at Gettysburg*. Chapel Hill, NC: The University of North Carolina Press, 2001.

Hessler, James A. *Sickles at Gettysburg: The Controversial Civil War General Who Committed Murder, Abandoned Little Round Top, and Declared Himself the Hero of Gettysburg.* El Dorado Hills, CA: Savas Beatie, 2009.

———, Wayne E. Motts, and Steven A. Stanley. *Pickett's Charge at Gettysburg: A Guide to the Most Famous Attack in American History.* El Dorado Hills, CA: Savas Beatie, 2015.

Heverly, C.F. *History of the Towandas, 1776-1886.* Towanda, PA: Reporter-Journal Printing Co., 1886.

Hewitt, William D. "'The General Plan of Attack Was Unchanged.' Robert E. Lee and Confederate Operations on July 3." *Papers of the 2008 Gettysburg National Military Park Seminar.* National Park Service (2010): 40-65.

Hill, Patrick, Perry Tholl and Greg Johnson. "'On This Spot…' Locating the 1st Minnesota Monument at Gettysburg." *Gettysburg Magazine*, No.32 (January 2005): 96-114.

Himmer, Robert. "A Matter of Time: The Issuance of the Pipe Creek Circular." *Gettysburg Magazine*, No. 46 (July 2012): 7-18.

Hogan, Edwin P. *Waiting For Jacob: A Civil War Story.* Latrobe, PA: Saint Vincent College Center for Northern Appalachian Studies, 2000.

Hoke, Jacob. *The Great Invasion of 1863; or, General Lee in Pennsylvania.* Dayton, OH: W. J. Shuey, 1887.

Holstein, Anna M. *Three Years in Field Hospitals of the Army of the Potomac.* Philadelphia, PA: J. B. Lippincott & Co., 1867.

Hood, John B. *Advance and Retreat.* Blue and Grey Press, 1985. Reprint of the 1880 edition.

———. "Letter from General John B. Hood." *Southern Historical Society Papers*, 4: 145-150.

Howard, Oliver Otis. *Autobiography of Oliver Otis Howard.* New York: The Baker & Taylor Company, 1907.

Humphreys, Henry H. *Andrew Atkinson Humphreys: A Biography.* Gaithersburg, MD: Ron R. Van Sickle Military Books, 1988. Reprint of the 1924 edition.

Hunt, Henry. "The Second Day at Gettysburg." *Battles and Leaders of the Civil War*, 3:290-313.

Hunt, Roger D. *Colonels in Blue: Union Army Colonels of the Civil War: The Mid-Atlantic States: Pennsylvania, New Jersey, Maryland, Delaware, and The District of Columbia.* Mechanicsburg, PA: Stackpole Books, 2007.

Hutchinson, Gustavus B. *A Narrative of the Formation and Services of the Eleventh Massachusetts Volunteers, From April 15, 1861 to July 14, 1865.* Boston, MA: Alfred Mudge & Son, 1893.

Hutton, Paul Andrew, editor. *G. M. Sorrel: Recollections of a Confederate Staff Officer From Manassas to Petersburg – an insider's view of the Confederate high command.* New York: Bantam Books, 1992. Reprint of the 1905 edition.

Hyde, Bill. "Did You Get There? Capt. Samuel Johnston's Reconnaissance at Gettysburg." *Gettysburg Magazine*, No. 29 (July 2003): 86-93.

———; editor. *The Union Generals Speak: The Meade Hearings on the Battle of Gettysburg.* Baton Rouge, LA: Louisiana State University Press, 2003.

Imhof, John D. *Gettysburg Day Two: A Study in Maps*. Baltimore, MD: Butternut & Blue, 1999.

Isenberg, Britt C. *The Boys Fought Like Demons: The Untold Story of the Wildcat Regiment During the American Civil War*. Charleston, SC: Createspace Publishing, 2016.

Johnson, Robert U. and Clarence C. Buel. *Battles and Leaders of the Civil War*. New York: Castle Books. Reprint of the 1887 edition.

Johnson, Rossiter. *Campfire and Battlefield*. Slovenia: Trident Press International, 1999. Reprint of the 1894 edition.

Jomini, Baron de. *The Art of War*. Westport, CT: Greenwood Press. Reprint of the 1862 edition.

Jones, J. Keith. *Georgia Remembers Gettysburg: A Collection of First-Hand Accounts Written by Georgia Soldiers*. Gettysburg, PA: Ten Roads Publishing, 2013.

Kirkley, Joseph W. *Itinerary of the Army of the Potomac and Co-operating Forces in the Gettysburg Campaign, June and July, 1863; Organization of the Army of the Potomac at Gettysburg; And Return of Casualties in the Union and Confederate Forces*. Washington DC: 1886.

Knudsen, Harold M. *General James Longstreet: The Confederacy's Most Modern General*. Girard, IL: USA Publishing Services, 2007.

Krick, Robert E. L. *Staff Officers in Gray: A Biographical Register of the Staff Officers in the Army of Northern Virginia*. Chapel Hill, NC: The University of North Carolina Press, 2003.

Krick, Robert K. "'If Longstreet… Says So, It Is Most Likely Not True': James Longstreet and the Second Day at Gettysburg." *The Second Day at Gettysburg*, 357-380.

———. *Parker's Virginia Battery C.S.A.* Wilmington, NC: Broadfoot Publishing Company, 1989.

Ladd, David and Audrey, editors. *The Bachelder Papers: Gettysburg in their Own Words*. Dayton, OH: Morningside House, 1994.

Lader, Paul J. "The 7th New Jersey in the Gettysburg Campaign." *Gettysburg Magazine*, No. 16 (1997): 46-67.

Laino, Philip. *Gettysburg Campaign Atlas*. Gettysburg, PA: Gettysburg Publishing, 2009.

Lake, D.J. *Atlas of Adams Co., Pennsylvania*. Philadelphia, PA: I.W. Field & Company, 1872.

Lash, Gary G. "'A Pathetic Story': The 141st Pennsylvania (Graham's Brigade) at Gettysburg." *Gettysburg Magazine*, No. 14 (January 1996): 77-101.

Law, Evander M. "The Struggle for 'Round Top'." *Battles and Leaders of the Civil War*, 3:318-330.

Lee, Jr., Robert E. *Recollections and Letters*. New York: Barnes & Noble, 2004. Reprint of the 1904 edition.

Lewis, George. *The History of Battery E, First Regiment Rhode Island Light Artillery*. Providence, RI: Snow & Farnham, 1892.

The Life and Death of Fanny White: Being a Complete and Interesting History of the Career of That Notorious Lady. New York: 1860.

Long, A.L. *Memoirs of Robert E. Lee*. Secaucus, N.J.: Blue and Grey Press, 1983.

Longacre, Edward G. *General John Buford: A Military Biography*. Da Capo Press, 1995.

Longstreet, Helen D. *Lee and Longstreet at High Tide*. Gainesville, GA: 1905.

Longstreet, James. "The Battle of Fredericksburg." *Battles and Leaders of the Civil War*, 3: 70-85.

———. *From Manassas to Appomattox*. Cambridge, MA: Da Capo Press, 1992. Reprint of the 1895 edition.

———. "General James Longstreet's Account of the Campaign and Battle." *Southern Historical Society Papers*, 5:54-85. Originally published in *Philadelphia Weekly Times*.

———. "Lee's Right Wing at Gettysburg." *Battles and Leaders of the Civil War*, 3:339-354.

———. "The Mistakes of Gettysburg." *Philadelphia Weekly Times*, 23 February 1878.

Loring, Wm. E. "Gettysburg. The 141st Pa. At the Battle. A Graphic Narrative by a High Private." *Fighting Them Over: How the Veterans Remembered Gettysburg in the Pages of the National Tribune*, 308-309.

Lowe, David W., editor. *Meade's Army: The Private Notebooks of Lt. Col. Theodore Lyman*. Kent, OH: The Kent State University Press, 2007.

Luvaas, Dr. Jay, and Col. Harold W. Nelson, editors. *A Communicator's Guide to the Gettysburg Campaign*. San Bernardino, CA: Self-Published, 2016.

Mahan, D. H. *An Elementary Treatise on Advanced-Guard, Out-Post, and Detachment Service of Troops, and the Manner of Posting and Handling Them in Presence of an Enemy*. New York: John Wiley, 1861.

Maine Gettysburg Commission. *Maine at Gettysburg*. Gettysburg, PA: Stan Clark Military Books, 1994. Reprint of the 1898 edition.

Marbaker, Thomas D. *History of the Eleventh New Jersey Volunteers: From Its Organization to Appomattox*. Trenton, NJ: MacCrellish & Quigley, 1898.

Marcot, Roy. "Berdan's Sharpshooters at Gettysburg." *Gettysburg Magazine*, No. 1 (July 1989): 35-40.

Martin, David G. *Confederate Monuments at Gettysburg*. Conshohocken, PA: Combined Books, 1995.

———. *New Jersey at Gettysburg Guidebook*. Hightstown, NJ: Longstreet House, 2012.

Martin, James M., R.G. Madge, E.C. Strouss, R.I. Campbell & M.C. Zahniser, compilers. *History of the Fifty-Seventh Regiment Pennsylvania Veteran Volunteer Infantry*. Kearny, NJ: Belle Grove Publishing Company, 1995. Reprint of the 1904 edition.

Martin, Rawley. "Rawley Martin's Account." *Southern Historical Society Papers,* 32: 183-189.

Mayo, Joseph. "Pickett's Charge at Gettysburg." *Southern Historical Society Papers*, 34: 327-335.

McCalmont, Robert. *Extracts from Letters Written By Alfred B. McCalmont*. Franklin, PA: Printed for private circulation by his son, Robert McCalmont, 1908.

McConnell, Edward N. "A Brief History of Company A 139th Regiment, Pennsylvania Volunteers." *The Western Pennsylvania Historical Magazine*, (October 1972): 307-318.

McDonald, Archie P., editor. *Make Me a Map of the Valley: The Civil War Journal of Stonewall Jackson's Topographer*. College Station, TX: Texas A&M University Press, 1973.

McGrath, Thomas A. "The Browne Brothers: Killed at Gettysburg." *Gettysburg Magazine*, No. 35 (January 2006): 101-108.

McKee, James W. "William Barksdale and the Congressional Election of 1853." *Journal of Mississippi History,* No. 34 (May 1972): 129-158.

McLaws, Lafayette. "The Federal Disaster on the Left." Philadelphia *Weekly Press*, August 4, 1886.

________. "Gettysburg." *Southern Historical Society Papers*, 7: 64-90.

McMillan, Tom. *Gettysburg Rebels: Five Native Sons Who Came Home to Fight as Confederate Soldiers.* Washington, DC: Regnery History, 2017.

McNeily, J.S. "Barksdale's Mississippi Brigade at Gettysburg." *Publications of the Mississippi Historical Society*, Vol. XIV (1914): 231-265.

Meade, George. *Gettysburg.* Gettysburg, PA: Farnsworth House Military Impressions, 1988. Reprint of the 1924 edition.

________. *The Life and Letters of George Gordon Meade.* New York: Charles Scribner's Sons, 1913.

Messent, Peter, and Steve Courtney, editors. *The Civil War Letters of Joseph Hopkins Twichell: A Chaplain's Story.* Athens, GA: The University of Georgia Press, 2006.

Minnigh, Luther W. *Gettysburg "What They Did Here".* 1905.

Moore, Frank. *Women of the War; Their Heroism and Self-Sacrifice.* Hartford, CT: S.S. Scranton & Co., 1866.

Moran, Frank. "A Fire Zouave. Memoirs of a Member of the Excelsior Brigade." *The National Tribune,* November 6, 1890.

Morton, Joseph W. *Sparks from the Campfire, or Tales of the Old Veterans.* Philadelphia: Keystone Publishing Co., 1892.

Moyer, H. P., compiler. *History of the Seventeenth Pennsylvania Cavalry, or One Hundred and Sixty-Second in the Line of Pennsylvania Volunteer Regiments: War to Suppress the Rebellion, 1861-1865.* Lebanon, PA: Sowers Printing Company, 1911.

Muffly, J. W., editor. *The Story of Our Regiment: A History of the 148th Pennsylvania Vols.* Des Moines, IA: Kenyon Printing & Mfg. Co., 1904.

Mulholland, St. Clair A. *The Story of the 116th Regiment Pennsylvania Volunteers in the War of the Rebellion: The Record of a Gallant Command.* Philadelphia: F. McManus, Jr. & Co., 1903.

Murray, R. L. "The Artillery Duel in the Peach Orchard July 2, 1863." *Gettysburg Magazine,* No. 36 (July 2007): 69-85.

________. *E.P. Alexander and the Artillery Action in the Peach Orchard.* Wolcott, NY: Benedum Books, 2000.

________. *Letters from Gettysburg: New York Soldiers' Correspondences from the Battlefield.* Wolcott, NY: Benedum Books, 2000.

________. *The Redemption of the 'Harper's Ferry Cowards': The Story of the 111th and 126th New York State Volunteer Regiments at Gettysburg.* Self-Published, 1994.

Nicholson, John, editor. *Pennsylvania at Gettysburg.* Harrisburg, PA: W. M. Stanley Ray, 1904.

Nelson, A. H. *The Battles of Chancellorsville and Gettysburg.* Minneapolis, MN: 1899.

New York Monument Commission for the Battlefields of Gettysburg and Chattanooga. *Dedication of the New York Auxiliary State Monument on the Battlefield of Gettysburg.* Albany, NY: J.B. Lyon Company, 1926.

———. *Final Report on the Battle of Gettysburg*. Albany, NY: J.B. Lyon Company, 1902.

Newton, George W. *Silent Sentinels: A Reference Guide to the Artillery at Gettysburg*. El Dorado Hills, CA: Savas Beatie, 2005

Norton, Henry. *Deeds of Daring or, History of the Eighth N.Y. Volunteer Cavalry, containing a complete record of the battles, skirmishes, marches, etc., that the Gallant Eighth New York Cavalry participated in, from its organization in November, 1861, to the close of the rebellion in 1865*. Norwich, N.Y.: Chenango Telegraph Printing House, 1889.

Norton, Oliver Wilcox. *The Attack and Defense of Little Round Top*. Gettysburg, PA: Stan Clark Military Books, 1992. Reprint of the 1913 edition.

O'Brien, Kevin E. "'To Unflinchingly Face Danger and Death': Carr's Brigade Defends Emmitsburg Road." *Gettysburg Magazine*, No. 12 (January 1995): 7-23.

Oeffinger, John C. editor. *A Soldier's General: The Civil War Letters of Major General Lafayette McLaws*. Chapel Hill, NC: The University of North Carolina Press, 2002.

Owen, William Miller. *In Camp and Battle with the Washington Artillery of New Orleans*. Baton Rouge, LA: Louisiana State University Press, 1999. Reprint of the 1885 edition.

Peatman, Jared. "General Sickles, President Lincoln, and the Aftermath of the Battle of Gettysburg." *Gettysburg Magazine*, No. 28 (January 2003): 117-123.

Pennsylvania Commission. *Fiftieth Anniversary of the Battle of Gettysburg*. Harrisburg, PA: William Stanly Ray, State Printer, 1914.

Petruzzi, J. David. "John Buford at Gettysburg: A Study in Maps." *America's Civil War* (July 2008): 33-37.

Pfanz, Harry W. *Gettysburg: Culp's Hill and Cemetery Hill*. Chapel Hill, NC: The University of North Carolina Press, 1993.

———. *Gettysburg: The First Day*. Chapel Hill, NC: The University of North Carolina Press, 2001.

———. *Gettysburg: The Second Day*. Chapel Hill, NC: The University of North Carolina Press, 1987.

Phister, Frederick. *New York in the War of the Rebellion*. 3rd ed. Albany, NY: J. B. Lyon Company, 1912.

Pickerill, William N. *History of the Third Indiana Cavalry*. Indianapolis, IN: Aetna Printing Co., 1906.

Piston, William Garrett. "Cross Purposes: Longstreet, Lee, and Confederate Attack Plans for July 3 at Gettysburg." *The Third Day at Gettysburg & Beyond*, 31-55.

———. *Lee's Tarnished Lieutenant: James Longstreet and His Place in Southern History*. Athens, GA: University of Georgia Press, 1987.

———. "Petticoats, Promotions, and Military Assignments: Favoritism and the Antebellum Career of James Longstreet." *James Longstreet: The Man, the Soldier, the Controversy*, 53-76.

Platt, Barbara. *This is Holy Ground: A History of the Gettysburg Battlefield*. Self-Published, 2001.

Powelson, B. F. *History of Company K of the 140th Regiment Pennsylvania Volunteers*. Steubenville, OH: Carnahan Printing Company, 1906.

Quay, W.H. "Still in Error. A Pennsylvania Comrade Corrects Capt. Hart." *Fighting Them Over: How the Veterans Remembered Gettysburg in the Pages of the National Tribune*, 306-307.

Rafferty, Thomas. "Gettysburg." *Personal Recollections of the War of the Rebellion*, 1: 1-32.

Raus, Edmund J. *A Generation on the March: The Union Army at Gettysburg*. Gettysburg, PA: Thomas Publications, 1996.

Rauscher, Frank. *Music on the March. 1862-1865, with the Army of the Potomac. 114th Regt. P.V., Collis' Zouaves*. Philadelphia: Wm. F. Fell & Co., 1892.

Rice, Edmund. "Repelling Lee's Last Blow." *Battles and Leaders of the Civil War*, 3: 387-392.

Rittenhouse, Benjamin F. "The Battle Seen From Little Round Top." *The Gettysburg Papers, Two Volumes in One*, 517-529.

Robertson, James I. editor. *The Civil War Letters of General Robert McAllister*. Baton Rouge, LA: Louisiana State University Press, 1998.

Robertson, William Glenn. "The Peach Orchard Revisited: Daniel E. Sickles and the Third Corps on July 2, 1863." *The Second Day at Gettysburg*, 33-56.

Rollins, Richard. *"The Damned Red Flags of the Rebellion": The Confederate Battle Flag at Gettysburg*. Redondo Beach, CA: Rank and File Publications, 1997.

———. *Pickett's Charge: Eyewitness Accounts*. Redondo Beach, CA: Rank and File Publications, 1994.

Rusling, James F. *Lincoln and Sickles*. Third Army Corps Union, 1910.

———. *Men and Things I Saw in Civil War Days*. New York: Eaton & Mains, 1899.

Sauers, Richard. *Advance The Colors! Pennsylvania Civil War Battle Flags*. Lebanon, PA: Sowers Printing Co., 1991.

———. editor. *Fighting Them Over: How the Veterans Remembered Gettysburg in the Pages of the National Tribune*. Baltimore, MD: Butternut and Blue, 1998.

———. *Gettysburg: The Meade Sickles Controversy*. Dulles, VA: Brassey's, 2003.

Sawyer, Gordon. *James Longstreet: Before Manassas & After Appomattox*. Gainesville, GA: Sawyer House Publishing, 2005.

Scott, Kate M. *History of Jefferson County with Illustrations and Biographical Sketches of some of its Prominent Men and Pioneers*. Syracuse, NY: D. Mason & Co., 1888.

———. *History of the One Hundred and Fifth Regiment of Pennsylvania Volunteers*. Philadelphia: New-World Publishing Company, 1877.

Sears, Stephen W. *Gettysburg*. New York: Houghton Mifflin Company, 2003.

Seigler, Robert S. *South Carolina's Military Organization During the War Between the States: The Lowcountry & Pee Dee*. The History Press, 2008.

Select Committee Relative to the Soldiers' National Cemetery. *Report of the Select Committee relative to the Soldiers' National Cemetery together with the accompanying documents as reported to the House of Representatives of the Commonwealth of Pennsylvania, March 31, 1864.* Harrisburg, PA: Singerly & Myers, State Printers, 1864.

Shaara, Michael. *The Killer Angels.* New York: Ballantine Books, 1974

Sherfey, William Emory, compiler. *The Sherfey Family in the United States: 1751-1948 (Scherffig in Germany), An Historical and Genealogical Record.* Greensburg, IN: H. E. Sherfey, 1951.

Shultz, David L. and Scott L. Mingus. *The Second Day at Gettysburg: The Attack and Defense of Cemetery Ridge, July 2, 1863.* El Dorado Hills, CA: Savas Beatie, 2015.

Sickles, Daniel E. "Further Recollections of Gettysburg." *North American Review* (March 1891): 257-271.

————. "Leaves From My Diary." Reprinted from *the Journal of Military Service Institution of the United States,* Vol. 6, No. 22-23: 1-30, New York Public Library, Astor, Lenox and Tilden Foundations.

————. *Oration Delivered by Maj-Gen. D. E. Sickles, USA Before the Society of the Army of the Potomac at Fredericksburg, VA, May 25, 1900.* Society of the Army of the Potomac: 1900.

Skelly, Daniel Alexander. *A Boy's Experiences During the Battles of Gettysburg.* Gettysburg, PA: 1932.

Small, Cindy L. *The Jennie Wade Story: A True and Complete Account of the Only Civilian Killed During the Battle of Gettysburg.* Gettysburg, PA: Thomas Publications, 1991.

Smith, Gerald J. *"One of the Most Daring of Men": The Life of Confederate General William Tatum Wofford.* Murfreesboro, TN: Southern Heritage Press, 1997.

Smith, James E. *A Famous Battery and Its Campaigns, 1861-'64.* Wolcott, NY: Benedum Books, 1999. Reprint of the 1892 edition.

Smith, John Day. *The History of the Nineteenth Regiment of Maine Volunteer Infantry 1862-1865.* Minneapolis, MN: The Great Western Printing Company, 1909.

Smith, John Holmes. "Captain John Holmes Smith's Account." *Southern Historical Society Papers,* 32: 189-195.

Smith, John L., compiler. *History of the Corn Exchange Regiment 118th Pennsylvania Volunteers.* Philadelphia, PA: J. L. Smith, 1888.

Smith, Karlton D. "'To Consider Every Contingency': Lt. Gen. James Longstreet, Capt. Samuel R. Johnston, and the factors that affected the reconnaissance and countermarch, July 2, 1863." *Gettysburg Seminar Papers, Programs of the Ninth Annual Gettysburg Seminar.* National Park Service (2002): 99-120.

————. "'We drop a comrade's tear': Colonel Edward Lyon Bailey and the Second New Hampshire Infantry at Gettysburg." *Papers of the 2006 Gettysburg National Military Park Seminar.* National Park Service (2008): 101-121.

Smith, Timothy H. *Farms at Gettysburg: The Fields of Battle.* Gettysburg, PA: Thomas Publications, 2007.

Sorrel, Moxley. *At the Right Hand of Longstreet.* Lincoln, NE: University of Nebraska Press, 1999. Reprint of the 1905 edition, *Recollections of a Confederate Staff Officer.*

Spear, Abbott, editor. *The Civil War Recollections of General Ellis Spear.* University of Maine Press, 1997.

Stahl, Joseph. "Pvt. Charles Clough Company C, 12th New Hampshire Infantry." *Gettysburg Magazine*, No. 48 (2013): 28-30.

Stevens, Charles A. *Berdan's United States Sharpshooters in the Army of the Potomac, 1861-1865.* St. Paul, MN: Price-McGill Company, 1892.

Stevens, George T. *Three Years in the Sixth Corps.* New York: D. Van Nostrand, 1870.

Stevenson, Jas. *History of the Excelsior or Sickles' Brigade.* Paterson, NJ: Van Der Hoven & Holms, 1863.

Stewart, Robert Laird. *History of the One Hundred and Fortieth Pennsylvania Volunteers.* Chairman Pub. Co., 1912.

Storrick, W. C. *Gettysburg, The Place, The Battle, The Outcome.* Harrisburg, PA: J. Horace McFarland Company, 1932.

Strausbaugh, John. *City of Sedition: The History of New York City During the Civil War.* New York: Hachette Book Group, 2016.

Styple, William B., editor. *Generals in Bronze: Interviewing the Commanders of the Civil War.* Kearny, NJ: Belle Grove Publishing Co., 2005.

———. *Our Noble Blood: The Civil War Letters of General Regis de Trobriand.* Kearny, NJ: Belle Grove Publishing, 1997.

Swinton, William. *Campaigns of the Army of the Potomac.* Secaucus, NJ: The Blue & Grey Press, 1988. Reprint of the 1866 edition.

Sword, Wiley. "Capt. William C. Morgan, 3rd Maine Infantry: Hero or Scoundrel at the Peach Orchard." *Gettysburg Magazine*, No. 25 (January 2002): 75-81.

———. "Personal Battle Weapons of the Civil War: Defending the Codori House and Cemetery Ridge. Two Swords with Harrow's Brigade in the Gettysburg Campaign." *Gettysburg Magazine*, No.13 (July 1995): 43-49.

———. "Personal Battle Weapons of the Civil War: Lt. Col. Caspar Trepp's Colt's Revolver and the Reconnaissance to Pitzer's Woods." *Gettysburg Magazine,* No. 14 (January 1996): 46-51.

Sypher, J. R. *History of the Pennsylvania Reserve Corps: A Complete Record of the Organization; And of the Different Companies, Regiments and Brigades.* Lancaster, PA: Elias Barr & Co., 1865.

Tagg, Larry. *The Generals of Gettysburg.* Cambridge, MA: Da Capo Press, 2003.

Tap, Bruce. *Over Lincoln's Shoulder: The Committee on the Conduct of the War.* Lawrence, KS: University Press of Kansas, 1998.

Tapscott, V.A. "One of Pickett's Men." *Fighting Them Over: How the Veterans Remembered Gettysburg in the Pages of the National Tribune*, 413-414.

Taylor, Michael W. *To Drive the Enemy from Southern Soil: The Letters of Col. Francis Marion Parker and the History of the 30th Regiment North Carolina Troops.* Dayton, Ohio: Morningside House, Inc., 1998.

Taylor, Walter H. *General Lee: His Campaigns in Virginia, 1861-1865, with Personal Reminiscences.* Brooklyn, N.Y.: Braunworth & Co., 1906.

Teague, Charles. *Gettysburg by the Numbers.* Gettysburg, PA: Adams County Historical Society, 2006.

Thacher, James. *The American Orchardist; or a Practical Treatise on the Culture and Management of Apple and Other Fruit Trees...* Plymouth, MA: Ezra Collier, 1825.

Thomas, Dean. *Round Ball to Rimfire: A History of Civil War Small Arms Ammunition.* Gettysburg, PA: Thomas Publications, 1997.

Toombs, Samuel. *New Jersey Troops in the Gettysburg Campaign.* Orange, NJ: The Evening Mail Publishing House, 1888.

Townsend, Thomas S. *The Honors of the Empire State in the War of the Rebellion.* New York: A. Lovell & Co., 1889.

Tremain, Henry Edward. *Two Days of War – A Gettysburg Narrative and Other Excursions.* New York: Bonnell, Silver, and Bowers, 1905.

Trimble, Tony L. "Paper Collars: Stannard's Brigade at Gettysburg." *Gettysburg Magazine*, No. 2 (January 1990): 75-80.

Trowbridge, John T. "The Field of Gettysburg," *Atlantic Monthly*, No. 16 (November 1865): 616–24.

Trudeau, Noah Andre. *Gettysburg: A Testing of Courage.* New York: HarperCollins, 2002.

Tucker, Glenn. *High Tide at Gettysburg.* Gettysburg, PA: Stan Clark Military Books, 1995. Reprint of the 1958 edition.

Tyler, Lyon G., editor. *Men of Mark in Virginia.* Washington, DC: Men of Mark Publishing Company, 1906.

The Union Army: A History of Military Affairs in the Loyal States, 1861-65 - Records of the Regiments in the Union Army - Cyclopedia of Battles - Memoirs of Commanders and Soldiers. Eight Volumes. Madison, WI: Federal Publishing Company, 1908.

United States Christian Commission. *Second Annual Report for the Year 1863.* Philadelphia: 1864.

———. *Second Report of the Committee of Maryland, September 1, 1863.* Baltimore, MD: Sherwood and Co., 1863.

Van Santvoord, C. *The One Hundred and Twentieth New York State Volunteers.* Rondout, NY: Press of the Kingston Freeman, 1894.

Vanderslice, John M. *Gettysburg, A History of the Gettysburg Battle-field Memorial Association, With an Account of the Battle, Giving Movements, Positions, and Losses of the Commands Engaged.* Philadelphia, PA: The Memorial Association, 1897.

———. *Gettysburg Then and Now.* New York: G. W. Dillingham Co., 1897.

Vandiver, Frank Everson, editor. *The Civil War Diary of General Josiah Gorgas.* University of Alabama Press, 1947.

Waitt, Ernest Linden, compiler. *History of the Nineteenth Regiment Massachusetts Volunteer Infantry 1861-1865.* Salem, MA: Salem Press, 1906.

Walker, Francis Amasa. *History of the Second Army Corps in the Army of the Potomac.* New York: C. Scribner's Sons, 1886.

Walters, Don. "In Defense of Maj. Gen. Richard H. Anderson and His Division at Gettysburg." *Blue & Gray*, Volume XXI, Issue 1 (2003): 16-21.

Walton, James B. "Letter from Colonel J. B. Walton." *Southern Historical Society Papers*, 5:47-53.

Warner, Ezra J. *Generals in Blue: Lives of the Union Commanders.* Baton Rouge, LA: Louisiana State University Press, 1963.

Warren, Charles. *History of the Harvard Law School and of Early Legal Conditions in America, Volume III.* New York: Lewis Publishing Company, 1908.

Welch, Spencer Glasgow. *A Confederate Surgeon's Letters to His Wife.* New York: The Neale Publishing Company, 1911.

Wert, J. Howard. *A Complete Hand-Book of the Monuments and Indications and Guide to the Positions on the Gettysburg Battle-Field.* Harrisburg, PA: R.M. Sturgeon & Co, 1886.

Wert, Jeffry D. *General James Longstreet: The Confederacy's Most Controversial Soldier.* New York: Simon & Schuster, 1993.

———. *Gettysburg: Day Three.* New York: Simon & Schuster, 2001.

Wilcox, Cadmus M. "General C. M. Wilcox on the Battle of Gettysburg." *Southern Historical Society Papers,* 6:97-124.

Williams, J. C. *Life in Camp: A History of the Nine Months Service of the Fourteenth Vermont Regiment, From October 21, 1862, When it was Mustered into The U.S. Service, to July 21, 1863, Including the Battle of Gettysburg.* Claremont, N.H.: Claremont Manufacturing Company, 1864.

Wilson, Arabella M. *Disaster, Struggle, Triumph. The Adventures of 1000 "Boys in Blue".* Albany, NY: The Argus Company, Printers, 1870.

Wilson, James Grant and Titus Munson, editors. *Personal Recollections of the War of the Rebellion.* Wilmington, NC: Broadfoot Publishing, 1992. Reprint of the 1891 edition.

Wingert, Cooper H. "Masters of the Field: A New Interpretation of Wright's Brigade and Their Assault at Gettysburg." *Gettysburg Magazine*, No. 47 (July 2012): 52-60.

Winschel, Terrence J. "To Assuage the Grief: The Gettysburg Saga of Isaac and Mary Stamps." *Gettysburg Magazine*, No. 7 (July 1992): 77-82.

———. "Their Supreme Moment: Barksdale's Brigade at Gettysburg." *Gettysburg Magazine*, No. 1 (July 1989): 74.

Wise, Jennings Cropper. *The Long Arm of Lee: The History of the Artillery of the Army of Northern Virginia.* New York: Oxford University Press, 1959.

Wittenberg, Eric J. *The Devil's to Pay: John Buford at Gettysburg. A History and Walking Tour.* El Dorado Hills, CA: Savas Beatie, 2014.

———. "The Truth about the Withdrawal of Brig. Gen. John Buford's Cavalry, July 2, 1863." *Gettysburg Magazine*, No. 37 (July 2007): 71-82.

Woods, James A. "Defending Watson's Battery." *Gettysburg Magazine*, No. 9 (July 1993): 41-47.

———. *Gettysburg, July 2: The Ebb and Flow of Battle*. Gillette, NJ: Canister Publishing LLC, 2012.

———. "Humphreys' Division's Flank March to Little Round Top." *Gettysburg Magazine*, No. 6 (January 1992): 59-61.

Wray, William J. *History of the Twenty Third Pennsylvania Volunteer Infantry Birney's Zouaves*. Philadelphia, PA: Survivors Association Twenty Third Regiment Pennsylvania Volunteers, 1904.

Wycoff, Mac. *A History of the 3rd South Carolina Regiment: Lee's Reliables*. Wilmington NC: Broadfoot Publishing Company, 2008.

———. "Kershaw's Brigade at Gettysburg." *Gettysburg Magazine*, No.5 (July 1991): 35-46.

Zuber, Richard L. *North Carolina During Reconstruction*. State Department of Archives and History, 1969.

Newspapers

The Aberdeen Examiner (Aberdeen, MS)

Adams County News (Gettysburg, PA)

The Adams Sentinel (Gettysburg, PA)

Altoona Tribune (Altoona, PA)

The Apollo Daily-Record (Apollo, PA)

Asbury Park Press (Asbury Park, NJ)

The Baltimore Sun (Baltimore, MD)

The Bradford Star (Towanda, PA)

The Brooklyn Daily Eagle (Brooklyn, NY)

The Brooklyn Evening Star (Brooklyn, NY)

The Buffalo Commercial Advertiser (Buffalo, NY)

The Buffalo Daily Republic (Buffalo, NY)

Buffalo Morning Express and Daily Democracy (Buffalo, NY)

The Cincinnati Daily Enquirer (Cincinnati, OH)

Cincinnati Gazette (Cincinnati, OH)

Daily Patriot and Union (Harrisburg, PA)

Daily State Journal (Raleigh, NC)

The Democratic Chronicle (Shippensburg, PA)

Denton Journal (Denton, MD)

Detroit Free Press (Detroit, MI)

The Evening Post (New York, NY)

Evening Star (Washington, DC)

The Evening Sun (Hanover, PA)

Flushing Journal (Flushing, NY)

The Gettysburg Compiler (Gettysburg, PA)

Gettysburg Times (Gettysburg, PA)
Harper's Weekly (New York, NY)
Harrisburg Star Independent (Harrisburg, PA)
Harrisburg Telegraph (Harrisburg, PA)
Hartford Courant (Hartford, CT)
The Inter Ocean (Chicago, IL)
Janesville Daily Gazette (Janesville, WI)
Lewisburg Chronicle (Lewisburg, PA)
The Louisville Daily Courier (Louisville, KY)
Martinsburg Statesmen (Martinsburg, WV)
Miami Herald (Miami, FL)
Montgomery Ledger (Montgomery, AL)
The National Era (Washington, DC)
National Republican (Washington, DC)
The National Tribune (Washington, DC)
New York Herald (New York, NY)
The New York Times (New York, NY)
New York Tribune (New York, NY)
Newport Mercury (Newport, RI)
The News (Frederick, MD)
The News (Newport, PA)
The North American Review (Boston, MA)
The North Platte Semi-Weekly Tribune (North Platte, NE)
Philadelphia Inquirer (Philadelphia, PA)
The Pittsburg Daily Headlight (Pittsburg, KS)
Pittsburgh Dispatch (Pittsburgh, PA)
Pittsburgh Post-Gazette (Pittsburgh, PA)
Pittsburgh Weekly Gazette (Pittsburgh, PA)
The Providence Journal (Providence, RI)
The Semi-Weekly Mississippian (Jackson, MI)
Semi-Weekly Standard (Raleigh, NC)
The Shenango Valley News (Greenville, PA)
Southern Standard (Columbus, MI)
The St. Louis Republic (St. Louis, MO)
The Star and Enterprise (Newville, PA)
The Sun (New York, NY)
The Times (Philadelphia, PA)
Times-Republican (Marshalltown, IA)

The Waco Herald (Waco, TX)

Weekly Press (Philadelphia, PA)

The Weekly Kansas Chief (Troy, KS)

The York Daily (York, PA)

Internet

American Civil War Research Database. Retrieved from http://www.civilwardata.com.

Battlefield Rehabilitation at Gettysburg National Military Park. (2015, February 26). Retrieved from https://www.nps.gov/gett/learn/news/gett-battlefield-rehab.htm.

Biographical Directory of the United States Congress: William Barksdale. Retrieved from http://bioguide.congress.gov/scripts/biodisplay.pl?index=B000147.

Congressional Medal of Honor Society. Retrieved from www.cmohs.org/recipient-archive.php.

Cozzens, Peter. (2012, January 12). *Fearless French Mary*. Retrieved from http://www.historynet.com/fearless-french-mary.htm.

Franks, Sammy, "Colonel James D. Nance South Carolina's Civil Wars 'Proper Commander'" (2012). Retrieved from All Theses. 1507. https://tigerprints.clemson.edu/all_theses/1507.

Heiser, John. (2017, March 10). "'The enemy were on the gun and limber...' Gunner John Norwood's narrow escape at Gettysburg." *The Blog of the Gettysburg National Military Park*. Retrieved from https://npsgnmp.wordpress.com/2017/03/10/the-enemy-were-on-the-gun-and-limber-gunner-john-norwoods-narrow-escape-at-gettysburg/.

"June 30." *Robert I. Boyington's Army Life Journal (1861-1863)*. Retrieved from http://www.robert-ford.ws/105%20PA%20Intro.htm. (Archived URL.)

Stoudt, John. (2012, May 10). "The Cavada Brothers: Two Soldiers, Two Wars." *The Blog of the Gettysburg National Military Park*. Retrieved from https://npsgnmp.wordpress.com/2012/05/10/the-cavada-brothers-two-soldiers-two-wars/.

Swain, Craig. (2016, June 16). "Wreck at the Fat Nancy." *The Historical Marker Database*. Retrieved fromhttps://www.hmdb.org/Marker.asp?Marker=41517.

Index

Acknowledgments

We humbly thank everyone who offered their insight into the completion of this project. The final interpretations are ours to agree or disagree with. Just have your citations handy if you are going to challenge us.

Archival assistance and permissions were essential to the completion of this project. Foremost among these was John Heiser and Greg Goodell at Gettysburg National Military Park. Thanks also to Ben Neely, Tim Smith, Andrew Dalton, and Roger Heller at Adams County Historical Society; L. Eileen Parris at Virginia Historical Society; Michael Ridderbusch at West Virginia and Regional History Center; the Mississippi Department of Archives and History; Matthew Turi at University of North Carolina Library; Kaitlyn Pettengill at Historical Society of Pennsylvania; Genevieve Coyle at Yale University Library; Anna Smith at Charleston Library Society; Dana Signe K. Munroe at the Rhode Island Historical Society; and David Kern at Pottstown Historical Society.

Many friends generously offered us their own research, support, and access to personal collections. In some cases, this included previously unpublished information. Thanks to Chris Army, Doug Ashton, Sam Beeghley, Sue Boardman, Jim Bowback, Maria Brady, Scott Brown, Anne Cody, the late Don Cody, Kendra Debany, Erik Dorr, Doug Douds, Jack Drummond, Tim Fulmer, Bob Gale, Bob George, Ellen Gonsalves, Rich Guidekoop, Fred Hawthorne, Lynn Heller, Arthur House, Jeff Kawalis, Mike Kilmer, Rich Kohr, Rich Landwehrle, Eric Lindblade, David Malgee, Tom McMillan, Wayne Motts, George Newton, Deb Novotny, Mike Osiol, Ronn Palm, William Parry, Tim Pierce, Janice Pietrone, Richard Rigney, Richard Sawhill, Steve Slaughter, Tonia Smith, Phil Spaugy, Andy Ward, and John Zervas.

Books benefit from peer review. The unique inhabitants of Gettysburg, those who physically reside here and those who consider it to be their home, remain the most qualified peer reviewers on this topic. Several friends and colleagues read early drafts. They offered considerable amounts of commentary, insight, and criticism. Our sincerest thanks to Alan Brunelle, Steve Floyd, Jerry Hahn, John Hoptak, Steve and Judy Mock, Dave Powell, Carol Reardon, and Susan Stromello. Jeff Prushankin then painstakingly edited on behalf of

Savas Beatie. Several members of this group also shared information from their personal libraries and collections. To this group we dedicate every active verb, reference to the "Gallant Second," and the 300 emails that were exchanged on the exact position of Hart's right section.

Thanks to Ted Savas and the entire team at Savas Beatie, including Sarah Keeney, Sarah Closson, Donna Endacott, Stephanie Ferro, Lisa Murphy, and Renee Morehouse for their production and ongoing support of this book.

Finally, to our families for their tireless support and patience over endless nights spent writing, editing, and producing maps. To Michele Hessler, Snezana Isenberg, Alex Hessler, Aimee Hessler, and Una Isenberg, our gratitude for accepting that the financial reward will never match the long hours that went into this project.

James A. Hessler and Britt C. Isenberg
Gettysburg, Pennsylvania
March 2019

About the Authors

James A. Hessler is a Licensed Battlefield Guide at Gettysburg. He is the award-winning author of *Sickles at Gettysburg* (Savas Beatie, 2009), the recipient of the Bachelder Coddington Award and Gettysburg Civil War Round Table Distinguished Book Award, and co-author of *Pickett's Charge at Gettysburg* (Savas Beatie, 2015). His media appearances include Travel Channel, NPR, PCN-TV, Breitbart News, Civil War Radio, and *Gettysburg Daily*. He was a primary content designer for the American Battlefield Trust's mobile Gettysburg application and has written many articles for publication. He lives with his wife and family in Gettysburg.

Britt C. Isenberg is a full-time Licensed Battlefield Guide at Gettysburg National Military Park since 2014. He has been published in several Civil War periodicals through writing and photography, and is the author of *The Boys Fought Like Demons* (2016), a regimental history of the 105th Pennsylvania Infantry. His tours at Gettysburg have also been featured on PCN-TV. Originally from Millersburg, PA, he resides with his wife and daughter near Gettysburg.